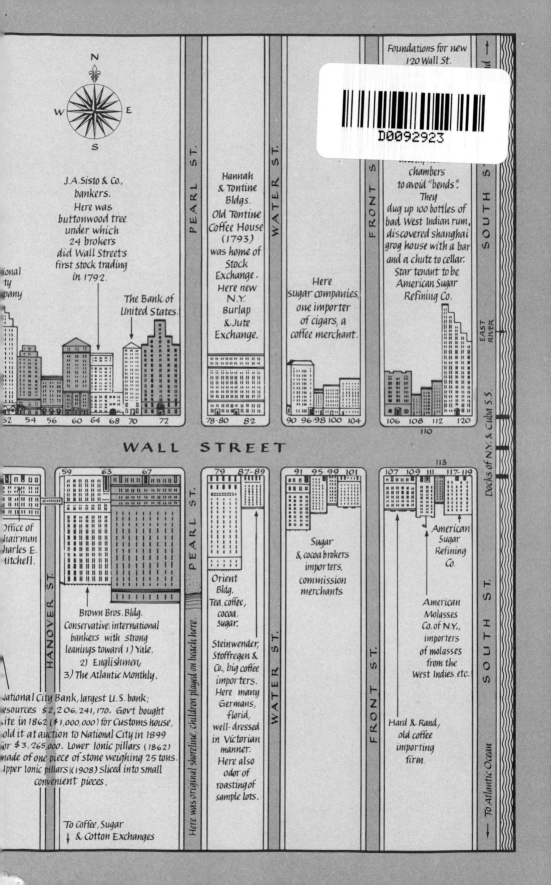

THE DAY THE BUBBLE BURST

THE DAY
THE BUBBLE
BURST

A Social History of the
Wall Street Crash of 1929

Gordon Thomas and Max Morgan-Witts

Doubleday & Company, Inc., Garden City, New York
1979

Library of Congress Cataloging in Publication Data

Thomas, Gordon.
The day the bubble burst.

Bibliography: p. 454.
Includes index.
1. Depressions—1929—United States.
2. United States—Social conditions—1918–1932.
I. Morgan-Witts, Max, joint author.   II. Title.
HB3717   1929.T54   338.5′4
ISBN: 0-385-14370-2
Library of Congress Catalog Card Number 79–7122

CONTENTS

x   *Contents*

AUTHORS' NOTE

The Wall Street Crash of 1929 was the most climactic financial disaster in history. It still affects all our lives today.

Periodically, when the market declines, the question is asked whether history will repeat itself. For a decade or more those warning of a likely repetition have been ably led by Professor Kenneth Galbraith, whose own book on the economic background to the Crash has become a standard work of reference.

That other doyen of American economics, Professor Milton Friedman, sees monetarism as our financial salvation.

Both agree the 1929 Crash was a financial turning point. Prior to that, the business of money was held to be the prerogative of businessmen. The Crash showed how widely that prerogative had been dispersed. The Crash affected everyone; it was the precursor to the Depression; as such it was not only a financial collapse but a human, family tragedy. In a way it was worse than war. One of those hurt explained: "In war, Dad goes off, a hero. But soon after the Crash, Dad was always at home. Nagging doubts were raised: wasn't he smart enough to get a job? Was he really trying to get work? Doubts about Dad as a person grew and remain to this day."

How such a situation came to be we have tried to explore and include. Our intention is to present, for the first time, a full social history of the Crash and its global impact; while the boom was essentially American, the ramifications of the Crash were worldwide.

It is our contention that the story of the Crash is best told through the lives of people; among them the people who sowed the financial whirlwind that would scatter not only them but untold others in penury.

They were the victims of a financial pandemic the like of which the world has never before, or since, seen.

Previous works have tended to restrict themselves to the New York market and its immediate environs—an admirable enough decision, but one that inevitably reduced the horizon. Our journeying into the hinterlands far beyond Wall Street produced a wealth of information buried in arcane documentation, private reports, and the accounts of eyewitnesses hitherto unrecorded.

While ours, too, is "a financial story," it is also a social study of a unique period in history, peopled with characters rich in every sense of the word.

There is Jesse Livermore, archmanipulator and nemesis of the Great Bull Market, locked in financial combat with great bulls like John J. Raskob, Billy Durant, and Charles Mitchell. Against the background of their wheeler-dealing, enough to keep most men fully occupied, Raskob is preparing his own monument, the Empire State Building; Durant is running a single-handed campaign to overthrow the policies of the Federal Reserve Board; Mitchell, chairman of America's biggest commercial bank, is, like the Artful Dodger, creating a scheme to avoid paying income tax on his millions.

There is A. P. Giannini, founder of the Bank of America, hurtling around California in a Rolls-Royce dressed up as a fire truck, planning his latest moves in another great conflict—this one with the most powerful private bank in the world, the House of Morgan. There is Joe Kennedy, founder of a dynasty, self-made millionaire, determined to revenge himself on Jack Morgan—whose virtually last public appearance is with a midget in his lap.

There is Henry Ford, avowed enemy of Wall Street, unwittingly providing the fodder for Hitler's anti-Semitism. There is Clarence Hatry in London, whose ambition some believe contributed to the Crash. There is Mike Meehan, who put Wall Street on the Atlantic.

Talking to the sons and daughters of these men, studying their contemporary writings—their diaries and office papers—the unsuspected connections between them, the tangled web of high finance, became clear. Often publicly distanced from each other, they are, in the end, drawn together into Wall Street by the mesmeric effect of the market.

Their decision-making touched not only almost everybody in America but also countless millions around the world.

Charles Mitchell's decision to float a new bond affected the lives of Brazilian peasants; a loan from Jack Morgan helped to prop up Mussolini; Nazism grew in part because of the decision of American financiers to support the ailing Weimar Republic—for profit.

We have tried to look at the effects on all strata: On the one hand there is Winston Churchill, who lost money, and a member of J. P. Morgan and Company whose wife dismisses the Crash as no more than the rattle of teacups; on the other, there is a young flapper and a vivacious bootlegger—both in a sense "in the market"—who, like so many others, are scarred forever by men they never met and decisions over which they had no control.

Few man-made events, short of the World Wars, created so much pain and bitterness, and the fear it could occur again.

Perhaps the only real protection against that happening is to have an understanding not only of *why* it happened but of what it was like to be there *when* it happened.

It began so promisingly, the events leading up to the day the bubble burst. . . .

GT/MMW

April 1979
Ashford,
Ireland

October, this is one of the peculiarly dangerous months to speculate in stocks. The others are July, January, September, April, November, May, March, June, December, August and February.
—PUDD'NHEAD WILSON (Mark Twain)

The most disastrous decline in the biggest and broadest stock market of history rocked the financial district yesterday.
—THE NEW YORK TIMES, October 25, 1929

The fundamental business of the country, that is the production and distribution of commodities, is on a sound and prosperous basis.
—PRESIDENT HERBERT HOOVER, October 25, 1929

I appeal to movie exhibitors to show pictures that will reinstate courage and hope in the hearts of the people.
—JIMMY WALKER, mayor of New York, October 29, 1929

Stock prices virtually collapsed yesterday, swept downward with gigantic losses in the most disastrous trading day in the stock market's history.
—THE NEW YORK TIMES, October 30, 1929

There is nothing in the business situation to warrant the destruction of values that has taken place in the past week, and my son and I have for some days past been purchasing sound common stocks.
—JOHN D. ROCKEFELLER, SR., October 30, 1929

Sure he's buying. Who else has any money left?
—EDDIE CANTOR, October 31, 1929

On Fifth Avenue, police found a parrot screaming "More margin! More margin!"
—WIRE SERVICE REPORT, undated, unverified

The situation has been reached in New York hotels where the clerk asks incoming guests, "You wanna room for sleeping or for jumping?" And you have to stand in line to get a window to jump out of.
—WILL ROGERS, November 20, 1929

THE DAY THE BUBBLE BURST

CHAPTER ONE

THE RAMPAGING BULL

One whang of his hand-tooled gavel against the fluted gong would stop everything.

It would end the action at Post Two, one of the stockade-shaped trading counters that had been under siege by brokers since early afternoon as U. S. Steel continued its giddy climb; it would quieten the harassed clerks inside Post Nine, where Standard Oil of New Jersey, after a slow start, had suddenly outpaced the trading in Sears Roebuck, another of the post's lively stocks; it would still the flashing numbers on the black annunciator boards which called traders to their posts for urgent messages from their offices.

The gong would herald a pause for 1,145 telephonists. It would ease the pressure on 500 page boys, 280 tube attendants and quotation clerks, 80 bond clerks, and 200 specialists' clerks, essential support troops for the delicate financial maneuvers performed every minute in and around the trading posts.

Walking steadily, watchful, freezing with a glare any overactive page, nodding to the famous, proud of all he could see, William R. Crawford, superintendent of the mechanical department of the New York Stock Exchange, was acutely aware of the power embodied in his gavel. His progress across the 16,000 square feet of recently felt-padded floor—insulation that effectively reduced the noise level in the cavernous room—had all the quality of a ritual. It once led a reporter to describe Crawford as "Mammon's Lord Chamberlain." The superintendent had not been amused.

But he still liked to believe that the moment he used his gavel, the business of America would be fixed and frozen until the following morning.

Now, as he made his measured way across the more than quarter acre of sacrosanct floor, his experienced eyes could see that it had been another highly satisfactory day for the elite in the room—the nine hundred brokers, each a member of the Exchange and the only persons on the floor permitted to trade.

At Post One, United Aircraft was up a few points—a sign of the growing public enthusiasm for air travel. Chrysler and General Motors were trading strongly at Posts Two and Four. Shares in the railroads— Pennsylvania, Rock Island, New York Central, New Haven, and Union Pacific—were being bought and sold briskly, as they had been for months now, every sale marking a heady profit for some investor.

As usual, the biggest crowd was gathered around Post Twelve, the "Radio Post" where the whiz kid of Wall Street, Michael J. Meehan, presided over the wheeling and dealing in RCA shares.

Crawford was fond of saying that anybody wishing to check the pulse, or the mood, of America need only walk among the eighteen posts. Each with its group of designated stocks reflected the unprecedented boom sweeping the nation. He believed that "seeing these posts would reassure anybody that the millennium's arrived."

Stocks in Woolworth, Macy, Montgomery Ward, Safeway Stores, and General Foods were up, reflecting the mass-marketing techniques sweeping the United States. The very name of some of the shares indicated America's belief in her global destiny: International Nickel, International Tel and Tel, International Match, International Harvester.

Crawford and many others who spent their working days on the Exchange floor were firmly convinced that the world outside their heavily draped sanctum depended for its prosperity on the financial juggling performed there Monday through Friday from 10 A.M. to 3 P.M., and on Saturdays until noon.

This Monday at 2:59 P.M., exactly on schedule, the superintendent reached a small rostrum, projecting in midair from the south wall. Above him an annunciator board continued flashing up white numbers. Flanking the board were the Stars and Stripes and the blue banner of New York State. Similar flags hung at the other end of the room. Limp and lifeless, collecting dust, the emblems were unruffled by the ebb and flow of groups of traders forming and re-forming, scurrying, even at this late stage, from one post to another, buying and selling at a nod, on trust.

From his pulpit, Crawford could see the strategically placed stock tickers. Recently he had supervised the installation of ingenious reflecting devices which threw the magnified quotations from the paper tape onto large screens visible to everyone. It was the latest in a long series of improvements that had made the New York Stock Exchange the most modern in the world.

His gavel would not immediately silence the tickers; they would continue to run for some minutes afterward—how long would depend on the volume of trading in these closing seconds.

Each ticker, like thousands of others linking the New York Exchange with other exchanges and brokerage offices throughout America, was under a round glass dome, not unlike the one that used to encase the wax flowers on the parlor table of Crawford's grandmother.

Her grandson was responsible for the maintenance of the small brass mechanism under the glass. It was a simple enough device: two little rollers pausing as they passed through printer's ink before beating a light tattoo on the narrow strip of white tape running through a slot in the side of the dome. All over America eager eyes perused the identical spirals of paper falling to the floor which spelled out new highs in railways, oils, and metals. Five hundred miles of tape, Crawford would recite to visitors, ran over the spindles of the tickers for every million shares traded.

From time to time this past year, the tickers had given news of setbacks in the market, to be swiftly followed by an even greater upsurge in value, sometimes as a result of "the pools"—syndicates of powerful investors—putting their huge financial resources behind a stock, spiraling it to new and dizzy heights.

Day after day a vast, and growing, public continued to register its faith that what goes up need not come down. The clicking of tickers had shown Americans a quick and easy road to wealth.

Now, at precisely 3 P.M. this Monday, December 31, 1928, William Crawford temporarily halted their progress down that road with a single strike of his gavel against the Stock Exchange gong.

Another market day had ended.

But this afternoon, instead of going back to their offices or to their homes, the great mass began to move purposefully across the floor, treading through thousands of canceled calculation slips and miles of discarded tape. Eagerly anticipating what lay ahead, some of the younger men broke a strict rule of the Exchange. They began to run toward the doors leading to the visitors' gallery.

For the past three hundred minutes—the five hours of trading—the gallery, running along the Broad Street side of the Exchange, had received a steady stream of visitors. In spite of the bitterly cold and damp weather, hundreds of people, native New Yorkers and visitors to the city, came to peer down on the trading floor, to witness for themselves

the most extraordinary economic happening in the history of America
—the bull market at full rampage.*

Throughout 1928 the double sensations of the stock market—
unprecedented volume and soaring prices—had been front-page news.
There had been two major breaks, in June and December, but they
were quickly forgotten. Day after day, month after month, the market
had surged upward, carrying favorite stocks into the empyrean. Radio
Corporation of America had gone from 85 to an incredible 420 during
the year; soon it would be due for a split-up.† An obscure company
called Western Warehouses had leaped in similar fashion. They, and
the shares of a hundred companies like them, rose mainly because, in
Crawford's opinion, "the titans of the market wished them to rise."

It was to catch a glimpse of those titans at work that most of the
spectators in the gallery had come to the Exchange.

On this last day of the year they stared down on the floor, trying to
spot the men whose boldness and daring had turned them into new authentic American heroes. The gray uniformed guides had patiently
pointed out Michael Meehan by the Radio Post where the trading in
RCA shares had made men, including Meehan, millions overnight, or
Frank Bliss, known for his sudden unexpected forays into the market
and immortalized by the media as "the silver fox of Wall Street." And
everyone wanted to learn whether the infamous Jesse Livermore was
playing the market that day; for years the taciturn, chain-smoking New
Englander, dubbed the "boy plunger" by the media, had been a living
legend because of his reputation for single-handed attacks on certain
stocks, pushing their price down.

All day the gallery buzzed with informed gossip. Spectators, who a
year ago did not know the difference between a bear‡ and a bull, now
talked knowledgeably of selling short* as practiced by the great Liver-

* *Bull market:* one in which the majority of share prices have been, and continue
to be, rising.
† *Split-up:* When the value of a company's stock goes very high, market dealings
are made easier if the value of the stock is reduced and the number of shares
correspondingly increased in a split-up.
‡ *Bear:* a person who believes prices will soon fall; a bull is one who expects
them to rise. Livermore was thought to be a bear.
* *Selling short:* a favorite device of bears; believing a stock's price is about to go
down, the bear sells stock he does not yet own, but knows he is able to borrow
for a time from a broker for a fee. He then delivers these borrowed shares to the
buyer, collects payment, and waits for the price to fall. Once it has done so, he
buys shares at the lower price and gives them to the broker to replace those he
borrowed. The bear's profit is the difference between the price at which he sold
the borrowed shares to the buyer and the price he paid for the replacement
shares to give the broker, less the broker's commission. There are many refine-
ments to this basic scheme, all of which are bad for the bear if prices unexpectedly go up instead of down. Since the 1930s, rules governing short selling
have been imposed aimed at obviating the possibility of such sales actually
causing prices to fall.

more himself. They endlessly analyzed the latest moves made by other market giants—Arthur W. Cutten, Charles Topping, the Fisher brothers. Every word these operators uttered in public was slavishly reported in the press and on the radio.

The Stock Exchange guides were used to dealing with the blandishments of attractive female investors anxious to meet famous traders; a woman's magazine had recently reported that stockbrokers equaled movie stars in sex appeal. To avoid the risk of a "sexy siren" waylaying a trader, on this last day of the year the guides had cleared the gallery well before William Crawford's gong ended trading.

When 3 P.M. was announced, a five-piece orchestra began to play at one end of the gallery. The guides opened burlap bags of confetti, ticker tape, paper hats, and noisemakers.

From the Stock Exchange Luncheon Club on the seventh floor, waiters filed out of the kitchen, carrying silver tureens. The club was one of the most exclusive in New York; few nonmembers had ever been inside the spacious room to admire its collection of early American prints, let alone to dine off one of the most sumptuous menus in the city. An outsider needed eight favorable votes to be admitted; two blackballs meant exclusion. The credit limit was one hundred dollars, even for members like Percy Rockefeller and Jack Morgan who were individually worth millions.

In solemn procession the waiters marched into the gallery with tureens of clam-juice cocktail that for the past twenty years had been a favorite beverage among brokers. The cocktail's fame had spread across America. This afternoon it would serve as the official aperitif at the Stock Exchange's traditional New Year's Eve party.

The members, their staff, wives, and mistresses had all been invited. Nevertheless, there would be some notable absentees. The elder John D. Rockefeller, who still owned a seat on the Exchange, had not visited the building for years. Jack Morgan, son of the legendary J.P., was a member, but had *never* entered the Exchange to do business—let alone sip clam juice with clerks in a drab public gallery. Many of the senior members—veterans who had traded for fifty years and who still talked mistily of the great stock market panic of 1893—had slipped away before the end of trading to reminisce in one of the speakeasies tucked away in side streets around the Exchange. Several of the affluent younger brokers decided to miss the party because there were more promising celebrations to attend uptown. Mindful of their mystique and social position, they knew it would be easy for them to pick up glamorous flappers at one of those parties.

Some of the biggest market manipulators would be absent because they were not members of the Exchange, preferring to mastermind their financial operations from outside. They were, therefore, not eligible to be invited to what was in essence a glorified office party.

Like all such gatherings, shop talk predominated. Almost everybody had a story to tell of a spectacular killing. An actor had made $40,000 from Vanadium Steel, Schulte Cigar Stores, Public Utilities of New Jersey, and Wright Aero. A waiter at the Exchange's Luncheon Club had resigned, $90,000 better off, as a result of tips passed on by his customers; he had successfully plunged into the market with $5,000 saved from ten- and twenty-five-cent tips. A stenographer was $15,000 richer through selling General Motors stock she had only had for two days; the girl promptly bought a fur coat and reinvested the balance in Anaconda Copper, a stock widely tipped to rise spectacularly in early 1929.

Everybody in the gallery knew what a tip could do. Only last March, John J. Raskob, a director of General Motors, had uttered a few sentences of optimism about the automobile industry, and his company's stock had driven upward twelve points. Raskob was a man to watch. So was Arthur Cutten. Six months earlier Cutten had moved his operations from Chicago to Wall Street. He was dealing in 200,000 shares a day— Armour & Co., Radio, Montana Power, United States Cast Iron Pipe. His takings so far were put at $100 million.

It was this sort of talk that made an otherwise dull party hum. An impromptu cabaret spot by a group of page boys caught the mood, their piping voices summing up a national attitude:

> *O hush thee, my babe, granny's bought some more shares,*
> *Daddy's gone to play with the bulls and the bears,*
> *Mother's buying on tips and she simply can't lose,*
> *And baby shall have some expensive new shoes.*

In a corner of the gallery, a group of young traders stiffened their clam cocktails with shots of potent homemade whiskey and listened eagerly to the words of Michael J. Meehan.

Just fifteen years before, Meehan was selling theater tickets at 71 Broadway and making about $5,000 a year. Now he was possibly the best known broker in America and president of his own firm, with eight Stock Exchange seats, the largest number ever held by a commission house. In 1920, when he had bought his first seat, he had two employees; now he had some 400, with an annual payroll of around $600,000.

When Meehan had become a broker, he had made only $18 profit his first month; he fell back to selling theater tickets to augment his income. Two years later he had saved enough to lay out the $90,000 needed to buy his first seat on the Exchange; his latest had cost him close to $500,000. He hadn't blinked when he'd written his check; money, Meehan was fond of telling newspapermen, was "there for the spending and making."

Short, with the first hint of a potbelly, he wore steel-rimmed spectacles that made him look older than his thirty-eight years. He worked hard to maintain his casual, off-beat image; he loved it when the media called him "one of the boys," when they reported he still wore soft shirts and did not "care a whoop whether his tie is the latest thing from London or whether it is knotted at just the proper point under his Adam's apple."

That sort of publicity helped to divert interest from his tough, ruthless style of operating, typified by the way he had speculated in, and made a fortune from, one of the most glamorous of all new stocks—RCA.

Mike Meehan was the Exchange's specialist in Radio; most buy or sell orders of the stock had to be made through him or members of his firm at Post Twelve. During 1928 he had helped engineer Radio's meteoric rise and made for himself an estimated $25 million.

Now he was preparing for a fresh foray—on the conservative Anaconda Copper stock.

In great secrecy, Meehan was planning to organize a pool with funds from such financial giants as Percy Rockefeller, the Fisher brothers, and John J. Raskob. He expected he would have no difficulty in finding other participants whose money would swell that available to over $30 million. Then they would act.

There were still weeks of careful groundwork to be laid before the first moves in the market would be made. But now Meehan was able to relax, sip a drink, and be glad that this New Year's Eve the orchestra had not singled him out by playing an Irish melody. He hated "all that ethnic nonsense."

Down on the Stock Exchange floor, there was now a milling crowd of men and women, some of them dancing, many of them fortified from hip flasks, the fashionable answer to Prohibition, now in its eighth year.

Two men moved ostentatiously and ceremoniously among the guests. Each was aware of his own importance.

The elder was Edward Henry Harriman Simmons, president of the New York Stock Exchange these past five years. The spiteful said that Simmons would really have preferred canonization, election to the papacy, or the role of lord mayor of London; that he had accepted only as a poor alternative the most important electoral office in the financial world. His few friends said that he was born for his exalted and unsalaried post. For them he epitomized the puritanism of those twenty-four brokers who in May 1792 gathered under a buttonwood tree and drew up a written agreement to deal only with each other on a common commission basis, so forming the Exchange Simmons now presided over.

His few public pronouncements on the market were predictable and ponderous. The press preferred to quote his companion.

Richard Whitney was vice-president of the Exchange, and probably the most unpopular man among the rank-and-file members ever to hold that office. They resented the way he calculatingly charmed reporters while treating his colleagues in cavalier fashion. With representatives of the media he talked shamelessly of his fine athletic record at Harvard and his impressive business and social contacts; in the Exchange he was invariably imperious, rude, or icily disdainful to virtually everyone. Most members of the Exchange found Whitney an insufferable snob.

Money and the right connections had swept him to office. His brother George was a Morgan partner, and Richard himself was known as "the Morgan broker"; when the gods of 23 Wall—the address of the headquarters of the House of Morgan and the only identification on its entrance door—had business to transact on the Exchange that they themselves so fastidiously avoided, they assumed the bodily form of the broad-shouldered, bullnecked Whitney. His own firm, Richard Whitney and Company, was a bond house, with no interest in that stormy side of the market where stocks are traded. Everything about him—his suits, his cars, his homes, his associates—suggested he was a pillar of America's financial establishment.

Yet behind Whitney's carefully burnished image of huntsman, yachtsman, and patrician was another, altogether less successful man.

For years he had been borrowing heavily from his brother George and a broker friend to finance recklessly speculative personal investments in the stock of, among others, a fertilizer business in Florida and an applejack distillery in New Jersey. In the year just ending he had borrowed $590,000, gambled, and lost.

No one dared protest at his actions: Whitney's Morgan connections were too powerful to upset. For many years the Exchange had been dominated by the great banking and investment house which was its neighbor—and the most powerful nexus of capitalism in the world. The House of Morgan annually gave out millions of dollars in gifts to "favored clients," often to the benefit of Exchange governors. The cynics of Wall Street said that "whenever a string was pulled across the Street at Morgan's, the Exchange jumped."

Whitney was confident that the overpowering influence of J. P. Morgan and Company would help him achieve his ultimate ambition—to take the place of the man he now walked with through the throng of partygoers.

What none of them could know was that the splendidly handsome Whitney, the obvious heir apparent for the position of president of the Stock Exchange, was in fact with every day that passed becoming ever more deeply and dangerously in debt.

The departure of Simmons and Whitney marked the formal end of the celebrations. By early evening there were only a few stragglers left. Some of them were planning a surreptitious visit to the House of Morgan—not J.P.'s, but Helen's.

Miss Morgan ran the most popular speakeasy in midtown Manhattan, if not in the entire Prohibition-dry city of 32,000 similar establishments; Police Commissioner Grover Whalen's men had just done a count and admitted that figure was probably low.

Speakeasies operated in the basements of fashionable Fifth Avenue mansions, in Park Avenue penthouses, in Greenwich Village cellars, in two-family dwellings in the Bronx, in the back of Bay Ridge hardware stores, even in Wall Street office buildings. They flourished behind facades of soft-drink parlors, restaurants, and tearooms. There was one on the East Side with an exterior that looked like a synagogue.

None was as well appointed as the House of Morgan with its blues-in-the-night music, snazzy decor, and bootleg liquor with the kick of a mule. Helen's was also the place where a broker could pick up some of the youngest and most delectable whores in town.

Both Houses of Morgan—Jack's and Helen's—flourished, in part, because it was the hey-day of easy money. Both required introduction before entry. But once inside, the specialist facilities offered by each House were at the disposal of their privileged clientele.

In the offices of the New York *Times,* reporters prepared end-of-year stories.

The main foreign news concerned the vigil Londoners were keeping outside Buckingham Palace, where King George was gravely ill.

Almost equal space was given to an account of Berliners preparing to hail 1929 "with old-time joy," when they would consume some 9 million "holeless" doughnuts, drink 500,000 gallons of beer, and set off tens of millions of fireworks.

On the home front, the impending inauguration at noon on January 1 of Franklin D. Roosevelt as governor of New York, taking over from the much loved Al Smith, would be front-page news. But it would be Wall Street that would again dominate next day's newspaper.

Working steadily, financial editor Alexander Dana Noyes laid out his pages, editing copy brought to his desk.

One story noted that "violent advances in the last hour by a handful of market leaders featured yesterday's extremely large operations on the Stock Exchange. The volume of trading was the heaviest since December 10." This, the paper would report, came as a "surprise to Wall Street, where the last day of the year is often, by tradition, given over to a few cash sales."

Another page recorded the day's sales at 4,887,700 shares, bringing the total for 1928 to 920,550,032 stocks traded—a new record.

The money market had also closed on a brisk, hopeful note. The foreign markets, especially London and Berlin, had made modest gains.

Noyes was a veteran financial editor, respected and even feared in Wall Street.

Twice during 1928—in the market breaks of June and December— he had predicted that the bull market was over. Though proven wrong, he had doggedly clung to his belief that it would only be a matter of time before the boom ended. In his view there was no way the present spiraling trend could continue.

He had told his reporters: "Something has to give. It's like an earthquake. The further you are from the last one, the closer you are to the next."

Noyes's instincts told him not only that a stock market crash was coming but that when it came it would flatten Wall Street. That would be the day the bubble burst.

Superintendent William Crawford would not leave the Exchange until the gallery and floor were completely clear of revelers. Then, his gavel safely locked away in his office, he put on his topcoat, said "Happy New Year" to a watchman, and walked out of the building.

Crawford found himself in an almost deserted Wall Street. It was now dark, and "the money"—his generic term for brokers, bankers, and financial men of all kinds—had departed, leaving the area to a few clerks working late on their ledgers. It was the time of the day Crawford found most witching: There were few people abroad to detract from the "awesome power" he sensed around him.

From where he stood, looking directly east past the six short blocks to the river, even in the gloom Crawford knew that Wall Street was not quite straight; it had a slight kink in it.

Diagonally across the street from Crawford was the old Subtreasury Building; for the past nine years it had housed minor government offices, including some of the two hundred federal agents responsible for enforcing Prohibition in New York. Next door was the U. S. Assay

Office. On this New Year's Eve the depository held more gold than anywhere else on earth. Daily a trickle of refiners, pawnbrokers, and dentists added to that hoard by turning in gold. Occasionally, Assay officials received a reformed burglar, anxious to make amends by cashing in his loot; nobody asked any questions or called the FBI: The stolen gold was merely bought at market value.

Farther east, on the north side of the street, beside the Assay Office, stood the Bank of Manhattan Company Building, the second highest skyscraper in New York, its pinnacle now lost against the darkened sky. Alongside, on the corner of William Street, stood the more modest Bank of America. Running down toward the river were the offices of the other eighty-nine major banks in the district, the twenty-five trust companies and the fiscal offices of 130 railroads. Sandwiched in between were 57 life insurance companies, 209 fire and marine insurance companies, and over 100 other types of insurance companies. In the side streets with their so-English names—Nassau, Pearl, Water, Front, and South—were also the offices of 15 safe-deposit companies, 20 cable and telegraph companies, 50 coal and iron companies, and hundreds of powerful industrial corporations. Close by were the other exchanges: the Curb Exchange, the Produce Exchange, the Cotton Exchange, the Metals Exchange, the Sugar Exchange, the Maritime Exchange. None was so powerful, so ornate, as the Stock Exchange, yet each had its part to play in maintaining Crawford's long-held belief that he worked in the financial capital of the world.

Visible proof that this was still so was there for the superintendent to see. The lights at 23 Wall were ablaze. Limousines were parked from that famous entrance to the House of Morgan, past the Equitable Company at Number 35—the home of some of the largest law firms in America—beyond the U. S. Trust Company, whose chairman, John Stewart, had died in office, aged 104. The cars were parked the length of the block down to the Atlantic Building.

Beyond, on the south side of Wall, its frontage filling a whole block, was the massive edifice of the National City Bank, the wealthiest in the country with resources in excess of $2 billion. Bought by the government in 1862 as a site for a customs house at a cost of $11 million, it had been acquired by National City in 1899 for over three times that amount—an indication of how property even in those days had been at a premium in Wall Street. The bank was one of the most beautiful buildings in the street, with its colonnade of pillars, each carved from a single piece of stone and weighing twenty-five tons.

Next door stood the Brown Bros. Building, sometimes known as "little England beyond the sea" because the conservative international bankers who owned it had a weakness for Englishmen, Yale, and the *Atlantic Monthly*.

Still farther down Wall, between Pearl and Water streets, was the Orient Building, next to the home of Steinwender, Stoffregen and Company, coffee importers. Those who worked there quickly became permeated with the odor from roasted sample lots. A similar problem faced those at Number 90 (cocoa) and 109, home of the American Molasses Company.

Tonight, these buildings appeared merely as dark shapes from where Crawford stood. He turned and began to walk briskly west along Wall Street toward Broadway.

His footsteps echoed on sidewalks that were part of the most valuable real estate in the world—a square foot fetched $700. Crawford passed the site for the new Irving Trust Building, which would rise between New Street and Broadway this coming year. Since 1650 only three other buildings had ever been erected on the site. When completed, the Irving skyscraper would dwarf the dingy, decrepit building opposite, housing the First National Bank.

Ahead lay Broadway, where at Number 26, John D. Rockefeller maintained an office he now never visited. Nearby was the historic graveyard of Trinity Church, whose dark Gothic spire rose majestically in the concrete canyons of Wall and Broadway.

The church, like many others in the city, had grown rich from the market; investment had allowed it to become a large Manhattan landowner, with properties whose book value stood at over $15 million bringing in annual rentals of $1 million.

Not for the first time did it occur to William Crawford that Wall Street was the perfect example of how religion and big business could be compatible.

Over three thousand miles away, in the late afternoon sun of northern California—in a time zone three hours earlier than New York—a cloud of dust whirled past a far more simply built church than the gloomy splendor of Trinity. It was one of the white-bleached adobe structures Catholic missionaries had erected last century along the Pacific Coast.

A glowing red light and familiar wailing came from within the moving cloud. Ahead, in the small town, children were running excitedly toward the approaching noise.

In the heart of the traveling dust storm, Joe Garcia changed gear. The grimed Rolls-Royce, a 1926 model, reduced speed and purred down the town's main street.

The fire-alarm light welded onto the car's classically styled hood continued to glow, the siren to wail.

This regulation-type equipment, purchased from the San Francisco Fire Department six weeks before, still troubled chauffeur Garcia. Such a desecration, he felt, "was enough to make Misters Rolls and Royce wish the wheel had never happened."

No one except his passenger, Garcia contended, would have ruined the styling of the car simply to facilitate his business interests. But the chauffeur knew that his employer had "no feel for the Rolls tradition— he didn't even know where the gas went in. He only had one interest— his work."

With the approval of the California State Legislature, the handmade Rolls-Royce had been classified a fire truck and Garcia's employer, banker Amadeo Peter Giannini, designated an honorary fire marshal.

The idea was suggested by the impatient Giannini as the easiest way to overcome a state law restricting all but police and fire department vehicles to thirty-five miles an hour. It was only proper that the transportation used by a fire marshal carried at least a siren and light. When Garcia had suggested the light be kept inside the car, the banker had shaken his massive Roman emperor's head and insisted that it be mounted on the hood.

During the past weeks the towns of northern California had witnessed the extraordinary sight of the Rolls racing down their streets as if it was on its way to a three-alarm call.

Giannini felt he needed to travel at a speed of eighty miles an hour because it was the only way he could keep pace with his expanding financial empire.

Even on the road he had no time to relax. As the Rolls sped effortlessly over the dusty, bumpy dirt tracks linking one settlement to another, its owner pored over paper work—a penalty he cheerfully paid for being one of the most important bankers in America.

On the last day of the year, they had been on the road since dawn, traveling from one bank to another. Lunch had been hurried because Giannini had an important appointment to keep in a small town north of San Francisco. When they reached it, on time, the banker learned the meeting had been canceled. He had given vent to his anger with a few well-chosen expletives; fully aroused, the multimillionaire could outcurse a longshoreman.

Only Garcia would have dared intrude on Giannini's brooding silence as they sped back toward the city. The chauffeur reminded his employer that Giannini was to preside over the family's traditional New Year's Eve dinner that night.

"Boss, you'd better get a shave; otherwise Mrs. A.P.'s gonna be mad at me."

Giannini grinned, his anger gone. The thought of Clorinda mad at anyone, let alone the devoted Garcia, was impossible for him to contemplate. His wife, the same age as himself, fifty-eight, had during all their marriage shown a forbearance and tolerance he marveled over. Clorinda had never raised her voice or complained; she had always loyally supported him in every risk he took; she was, he confided to his friends, "the perfect Italian wife."

The Rolls stopped outside the town barbershop.

Garcia hoped it was empty, the barber ready.

Giannini had not shaved himself for twenty years—regarding it as "non-productive and time consuming." He had told Garcia: "In the time I would take to shave, I could read a company report—and make a decision that could, maybe, bring in a million dollars. Maybe more."

Impressed, the chauffeur had set up a unique tonsorial network. During the past year, as Giannini expanded his banking enterprises throughout California—in between entrenching his position in Wall Street—Garcia briefed every barber he came across that whenever he pulled up in a Rolls, the barber must be prepared instantly to attend his master. The chauffeur promised a quarter tip on top of the ten-cent charge for the shave.

Escorting his master into the shop, Garcia was relieved to see it was empty; there was no risk of anybody pestering the banker for advice about the stock market, something that frequently happened nowadays as Giannini became one of the most quoted figures on the state of the American economy. His shaggy eyebrows, bristling mustache, and bruiser's nose stared out of hundreds of newspapers, the photographs accompanying stories about his predictions and financial moves. The fiercely proud Garcia felt that no newspaper photo conveyed the most striking of all Giannini's features—his eyes: "They could see through a person, into his heart and mind. And they were the mirror of A.P.'s own soul."

Seated in the tilted barber's chair, Giannini's eyes were now closed, his face smothered by hot towels.

Garcia watched the barber carefully whet a razor. The chauffeur had an abiding fear that someday a crank would harm the man he loved with that special affection only one Italian man has for another. Distanced by money and power, the two men were nevertheless closely linked by their similar backgrounds. They shared the same pride in family, Church, and America.

To protect Giannini, the chauffeur carried a Colt .38 in an armpit holster. Every weekend, at the San Francisco police armory, Garcia practiced shooting. He was skilled enough to kill a man at fifty feet. He hoped he would never have to shoot. Yet he knew that if it came to "a choice between A.P. and anybody, then I wouldn't hesitate to kill."

Giannini had always commanded such loyalty.

Perhaps it stemmed from that day in October 1904, when, barely thirty-four years old, Giannini had quit the produce business in order to found the first "people's bank" in America. The odds were stacked against him: he had no real banking experience, no connections "in high places." San Francisco had a history of "big banks for big people." In spite of being the financial capital of the West, its banks really only catered for the wealthy—upstate ranchers and the like—and mines, lumber mills, and city developments. A bank would loan a million dollars to buy a ranch or extend a railroad as quickly as it would refuse a man fifty dollars to improve his home. The poor were driven to the loan sharks who charged them exorbitant interest.

Giannini decided to change that, opening the Bank of Italy for the masses. Three thousand shares of stock were issued. No stockholder, including Giannini, held more than one hundred shares. Over half the shares were in the hands of 1,620 stockholders; among them were a grocer, a fish dealer, a teamster, and a druggist. Many held no more than two or three shares.

Every day Giannini tramped the Italian district of North Beach, where he had grown up, touting for business. Within eighteen months he had persuaded a stream of small investors to put their money in the Bank of Italy, where it earned 3½ per cent interest, rather than to leave it in a tin on a shelf in the back parlor.

The other city bankers—aristocrats raised and nurtured in the timeless traditions of the Rothschilds of London and Lazard Frères of Paris—looked with contempt at Giannini scrabbling for business. To some it was no better than they expected of an Italian who had once sold vegetables, and was now treating the serious business of banking as if it were the same as peddling grapefruit. They talked disparagingly of the "Dago Banker," a man never to be admitted to that intimate circle dominated by the American National Bank and the men of Wells Fargo.

Then, at 5:13 A.M. on April 18, 1906, came the great leveler. Earthquake devastated San Francisco, swiftly followed by a raging inferno.

The city badly needed a calming gesture. Giannini provided it. While other bankers, their money sealed in vaults inside buildings too dangerous to enter or buried beneath tons of rubble, were reduced to sending reassuring telegrams to the stock exchanges in New York, London, Paris, and Berlin, Giannini executed a financial coup. He had rescued $80,000 in cash from his bank at the height of the fire. It was all he had to cover deposits of $846,000. If there was a "run"—if depositors decided to withdraw their savings in full—the Bank of Italy would face a crisis from which it could probably never recover.

Giannini decided on a calculated gamble. He would use the $80,000, hidden in his living room fireplace, for loans to help people to restart businesses and rebuild their homes. The bank would lend at a fair interest; and by doing so, Giannini hoped also to attract enough new depositors to balance the loans. The risks were huge. The loans would have to be carefully parceled out. He could not be certain he would be repaid. He had no guarantee he could attract new depositors.

But the rewards, if the plan worked, would be substantial. They were —and the Bank of Italy prospered.

A year later, during the financial panic of 1907, which J. P. Morgan finally quelled, Giannini laid in so much gold that he had to hire storage space; his was the only bank in California able to meet all the demands of its customers. Thousands more new depositors flocked to the Bank of Italy.

The dream that had sustained Giannini for years began to come closer. He was sure the day could not be far off before branch banking became a reality, when it would be possible to find Bank of Italy branches in every state and eventually in every city and most towns.

World War I temporarily ended that hope. But by 1919 it had returned, stronger than before, driving Giannini to break into the New York banking world.

Characteristically, he went first to the East Side, with its modest family homes and small shops. For the moment he ignored Wall Street, and, as they had done in San Francisco fifteen years earlier, the great banking houses of New York looked down their noses at this upstart. The betting in the smoking and club rooms was that the "Eyetie" would not last a year.

Giannini bought two banks, the East River and the Bowery National. He amalgamated them and founded the Bancitaly Corporation as a holding company. Ten years later its assets totaled $250 million and its stockholders numbered 75,000.

Mastering corporate procedure—Giannini claimed he had "more corporate balls whirling in the air than a juggler at a county fair"—he incorporated and consolidated in a series of virtuoso performances that brought bank after bank into his fold.

In 1927 he engineered the greatest merger in U.S. banking history, when, in one fell swoop, the 174-branch Liberty Bank of America *and* the substantial Italian American of San Francisco were absorbed by the Bank of Italy. It put Giannini on a par with the biggest banks in New York. It put Wall Street on notice. The New York *Times* issued its seal of approval on October 30, 1927:

SON OF IMMIGRANT INTERESTS BANKERS
Success of A. P. Giannini,
Who Founded Bank of Italy, an International Marvel

HIS METHODS ALL HIS OWN
Ignoring Precedents, San Francisco Man
has Developed a $500,000,000 Institution

From that day on the press never left him alone. They, and millions of their readers, watched open-mouthed as Giannini executed a series of complex and interwoven deals which allowed him to invest $162.5 million in foreign stocks and bonds, "as a cushion against the time when depression could affect domestic conditions."

Everybody thought that was Giannini's little joke, the "Dago Banker" allowing his background to show. Everybody, said the pundits, knew that this was late 1927 and America was already firmly gripped in the beginnings of a boom.

Giannini continued to invest abroad, choosing such gilt-edged stocks as those of the Bank of England, the Bank of Ireland, the Banque de France, the Reichsbank, and the Suez Canal.

By January 1928 he owned 289 banks, including the relatively small but prestigious 116-year-old Bank of America.

Lauded by the world's press—reporters traveled from all over Europe to interview him and he was attracting more coverage than many of the stars of the Hollywood studios he had invested in—Giannini recognized that the enemy was at the door. He identified them, correctly, as Wall Street speculators, boosting his bank's shares beyond their true worth in order to make a killing for themselves. In one day he saw Bancitaly stocks soar ten points—ten dollars—on the San Francisco and New York stock exchanges.

He fought back, mobilizing his considerable talent for publicity; in February 1928 he served historic warning on the public not to buy his stocks as they were overvalued.

The speculation continued. "The Great Bull of Wall Street was in the corral and everybody was trying to hitch a ride" was how Joe Garcia saw it.

The chauffeur remembered how "bitterly angry" Giannini was as he prepared to depart on a planned business and vacation trip to Europe.

That was in April 1928.

Six weeks later, on June 11, a cablegram reached Giannini in Milan. It brought the first news of "Blue Monday." Shares in Bank of Italy had fallen 160 points; Bank of America was down 120 points; Bancitaly Corporation had plunged 86 points; United Security 80 points.

To Garcia, "the speculators had made their killing, packed their tents and left A.P. bleeding to death."

Six thousand miles away in Italy, Giannini gave the first orders to transfuse stock from one company to another. Then, as he was packing his bags to come home, he was struck down with polyneuritis. Hospitalized in Rome, he spent the next two painful months waging a relentless fight to recover his health and financial fortune.

On September 5, 1928, fit again, but considerably thinner, his face lined and gaunt, he reached San Francisco. His first words to Garcia were: "Those bastards will never do this to us again."

The chauffeur couldn't trust himself to speak.

In silence they drove to Giannini's office in midtown San Francisco. Hundreds of people overflowed the bank and onto the sidewalks to welcome him. Thousands of floral tributes turned the austere building into a gigantic florist's; it would be days before the sweet fragrance disappeared.

Close to tears himself, Giannini had choked: "It's good to be back."

Those were his last public words for a month. He moved from his modest family home in San Mateo to a room in the Mark Hopkins Hotel in the city. To Garcia "this was a sure sign something big was brewing."

Even the prescient chauffeur could not have guessed how big. The financial world was itself stunned when, on October 11, Giannini announced he was consolidating his multifaceted organization under one speculation-tight umbrella. It would be the greatest holding company in the world, inviolate he hoped, from the attention of even the most rapacious of the Wall Street bears. Giannini named it Transamerica Corporation. It was capitalized at $217.5 million, "a mere pittance just to get things started."

Tucked away from the "grubby speculators" Giannini so despised, behind the shiny-new Transamerica shield, were: Bank of Italy, Bancitaly Corporation, National Bancitaly Company, California Joint Stock Land Bank, Bancitaly Agricultural Credit Corporation, Bancitaly Mortgage Company, America Commercial Corporation, Pacific National Fire Insurance Company, and the Capital Company.

From now on only Transamerica stock would be dealt with on the open market. It was first listed on the San Francisco Exchange on November 15, and was an immediate success.

The very next day Giannini had the fire-alarm light mounted on the Rolls-Royce which was now outside the barbershop and attracting a growing crowd of children and adults.

When Garcia and Giannini emerged, a man shouted: "What kind of a fire truck is this?"

"A special kind. It puts out speculative fires!"

Grinning hugely at his jest, Amadeo Peter Giannini climbed into the back and instantly returned to his paper work. He was glad to see that an East Coast newspaper had given prominence to the news that he had divested himself of some $1.5 million, the bulk of his personal fortune, in favor of an agricultural research program at the University of California. The paper had approvingly reported: "He retains only that amount necessary comfortably to maintain and educate his family. He has not, and never had, an ambition to make or save money for himself, but has devoted his time toward the building up of a great bank system which his employees eventually will own."

Giannini was further pleased with a syndicated Scripps-Howard report calling him the "J. P. Morgan of the Pacific." The reporter was the first to note that Transamerica included only a part of the total Giannini empire. Outside the paling was the Bank of America with its 30 branches in New York, the 73 branches of the United Securities Bank, the 28 branches of the Merchants' National in Los Angeles, and the 290 branch banks he controlled in California. All were deemed to be strong enough to withstand any speculative pressures. The writer lauded Giannini as "the father of the branch-bank idea."

What nobody knew in these closing hours of 1928 was just how far Giannini was willing to go to ensure his idea grew to maturity.

He leaned forward and shouted at Garcia.

"Morgan and the Fed are in for a surprise or two next year."

"Yes, boss."

Garcia knew who Morgan was: "that snotty bunch in Wall Street who didn't like Catholics or Jews." But the reference to the "Fed" puzzled him. He could not imagine how his employer was going to surprise the FBI.

The chauffeur was about to ask. But Giannini was once more immersed in paper work. It never occurred to Joe Garcia that his passenger was referring to the Federal Reserve Board—or that he had just heard a declaration of war.

A different declaration—but equally portentous—was made in New York that evening by John Jacob Raskob, a forty-nine-year-old millionaire who had boosted his already huge fortune by successfully speculating in Giannini stock.

For months the cherubic-faced Raskob, who was born in the slums of New York's Hell's Kitchen and went on to help develop General Motors, had kept the staggering plan to himself.

Tonight Raskob was ready to unveil his dream to the man he had chosen to make it possible.

William Lamb had a considerable reputation as one of the architects changing the skyline of midtown Manhattan. Every day one tall building followed another into the air, many of them rising from Lamb's blueprints.

He had not been surprised to be summoned to Raskob's palatial suite at the Carlton House, but once inside, he felt he had walked into a library; every available wall was lined with books. They overflowed from tables onto the floor. The architect's trained eye noted the absence of clocks; the financier had an aversion to timepieces of any kind. The brightly colored shirt Raskob wore was a further pointer that here was one more of that eccentric new breed of millionaires who manipulated in Wall Street with consummate ease.

Lamb had grown rich catering to their whims. He'd given Jesse Livermore a new office, refurbished William Crapo Durant's apartment, advised a dozen other big market men on their new homes or office towers.

He had found it profitable to study his clients. Consequently Lamb already knew a great deal more about the secretive Raskob than the short and burly millionaire would have cared to reveal. The architect knew that Raskob abhorred smoking, though his father was a noted cigar maker in Alsace; that the financier hated to drive, in spite of having made his initial fortune from automobiles. Raskob kept two Cadillacs and a chauffeur but insisted on walking everywhere in New York. His wife refused to live in the city, preferring to remain in Wilmington, Delaware, with their eleven children. There Raskob owned a palatial manor house, Archmere, on the Delaware River. In summer the family moved to their rustic retreat, Pioneer Point, Maryland, where they grew flax and tended their splendid stable of horses. The only blight on this idyllic life-style came in the summer of '28 when the Raskobs' second son, William, died in an auto accident.

None of this knowledge had prepared Lamb for what Raskob wanted.

The two men walked to the Waldorf-Astoria Hotel, on the corner of Fifth Avenue and Thirty-third Street.

"It's coming down," said Raskob casually. "You're going to see to that. Just as you're going to put in its place the tallest building on earth."

Too stunned to reply, Lamb followed the financier into the 450-

room red-brick-and-sandstone structure, patterned after the German Renaissance style and built at a cost of $5 million in 1893. During the subsequent thirty-five years, the hotel had firmly established itself as a magnet for New York society.

Tonight, extravagant costume balls and bacchanalian feasts were scheduled for the gold-and-burgundy-draped restaurants and ball-rooms.

Yet, in spite of all its outward spendor, the hotel was an expensive anachronism; taxes and esclating operating costs ate away the profits.

Weeks before, having failed to have former New York governor Alfred E. Smith elected President of the United States—Herbert Hoover had trounced Smith in the election—Raskob, back to wheeler-dealing in Wall Street, had heard a whisper that the hotel was up for sale.

Working from the twenty-third-floor offices he shared with Pierre Du Pont at 230 Park Avenue, Raskob had sounded out trusted friends, among them James J. Riordan, president of the New York County Trust Company. Their inquiries confirmed that the hotel could be bought cheaply.

Now, pausing in the cavernous lobby with its potted palms and uniformed flunkies, Raskob repeated he would shortly buy the hotel, raze it to the ground, and that in its place Lamb would design and supervise the erection of the ninth wonder of the world. It would be a permanent monument to "the American way of life that allowed a poor boy to make his fortune in Wall Street."

John J. Raskob already had a name for the superstructure. He would call it the Empire State Building.

Claire Giannini could relax. Her contribution to the New Year's Eve family dinner had not provoked criticism. Her father merely glanced at the gleaming new silverware that Claire had purchased to replace the worn bone-handled flatware used since she was a child.

Tonight, Giannini had not unbuttoned his collar or removed his jacket before sitting down to the meal. His daughter was pleased at these small signs of propriety in her father; she dearly loved him but silently despaired whether he would ever develop the sartorial elegance of the men in those fashionable houses back East. She had often wondered what they would think of the two-story Giannini family home in San Mateo, seventeen miles from San Francisco. She still found it difficult to explain to even the most understanding of her wealthy friends that "Papa isn't interested in worldly possesions."

As long as she could remember, her father had firmly resisted any attempts to make him dress or live in the style of one of the world's most successful bankers. He had rejected any suggestions that he should have his suits tailored, even though nowadays he was regularly meeting such men of influence as the Pope, President-elect Hoover, and dictator Benito Mussolini. The last time she had raised the question, on the eve of their visit to Rome, he had angrily shaken his head and reminded Claire that he had not given her a fine education to worry about such trivial matters.

For years she had known that "Papa was grooming me to take over some of his responsibilities." While other teenagers concerned themselves with clothes, Claire studied balance sheets. She now knew more about corporate matters than many of the lawyers who advised her father. She could spot the faults in even the most polished prospectus, and had an unerring instinct for an overinflated budget. She took quiet pride in being called "a chip off the old block."

Claire knew that her aggressiveness and command of boardroom strategy frightened off many men; other potential suitors were shown the door because her father suspected they were fortune hunters. Her mother had told her that when "the right man comes along you will have our blessing."

Having failed to persuade her father to improve his wardrobe—he still owned only five ready-made suits bought in a local department store—Claire had tried to titivate the family home.

Most of the furniture was bought the year she was born, 1904. Twenty-four years later it showed increasing signs of wear and tear. But Giannini stubbornly insisted that nothing should be replaced without his sanction.

Claire still vividly recalled the time she suggested that the dining room suite be replaced.

"I'm not made of money," her father had said.

"But you make so much!"

"For others, Claire, for others."

Giannini had been trying for years to convince not only his family but the whole world that he had no wish to be a millionaire or adopt the life-style of one. In 1924 he had announced that he would no longer draw a salary as president of the $115 million Bancitaly Corporation. He told a banking magazine: "I work without thinking of myself."

Claire found it hard to accept the frugality her father preached. She still felt the need to protest his refusal to spend money on the family when the newspapers were reporting a new bequest to some school or university. After hearing her out, Giannini would invariably say: "Look how unhappy money can make you! Be like me and have no interest in it for yourself, and you'll be a lot happier."

She had yet to find an answer to that argument.

Nor could she now think of a suitable reply when her father finally commented on the new silver.

"Very nice," he pronounced. "But it's going to need regular polishing. Another job for you, Claire!"

The meal was barely over when the family's privacy was interrupted. The wire services wanted Giannini's financial prediction for the coming year. He reminded reporters that in this era of unbounded prosperity over four thousand banks had failed during the past six years. It was a sign that something was wrong. If things didn't improve, there could be serious trouble ahead.

It was meaty copy for turn-of-the-year stories from a banker who knew the value of publicity—even though it would bring him growing resentment from within the walls of the single most powerful financial house in the world, one that preferred to conduct its affairs in the closest secrecy. Only in the direst emergency would any public utterance be considered by the House of Morgan.

Engines idling, the line of limousines stood guard along Wall Street, their liveried chauffeurs sensing that the hallowed ritual inside the squat, fortresslike building was coming to an end. By tradition the first car was parked immediately outside the doors of 23. It belonged to John Pierpont Morgan, Jr.; "Jack" to members of the British royal family and a few other intimates; "Mr. Morgan the Younger" to bankers around the world; "Sir" to almost all his partners and staff.

The second car in the line belonged to Thomas Lamont, senior partner and acknowledged deputy to Jack Morgan. Lamont was the firm's diplomat. His charm had won over financiers in Peking, brokers in Berlin, and corporate presidents in all those many countries that had been Morganized—a term that brought pain to the well-bred faces in the House of Morgan.

The other cars, uniformly black apart from discreet chrome trim, belonged to the other partners, able financiers like Parker Gilbert and George Whitney, the elder brother of the Exchange vice-president.

Late though the hour was, they waited at their desks in an otherwise deserted building; the clerks and stenographers had long gone. The heavy outer doors of 23 and its walls bore no identification, offered no clue that from here, from the time it was built in 1914, Morgans had been quietly financing governments and the business interests of the world.

Tonight, as he did every New Year's Eve, Jack Morgan was calculating the accrued profits from the past twelve months. All day—from Europe, from Japan, from Australia, South Africa, from anywhere and anybody that the House had financed this past year—had come details of the interest and other payments due for such help.

By custom, Jack Morgan would retain 50 percent of the net profits. The other half would be divided among his partners.

The autocratic articles of partnership had been established by the most celebrated of the Morgans, Pierpont, Jack's father. Any dispute between the partners must be settled by the senior Morgan in the firm. His decision "shall be final." The senior Morgan could compel any other partner to resign by dissolving his partnership. There was no redress or appeal; no capital contribution was asked of new partners.

The philosophy of old-fashioned hierarchical private banking was laid down by an even earlier Morgan, Junius Spencer Morgan, and refined by Pierpont to a total reliance on economic trust enforced by social status. A Jew would never be invited to become a partner. No statement of the firm's financial condition would ever be issued to depositors. The House would never lend money to anyone who could merely provide sufficient collateral. It would only do business with those with whom it chose to do business. The same guiding principles applied to the House's acceptance of depositors: they must be clients before being allowed to place their money with the firm. To become a client required an introduction—from another client, a person, in Jack's view, who was "a good, straight fellow."

Seated at his rolltop desk, in the same anteroom by the front entrance where all the senior partners sat at identical individual rolltop desks, each with a gleaming brass spittoon by its side, Jack Morgan epitomized all that he himself sincerely believed was "good" and "straight."

He had aged gracefully; now at sixty-two, he had an avuncular twinkle, a snow-white mustache, and startling black eyebrows. He dressed like his friend, England's Prince of Wales: somberly for the office, tweedily for the country estate he kept at Glen Cove on Long Island, stylishly for the mansion he maintained at 231 Madison Avenue. There was another town house in London, and a shooting lodge in Scotland to which Morgan invited the royal family from time to time for a spot of grouse shooting.

Since April 1, 1913, the day his father died, Jack had run the firm. His first innovation was to introduce the nineteen other partners to afternoon tea, English-style. From then on, bone-china cups and saucers for tea and plates of cucumber sandwiches and scones would be served to the partners in their private offices on the second floor. The ritual enhanced the impression that the House of Morgan was the most exclusive and influential club in the American financial world. Afternoon tea blended with the woodburning fireplaces, the sofas and easy chairs, creating the feeling that big business was the province of gentlemen.

When death created a vacancy, Jack Morgan chose a new partner with care. Born to the purple—the unkind said that when he died Jack would render separate accounts to Caesar and to God—he was determined that all his partners would fit his concepts of physical and mental perfection.

Physically they tended to be tall, slim, handsome, fair with copious heads of hair that turned impressively white. Twenty years earlier a Wall Street wag had coined the adage that "when the angels of God took unto themselves wives among the daughters of men, the result was Morgan partners."

This still held true in 1928. The Morgan partners, like thoroughbred dogs or horses, shared not only physical kinship but a similar mental outlook which was a carefully controlled mix if puritanism, class-consciousness, and the solemn self-righteousness of late nineteenth-century American Protestantism. No partner, or employee, could work for the firm if he was divorced; sins of the flesh, if discovered, meant dismissal. Jack Morgan's favorite maxim was: "Do your work; be honest; keep your word; help when you can; be fair; be a good, straight fellow."

That dogma had carried him through a number of tribulations. There was that dreadful day in 1915 when Jack had encountered a would-be assassin at the Glen Cove estate. The man was armed with two primed revolvers and a stick of dynamite. Jack had not hesitated to tackle and overpower him. The resultant publicity had been more painful to face than the potential killer. There was that even worse moment when on September 16, 1920, a bomb had exploded outside the firm. Jack had been on vacation in England. His eldest son, Julius, had been one of the five partners in the building; all escaped unhurt except Julius, who suffered a minor cut. But the ensuing publicity lasted for weeks. Only the iron control his own father had taught him enabled Jack Morgan to cope with the excesses of the press.

The death of Pierpont Morgan grieved Jack greatly, though it would have been unthinkable for him to show public sorrow. Morgan the Elder was a capitalist in the accepted mold—often ruthlessly energetic in his dealings. His son preferred a low-key role as organizer and executive, willing to deputize, content to retain overall policy control while leaving the daily operations to his partners.

Yet sadness continued to blight his private life. In 1924 his mother died; a year later, his wife, Jessie, succumbed from sleeping sickness.

Not even Julius really suspected how deep the pain penetrated his father's mind. By the time Jack Morgan buried Jessie he had developed such self-control that nothing could shake it. He believed this was expected of a gentleman.

In the fifteen years he had led the firm, it had lost some of its temporal power in domestic affairs. The Federal Reserve Act of 1913 had heralded the end of Morgan and Company's *de facto* status as America's central bank. Since 1920, the emergence of gigantic corporations, able to finance their own growth from retained earnings, had eroded the Morgan purse-strong power over U.S. business.

Even so, the Morgan style, with Jack at the helm, had been evident with the acquisition, jointly with the Du Ponts, of control of General Motors in 1920.

Abroad, Morganization was as potent as ever. In 1921 the House floated a substantial French Government bond issue in the United States. Next, it backed and sold a Chinese bond issue. The Polish and Romanian governments were financed in 1922. The following year, Morgan kept the Cuban and Austrian governments solvent. In 1924 the firm loaned $100 million to the Bank of France—and gave Japan a badly needed injection of capital. Between 1925 and 1928, the House loaned so much money, selling bonds, to so many countries that it inevitably brought unwelcome publicity.

After Morgan had loaned Cuba money, the Havana regime threatened tax measures that would discriminate against Americans. Jack sent a man to Havana. The Cubans backed off. From Moscow came an orchestrated cry that "Morgan capitalism was trying to run the world." In 1925 Thomas Lamont spent weeks in Rome with Mussolini and his finance minister, Count Volpi. Lamont returned home to recommend that the House undertake the sale of $100 million in bonds, plus another $50 million in loans. A syndicate was formed, Morgan taking $250,000 for managing it, and lending its name to sell bonds. The syndicate—of which the firm was the linchpin—made a profit of $4.5 million. The stormy publicity that ensued genuinely puzzled Jack Morgan; to him propping up Italy's Fascist regime was good business.

This past year had been mercifully free of headlines for a man who cringed every time he read his own name in the press; he devoutly hoped the coming year would be the same.

On the filial front he had promising expectations for the next twelve months. Julius was showing signs of real business acumen; he was now handily placed on the board of General Motors and United States Steel. His second boy, Henry Sturgis, was about to become a partner. Soon he, too, would be acquiring the directorships which allowed the firm to keep its fingers firmly on the financial pulse of the world.

Between them the partners held directorships in a list of companies that filled thirty-five pages of closely typed foolscap.

On this the last day of 1928, Jack Morgan truly believed that the House was at its financial zenith.

Yet, in spite of its continuing rock-solid base, there had been changes he and his partners had so far failed to appreciate. In the era of Pierpont Morgan, respect and admiration formed the basis of the American public's attitude toward the House of Morgan. But now, under Jack, there was a mounting feeling of awe and distrust that such vast wealth and power should be invested in so few hands.

With Amadeo Peter Giannini winning increasing public praise for his rejection of amassing a private fortune, Jack Morgan, it was also widely reported, was himself now worth $500 million. Nobody really knew because, as in all things, Morgan kept his own financial affairs closely guarded from prying eyes.

Nevertheless, on this New Year's Eve, he was about to increase his income by a sizable amount.

His calculations complete, Jack Morgan rose to his feet, clutching a handful of envelopes.

Moving from one rolltop desk to another, he handed an envelope to each of his partners. They murmured words of gratitude. Each envelope contained a bonus for the year's work—a check for not less than $1 million.

Soon afterward the limousines left Wall Street to the care of a patrolling policeman, shivering in the first snow flurries of 1929.

CHAPTER TWO

A VIEW FROM ABROAD

Across the Atlantic, the people of Great Britain began the new year with the feeling that, whatever it brought, it could only be an improvement on the one just ended; 1928 had been disappointing, with the newspapers constantly having to report that the hoped-for recovery in trade had not happened.

Even so, for Clarence Charles Hatry in London, 1929 had got off to a good start. There was so much happening to catch the attention of reporters that the mercurial financier doubted if even the most intuitive of the new breed of muck-raking journalists in Fleet Street would inquire into what he was planning.

The popular press, long his enemy, was too busy describing the latest police raids on the capital's nightclubs, where guests had been booked for drinking out of hours, "that strange sin whose enormity is only exceeded by paederasty in Anglo-Saxon countries," one reporter declared. Male inversion was also under the fullest police persecution and newspaper scrutiny. Once homosexuality had been something scarcely comprehensible; it was King George V himself who had said in 1914 with genuine astonishment that "I thought men like that shot themselves." Now, homosexuals, with their brittle humor and elegance, encouraged by Freud, Jung, Havelock Ellis, and Edward Carpenter, broke cover, congregated in certain pubs, and were driven from bar to bar across the City.

Certain sections of the press found it boosted their circulation to be moral and sensational at the same time. The arts were still a favorite target; the *Daily Mail,* apostle of conservatism, regularly worked itself up into a fury over some book or play.

Typically, on this first Thursday morning in January, the *Daily Herald* had burst the great new cumulus of rumors building up around Thomas Edward Lawrence, a man many regarded as Britain's quintessential hero of the desert. For months now, fresh from his escapades in Arabia, T. E. Lawrence had been in Karachi, translating Homer. But the *Herald* doubted if he was engaged in such a peaceful pastime. Calling Lawrence the "arch-spy of the world," the Socialist newspaper suggested that Lawrence was in Karachi to organize a right-wing revolution.

Hatry, an astute judge of such matters, knew that the rekindled interest in Lawrence could last for weeks. He also knew too well how savage the press could be.

The scar tissue, the result of a hundred printed barbs, was still there from a decade before, concealed beneath Hatry's Savile Row suit, striped shirt, and carefully knotted tie.

His specialty then, and now, was stock speculation on a massive scale combined with a flair for promoting large company amalgamations, which Hatry liked to call part of his grand strategy for the "rationalization of industry." Along the way he had made and lost a number of fortunes.

Hatry's first windfall came in 1912 when he had devised a scheme for emigrants traveling from Central Europe to the United States and Canada. Hundreds of thousands of Poles and Russians passed through the hands of Hatry's agents, whose job it was to ensure them against the risk of rejection when they reached the New World. Hatry's own encounters with "these poor wretches, many drawn from the lower strata of European civilisation," affected him, he would insist, deeply. He felt they would be better directed to the underpopulated areas of the British Empire. The benefits for Britain would be obvious; the emigrants could be put to work developing the "unlimited potential wealth" of the Empire, thus ensuring Britain's continuing preeminent role in the world. As yet, Hatry had not made public this vision.

From 1919, when he formed British Glass Industries, he had fathered a number of industrial mergers; yet, in spite of his undoubted brilliance, the newspapers said that the slightly built company promoter had a habit of overreaching himself, pointing to the 1923 liquidation of his Commercial Corporation of London, and the collapse, in 1926, of British Glass.

Publicity over that unhappy venture was swiftly replaced by a vastly more important event, one that shook not only Hatry but also hundreds of thousands of his fellow countrymen.

One sunny morning in May 1926, long lines of armored cars and thousands of armed troops poured into London. The Conservative

Government had mobilized all its resources to defeat "the enemy"— British organized labor. The Trades Union Congress had called a general strike, and 3.5 million union members stopped work on May 3. Public transport was halted. Factories, mines, and mills were shut. Most newspapers stopped production. In the days that followed, Hyde Park became a vast food storage center, protected, the New York *World* reported, "by enough artillery to kill every living thing in every street in the neighborhood." Battleships were anchored off great ports like Liverpool and Southampton, guns trained on the quayside. These ominous military warnings were matched by equally belligerent policies. The Chancellor of the Exchequer, Winston Churchill, editing the official *British Gazette,* warned that any action taken by the armed forces "will receive both now and afterwards, the full support of His Majesty's Government." Within hours, 30,000 more special constables had been enrolled to swell the total to 200,000. Police measures became draconian; in six days 4,000 strikers were arrested. There were ugly riots in a dozen cities. The *Flying Scotsman,* the nation's most famous rail express, was derailed by saboteurs. Novelist Arnold Bennett, a close friend of Hatry's, confided that the fight would be "short but violent." It was; it lasted nine days, bringing Britain to the brink of revolution. It took a long time for the charm of the Gay Twenties to reassert itself.

The strike over, Hatry prospered. His huge Drapery and General Investment Trust became a part of Debenhams. His other front-runner, Corporation and General Securities, issued £37 million in municipal loans.

But all this was "small beer" for the venture the thirty-nine-year-old Hatry was about to embark upon. He planned to acquire the securities of the United Steel Companies for around £8 million; the companies controlled about 10 percent of Britain's iron and steel industry. Hatry then intended to amalgamate this group with still other independent iron and steel companies in a series of takeovers that would "rationalize" and modernize the entire industry. Eventually, he would resell the bumper merger to the public—earning for himself a handsome profit while at the same time, in his view, doing the country a great service.

Hatry's timing was impeccable. The steel industry was at a low ebb, as were other of the national export industries—coal, textiles, shipbuilding. Foreign competition and contraction of world markets were thought to be causing the increasing unemployment and decreasing profits.

This recession in Britain was a major political issue. Hatry was not alone in believing that a general election must soon be fought on the crucial question of domestic policy. And already Britain's Labour party leader, Ramsay MacDonald, was giving broad hints that his platform would have two basic planks: the end of unemployment and the restoration of national prosperity.

And yet the shrewd, farsighted Hatry could also detect other indications that suggested this was the time to buy into the steel industry. There were hopeful signs for the country's economy, and the social advances of 1928 were continuing; 1929 would see new industrial consolidations, new suburbs created, and above all an increase in the standard of living for everyone in work. The Central Electricity Board, a monopoly just three years old, would continue to replace the large number of small and inefficient power stations with superstations linked to a national grid, scheduled for completion in 1933. Already the consumption of electricity in Britain had increased dramatically. Ten years before only one house in seventeen was wired; now it was one in four, with another 250,000 consumers expected to be added during the year.

Hatry believed, correctly, that the spread of electricity would mark an upturn for the steel industry as other businesses were reallocated in "greenbelt" areas, especially around London. The auto and aircraft companies were already announcing expansion plans.

The financier had also noticed that important developments were beginning to merge in patterns of trading and marketing. Goods were being prepackaged by the manufacturers rather than the shopkeepers. A retailing revolution, born in America, was starting to spread across the country; its flag bearers were Woolworth, Marks & Spencer, Lipton, and Sainsbury. That, too, augured well for the future of the steel industry, which would supply all the tin for millions of cans of meat and fruit coming onto the supermarket shelves. Advertising—the importance of which Hatry was one of the quickest to spot—and the press, linked in a symbiotic relationship, each feeding off the other, were creating a demand for all kinds of consumer goods. And for those who could not afford to pay at once, credit facilities—"tick," "the slate"—were becoming more readily available in even the depressed steel towns.

All these were merely pointers. But to Hatry they confirmed that "now was the time to move into steel."

Yet there was a fatal flaw in his plan—a lack of ready money to achieve his ambitious goal. He would have to raise finance—by one means or another.

Raising money, though not for his private use, was relatively easy for Winston Churchill. As Britain's Chancellor of the Exchequer he could do so merely by introducing new fiscal measures. Since 1924 he had produced four budgets, competently, but without his usual élan. He confided to friends of being mired "in a bog of sums."

Churchill had also brought Britain back onto the gold standard,* suspended since 1919, because he believed it was essential for Britain's prosperity that the "old economic values" be restored. The Bank of England had warmly endorsed the decision. Germany and the United States had already returned to gold parity by the time Britain followed in 1925.

His key role in the general strike embittered many workers. Churchill had defended his actions with a swingeing, "I decline utterly to be impartial as between the Fire Brigade and the fire." In some union quarters, hatred for him still persisted. But for Churchill the strike was now history, material for his memoirs; other matters of state crowded his days.

The groundwork for his fifth budget, to be unveiled on April 1, had to be laid. Churchill knew that a general election was in the offing. Therefore he must deliver a "fighting Budget" which contained a set of vigorous new policies designed to appeal to the voters. If those proposals were favorably received, Prime Minister Stanley Baldwin could go to the hustings with confidence.

The prospect of public political jousting always excited Churchill. Colleagues wondered if this was because of his American heritage; his mother was the daughter of a self-made New York businessman. Churchill greatly admired most things American, more so since his U.S. publisher had established him as a successful author; nowadays he earned more in America from his writing than he did as a cabinet minister.

Almost thirty years had passed since he had last visited his mother's homeland. He was nearly fifty-five years old, a time for one of his periodic stock-takings. Politics was still his first love. But if he should lose office at the next election, then he would have a chance to indulge his next passion—travel. He would go to America to see old friends and to ask them to explain something he found fascinating as a politician, and enticing as an investor—the spiraling bull market of Wall Street.

Some nine hundred miles east of London, in the cramped offices of the Berlin bureau of the Associated Press, reporter Louis Paul Lochner came to the conclusion that the countries of Europe shared almost a common view of what was happening on the American stock market—

---

* *The gold standard:* Stated simply, this is a means whereby the exchange rates between the currencies of participating countries are virtually fixed, due to each country agreeing to tie the value of its currency directly to the value of a fixed weight of gold; the system requires gold to be transported from one participating country to another in order to maintain the existing rate.

either unawareness or indifference. He knew this was not the story his editors in New York wished him to file; their cable was quite specific— he was to collate reactions around Europe to booming Wall Street for a feature that would be a powerful reminder of how the Old World was agog at what was happening in the New.

From the outset Lochner had trouble making facts fit that premise. Apart from Switzerland, almost every country was either beset by its own problems or preoccupied with the political and economic maneuvers of its neighbors.

Russia was in its fifth year of Stalin's New Economic Policy, the Politburo, for the moment, content to accept Stalin's slogan of "Socialism in One Country." There was no other alternative; Russia simply lacked the resources to carry the Bolshevik cause past other frontiers. The Soviets had barely returned to pre-Revolution production. Food shortages were still rampant—the 1928 harvest was short by 2 million tons of the minimum amount of grain needed to feed the urban population. Reports reaching Lochner from Moscow showed Stalin far more preoccupied in January 1929 with having Trotsky exiled to Turkey than with the fluctuations of the Dow Jones Index.†

Lochner doubted whether anybody in Madrid had even heard of the Index. He pondered that the only bulls Spaniards would be interested in were those that died in the Sunday afternoon *corridas*. Those spectacles were welcome relief from the political inertia that paralyzed the country. But if the parliamentary system had been badly bruised under the dictatorship of General Primo de Rivera, Spain was still undergoing economic expansion, financed in part by funds from France. The insular Spanish press devoted most of its space to covering dictator De Rivera's patriotic public speeches—and carefully avoided mention of his private excesses, his drinking and lovemaking with gypsies, his stalking through the streets of Madrid in the small hours, swathed in an opera cloak and alcohol fumes. De Rivera was a tragicomic figure who would make an amusing character sketch on a dull news day for the energetic Lochner.

The experienced reporter hadn't bothered to inquire about Wall Street in the Balkan States. The only time foreign journalists made inquiries among the Slavs, Croats, Slovenes, and Magyars was when their perpetual feuding turned toward full-scale war.

Yugoslavia was gripped in yet another constitutional crisis; King Alexander had just appointed himself dictator.

Italy, under Mussolini, was faced with growing problems that left no

† *Dow Jones Index:* the average daily price of sixty-five selected stocks, all traded on the New York Stock Exchange. It can be misleading: Based on this index, it is possible for the market to be said to be up, when in fact the price of the majority of all stocks traded may be down.

time for thoughts about a boom in Wall Street, or anywhere. Industry and agriculture were already in recession. The prices index had started to fall. A series of currency revaluations had not stemmed the national mood of impending collapse. The few who held them could change a dollar for 19.07 lire. On the Milan Stock Exchange—a majestic six-story brownstone building near the city center—the 177 listed stocks moved sluggishly; only eight of them were foreign shares, none was American.

Austria, in spite of a remarkable economic recovery from the World War, was still riven by a political crisis that had begun in July 1927 when leftists burned down the Palace of Justice in Vienna. The first Austrian Republic died in the flames. Since than armed bands roamed the country, gathering numbers. In reporter Lochner's estimation, it would only be a matter of time before bloody civil war would engulf his favorite city, Vienna.

He had not been surprised to learn that Swiss journalists were following attentively, and commenting with lively interest on, the events in Wall Street.

This was in marked contrast to the attitude of his colleagues in the press which served 40 million French people. Events on the New York Stock Exchange were not mentioned, nor was American stock listed in any of the Republic's newspapers. In this first month of 1929, France was an economic fortress, with a balanced budget, an appreciable foreign trade surplus, full employment, a rise in living standards of 33 percent in the past fifteen years, and the world's second highest gold reserves. Ruefully, Louis Lochner admitted that an insular France could indeed afford to be indifferent to events in Wall Street.

That left Germany.

During his five years in Berlin, Louis Lochner had come to know Germany and its people as well as any foreign correspondent. His connections ranged from Foreign Minister Gustav Stresemann to lowly officials in far-off Bavaria. It was one of those who had tipped Lochner to keep a wary eye on a rabble-rouser in Munich named Adolf Hitler. But stories about a group of fanatics calling themselves Nazis and chanting anti-Semitic slogans were thought hardly newsworthy by Associated Press standards.

Lochner had reported all the great milestones along Germany's road back to cautious acceptance after the World War. First there had been the so-called Dawes Plan of 1924, which required the Germans to pay the Allies about $600 million every year in war reparations, for an indefinite period. As security, the Allies assumed partial control of the German railroads and received part of the tax revenues on tobacco, sugar, beer, and alcohol. Now, in January 1929, Lochner had received a hint that the Germans planned to attend a meeting at The Hague with their former enemies to try and negotiate a more favorable final settlement. There was talk in Berlin of reducing the annual payments and letting them run for a set period; the year to end all reparations being mooted in Reichstag circles was 1988.

The economic-type stories that Lochner filed reflected the dramatically changing conditions Germany had experienced. His arrival in Berlin coincided with the peak of inflation. In 1923 the German mark reached the dizzy figure of 4.2 billion to the dollar. Four years earlier the exchange rate had been 8 to the dollar. As inflation soared, over 300 paper mills and 2,000 printing houses worked round-the-clock to supply the Reichsbank with paper money.

Yet, in one of the most spectacular recoveries in economic history, a year later Germany was one of the great industrial nations of the world.

The short reason for this miracle was that the country had become a prime field for foreign investment. An unprecedented flow of capital, mainly from the United States in the form of short- and long-term loans, enabled German corporations to build new factories and assembly lines. State and city governments floated loans to subsidize parks and theaters; even churches borrowed to build more churches. Some foreign investors were beginning to withdraw their money from Wall Street in order to invest it in Germany, where interest rates were far higher than those prevailing in the United States.

One of Lochner's early reports had shown how the country had absorbed not only American capital but American know-how in management and efficiency. Productivity increased and wages rose.

The latest figures showed unemployment at an insignificant 650,000. But the nation's foreign debt had swollen to $7 billion, much of it in short-term, high-interest loans. To pay that off, Germany was even now looking for more money abroad.

The warning to Wall Street was clear. Reporter Lochner began to type his story.

Directly south of Berlin, in the graceful village of Berchtesgaden, deep in the snowbound Bavarian Alps, Adolf Hitler had received further evidence to support the two most ingrained convictions that sustained him—the danger from Jews and Germany's need for *Lebensraum,* increased living space.

Nazi party membership now stood at 100,000, attracting anti-Communists and all those who believed the Reich must acquire new territory—or "perish at the hand of the Jewish menace."

Looking out of his villa window to the twin mountain peaks that dominated the view, Hitler had come to the conclusion that the principal tasks that faced him were really interwoven: He must obtain *Lebensraum* in the East and at the same time annihilate the Jews.

His recent speeches had increasingly raised the specter of racial degeneration unless those aims were achieved. Now he had something further to fan the flames. His faithful Joseph Goebbels had obtained from America evidence that the Nazis were not alone in castigating world Jewry. For years one of the most distinguished of all Americans had waged a bitter and relentless public campaign against the Jews; his anti-Semitism was only equaled by his hatred of Wall Street. His name was Henry Ford.

CHAPTER THREE

THE DEALER WHEELERS

Standing in a works manager's office, Henry Ford, the unsuspecting recipient of Hitler's gratitude, looked down on a scene that provided him satisfaction. It afforded living proof that the automobile industry was thriving, that the newspapers were not exaggerating when they said there were more cars on the streets of New York than there were in the whole of Europe.

Beyond the gates, guarded by his own private police force, thousands of men were corralled in an open parking lot. Ankle-deep in icy slush, they shuffled toward the entrance to the Rouge plant, the largest of the Ford Motor Company factories in Detroit.

Some of them had been coming to the lot since January 2, 1929. On that day, Ford announced he would begin hiring the first of the thirty thousand additional workers he needed at the Rouge; four hundred men every day would be taken on to meet an unprecedented demand for his cars and trucks. Tens of thousands of workless had hurried to Detroit. The response was another sign of the city's reputation as the mecca of high wages—and an omen that elsewhere in the nation, in spite of the booming stock market, employment was falling.

Those fortunate enough to be hired—at 62.5 cents an hour they were among the highest paid manual workers in the land—found themselves in the most spotless auto plant in the world. Cleanliness was one of Ford's many obsessions. Five thousand men were engaged continuously in keeping the plant spick-and-span. Every month they used eleven thousand gallons of eggshell white and five thousand gallons of machine-blue paint; the colors were chosen by Ford, who believed them beneficial for maintaining "order and morale," another of his fixations.

He also specified the amount of soda to be mixed with the boiling water for scrubbing floors. Trash cans were emptied, on his orders, every 120 minutes, on the dot, around the clock. An intricate network of suction pipes kept the Rouge air dust-free.

Another obsession—one that even brought grudging admiration from the unions, still trying unsuccessfully to force Ford to declare a closed shop—was his attempt to reduce the hazards of the assembly line. From the day he had introduced mass production, Ford was aware that the steady clack-clack of machinery and the soothing whir of wheels as men performed repetitive motions could induce carelessness. A multiplicity of bells, locks, shields, signs, and blood-red paint warned of danger on all machinery capable of cutting or crushing a worker. While Ford had not been able to ban the fatigue and monotony of the shop floor, he had the best safety record in the industry, and probably in the whole country.

Another of his fears was that suddenly an epidemic might halt production—one infected worker could spread illness like wildfire. For years now all telephones, goggles, respirators, "and like sources of infection" were sterilized every day. Company regulations insisted that the slightest scratch or pin prick, "or even a trifling indisposition," be reported immediately to one of the first-aid stations dotted around the plant; a worker returning from the World War said there were more casualty stations at Ford's than he'd seen on the battlefield of France.

A well-staffed hospital, the envy of any outside community, was on permanent standby close to the assembly lines.

Even the natural elements came under Ford's scrutiny. He ordered a uniform temperature for all drinking water: between 55° and 60°. Ford also calculated that every worker needed thirty cubic feet of fresh air each minute in order to work at full capacity. Ducts ensured the Rouge atmosphere changed sixty times an hour.

Well arranged, managed, and maintained, the plant was an extension of its owner, still intently watching the men in the parking lot.

Sharecroppers from Georgia, Mexican beet pickers, unemployed coal miners from Kentucky, and farm workers from all over the Midwest had arrived at 4 A.M., hoping to be hired.

Whether they would be depended on what the New York *Times* compared to a lottery. Ford's hiring agents resorted to a "ten in, ten out" method of selection. The ten men closest to the factory door were taken in for inspection, the second ten arbitrarily told to go away, the third ten, admitted. The rejection of every "even" ten men cost them, for no apparent reason, the chance to work that they had won by standing in the snow most of the preceding night.

On the first days, fighting had broken out as the desperate men strove to be in the right position when they reached the gates; the guards doused them with fire hoses. Some of the men began to freeze where they stood. They were either taken to hospitals or struggled to a local ten-cent movie house where, the *Times* man noted, they were "not so much interested in the show as in keeping warm."

After thawing out, they would return to the car park, once again hoping to be hired.

Henry Ford was pleased to see that on this morning, order was being strictly maintained by the guards. He congratulated the bouncy little man at his elbow.

Harry Herbert Bennett was listed on the company's books as head of personnel. In reality, he ran one of the largest private armies in the United States, some three thousand handpicked guards, capable of instilling fear in even the toughest of workers. Bennett himself had an infallible way of dealing with an uppity employee: He simply beat him senseless. He could flatten a man twice his size.

This morning the bantam-cock Bennett had left his closely guarded bunker near the main gates to join his master. As usual he wore a bowtie, a legacy of the day he was nearly strangled in a fight by his own necktie. In his waistband he carried a brace of pistols. Recently he had shot a cigar from the mouth of a visitor who had ignored a warning that smoking was forbidden at the plant. On another occasion he put a couple of bullets through a visitor's boater because Bennett didn't like straw hats. To keep up his marksmanship he regularly sat behind his desk and blasted away at a six-inch steel target set up on a filing cabinet at the opposite end of the room. For weeks he had kept a pair of caged tigers in his office—and threatened to feed them with any employee who proved too recalcitrant.

Ford adored his thuggish henchman because "If I want something done, he will do it. I don't have to tell him twice."

His salary, paid out of Ford's own pocket—no hardship for a man whose personal income in 1928 had reached $136,000 a day—ensured that Bennett was answerable only to Ford. In his service, he had recruited convicts and professional bruisers to join the retired athletes who completed his battalions. Between them they spied and informed on and bullied the company's ninety thousand other employees.

In his perennially blue shirt, Bennett seemed to be everywhere, quelling the first hint of trouble, driving on the assembly workers, "getting things done." When he was not prowling the plants, Bennett flitted between the five mansions he maintained around Detroit. At the one on Grosse Isle—a pseudo-oriental palace—he had a covered dock. Moored inside was a steel-hulled yacht, prepared for a quick getaway should Bennett ever meet more trouble than even he could handle.

Today, there was no sign of trouble. The lines of unemployed continued meekly to move forward.

Dressed in his regular gray wool suit, his feet enclosed in expensive shoes—one of the few luxuries he permitted himself—Henry Ford could view with satisfaction the columns of men in the car park. His instinctive flair for publicity had again worked. Already it had made him the most widely discussed man of his time. Fifteen full-length books on his life and work had appeared in the past nine years; a further fourteen had been largely devoted to him. No other American had ever received such attention during his life. Ford's own name appeared as an author on the title page of three volumes. The most successful was: *Good Morning: After a Sleep of 25 Years, Old Fashioned Dancing Is Being Revived by Mr. & Mrs. Henry Ford.* It had sold fifty thousand copies and become a standard work in its field. With the same folksy and, said his enemies, foxy approach that had made him a hero to the dance masters of America, Ford had now reaffirmed himself as the media's favorite answer to the workless.

Firmly entrenched where he believed he belonged—center stage, leaving all his rivals in the auto industry trailing by thousands of column inches of invaluable free publicity—Henry Ford could, for the moment, turn away from work problems to ponder more relaxing thoughts.

His dream of creating a memorial to those he most admired in the evolution of America was soon to come true. Two years had passed since he announced his decision to build an "industrial museum" in Dearborn for his collection of cars. A year later he revealed plans to supplement the museum with an early "American village," where he would exhibit "original buildings and inventions" spanning several stages of American life or linked with important events and persons—including himself.

For a man who thought the only way to preserve his sturdy growth of hair was to comb it with salt water, that granulated sugar was dangerous because "the sharp edges of its crystals cut into the blood vessels," that jails and hospitals would be made obsolete once people learned "to eat the things they should," the idea of creating what would be one of the world's largest private monuments was not unreasonable. Greenfield Village, at its planned public opening October 21, would cover over two hundred acres, testimony that money, as Ford often said, could buy anything—except a way to rid himself of enemies. Over the years these had been many, but two remained constant at the top of his hate list—Jews and Wall Street.

Perhaps Ford's anti-Semitism had always been there, an extension of those other phobias that had riddled him from childhood on that ninety-acre farm near the village of Dearbornville, Michigan. He was born July 30, 1863, into a world where the dead of the Civil War were still being buried. His hatred of war, claimed the mythmakers, stemmed from that accident of birth. His health fads were rooted in his sickly childhood, when he was frequently gripped with "the ague." His dislike of farming was a direct result of having to shovel manure. Coddled by his mother, indulged by his hardworking father, Henry went his own way. His mechanical bent was evident early on, but his turbulent emotions, his desire for revenge, his habit of making judgments based on obsessions rather than facts, began to grow as his fame grew.

His wife, Clara, whom he married in 1888, remained totally loyal to his whims and caprices. She bought his clothes, soothed his ego, listened as he waged verbal war against those he imagined had wronged him.

Somewhere along the way, his enemies became epitomized by Jews. He first publicly attacked them in 1916, suddenly accusing them of starting the Great War: "they have cornered all the basic materials needed to fight the war and all that—and until the Jew stops the war it cannot be stopped."

The 1918 armistice did not end Ford's intolerance. He blamed the Jews for the postwar crime wave, for the inefficiency of the peacetime Navy—even for the poor state of the candy bar industry: "The Jews have taken hold of it; they're cheapening it to make more money out of it."

Above all it was the Jews who were wrecking his idea of what the American way of life should be, particularly by their "obnoxious" use of credit. The fact that installment buying had created an almost insatiable demand for cars did not interest Ford. Borrowing money was bad —and that was that.

In November 1920 Ford bought a local weekly, the Dearborn *Independent,* which gave him a platform to wage an unfettered virulent attack against the Jews and their front men—"the greedy bankers of Wall Street." Under such inflammatory headlines as:

THE INTERNATIONAL JEW: THE WORLD'S PROBLEM

the *Independent* set out to disrupt the lives of 3.3 million Jews living in North America in rare tranquillity. Week after week the Jew-baiting continued. The Jews retaliated with a boycott of Ford cars, trucks, and tractors. Many Gentiles joined the boycott out of sympathy. Their action, said Ford derisively, was "a bit like rearranging the deck chairs on the *Titanic* after it had been holed." Sales of the *Independent* soon reached 500,000. Copies found their way to Germany, where Hitler was writing *Mein Kampf*. The future Führer must have been much encouraged by the despot of the auto industry.

In Detroit, watching the stock market booming in Wall Street, the *Independent* lashed out at this further "evidence of Jewish knavery."

Seeking new targets for his venom, Ford launched his most inflammatory attack. He accused the Jews of "plotting" to seize control of the nation's agriculture. The *Independent* named a Chicago attorney, Aaron Shapiro, as the archconspirator.

Shapiro sued for libel.

After an aborted first trial—Bennett's goons produced affidavits that a juror was connected with a speakeasy and had accepted a bribe from the plaintiff's side—Ford agreed to an out-of-court settlement.

The Jewish boycott was wrecking his profits.

Ford agreed to pay Shapiro $140,000 legal fees, recant his anti-Semitism, close down the *Independent,* and publicly issue a groveling apology. Officially, the matter was closed. Privately, Ford's hatred for Jews now focused on Wall Street. There was always a fear in his mind that a Jewish-engineered coup could somehow gain control of his company. Then, waiting in the wings, ready to take over, could be William Crapo Durant—a powerful bogeyman in Ford's box of monsters and goblins.

At a mile a minute, the *Wolverine* roared toward Detroit, a swaying streak of green Pullman cars against the Michigan snowscape. From the cars, passengers glimpsed the approaching city, dominated by the huge gray bulk of the General Motors Building. At this speed and distance no one aboard the express could detect the small decorative stones in the walls near the roof, let alone the repetitive letter "D" inscribed in the stonework.

For the past fourteen hours the owner of that initial had remained in solitary isolation in a private suite aboard the crack train of the New York Central Railroad as it thundered northward through Albany, Buffalo, across the Canadian border into lower Ontario, and on to Detroit. Waiters had served him dinner and breakfast in the suite's drawing room; the porter had turned down the bed, its mattress made from "the finest horse hair with pillows stuffed with goose feathers."

Neither food nor sleep had refreshed William Crapo Durant.

The soft-spoken, immaculately tailored little man traveling in regal splendor had a deserved reputation as the greatest living promoter outside prison bars. Few of his schemes equaled in audacity the offer he had made in 1909 to buy out Ford for $8 million and amalgamate the company into General Motors. Ford, at that time plagued by debts and a bout of "nervous dyspepsia," a recurrent affliction, accepted terms:

$2 million cash, the balance payable over two years. At the last minute Durant's bankers refused to back the deal because they felt "the Ford business is not worth that much money."

Now on this icy morning in mid-January, Durant doubted whether any consortium could buy out Ford. It always made Durant chuckle when he heard about Ford's fears that the "kosher robber barons" of Wall Street were planning such a move.

Durant knew only too well the industries, companies, stocks, and shares targeted for such attention in 1929. He was responsible for selecting many of the plums to be attacked. For the past four years, Durant had been one of the dominant men in Wall Street, portrayed in the press as "the most picturesque, the most engaging, the most audacious operator in this present market." He brushed aside such flimflam. He knew how easily the press could turn. Even now there could be reporters assembling at Detroit's Central Station to ask him why he had just quit Durant Motors, the company he had founded for a final fling at recapturing those days of glory when he had helped to propel America into the automobile age. Without him there would have been no General Motors, no mass-selling Chevrolet, no Buick, Oldsmobile, Pontiac, or Cadillac. All those cars owed their genesis to his genius. Without Durant's persuasion, Walter P. Chrysler would still be in railways, Charles Nash would not be running his own company, and Alfred P. Sloan would not be sitting in Durant's old office in General Motors—the one he had used as company president.

The reporters, of course, would not be interested in history. They would focus on the latest collapse of Durant Motors and its affiliates, probing for evidence that Durant prospered while his companies foundered. It would be difficult to deny the charge that their failure occurred because Durant had not devoted enough time to running them. Already some of the financial journalists had written speculative articles on whether he had succumbed entirely to "the charms" of Wall Street. And, as any newspaper reader knew, since 1924 Durant had led one of the most powerful syndicates the market had ever seen.

Before Durant left New York, John J. Raskob—whose own fortunes down the years frequently intermingled with Durant's—had offered him financial participation in the erection of the Empire State Building. Durant wasn't sure that a 36-million-cubic-foot building could be fitted onto an acre of midtown Manhattan. And his fear that now was not the time to invest in such a project was colored by his view of the Federal Reserve Board in Washington. He sensed the board could be planning an attempt to reduce stock market speculation; that it could raise interest rates and cut off the flow of easy money with which the general public was increasingly playing the market. It was a worrying thought. The wily Durant depended on public participation in his schemes.

Throughout the train journey he had alternated between preparing press releases explaining the collapse of his companies, and others attacking the Federal Reserve Board.

His mind was filled with problems and possibilities, so interconnected that even he had difficulty in unraveling them. He had hoped that the overnight journey from New York would have prepared him for the swift decision-making that had characterized his rule at General Motors; those were the days when the monolithic GM Building had been named the Durant Building. Then, as now, it was the world's largest office block, fifteen stories of limestone, its four wings housing seventeen hundred offices, needing a total floor space of thirty acres. It cost $20 million to erect in 1919. Durant had opposed such extravagance. He wanted to use General Motors cash only to build more cars, to carry the fight to Ford. John Raskob, then on the Board of GM, had pushed hard for the building. He argued it would be a fitting headquarters for the expanding conglomerate of 86,000 employees in the scores of subsidiaries and divisions that made up General Motors. Flattery bought acceptance. Durant agreed to the edifice.

The building bore witness to the fact that the historic boner of ten years earlier—when the bankers missed a golden chance to buy Ford's —had not affected Durant's expansionist ambitions. The crucible for those dreams had been between 1910 and 1915. Prior to that, Durant had borne the costs of developing General Motors largely with his own money, but finally, short of $10 million, the bankers had pried the company from his grasp.

Sacked from the Board by the financiers, Durant decided to study their methods. General Motors became listed as a publicly owned company. Durant quietly bought up the company's voting certificates in the open market, using profits from the Chevrolet Car Company, which he had founded after being removed from control of General Motors. Too late did the bankers recognize Durant's strategy. On September 13, 1915, he recapitalized Chevrolet at $20 million; within weeks he had increased that yet again—this time to $80 million. He then made an offer few General Motors stockholders could refuse—five Chevrolet shares for one GM. On a sunny September morning he walked into the GM boardroom and calmly announced that he had acquired enough GM stock to take control again.

In the five years that followed, Durant had ruled serene and supreme. Then in 1920, with the Durant Building topped out, he found himself once more in financial trouble, caught in a vise of a heavy expansion program on the one hand and the refusal of banks to support him on the other. Durant turned to Wall Street for help. He offered $64 million worth of common stock for underwriting. In a declining market the gamble failed. Durant then decided, without consulting anybody, to try to support GM stock—and his own equity in it of $105 million—by engaging in what were later referred to as "personal market operations." As large blocks of GM stock were offered for sale, he and a few wealthy friends purchased them privately; Durant used his own personally endorsed notes to pay for these purchases. But GM stock continued to plunge. His friends pulled out. Alone, unsupported, groggy from the drubbing he was taking but still mulishly hanging on, Durant watched the stock fall to 12¼ a share. At that price he became a ruined man, reduced from one worth over $100 million a few months earlier to a pauper owing $20 million. This time he did not wait for the bankers to oust him. He resigned from General Motors on November 30, 1920.

Next day, in a futile attempt to remove all traces of Durant, the new Board renamed their headquarters the General Motors Building. Now, over eight years later, only the repetitive "D" in the stonework served as a reminder of his association with the company. That did not trouble Durant. The day he walked out of General Motors he had expressed his philosophy on the vagaries of fortune: "Money is only loaned to a man; he comes into the world with nothing, and he leaves with nothing."

Freed from the burdens of running a vast business, Durant plunged into the stock market, encouraged by his many friends in Wall Street. They arranged the finance to start him speculating. He found it was his natural métier. He made a million dollars in a month; ten in two months; fifty in three. *Collier's* magazine reported in the January 19, 1929, issue that "in Wall Street it is believed that he has made more money out of this market than any other operator. The estimates run all the way from 100 millions up."

If that was inspired journalism, there was no disputing the fact that since 1924 Durant had headed a syndicate that had plunged up to $4 billion into selected stocks. Millions of Americans followed, pouring money into these shares, boosting the fortunes of the syndicate still further. Their investment fund was probably the largest block of money ever to be devoted to stock manipulation by a single syndicate.

The only possession Durant had taken with him from General Motors was his portable barber's chair. It accompanied him everywhere. It stood in a corner of the Pullman car suite, a magnificent contraption of rich velvet padding and carved wood. Like his good friend A. P. Giannini, Billy Durant didn't like to waste time shaving.

Waiting for him on the platform at Detroit station was a barber, one of a team who attended Durant's tonsorial needs across America. The

barber carried the chair into a private waiting room and shaved his illustrious client. Only then did Durant meet the press.

He accepted liability for the collapse of Durant Motors and its
affiliates. But he was happy to reveal that he hoped to raise $10 million
to reimburse stockholders. He expected the money to be available by
1930.

Before there could be any awkward questions, he moved on to attack
the Federal Reserve Board as an "autocratic group," whose "power is
beyond that of any constituted authority of the United States."

Now the reporters did not wait to ask questions. They already had a
story that would be front-page news.

Satisfied, the diminutive promoter walked to his waiting chauffeur-
driven limousine to continue the sixty-mile journey to Flint. He had
hated trains from that January day three years earlier when his private
car, "Patriot," had been crushed by an oncoming express. Three people
had died and thirty were injured in the accident. Durant, although
badly bruised, suffered only minor cuts, but so extensive was his
influence in Wall Street that the market was immediately shaken. It
recovered balance when Durant announced he felt "bullish" and was
off on a share-buying spree.

The journey to Flint, in a way, was a pilgrimage for Durant. His ma-
ternal grandfather, H. H. Crapo, had been a governor of Michigan, and
Durant, though born in Boston, had spent his boyhood in Flint. Whenever he felt a need spiritually and physically to recoup, he returned to
the old lumber town. He was confident that after a sojourn there he
could return to the fray of Wall Street with renewed vigor. Already, in
his mind, new schemes to make a fresh fortune were starting to evolve.
To succeed he must somehow contain the Federal Reserve Board. That
in itself was not an insurmountable task for a man who knew that he
could walk in unannounced on Herbert Hoover, the President-elect of
the United States.

News that Billy Durant was heading for Flint reached Charles Stewart Mott via a secretary. General Motors' chief of advisory staff—a
post that made Mott the second most important executive in the corporation—displayed no reaction. He had always been careful to conceal whether or not Durant's presence in Detroit made him uncomfortable. Mott owed much to Durant. It was Durant who, in 1905, had
persuaded Mott to move his wheel-and-axle business from Utica, New
York, to Flint, a transfer that soon helped make Mott one of the first
auto industry millionaires. Durant brought Mott into General Motors
as a vice-president, supported his election to mayor of Flint in 1912,
encouraged Mott's membership of the Elk, Moose, Lions, and Kiwanis

clubs, applauded all those well-publicized moves of Mott to support numerous Flint community projects. Mott's charity was formalized in 1926 by the establishment of the Mott Foundation, a tax shelter as well as a philanthropic platform. Finally, it was Durant who sowed the seeds for the media to turn Mott into another of those living legends: "Mr. Flint."

Nobody, least of all Mott, knew why Durant had done all this. For years he had expected to be asked to provide some service in return, perhaps even to play a part in a third bid by Durant to take back General Motors. But Durant had made no request for help. Mott relaxed, content to bask in the limelight that his charity brought him. He ignored those who sniped that his foundation was really only a means to sidestep income tax. He preferred instead to look upon the foundation as "a way of organizing help to the community and making it businesslike." And, with justification, Mott could argue that the tax laws encouraged such private giving.

Inside General Motors these past eight years, Mott had maintained a carefully neutral position toward the still existing pro- and anti-Durant factions. He was, in his own phrase, "in the good graces of the whole outfit."

It was an uncharacteristic position for a man who thrived on the infighting of big business, and coped with the machinations of Wall Street speculators, determined that they would never have a chance to "play games with GM stock."

There seemed little chance of that now happening. General Motors was set for another year of success under the guidance of the long-nosed, cold-eyed presidency of Alfred Sloan and the tall, ramrod-straight Mott. Even the resurgence of Ford in 1928 as a market leader had not fazed them. They evaluated his new Model A as a "fine little car—but another expression of Ford's concept of a static-model utility car." They dismissed the initial success of the Model A as "a splurge —not the sign of a trend."

In the past decade many of the industry's trends had evolved in Mott's office suite in the General Motors Building, immediately below the "D" motif in the stonework. Here, from 1923, the year of the first 4 million car and truck output, market strategy was hammered out, blueprints for new models dissected, the promise of the drawing boards harmonized with "the nuts and bolts of car economice." Mott and Sloan were a formidable team. Their engineering backgrounds made them methodical; neither man relied on hunches: "We leave all the glory of that kind of thing to such men as like to be labeled 'genius' "—a sly dig at Henry Ford.

The polluted air of downtown Detroit was regularly filled with such whiffs of sour-grape shot. So far everybody had failed to sniff out a choice tidbit to enliven the city's already pulsating social scene—fifty-three-year-old Mott was hopelessly in love yet again. In a city where the amours of motorcar magnates were of consuming interest, Mott's romancing with Dee Van Balkom Furey—the vivacious twenty-nine-year-old editor of the local *Bridle and Golfer* magazine—had remained a closely kept secret.

Even to their intimate friends they seemed an outwardly ill-matched couple: he, with the sartorial elegance of an office clerk and a penchant for childish practical jokes; she, with a sophisticated wit and an inborn flair for clothes. A mutual interest in horses had kindled their friendship.

Mott soon became spellbound by Dee's tales of her early life in Sumatra and her later experiences as a newspaperwoman in New York and Toronto.

She had arrived in Detroit in 1923, a year before Mott's first wife, Ethel, ill for some time, mysteriously fell from her bedroom window at Applewood, the family home in Flint. Ethel died soon afterward, leaving two daughters and a son for Mott to rear.

He tried hard to be a better father than he had been a husband: In the last years of the marriage, he had established a reputation as a womanizer, making little attempt to keep his philanderings from Ethel. After her death, he became one of the gayest widowers in Michigan society. Women invited to Applewood dinners had difficulty, in the words of one, "from keeping his hands off our panties' elastic."

Before long, he was smitten by Mitties Butterfield Rathbun, the divorced daughter of a local impresario. On July 12, 1927, they married. The next year, in February 1928, the second Mrs. Mott died from a sudden throat infection at her husband's remote ranch in Arizona. Mott's grief was short-lived. Eight months later he had taken up with Dee.

She, like the other women in his life, was captivated by tales of how he had turned Flint from a hick town into one of the main centers of automobile production; how, when the World War came, he had resigned from being mayor in order to join the Army. Mott did not stress that he had enlisted three days before peace was declared. He was an endless fund of stories, which from anybody else would have been boring, but in Mott's telling took on all the glamour a woman could want.

He, in turn, was enchanted by Dee's attention, the way she sat very still and stared round-eyed at him, often only speaking to ask a question which unleashed yet more yarns from Mott's bottomless memory bank. Then, when he would pause, she would tell him of her life, of her divorce from Nicholas Furey on the grounds of "nonsupport and abusive conduct," of her daughter, Denise, aged nine. And so, under the gentle gradual exploration of courtship, Mott came to believe he was once more in love, with a woman almost half his age, and, so it seemed to their friends, with none of his burning business interests.

That did not unduly trouble Mott. Coping with a younger woman and a marriage would not be nearly so demanding, he thought, as running General Motors. Sometimes he wondered why he put in those long exhausting days there, often stretching to fourteen hours. He knew he had achieved more than most men could acquire even in their dreams. He was wealthy beyond count; he had social and political power that made him a kingmaker in Michigan politics. No door in the land was closed to him. Yet the need to go on was deeply embedded.

And Mott knew that should he ever want to quit the auto business, he could always go into banking. He might even attempt to emulate one of the few financiers he admired—A. P. Giannini. Mott had already laid the ground for such a possibility by becoming chairman of the Board of the Union Industrial Bank in Flint. He was now the largest single stockholder on a board he had filled with friends. It was, he confided to Dee, a nice feeling to be a banker. It sounded so much more respectable to some people than being a leader of the auto industry. And so far the prestige of being a banker had cost him little of what he prized above all—time.

Mott had not attended a bank board meeting for many months. This did not concern him, because "after all, bankers are the last persons you need to keep an eye on."

It was a fashionable view. But in the case of the Union Industrial Bank in Flint, it was wrong.

CHAPTER FOUR

PEAKS AND TREMORS

Looking out of the third-floor window in the Bank of America Building, Claire Giannini thought how short was Wall Street, a mere six blocks running down to the river. To her right, where Wall began at Broadway, the twenty-story-high spire of Trinity Church was lost against the leaden, early February sky. Claire wished she was back in San Francisco. But that was unthinkable until her father "settled matters once and for all" with the Federal Reserve Board, the Federal Reserve Bank of New York, and with J. P. Morgan and Company, who acted as advisers to the Giannini empire.

Staring kitty-corner across Wall, toward Number 23, the "Corner," Claire wondered how long Morgan would remain in that position.

The rumble of her father's voice rose again. Giannini's fury had sustained him during the four-day train journey from California; it showed no signs of abating.

Claire and her brother Mario, together with Giannini's longtime confidant, Prentis Cobb Hale, had spent most of the trip trying to placate A.P. They discussed the ancient Order of Malta, one of the highest secular honors the Catholic Church confers, which the Pope had just bestowed on Giannini. With the papal congratulations came a fulsome invitation from Mussolini to again visit Italy. Giannini was in no mood to discuss the trip. Claire had raised another topic close to her father's heart, his huge financial investments in Hollywood. Sam Goldwyn, Charlie Chaplin, Douglas Fairbanks, Mary Pickford, Eric Von Stroheim, and Harold Lloyd were among the scores of stars and producers whose fortunes had been assured because of Giannini's backing. Claire wondered what effect the advent of "talkies" would have on the silent productions still going through the studios. Her father refused to be drawn, except to prophesy that Walt Disney's Mickey Mouse would survive far longer than any of the present crop of human stars.

Doggedly, Hale reviewed the brief, bloodless coup Giannini had just engineered to support John D. Rockefeller, Jr. The proxies of 32,000 shares in the Standard Oil Company of Indiana that Transamerica owned had been voted to Rockefeller to oust Robert Stewart as the oil company's chairman. Stewart had been exposed by a Senate committee investigating financial scandals.

Giannini seized on the subject as an example of what was wrong with present-day business ethics, bringing the conversation back to the purpose of their journey—a confrontation with J. P. Morgan and "the Fed."

The train pulled into New York with his companions still trying to persuade Giannini out of his intention. But pausing only for a quick shave, the banker had been driven to his office in the Bank of America Building at 44 Wall Street, bent on a showdown.

Even with her considerable understanding of financial matters, twenty-four-year-old Claire found it difficult to grasp the full complexities of an issue that had simmered for months. She doubted whether anybody, apart from her father, would ever be able to re-create the exact sequence of events and apportion responsibility properly for each of them. But, stripped of the prevarications and qualifications that Claire now recognized were routine in business wrangles, the issue boiled down to the Federal Reserve Board in Washington and the Federal Reserve Bank of New York opposing the quotation of Transamerica stock on the New York Exchange. J. P. Morgan supported them. Their reasons amounted to a charge of impropriety in the way Bank of America stock had been transferred to Transamerica during the involved moves Giannini was still making to consolidate Transamerica's position.

Claire shared her father's view that this was yet another transparent maneuver to keep him out of New York's financial world. She did not share his astonishment that the House of Morgan should have thrown its weight behind the board and bank; she had always felt it only a matter of time before there was "a falling out" between her father and the firm.

Totally preoccupied at present with attempts to curb overspeculation, neither the board nor the bank was represented at the meeting with Giannini. Morgan sent an emissary, the urbane, elegantly dressed Frank Bartow.

Giannini reiterated that Transamerica was designed to do more than ward off speculation in his company stock. He had also created it to bring the Bank of America into line with all his other banks. Even though he now owned the Bank of America, it still lacked "the originality, the purpose, the verve, the savvy, the good-natured drive to win friends and get business, no matter how large or small." He reminded Bartow that Morgan had "an interest" in the Bank of America, yet did not seem to approve of the idea of strengthening its position.

Bartow then defended the view of Morgan, the Federal Reserve Board and Bank. His crisp, cutting voice insisted that "the Fed" was right and that there had been "a violation."

Giannini erupted.

Nostrils flared, blue-jowled jaw thrust pugnaciously toward Bartow, the banker roared like an Italian trucker.

"I will fight this to the last ditch! We are absolutely right! We have been treated badly. Badly!"

Hale tried to intervene.

Giannini brushed him aside, addressing Bartow.

"J. P. Morgan ought to uphold us!"

Claire watched her father, towering over the table, glaring formidably at Bartow. She sensed that the unfortunate Morgan broker epitomized all that her father hated in the "eastern establishment."

"Please, A.P.," implored Hale.

Jabbing a finger toward Bartow, Giannini ignored Hale.

"Well, Mr. Bartow?"

Staring fixedly at Giannini, Bartow delivered a stinging ultimatum.

"Right or wrong we are for the Federal Reserve Bank. You can either do what the federal people ask or take your account away from J. P. Morgan and Company."

Hale tried desperately to defuse the situation.

"Gentlemen, gentlemen, please. We can resolve this—"

"No!" roared Giannini.

Hale stood his ground.

"Yes, A.P.!"

The silver-haired Hale then addressed Bartow.

"We'll be in touch and let you know our plans in a few days."

With an icy farewell Bartow left the room. He could not remember when a Morgan man had been so humiliated.

His departure brought a fresh broadside from Giannini. Morgan, the board and bank were acting in "a high-handed, improper and unlawful" manner; legally and morally he was in the right.

The others agreed, but pleaded that this was not the time to challenge Morgan.

"We need them," insisted Hale.

"We need somebody else," thundered Giannini. "Morgan is out from now."

"Good God, nobody's ever fired Morgan," said Hale. "Not even a government—."

"Then it will be a new experience for them!"

Turning to a secretary, Giannini dictated a letter of two short sentences, withdrawing all Giannini accounts from Morgan.

Later a second letter was drafted, to Gates McGarrah, the chairman of the Federal Reserve Bank in New York. It was also short and to the point. It contained a blunt warning that Giannini intended to resist to the bitter end any attempt to impair "my lawful right to operate unmolested in the second Federal Reserve District."

He turned to his apprehensive colleagues.

"One of two things will happen. We'll either be out of New York. Or we'll stay. My bet is that they'll leave us alone. Bully boys always do when you stand up to them."

Then he took Claire and Mario to lunch at an Italian restaurant, confident that "the Fed and Morgan will have indigestion" when they read his letters.

Afterward, when her father and Mario returned to the office, Claire wandered through the financial district, familiarizing herself with the ground on which her father had chosen to do battle.

A keen student of history, she probably already knew more than most about this haphazard maze of streets with names common to the early American colonies: Maiden Lane, Old Slip, Liberty Street. Even before the first cobblestones were laid, the colonial Dutch had put a fence around what was then pasture to keep their cattle from straying onto a footpath that became Broadway. Governor Peter Stuyvesant put up a wall; later, when the grazing land was built over, the name of Wall Street was given to a row of modest houses and shops, shaded by a buttonwood tree, under which those brokers in 1792 had agreed to establish a stock exchange.

The street was already infamous for its pillories and whipping posts where transgressors were publicly chastised. Slave auctions were regularly held in Wall. And it was there, in 1789, on the second-floor balcony of Federal Hall, that George Washington was sworn in as first President of the United States.

But the arrival of the Exchange established Wall's financial position. By 1802 forty banks had offices there; in 1815 the New York newspapers began to list stocks. In 1857 the first real financial panic gripped the market; it was resolved largely because the Exchange helped to ensure shares were traded "in a stable atmosphere." In 1869 the Exchange increased its membership. Two years later, it was decided to charge for a "seat"; in those days it literally was a chair, allowing a member to sit and trade in comfort. In 1870 the price of the seat was $2,000. In 1929 it was more than $500,000—and there was no room for chairs on the crowded floor.

Now, apart from the street names, there were no traces of old New York; the district was a series of concrete canyons, walled by towering office blocks; the sun shone on some sections of pavement less than twenty hours in a year.

Claire returned to the Bank of America Building and made her way to a top-floor office. From its window she could glimpse the great harbor to the south where, in the late nineteenth century, ships brought two out of every three persons immigrating to the United States.

Closer, Claire's vantage point allowed her to see sights seldom noticed or imperceptible to those who spent their days in the banking halls below, at street level. The tops of Wall Street's towering buildings were a mass of bas-reliefs, brass sculptures, stone statues, and gargoyle figures, many forty feet tall, cut into the stone. From her window, Claire could count six of the nation's ten largest banks, each within a few blocks of each other. Hemming them in were dozens of smaller banks, many with assets barely in excess of a billion dollars.

But, as Claire knew, the real business of Wall Street was conducted in the upper floors of the towers, where bankers decided how to invest the capital on which industry had expanded at an incredible rate in the last two years.

Claire, like everyone else, could reel off the milestones that accompanied this expansion. A new record for the Atlantic crossing was being chased by the *Bremen;* United Airlines had just launched the first coast-to-coast passenger flight: a trimotor took twenty-eight hours to fly from New York to Los Angeles. Airmail flights were now in their fifth year. On the ground a bitter war had broken out between the railroads and trucking companies for the lucrative freight-carrying transcontinental hauls. One company had just claimed a "world record," from Los Angeles to New York by road in thirteen days, five hours. The railways trumped that they could maintain mile-a-minute schedules across the country.

Cars were being equipped with radios—a further sign that Americans were starting to accept the motorcar as a necessity rather than a luxury.

The ten-year-old radio industry was in the midst of an extraordinary boom. Two years before, in 1927, so many stations were in operation that the Federal Radio Commission was formed to issue licenses and assign airwaves. NBC, founded in 1926, was locked in combat with CBS for listeners.

Labor relations had never been smoother; trade union membership had declined from the 1920 figure of 5 million to its present 3.4 million; the workingman seemed content to give management a free run. And, for the average worker, goods and services had never been more varied or of better quality.

All this was reflected on the New York Stock Exchange. The number of shares traded had grown from 493,449,000 in 1925 to over 900 million in 1928; already the Exchange had enjoyed its first 4-million-share day.

But Claire knew her father was worried about how long the boom could last. There had been a sharp break in the market in January—the third in seven months—when issues lost scores of points in a single day's trading. Precisely why this happened or why the market had promptly recovered was a question quickly forgotten by most people. Giannini had analyzed the break and told his daughter why it occurred. "Small folk," who were investing by borrowing to the limit from their brokers, had suddenly been caught by a demand for more collateral as the market went into one of its regular bouts of nervousness. Unable to provide the extra cash, they were sold out—their stocks put on the market by brokers in order to recover their loans. This had the effect of accelerating the price drop—perpetuating the break. One day, Giannini warned, buying support might come into the market too late—with what result no one could predict.

Even now he felt the market was edgy and overstimulated. There was a new hysteria in the printed newsletters brokers supplied to their customers; many of the prospectuses containing "facts" about new securities smacked of fairground huckstering; company reports were tricked out with fancy covers—and often even more fanciful claims on future growth.

Peering down into Wall Street, Claire Giannini wondered what would happen to its occupants, and her father, in a full-scale crisis.

Preparing for such a prospect was an abiding concern of Joseph Kennedy. For seven years this wickedly handsome six-footer, exuding vitality and roguish charm which masked a steel-trap mind, had profitably played the stock market. It suited him. Joe Kennedy reveled in games without rules. Operating alone, he had regularly struck ruthlessly and pitilessly. His successful deals became as well known as his temper. He could switch from warmth to malice in the flicker it took his blue eyes to frost the color of an icy lake. In the rough and tumble of business, friendships were broken and acquaintances discarded as Kennedy moved still further away from the beachhead that Irish immigrants had set up in Boston after being washed up on New England's shores. Joe Kennedy had learned one unforgettable lesson during his childhood in a community surrounded by inhospitable boundaries. Only the fittest could break out and survive in a world of "Yankees who had stepped on faces to get what they had."

Kennedy absorbed the punishing logic of that lesson and prospered. But he would not be satisfied until he had achieved his consuming ambition—the establishment of a Kennedy dynasty. His progenitor's sense drove him on; to him his children were an extension of himself; whatever he did, it was with them in mind.

Now, against advice and accepted opinion, he had made a major decision: He would begin to liquidate his stock holdings and gradually get out of the market. His instincts smelled trouble; his cold professional judgment told him he should bet against the crowd.

But before quitting he wanted to discuss the state of the market with the one man in Wall Street who still overawed him—Jack Morgan.

For days Kennedy contemplated his planned visit to the House of Morgan. He intended to arrive unannounced and uninvited—that was part of his style. Kennedy was certain that his name and reputation would gain him swift access to the inner sanctum. He discussed the matter with his wife, Rose, whom he had married fourteen years earlier, and who, so far, had borne him eight children and shared his burning ambition for the advancement of the Kennedy family.

Rose approved of his proposed heart-to-heart with the single most important man in the financial world.

Joe Kennedy had decided that this February morning was the time for the meeting of what he firmly believed were two like minds; the encounter would mark the moment when he would finally throw off the last vestiges of his past and become part of the Establishment.

Joe's father, Patrick, began as a docker. It was no job for a man who preferred brain to brawn. He seized the first opportunity to enter politics, a calling in Boston which attracted spirited Irishmen like the wail of a fiddler's flute. Patrick was a state senator at thirty-two, put there by his fellow Irish, and director of a small Boston-Irish bank. It was all very ethnic.

To break the pattern, Patrick kept Joe away from traditional Catholic schools and sent him to a Protestant academy. Later, instead of completing his education with the Jesuits at Boston College or Holy Cross, Joe went to Harvard. He did well, got good final grades in history and economics, and showed his first flair for business by making $5,000 running summer tourist buses.

Using his father's influence, Joe became a state bank examiner at $1,500 a year. The low salary and long hours were more than compensated for by all he learned about banking.

At night he courted Rose Fitzgerald, the daughter of Boston's mayor.

In 1913 his father's bank was threatened by a series of bank mergers. Joe led a counterattack. He put to good use the time spent poring over other people's ledgers. He borrowed money. Then he rallied proxy votes among his Irish friends. Finally, at twenty-five, he was elected president of the bank, the youngest to hold such office in the country. It brought him his first taste of national publicity. He liked the taste and set out to cultivate a distinctive Kennedy "image." He dressed and spoke like a banker and often behaved like one—quick to foreclose on any mortgage that fell behind.

His striving for success intensified with his marriage to Rose in 1914. It failed to bring him what he openly longed for, social acceptance in a class-conscious community. He was still "bog Irish" to the aristocrats of Boston. They shrugged and nodded knowingly when they heard Kennedy had borrowed heavily to buy his first home; they tittered when it soon grew too small to house his rapidly expanding family; Rose was giving birth regularly every eighteen months.

Recognizing that his background would never gain him position in the city of the Cabots, Lowells, Lodges, Peabodys, Adamses, and other first families, Kennedy set out to win respect in business.

The World War found him earning $20,000 a year as assistant general manager of Bethlehem Steel's yard at Quincy, Massachusetts. He also ran a profitable sideline—a restaurant near the yard which fed 22,000 workers a day. By 1918 he had a healthy bank balance and his first stomach ulcer. The end of the war made Kennedy eager again to achieve his deep-seated craving for status. He took a 50 percent cut in salary and went to manage the office of the brokerage firm of Hayden, Stone & Co. There, Kennedy swiftly acquired the skill to go with his instinct of how best to manipulate the tricky postwar market.

At the end of 1922, aged thirty-four, filled with confidence, he decided to strike out on his own. He moved in on Wall Street, soon locking horns with all the other tipsters and manipulators, relying on his own abilities to survive the dangers of financial combat.

Kennedy showed that his icy, appraising mind and iron nerves admirably suited him for his chosen role.

His first major coup was against fellow operators who were driving down the stock of the Yellow Cab Company. Kennedy persuaded the company to let him mount a defense. From a room in the now-doomed Waldorf-Astoria, after four weeks and a bewildering series of buy and sell orders, Kennedy brilliantly drove off the raiders and stabilized Yellow Cab's stock. He also made a substantial profit for himself. From then on, he went from strength to strength. Eventually, in 1926, he chose to operate in that most spectacular and slippery of all fields—show business.

Kennedy formed a syndicate and purchased a small, ailing Hollywood film-producing company and its distribution affiliate for $10 million. He renamed the company F.B.O. and breathed life and money into it. Four banks pledged $500,000 credit—the working capital to mass-produce Westerns and melodramas starring Fred Thompson and Red Grange. A feature a week was cranked out on $30,000 budgets. They earned Kennedy substantial profits in a movie-mad era. But he was far too ambitious to remain merely the head of a thriving but still-small studio. He wanted to be "among the majors." He persuaded Radio Corporation of America to invest $500,000 in his studios—giving R.C.A. a film-producing outlet to go with its chain of theaters.

Still not satisfied, Kennedy quietly gobbled up the long-established Keith-Albee vaudeville circuit for $4.2 million. By 1928 he was going through the anything-but-scatty world of show business like "a figure in an absurdly speeded-up movie." He drew a salary of $2,000 a week for each company he had a stake in, and profited from the stock options on everything he controlled. He was making more money than his movie stars.

Now there was no stopping him. For months he laid his plans carefully. First he acquired another movie company, Pathé Exchange. Next he became financial adviser to First National Pictures at $3,000 a week. He was an empire builder on a scale that even Clarence Hatry in London would admire. Then, in October 1928 he "shot for the big pot." He merged all his own companies to form R.K.O—the new giant of the movie industry. Then he promptly cashed in his stock for $5 million and pocketed another $150,000 for "supervising the merger."

He flew back from Los Angeles to his old stomping ground in New York.

Outwardly, nothing had changed in Wall Street. Yet despite the familiar scene, Kennedy sensed danger in the runaway market where everybody was compulsively bullish. He decided to pull out, to go to Florida and sit in the sun with Rose and the children. But first he would talk to Jack Morgan.

It was late morning when the immaculately dressed Kennedy arrived in the Street.

The first of the lay preachers was at his sidewalk podium, which he had draped with the American flag and illustrated biblical texts. Farther down the street other missionaries prepared to mount their soap boxes and warn of the perils of Mammon. For the next hour their voices would bravely harangue the lunchtime agnostics whose meal break was enlivened by the presence of the itinerant ministers. On important holidays a Salvation Army band serenaded.

Loud and clear above the traffic, organ music floated out of the open doors of Trinity Church, where the daily recital had begun. People of all denominations crowded the pews for the concert.

Yet in spite of this apparent religious harmony, Wall Street, as Joe Kennedy knew, was a bigoted place, filled with prejudices.

Kennedy had been appalled by its anti-Semitism. Virtually the only hope a Jew had of employment was at Goldman, Sachs; Kuhn, Loeb; or Lehman Brothers. Whenever the market dipped, racism escalated and there was talk of "shylocking" and "Jewish-style deals."

Wall Street was still three-quarters white Protestant, a WASP enclave in a city where nine tenths of the population were Catholic, Jewish, or black. Negroes, of course, were rigidly excluded from the Street. Not even Kennedy at his most radical wished to change that situation. But he did believe the time had come when family, school, university, and church—the interwoven threads binding together the Protestants of Wall Street as tightly as money or business—should no longer be the governing factors. He failed to appreciate that for Morgan men the means were the end; being in the team was more important than the game, provided always they could play together with men like themselves.

Perhaps, if the opportunity arose, Kennedy might even raise the whole issue with Jack Morgan, and appeal to him to give a lead. Morgan was reputed to be considerably less anti-Semitic than his father, though Jack still bridled at the idea of admitting Jews to the Yankee clubs and drawing rooms he patronized.

Still pondering such thoughts, Kennedy walked up the six broad granite steps and through the double doors of 23 Wall.

His progress was immediately blocked by a doorman.

"Mr. Joseph P. Kennedy to see Mr. J. P. Morgan."

The doorman asked if Kennedy had an appointment.

"No. But I'm sure he'll see me."

The doorman remained firm. Every day he faced similar situations. Nobody was seen at Morgans without an appointment.

Kennedy switched on his grin. The voice that had charmed a thousand businessmen spoke loudly and firmly.

"Tell Mr. Morgan it's Joe Kennedy back from Hollywood."

The doorman still hesitated.

Kennedy spoke sharply. "Be quick, man. I haven't all day."

The doorman walked toward the small cordoned-off area to the right of where Kennedy stood. The area was where the Morgan partners sat at their rolltop desks.

Kennedy's eyes swept the huge saloon in front of him. Some 250 feet long by 200 feet wide, the room was a tasteful blend of paneled woods, leather upholstery, pink marble floors, and heavy drapes. There was an air of muted magnificence.

He watched the doorman reach the low gate rail leading into the partner's enclosure. A secretary was waiting. Whispered words were exchanged. The secretary turned and moved past the rolltops. Kennedy knew some of their occupants: Thomas Lamont; his son, Thomas Stilwell; Henry Sturgis Morgan; Henry Davidson. All were busy, all were aware of this highly unusual interruption.

Even from this distance, Joe Kennedy could recognize the distinctive features of Jack Morgan, seated squarely at his desk, reading reports.

The secretary bent and whispered in his ear.

Without raising his head, Jack Morgan murmured his response.

The secretary backed away. She repeated the message to the doorman.

Turning, his resolve stiffened, the man advanced on Kennedy.

"Mr. Morgan's too busy to see you."

Kennedy's cheek twitched—then some inner force stilled the tic.

Without a word, Joe Kennedy walked out of the House of Morgan, determined never to forget or forgive the public slighting he had received.

News of Kennedy's humiliation reached Jesse Lauriston Livermore shortly after the Irishman left the Street. The fifty-two-year-old Livermore liked to boast to the mistresses he kept in villas around the world that nothing happened in the financial district that he did not soon know about.

Livermore recorded Kennedy's discomfiture in a notebook. He had notebooks for everything: One recorded the general state of the market; another the rise and fall of selected stocks; a third his feelings about such fluctuations. Sometimes, when a reporter was lucky enough to catch him, Livermore would reach for a notebook and, in his flat, nasal Boston accent, read from it "a thought"—and get himself a splash on the financial pages. But the slim, blond Livermore was not keen on publicity. He liked to operate secretly. His dealings were not popular with the public; he was believed to be a bear in a world of bulls, pushing down stock prices by short selling in order to increase his fortune.

He had designed a most remarkable office complex in which he painstakingly prepared for his infrequent, but always devastating, raids, which often netted him several million dollars a time.

The Livermore suite in the Heckscher Building on Fifth Avenue was protected at street level by a doorman who denied its existence. Only those whose names appeared on an approved list were allowed past, and then they were whisked up by elevator to the eighteenth floor. All visitors were there further screened by a burly Irishman, famed for his ham-sized fists, before being allowed to enter the unnumbered door of Livermore's citadel.

Twenty clerks, personally handpicked by Livermore for their ability to keep their mouths shut, ran an operation requiring scores of private telegraph wires and dozens of unlisted telephones; they were also responsible for keeping up to the minute a large quotation board. In addition, a team of statisticians, culled from some of the best business schools in America, provided instant trend analyses based on the prices a bank of ticker tapes spewed out. In all, with telephonists, tipsters, and secretaries, some sixty people were on Jesse Livermore's payroll—for no other purpose than to assist him with his personal investments.

Livermore worked for nobody, and nowadays, seldom with anybody; he rejoiced in his image of "the loner—the market's biggest single titan."

On this morning of February 14, 1929, already a multimillionaire, he was still obsessed with increasing his fortune. Nothing else mattered; he lacked social polish and despised culture in any form. His braying laugh would punctuate his favorite story of a dealer who asked him what he thought of Balsac. Livermore had replied: "I never trade in them stocks."

Single-minded and simplehearted, he was a curious mixture of New England Calvinism and lecher; he could recite the Bible, yet liked to cruise through Manhattan at night in his canary-yellow Rolls-Royce, chasing girls to satisfy his considerable sexual appetite.

But nothing excited him more than the chance to make a killing in the market.

Livermore now sensed a further opportunity was coming. On February 2 the Federal Reserve Board in Washington had sent a confidential letter to its reserve banks throughout the country—including its main one in New York—asking them to refuse loans for financing speculation on the stock market Then, on February 7, the board issued a statement to the press in which it warned of "the excessive amount of the country's credit absorbed in speculative loans."

Jesse Livermore guessed, correctly, that the well-meant words would have little effect on the general public. It seemed to him also a sign that the Fed was relying solely on simple persuasion to reduce the amount of money available "on call."*

---

* *Call money:* loans secured by stocks and bonds as collateral, repayable at the option of lender or borrower on demand. The "call money market" was closely connected to the use of *margin:* the amount of credit a broker allowed an investor

What even Livermore, with his carefully nurtured network of paid informants, could not know was that on this St. Valentine's Day, the Federal Reserve Board and its New York bank were locked in violent disagreement. Both well understood the need to stop unwarranted speculation. But the Federal Reserve Bank of New York believed that the only way to do so was by increasing the cost of money borrowed for speculation. The bank thought the rediscount rate should be raised from 5 to 6 percent in "one sharp, incisive action." It proposed to do so unilaterally. After a day-long wrangle, the board overruled the bank, partially as a result of pressure from the governor of the Bank of England, who was concerned that the high interest rates in New York would draw even more money from Great Britain. Indeed, just a week before, on February 7, 1929, the U.K. bank rate had been raised to 5½ percent, largely in an attempt to stem the flow of funds to Wall Street.

In future, the opposing views of the Federal Reserve Board in Washington and its Federal Reserve Bank in New York would continue to cancel each other out, nullifying fiscal action which might well have altered all that was to come.

Although Livermore was unaware of these crucial internal deliberations, he could see for himself that the world situation was becoming "uneasy." Throughout January, foreign funds had flowed into the United States, as nearly every European exchange rate declined through the month. Gold imports were $48,577,000 while exports amounted to a trifling $1,378,000. Over $38 million worth of gold came from Canada, whose currency, Livermore observed, "had been weak for some months"; $7.3 million worth of gold came from England.

There had also been a continuous advance in stocks; during January the "averages" had risen 17 points, or 7 percent. The month's transaction of 110,803,940 shares was double that of January 1928. Call money had declined early in the month from 12 percent to 6 percent, but had soon risen to 9 percent, and evened out at 7 percent—a little high for some bulls, but people were happy to pay.

Now, in mid-February, despite the Federal Reserve's public warning of a week before, the speculative fever, far from subsiding, showed every sign of increasing.

---

to buy shares. In 1929 it was not uncommon for a speculator to buy stock with only 10 percent cash, the remaining 90 percent "margin" borrowed from the broker, who, in turn, borrowed it in the "call money market." High interest rates were gladly paid because investors believed the stocks they bought with the borrowed money would so increase in value that when they were sold, the profit would make the interest negligible. However, if the value of the stocks fell, the investor would be required by the broker to put up more margin—more cash— or the shares would be sold by the broker so that the broker himself would have the necessary cash to pay back the money *he* had borrowed.

Jesse Livermore correctly assessed the dilemma facing the federal authorities: If they raised the interest rate, it would seriously handicap the nation's industry, while not necessarily halting speculation. Further, such a hike would force the government to pay more on its own borrowings—and that would not please the incoming Hoover administration. Finally, an increase of even 1 percent would bring millions more dollars into the United States which could have a disastrous effect not only on Britain but on world trade generally.

Like Giannini and Kennedy, Livermore could sense the market growing restive. But to him, the danger seemed much closer, for Livermore could see no way to deflation except through an imminent disaster.

He was ready to exploit such a calamity—just as he had done many times before.

At the age of fourteen, Jesse Livermore began his career, appropriately, in the offices of a brokerage firm in Boston. For a dollar a week, he marked quotation prices on a display board. In no time he was able to calculate in his head to a fraction the average rise or fall of a stock. He came to realize that analysis was the key to success.

At the end of a long day, Jesse would remain alone in the office, standing before the quotation board and carefully copying into a notebook all the closing prices. Then he would compare them with the previous day's figures. Soon he was able to detect a pattern. Using those patterns as guidelines, the baby-faced Livermore began to tour the Boston bucket shops in his lunch hour.

The city was filled with such shops; they were the bookmakers of the stock market, ready to part gamblers from their cash. No shares were bought or sold in many of these establishments. Customers bet on prices as they were chalked up on the shop's quotation board. If a client bet on the stock going up, and it did, he won. If the stock dropped, he lost. With his uncanny memory, his notebooks of data and ability to anticipate price fluctuations, Livermore began to clean out the bucket shops.

Their owners tried to cheat him, faking prices to lead him on. Livermore refused to be conned. He continued to win. The bucket shops banned him. He disguised himself—and collected. The shops discovered his ruse. He was forced to operate in the city's suburbs. Finally, banned from every bucket shop in the Boston area, he was ready to play the stock market proper.

Barely twenty-one, with the innocent face of a ten-year-old, Livermore went to New York with a stake of $2,500. There he quickly learned iron-clad control and never to panic. He began to use his country-boy guile to realize every tinhorn's dream of outsmarting his elders and betters. He played at being a bull or a bear, ready to snatch a profit as shares rose or fell.

The growth of his bank balance made possible the realization of his other dreams. He soon had expensive cars, racks of suits, drawers of shirts, gallons of eau-de-cologne, and mistresses in Florida and Europe.

Then, one evening in 1906, vacationing in Atlantic City with a girl friend, he dropped into a brokerage office to check on the market. It was bullish. Livermore noted that the shares of the Union Pacific Railway, which served San Francisco, were particularly high and rising. Nevertheless, believing they would soon fall, he gave an order to sell short some 3,000 shares. He was responding, he told his girl, to a "gut reaction."

Union Pacific continued to climb.

Even so, next day, Livermore sold 2,000 more shares short. Kissing good-bye to his girl, he returned to New York. That night he slept alone, deeply, untroubled.

Next morning, his valet awoke him with the news that San Francisco had been devastated by earthquake—and that Union Pacific's network of track lay buckled and twisted in the disaster area. Within hours the stock market began to slide to full-scale panic. The value of Union Pacific's shares plummeted. The lower the price fell, the more Livermore collected. By nightfall he was a millionaire.

He had established his name as the market's leading short seller, a master manipulator. The San Francisco earthquake had provided him—as it had A. P. Giannini—with a springboard into the future.

Less than a year later Livermore struck again. He had studied the country's economic conditions and concluded that the "money outlook" was poor. Interest rates were rising, unemployment was on the increase: the ingredients for a fall were there. He began again to sell short. The stocks he borrowed to sell rose again. But his "gut reaction" was so well developed that nothing could budge him. He arranged to borrow even more shares, and then immediately sold them in the hope he could later buy the replacement shares at a lower price. The great stock market crash of 1907 allowed Livermore to do just that. On one day alone, October 24, he showed a profit of $250,000. Altogether he made over $1 million. It was then that the press dubbed him the "boy plunger."

He became unstoppable. During the World War, he made several million more dollars—some reports put it as high as $25 million; a more realistic figure would be $5 million—speculating in steel and petroleum shares. He became a temporary bull, believing, rightly, that the market would react upward to the booming war economy. But, in 1918, he returned to his bearish ways. He filled his notebooks with jottings predicting a stark future: "Too many war contracts unfulfilled because of Peace. Returning soldiers: no jobs."

He sniffed another period of deflation. Once more he sold short; when the 1919 collapse came, he raked in an estimated $15 million. By now he had become the bear the press loved to bait. They attacked his methods, his lack of patriotism. He was scourged as the man who had profited at the expense of small investors who had gone to the wall. One tabloid called him "the man with the evil eye." He was accused of shortchanging America. In financial terms he was Public Enemy No. 1.

He ignored the clamor and continued through the early 1920s to operate in big-action stocks like Baldwin Locomotive and Crucible Steel. He made one killing on American Sumatra, another on Mexican Petroleum, selling short at from 160 to 180 and covering at an average of 92.

Livermore always seemed to know the high point in a stock and he went short as near to it as he could.

His private life-style matched his successful market strategy. He owned several mansions, a yacht, a rail car, a private plane, and courted some of the most beautiful women in America. He bought champagne by the truck, caviar by the case, suits by the dozen. He flitted between Nice, Gleaneagles in Scotland, Maxims in Paris, and his office complex on Fifth Avenue.

For a while he teamed up with Billy Durant. Between them they put on a display of financial fireworks that would probably never be equaled. Livermore's "take" from these deals was estimated at $20 million.

Now he was back in his favorite role, alone, plotting and scheming.

All day he related the market trends to the Federal Reserve Board's press announcement. He pored over the precise words in the statement; it was too mild in its warning about "speculative loans." The wording suggested uncertainty when firmness was required to take in hand a market that was shaky.

He turned again to study the situation in Europe. The French market, as he expected, was steady. Elsewhere, things were sluggish. The Bank of England had ordered that more than $22 million worth of British gold be shipped to New York. Close to $4 million worth was coming down from Canada. It all added up, in Livermore's view, to a precursor of trouble; the world's economy was being tilted out of true.

Alone in his inner office, insulated against the clatter of his communications center—which linked him to Chicago, San Francisco, London, Paris, Berlin, and Milan—Jesse Livermore continued to ponder the situation.

Outwardly he looked as calm as ever, fielding calls from favored associates around the nation, issuing orders, and absorbing the latest ticker assessments. With his ash-blond hair, glowing cheeks, and unlined face, he looked far too young to be smoking the torpedolike Havana cigars that were specially rolled for him in Cuba. He smoked nearly three hundred a month—the only outward sign of the inner tensions that gripped him.

Whichever way he looked at it, the state of the market was becoming perilous.

Slowly, with all the certainty of his long experience, Jesse Livermore felt intuitively that another crash was coming. He thought it would happen within a month—two at the most. He began to plan.

CHAPTER FIVE

BUY UNTIL IT HURTS

The prospect of a crash was beginning to haunt architect William Lamb. In his nightmare it flattened a square mile of Manhattan and left up to a million people dead or injured, buried beneath tens of thousands of tons of steel, concrete, and limestone or shredded by the glass fallout from thousands of windows—all because he had miscalculated the structural strains involved in erecting the world's tallest building.

In reality, the experienced Lamb knew he would never make such a mistake. But the fear persisted—a reminder of the awesome task he faced.

Lamb knew better than to share his misgivings with John J. Raskob. The proposed Empire State Building was an obsession with the financier; not even a dream would be allowed to threaten it. The project also provided welcome relief from all Raskob's other involvements; he was a member of numerous Wall Street syndicates feeding off radio, oil, and transport stocks.

Unlike Livermore, Raskob was confident that the market would soon even out. He heartily endorsed the slogans he heard in the Street: "Be a Bull on America" and "Never Sell the United States Short."

Raskob confided to Lamb that this jingoism mirrored his own optimism in the economy. He saw the Empire State Building as a reflection of his faith in America's future. He also told the architect that he had still another plan to express that belief—one that he would unveil after they studied the initial plans for the tallest building in the world.

On this February night the two men were alone in Raskob's penthouse office at 230 Park Avenue. Below them, the city sparkled and twinkled. For a while they stood and contemplated the view they planned to enhance. Then they returned to the first rough sketches Lamb had created.

Raskob saw that even in the crude drawings, the sheer elegance of the architect's concept was breathtaking.

Lamb held up a pencil. "It'll look like this."

Raskob looked at the pencil and nodded happily. Lamb's vision was not another version of the multitiered wedding-cake-style skyscrapers that dominated New York—"giant birdcages decked out with trivial and inapposite concrete ornaments" was how Lamb described them.

The architect had designed a soaring, uncluttered structure.

"It'll work," murmured Raskob. "It really will."

"It'll cost money," reminded the practical Lamb.

"It's there," promised Raskob. "Just deliver on time."

Both men realized that time and money were the key factors, coupled, for the moment, with secrecy.

Rumors that the site they had chosen for the building was up for sale had surfaced, raising speculative interest in Wall Street. Several consortiums were looking for finance to purchase the site on which, at present, stood the Waldorf-Astoria Hotel. Typically, Raskob had gone into partnership with the Du Pont brothers and appointed former New York Governor Alfred E. Smith as front man. It was an unbeatable trio—Du Pont's money, Smith's charisma, Raskob's business acumen.

Raskob had approached the hotel owners. There was no haggling. They named a price. He wrote out a check—for $16 million. The two-acre site was his.

No outsider yet knew that the deal was made. It gave Raskob great amusement to hear and read of the frantic maneuverings going on in Wall Street to buy a property he already owned lock, stock, and barrel.

He intended to keep his acquisition secret while Lamb quietly worked out the technicalities of the task ahead. Publicity at this stage could only bring city officials poking to see that all the regulations involved in building such a skyscraper were enforced.

The first problem that Lamb faced was the rigid New York building code which was unyielding on the height-to-land ratio for skyscrapers. This meant that buildings could only go to a certain height before their structures became so narrow as to be commercially unviable. Raskob wanted every floor of the Empire State Building to provide profitable rental accommodation.

Lamb's pencil-slim design would solve the basic problem of fitting a 100-plus-story, 36-million-cubic-foot structure on a one-acre site; the other acre would be used to help support from underground the towering elevation.

Raskob's advisers had estimated that the structural costs would come to $60 million. Borrowing the money was no problem—the financier already had promise of ample funds. The critical question was how much would be paid in interest on such a huge sum. To keep that to the minimum, Raskob's accountants informed him the entire project should be completed eighteen months from the day wrecking crews moved in to tear down the Waldorf-Astoria. It would mean working to an unprecedentedly tight timetable, in which the time taken to remove each cubic yard of earth would be costed.

When he finished perusing the drawings, Raskob raised further questions. Had Lamb allowed for bad weather delaying the project? What about late delivery of materials? Contingency plans to cover traffic snarls on one of the busiest streets in the world, Fifth Avenue?

The architect promised all such problems would be taken into account.

For the moment the financier was satisfied. He turned to a leather folio containing portraits of his children and told Lamb that the building would be "their legacy—and for all who follow."

Then, slumping in his massive, padded chair, hands locked behind his head, Raskob unveiled his other plan.

It was "a way of life to embrace the whole nation."

He was going to launch an investment trust specifically designed to allow "the poor man" to increase his capital, "just as the rich man is doing."

Reading rapidly from notes, Raskob outlined his theory of "intelligent debt," which was somewhat akin to buying a home on the installment plan.

His concept was altogether grander, one in which "public ownership of our large industries becomes a reality."

Lamb was stunned. Here was one of the apostles of capitalism talking socialism—or even worse, communism.

Sensing his reaction, Raskob insisted that he was speaking of "opportunism." He wanted everybody, however humble, to share in the boom that "has just begun."

To help them, he planned to put $5 million into an "Equities Security Company," the purpose of which would be to buy stocks for "proletarians who could invest $200 a head."

The company would then buy a stock in $500 blocks. The $300 deficiency would be loaned to investors by a financial subsidiary, in which the stock would be posted as collateral. They would pay off their $300 debt at $25 a month—the money coming from what Raskob believed would be the "assuredly increased value of the stock."

He foresaw the day when "we will tell the people 'invest your money with us, under proper legal safeguards, and we will make money for you.' There is no excuse for a man who can save a little money and does not compel that money to work for him."

Lamb felt he had just been given a "privileged glimpse into a practical Utopia, whose portals would be guarded by the Empire State Building."

Evangeline Adams was a regular traveler to Utopia. She had only to look into her crystal ball or shuffle her tarot cards. Sometimes she reached it through studying palms. She was America's most famous fortuneteller. Since 1927, coinciding with an upsurge in the market, Evangeline had concentrated on predicting its future. It had made her even richer, even more sought after. Four thousand people a day wrote to her. At twenty dollars a reading, she claimed to predict how the Dow Jones Index and the New York *Times* Industrial Averages would behave.*

Her clients numbered some of the most famous in the land. Movie queen Mary Pickford always consulted Evangeline before investing; steel tycoon Charles Schwab was said to base his buy and sell orders largely on her predictions.

For those who could not visit her studios above Carnegie Hall, Evangeline produced a monthly newsletter, explaining how the changing position of the planets would affect stocks and shares. Over 100,000 people paid fifty cents each for these forecasts, advertised as "a guaranteed system to beat Wall Street."

There were scores of other "systems" offering similar advice. One was based on the premise that no bull market would collapse in a month that did not have an "R" in it. Another depended on sunspots. A third system used a complicated code which was rooted in the dialogue of popular comic strip characters; their speech was broken down and reassembled to form the names of shares which investors should buy. Thousands swore by this method. Then there was the Oyster Theory, which claimed that the market would peak during the oyster season. No reason, valid or otherwise, was advanced for this theory. Still, thousands believed it.

Many thousands more Americans believed Evangeline Adams. They were confirmed in their faith by the knowledge that Morgan the Elder was said to have sworn by her prophecies. There was a lovingly retold legend that the financier had once loaned $100 million simply because Evangeline said his rising sign, Aries, was favorably positioned. Morgan was rumored to have made a handsome profit from the loan. Soon afterward, he took Evangeline on his private yacht for an extensive

* *New York Times Industrial Averages:* less well known than the Dow Jones Index, these are the average of the prices of twenty-five specially selected stocks.

cruise to conduct "scientific investigation" into her powers. Whatever Morgan discovered, he kept to himself.

Evangeline's own horoscope had told her to come to New York on a certain day in March 1899. She did, putting up at the Windsor Hotel on March 16, and that very evening consulted the stars of the hotel's owner, Warren F. Leland. As she wrote later, "I hastened to warn him that he was under one of the worst possible combinations of planet conditions, terrifying in their unfriendliness."

The next day the hotel burned to the ground. Leland's family perished in the fire.

Fortunately for Evangeline, he was not too distraught to tell the newspapers about her prediction.

From that moment on her success was assured.

Not only Pierpont Morgan, but European royalty consulted her; the more she charged, the greater her fame grew.

This morning, as usual, the studio waiting room resembled a broker's office, with its ticker tape machine, and copies of *The Wall Street Journal* and other financial newspapers. Every chair was occupied either by men in expensive topcoats or women in even more expensive furs. They talked incessantly of the market as they waited their turn to enter Evangeline's office.

Its walls were lined with portraits of the famous. Enrico Caruso (Pisces) hung next to England's King Edward VII (Scorpio). A faded photo of Pierpont Morgan shared wall space with a fellow Arien, Mary Pickford. Steel tycoon Charles Schwab (Aquarius) had a wall to himself.

Seated firmly behind her desk, dressed in a severe black suit, the bespectacled, lantern-jawed Miss Adams dispensed predictions in a confident voice. She reminded some clients of their psychiatrist. Others thought she resembled a benign attorney imparting news of an unexpected windfall. Still others detected a religious fervor about her; perhaps it was the way Evangeline continually stressed that God's hand was guiding the market ever upward. Not short on optimism, she herself was heavily into the market, and intended to remain so, she told friends, until her self-predicted death in 1932.

Now, February 15, 1929, she was content to inform clients that call money would soon climb, and that a "violent upswing" was indicated around the end of the month.

The message from the medium was clear: invest now.

Nowhere was this exhortation being so enthusiastically followed than in a private suite of the condemned Waldorf-Astoria Hotel. Only women were allowed inside the suite, which was permanently rented by a Stock Exchange firm and decked out as a club. The lighting was discreet, the drapes permanently closed, the davenports cavernous. Deep Florentine armchairs, bronze statues, and side tables to which waitresses brought coffee and drinks, added to the illusion.

A dozen customers of all ages lounged around the suite, drinking and smoking fashionable Turkish cigarettes in long holders. Their eyes moved between the cabalistic symbols gliding across a narrow screen fixed to one wall and a blackboard on which two blue-smocked girls chalked an ever-changing variety of similar figures. The staccato noise from half a dozen tickers banked along another wall was sometimes lost in the shrill voices of the onlookers.

The suite was one of the dozens of "speciality shops" in New York catering exclusively for women investors. There were an estimated 5,000 more in other cities throughout America.

Nobody knew exactly when women had begun to invest on a mass scale. Some dated it from the World War, when the number of workingwomen increased. Others said it was a spin-off from the fact that a large percentage of the depositors in U S savings banks were female. There had been a great increase in joint bank accounts, resulting, said one survey, in "an awareness of money among women."

Another poll concluded: "The number of families in which the wife assumes the leadership and direction in the care of funds is growing. Many professional men—professors, ministers, doctors, writers—who have never had any contact with financial matters, have married young women who have gone through the training of secretarial posts in business offices; these men have come to lean upon their training when it comes to investments."

A third survey noted "the marked upsurge in the number of cases in which stocks are bought in the name of the husband but where all the correspondence and dealings are with the wife."

Surveys like these played their part in encouraging women to invest. Newspaper stories further fired their interest; it was reported that in 1928 forty-four women paid tax on incomes in excess of a million dollars. There were not only more women millionaires in the United States than ever before, but there were more women than men paying taxes on incomes over $100,000. The banking house of Lawrence Stern and Company had concluded that women possessed 41 percent of the total wealth of the nation.

Nowhere was this more evident than in corporate share holdings The United Steel Corporation had 59,688 woman stockholders—about 37 percent of all its shareholders—and the number was increasing every week. General Motors had 36,900 woman shareholders as against 59,700 men; the women controlled 3,958,570 shares—enough to have a decisive effect on company policy. Forty-four percent of the Baltimore and Ohio Railroad—15,826 stockholders—were women. Pennsylvania Railroad had 79,275 woman stockholders, a little more than 50 percent; the company was unkindly referred to by Wall Street chauvinists as "the Petticoat Line."

But women's influence was most evident in the American Telephone and Telegraph Company where 250,000 women held 55 percent of the company's shares.

Local and national surveys showed that 90 percent of salaried women had bank accounts, and that of them, 80 percent held securities. Naturally, the media became interested.

Eunice Fullar Barnard, a writer on the *North American Review,* decided to visit the suite in the Waldorf. She was preparing an article on "ladies of the ticker," a title that the genteel Eunice preferred to the brasher one a tabloid had coined: "Ladybulls." A perceptive reporter, she filled her notebook with cameos of the ladies lounging and smoking.

"Almost noon!" yawned the domestic-looking young woman. "How the time does go in here! That RKK ought to start pretty soon. She generally runs toward the middle of the day."

"But look how Steel is breaking!" countered a firm, middle-aged voice. "That ought to mean something. A big market by the first of the week. I have a tip, but I always watch them awhile first. Now Copper, I wouldn't—"

The nervous little gray-haired person in front dropped her tip sheet. "Did you say Copper?" she faltered.

On the other side, the voice of the woman in the fur coat cut across. "Even if I have to sell short," she was protesting. "And I promised my husband I'd never do that."

These impressions would enliven the thorough research Eunice conducted in the many establishments outside which hung the telltale sign: "Women Customers Only." Her overall feeling was that "day in, day out, through a long five hours, aggressive, guttural dowagers, gum-chewing blondes, shrinking spinsters who look as if they belonged in a missionary-society meeting, watch, pencil in hand, from the opening of the market till the belated ticker drones its last in the middle of the afternoon."

Her investigations had drawn her to stuffy back rooms in brokerage houses, ticker-tape-strewn private parlors—one with a beauty salon attached—and to specially created ornate suites like the one in the Waldorf. She had spoken to a variety of customers—typists, housewives, a few heiresses among them. And, like any good reporter, she had collected picturesque examples of feminine luck in the market. Eunice liked particularly the tale of a woman farmer in the Midwest who had phoned an order to her woman broker in New York to buy one hundred shares of auto stock at a certain price. By the next day the stock had gone up twenty points. The lady farmer had made an overnight profit of almost $2,000 at a cost of $6 for the telephone call.

Another broker told Eunice about a scrubwoman who had made $15,000 on the market, and came into his office with the cash for reinvestment. It was a typical enough story—the market was filled with waitresses, telephonists, cooks, and maids investing their mites to accrue modest fortunes. A few, like the wife of an Indianapolis banker, made huge killings. She had bought stocks in a large mail-order house; her ultimate profit was $500,000.

The reporter discovered that an estimated 85 percent of the spending in America was done by women, and had found enthusiastic support for the idea that still more women should buy securities. Bankers, brokers, and insurance company officers told her that women made better investors than men because, in the words of one banker, they had "more common sense." Eunice also learned that the New York Stock Exchange still had "certain discriminations" against women. Technically, she was told, stock in a married woman's name was a bad risk; the Exchange insisted this was not an arbitrary distinction on its part, but a provision to protect investors in states where the laws did not recognize a married woman as party to a contract. And, while there was no formal ban, the floor of the Exchange was "better protected against women members than that of Congress." No woman—or man for that matter—could buy a seat unless he or she received enough votes from the membership committee. The committee had never yet seen fit to favor the admission of a woman.

An early feminist, Eunice could nevertheless see that the hurly-burly of the floor was no place for a lady. But she failed to understand why they had to buy their stocks segregated from men, in places like the hotels she had toured. The manageress of the Waldorf-Astoria suite offered her an unexpected reason: "We do not want a lot of men smoking cheap cigars in here!"

It was just the sort of quote Eunice needed to wrap up her conclusion that in future, lady investors would probably "do more to raise the level of the common respect for women as a class than all the hard-fought suffrage campaigns."

Eunice Barnard's article was a serious attempt by a respected writer to try to explain one aspect of the bull market. Hundreds of other journalists tried, with varying degrees of success, to report other factors. Few of them recognized the increasing influence of advertising as related to Wall Street.

Thirteen years earlier, in 1916, Adolph S. Ochs, publisher of the New York *Times,* offered $100 for information leading to the conviction of anyone placing a false or misleading advertisement in his newspaper; subsequently, the *Times* rejected millions of dollars' worth of advertising. Other newspapers followed, often boasting in their columns of their honesty.

But now, the *Times,* in common with the rest of the media, accepted advertisements that would never have passed the scrutiny of Ochs—and might well have earned that $100 had the reward still been in existence.

Many of the dubious advertisements appearing in the U.S. press urged readers to invest in bonds and stocks. The circle between Madison Avenue and Wall Street was complete; they were inexorably linked, in a relationship developed in ten short years, during which the ad men had created an ambience invaluable to the continuing popularity of stock speculation. The limitless, desirable, and expensive goods coming onto the market—often products of companies quoted on the Stock Exchange—could only be sold by determined advertising campaigns. If those campaigns failed, the market would slump.

To maintain his place in consumer society, a man was told he needed a car, radio, icebox, and refrigerator; his wife required a washing machine, automatic furnace, and one of the modish pastel-hued toilets. To complete their domestic bliss they would have the latest in bathrooms: a shrine of stunning magnificence, containing, among other items, "a dental lavatory of vitreous china, twice fired." To buy it would cost the average American six months' salary. But paying was no problem; there were the installment plans. It was also part of the advertising philosophy that it was no longer enough to buy a car, radio, or refrigerator. People must have the *latest* model—junking the old one, even though it was still useful. Failure to do so would cause factories to close from the Atlantic to the Pacific, ending what some newspapers called "the golden era." To protect it, they told their readers, was the patriotic duty of every American; one way to express that was, "to buy until it hurts."

The farsighted were even encouraged to spend while alive to ensure a better hereafter. They could, for instance, find in the current issue of *The Saturday Evening Post* this advertisement from a New York casket and vault manufacturer: "How often we find cause only for regret in our memories of the manner in which we disposed of the remains of our loved ones. We were thoughtless, perhaps. It would have been so easy to provide adequate protection against the elements. However, it is idle to dwell on things past. Let us look into the future calmly and follow the examples of thousands of families who rely upon the Clark Graves Vault to defeat Nature's destructive forces. For never yet has this vault failed to protect its contents from the hurtful elements of the earth."

And so, with that promise of bodily immortality, the forward-looking would not just be buried in old-fashioned graveyards; they would be "lovingly interred" in Gardens of Rest and Vaults of Sleep, "resting" in silver- or gold-plated coffins in sepulchers resembling Greek-pillared mausoleums, equipped with specially sealed boxes in which, if one wished, the departed's stock certificates might be placed. The boxes would be hewn from "immortal" granite. If that was too expensive, the Rock of Ages Corporation offered sculpted headstones, with extra angels available on demand. For those who could not afford even that, a range of cut-price funeral parlors offered "a Repose Room, Free, and use of Twenty Palms."

The twin pillars of American civilization were now the copywriter and the salesman. Between them they supported the stock market. To do so they committed many sins in the name of prosperity. But the age of plenty seemed destined to go on forever as the manipulators continued to think of new ways to create still bigger gains in the Dow Jones and *Times* "averages." The nation was being coerced and cozened by forces it blindly trusted—business, advertising, and journalism. The few voices that protested were ignored.

Wall Street constantly encouraged Madison Avenue to persuade the public to extend its mortgage on the future. If it was necessary to buy a new car every year, it was far better to purchase *two*. A home should not merely have one bathroom—preferably with a dental lavatory—it needed a *second*. A radio was essential for *every* living room. Even the American Association of Wholesale Opticians had joined the clamor, urging people to wear one style of glasses for work, another for leisure, a third for sport. The jewelers urged brides to insist on platinum wedding rings, preferably encrusted with diamonds. If they had any doubts about the wisdom of not wearing plain old-fashioned gold bands, the advertisements informed them that by buying fancier and more expensive rings, they were giving employment to more American craftsmen than would otherwise be working. Patriotism was always a clincher. And it all helped to keep the market booming.

By 1929 the Greeting Card Association of America was ready to play its part. In a few sickening verse-years, the association had come a long way from simply selling birthday and Christmas cards. Now they had get-well cards, sorry-I-forgot-your-anniversary cards, and even sorry-you-have-been-run-over cards. Under the benevolent gaze of the stock market, the association was out to make America anniversary conscious. And so it became necessary to create new ones.

Mother's Day was born.

Combining the talents of the card makers, the candy manufacturers, and the florists, Mother's Day became the perfect rip-off. Florists had always been in the van of advertising; they had also mounted a successful campaign to remove the unhappy phrase from newspaper death notices: "No flowers by request." It had been replaced by the far more positive—and profitable—slogan: "Say Farewell with Flowers."

In a mother-orientated nation, no son, however cynical, could refuse to send flowers on that special day; the many florists in and around Wall Street—established originally to provide the carnation boutonnieres favored by fashion-conscious brokers—did a record business during the week before the bogus anniversary. As the day drew closer, the price of blooms soared—a practice perfectly understood in the countinghouses; it was known as pushing the price as high as the market would bear. In fact, candy manufacturers saw the price of their shares rise as a result of Mother's Day. Western Union and other telegraph companies witnessed similar results. Western Union even prepared a selection of messages for those unable to think of what to say. The most popular one in 1929 was: "I send a blessing for every thread of silver on my mother's head."

There was also a determined effort to sell Culture; 1929 was the year when the *nouveaux* were told it was not enough just to be *riche*. They had to have Knowledge, Conversation, Etiquette, Poise, and Language, especially French. Americans—"ordinary folk whose investments have come home"—were told to make themselves "worthy of Paris." The risks of social discomfiture were stressed. An advertisement showed a young broker, "a big success in Wall Street," humiliated by his inability to explain the menu to his date. Other advertisements stressed the need to speak "proper English." The senior partner in a Wall Street brokerage firm was depicted at his desk rejecting a man for promotion because he had committed the cardinal sin of saying "can't hardly."

Many Wall Street firms recognized the benefits of such campaigns and began to style their house ads along similar lines. In these, a man-to-man approach was adopted: a bank manager was depicted as a friendly fellow with unlimited cash to alleviate any anxiety; a broker was the middleman, there to "help you make your fortune." Big business took on human characteristics: friendliness, tolerance, and sympathy—all to attract more investors.

It worked; money flowed into Wall Street.

With few exceptions, the press doted on the upward sweep of the market. Nobody suspected that some journalists were taking regular kickbacks for writing favorable comments about questionable companies. Among them was a columnist on the *Daily News,* who signed himself "The Trader." A radio commentator, William J. McMahon, received a secret stipend of $250 a week from stock manipulator David M. Lion. McMahon praised shares in which Lion had an interest, duping his listeners into buying them.

A few newspapers tried hard to maintain not only their ethics but a sense of reality about the market; they included *Poor's Weekly Business and Investment Letter,* the *Commercial and Financial Chronicle,* and in spite of its advertising lapses, the financial pages of the New York *Times,* edited by the veteran Alexander Dana Noyes.

But even to his colleagues Noyes was becoming something of a joke, his warnings shrugged aside by the euphoria of the New Age.

Grimly, he held to his position. A crash was coming.

CHAPTER SIX

BANKERS OF A KIND

Billy Durant was angry. The telephone connection with New York kept fading, and what he had managed to hear did not improve his temper.

Charles Edwin Mitchell, president of the National City Bank, the largest in the country, repeated that the action of the Federal Reserve Board in requesting banks throughout America to curb brokers' loans was already having an effect. Call money had jumped 3½ percent in forty-eight hours. Now, on February 16, it stood at 10 percent, and there had been a break of twenty-one points in certain stocks.

Mitchell paused between each sentence of bad news; he reminded Durant of an attorney bullying a witness with inessentials before slipping in a loaded question.

The banker framed his adroitly: Who would tell the incoming President of the United States, Herbert Hoover, that the financial health of the nation was based on credit, and that the "Fed's killing the goose which laid the golden egg"?

Mitchell knew that Durant had already given several widely quoted interviews saying precisely that. He was also aware that Durant had easy access to Hoover; theirs was a long friendship, transcending politics.

The relationship between Mitchell and Durant was a shorter one, based largely on business. Some of the millions of dollars' profit Durant had made in Wall Street these past five years had passed through the National City.

Durant promised Mitchell he would consider the best approach to Hoover.

The call over, Durant resumed pacing his suite in the Flint hotel which bore his name. Like the "D" on the GM Building in Detroit, the Durant Hotel in Flint was a reminder of the immense debt that city owed the promoter. But nowadays Flint was becoming ever more associated in the public eye with Charles Mott, mainly through Mott's well-publicized munificence. His generous gifts to the community were matched by the lavish space the Flint *Journal* gave to his bequests. So far he had successfully kept from the paper's pages his love for the young Dee Furey.

From his hotel window, Durant looked down on one of the more obvious assets that Mott had helped develop. The Union Industrial Bank Building was across the street. Mott had once invited him to invest in the bank. Durant had declined; he did not trust small banks. He knew that the caliber of their staffs frequently made them susceptible to temptation; the history of American banking this past decade was cluttered with tales of tellers who had stolen. Eighty percent of them had worked in what Durant regarded as small banks—those with assets of less than $100 million.

He turned back to his own problems. Mitchell's news was disturbing. It was not the twenty-one-point drop that alarmed Durant. His market sense told him there would be a rally in a day or two. And he had been given a number of pointers to confirm this view. A source in the Commerce Commission in Washington had phoned with news that the Baltimore and Ohio Railroad and the Chesapeake and Ohio planned between them to take over twenty-seven smaller railroads. An announcement was expected in a few days. Durant had thanked his informant, but decided not to buy rail stock. That sort of quick killing no longer appealed. Of much more interest was the rumor that Guaranty Trust and the National Bank of Commerce were planning a merger. That was bound to have a beneficial effect on the market. So, too, would the outcome of the next meeting of the Board of U. S. Steel. Durant's source in the company predicted that the directors would vote to increase the common stock from its present 7,533,210 to 12,500,000 shares, each of $100 par value. The new issue would add nearly $500 million to its working capital. Durant knew this would steady the market and perhaps call money would drop a percent or two.

But it was the long-term efforts over the period leading into the summer that troubled Durant. He felt that if the Federal Reserve Board continued what he saw as public nagging, the market could become seriously depressed.

He turned again to his files on the Federal Reserve, studying the board's arguments, looking for means to destroy their credibility.

Charles Mitchell's proposal that Durant should beard Herbert Hoover once he was installed in the White House was only part of his campaign against the Federal Reserve. From his second-floor office, one of the largest and plushest in Wall Street, the president of National City had mobilized other forces to his bidding.

Telephone calls had alerted obliging editors to start a campaign against the Reserve Board. Soon Mitchell could expect to see a familiar photograph—the one with his shaggy eyebrows raised over his wide, confident grin—across the financial pages, accompanying appeals for "business to be left to businessmen." Doubtless the editorials would again laud Mitchell as the banker of bankers, the genius of the New Economic Era. He had spoken to Richard Whitney, and the Stock Exchange vice-president—who had a personal vested interest in maintaining a rising market—promised to arouse Wall Street's many friends in Congress; in the next few days the first barbed attacks would be launched against the Federal.

Mitchell also spoke to Secretary of the Treasury Andrew Mellon, an old friend who was largely responsible for the benevolent attitude Washington displayed toward commerce and industry. Mellon had resigned directorships in fifty-one corporations to become Secretary, first under Harding and then Coolidge, and soon, he hoped, under Hoover. He had never lost his passion for big business; he liked nothing better than to hear details of some merger or boardroom battle. His policy hinged on a belief that high corporate taxes were not only economically unsound but morally wrong. But he seemed to see nothing wrong in the fact that there was now a vast concentration of wealth in a small section of the community. A recent survey showed that the 60,000 families at the top of the economic scale were worth the same in financial terms as the 25 million at the bottom; and the wealthy were steadily growing wealthier. Income from dividends, under a series of tax cuts introduced by Mellon, had risen 65 percent in nine years. Higher dividends attracted more investors. Up went the market.

Mitchell knew that at the first signs of an economic downtrend, at the faintest hint of pessimism in Wall Street, Mellon could be counted on to make a suitable public statement which would send the market flying again. His tenure in office was signposted by such statements, each as optimistic as the previous one. So it was now. Mitchell's telephone call elicited the helpful promise that, while Mellon could not publicly chastise the Federal Reserve, he could pass the word along that this was not the time to halt the full flow of America's industry or the national desire to absorb consumer goods.

These were all shrewd tactical moves in what Mitchell now regarded as open warfare between his National City and the Federal Reserve Board.

One of the reasons for the conflict could be stated simply. Commercial banks borrowed money from the Federal Reserve Banks at one rate, then reloaned it to customers in the call money market at a higher rate. The present call money rates—averaging around 8 percent—meant that National City, borrowing at the fixed 5 percent from the Federal, made a handsome profit. Mitchell, like other bankers, saw this as one of the perks of banking. And, if the Federal raised its discount rate by 1 percent, he could follow suit, and raise the interest he charged by a similar amount. But the board, by requesting its reserve banks to refuse altogether loans to commercial banks who intended to use the money to finance speculation, had initiated an action to which Mitchell had not yet found a solution; if he informed the Federal Reserve Bank in New York that his National City wanted to borrow in order to finance stock market loans, the bank would likely refuse his request.

To the blunt, beefy Mitchell, for professional—but also personal—reasons the Federal Reserve had become a dangerous meddler. Nevertheless, he sensed a certain weakness in their resolve, and a sign of weakness always brought out the bully in Charles Mitchell. He felt he needed to teach the board in Washington a lesson it would not forget, to deliver a coup de grace which would bring gasps of admiration from even those hard-nosed Wall Streeters who did not always like his methods. The more he thought about it, the more he could see the glimmer of a plan. And it had the one quality he was famous for—brazen cheek.

There were other characteristics that molded Mitchell: inexhaustible energy, vivid imagination, a surprisingly foul tongue for a banker, powerful concentration, a talent for organizing and stimulating others, a natural gift for commerce, and, above all, a flair for salesmanship. Together, they had made him, at fifty-three, a colossus of banking and a living example to every poor boy that America really was the land of opportunity.

He was also a tax dodger and share manipulator.

Born in the rundown Boston suburb of Chelsea, a few blocks from Joe Kennedy's Irish immigrant quarter, Mitchell paid his way through college by teaching public speaking. He had a mellifluous voice, able to charm anybody, and was quick to make use of his talent. It got him a job with Western Electric in Chicago; at night he studied commercial law and bookkeeping. In a few years he was the company's credit manager. Always on the lookout for a situation to exploit, he spotted the possibility of bringing together a number of small companies making telephone switchboards, for whom Western Electric supplied the parts. It was too good an idea to put to his employers. Mitchell took his scheme to New York and presented it to Oakleigh Thorne, president of the Trust Company of America. Thorne did not take up the plan, but he was so impressed by Mitchell that he offered him a post as his personal assistant. That year, 1907, in the same financial panic that had given Jesse Livermore the chance to make his name, Mitchell was offered an opportunity of a different sort. The Trust Company found itself in the midst of the vortex; Mitchell worked twenty-hour days, catnapping on the floor of Thorne's office. The panic passed, but the experience Mitchell gained was invaluable. Four years later he founded his own investment house. Five years after that—1916—he accepted the presidency of the National City Company, a wholly owned subsidiary of the National City Bank. Its main function was to deal in securities that the bank was forbidden by law to handle.

In 1921 Mitchell became president of the bank as well.

When he started with the National City Company, its staff consisted of a typist, a clerk, and an errand boy. By 1929 Mitchell had transformed it into an organization with a staff of 1,400—350 of which were salesmen—and branch offices in fifty-eight cities.

He was in his element, a financial emperor, dynamic, optimistic, and insolent. Mitchell sent out his salesmen in all directions. He preached at them, bullied them, bribed them. He taught them to lay in wait outside bucket shops, nightclubs, and inside railway terminals, arguing that a good salesman could sales-pitch a customer between the time he bought his ticket and boarded the train. Some salesmen even worked the transcontinental expresses.

Mitchell had them knocking on the doors of rural homesteads as if they were selling Fuller brushes or vacuum cleaners. He devised contests that set them at each other's throats. And above all, he held over their heads the threat of dismissal if they failed to meet their quotas.

Fearful of failure, the salesmen resorted to faking orders to inflate their figures; to do so they sometimes invested their own salaries in securities about which they knew as little as the people they sold them to.

Driven ever on by Mitchell, his salesmen sold the American public $15 billion worth of securities in nine years. They sold the stocks of automobile companies which almost immediately went broke; they sold the bonds of South American republics on the verge of insolvency and revolution; of Bavarian community schemes that had no hope of materializing; in companies launching cloud-cuckoo-land plans in Switzerland, Austria, and the Benelux countries.

And they sold stock in their parent company, the National City Bank —making a mockery of the law expressly forbidding that.

To one of his employees, the exhortations of Mitchell "sounded as if

Attila the Hun had coupled with one of the Borgias to create their own Nero."

When bond salesmen dared suggest to Mitchell that buyers were becoming difficult to find, he took them up into the Banker's Club in New York, if he was in a jovial mood, and delivered them a familiar sermon. Leading them to one of the club's windows, he would boom: "Look down there! There are six million people with incomes that aggregate thousands of millions of dollars. They are just waiting for someone to come and tell them what to do with their savings. Take a good look, eat a good lunch, and then go down and tell them."

It never failed to work.

And even abroad, from the Balkans to the Falkland Islands, on this February morning salesmen were peddling Mitchell's wares.

It made him:

Wealthier—his 1928 income from the bank alone was $25,000 in salary plus a whopping $1,316,634.14 in profits; 1929 promised to be even better.

Fatter—his weight bothered him; in an effort to control it, most mornings he walked from his mansion in the East Seventies to his Wall Street office.

Meaner—recently, when barnstorming through the bank headquarters urging people to work harder, a young salesman asked to speak to him privately. Mitchell scowled. The young man politely pressed his president to step aside. Still scowling, Mitchell complied. The young man whispered discreetly: "Sir, your trousers are unbuttoned."

Mitchell fired him on the spot.

The banker was not the sort of man to accept criticism.

Nor, for that matter, could he allow the Federal Reserve to commit *lèse majesté* by its actions to curb speculation in shares. He had thought long and hard about the problem. And now Charles Mitchell knew exactly what he would do to the faceless men of the Reserve Board in Washington.

Having reread his files on the Federal Reserve, Billy Durant decided he should return to New York for consultation with Mitchell and others. Basically a cautious and conservative thinker, Durant did not favor "a bull in a china shop approach" to Herbert Hoover.

Once Hoover was installed as thirty-first President of the United States, Durant believed he could persuade him to intervene favorably. Hoover's entire election campaign had been fought and decisively won on a platform that was simple and sweet. He had spoken of two chickens in every pot and a car in every garage. He had no fears for the future of the country: "It is bright with hope." Based on such banalities, Hoover had collected 21 million votes—the third largest number in history. His opponent, Al Smith, had quietly gone into partnership with John J. Raskob to raise the Empire State Building. Hoover would assume office on March 4.

Durant knew the President would need time to settle in, to familiarize himself with the trappings of power. And, in spite of their friendship, Hoover could be embarrassed by a preannounced visit from Durant; it would not take the press long to ferret out the reason. The ensuing publicity would act against what Durant intended, to "have Hoover make the Federal Reserve toe the line."

His decision made, he had booked a private compartment on the 6:21 P.M. Père-Marquette Railroad express to New York.

With time in hand before departure, Durant set off to enjoy himself, walking through the streets of Flint, dropping in on old friends. He had a trick of immediate intimacy, an intensity of recall that made him both a clown and character assassin. Recently a tabloid had called him "a Robin Hood of memory, robbing the past to pay for the present," journalism that Durant dismissed as "bullshit." Nevertheless, he did have a way of describing the Flint of his youth, of recalling the flavor of a time gone. It was an expression of love for the city and its founders, and it was a side of Billy Durant that he kept carefully hidden from his associates in Wall Street.

With his quick, distinctive, bouncing gait, Durant walked across the city's main intersection, Saginaw and Kearsley streets, where all those years ago a friend had picked him up in his new two-wheeled cart—and fired Durant's first interest in transport.

Everywhere he turned, memories were stirred. Passing the Citizen National Bank, he remembered the day he had persuaded the manager to loan him $2,000 to found what would eventually become the largest auto company in the world, General Motors.

The cars his organizational genius had created changed not only the physical but the social structure of Flint. The city expanded and was still doing so; Durant often said that only New York seemed to be as frenetic about building as Flint. The dominant structures were the auto plants, and the factories—big and small—that supplied them with parts; the plants dwarfed the drab streets with their clapboarded houses and shops. Beyond the augean work areas were the suburbs, greener and cleaner, where the managers lived. Once they had either walked or come by horse carriage into the city. But the buggies had disappeared, most of the stables were closed, and the horses auctioned off at the Chicago rendering plant. In his nostalgic moments, Durant regretted the passing era, when men hitched a wagon and team to take courting couples for picnics in the country, when youths drove a pony and trap to the cockfights held on Friday nights in out-of-town farm barns.

And yet, whenever he became too sentimental, he reminded himself that the auto industry had brought untold prosperity to Flint.

From the People's Furniture Company (advertising a new line in imported tinware) to Thomas Doyle, coal merchant ("handling the world famous Lehigh coal") the signs of prosperity were even more striking to the perceptive Durant than they were in New York.

Customer credit in Flint was easy to come by; the shops, in turn, extended their credit with the wholesalers, who in turn kept the factories waiting. But as one trader assured Durant, everybody got paid in the end. Industrially, the city was at peace. The unions were making no demands; they would have found it difficult to improve on working conditions. The Negroes knew their place, and if they did not, the local chapter of the Ku Klux Klan could soon put them there.

Road transport, which Durant had been so instrumental in helping to create, meant that the New Orleans Fruit House could import fruit from California, and even expected to do a brisk trade this summer with pineapples "all the way from Hawaii." The Economy Shoe Store had on display the identical shoes imported from Europe that Durant saw on Fifth Avenue. William Lederbach, butcher, bought meat in Chicago and had it rushed to Flint by truck, enhancing his published boast that he "followed the cow from the pen to the ice chest with a skillful hand." The Grand Union Tea Company brought to Flint housewives "the best that the world produces at prices better than the average." Only the Flint Brewery Company stood closed and silent—a mute reminder that Prohibition had just entered its ninth year.

This evening, as usual, fair-haired Jolan Slezsak was at the railway station to watch the night express depart for New York. Though she had never made the journey, she knew the route by heart: Detroit, Toledo, Youngstown, Pittsburgh, Washington, Baltimore, Philadelphia, and on into Grand Central Terminal—faraway places with romantic-sounding names which Jolan dreamed of seeing one day. Meanwhile, she shared with other onlookers the vicarious thrill of watching passengers board the train.

Even in her hand-me-down clothes—cut, patched, and darned by her mother—the well-developed fifteen-year-old knew she attracted the interest of the men around her. She blushed and busied herself, fussing over her baby sister Margaret, plonked in the battered baby carriage. Jolan hoped nobody would come close enough to smell the fumes rising from the buggy. One of the bottles of home-brewed gin carried in its false bottom had broken, and the liquor was seeping out onto the ground.

The chubby-cheeked six-year-old Margaret giggled happily; Jolan suspected her sister was becoming intoxicated by the aroma. Her own clothes were permanently permeated by a blend of whiskey, gin, and the Hungarian schnapps her mother and stepfather produced. They had cautioned Jolan never to stand too close to an open fire for fear she ignited in a blaze of alcohol.

It was just one of many hazards for the youngest and prettiest bootlegger in Flint. There was the risk that a police patrol might stop and search the baby buggy; or worse, that a special Prohibition agent might arrest her. The agents had arrived in the town a year ago determined to sniff out the stills that made Flint famous throughout Michigan. The men were uniformly despised. And even if Jolan avoided their clutches, she still faced the danger of having her liquor stolen by a street gang.

Yet the excitement "of doing something wrong but not criminal" made it fun for Jolan. And without her regular liquor-delivery run, she would have no excuse for this visit to the rail station each night.

Standing beside the locomotive, enjoying the warmth from its boiler, Jolan watched the last passengers board.

She recognized William Crapo Durant from his newspaper photographs. He looked very small, surrounded by strapping porters manhandling his baggage. Jolan was puzzled by the folding chair one carried so reverently. Surely, she thought, the train seats were not so uncomfortable that he had to bring his own. It was beyond her imagination that one of Durant's pleasures in life was having his own barber's chair with him wherever he went.

Jolan watched, round-eyed at the quarter-dollar tips he dispensed. In a few minutes Durant casually gave away more money to the porters than her stepfather profited from a night's distilling.

She promised herself that one day she, too, would be in a position to tip people, command service, be "somebody."

For a moment Jolan imagined the baby carriage she had yet to push for several more hours was really a luxurious limousine, and the decidedly tipsy Margaret a chauffeur. Caught up in her fantasy, she ordered Margaret to take her to the Union Industrial Bank headquarters in downtown Flint. Margaret joined in the game, making car noises while Jolan ran, pushing the buggy, scattering onlookers, leaving them sniffing the air in her gin-sodden wake.

Coming to a halt, she saw herself outside the bank. In quick succession, Margaret became a doorman and then a teller. Imperiously, Jolan demanded her money, the $400 her father had left in trust for her just before he died in a coal-mining accident.

This was always the part of their game that nonplussed Margaret. She didn't know what banks were for, and had no idea what a trust fund was. And she simply could not comprehend how her sister came to have so much money.

She began to cry, her tears lost in the shunting of the departing express.

After soothing Margaret, Jolan continued to dream. She knew the $400 was in the bank, and that it *would* be hers when she reached eighteen, the day when the trust fund matured. Her stepfather had explained that every day the money stayed there, the bank added a few cents of its own to the nest egg. He called this "interest." Jolan could not understand it; she often wondered, if the bank gave "everybody money like this, then how did *it* make money?"

Nevertheless, her money was there, and seemingly growing every day.

Her delivery round took her past the headquarters of the Union Industrial Bank. The lights were on, and through the ground-floor windows Jolan glimpsed the impressive banking hall and tellers' cages. There was nobody to be seen, and her first reaction was that the bank had no business wasting money on electricity when they could use it to give her more of "that interest."

The thought occurred that maybe the lights were being left on to frighten off thieves. Then she remembered her stepfather saying her money was locked away in a vault that nobody could open, "without a special key."

So maybe, after all, there were people still working late, earning more interest for her.

It was a thought that sent Jolan singing on her way.

If her piping voice penetrated the oak-paneled boardroom at the rear of the Union Industrial Bank, none of its occupants gave any sign of hearing. They were preoccupied with other matters.

Fifteen men sat around the long polished table under a portrait of the chairman of the Board of Directors, Charles Stewart Mott. He had not been invited to this extraordinary gathering. And all those present were in no doubt that if Mott knew of their discussions, he would have them arrested.

They were the officers and tellers of the bank, trusted employees. Each one of the men was also a practicing embezzler.

As if to establish this was not a normal bank occasion, some of the men sat in shirt sleeves, smoking, using brass spittoons as ashtrays.

Frank Montague, one of the bank's vice-presidents, a tall, cadaverous man, did not approve of such lapses. But he said nothing, sitting attentively in his blue serge suit, uncomfortably aware that the discussions increasingly placed him outside the law. Yet the others sounded so confident, so certain of success, that Montague felt "obliged to go along."

He did not think he was stealing; he preferred instead to regard it as "merely borrowing money without approval." And, he kept telling himself, he had every intention of replacing all the money. Even so, the risk of discovery was beginning to cause Montague sleepless nights. He worried about how his wife, Louise, and children would manage if he were caught and sent to prison. Yet it was to ease his financial problems that Montague had become a thief in the first place. Ever since his marriage, he had been short of cash; the demands of a growing family had exacerbated the situation. On Montague's salary, he went into debt a little more each month. When he was invited to join the other embezzlers, it seemed a solution to all his problems. But the fear of arrest had now dampened his enthusiasm.

Milton Pollock, a handsome thirty-nine-year-old, and also a vice-president, had learned to put such unpleasant thoughts from his mind. He, too, was a family man, with a sick wife, Elizabeth, and growing children. He knew he could never tell Elizabeth what he was doing; the shock might kill her. The doctor had repeatedly told Pollock that his wife was "very fragile"; and treatment was proving a slow and expensive process. A desire to get extra money for drugs had drawn Pollock into the syndicate. Once in, he had worked especially hard to make sure no bank examiner would ever be able to detect his chicanery.

Ivan Christensen, the bank's assistant cashier, was stealing to maintain a life-style that his $375 a month salary could not support. He and his wife, Betty, belonged to several country clubs, moving easily amid the upper strata of local society. Gay and vivacious, Betty was one of the smartest-dressed women in town; in his fine suits and hand-laundered shirts, her husband looked more like a bank president than a junior officer. The Christensens were having built a $75,000-dollar mansion in the most expensive part of town. Their neighbors would include some of Flint's most distinguished first families. Christensen planned to pay for the house by speculation.

He had started stealing money from the bank early in 1928, working alone, using the money to play the New York stock market. The shares he first bought achieved modest gains; he sold them, replaced the stolen money, and kept the profit. Encouraged, Christensen embezzled and invested again. This time he made a loss, having sold short on a rising market. To cover his loss he stole more. Investing again, he had been partially successful, but was still in debt to the bank and his stockbroker. Christensen hoped to solve that by committing another theft of bank money. Luck was with him—this time he made enough to cover his debts and provide a profit for himself. He had been bitten by the bug. From then on he had systematically plundered the bank.

Sometime in 1928, it gradually dawned on him that others in the bank were doing the same. The conspirators had ganged together, their confidence growing with their numbers.

Christensen was now their acknowledged leader, buying and selling securities on the private phone connecting his desk to Wall Street. Over $2 million of the Union Industrial Bank's money had already been stolen to play the market.

This weekly meeting of the conspirators was Christensen's latest innovation. The boardroom was the only one big enough to accommodate all those engaged in what had become the biggest bank swindle in history. The gatherings were a chance to pool ideas and plug any gaps in their system.

Montague was not keen on the meetings. He would have preferred to "operate alone," without the risk of somebody else making a mistake that could incriminate him.

Equally, though he would never have admitted it to anybody, he felt he had little in common with members of the group that had come to regard itself as "a league of gentlemen."

Christensen, for instance, was "too flashy"; Clifford Plumb was "utterly boring"; some of the other tellers were "just not the sort of people I would associate with normally."

Only the presence of John de Camp among the conspirators made Montague relax. The bank's senior vice-president, in Montague's view, was "class."

De Camp sat in his accustomed chair at one end of the table, expensively suited, a solid gold fob watch tucked in a vest pocket. Stocky and bespectacled, he looked like a church deacon, one of the many roles that he, in fact, relished; he enjoyed being introduced to strangers as a banker and "pillar of the church." Married, with four children, he planned to move his wife, Edna, and family into a spacious new home on Flint's most prestigious street, Circle Drive. Yet it was not a shortage of money to pay for the house that had turned De Camp into a thief. Although not rich, he was comfortably off. For the past year he had been helping steal money he did not really need. He was not even sure himself why he was involved. The nearest he had come to explaining it was in an unguarded remark to Montague that the "bull market game has gotten to me and there's no way I can stop."

He and Montague were shareholders in the bank they were looting. The only other officer to hold stock was the bank's president, Grant Brown. His son, the boyish-faced Robert Brown, a twenty-eight-year-old teller and member of Montague's church, was one of the conspirators.

Montague knew that Grant Brown had no inkling that his son—or indeed any member of the staff—was an embezzler. Nowadays, the fifty-six-year-old chief executive spent a great deal of time away from the office, traveling or mixing in Michigan society. Grant Brown insisted such socializing was important to preserve the position of the Union Industrial Bank as the most thriving in Flint. During the past fourteen years, in partnership with Chairman Mott, President Brown had guided the bank to its present preeminent position—deposits of over $32 million in ten branches.

It was Grant Brown who had created the slogan "The Bank of Personal Service" and written the advertising copy that marked the bank's move to its present headquarters:

"The bank is a human sort of place. It has its own club, 'The Industrial Bank Club,' which has for its object the development of its members along educational as well as social lines. Regular business meetings bring out helpful discussions on the problems of banking— friendly gatherings that promote acquaintance and good fellowship. The bank is a bank with an unusual warmth and friendliness. Too much credit cannot be given to those in our ranks who come in daily contact with the general public. These men and women, by their courtesy and careful attention to the wants of our customers, have made our slogan a real working principle."

Frank Montague sometimes wondered what the author of those words would say if he knew how his pious sentiments were being subverted. And knowing the family's background, the vice-president also wondered what had made young Robert succumb to temptation.

The Brown family, in Montague's view, was "a Flint first family," not only wealthy but respected across the community for their moral leadership. Grant Brown had become the bank's president after a stint as a state bank examiner. One of his tasks then was to detect embezzlers in Michigan banks.

A nonsmoker and teetotaler, Brown ran the bank as an extension of his private life—infusing in the staff the same "strong Christian principles" that he tried to instill in his children.

Gail, the eldest, had married in 1923. Two years later, Grant Brown's wife suddenly died. By then Robert was working in the bank as a teller and had married the daughter of a judge.

Everybody expected he would one day become bank president; in the meantime Robert and his wife were leading members of their church congregation.

In 1926 Grant Brown caused a minor sensation in Flint by announcing he was marrying an old school flame, Marie Bailey, a buxom forty-eight-year-old. Theirs was a head-turning romance; two middle-aged people caught in the full flush of new love. They married in the spring of 1927. Not long after, Robert started to pilfer the bank's money.

Now, for this mid-February meeting, the other tellers had grouped themselves around Robert Brown. There was Russell Runyon, a quiet man with a natural flair for figures. Runyon, in Montague's opinion, could trace a mistake "quicker than any man alive"; or, as he had been doing this past year, bury the evidence of his embezzling deep in the neat ledgers he kept.

James Barron, Farrell Thompson, Robert McDonald, George Wood-house, Clifford Plumb, Mark Kelly, David McGregor, and Arthur Schlosser were the other tellers involved in the swindle. Montague believed it was "simply a desire to live a little better" that had originally enticed them.

Now, like him, they were all "in so deep" there was no escape.

Montague doubted if Elton Graham, the bank's senior cashier, a sober-faced man in a black suit, would want to escape even if he could. He had stolen more money than any of the others; his market speculations had been disastrous. He had repeatedly backed the wrong stocks, selling short and being sold out.

There was painful silence when Christensen announced that Graham was down by almost $70,000—a fortune for a man earning just $300 a month.

The grim-faced Graham agreed to accept advice from Christensen before speculating further.

Milton Pollock also revealed that he was down, by some $50,000. Like Jesse Livermore, he was a short seller, but Pollock was no Livermore.

So far, Montague reported, he was "slightly ahead." For the money to invest, he relied "on the call market game." Like all good cons, this one was strikingly simple, and each man around the table favored it.

They merely took advantage of the considerable flow of cash that was deposited every day by customers anxious to have the bank place their money in the lucrative New York call money market. Banks all over the world were doing that for their clients.

At the Union Industrial, each customer was given a proper receipt for his money, which was then sent to New York. A careful entry was made in bank records showing the amount transferred. To even the most vigilant bank examiner it would appear the money was in New York, earning interest.

In reality, the conspirators recalled the money from New York only hours after it reached there. But no record showed that the money was back in Flint.

It was now available for the embezzlers to recycle into Wall Street for their own purposes. When they made a profit, they used it to replace the pilfered money and the interest it would have accumulated on the call market. The balance they kept.

If a customer suddenly demanded his money, other bank funds were diverted. To conceal that, a further juggling of the books was necessary.

The system was almost foolproof, providing there was a regular flow of profits from Wall Street.

But now, an unexpected break in the market, coupled with not too clever investing, had once more plunged the embezzlers into debt. They badly needed a killing to pay back what they currently owed to the bank.

The inventive Christensen suggested a new means of raising cash for them to invest. Women customers tended to leave their safe-deposit keys with the bank "for safe keeping." It would be a simple matter to open those boxes and use the contents to play the market.

After a lively debate, it was decided to hold over this scheme for future consideration; there were already a number of ploys in daily operation.

The tellers were making use of one of the oldest tricks in banking. They simply pocketed the cash deposited at their cages and placed it on the stock market. If they won, they replaced the money. If they lost, they pocketed some more and invested that. If a customer wanted to withdraw his cash, he was paid out in money purloined from someone else.

Another dodge was known as "FNS"—the faked note scheme. FNS required close teamwork and careful forgery. Both were supplied by the embezzlers.

Like any bank, the Union Industrial daily received bills and drafts of all kinds to be sent to other parts of the country. Some of these transfers involved the routine movement of share certificates from one city to another.

In 1928 the embezzlers had begun diverting those certificates into their own hands. They then set their scheme in motion.

First they wrote out promissory notes in the name of prominent local figures, stating that those personages owned the shares and that the certificates were lodged with the bank as collateral against loans. The share certificates were attached to the promissory notes as proof. Then the notes were signed with forged signatures. To complete matters, the

Union Industrial Bank made available the loans, not to the persons whose names had been forged, but to the embezzlers.

For months, the name of the bank's chairman, the unsuspecting Charles Mott, had appeared on forged notes. Recently, running out of local dignitaries, the forgers had looked further afield. Deposited now with the bank were faked notes in the name of William Crapo Durant, Henry Ford, and George F. Baker, the president of the First National Bank of New York.

And yet, in spite of all this hard work, the embezzlers continued to show a worrying inability to make money in the market.

Ivan Christensen brought the meeting to a close on a hopeful note. He told the men around the table that it would not be long before they all were out of trouble, and individually rich. The stock market, said Christensen, was about to climb to the moon.

CHAPTER SEVEN

MARRIAGE ARRANGEMENTS

Henry Ford warmed himself before the huge fieldstone fireplace. The flames picked out the Thoreau quotation carved on his orders into its mantel: "Chop your own wood and it will warm you twice."

Head cocked to one side, dwarfed by the fireplace, Ford looked frail and vulnerable.

Glancing nervously at his employer, Charles Sorensen continued to read aloud. The heavy Danish accent of the production chief was in abrasive contrast to the room's chintzy furnishings. Not even a hand-tailored suit and expensive shoes could disguise that Sorensen was blue-collar, a man used to action, not words.

He was uncomfortably aware of the ever-watchful Harry Bennett. Ford's troubleshooter lounged in an armchair, sipping carrot juice, a new fad of his master. Ford believed the juice helped to purify the body.

Bennett reminded Sorensen of a guard dog awaiting the command to attack. Even when relaxed, Bennett's muscles strained against his suit.

Edsel Ford sat well back in his armchair, listening carefully, saying nothing. Henry's son and heir knew from bitter experience that this was the safest policy. A shy, sensitive man in his mid-thirties, lacking any formal commercial training, Edsel was locked into an organization geared entirely to the unpredictable whims of his father. Nominally company president and treasurer, Edsel found himself too often the whipping boy. He was now accustomed to being publicly humiliated by his father. But Edsel still bravely raised issues that he knew must be faced if the company was to progress.

Edsel was the Ford in touch with reality, painfully aware that his father was growing increasingly insulated by his ego, his money, and the web of intrigue that Bennett continued to weave. He also knew that in practical terms, he had less power than either Bennett or Sorensen; both men swiftly exploited any chance to influence his father.

And yet, listening to Sorensen now, Edsel could feel quiet satisfaction at the role he had played in revamping Ford's future.

In a voice more suited to the factory floor than to Fair Lane—the fifty-six-room Ford mansion ten miles outside Detroit—Sorensen rumbled on with his presentation.

While stressing that American cars still dominated global sales—out of 5.2 million produced in the entire world in 1928, 4.36 million were built in the United States—Sorensen carefully glossed over the fact that Ford's share of the market had seriously declined. Indeed, General Motors' Chevrolet had cornered the major portion of home sales, while abroad, it was biting deeply into traditional Ford markets in Spain, Sweden, Iraq, and the Philippines. Only South America remained a secure Ford fief—though nobody could be sure for how long. In Britain, Austin and Morris were drawing customers from Ford; in France it was Citroën; Fiat in Italy.

Edsel, Bennett, and Sorensen all realized it was not just competition that was accelerating; speed itself had now overtaken dependability as the main selling factor.

It was still dangerous to utter such heresy in front of Henry Ford; he had been known to set Bennett on to a man who even hinted at such thoughts. Ford's coveted Model A relied for its success on that one quality—dependability. It was there in her sturdy hood, her rugged four cylinders capable of producing forty horsepower and a top speed, if pushed hard, of sixty-five miles per hour; it was there in the way she could bounce over fields, climb steep slopes, traverse streams.

But Henry Ford failed to accept that the increasing number of surfaced roads was making such feats of endurance largely unnecessary.

Sorensen was careful to avoid any criticism of Ford products, merely telling his listeners that the General Motors and Chrysler models were attracting many customers who apparently preferred to choose their cars from a selection sprayed in almost every color of the rainbow. The Model A was still painted a durable black.

There was no need for Sorensen to remind the group of Henry's famous maxim: A customer could have any color he liked—so long as it was black.

Then, striking an optimistic note, Sorensen recalled that the company was about to enter a new phase, its worldwide production and distribution to be concentrated mainly in three centers: Dearborn, across the Canadian border in Windsor, and at Dagenham in England.

The Rouge plant would produce parts for assembly in Japan and South America; the Ontario factory would distribute principally to countries of the British Empire and Commonwealth. The Dagenham plant would look after Europe, Turkey, the Middle East, and Africa as far south as Rhodesia. From the frozen north of Norway to the deserts of Africa, over the peaks of Afghanistan, across the plains of India, down through Malaya, Singapore, the great outback of Australia, and on to the rugged roads of New Zealand—this huge domain would be served by the new English plant.

Henry Ford had personally selected the Dagenham site—a low, five-hundred-acre, water-soaked tract of the Essex marshes, immortalized by Dickens in *Great Expectations*. Never short of an apt phrase, he had told the British press in 1928 that he, too, had high expectations for the factory. Just as he hoped his tractor plant in Cork, Ireland, would reduce the flow of Irish emigration to the United States—another of Ford's aversions—so he wished with the Dagenham plant to alleviate the chronic unemployment in London's dockland.

To launch the British segment of his expanding empire he had established a new English company. It embraced the other plants he owned in ten European countries and had a nominal capital of £7 million; £4.2 million was jointly owned by Henry, his wife, Clara, and Edsel.

The balance of £2.8 million had been offered to the public.

Sorensen described how Wall Street sharks had seized their chance to exploit the English issue of Ford stock, setting up brokerage houses solely for that purpose. They had bought large blocks of the shares knowing that American investors, unable to purchase stock in the Ford Motor Company of the United States, would be eager to buy into the British company. The issue was oversubscribed. Shares were at a premium. Their price rose. The result, entirely contrary to what Ford wanted, was that American investors had been able to purchase almost five times more shares than British investors, who were left with only a minority holding.

The goblins at the back of Ford's mind swiftly made themselves known; perhaps it was part of a plot inspired by the Jews, mounting a fresh onslaught from Wall Street.

He began to issue orders. If he could not legally restrain "these Wall Street pariahs," he would fight them in the media. The world must know that the bucket shops had no authority to trade in Ford stock like this; further, he intended to restrict the sale of Ford shares in future to no more than one or two per purchaser.

Nobody asked how he intended to achieve this.

He would speak to the Attorney General, and if necessary to the

President. Dredging among his limitless collection of clichés, Ford found the one he was looking for: No stone must be left unturned to scotch the plot.

Suddenly tired, he waved for his son and Sorensen and Bennett to leave. It was ten o'clock and close to Henry's bedtime.

After his visitors had left, Ford prowled listlessly through the $2 million house that bore the unmistakable stamp of his thinking. Obsessed with privacy, he had sited Fair Lane at the end of a drive that wound for a mile from the guard post by the entrance gates on Michigan Avenue. The mansion's limestone walls were almost a yard thick; the decor inside was what Ford fondly imagined a laird's castle in Scotland looked like. The rooms were a curious mishmash of paneling, concealed doors, oak beams, floral wall coverings, and drapes. The overall effect owed more to Walt Disney than to the Highlands.

And Fair Lane had extras that no castle possessed. It had its own private dam, providing water to run the four-storied power station he had built to light and heat the house. The station had enough reserve capacity to supply a large part of Detroit with electricity.

There was an Olympic-sized swimming pool surrounded by solid marble benches. Inserted into the seats were electric rods to warm them when Henry and Clara lounged by the pool. It had been Clara's idea to have all the birdbaths dotted around the landscape fitted with tiny electric heaters to keep them ice-free in winter.

Ford had built an artificial lake, big enough, some said, for a warship to maneuver on; it was meant to attract wild fowl.

Bird watching was one of Ford's favorite pastimes. Since their courtship, he and Clara had beckoned each other by birdcalls. They warbled at one another from different parts of the house; the servants said it made them feel they were living in an aviary.

At night, when Ford was troubled, as he was now, he went to his sanctuary, a porch room filled with bric-a-brac. In the drawer of a desk he kept a pile of well-thumbed notebooks, containing aphorisms culled in the main from *The Old Farmer's Almanac*. He enjoyed reading the one-liners he had copied out so laboriously: "Don't find fault: Find a remedy"; "Anybody can complain."

Ford slowly realized that complaining about the way speculators were trading in his stock would do no good; that, in fact, nothing could be done.

That conclusion reached, his gloom lifted. It was one of Ford's traits that he would swiftly switch from despair to almost boyish happiness. He turned to more pleasant thoughts. For a week he had secretly treasured a letter from the one man he hero-worshiped, Thomas Edison. Edison had written accepting Ford's proposal to reenact that magical moment when he had first created electricity in his laboratory at Menlo Park, New Jersey. Edison would reproduce the experiment at the opening of Ford's "American Village" this coming October.

Ford began to draft a press release announcing the news. It took time to shape the words—for there were no paid sycophants on hand to polish his prose. In the end, he was satisfied. He marked the handout for release the following morning, February 20.

Content, he retired to the bedroom he shared with Clara.

It was there that Clara performed her last wifely duty of the day— reading aloud to her husband from one of the library of leather-bound books she had collected.

It had taken considerable patience to get Henry to accept into their home literature of any kind that was a cut above his farming *Almanac*. He had always insisted that "books only mess up the mind"; that people only read "to escape thinking"; that "reading can become a dope habit"; besides, "no one has ever yet found it worthwhile to know everything."

This night, at least, Henry Ford could fall asleep knowing one thing: The celebration he planned this coming October would surely be the most spectacular event of the decade. And he would mount it entirely with his own money, without a cent's help from Wall Street.

News of Ford's plans was just one of the conversational tidbits smoothly injected by twenty-six-year-old Charlton MacVeagh to cover a lull in the conversation at the Merrill family's dinner table. He felt that Ford would undoubtedly "put on a good show." The thought was eagerly taken up and developed by members of the Merrill family.

Adele Merrill, the vivacious nineteen-year-old eldest daughter, smiled appreciatively at Charlton. She admired his ability to keep people talking, egging them on with his splendidly English phrases, a relic of two years spent at Balliol College, Oxford. His worldliness, his good manners, his sartorial elegance, his innate sense of always doing what was "right"—Adele admired all these qualities. They helped make her even more confident that he was the man she wanted to marry.

They had met at this very table almost a year ago. Adele could remember the occasion vividly. Her elder brother, Edwin, brought Charlton home for supper; they had been classmates at Harvard, and had met again after a gap of several years.

Now, during this meal, she sat next to Charlton; her younger sisters, Priscilla and Elizabeth, spent most of their time staring enviously at her. Her father and mother, Edwin and Adelaide, were captivated by Charlton's fund of stories. Even Adele's brother, Dudley, the acknowledged humorist of the family, sat back and listened and laughed.

Charlton had just joined J. P. Morgan, one of the bright young men taken on by the firm each year to help sell new issues of stock.

Adele's father, a banker, nodded sympathetically at Charlton's vivid description of the trials of prospectus writing. The entire family were convulsed by his impression of one of his Morgan colleagues, a Danish count with the unlikely name of Ben Oliphant. Every afternoon Ben had his tea served at a desk surrounded by little Danish flags.

When he was being serious, Charlton could make even the most complex financial details easy for Adele to understand. For the first time she had begun to comprehend something of the ramifications of the stock market. And in the time they had known each other, she had come to realize that Charlton was one of the most promising young men employed at Morgan's. That, probably above all else, made him, in her father's eyes, an ideal match for his daughter. Edwin Merrill was president of the small, but prestigious, Bank of New York.

Adele's mother had deftly questioned Charlton in the months following that first supper meeting, and had learned a great deal that made him seem the sort of son-in-law she, too, had always hoped for.

He was the son of Charles MacVeagh, a partner in one of the most eminent law firms in New York. MacVeagh's clients included U. S. Steel and J. P. Morgan. Young Charlton's education had been as carefully prepared as any of his father's briefs. First he went to Fay School in Massachusetts; then he moved to Groton, one of America's most exclusive boarding schools. After that he went to Harvard, graduating 1924 magna cum laude and Phi Beta Kappa in history. He was the third generation of his family to go to Harvard, and probably the most distinguished. He received the DAR history award, the Charles Elliot medal, and was editor of *The Crimson* and head of *The Advocate,* the poetry magazine.

The group were having coffee when Adele's father asked Charlton about his days in England. Charlton said that his most memorable experience had been during the general strike.

"You supported Churchill, of course?" asked Edwin Merrill.

"No, sir, I did not!"

"No?"

"No, sir, I helped run a newspaper opposed to him!"

"Good God. But Churchill's one of Britain's great heroes."

"Not to the strikers, sir," said Charlton, clinging to his ground.

"I think you had better explain what you mean," encouraged Adelaide.

In thoughtful silence they listened as Charlton told how, during the 1926 strike, he had helped to edit a "worker's newspaper," directly opposed to the official *British Gazette* Churchill was producing.

Charlton graphically described driving around the north of England, distributing the sheet, feeling like "a latter-day Don Quixote."

Only two issues of the newspaper were produced before the government silenced it. Soon afterward Charlton received a letter from Harvard canceling a post as history professor which the university had previously offered him.

"I guess I was just too radical." Charlton smiled at the Merrills.

Adele's parents looked at him, suddenly worried.

Edwin Merrill asked him what he had done after the Harvard rejection.

"I did what any boy would do—went to see my dad."

Charles MacVeagh had temporarily forsaken law to become the United States ambassador to Japan. His son joined him in Tokyo. His father advised him to return to New York and try his hand in the financial world.

By chance he met Thomas Lamont of J. P. Morgan. Charlton explained to Lamont that he believed he had lost the Harvard job because "it was thought I had become a Bolshevik."

The financier chuckled and said Morgan "needed more Bolsheviks."

Charlton was hired at $1,000 a year.

Edwin and Adelaide were relieved to hear such a satisfactory outcome to the story; they did not want an upset now to mar what was clear to them both: Charlton and Adele hoped to marry.

But Adelaide Merrill had explained to her daughter: "These things must be done properly."

Tonight's dinner party, for the family only, was the first step in formalizing the ritual. The men wore tuxedos; Adelaide and her daughters long evening gowns.

The family's cook had spent the entire day preparing the meal. It was served by a uniformed waitress; Adelaide preferred a woman to wait at table rather than the butler usually found in such households.

The other below-stairs staff—chambermaid and chauffeur—were also aware that this was an auspicious moment in Miss Adele's life.

They could remember, "as if it was only yesterday," Adele being packed off to Brearley, one of New York's finest private schools for girls. Later she went to Bryn Mawr. Halfway through her first year there, she had left college to prepare for marriage.

There would be no discussion tonight of wedding plans; that would come later, and be a matter for Adelaide and her daughter. Tonight was to make Charlton feel he was now part of the family.

As usual he was full of Wall Street gossip. The talk at Morgan's was still about the way Giannini had so precipitately sacked the firm as his representative. It was said the decision had even momentarily rocked

Jack Morgan. The conversation moved on to Wall Street's reaction to the Federal Reserve's pegging of interest rates, and the effect the influx of foreign gold could have on world trade.

Adelaide and the girls listened politely, not really understanding what they regarded as "man's talk."

But by the time Charlton said good night, it was clear to everyone that Adelaide could confidently go ahead and begin to plan a full-scale society wedding for her daughter in the summer.

Kissing Adele good night, her mother explained that, "in our world, this is the way things are done."

Already, in her mind, she could see those giants of Wall Street who must be on the invitation list.

Seated at the plain wooden kitchen table around which all the most important family decisions were made, Andrew Arvay, Jolan Slezsak's stepfather, and Barbara, her mother, were settling Jolan's future.

Barbara Arvay insisted that her fifteen-year-old daughter was now old enough to "get work." Ephraim Goldberger had promised to help. He was the Jewish lawyer who, by common consent, was "Mr. Fixit" for the Hungarian community in Flint. Goldberger had arranged Andrew Arvay's divorce—a protracted business as his wife still lived in Budapest—and afterward had smoothed the way for Barbara and Andrew to marry in Church. Whenever there were layoffs at "the Buick," it was Goldberger who found temporary farm work for his Hungarians; when they died, he settled their affairs. He charged them all modest fees; it had made him a wealthy man with a large house on the fashionable west side of Flint. Goldberger had told Barbara he could probably place Jolan as a maid for a neighbor, "a nice Jewish lady."

Andrew Arvay was not keen on the idea; he felt his stepdaughter would be more useful as a liquor runner. She knew the ropes; the police never bothered her.

Jolan could do both, urged her mother: work during the week as a live-in maid, come home at weekends and trundle the baby carriage to customers.

Neither of them felt their attitude toward Jolan was inconsiderate. They had both been conditioned to work from childhood; they felt their children should do the same.

Jolan's stepfather was toughened like pig iron from a lifetime on the Buick production lines; all that remained from his youth was a curiously innocent gaze. Her mother, upon whom the years of marriage and hard work had left their mark, also had that clear, trusting look.

Shortage of money had always been a problem. Barbara could never understand why her first husband had insisted, shortly before he was

The Age of Illusion in Wall Street. The Great Crash is still months away. Brokers and clerks sense nothing amiss, believing that the millennium can be witnessed every day inside the monolithic New York Stock Exchange (left). Trinity Church stands guard at the top of Wall, a reminder that Mammon and God have come to live in easy fellowship. *United Press International.*

The trading floor of the New York Stock Exchange on a typical boom day in 1929. Here fortunes were made in minutes in a cavernous room covering more than a quarter acre of sacrosanct floor. From opening to closing gongs, there was a nonstop swirl of trading activity around the eighteen posts. On an average day 5 million shares were exchanged— heightening the impression among the 2,000 people who worked on and around the floor that the world outside their heavily draped sanctum depended for its prosperity on their financial juggling. *The Bettmann Archive, Inc.*

Buy at the market! A familiar cry inside any broker's office. The smiles of customers reflected the prospect of new fortunes from the ever-climbing quotations being chalked up. This was the heyday, when men threw up safe jobs to spend their time, and money, in customers' rooms. Day after day a growing number of people believed the symbols on the quotation boards guaranteed a quick and easy road to wealth. *United Press International.*

All over America eager eyes scanned the spirals of paper that spelled out new highs in hundreds of stocks. Five hundred miles of tape ran over the spindles of the tickers for every million shares traded. *United Press International.*

Inside the most hallowed doors in Wall Street—the entrance lobby to the House of Morgan. It was through these doors in 1929 that a confident Joe Kennedy walked in, unannounced, uninvited—and, as it turned out, unwanted. He suffered a snub he would never forgive. *Courtesy J. P. Morgan & Company, Inc.*

Partners' Row in the House of Morgan. Here, on New Year's Eve, 1928, Jack Morgan handed an envelope to each of his partners seated at the identical rolltop desks. They murmured words of gratitude: Each envelope contained a bonus for the year's work—a check for not less than $1 million. The recipients had every expectation that 1929 would earn them yet more profits. Even their great financial skills could not predict the Crash which was coming. *Courtesy J. P. Morgan & Company, Inc.*

The inner sanctum, the nerve center of the House of Morgan, the area where Jack Morgan worked and controlled a worldwide financial empire. It was in this room that decisions were taken which affected the fiscal policies of governments, the solvency of nations. And it was here, on October 24, 1929, that a crucial meeting took place to try to stem the Great Crash. *Courtesy J. P. Morgan & Company, Inc.*

Panic in the Street. Thousands of investors converged on Wall Street on "Black Tuesday," October 29, 1929. As the hours passed, their unease turned to panic, to abject terror, and in the cases of a few, to actual suicide. *United Press International.*

Like mourners, they waited, stunned, not believing. For many of them, "Black Tuesday" was the day their fortunes were wiped out, their life-styles changed forever. Ahead lay the breadlines of the Depression. *United Press International.*

killed, on placing $400 with the Union Industrial Bank in a trust account for Jolan.

Even Mr. Goldberger had found it impossible to get the money out. Under the terms of the trust, the money would be paid on Jolan's eighteenth birthday, or on the day she married, whichever came first. Her brothers and sisters had similar conditions attached to the modest trusts their father had also set up for them.

The question of Jolan marrying had become a serious matter for her mother. Even with the combined wage packets of her husband and eldest boys, Julius, seventeen, and Michael, sixteen, there was still not enough money to feed and clothe the family. Mainly they ate stews made from cheap cuts and vegetables grown on the patch at the back of the house. Jolan, like the rest of the girls, wore underpants made from flour bags.

It was in the hope of having more money that Barbara had agreed to her husband becoming a bootlegger. The smells of cooking and scrubbing were joined with, and then overpowered by, the heady aroma of mash being turned into whiskey. Over the years the fumes had seeped into the ceilings and floorboards, permeated the furniture and drapes. The smell of fermentation lingered in every room, touching the few precious treasures that had survived the years: photos, dime-store prints. Even the cheap six-day clock from the old country had a face that matched in color the pale amber liquid distilled in the cellar.

But the brewing had not brought in enough extra cash; the family still owed money in various food and clothing stores in the district. Even Jolan's salary as a maid and her absence from home during the week would leave the household budget hopelessly unbalanced.

"The girl eats like a man," said Barbara. "At weekends she'll be back and eat us out of house and home."

There was, argued Jolan's mother, only one solution. Her daughter must be married off as soon as possible, so that she could claim the $400 in the bank. The money would be an attractive dowry for any prospective husband.

"But she doesn't even know what boys are for!" protested Andrew.

"She'll learn," promised Barbara. "We all do."

"But who . . . ?" Andrew shook his head, unable to offer suggestions.

"I could ask Mr. Goldberger."

"To find a husband for our daughter? What would the neighbors say!"

"Never mind them! They don't have such hungry children to feed!"

Ending further argument, Barbara outlined her plan. Andrew, Julius, and Michael would look for "a likely prospect": a young Hungarian, in work, in a steady job. Suitable suitors would be invited to the house. The one Barbara approved would be introduced to Jolan. Jolan would take it from there.

Andrew made one last attempt to dissuade his wife.

"Supposing she doesn't love the boy?"

Barbara Arvay shook her head decisively. Love, she said, had nothing to do with it. What had to be done was to get the money out of the bank as quickly as possible.

Homer Dowdy was pleased he had placed his savings in the Union Industrial Bank. It was a comforting thought for the thirty-four-year-old postman to know that "the money was safe and growing," faced as he was with a sick wife and three small children to rear.

Ferne and Doris and their seven-year-old brother, Homer, also had accounts with the bank. The Union Industrial had persuaded the Flint school board to encourage all the city's children to open savings accounts. Every week the Dowdy children handed over nickels and dimes at school and the money was then taken to the bank.

But with Gladys bedridden and needing frequent and costly house calls from the doctor, Homer Dowdy was not sure how long he could go on giving the children money to save. Most troubling of all, the doctor did not seem to know what was the matter with Gladys; he spoke vaguely of "more tests" and in the meantime had placed her on expensive medicine to ease her pain.

Even with his postman's salary of $2,100 a year, "things were tight." Dowdy suspected that his hard-saved money in the bank might have to be withdrawn for drugs for his wife.

He did not know how he could tell his children that life could get tougher; it was hard enough for them already. When other children played, the girls and their brother tended house, shopped, and nursed their mother until their father got home from work. At night the family gathered around the sickbed and sang and read from the Bible until Gladys went to sleep.

Homer had come to envy those people on his delivery route who regularly received checks from their stockbrokers in New York.

He had learned that the slim buff envelopes contained money the morning a woman, waiting impatiently on her doorstep for mail, ripped open the envelope in front of him, "and then danced up and down with excitement." She explained to Homer she had "just made a killing in General Motors."

Several times since, the woman had received similar good news, and the postman, judging from the buff envelopes, knew that many other people on his route were also successfully playing the stock market.

But Homer Dowdy was old-fashioned. He knew the value of money earned by honest sweat; he suspected cash acquired by any other means.

All his life he had scrimped and saved. Once it had been to buy a new plow when he had farmed in Missouri at the turn of the century. Next it had been for the means to marry Gladys. He had saved before the arrival of each child. Then, realizing his small holdings could never support them, Homer had sold it and brought the family to Flint. He was attracted, like so many migrants, by the high wages Billy Durant offered at "the Buick."

Homer had hated life on the assembly line: the noise, the heat, the hire-and-fire mentality, the sudden, unexpected layoffs.

But he saved enough from his sixty cents an hour wage to put a deposit on their home. And he had studied at night for the Civil Service Examination. In 1925 he had passed it and joined the postal service.

The great thing about being a postman, he told Gladys, was that "it's a permanent job." As he saw it: "Everybody else can get laid off, but they still like to get letters."

And he built up a nest egg at the Union Industrial. Homer chose the bank partly because Charles Mott was behind it and partly because the Union Industrial's advertising "had a solid sound." The bank's posters were a familiar sight on billboards in Flint. Their slogans claimed that people who banked with the Union Industrial were "happy and carefree." The public were urged to "give your dollars employment and earn interest— Save."

It had taken four years' hard saving by Homer for his account to reach its present healthy position.

The money, he told Gladys, "is for any need that may arise." He did not tell her how close he felt that need was.

Charles Stewart Mott had decided to become a husband for the third time. He had set March 1, 1929, as the day he would marry one of Detroit's gayest divorcees, Dee Van Balkom Furey. The executive vice-president of General Motors and chairman of the Union Industrial's Board laid his plans with one thought in mind—to keep news of his forthcoming wedding secret for as long as possible.

It was a surprising decision for a man normally so keen on publicity. But Dee Furey, herself a journalist, had insisted that Mott keep the press at bay. With just a week to go, he was confident his scheme to send the media off on a wild-goose chase would work.

There was nothing Mott could see on the horizon to impede his wedding plans.

The last time he had spoken by telephone to Grant Brown in Flint, the Union Industrial's president had reported that the bank's business was booming. Both men agreed the stock market was responsible. The brief call was virtually the full extent to which Mott showed his interest and exercised his responsibility as board chairman. He had not been to Flint for months. Dee did not like the city; it was much too "small town" for somebody who was a dominant figure in Detroit society. She had also vetoed Mott's idea that after their honeymoon they would spend weekends at his Flint manor house. Dee told him firmly they would spend all their time in Detroit.

Charles Mott did not really mind. In some ways it would be pleasant to be close to his main work; General Motors was continuing on its serene way. The Chevrolet Division had doubled its sales in four years; the new Pontiac, for the introduction of which Mott himself was largely responsible, was making a name for itself. Abroad, Vauxhall in England and Opel in Germany were already showing signs of being valuable acquisitions. The corporation's substantial investments in the aviation and diesel fields also looked promising.

Three years before, Mott had authorized a huge increase in plant investment—from $287 million to $610 million. But the net income for 1928—a record $267 million—showed his gamble was paying off.

From his office window he could look down on ample evidence to support these figures; a constant stream of General Motors vehicles passed along the street below.

Mott had no patience with critics who said the new highways were beginning to create their own junkyards—the ribbon development of filling stations, roadside diners, hot-dog stands, peanut, fruit, and vegetable stalls and the used-car lots starting to litter the edges of many thoroughfares.

He preferred to point to the positive benefits. He could argue, with great truth, that motorization had made the countryside accessible to the masses. It meant that ordinary families could now live in pleasant open surroundings for the first time, while the breadwinners drove in daily to work. And motorization ended the isolation of the farmer.

Mott heartily endorsed the sentiments of one reporter: "The American who has been humbled by poverty, or by insignificance in the business order, or by his racial status, or by any other circumstance that might demean him in his own eyes, gains a sense of authority when he slides behind the wheel of an automobile and it leaps forward at his bidding, ready to take him wherever he may personally please. If he drives a bus or a huge truck trailer his state is all the more kingly, for he feels himself responsible for the wielding of a sizable concentration of force."

It was a killing force. In 1922 less than 15,000 people had died on the roads; now, at the end of the second month of 1929, the annual rate was running at close to 30,000.

Mott, understandably, preferred to publicize reports that the auto industry was improving the life-style of the nation. He believed it was making everyone happier—and richer.

It did not need much to be classified as rich in 1929: An income of $6,000 a year was sufficient to put an individual among the top 5 percent of the population.

There were also the very rich, of which Mott was one. In 1928 he was included in the record 513 individuals who had an annual income of over $1 million. He was a shrewd player of the market, and his salary had been boosted by profitable stock dividends.

All the signs indicated that 1929 would be an even more satisfactory year for Mott, both on Wall Street and at the company. His stock market investments were always gilt-edged. The latest General Motors figures showed that, on present trends, even allowing for depreciation and new plant expenditure, the stockholders could expect to receive 60 percent of the company profits shared among them. As one of the corporation's largest shareholders, the news was a perfect wedding present for Mott.

CHAPTER EIGHT

THE POOL

The sound of the first stirring bars of music rolled past the open suite door and down the corridor of New York's Ritz Hotel. Moments later the richly powerful, and surprisingly musical, baritone voice of Amadeo Peter Giannini accompanied his piano playing.

Other guests and staff of the hotel began to congregate at the door, listening to Giannini's impromptu concert. Most nights, if he was not at the movies or involved in a business meeting, he would play for an hour or so, sitting at the keyboard, in his braces, tie undone. He managed to sound like a singer at the Met while looking like a piano player in a Broadway dive.

When he was happy, he played and sang Neapolitan love songs; angry, he attacked Wagner; excited, it was Italian operatic arias.

Tonight he was excited—more so than he had ever been on previous visits to the city.

Spontaneous applause came from those grouped in the doorway. They had never heard Giannini perform better.

Only Clorinda knew the reason, and she was content to sit back and listen, pleased that her husband was in such good spirits. She was glad they had chosen to stay at the Ritz. During the past year it had been the Giannini's base whenever they were in New York. The management did everything possible to make the family feel at home. They had arranged for Claire to have a comfortable bedroom adjoining her parents' suite, and had installed at Clorinda's request the full-sized concert grand for Giannini to play.

Now, with a final flourish, he rose from the keyboard, bowed to his audience, and hurried into the bedroom to change, anxious not to be late for his important dinner appointment.

The breach with J. P. Morgan had left Giannini "looking for talent that knew the ways of Wall Street, had the proper entree there and a sympathetic understanding of nationwide banking."

After two weeks of discreet but intensive searching for the right "talent," Giannini's interest had focused on the private banking and investment house of Blair and Company.

Blair himself, he discovered, was old, blue-ribbon, rich, eminent, shrewd but not soft. He spent most of his time at his Bermuda estate, keeping in touch by telephone with the company at its palatial offices on Broad Street.

Effective control of the firm was in the hands of Elisha Walker.

Giannini had researched Walker as thoroughly as any private detective. Before their first meeting, he thought he knew everything about the forty-nine-year-old native New Yorker, a graduate of Yale and the Massachusetts Institute of Technology.

Giannini had been surprised. He had expected Walker to be cold and inscrutable; instead he found him frank and open-minded, showing "none of that cold aloofness which we are accustomed to associate with men of Wall Street."

Their first exploratory meeting had led to others. Giannini had been characteristically forthright, telling Walker: "I need financial ability. Your company has it. I want your company."

Walker had traveled to Bermuda to discuss the matter with Blair. He had just returned and immediately invited Giannini to dinner.

Sharp at eight o'clock, wearing his best suit, a charcoal-gray pinstripe, Giannini was let into the Blair Building. A footman led him across the deep-pile carpeted hall to the boardroom, its table laid for dinner.

Elisha Walker and the eleven other partners greeted their guest warmly.

Giannini saw that his tastes had been catered for—a sign that he, too, had been "researched." His favorite Italian wine was offered, along with nuts and olives imported from Rome. He detected the faint but unmistakable aroma of Italian cooking. He felt that anybody who could go to this trouble must be the sort of person he "liked to do business with."

Walker introduced him to the other Blair partners. Most of them were young, in their thirties, self-made, unlike the men at Morgan's who had background, influence, and wealth.

Giannini was especially glad to meet Jean Monnet, a Frenchman who had been a brilliant industrialist and later deputy secretary-general of the League of Nations. Monnet was known as a pacifist, but more important to Giannini, also as an internationalist; he would be the ideal choice to mastermind his plans to expand in Europe. The story had already broken that Giannini intended to form a Transeurope Corporation, capitalized at $50 million. Its offices would be in London; it would be responsible for the Banca d'America e d'Italia in Milan and Giannini's financial interests in France.

Blair and Company would of itself provide impetus for Giannini's expansion plans. Its partners sat on the boards of nearly two hundred American and foreign corporations and regularly arranged loans for foreign governments. Recently, it had set up a $55 million investment trust known as the Petroleum Corporation of America.

The dinner table conversation was relaxed and informal. Giannini revealed that he was making a gift of $50,000 to the American Institute of Banking to improve the standard of public speaking among its younger members. He felt that with the stock market creating an unparalleled interest in all matters financial, it was essential that the public should receive clearly stated views from the banking fraternity.

One of the partners asked if press reports were true that King Victor Emmanuel wished to present Giannini with a gold medal in recognition of his efforts to establish a chair of Italian culture at the University of California.

Giannini replied that the reports were true, but he would not be attending any formal ceremony to receive the medal; he did not feel it was proper for an American to accept awards from foreign governments.

Someone else opened a discussion on Giannini's recent reaction to the latest Henry Ford widely quoted pronouncement: "No successful boy ever saved money."

As usual, the press had sought Giannini's view. He had responded in vintage fashion: "I don't wholly agree with Mr. Ford. Saving money does seem to me the least vital pursuit to which a boy can devote his energy. Even making money is not to be taken too seriously. The making or saving of money represents only by-products of one's work. The important thing is that any young man should work hard at whatever interests him most."

After dinner, Walker and Giannini adjourned to a side room. There, Walker told the banker what he had been waiting to hear; Blair and Company was ready to be absorbed into the Giannini empire.

Giannini now had an unchallengeable beachhead in Wall Street. He was ready to fight off anybody who tried to attack him.

By the late evening of February 28, thirty-eight-year-old Michael Meehan—the Stock Exchange specialist in Radio—had come to the conclusion there were at least three good reasons why he should launch another big pool in RCA stocks.

A few days ago, the Radio Corporation of America's directors had announced a split-up of their shares on a five-for-one basis. Although the stock had reached a high of 420 during 1928, after the share split it was now hovering around 70. Meehan thought the price was too low. It was time for the stock to be "taken in hand."

The pool in Anaconda Copper, which Meehan had helped form in late January, was now in full operation, its management in the trusted hands of two of Wall Street's most high-priced master manipulators, Ben Smith and Tom Bragg of W. E. Hutton and Company. The two men, who almost always worked closely in tandem, had such faith in the Anaconda pool's prospects that each had put $500,000 into the kitty; with the money added by such other great market players as Percy Rockefeller, Billy Durant, and Charles Mitchell, Bragg and Smith had funds in excess of $32 million at their disposal. So far the signs were good. The price of Anaconda Copper was creeping up. Meehan could confidently leave the operation to them.

Another reason the Irishman felt the time right to start the new Radio pool was, typically, purely sentimental; in just a few days it would be exactly one year since he had helped engineer the start of the big 1928 boom in RCA shares. In one twenty-four-hour period, from the morning of March 12 to the morning of March 13, Radio had gone up an astounding 40 points.

After that, the spiral had continued upward to its record high of 420. Many dated the inauguration of the present bull market from that March 12. Now, with the first anniversary of that dramatic beginning less than two weeks away, Meehan was planning a repeat performance.

All evening he had made, and received, telephone calls in the study of the Meehan family apartment on New York's East Sixty-seventh Street. Whenever he could, Meehan liked to work among the comfortable clutter of family living rather than in his offices at 61 Broadway. If nothing else, it allowed him to see his two young daughters; his teenage sons were both away at prep school. The girls loved having their father at home; he was always ready with a joke, a dollar to buy candy, or a seat at the movie matinee.

Before moving into the apartment the family had lived in an expensive suite at the Sherry Netherland Hotel. That was early in 1928 when Meehan was often so busy operating in Radio that he did not return from the office until midnight. His wife, Elizabeth, whom he had married in 1911 when she was eighteen, had insisted they move into the city. It was impossible for Meehan to commute from their "country home" at Forest Hills. Now that they were settled in their new fourteen-room apartment, the mercurial Meehan could relax. But work was never out of his mind for long. He was acutely aware that in Wall Street he had to live by his wits; he feared that if he let up for a moment, he could lose all he had attained.

Sometimes he would talk to Elizabeth about his impoverished background. It was that, she thought, which gave him his incredible drive.

Meehan was born in Wales of poor Irish parents. When he was still very young, they moved to America, where his father found work in a hospital on Staten Island. Meehan grew up in a devout Catholic household where a dime for the Sunday collection plate came before most things. He had barely finished grammar school when he took his first full-time job: selling cigarettes for the United Cigar Store Company. By the time he was eighteen, he was a store manager. That was the beginning of the long road that had taken him to the theater ticket agency, to the Curb Exchange, and finally, in 1924, to the New York Stock Exchange.

He became Radio's first bull. Meehan had arrived on the floor the same year the stock was listed on the Big Board. From the beginning, the two seemed made for each other.

It had not been easy to push the stock in those first years. But by charm, drive, and sheer perseverance, Meehan had taken it from 25 in 1924 to nearly 200 during his Radio pool of March 1928, and eventually on to 420.

And now, he had sensed the time was ripe to strike again.

He well knew the dangers: the bears would crush him if he made one false move. Meehan had carefully mulled over in his mind those he should invite to partake in the pool. He decided the "old faithfuls"— the big operators already in the Anaconda pool—should again form the core. Percy Rockefeller, John J. Raskob, Billy Durant—Meehan knew he could count on them for a substantial commitment. He ruled out inviting Joe Kennedy. The relationship between the two Irishmen was not good.

The question of who should actually manage the pool's operations on the Stock Exchange floor—who would in fact be buying and selling through Meehan—was a worrying one. If only a way could be found to release the pressure on Bragg and Smith, now so busy with Anaconda Copper, then possibly they could also take over this pool. Meehan knew there were no men alive who were such skilled market manipulators as this pair. The Anaconda pool was planned to run for many months. Meehan had decided the Radio pool would be a short, sharp attack, lasting perhaps only a week. In that case, Bragg and Smith might be able to handle the operation. He decided he would "feel them out."

There was another question that exercised Meehan. Under the rules of the Exchange, he could not hold shares in any stock he traded. But there was no law forbidding Elizabeth from speculating in RCA stock. His wife had done so before. Meehan decided she would do so again.

Finally, he had to decide when the pool should be activated. It was a bit too soon to be certain, but Meehan thought it would be a nice touch if he could initiate operations on March 12, one year to the day since that 40-point rise of 1928. He resolved to work to that end.

Far to the west, in the small town of Toledo, Ohio, Charles Stewart Mott received a sign shortly before midday on March 1 that his plan had worked. Hamish Mitchell, his son-in-law, standing in the church porch, quickly raised and lowered his hand. It was a prearranged signal that there were no reporters outside the tiny Trinity Episcopal Church.

Mott slid out of the hired car and hurried into the church, relaxed and confident, knowing that, as part of his plan to avoid the press, newsmen in Detroit had been told that at this moment he was being married in New York before embarking on a honeymoon in Europe. Even so, Mott guessed the brief announcement from his office at General Motors would galvanize reporters to try to track him down.

He doubted if they would ever think of looking for him in Toledo. He and Dee Van Balkom Furey had slipped into town and stopped the night as house guests of Mott's close friend, Earle P. Halliburton, an oil magnate and director of Southwest Airline.

Early in the morning, Mott's married daughters, Aimee and Elsa, had decorated the altar with spring flowers. Later, their husbands ferried the handful of guests to the church.

They were now clustered before the altar, virtual strangers to one another. On the bride's side were Dee's small daughter, Denise, her cousin Lila Chappell, and her mother, Mrs. Annie Deeble, flown in specially from Canada in Halliburton's private trimotor plane; the aircraft was being readied to fly the newlyweds off on their honeymoon at Mott's secluded ranch, where his second wife had so suddenly died just a year before.

Dee's only other guests were Mr. and Mrs. Prewitt Semmes. He was her attorney.

Mott's two daughters moved closer to their father as he took up his position before the Reverend Charles Bentley.

Moments later Dee appeared from the vestry. She looked pale and tense.

The ceremony was brief and simple. There were no hymns or music.

The bridal couple, perhaps fearful that a reporter might chance by and discover their presence, hurried from the church to a private reception at the Halliburton home.

At 2 P.M., luncheon over, they waved good-bye to their guests and climbed aboard the trimotor for the long flight to Arizona.

The aircraft was barely airborne before the new Mrs. Mott began to complain: the ride was too bumpy; her seat was too hard.

Mott tried to calm his wife. He brought out his fund of funny stories. Dee did not respond.

Rejected, he slumped back in his seat. They traveled on in sullen silence.

Suddenly, over Anderson, a small township in Indiana, a snowstorm swirled around the plane. It began to career about the sky, then slipped sickeningly toward the ground.

Dee sat icy calm.

The pilot shouted he was lost.

Dee turned to her husband and said it was all his fault.

Mott ordered the pilot to fly lower and try and locate a landmark.

The plane roared over Anderson and, seven miles north of the town, dropped down into a plowed field, its landing gear deeply bedded in the soil.

Mrs. Mott stumbled from the damaged plane and hurried to a nearby farmhouse. From there she telephoned Prewitt Semmes.

When her husband joined her, she rounded on him, complaining about "the accommodations" at the farm.

Once more Mott tried to placate her. He persuaded the farmer to drive them into Anderson where they could stay at the town's only hotel, a small, simply furnished establishment.

Again, Dee lashed out, this time complaining bitterly at the lack of service.

Baffled, Mott shied away from her, feeling that "she was beginning to find fault with everything I did, no matter what the circumstances."

Troubled and upset, he was starting to realize that running General Motors was easy compared to managing his third bride.

Jesse Livermore's "problem" with his wife, Dorothy, left him exhausted and quite unable to cope with the swiftly developing situation in Wall Street.

There had just been time, during a lull on the home front, for him to jot in a notebook that "market rises violently under leadership Adams Express, up 60½ points. Call money 10 percent." That was on February 28. On March 1, before the latest domestic crisis broke, he hurriedly noted that it had been a 6,021,300-share day, the largest so far of the year, "exceeded only in November and December, 1928. Gains of up to 25 points."

But there was no time for him to evaluate properly the market developments, to assess whether they really were the vanguard of a still bigger boom, or whether they could be the precursor to a market collapse.

Dorothy's "problem" had once more forced him temporarily to abandon his office complex in the Heckscher Building and leave his staff and expensive trappings to their own devices.

His wife was losing her battle with the bottle.

Drink had already removed most traces of the clear-skinned eighteen-year-old, the daughter of a rich Brooklyn merchant whom Livermore had married in a simple ceremony at the St. Regis Hotel on December 2, 1918. On that day, he had slipped a wedding ring on her finger inscribed with the dedication: "Dotsie, for ever and ever. J.L." Ten years later, Dotsie was growing plump, slovenly, coarsened by whiskey; she was alternatively garrulous and maudlin. She blamed him for her condition.

It was Livermore's second marriage; he had once told the press it was the "love of his life."

And for a while, they had been happy. Two children were born: Jesse, Jr., now nearly ten, and Paul, a jolly eight-year-old.

At some point—Livermore could never put a date to it—Dorothy began to drink too much. Perhaps it was after one of those endless cocktail parties he gave or attended to mark some spectacular killing in the market. Prohibition, he was fond of saying, was a condition for those who didn't have "connections."

Perhaps Dorothy's drinking stemmed from the day she first challenged him about "romancing in hotel rooms with other women while you should be working."

Livermore had brushed aside the accusation, and continued with his extramarital entanglements.

Dorothy raised the issue time and again. A proud and possessive woman, she loved her husband deeply; the thought that he found sexual solace elsewhere was a cruel blow, one she could not cope with. She would never have understood that Livermore's complex personality required him regularly to pursue his sexual peccadilloes outside the marriage bed. He had a roving eye, a fat wallet, and he did not see why marriage should hamper his freedom.

The rows between Dorothy and her husband became increasingly frequent and bitter. She drank more and more, a sad, lonely figure, unable to grasp the fact that her only chance of retaining her husband's interest was to cut down drinking and try to return to those early years of their marriage when she was a vivacious fun-lover.

Instead, her behavior had driven "J.L."—as Livermore liked everybody to call him—to the sanctuary of his office and the arms of other women.

A first, Dorothy had pursued her husband by telephone and with visits to the office. Angry at being embarrassed in front of his staff, Livermore had now managed to confine the marital battles to their luxurious apartment at 817 Fifth Avenue. He remained with his wife while she reeled through a familiar charge sheet: affairs with other women, disregard for her needs, neglect of his children.

That was the point at which his own fury boiled over. He loved his boys and he believed they adored him. He felt that any charge of neglect toward them was a monstrous travesty of the truth.

Battle was joined; the verbal recriminations were painful for the young children to hear.

On this March morning the latest row had only stopped when Dorothy and the boys returned to the family's country estate at Great Neck, New York. The house was called "Evermore."

Left alone with the servants in the apartment, Livermore brooded over another problem that threatened to engulf him.

He had heard a rumor that the ghost of some dubious property promoting he had done in Florida back in 1926 was about to return to haunt him; his lawyer had picked up a whisper that a group of dissatisfied investors were organizing to sue Livermore in the New York courts.

Livermore knew what that meant: endless legal conferences and the sort of unwelcome publicity that could severely hamper his standing.

Not for the first time he wished he had the comfort and security of a balanced family life.

To Rose and the children, Joe Kennedy was the ideal husband and father, their home in Palm Beach, Florida, a bastion of joyous laughter. She wished that those who found him "hardheaded" and "tough" could see him now: "warm and gentle, absolutely devoted to his children, loving them, letting them absorb the understanding of his love in the most demonstrative ways."

Every morning Rose sent one of the children into bed with Joe and left the two of them propped up on pillows, conversing about anything and everything.

The children were carefully rotated so as to ensure that each of them had an equal opportunity to share in the experience; the greatest punishment was to be made to miss a turn. Afterward, most of the day was spent outside in the balmy Florda air, playing games, acquiring suntans.

At lunchtime, Joe would summarize for the family the world's news, culled from the New York *Times*. Items triggered off explanations. The newspaper reported a Joan of Arc anniversary celebration in France; he gave the children a concise history of the saint. A paragraph about aviator Charles Lindbergh flying from Texas to Mexico City to see his fiancée, Anne Morrow, produced the theory that global flight was only a matter of time.

Once the children had gone off to play and while Rose was clearing the table, Joe Kennedy daily took an hour to peruse the financial pages. His fury over the Morgan slight had abated; his determination to avenge it was as strong as ever. But the main reason why he wished to keep abreast of the market was his unquenchable desire to make yet more money to broaden the social and political base of the family dynasty he wanted to found.

He read swiftly, absorbing a prodigious amount of information. Then he made telephone calls to New York. By the end of the last one, he was as fully conversant with stock market trends as if he had been sitting in his office.

Kennedy's interest nowadays centered on the foreign exchanges. Already an internationalist in his thinking, he knew that the bourses of Europe could have an important effect on America's fortunes. And the rumor in New York was that the Dutch and Italian central banks would soon be raising their discount rates in an effort to lure more money to their countries. Further, the flow of foreign gold into the United States was undiminished. It now appeared as if substantial German shipments would soon join those coming from Britain, Italy, and Canada. That could tilt the world economic equilibrium a little more out of true.

Nevertheless, from all quarters Kennedy had been assured that the domestic market would continue to rise. The temptation for him to invest was great.

But Kennedy decided he would wait awhile yet. He knew his time would come.

The changeover of executive power went smoothly in Washington, D.C. A large crowd stood patiently in the rain to see Herbert Hoover become the thirty-first President of the United States on March 4, 1929.

Thirty airplanes, the dirigible *Los Angeles,* and four blimps hovered overhead, filming the scene.

Hoover urged law enforcement in his inaugural address. It was a popular theme: The cities of America were becoming ever more lawless.

Even as he spoke, the wire services were breaking the news that thirteen people had been poisoned to death in Peoria, Illinois, victims of bootleg liquor brewed by local hoodlums. The streets of Chicago, New York, San Francisco, and Detroit seemed almost daily to be smeared with the blood of slain gangsters.

The fight against Prohibition was being lost on all fronts; the Treasury had just announced it had fired 706 agents and would prosecute another 257 for taking bribes from speakeasy owners.

A government estimate put the annual income of the nation's Public Enemy Number One, Al Capone, at: $60 million from bootlegging, $25 million from gambling and dog tracks, $10 million from brothels and dance halls, and a further $10 million from "miscellaneous rackets." His "expenses" were thought to be running at around $75 million a year.

Capone happily admitted he had lost $10 million gambling, but his income, he solemnly insisted, had been made as a result of "good business principles."

One of those principles involved "rubbing out" all possible competition. Just over two weeks ago, on February 14, during what had come to be known as the St. Valentine's Day Massacre, Capone's hit men had gunned down seven members of the rival Bugs Moran gang in a classic underworld execution.

Carefully sidestepping that sensitive issue, he told reporters—as with other public figures, Al liked occasionally to burnish his image for the media—that he saw no point in playing the stock market: It was much too unpredictable for a man who liked all his investments to show a surefire profit.

With his 11½-carat diamond ring, his steel-plated custom-built $30,000 limousine, his mansion in Chicago's Grand Crossing District, Capone was undoubtedly underworld supremo.

He would not be for long. One of President Hoover's first orders would be to break Capone's iron hold on Chicago.

Hoover, a Quaker, an engineer, an enemy of immorality and waste, a self-made millionaire and cosmopolitan thinker, was also a shrewd assessor of the domestic pulse. Probing just beneath the superficial surface, he found that, in many ways, the country was still trapped in the aftermath of the Great War. "Return to normalcy," the slogan of 1919, had ten years later led to widespread disillusion and corruption, "the noble experiment" of Prohibition had spawned drunkenness and Capone. For the first time since the founding of the Republic, serious thinkers were challenging the efficiency of the democratic process. H. L. Mencken castigated the *"Homo boobiens"* who had voted

Hoover into power. Sinclair Lewis pilloried big business in *Babbitt*. *The Army Training Manual* for 1928 listed the effects of democracy as "demagogism, license, agitation, discontent, anarchy." Church attendance dropped; now, in 1929, more people went to the movies than to places of worship. The United States, said intellectuals, lacked a cultural tradition and was suffering from commercialism. And the popular mind of the American public, according to Walter Lippmann, was "irrational, gullible, easily misled."

Nowhere, Hoover knew, was this more evident than on the stock market.

Yet his predecessor, Calvin Coolidge, the man who was said to have used the White House "mainly for sleeping purposes," had once phrased it succinctly: "The business of America is business." Hoover personally preferred the more elegantly phrased and time-honored McKinley principle: "Less government in business and more business in government."

Standing before the bank of microphones, reaching a radio audience estimated at 63 million, Hoover knew that in the end, the real people who mattered, in economic terms, were that handful of men who controlled some two hundred companies that made up about 50 percent of the nation's corporate wealth. These were the people he had carefully wooed and courted to become President. These were the people who would expect him to redeem his campaign promises of continued prosperity, who could expect him to continue Coolidge's benign rule.

Hoover realized Coolidge had little grasp of finance; he had preferred to leave "such matters" to Andrew Mellon, the astute Secretary of the Treasury who was wedded to the idea that government should keep its hands off business. Hoover had asked Mellon to stay on. The new President approved of Mellon's policy.

After bidding farewell to Calvin Coolidge on the Capitol's east portico, Hoover repaired to the Oval Office in the west wing of the White House.

He was entering the presidency with a spotless record and massive public support. His wartime work as chairman of the Belgium Relief Commission and postwar role as U. S. Food Administrator had made him a world-respected figure. His seven years as a successful Secretary of Commerce had given him high standing at home. He believed in the individual, in open opportunity, and in profit. He thought the American people were "engrossed in the building for themselves of a new economic system." He promised to push "the direction of economic progress toward prosperity and the further lessening of poverty." He was honest, sincere, and clever—assets that could help make him a distinguished President. Already the newspapers were calling him "the Great Engineer."

Alone in the Oval Office, Hoover studied his papers. The reference to poverty in his inaugural address had been well founded. In spite of the booming stock market, less than three out of every hundred Americans had incomes of over $10,000 a year; only eight in every hundred earned over $5,000. Sixty percent of the population earned less than $2,000.

Hoover did not have to be an economist to know that in this, the "golden year" of which newspapers spoke, those 60 percent of American families living on less than $2,000 a year had enough only to buy the basic necessities. They were, in fact, living below the poverty line.

The President would have been less than human not to be dismayed. Such statistics made a mockery of his campaign pledge of "four more years of prosperity." Yet it was hardly the sort of information to be made public.

Besides, Hoover had only to turn to the summary of yesterday's stock market to see that the news there was reassuring. In the previous day's trading, General Motors had opened at 139¾ and risen in two short hours to 144¼. Other major shares had also been bullish.

Yet Wall Street, as Hoover well knew, had its faults. There were those company mergers in which "insiders" had a unique opportunity to profit. There were the holding companies, piled one on top of the other, designed to allow profits to be drawn off largely by those who had built the huge pyramids. There were the "security affiliates" of the commercial banks, such as Charles Mitchell's National City Company, which allowed the bankers to play the market with their depositors' funds. There was the unfettered practice of short selling. There were the stock market "pools." And there was the increasing specter of public overspeculation.

Collectively, they suggested possible derelictions of fiduciary duty and a clear need for reform.

But Hoover felt hemmed in. Only a few days before, Calvin Coolidge had told the American public that shares "were cheap at current prices." Hoover now thought it would be futile for him to "ask Congress for powers to interfere with the stock market." In any case, he believed it might be unconstitutional for a President "to dictate the price of stocks." Further, he wondered whether the entire matter of controlling the runaway market was not more properly the province of the governor of New York, Franklin Roosevelt, who in Hoover's mind, was unfortunately showing a distinct disinclination to help.

Mindful of all this, Hoover chose to take a circumlocutory route in search of solutions. He would ask influential editors to "warn against gambling and the unduly high price of stocks." He would send someone suitable to New York "to talk in my name to the promoters and bankers behind the market." He would invite Richard Whitney to the White House and urge that the New York Stock Exchange itself "act to curb the manipulation of stocks." And he would order Treasury Secretary Mellon to issue strongly cautionary public statements.

Having read through his papers and made his decisions, the President left the Oval Office to change for the Inaugural Ball. It was to be one of the largest Washington had yet known.

On the radio, the financial reporter announced that there had been a break in the market: the New York *Times* Industrial Averages had declined during Hoover's first day in office by 5½ points.

Mike Meehan dressed particularly carefully this Tuesday morning of March 12, avoiding anything green. Once he had worn a green necktie for several days and suffered heavy losses. He burned the tie; his losses turned to gains. The superstitious, highly strung Irishman firmly believed from then on that green was, for him, an unlucky color.

Today Meehan wanted nothing to endanger his fortunes; at ten o'clock sharp, when the stock market opened, the operation of the Radio pool would be put fully in action, just as its predecessor had been precisely one year ago to the day.

Meehan kissed his wife, Elizabeth, good-bye—she would again stand in for him as one of the principal members of his pool—and patted his two young daughters on the head. At street level, John, his longtime chauffeur, had the Rolls ready, its engine running. Chain-smoking, Meehan was driven downtown to his headquarters at 61 Broadway.

For the past two weeks he had been laying the groundwork for this day. Most important, he had engaged Tom Bragg and Ben Smith to manage the pool. To do so, Meehan had to bring in a third broker, Bradford Ellsworth, who would help relieve the strain on Bragg and Smith, already heavily committed as comanagers of the ongoing Anaconda pool.

Meehan had not been surprised when the market dipped on March 4, the day of Hoover's inauguration. Two days later call money had soared to 12 percent and the market had slipped a further 16 points. On the seventh there had been a rally; Radio went from 74 to 81¾. That was the day Meehan chose to circulate the three-page document which was the basis for the pool. The circular went to favored clients not only of Meehan's own company, but also to those of W. E. Hutton and Company, and Block-Maloney and Company, who had recently agreed to take part.

The document was marked "Private and Confidential." Under the

Meehan company letterhead, stating that the firm was a member of the New York Stock Exchange was the typed heading:

Radio Corporation of America.
Common Stock Syndicate
New Stock

The circulars, carefully written in legal language, set out the terms of the pool. The syndicate would be limited "at any time" to not more than 1 million shares, "either long or short"; all transactions would be "in accordance with and subject to the rules and regulations of the New York Stock Exchange." The charge for operating the pool was to be "10% of the profits, said payment to be made prior to the distribution of the profits among syndicate participants."

Sixty-eight eager investors took up the offer and signed acceptance of the terms.

Among those who agreed to deposit $1 million was John J. Raskob. He also persuaded his old friend, James Riordan, to join in. Walter Chrysler put up $500,000. So did Bradford Ellsworth, who clearly had faith in what he and Bragg and Smith were about to do. But unlike them, Ellsworth deposited his half million in his own name.

To keep everything legal, Bragg had decided that, "as it was a rule of the Exchange that a broker cannot be at the same time also a principal," he, like Smith, would invest most of his money in the name of his wife. On the pool's books, both Gertrude Smith and Vera Bragg were shown as putting up $100,000; they also had a "joint account" in which an extra $300,000 was deposited. Bragg himself had a further $150,000 invested under cover of a company that he wholly owned, Cliffwood Corporation. Elizabeth Meehan was on the books for $1 million; Billy Durant for $400,000; Percy Rockefeller for only $75,000, but he had the possibility of additional investment through a joint account with Smith and Bragg left over from a previous, now dormant, pool operation.

All told, the pool managers had $12,683,000 to play with.

The day after the secret invitation to participate was sent, Radio moved up from $81.75 to $89.

Next day, Saturday, March 9, *The Wall Street Journal* ran the enticing item: "Radio Corporation of America to extend activity abroad. Corporation is financially better off than ever before in its history."

It sounded like an inspired leak; the paper neglected to mention that Radio had never paid a dividend.

By the close of trading at noon that day, the stock had gone to 92.

On Monday, March 11, "The Trader" in the New York *Daily News,* one of the journalists regularly accepting payola for pushing certain stocks, ran a paragraph stating that he was tipping Radio to rise to 100 "very soon," because "its original sponsors are behind it. . . . Tuesday it should be a real buy."

Now, on Tuesday, before the market opened, Smith and Ellsworth met Bragg in his private office at W. E. Hutton and Company. They were there to confirm the plan of action for the day. Bragg was in charge of overall strategy. Refreshed after a vacation in Florida, he would remain in and issue orders from his office. Smith would operate on the Stock Exchange floor, buying and selling the RCA shares on Bragg's instructions, mainly through the staff of M. J. Meehan and Company at Post Twelve. Ellsworth would assist either Bragg or Smith, depending on need.

Bradford Ellsworth, quiet and studious, listened carefully, taking notes. The broker looked older than his thirty-eight years. He dressed and behaved more like a conservative banker.

Tom Bragg looked, sounded, and frequently behaved like a prizefighter. He drank, swore, and, his many enemies said, only smiled when he collected a check from them. Handsome and in his prime at forty, he was a veteran manipulator of a score of pools.

Ben Smith was three years older than his partner, shorter and heavier. Smith *never* smiled. Soberly dressed with manicured nails and well-groomed hair, he showed not a trace of his upbringing in the slums of Hell's Kitchen. Nor did many know that he owed his position to Percy Rockefeller. Smith had once been his chauffeur, and it was Rockefeller who had purchased for him his seat on the Exchange.

The three men agreed that Ellsworth should be on the floor this morning with Smith, but that they should take care not to be seen together.

Already at Post Twelve in the Exchange, Mike Meehan was also in conference. Although tense and nervous inside, he was outwardly calm. He spoke reassuringly to his main Radio clerk, twenty-three-year-old Edward Schnell, and to Esmonde O'Brian. O'Brian would be a key man in the operation ahead. A senior partner in M. J. Meehan and Company, he would execute most of the buy or sell orders in Radio that either Smith or Ellsworth requested. Meehan would be free of direct involvement, able to ensure everything went according to plan.

At precisely 9:30 A.M., Superintendent William Crawford began his ritualistic morning round. It was his responsibility to make certain that "the mechanics"—the hundreds of miles of wires and cables and equipment they were connected to—were in order before his gavel struck the big brazen gong to open another day on the capital security market of the greatest creditor nation on earth.

Stepping into the spacious lofty chamber, six stories high, walking between the trading posts, he was immediately engulfed in the familiar and comforting sounds of premarket activity.

The superintendent's experienced eyes told him there were already about four hundred members assembled in the room, many busy making notes of orders being sent in from all over the country. There were also orders that had accumulated overnight from as far away as Shanghai, Sydney, and Tokyo as well as all parts of Europe, even including Lithuania; there a sizable colony of retired Americans continued to invest their savings in Wall Street. Hugh Fullerton, the United States consul in Lithuania, who himself owned $40,000 worth of American shares, was surprised by the number of expatriates who relied for their living largely on regular dividend payments from the United States.

In the main, the orders—wherever they originated—came to brokerage houses in and around Wall Street; they were then relayed by privately rented wires directly to the floor of the Exchange.

Hundreds of telephone clerks sitting in cramped booths around the edge of the floor took down the orders. Crawford always marveled at their speed and the way they never made a mistake while each day transcribing messages which involved millions of dollars; the slightest lapse in their concentration could cost firms huge losses.

For the next five hours, they would be rigidly confined to their cubicles. If Crawford spotted a telephonist on the actual trading floor, the man would be ordered out of the Exchange and fired by his firm.

The link between the booths and the trading posts were the page boys. They all had high school diplomas and many were college graduates. They wore military cadet-style uniforms, known as "Wall Street West Pointers," and earned a salary of fifteen dollars a week.

Crawford frequently reminded them they were constantly under the scrutiny of Exchange members; keen and alert boys who demonstrated high intelligence and good judgment might find themselves promoted to the position of telephone clerk. And many clerks eventually had seats on the Exchange bought for them by a brokerage house. Some even became partners.

It was a possibility heady enough to spur on any ambitious boy.

Crawford paused to watch a page working with a telephonist. The superintendent knew his presence helped "to keep everybody on their toes." The telephonist, headset clamped over his ears, hands free to write, handed a slip of paper to the page. The boy took it to a nearby bank of pneumatic tubes, inserted it into one of them, and the buy or sell order was then shot to the appropriate post.

In the final fifteen minutes before the opening of a new day, often more than 25,000 of these order slips were rushed through the tubes; others were hand-carried by the pages from the booths to the posts.

An assistant informed Crawford that all circuits and systems were working properly; the Exchange was now fully operational and electrically linked to the world outside. A complex network of wires and cables, running under the floor and buried in the walls, ran to scores of brokerage houses in the financial district. They, in turn, were linked by telephone and private wire to thousands of cities, towns, and hamlets across America; it was one of Crawford's proud claims that "a big frog in a little pond, maybe Willow Bend, can place an order with his broker and have it executed on the Exchange floor in seconds."

Still other circuits tied in the rest of the world: A Japanese in Tokyo could, if he wished, place an order and have it processed within three minutes. It took little over a minute for orders from London, Paris, or Berlin to be executed. It was all part of the service provided by what Crawford called "the greatest financial market-place in the world."

As usual, the superintendent paused at Post Five to exchange pleasantries with William Wadsworth, the oldest broker on the floor, who had been trading in railroad stock for sixty years. Nearby, at Post Eleven, a group of three Bouviers were in conference. The eldest, eighty-two-year-old Michael Bouvier, had been a member of the Exchange since 1869, and was founder of the flourishing brokerage firm of M. C. Bouvier and Company. His nephew, John Bouvier, was senior partner in the firm. And John's son, Jack Bouvier, expecting his first child in July, was the specialist at Post Eleven. Almost all of the Bouvier clan's considerable wealth was tied up in securities.

Moving purposefully—through the groups of commission brokers, floor traders, and specialists; past the odd-lot dealers, who only handled orders for fewer than 100 shares; past the "two-dollar men," so called because that sum was once their compensation for buying or selling 100 shares for a commission broker, though now it was $2.50—William Crawford finally climbed onto the podium. On rare occasions—a declaration of war or peace, the death of the President, a full-scale financial calamity—the president of the Stock Exchange would use the rostrum to address members.

From his vantage point, Crawford could see Simmons and Richard Whitney beginning their morning tour of the trading posts.

Crawford also spotted, away down to his left, at Post Twelve, Mike Meehan. More and more brokers were converging on the Radio post.

The superintendent glanced toward the big clock on the far wall. It was almost ten o'clock. He looked down at the finely adjusted chronometer built into the rostrum's railing. He would take his cue from that instrument. Its second hand ticked silently on. When it reached 10 A.M., Crawford gave the gong a resounding thump with his gavel.

Instantly the hum of conversation rose to a roar.

To the experienced ears of Mike Meehan, to the seething mob on the floor, the roar had a satisfying ring to it; already the high, shrill sound was being punctuated by yells and cheers as the first prices leaped upward under the stupendous buying pressures unleashed by Crawford's gavel. In a market break, the moment a great selling wave set in, the sound would be deeper—broken by raucous cries of "Boo! Boo! Boo-ooo!"

This morning there was no booing as the wave of buying orders rolled in.

The gong's echo had barely faded before the Radio pool was in action.

First the unsmiling Smith, then Ellsworth, moved unobtrusively to Post Twelve. There they gave their initial orders for RCA stock to Meehan's Radio clerk, Ed Schnell, or to Esmonde O'Brian. They were not yet large orders, averaging only 500 or 1,000 shares. They joined other orders coming in from all parts of the country, some of them no doubt as a result of the paragraphs in *The Wall Street Journal, Daily News,* and other syndicated financial columns.

Surrounded by his team at Post Twelve—which included price reporters whose function it was to keep updating the price recording dials of all shares traded at the post—Meehan could see at once that Radio was moving up from its closing price yesterday of 90⅛.

Within minutes of trading beginning, the ticker tape was carrying the news. It would be noted in brokerage offices all over the country. The word would be phoned by local brokers to their customers that now seemed a good time to buy into Radio. The reaction would not be immediate, but Meehan could feel confident that within a few days, an avalanche of orders would be on the way further to engulf his post in thousands of slips of paper.

Many of those slips would pass through the hands of Edward Schnell, standing inside the post. Schnell was one of the young men who had started as a page and was now on his way up; having been with M. J. Meehan and Company for less than a year, he was already showing great promise.

The Radio clerk respected Mike Meehan above all other brokers on the floor. To Schnell, his employer was "dynamic, courageous and fair —one hell of a guy." And, when he had a moment to spare, Schnell enjoyed watching Meehan exhibit his most famous mannerism, now almost a personal trademark: When excited, Meehan would roll five or six pencils together between his hands. They made a satisfying sound. They released tension. They were also a signal things were going well.

This morning, Meehan was rolling his pencils.

At about 10:30, the pool's managers fed in their first big buy order. It was for 5,000 shares.

Thirty seconds later, news of this blockbuster order was flashing across the ticker.

Soon afterward, Bragg spoke by phone to Smith on the floor. He ordered him to purchase a further 1,000 shares in the name of W. E. Hutton and Company. Smith bought them through Meehan's at 92⅞. On Bragg's books, they were shown as belonging to his wife, Vera Bragg.

Orders from as far away as San Francisco, Florida, Seattle, and Hawaii now began to come in.

The financial reporters of the Associated Press and United Press sent out flashes that Radio was on the move.

On receipt of the flashes, radio news directors slotted them into their next bulletins and city editors found space for them in their latest editions.

By eleven o'clock the ticker was showing almost continuous trading in Radio.

At regular intervals during the morning, Billy Durant checked the ticker in his Manhattan office at 250 West Fifty-seventh Street. His $400,000 investment in the pool looked like showing a healthy profit.

He turned back to his scratch pad, hunched over a desk in the corner of his hermetically sealed office.

Durant believed that fresh air contained impurities that could damage his health; whenever possible he worked in a room that was almost airless. Nor was he keen on strong sunlight.

At noon, another quirk manifested itself. His personal chef wheeled in a portable oven, broke the seal on its door, and produced Durant's lunch. The chef traveled thirty blocks every day in one of Durant's limousines to serve the meal; his master, like Henry Ford, did not trust the cooks of New York to prepare the sort of germ-free food he insisted on eating.

His meal over, Durant took another look at the ticker. Satisfied, he returned to his desk to resume preparing his notes for the meeting he planned to have with President Hoover. He intended to leave the President in no doubt as to his feelings: He would castigate the Federal Reserve Board as "a wrecking crew, draining the life blood of the nation."

At the San Francisco Stock Exchange, founded in 1883 and now the second largest in America, brokers received a spate of orders to buy

RCA stock. The Exchange had just been relocated in the U. S. Subtreasury Building on the corner of Pine and Sansome streets in order better to cope with the huge increase in trading on the West Coast. The volume of sales in 1928 had been greater than the total for the previous eight years.

In Chicago, on La Salle Street—the imposing stone canyon in Chicago's Loop that is the financial center of the Midwest—the news about Radio raced like a prairie fire through the stately gray buildings. The Chicago Exchange was already in the grip of an unprecedented boom. In the first three months of 1929, the total number of shares sold would come close to the combined figure for the entire period 1924–27.

On the sparkling new Twin Cities Exchange of Minneapolis–St. Paul, the surge in Radio was one of the first to be experienced since its opening in January.

Farther east, on the Baltimore Exchange, founded in 1838, the Hartford Exchange, founded in 1876, and the equally well established exchanges at Boston and Philadelphia, there was a steadily growing demand to "get into Radio."

In each of the twenty-two exchanges, from St. Louis to Los Angeles, the cry was the same.

A flood of orders—often for just ten, fifty, or seventy-five shares— was telegraphed to Wall Street.

When news that Radio "was taking off" reached Frank Montague in the Union Industrial Bank, Flint, he informed his fellow conspirators.

There was a hurried discussion as to whether more bank funds should be "borrowed" to invest in what "looked like a certainty."

Montague urged caution; it was early days yet. It was better to wait and see what developed.

The others agreed.

In Wall Street, the pool's managers, monitoring the ticker, noted the flow of small orders beginning to show on the tape. For the time being, they would cease their transactions. They wanted these modest orders to be given full play. Everything was going as intended.

William Lamb was having difficulty in holding John J. Raskob's attention. As the architect attempted to explain his latest plans for the Empire State Building, the promoter frequently leaped from his chair and hurried out of the office to a closet down the corridor. Inside the closet was Raskob's personal ticker; he kept it hidden there so that nobody would accuse him of being a slave to the market. Today, he was happy to be enslaved. The $1 million he had put into the syndicate was almost certainly going to prove a sound investment.

If the RCA stock continued to climb, Raskob joked to Lamb, he might consider renaming their project the Radio State Building.

There was only one cloud on the immediate horizon. Auto manufacturer Walter Chrysler, who had $500,000 in the pool, had just casually announced that he was planning to build the world's tallest building. It would rise on Lexington Avenue; it would be called, appropriately, the Chrysler Building.

The last thing Raskob wanted was to be pipped at the post in the skyscraper stakes. Yet the world still did not know of his plans.

Lamb relieved Raskob's fears. In the architect's opinion, there was no chance of Chrysler topping the Empire State Building.

Mollified, pleased the way Radio was trading, Raskob finally gave all his attention to Lamb.

Leading a small army of engineers and design experts, the architect was preparing for what would literally be a full-scale assault on Fifth Avenue.

Even now, before the Waldorf-Astoria had been bulldozed, his agents were scouring the world for materials. In French and Italian quarries, American stonemasons were selecting an entire year's output of the finest marble to pave the lobbies and corridors of the Empire State edifice. Steel mills in Pittsburgh were being alerted to produce girders and rivets for the building's skeleton. Glass factories were being checked for their capacity to produce thousands of windows. Lumber mills were being visited to ascertain their output; specialist companies were being canvassed. And it was all being done in the strictest secrecy.

Lamb had one final thought for Raskob: When their plans were finally unveiled, the world would get an even bigger kick than the financier now felt from watching his Radio stock climb.

Well before William Crawford ended the day's trading, Mike Meehan knew the pool had made a most promising start. All told, Smith and Ellsworth, during the five hectic hours of trading, had placed orders with his firm for 392,600 shares; in the same period they had also sold 246,000 shares. The price had risen during the day to close at 91⅝, not so great a gain as on the first day of the Radio pool of one year ago, but a picture of great demand was being created nationwide.

And the market had also been "cleaned"; the floating supply of stock had been swept into the hands of the pool. The syndicate managers now had irresistible power to force the stock upward.

By next day, Wednesday, March 13, readers of *The Wall Street Journal* knew that the RCA stock had gone "to fresh record levels on the activities of big operators who have sponsored Radio's market for the last several weeks." The paper seemed singularly well informed. The same day Radio went to 94.

On Thursday, March 14—a day during which President Hoover spoke to a group of editors about the excesses of the stock market—the pool managers sold 73,800 more shares than they bought. Among those they purchased were 2,000 "for the account of" Vera Bragg, and 2,500 for Gertrude Smith. By the day's end, Radio had climbed to $100.50 a share. Treasury Secretary Mellon, on Hoover's advice, suggested the public purchase bonds. The idea was buried on an inside page of most newspapers.

The following day, Friday, March 15, trading opened with Radio again advancing swiftly. On Bragg's orders the 2,000 shares purchased the previous day for his wife were now sold back to M. J. Meehan and Company. Sold back also were 5,000 shares previously bought in the name of Gertrude Smith. Bragg then instructed Ellsworth to buy that same number of shares—5,000—for the account of Ellsworth himself.

At the same time, Bragg also managed to arrange that 25,000 shares were bought, and 25,000 shares sold, at precisely the same price, both through Meehan's, for pool participants. It was masterful manipulation.

This was the day New York's first Federal House of Detention opened. The day closed with Radio standing at 107—and the jail filled.

By the midday close on Saturday, March 16, Radio had reached its peak, 109¼—although no one but the pool managers knew that. For on Sunday, after consultation, they confirmed their decision that next day they would "pull the plug."

On Monday, March 18, Radio gradually dropped back to 101 as Smith and Ellsworth carefully unloaded 238,600 shares on the market. The stock was eagerly snapped up by the unsuspecting public. Call money stood at 10 percent. Meehan could also be satisfied with the operation of his other pool, the one in Anaconda Copper, for its price during the day rose to 22 cents.

In Flint, the Union Industrial Bank's "league of gentlemen" decided yet again to throw caution to the winds. Using pilfered bank funds, they finally issued orders to buy Radio.

Three days later, the stock had dropped further to 92½ as the pool managers completed their divesting operations.

Frank Montague detected a feeling of "general unease" among his fellow embezzlers. But before selling their stock, they decided to hang on a little longer.

On Friday, March 22, *The Wall Street Journal* reported, entirely accurately, that "the large pool in Radio finished letting out its line Tuesday and, for the time being at least, has turned its attention to the copper group with most of its buying in Anaconda."

The men of Flint decided it was time to get out. Next day, their Radio shares sold for just 87¼. They had made another substantial loss; they were now in even deeper financial straits than before.

But, for the participants in Meehan's syndicate, the pool had been a huge success.

Its profits were made in the first crucial week, March 12 to 19. Altogether Smith and Ellsworth had bought and sold 1,493,400 Radio shares, involving a sum of $146,987,527. The pool's net profit was $4,924,078.68—which was divided among syndicate members according to the amount they had originally subscribed.

John J. Raskob got his $1,000,000 back—plus another check for $291,710.80. His friend, James Riordan, received $58,342.15—and Riordan had not even put up a penny to cover the 10,000 shares the pool managers purchased in his name. Billy Durant made $145,855.39; Bradford Ellsworth $282,635.34, which included his management fee.

Messrs. Bragg and Smith and their wives together amassed $634,631.40.

Mr. and Mrs. Meehan made $652,783.94 and their firm a further $580,000 in commission.

It was not a bad share-out for little more than a week's work.

And it was all done "in accordance with and subject to the rules and regulations of the New York Stock Exchange."

CHAPTER NINE

THE CORRALLED BULL ESCAPES

At every stop the *Overland Express* made in its journey from New York to Oakland, California, fresh newspapers were brought to Giannini's private Pullman compartment. They joined those scattered over the seats and floor, discarded by the industrious Clorinda. She was occupying the journey clipping all references to the family and her husband's business interests. Later, back in San Mateo, the clippings would be pasted into books. This obsession was one of the few things Clorinda shared with Henry Ford's wife, Clara. The other was a love of nature.

The very fact that the Gianninis were passing through its circulation area was enough for a newspaper to record the event. The more irresponsible ran stories that Giannini was in the vicinity to buy a bank or two. In reality he never stepped out of the train.

Clorinda had never known her husband so relaxed. Only she knew just how emotionally satisfying and important the acquisition of Blair and Company had been to him.

Yet there was something about Elisha Walker that bothered Claire Giannini. Walker would be the president of what would be known as the Bankamerica-Blair Corporation, and chairman of the Executive Committee of the bank. These dual posts would make him the most influential man after her father in the Giannini empire. In her meetings with him, she had found Walker charming, polished, and able to command respect.

She remembered the last night in New York when Walker took them to dinner at the Plaza. The maître d' had become immediately obsequious. And it was difficult, Claire agreed, not to be impressed by the man.

Even in the Plaza, accustomed to European royalty, state governors, and movie stars, eyes followed Walker everywhere. When they were seated, there was a flutter of menus, and her father had joked that the surrounding waiters and wine stewards reminded him of the old Wild West, Indians circling a wagon train.

Giannini tolerated the sycophantic behavior; Claire felt their host relished it. But that was not the reason for her misgivings. There was something in Walker's makeup, something about the man, that troubled her. She had puzzled over it after they left the Plaza. It was still nagging at the back of her mind when Walker saw them off on the long journey home. Walker had been courteous and solicitous. Then she remembered: He had shaken her hand—it had been a cold, brief handshake, not at all like one of the Italian embraces Claire was used to. That was it: Beneath all the outward poise, Walker was "cold as a fish."

Several times she thought to raise the matter with her father. But she realized to do so would only spoil his mood. She reserved her thoughts for herself, having resolved to "keep a weather eye on our new man."

While Clorinda clipped, her husband digested the financial news.

Transamerica stock was performing conservatively. His well-known policy advocating outright ownership and opposition to anyone buying Transamerica on margin, plus the lessons of the 1928 break in the stock, all combined to dampen enthusiasm for Transamerica as a good speculative risk. Though in healthy demand, the shares sold in the 130s, a modest increase over the price of Bancitaly when that stock had been withdrawn in December 1928.

Yet the overall behavior of the market still bothered Giannini. It was not because call money was climbing again, or that Secretary Mellon's advice to buy bonds was largely meaningless, or that Hoover was doing some deft, but futile public maneuvering in relation to the market. What troubled Giannini far more was the knowledge that everything seemed to be conspiring to create the illusion that, for the first time in history, the secret to an everlasting bull market had been found.

Giannini was not a man to sell America short or to issue alarmist press statements.

But he emphatically rejected the incessant newspaper stories that there was only one way for the market to go—up. He disliked even more the cheapskate journalists who actually duped their readers and employers by accepting bribes to propagandize in dubious stocks. Among those guilty of such practice were Richard Edmondson of *The Wall Street Journal,* William Gomber of *Financial America,* Charles Murphy of the New York *Evening Mail,* J. F. Lowther of the New York *Herald Tribune,* William White of the New York *Evening Post,* and W. F. Walmsley of the New York *Times.*

All received checks from Newton Plummer, a former publicist who was regularly hired by pool managers to plant items in newspapers. Bragg and Smith never used Plummer; they preferred to employ the contacts they personally made in the media.

The fact that supposedly incorruptible newsmen were being bribed concerned Giannini. He was worried even more by the trend whereby tipsters and confidence men, always a scourge of the financial district, were now becoming almost respectable and accepted as part of the Wall Street scene.

To Giannini it was another sign of how far things were slipping.

It was not until the train reached Chicago late afternoon on Monday, March 25, that he learned call money had shot up to 14 percent, the highest since July 1920. Transamerica, like most stocks, had dropped in a market break which averaged five points. Ninety stocks had plunged to their lowest point for the year. The ticker was running fifty minutes late.

The press was waiting for him at Chicago. The reporters had one question, posed by the man from the *Tribune:* "Has the bull been corralled?"

Giannini didn't know. But his face showed enough for some newsmen to file stories about "the world's greatest banker" being seriously concerned over what was happening in Wall Street.

Momentarily shaking off his marital problems, Jesse Livermore struck suddenly and unexpectedly at the market on Monday, March 25.

He had listened carefully to the morning news and then laid his plans. The broadcaster spoke of Hoover's latest "economic measure"—turning over the seven horses quartered at the White House stables to the War Department. The British and American governments were at odds over the sinking of a British schooner, thought to have been carrying contraband liquor, by the U. S. Coast Guard. In France, General Maurice Sarrail, "a military genius and hero of Verdun," had died. Lightning had struck the Canadian Parliament.

Livermore did not hear what he had been waiting for—a statement by the Federal Reserve Board. Everyone in Wall Street knew the board had been meeting for days behind closed doors in Washington. Livermore guessed the market was on the verge of breaking as a result of the uncertainty.

By eight-thirty he was in his office, completing his plotting.

Ninety minutes later, the moment Crawford's gong signaled the start of trading, Livermore began to feed a bewildering stream of buy and sell orders into the market. No one could know what he was up to. But whereas his were joined by a deluge of straightforward orders to sell from all over the country, Livermore was selling short, banking on borrowing the shares he was selling.

He struck first at Post Six, catching American Can, American Woolen and Corn Products before their prices began to tumble.

He then switched his attention to Post Nine, short selling the rail stocks traded there.

Avoiding A.T. and T. at Post Fifteen, Livermore launched himself against Post Sixteen, going short of Seaboard Oil just as it began to slip.

By eleven o'clock, experienced hands thought they could detect Livermore's imprint. The legendary bear was like a red rag to the bulls. But there was nothing they could do.

Hidden away in his retreat on Fifth Avenue, Livermore had issued his last instructions by noon. The rest of the day he spent watching the ticker.

Next morning, Tuesday, March 26, when the market opened, call money had skyrocketed to a staggering 20 percent—the highest it had been for over nine years. As if to mark the moment, just as the rate was posted on the Exchange's new electric announcement board, a fuse blew. According to one observer, it "caused even the worst crippled of the bulls to laugh."

There was no reason for laughter in the period that followed. Prices fell almost vertically. And still the Federal Reserve Board remained silent. Sell orders poured in at such a rate that by the close of the day, another record was set—8,246,740 shares had changed hands, far and away the greatest volume in the Exchange's long history.

By then, Livermore had returned to the fray, buying at rock-bottom prices to cover the shares he had previously sold short. It was later calculated he made a profit of $200,000—or a little over $1,000 a minute for the three hours he had actually been actively engaged in the market.

The serious break, which showed every sign of bringing the great bull market to an abrupt end, was just what Charles Mitchell, chairman of the National City Bank, was waiting for. His reaction was almost immediate. He announced to the press: "We feel that we have an obligation which is paramount to any Federal Reserve warning, or anything else, to avert any dangerous crisis in the money market."

Mitchell spoke not only with the authority of his own mammoth bank. As one of the senior directors of the Federal Reserve Bank of New York, it was well understood that he also spoke for them. Both banks meant to ignore the Federal Reserve Board's instruction about reducing the amount of money which they made available for speculation.

It was partly as a result of the cutback in loans demanded by the board that the call money rate had risen to its dangerously high level of 20 percent—an increase that made it impossible for many investors to continue buying shares on margin.

Now, early afternoon of March 26, Mitchell made it clear to the press that his bank, if no other, would be making money available in huge amounts for borrowers to use as they wished.

The announcement had a moral tone about it, a desire to put the welfare of the ordinary man above all else. It was reminiscent of Mitchell's memorable press release of January 1928 when he stated he had detected "microscopic signs" of manipulation in bank stock prices. This he solemnly considered to be "distinctly disadvantageous and probably at times might even be dangerous."

It sounded high-minded and idealistic. It was cant of the first order.

The law forbade any bank to purchase its own stock. Nor could banks lend money on their shares. The regulations were formed to stop the possibility of a bank becoming involved in the wilder side of the market; if a bank was subject to the advances and recesses of common stock, then it would gravely affect the stability and reputation of the institution. The law was specifically designed to avoid bank stocks becoming the "football of speculation."

In 1928 Mitchell withdrew his National City Bank from the market. By doing so, he publicly upheld the law.

Then, just as publicly, he had flouted it.

Using his bank's affiliate, the National City Company, of which he was also chairman, Mitchell began what even he would later concede was "an orgy of trading" in his bank's stock.

In January 1928 its shares sold at $785. By June 1928 Mitchell's company salesmen had boosted them to $940. By January 1929 they stood at $1,450. Now, at the end of March, they were close to $2,000 a share. And the National City Bank, which had supposedly removed itself from market rations "to prevent manipulation," was, through its wholly owned subsidiary, the principal trader in its own stock—willfully defying the law.

The company's success had been of benefit to its parent bank in other respects. In October 1928 it had quietly bought a $5,013,000 block of shares in the Boeing Airplane and Transport Corporation, a holding company controlling three subsidiaries successfully engaged in manufacturing airplanes and carrying mail and passengers. In January 1929 the company was renamed United Aircraft and Transport. Under that name its stock quickly became one of the most sought after on the New York Exchange.

Because it had been able to buy the initial block before it was offered to the public, Mitchell's organization had made, until now, a profit on the shares of over $1,659,000.

Two months before, he had ordered the company to acquire a further block of United Aircraft stock. This had cost $13 million. They, too, had been resold to the public, at a profit of $1,447,000.

Mitchell and a group of favored "insiders"—who included Percy Rockefeller, a director of the National City Company, and Frank Bartow, the Morgan broker who had clashed with A. P. Giannini—held 13,000 United shares, purchased privately from the company at a special price of $80 each. Two days after buying them on these terms, never offered to the public, the stock came on the market at $96 a share.

Mitchell's instant profit, if he had wished to sell his 1,000 shares, would have been $16,000.

He chose to wait. Now, in spite of the market break, United Aircraft was selling at $127 a share, offering an even larger profit for Mitchell.

Legally, there was nothing wrong in what he was doing—taking advantage of his privileged "inside" knowledge to line his own pocket. The morality of the action was another matter.

The stock market break had no effect on the $16.5 million bond issue the National City Company had recently launched on behalf of Minas Gerais, one of the states in the republic of Brazil. The issue was small by company standards, but the profit potential was enticing.

Until Mitchell moved in, Minas Gerais had been supported by French banks. They had been thankful to get out. French bondholders had to bring suit against Minas Gerais before obtaining payment in gold under the terms of their loans.

The National City had no illusion about the situation in Brazil. For an investor, the risks were appalling. A confidential company report stated "it would be hard to find anywhere a sadder confession of inefficiency and ineptitude than that displayed by the various state officials of Minas Gerais in respect of long-term borrowing."

But in the brochure that Mitchell authorized for the Minas Gerais bond issue, there was no mention of ineptitude or inefficiency. In the fine, flowery language he liked to see in his prospectuses, the venality of corrupt officials in a destitute South American province took on a new meaning. The brochures contained the fine declaration: "Prudent and careful administration of the State's finances has been axiomatic with successive administrations in Minas Gerais."

Later, "axiomatic" was changed to "characteristic."

The bond issue was one of the big successes of this past winter. So much so that Kuhn, Loeb and Company, recognizing the potential plush pickings, tried to become bankers for the Brazilian province.

They should have known better than to tangle with Charles Mitchell. In a short, sharp exchange, he saw them off with a warning not to attempt to "chisel in"; he sounded like Al Capone driving a rival gang from his patch.

Yet if Mitchell saw no possibility of the Minas Gerais bond issue being adversely affected by today's market break, he could not be so optimistic of a stock in which he took a special personal interest, Anaconda Copper. So far, with the help and careful supervision of pool managers Bragg and Smith, the shares were holding up well. But Mitchell knew that, as other stocks were falling so precipitately, it was only a matter of time before Anaconda, too, would have to give way.

It was a worrying thought. The National City Company was a principal investor in the Anaconda pool, and the National City Bank was itself banker to the Anaconda Copper Company.

Further, the National City was financing three smaller and separate pools in Anaconda subsidiaries. One was in Andes Copper, another in Chile Copper, the third in Greene Cananea.

So far, nearly 500,000 shares in these companies had been purchased by National City. Some 100,000 were retained as an investment; the rest were being profitably traded on the Exchange.

And finally, the company had accumulated 300,000 shares of Anaconda Copper which Mitchell had planned to begin selling to the public early next month. He realized that, if Anaconda's price fell, National City might well have problems in unloading this huge investment at a profit, if at all.

And so, with all these weighty considerations in mind, Mitchell held his press conference early this afternoon of March 26. As soon as his promise to loan money with no embarrassing questions asked reached Wall Street, the gloom there lifted. Call money began to drop back—at the close of trading it had fallen from 20 to 15 percent—and share prices began to rally. Charles Mitchell had saved the day, and himself.

By next morning, Wednesday, March 27, he had arranged, as he had promised, for his National City Bank to borrow $25 million from the Federal Reserve Bank of New York, in open defiance of the Federal Reserve Board in Washington. The board, which knew the money would be fed into the market, made no comment. Mitchell had won. The Great Bull Market would go on.

Mitchell found himself the hero of hundreds of editorials; he was hailed as the man who had assumed Calvin Coolidge's mantle as patron of the boom.

In the past forty-eight hours, the violent tumble in stocks had ruined uncounted thousands of small-time investors, those unable to meet their brokers' demands for more margin.

Now, under Mitchell's impetus, thousands of others—"financial lemmings" was how one jaundiced journalist saw them—rushed into the market to take their place.

Many stocks were back where they were before the fall and had started to climb higher—boosted by Mitchell's money. The total daily interest charge for the funds borrowed specifically to play the New York stock market was now running at $2,280,000.

In Washington, three senators demanded Mitchell's resignation as a director of the Reserve Bank in New York He did not resign, and the Federal Reserve Board, weak and vacillating, watching from the sidelines as the bull market broke out of its pen and resumed rampaging, uttered no word of public protest about the way in which the single most powerful commercial banker in America had behaved.

First, Billy Durant breakfasted with his wife, Catherine. They had married the day after Durant divorced his first wife in May 1908, a settlement that cost him $2,150,000 in cash and stock. Twenty-one years later, Billy and Catherine were still deeply in love. She tolerated his eccentricities, philosophically accepting that, after she had prepared dinner on their chef's night off, her husband might well suddenly disappear to play checkers with the elevator boy. The game was an obsession with Durant; he regularly interrupted important business meetings to invite colleagues to play. Catherine had also become used to the marathon poker schools which sometimes kept her husband out all night. But still she could not quite accept that he should so casually gamble $10,000 on the throw of a card.

Now, breakfast over, Durant returned to his dressing room, where his personal barber waited at the portable shaving chair. Afterward, sprayed and talcumed, Durant packed a small case, carefully choosing suit and matching attire.

Though he had once been a cigar smoker, he had recently given up on doctor's orders. Nevertheless, the habit died hard. His packing complete, Durant slipped a cigar into his vest pocket. Should the urge to smoke become too strong, he could always sniff the cigar.

Durant hoped his old friend, Herbert Hoover, would not mind if he did so. He also expected that the President would be far too interested in what he had to say than to comment on the foible.

Kissing Catherine good-bye, Durant slipped out of their home, 905 Fifth Avenue, in New York.

This morning, his chauffeur was not waiting. Apart from Catherine, Durant was determined nobody would know his destination. He took a taxi to the station. Unannounced and unexpected, Billy Durant was off to see the President.

By early afternoon he had settled into a room in the Carlton Hotel, a few convenient blocks from the White House.*

Throughout the afternoon he reviewed his arguments and consulted his documents. They included replies Durant had received to a series of telegrams he had sent out on March 31. The telegrams had gone to top executives of one hundred of America's most important companies whose shares were quoted on the New York Stock Exchange. Durant asked each man to let him know, confidentially, whether, based on their company's "present condition and plans for the future," they thought the market price of their common stock was too high—"yes or no."

Although he had not yet received replies from everyone, the majority of those that had come in had answered no. This bolstered Durant's confidence in the arguments he would put to the President. He knew there was a need to present a watertight case.

Although the market was recovering from the battering it had taken at the end of March, largely through the intervention of Charles Mitchell, the Federal Reserve Board had since become more vocal in its criticism of speculation. On April 4 it threatened that if its Reserve Banks did not "co-operate voluntarily," the board "may adopt other methods of influencing the situation."

Durant no longer felt this was yet another hollow threat. He now believed the board was both "thoughtless" and "dangerous."

When darkness fell, he strolled past the White House, ablaze with lights. It was still too early. Durant returned to his hotel, wondering how Hoover would react to his proposals.

President Hoover had spent his day dealing with the Cabinet, the sub-Cabinet, committees and subcommittees, the Supreme Court and the Congress. A great deal of his time was spent in formal and informal politicking.

But uppermost in his mind was concern over the plight of America's farmers. While the urban standard of living was increasing, farm prices were falling. As a result, a strong lobby had been raised in favor of imposing protective tariffs on foreign agricultural products coming into the country. Those voices had now been joined by others who wished to impose tariffs on all manner of imported goods. The danger, as Hoover knew, was that if such tariffs were introduced, it would not only make it difficult for foreign nations to export to the United States, but America itself would in turn find it difficult to export her goods to those same nations. And if that happened, investment would fall, and the stock market would inevitably be hit.

* Fifteen years later another financier, Alexander Sachs, would sit in the same hotel, waiting to see another President, Roosevelt, to discuss an equally momentous matter—America's secret atomic bomb. See *Enola Gay,* by the authors.

Hoover looked forward to going fishing for a few days when he intended to think over the problem.

But tonight he had to host a private dinner party for members of the Washington judiciary. He hoped it would not go on too late.

A little before nine-thirty, dressed in the suit he had packed in New York, cigar tucked in his vest, Billy Durant stepped out of the Carlton Hotel and got into a taxi.†

Five minutes later it drove past the entrance gates of the White House—apparently the guards thought Durant was a late dinner guest and waved him through.

A Negro footman spotted the cab and hurried forward. The servant was puzzled; his list showed all the dinner guests had arrived.

"I'm Mr. Billy Crapo Durant. I wish to see the President."

"Sorry, sah—"

"Fetch the butler," said Durant. He turned to pay the cabby.

The tail-coated, white-gloved butler emerged and stared imperiously at the little gray-haired man bounding toward him.

Durant had his own way of dealing with snooty servants.

"Mr. Durant to see the President."

Without waiting, he brushed past the dumbfounded butler.

The man caught up with him, told him to wait, and fetched the President's secretary, who began to question Durant.

"Mr. Durant—the financier?"

"Yes. This is important."

"Then tell me. I'll convey your message to the President in the morning."

Durant stubbornly shook his head. "You're wasting time. Go and tell the President his friend Billy Crapo Durant is here!"

The secretary bridled. Icily, he told Durant that President Hoover was in the middle of dinner, entertaining some of the most important judges in the land.

"Do what I say," commanded Durant. "Mr. Hoover will thank you later."

"Mr. Durant! You really can't come in here—"

Slowly and deliberately Durant ground out every word. "Go and get the President!"

The secretary left. The butler showed Durant into a spacious waiting room.

Minutes later Herbert Hoover joined him.

"Billy, this better be important."

"It is, Mr. President. It is."

† See Source Notes.

For the next ten minutes Hoover sat and listened as Durant warned that a major financial collapse was inevitable unless the Federal Reserve Board was forced to end its attempt to control brokerage loans and security credit. He spoke quietly, devoid of emotion, piling on the facts as he saw them. He ended his explanation with the words: "It's up to you now."

Hoover thanked him for coming and returned to his guests. Though the President had made no comment, Durant believed his mission had not been a failure. He had been allowed to make his points plainly. He was especially pleased that he had not once sniffed his cigar. Walking down Pennsylvania Avenue, he pulled the Havana from his vest pocket, waggled it under his nose, and tossed it away.

CHAPTER TEN

EVERYBODY'S DOING IT

Until he discovered Pat Bologna's shoeshine stand at 60 Wall Street, Charlton MacVeagh had a problem. Jack Morgan liked his keen young men to have gleaming shoes. It went with their sober suits, stiffly starched white shirts, and carefully knotted ties. But the subway journey from Charlton's bachelor apartment on Fifty-seventh Street downtown to Wall left his shoes scuffed and dirty.

For ten cents a shine, nineteen-year-old Bologna not only restored them to mirrorlike perfection but also passed on a nonstop barrage of stock market tips and astonishingly well informed gossip.

The short, well-built Bologna was the self-appointed shoe black to the titans of Wall Street. Joseph Kennedy, Charles Mitchell, Billy Durant, and Ben Smith were among a long list of impressive names who had their shoes burnished by Bologna.

From them he picked up useful financial tidbits which helped him invest sensibly in the market; like most small speculators, Bologna bought on margin, dabbling in a variety of stocks. Sometimes, when he was "on to a real winner," the gregarious young Italian liked to share his luck with his regular customers.

This morning, April 9, he had a hot tip that Woolworth was going to double its capital. He told Charlton now was the time to get into the chain-store stock.

The broker smiled and hurried up Wall, musing that if Bologna ever got inside the House of Morgan, his quick, fertile mind would likely glean enough information to set him up for life.

But Charlton knew that no shoe black would ever get past the doorman at Number 23 Wall without a special appointment. In any case, unlike the majority of employees who came to work by public transport, Jack Morgan and his partners never ran the risk of getting their shoes dirty. They were conveyed everywhere, from doorstep to doorstep, by chauffeured limousine.

Charlton arrived at 23 just as the first of their cars was turning in off Broadway. He hurried into the fortresslike building: It was one of the many unwritten rules at Morgan's that junior staff must always arrive before the partners.

In a stately, funereal procession, the gleaming black automobiles slid into the curb. Doormen rushed forward as the majestic Morgan partners alighted and began to ascend the stone steps of their citadel.

First, as usual, was Charles Steele. Black-suited, white-skinned, he possessed a piercing stare which had quelled many a boardroom argument.

Next came Frank Bartow; the loss of the Giannini account had not, outwardly at least, affected him; many years of training taught Bartow to conceal his feelings behind a bland, affable smile. He exchanged a few words with the doormen about the weather—a habit Bartow had acquired in London.

George Whitney arrived with Russell C. Leffingwell; the two men had breakfasted together, as they often did, reviewing over their bacon and eggs those aspects of the Morgan business for which they were directly responsible.

The imposing figure of Parker Gilbert, in a black topcoat, gray gloves and hat, hurried past the doormen. Gilbert always gave the impression of never having enough time in his day; he regularly worked late and left the building with a bulging attaché case.

E. T. Stotesbury—even his partners called him only "E.T."—arrived, overcoat collar turned up against the chill wind blowing off New York Bay and up Wall Street. Head thrust forward, he hastened into the building, every inch the aggressive banker.

Thomas Lamont, still strikingly handsome at fifty-nine, in his black pinstripe looked and behaved like a senior diplomat from some important nation.

He handed a doorman his attaché case and stepped out of the car. Tall and patrician, with an unblemished face and clear blue eyes, he was physically and mentally the quintessential Morgan partner; a favorite office saying was that "Mr. Morgan speaks to Mr. Lamont and Mr. Lamont speaks to the people."

This morning, as always, Lamont had pleasant words for the doormen. Though he was financially one of the most powerful men in the country, he still liked to retain the common touch. On his regular visits abroad—to England, Mexico, Egypt, Italy, Japan, China—he had been known to question people in the street about their way of life. It was said that this endearing trait was a throwback to those days when Lamont had been raised in a parsonage. The son of an impoverished Methodist minister in Claverack, New York, he had been taught that the views of his father's congregation were important. Or his inquisitive nature may have stemmed from the time he spent as a reporter on the New York *Tribune,* his first job after working his way through Harvard. He never lost his interest in journalism, and, in 1918, seven years after he had joined Morgan's, he could not resist the temptation to buy the New York *Evening Post.*

Pierpont Morgan saw in Lamont a natural ambassador for the firm. With his command of languages, his extraordinary grasp of complicated financial details, and his even more assured understanding of global politics, Thomas Lamont was now Morgan's chief emissary to the world.

Next to Jack Morgan, Lamont probably knew more kings, presidents, dictators, despots, and rulers than any other living financier.

Yet he could still stand at the top of 23's steps, chatting happily to the doormen, secure in the knowledge that they both served a common purpose: maintaining the House of Morgan's status as the world's most prestigious private bank.

The last car to arrive brought Jack Morgan, immaculate in wing collar, gray tie held in place by a pearl pin, black lace-up boots gleaming.

Together Morgan and Lamont walked through the unmarked outer doors and through the inner glass doors, distinguished only by the small legend—"J. P. Morgan and Company." Nothing indicated that the building, known in Wall Street as the House on the Corner, was a bank. The laws of New York forbade Morgan's, as a private bank, to advertise; they also allowed it to avoid various regulations to which ordinary commercial banks were subject. The arrangement suited J. P. Morgan and Company.

Seated in the large open area directly ahead of the entrance doors, Charlton MacVeagh had an uninterrupted view of the comings and goings of the partners, in their special enclosure just to the right of the entrance. There, at ten o'clock sharp, as they did every weekday, the nineteen men grouped themselves in a close circle around Jack Morgan. The daily partnership conference was an old custom, going back to 1907. No stenographer was present; no notes were taken of these highly confidential meetings which usually lasted no more than fifteen minutes.

Charlton suspected the meetings set the daily guidelines for the firm's worldwide interests.

This morning, the young broker knew those interests had never been more varied or complex. He doubted if there was now a country in the civilized world whose fiscal future was not in some measure influenced or controlled by J. P. Morgan and Company.

All the partners grouped around Jack Morgan were automatically profit-sharing members of Morgan Grenfell and Company of London and Morgan and Cie of Paris. Each of these European affiliates had distinguished resident members. The London office was jointly managed by E. C. Grenfell, a member of Parliament and a director of the Bank of England, and Vivian Smith, head of the Royal Exchange Assurance Corporation. The Paris office was similarly controlled by financiers who sat on other key French company boards. Nominally in charge of their local operations, the European affiliates were, for all real purposes, rigidly governed by Jack Morgan and his home office partners.

Here, at home, the House had in past weeks established an even tighter hold on the commercial bankers of America. Many of them had privately borrowed huge sums from Morgan at rates their own banks could not match, in order to finance personal stock market speculation. Charles Mitchell had borrowed $10 million; almost equally substantial amounts had been loaned to Seward Prosser, chairman of the Bankers Trust Company, and to William C. Potter, president of the Guaranty Trust Company. In total, some sixty of America's leading bankers were in personal debt to J. P. Morgan and Company. All of them, in Jack Morgan's view, were "friends of ours, good, sound, straight fellows."

He strongly resented any suggestion that, by putting these powerful and strategically placed financiers under considerable obligation, his firm now had a distinct advantage.

But had he known, even Jack Morgan might well have balked at the personal financing in which one of his senior partners was deeply involved. For the past eight years George Whitney had been loaning substantial sums to his younger brother, Richard, vice-president of the Stock Exchange.

The first loans, in 1921, were comparatively small, tiding Richard over the beginning of what were to become all-too-regular periods of embarrassment. George had lectured Richard on financial husbandry; Richard had gone on spending; George had continued to indulge him. In 1926 he had loaned Richard $100,000 to buy a new town house. In 1928 he had parted with $340,000—every cent of which was gambled and lost by the scapegrace Richard on madcap investments. All told that year, the younger Whitney had borrowed close to $600,000.

Now, in 1929, he was tapping his brother again. In February George had paid out $175,000 for Richard to invest in an obscure Florida company devoted to turning peat humus into commercial fertilizer. Its stock was one of the most speculative on the market, wide-blue-yonder shares which even the wildest of brokers tended to avoid. But Richard, the arrogant, self-opinionated heir to one of the most exalted positions in American finance, was firmly convinced that he could become forever rich through fertilizer.

And now, Richard Whitney had come begging again. This time he wanted $500,000 to buy an additional seat on the Exchange to cope with "the expansion plans" he had for his firm.

For days George had deliberated what to do. Finally, he had made up his mind. In his neat copperplate writing, he had sent Richard a note, again stressing the virtues of using money carefully. With the caution went a check to buy the seat.

George's main concern now was to ensure his partners did not discover just how deeply Richard, "the Morgan Broker," was in debt. He knew discovery of his brother's impoverished state could have far-reaching consequences.

It was to avoid just such potentially damaging situations that Jack Morgan, following his father's policy, had ruled that apart from exceptional cases, the bank should not do business with individuals; it was one thing to lend Charles Mitchell a few million dollars—Mitchell, because of his position, could reasonably be expected to repay the money —it was quite another matter for a Morgan partner to make loans from his own pocket to someone like Richard Whitney, who was almost in an employee relationship with the firm.

That was one of the reasons why Morgan's preferred to finance the giants of industry: the huge telephone and telegraph companies, the mighty railroads, the major oil and auto companies.

On this April morning, as on most days, some fifty of America's leading corporations each had on deposit over $1 million with the firm. All told, Morgan's had on deposit each day half a billion dollars.

How that sum was managed was at the discretion of the men Charlton MacVeagh could see gathered around Jack Morgan. And, ultimately, it was he who would decide how much of, where, and when this vast reservoir of hard cash would be used. He could do so without fear of interference; no government official could give him instructions; no bank examiner could check the books; nobody could demand an accounting. J. P. Morgan and Company was the most private of private banks.

Charlton MacVeagh watched the partners return to their rolltop desks. What he especially liked was the calm, unhurried atmosphere which pervaded not just their closed-off area but also the spacious salon he worked in; there were dozens of people around him, yet it was "like being in church."

Nowadays, the image of one church increasingly filled Charlton's mind. It was St. Matthew's at Bedford Hills, New York. There, on June 15 he would marry Adele Merrill.

Charlton was continuously bemused by the way his future mother-in-law was organizing everything. Without telling him, she had placed engagement announcements in the New York *Times* and *The Wall Street Journal*. When he had tackled her, Adelaide Merrill had simply smiled sweetly and said it was time to "formalize your relationship with my daughter."

It was only then that Charlton had actually proposed to Adele.

The wedding date set, Adelaide Merrill was now concentrating her efforts on a more immediate event—the formal engagement party to be held at the Colony Club on April 26.

She had told Charlton to choose "a nice group" of young men from among his business colleagues. It was not going to be easy; he liked them all.

For the past month, Charlton had been one of a group acting as promoters of corporate ventures that even a year ago would have been considered far too flighty and speculative for ultraconservative J. P. Morgan and Company.

Only once before—in 1901, when Pierpont Morgan had formed the United States Steel Corporation—had the firm been involved publicly in launching a new company.

In the past three months, it had promoted two such concerns, United Corporation and the Allegheny Corporation. Both were designed to cash in on the market boom.

Charlton had done some of the research for the prospectuses of the companies; now he was one of the men "helping to bring them to the market."

Shares in the United Corporation had "taken off like wildfire." It was a holding company; it did nothing but buy and then hold stock in other companies; its sole function was by this means to control those companies.

The companies controlled were among the leaders in the business of supplying electricity, gas, and heating. In turn these companies controlled, all told, 129 other companies. And some of the companies controlled by the "master" holding company were themselves holding companies. All of them were dominated by J. P. Morgan and Company through United Corporation.

In every way United itself was a mere shell; it had practically no staff. Its president, George Howard, maintained a pleasant office at 15 Broad Street, around the corner from Morgan's. United's books were written up and kept in one of the Morgan vaults. Its directors, with the exception of Howard, were either Morgan partners or members of companies closely cooperating with Morgan. To all intents and purposes, J. P. Morgan and Company now had control over a vast network of electric power companies "from Niagara to the sea." This network produced 20 percent of all the electricity used in America; in effect, fifteen out of every one hundred people were paying their electric and gas bills to Jack Morgan and his partners. From their rolltop desks they controlled a public utility empire whose gross revenue would soon amount to hundreds of millions of dollars each year.

Charlton MacVeagh knew there was no problem selling shares in the United Corporation. Every broker's office in America had investors eager to put money into "this great new Morgan company." In the past two months, United's common stock had risen from $22.50 to $70.

Allegheny Corporation had begun to sell on the New York Stock Exchange weeks before the company had even been formally organized. The opening price to the public had been $35 a share. But to those who were on the secret "preferred list" that Jack Morgan kept, the shares were offered at a substantially lower price.

There were about five hundred names on the list; most of them were powerful figures in financial, business, or political circles. Former President Coolidge was there. So was General Pershing, and Colonel Lindbergh. Charles Adams, Hoover's Secretary of the Navy, was listed. So was John J. Raskob amid a profusion of businessmen, financiers, and speculators.

Nor had Jack Morgan forgotten his fellow bankers. Every Morgan partner was on the list, as were Charles Mitchell and Albert Wiggin, president of the Chase National Bank. Bernard Baruch was there. And so was Richard Whitney.

His brother, George, had recently received a letter from Raskob who had been weekending in Florida, studying the first scale models of the Empire State Building. Raskob had sent a check of $40,000 for 2,000 shares of Allegheny, adding: "I appreciate deeply the many courtesies shown me by you and your partners, and sincerely hope the future holds opportunities for me to reciprocate."

It was on such future expectations that the Morgan empire, in part, was built.

Between them, Jack and his fellow partners held directorships in ten major railroads with total assets of $3,430,000,000. They held nineteen directorships in thirteen public utility companies with total assets of $6,222,000,000. They held six directorships in insurance companies whose total assets were $337,000,000. They had seats on the boards of thirty-eight industrial corporations with total assets of $6,000,000,000. In all, they had 126 directorships in eighty-nine corporations whose total assets amounted to $20,000,000,000. It was without doubt the greatest concentration of financial power in private hands in history.

And yet, what struck Charlton MacVeagh was that the partners "were just a bunch of regular fellows, bright as silver buttons. But regular."

If he had his way, he'd have them all along to the Colony Club for his engagement party.

Jolan Slezsak would always remember April 10.

It was spring, a time when, in the evening, her mother and stepfather talked of those plans that had lain dormant through the hard winter months: papering the painted plaster walls, replacing some of the oldest furniture. But everything depended on the familiar qualification: *if*. *If* her stepfather could get a cent or two more an hour at the Buick; *if* her mother could get a few more customers for the moonshine; *if* Jolan herself could get that summer job as a maid; then, *if* all that happened, the house improvements could be carried out.

The talk of money, or lack of it, had raised again the question of the cash held in trust for the children in the Union Industrial Bank. Jolan's mother had expressed her bitterness anew, railing that the money was "useless locked up in a bank."

It was then that her stepfather had quietly intervened.

Jolan was being shown by her mother how to black the stove, holding her body away from the metal to protect her clothes; her stepfather told her to leave the kitchen.

Mystified, Jolan had stepped into the backyard. On impulse, she crouched under the kitchen window. Though she could not hear all her stepfather said, she picked out certain phrases: "hardworking boy . . . Mr. Goldberger knows the family . . . coming in the morning . . ."

That had been last night. Now, after breakfast on April 10, she had been packed off, told to take her younger brother and sister, Frank and Margaret, for a walk in the woods beyond the city.

Rambling through the trees, aware of the strong stirrings in her body —her mother had brusquely warned her "to let no boy near"—fifteen-year-old Jolan was engrossed in romantic dreams that took her away from Flint, a city that seemed to be changing and growing daily around her. Every week more people came to the city, drawn by other, less romantic notions of making a decent living working in one of the auto plants.

Jolan could think of nothing more soul-destroying than spending the rest of her life on a production line. She had seen what it had done to her stepfather, aging him prematurely, sucking the very life out of him. She would not want that to happen to her husband—though the thought of marriage was something she had not even begun to contemplate.

Her mind still filled with escapism, she escorted Frank and Margaret home.

Mr. Goldberger's shining Chevrolet was parked outside the house. Almost magically, as if he had been waiting for her, the attorney suddenly emerged.

From a vest pocket he took out a quarter and told the younger children to go and buy themselves some candy at the corner store. Then, taking Jolan by the hand, he led her into the living room.

Grouped around the table were three strangers, interspersed between her mother and stepfather.

The woman was careworn like her mother; the man looked like her stepfather—old before his time.

Even if Jolan had not been told, she would have guessed the young man was their son; he had the same high cheekbones as the woman, the same distinctive eyebrows as the man. It was a good face.

It was also assessing her with open curiosity.

Jolan felt the skin tingle under her blushing.

Mr. Goldberger sat her down beside him at the head of the table, smiling affably at the serious faces around him. Jolan would later remember how he had patted his ample stomach before speaking. Then, in a surprisingly small voice—Goldberger always reminded her of a character in *Alice in Wonderland*—he introduced her.

"Jolan. This is Mr. and Mrs. Vargo and their son, Steve."

The couple nodded. Steve smiled; Jolan was surprised how white and even his teeth were. From where she sat she could smell soap; flakes of it were drying in his hair. She thought he looked a nice boy.

Jolan's mother sat, arms folded, staring at her. Her stepfather, too, was silent.

It had all happened so fast—less than a minute had elapsed from the time Mr. Goldberger sent the children off for candy—that Jolan hardly had time to collect her thoughts. But now she recognized Steve: He used to play with her elder brothers when they were growing up. And the Vargos—it was coming back now; they were the family who lived ten blocks away, kept to themselves. She wondered why they were here.

She looked at her stepfather. He sat bolt upright, eyes on Mr. Goldberger.

Swiftly, as if he was leading Jolan through a court examination, the attorney established her age and school grades.

Next he turned to Steve.

"You are nineteen?"

"Yes."

"And you work at the Buick?"

"Yes."

"For how long?"

"Three years."

"Never been laid off?"

"No."

"And you make?"

"Sixty-five cents an hour."

Goldberger nodded approvingly.

"And you know Jolan's elder brothers?"

"Yes."

"Well, you're almost one of the family!"

Then, for the first time, Jolan's mother spoke.

"You and Steve are going to get married."

The others looked at her, waiting for a reaction. Jolan felt her face go crimson; her skin seemed on fire.

"Married!"

Goldberger jumped in, no longer the lawyer, more the beaming uncle figure she had always known.

"Why not, Jolan, why not! Lots of girls get married at your age. It's a fine thing. You'll have a good life together."

Now her stepfather spoke. "She can't get married before the fall. She's got that summer job, Mr. Goldberger—"

"Quite so, quite so." He turned to the Vargos. "I'm sure the fall will be acceptable?"

They nodded.

Jolan thought they might have been deciding whether to buy a bag of peanuts; it all seemed so casual and matter-of-fact.

Goldberger rose to his feet, patting her on the head.

"I'm sure you are both going to be very happy." He looked at the adults. "I'll leave you to work out the details."

With a quick bow to the women he left the house.

Jolan sat dumbfounded. She was going to wed someone she didn't know; she was going to be plucked from school straight into marriage. The enormity of it made her want to weep.

In a daze she heard her mother and Mrs. Vargo beginning to talk about the wedding.

Steve spoke.

"You want a vanilla ice cream? They've got some good ones down at the drugstore. Wanta come?"

Jolan smiled. Vanilla was her favorite flavor.

Spring was a busy time for the Dowdy's; it was when Homer and the children laid the foundations for a further year of living. It was when they sorted out their clothes, tilled their small garden, spruced up the house.

Homer loved having the children around him. He had always hoped for a big family; now he knew there would be no more.

The last time the doctor called to examine Gladys he had looked more serious at the end of his examination than Homer could ever remember.

After the doctor washed his hands, the two men sat in the kitchen over coffee.

"She's real sick, Homer, real sick."

"Shouldn't she be in a hospital?"

"She's as well here."

The doctor said no more and left.

That night Homer spoke to Gladys about withdrawing the savings he had in the Union Industrial Bank and taking her to see the best specialist in Detroit.

Gladys smiled wanly and shook her head.

"Our doctor's doing his best. Keep the money for the children."

In that one awful moment, Homer knew his wife was telling him that she was going to die.

At five minutes to nine, Grant Brown began his customary morning inspection of the Union Industrial Bank's headquarters.

He was in an ebullient mood. From this morning he could count the days before he and the headquarters staff moved into an imposing new twenty-story building, scheduled to rise in the center of Flint.

The blueprints had been delivered to him the previous night by special messenger from Detroit. With them came a brief note from Charles Mott, approving the $1.5 million budget for the building. Mott had thanked bank president Brown for his congratulations on marrying, and regretted that pressure of work was still keeping him away from Flint. In one sense, the letter disappointed Brown: There was no way he could tell from it whether the rumors drifting out of Detroit that Mott's marriage was in serious trouble were true. Grant Brown hoped not; he was himself "deliciously happy" with his new wife, Marie, and he wished Mott the same good fortune.

Mott's continuous absence from Flint did not, in a professional sense, trouble the bank president. Much as he personally looked forward to Mott's visits as an opportunity "to catch up with the wider world of business," Grant Brown knew that some of his staff became tense in the presence of the industrialist. Brown put this down to "understandable nervousness." He was secretly relieved that Mott, for whatever reason, continued to stay away. Besides, Grant Brown felt his presence was not necessary because "things had never been better."

Only recently, his son Robert had assured him that the staff had "never been happier now that Mr. Mott stays in Detroit."

Grant Brown could see Robert now at his teller's window, checking the money he had drawn out for the day.

Robert's cage was the second from the end, far down the row of cages which began at the bank's entrance. His son was flanked by David McGregor, another paying and receiving teller, and Russell Runyon, the collection teller. Like all the men, except the officers, the tellers wore black alpaca jackets.

Walking slowly down the line, Grant Brown was pleased to see that this morning all the bars on the cages were highly burnished. On a recent return from one of his regular trips away, he had been upset to see how tarnished the bars were. A firm word with his deputy, John de Camp, seemed to have worked. Their entire relationship was like that: Grant Brown issuing peremptory orders for De Camp efficiently to implement. Socially, they had little in common and they rarely met outside the bank.

Socially, Grant Brown felt much closer to Frank Montague. They shared the same church, worshiping in adjoining pews every Sunday. He could see Montague now, bent over his desk, the model of industry. The president was pleased that young Montague was still showing his early promise of being a hard worker. Soon he must consider him for another promotion, perhaps manager of one of the branches.

He walked on down the line of cages, pausing at each one to have a friendly word with its occupant—and to check that everything was just so. Grant Brown lay great store on the "little things." A teller could expect a swift rebuke—and later a fuller dressing down from De Camp—if he had not positioned, exactly in their preordained places on the sloping desk, the little white roller on its stand—the moistener—and, to its right, the machine containing rows of half dollars, quarters, and dimes, ready to be released in the precise sum by the pressure of a key. To the left of the machine were neat piles of bills. The rest of the teller's money lay in separate compartments in his drawer. Every morning each teller drew $10,000 from Elton Graham, the chief cashier.

Satisfied that his frontline troops were in position and ready for action, Grant Brown moved on to inspect the rear echelons, the clerks and bookkeepers with their calculators and adding machines. They, too, passed muster.

He crossed the banking hall and entered the Trust Department, cut off from the public areas by a substantial oak railing. De Camp and the other officers were at their desks.

Grant Brown's own desk was strategically placed in a far corner of the department. From behind it, he had an uninterrupted view of the entire working area.

At exactly nine o'clock, the bank doors opened and customers began to arrive in a steady flow.

For a while Grant Brown watched the activity. Then, satisfied, he returned to the blueprints for the new headquarters. Even from the drawings, he could see that the building would be a fitting structure for the largest bank in Michigan outside Detroit.

Already, in a burst of enthusiasm which he carefully hid from the staff, the austere-looking president had penned some fine phrases for the brochure he planned to issue to mark the opening of the headquarters. It would be "Flint's most impressive building! Designed in the Greek style, the order of the Temple of the Winds is executed in variegated Indiana limestone."

Only his new wife, Marie, knew of his literary yearnings; she encouraged him, telling her husband that composing a bank brochure could be a start to a literary career.

At noon, he handed over control to John de Camp, and left for a leisurely lunch at home—yet another innovation in his life-style since remarrying.

The change his second marriage had worked on Grant Brown was a source of wonder among his relatives. His daughter-in-law, Beryl, Robert's wife, had never known him so "trouble-free." He behaved as if "life was for loving." Even his young nephew, Ed Love, could not previously recall his uncle being so "frisky. Once the bank was his life. His second marriage had given him new perspectives. He and Marie spent more time away from Flint than in the place."

Grant Brown had even dropped the pretense, at least among his friends, that these absences were all strictly on business. He fondly admitted he was indulging Marie's passion for travel. But he was quick to add that he had "the most trusty bunch of boys running the bank."

The "trusty bunch" were, in turn, relieved that domestic bliss was keeping their president away. Frank Montague felt there was always just a chance that Grant Brown might become suspicious. The owlish-looking Montague was increasingly worried by the possibility of the wholesale embezzling being discovered. The sums involved—well over $2 million of bank funds had by now been misappropriated—were so large, involving so many people, that Montague thought it was only a matter of time before the gang was discovered.

Ivan Christensen believed otherwise. He argued, with considerable force and persuasion, that there was safety in numbers; one man could indeed make a mistake; a team could cover for each other, checking and double-checking to make sure nothing was visible to the most prying eyes. And Christensen could always point to the fact that so far they had escaped detection.

Even Montague grudgingly admired the simple but effective method the assistant cashier had devised to cope with the one event that could unmask them—an unexpected visit by a team of bank examiners.

The examiners were based in Lansing; careful observation had shown Christensen that they liked to arrive in Flint for lunch, only afterward spending the afternoon going through a bank's books.

Normally, they dined at the Durant Hotel. A trusted bellboy had been put on a weekly retainer to act as a lookout. Later, concerned to appease the fears of men like Montague, the net had been spread to include staff at other hotels and restaurants in the city. There was now no way the examiners could arrive in Flint without the news being telephoned to the bank.

Yet, when the call came, Montague saw how those involved in the embezzlement "became very, very nervous indeed."

The Durant bellhop reported that three men were lunching in the restaurant; their names and descriptions fitted exactly those Christensen had thoughtfully provided for all the Lansing examiners.

The word was quietly passed around among the conspirators that they probably had two hours in which to prepare themselves.

At one minute to three o'clock, just as on previous visits, the examiners walked into the bank.

The doors were locked behind them; the staff were told to remain at their posts.

To Frank Montague, the examiners looked "grim and unfriendly."

He wished again that he had never become involved in "this mess."

Slowly his confidence returned as he watched De Camp and Christensen. Both were relaxed, happily cooperating with the examiners.

Once, as Christensen passed his desk, he had whispered to Montague that it was "just a routine check. Nothing to worry about."

Montague knew that all the banks in the state were checked once or twice a year for any signs of irregularity. From time to time an embezzler was discovered and put away in the Michigan Penitentiary. These convictions were widely reported; publicity was one of the weapons the examiners used as a deterrent. They liked to foster the image that, like the Mounties, they always got their man.

They had no chance against the league of gentlemen.

At the end of a thorough inspection, the examiners agreed that all was in order.

Their initial coldness gave way to cheery banter. De Camp pressed them to stay on and have dinner. Montague was relieved to hear the officials were anxious to get home to their families.

It was only after they had left that De Camp telephoned Grant Brown with the news that the bank had passed the inspection.

CHAPTER ELEVEN

WALL STREET AFLOAT

The sound of the nationally advertised and mass-produced alarm clock
—featuring a cathedral chime, intermittent alarm, and a luminous dial
—awoke Edith Stone. She found it amusing to be called by such a
splendid device; the clock was the latest model, marking its owner as a
social trend-setter.

The strikingly beautiful twenty-four-year-old divorcee stretched her
long legs and luxuriated in the warm midday sun streaming through her
open bedroom window. Edith wished she had removed her makeup
before retiring—it had smeared the black satin pillowcases and sheets
—but it had been almost dawn when she came home.

Fully awake now, she remembered the previous night. Her escort, in
spite of his good looks, had turned out to be utterly boring. At dinner
he had insisted on ordering only the most expensive items on the menu;
Edith suspected he did so to hide his ignorance of French, assuming
that anything that cost a great deal must be good. He took her advice
on the champagne, buying an imported magnum, but then he had
spoiled even that gesture by detailing the money his father possessed,
keeping up a monologue in an affected English accent as they moved
from one speakeasy to another. Finally, to blot him out, Edith had
started to drink heavily—although not so much she was unable to resist
his advances when they eventually said good night. The last thing she
did before going to bed was to pencil his name out of her address book.

She didn't have a hangover. Long experience had taught her always
to order French champagne; if her escort couldn't afford this extrava-
gance, he had no right to take her out in the first place.

Yet, in spite of her outward appearance as a fluffy, scatterbrained playgirl, one of the most sought-after flappers in a city filled with them, Edith was an articulate and strong-willed young woman. Had any of her dates managed to penetrate her art deco bedroom, he would have been surprised. As well as a wardrobe stocked with filmy dresses and gowns and jewelry boxes stacked with pearl necklaces and diamond-studded brooches, there were also shelves of books on psychology, the theater, and the arts. She had a keen inquiring mind for everything that interested her. Edith only wished there were more men who shared those interests; nowadays New York, or at least the group she mingled with, seemed to be "filled with chinless wonders who thought of nothing except how to become richer from playing the market."

The distant sounds of traffic in Central Park drifted into the bedroom, a reminder that her father, Edward Stone, like most people in the city, had already been at work for several hours.

Edith still wasn't entirely sure what her father did. But officially, for tax purposes, she knew he was classed as a millionaire. That, in itself, did not impress her; she had grown up with money and had a healthy disregard for it. Once she had asked him how he'd made his fortune; he had replied vaguely: "from wool and the market."

Edith had mentioned her father's involvement in the market to another of her beaux. It was a mistake, only spurring him also to bore her for hours with talk of investments. She had sat languidly blowing smoke rings from her cigarette holder, a trick that finally silenced him. He, too, had been scratched from her list.

Yet, in a way, the incident helped kindle Edith's interest in the stock market. She still thought it vulgar to talk so openly about money, but she began to listen and read about shares and bonds. Her father never talked business at home in front of the family; that would be unthinkable. Nevertheless, by piecing together overheard telephone calls, Edith had concluded "he was in the market to the tune of five million or so."

His wealth enabled her father to rent their luxurious custom-built apartment in one of New York's most fashionable addresses, the spanking-new San Remo block overlooking Central Park. It also allowed her mother to furnish the apartment without bother about expense; its eleven rooms were the epitome of quiet good taste. To run the apartment there was a retinue of three living-in servants plus a seamstress, laundress, and chauffeur—all immediately available at the beck and call of their employers.

Her father's money had cushioned Edith against the pain of a broken marriage. Ellwood Greene had been the "catch of the year, 1925." The marriage lasted three days and was never consummated: No sooner had Edith said her vows than she realized "it was all a terrible mistake." She had confessed to her parents; in no time her father had "bought me out of the mess almost as easily as he bought shares." It was the only time Edith was ever impressed with the power of money.

There had been other men since, but none serious. Edith sensed her mother wanted her to marry again, but she was now in no hurry "to marry simply for the sake of it."

Edith envied her parents their long and happy marriage. She admired the way her mother managed her father; by far the stronger member of the partnership, Mabel Stone was careful never to undermine her husband's role as head of the household.

Long ago Edith had learned that when it came to money, it was her father who decided how much she had. Now his money was comforting backup support for her consuming interest—writing plays which she hoped to get on Broadway.

The attraction of show business was the one constant in her life. Edith had sampled it as a singer and, briefly, as a movie actress. Now she had taken seriously to writing comedy. She had teamed up with another flapper, a pretty girl called Sylvia Lewis, and got "Brandt, the best agent in New York" to represent them. So far, in spite of their connections around the classier speakeasies of the city—they had met more directors and impresarios than Edith could remember—they were still awaiting their big break.

Edith was toying with the idea of doing a comedy about Wall Street; she had already started to clip newspaper items that might help with the script. There was the tale of a Boston dowager who, every morning, telephoned her broker just before the market opened, listened to his advice, and then bought a sizable list of stocks. She would then potter about all morning, write yet another letter to the *Transcript* denouncing petty gambling among street boys, and call her broker back each day after lunch.

"Sell everything," she would say, without bothering to find out the latest quotations.

Usually, the newspaper reported, she made a fat profit.

Edith thought the dowager had possibilities; the old lady could be developed into a major part in a dozen different ways.

Then there was the young man, scarcely out of his teens, who had put $2,000 into a stock that immediately jumped fifty points. As the young man pocketed his $8,000 profit, a senior member of the brokerage firm from which he had purchased the shares respectfully asked where he had received such good advice. The youngster pretended he could not remember; it was impossible for him to explain that he had bought the stock solely on information provided by a *junior* member of the man's firm.

Edith thought the young investor could also be used. She would give him sleek, shiny hair, dress him in fashionable looping knickerbockers, known as plus-fours, and have him tote a hip flask filled with Prohibition gin. She could lace his speech with the latest snappy expressions, such as "so's your old man," "he's the cat's meow," and "she's the bee's knees." He would have a flapper girl friend, complete with stockings rolled just below the knees, bobbed hair, bright red lipstick, and, most daring of all, the latest craze, no underwear, just a skimpy dress. That should set Broadway alight.

Edith had no doubt Sam Harris, the theatrical producer, would adore characters like this; recently he had been quoted as saying he felt Wall Street was ripe for the stage. Harris had begun his working life as a messenger boy there, before, as he put it, "switching to another branch of show business." In 1927, wealthy after producing a string of stage hits, he had invested $200,000 in twenty-five carefully chosen stocks; Harris had just sold them for $4 million. Maybe later, when she had a script, she would give him a call. And if he needed a lyricist, Edith had someone in mind: Ira Gershwin. She much appreciated Gershwin's advice to would-be writers like herself: "keep a sharp pencil."

Even Edith's haphazard clipping of the New York newspapers had given her the feeling that a "carnival of speculation" was sweeping the nation. And, she reminded herself, it was all centered on Wall Street, only a few minutes away from her home.

That decided her. After showering, she dressed carefully in silk underwear and chose a knee-length suit which made her look pencil slim; she covered her head in a helmetlike cloche hat. Checking carefully that her bust and hips were flattened out of all recognition, she left the bedroom, dressed in the height of fashion. In most women the effect was of boyish sexlessness; in Edith it was of enhanced desirability.

On a hall table, she glanced at her mail. This morning, as usual, there were half a dozen invitations to dinners and parties. Edith told the butler to refuse them all. Then she ordered the chauffeur to take her to Wall Street.

Thirty minutes later she was ensconced in the crowded visitors' gallery of the Stock Exchange, peering down onto the trading floor, impressed by the sheer size and noise of the spectacle.

Edith was used to asking questions; the knack had helped bridge many a dull moment with some young man in a speakeasy. She turned to a gray-uniformed guide for help. Edith had a reporter's gift for the essential or unusual. She asked him why so many of the traders were young; he explained the work was grueling. She spotted an old man; the guide quickly added that even so there were twenty-five men on the floor who had been members for forty years, six who had traded for fifty years, and even two who had been coming to the Exchange since

1869. She looked at the guide; he sounded like one of those speak-your-weight machines. She decided to shake him out of his routine responses.

"How many crooks do you think are down there?"

The guide looked scandalized.

Edith smiled sweetly. "Just once in a while doesn't somebody try and get away with something?"

The guide assured her that never happened.

Edith sauntered through the gallery; there was the same "avaricious look about many of the people as you find in a gambling salon."

She could not see much potential for comedy here, although perhaps it would come once she got to know the place better. Maybe it should be a tragicomedy, built around a broker who had to cheat to survive. The plot would need time to gel. But time was no problem. And writing a play about the stock market would be the perfect reason for refusing some of the more boring men who pestered her for dates.

Edith knew that her father would be pleased to hear she was at last going to write "something serious"; indulgent and generous though he was, she suspected he had become uneasy over her gadabout existence. He did not seem to understand how difficult it was for her to blow away the last remnants of her disastrous marriage. But now that she was finally getting the experience in perspective, she herself was becoming increasingly dissatisfied with her way of life and the New York social scene.

She was glad she was off to Europe shortly for the summer season; the conversation and the people were always so much more sophisticated there. And perhaps they would provide new ideas for her play.

Excited by the prospect and determined to immerse herself in the European scene—Edith could not understand those Americans who went to Europe expecting everybody to like ketchup—she left the Stock Exchange and told her chauffeur to take her to a newsstand selling foreign periodicals. She bought a pile of dailies and magazines and returned to the apartment, retiring to her bedroom to study them.

The London newspapers were full of Winston Churchill's latest budget, his fifth, a count reached previously only by Walpole, Pitt, Peel, and Gladstone, each of whom was at the time or later became Prime Minister. The papers said the Churchill speech had been brilliant, wittily presenting such measures as the abolition of the tea tax which had been in force since the days of the first Queen Elizabeth, the removal of betting taxes, the reduction of duty on motorcycles, and making more money available to equip rural post offices with telephones.

Edith thought "the whole thing sounded marvelously English." She wished she could be in London in time for the forthcoming election;

there were bound to be wonderful parties during the closing days of the campaign.

She turned to the French periodicals. President Raymond Poincaré was still displaying the three qualities she remembered from her last visit to Paris—honesty, xenophobia, and patriotism. She wondered why the French seemed so insular and arrogant. Perhaps it was the inevitable by-product of years of political instability; since 1920, sixteen governments had come and gone. Some ministers had held office only for a few months. One of them, in 1925 the newly elected Finance Minister, Anatole de Monzie, when making his inaugural speech forthrightly declared: "Gentlemen, the treasury is empty." It was a mistake. De Monzie survived this spark of lucidity by only a few hours; that afternoon he found himself removed from office.

But now, Poincaré, having picked up the pieces following the disastrous mid-twenties Cartel des Gauches—a coalition of radicals and socialists—had put France on her feet. He had balanced the budget, cut spending, devalued the franc to a dollar parity of twenty-five—promoting the export market—and rid France of foreign currency speculators. French money had flowed back into the country. Poincaré, the providential figure, firmly believed in gold as the only real security; further, it did not rust and could be cut into easy-to-handle bars. Under him, gold hoarding became official policy.*

Edith was tempted to ask her father for an ingot or two to tide her over in Paris; she decided it would probably be as easy to buy the bars in Europe. She looked critically at the French fashion pages and concluded that this year American women had nothing to learn from Parisian couturiers.

The German newspapers jolted her. On their front pages was the same photograph of a slight, mustachioed man standing before a bank of microphones in Nuremberg, addressing a large rally. Edith's German was fluent; she had no trouble reading the text. The newspapers approved of this new figure in German politics, Adolf Hitler. At Nuremberg he had promised a return to "the old ways," a rejection of the alarming postwar innovations that were "weakening" the country.

Edith read how national socialism "appealed to technicians, engineers, chauffeurs and the like." The blue-collar class welcomed Nazi talk of expansion; many were *Auslandsdeutsche,* who, under the Versailles Treaty, found themselves suddenly living in foreign countries and returned to Germany believing it was their only haven. Hitler was appealing to the most primitive mass emotions in a country where na-

* Thirty years later France was to know another providential figure who had the same monetary concept: Charles de Gaulle.

tional pride had been followed by the humiliation and bewilderment of the early 1920s.

Even from these days-old newspapers, printed over three thousand miles away and brought to New York on the *Bremen,* Edith could feel the menace in what Hitler said. The "strong" were the Aryan or German race; they must be further strengthened at the expense of the usurping weak—the Jews and other "unwanted populations." Time and again in these newspaper stories, Hitler linked the Jewish "menace" with the Communist threat, of which, Edith knew, most Germans were greatly afraid. She could see the appeal Hitler would have for them; to many a Geman the change from the discipline of imperial days to the outburst of what one newspaper called "dangerous decadence" was disturbing and shocking. From her last visit to Germany, she knew that the provinces were often outraged by the excesses of Berlin. But then, in 1928, the last time Edith had read a German newspaper, she could recall no mention of the Führer. He seemed to have come from nowhere, "like some evil genie released from a bottle."

Edith crumpled up the newspapers so that her parents would not see them. Her father, in particular, would not like what they said and might stop her from including Germany on her European trip. He was the only one in the family who felt devoutly Jewish.

One of the many qualities John J. Raskob liked in his friend, James Riordan, was a complete absence of religious, social, or political bias. A staunch Catholic, Riordan numbered Jews and Protestants among his closest friends. Born in poverty, Riordan now moved in New York society, yet still managed to be as relaxed with a garage man as he was with a Rockefeller or an Astor.

Of all the hundreds of men Raskob could have chosen to share this special evening with, he selected Riordan because "Jimmy would really understand."

He greeted Riordan with a favorite dry martini; cocktails were still an innovation and Raskob took great pride in mixing them from recipes passed on by trusted bartenders.

The two drank to "The Past—may it never be repeated," a veiled reminder that they had both risen from the slums of New York to their present positions. Then they toasted "our children"; Raskob's eleven, Riordan's four: James, Robert, Florence, and Elizabeth, who helped keep their forty-eight-year-old widowed father feeling young.

These ritual toasts to memory and family were an indication of the bonds that linked the two men.

There were others. They shared the same sardonic sense of humor; the same interest in golf and horses; the same taste in theater and movies; the same tailor. As they sipped drinks in Raskob's Carlton House apartment, their clothes and manners hid all traces of their humble background.

Only when Riordan became excited did his vowels flatten, his voice thicken, a vocal throwback to his youth when he had settled arguments in the Chelsea markets with a few well-chosen words, or, if they failed, a handy pair of fists.

Long ago, he had discarded brawn for brain—a decision that had made him wealthy and brought him the friendship of John J. Raskob.

The financier always held up Riordan as a shining example of why America "is the land of unequaled opportunity." Raskob knew Riordan's story by heart; he loved to retell it at lunchtime business clubs.

James Riordan had graduated from college, joined a bank, risen to be an assistant manager, realized he would never become president, quit, gone into the trucking business at the bottom, again worked his way up, and eventually founded the United States Trucking Corporation.

He had persuaded Alfred Smith, then New York's governor, to become company chairman. Smith introduced Riordan to the czars of New York politics. At a Democratic rally, Riordan met Raskob. They liked each other instantly. They had been friends ever since.

Over dinner, Raskob reminisced about their years of friendship, rare in that it had never been marred by a cross word.

Riordan recalled, in fond detail, how Raskob at this very table had given him a most valuable lesson in finance, ending with the words "money has to work for you, never you for money."

And he had benefited directly from Raskob's advice when the financier made him a fellow member of Michael Meehan's Radio pool. Riordan was at first hesitant about joining; although wealthy he was simply not in the same financial league as his friend. But Raskob had brushed aside his objections; Riordan need not even put up any cash for the shares bought in his name; pool operations were entirely legal, seldom lost money, and if this one did, Raskob, unknown to Riordan, had told Meehan he would meet any losses incurred by his friend.

Mike Meehan's Radio pool did not lose. Riordan had Raskob to thank for the $58,000 he had made.

Over coffee, the two men talked about the market. U. S. Steel had just offered $40 million worth of new stock in a share split; what interested Riordan more was the news that Giannini's Bank of America had recently acquired the Nassau National Bank. Riordan himself was president of the small but thriving New York County Trust Company, a bank on the edge of Greenwich Village which he had founded three years ago. Capitalized at $4 million, it now had deposits totaling over $20 million.

Riordan joked that Billy Durant would likely call that only a "piggy bank." Raskob doubted whether Durant was in the mood nowadays for jokes of any kind. A week before, on April 15, following his visit to Hoover, he had made a national radio broadcast bitterly attacking the Federal Reserve Board. Durant charged that the board was "alone responsible" for the "high money rates" in Wall Street, and demanded the New York bank rate be reduced to just 3 percent, the lowest ever fixed. After his broadcast, a resolution was put before the House calling for an immediate investigation of the Reserve Board. Riordan detected the hand of another business acquaintance, Charles Mitchell, behind the move.

But whatever the next few months held for banking, Riordan was certain that his establishment would continue to prosper.

Raskob was pleased; the success of his friend's modest bank meant almost as much to him as it did to his guest.

Warmed by brandy, they talked on. Raskob revealed that Joe Kennedy was back in town; Riordan said he looked forward to one of the sudden, unexpected visits Kennedy was famed for.

Riordan and Kennedy were friends, linked by similar ethnic backgrounds and the same determination to succeed. It was Charles Mitchell who had once told Raskob: "Your two buddies are the hardest workers I know. I wish I had them on my team."

Kennedy, Mitchell, and Raskob were united by a common quality: They were all devoted family men. They admired the way Riordan had coped with his wife's death, in 1917, and ever since had been both father and mother to his four children. They were now away at college, although the girls came back most weekends to Riordan's New York home on Twelfth Street. There Elizabeth and Florence were told by their father everything he had done during the week, the meetings he had, the shares he had bought, the property he had sold.

The Riordan house was a meeting place for all kinds of people. A guest like Percy Rockefeller might find himself seated at the family dining table beside a driver from Riordan's trucking firm. The girls particularly liked those evenings when Raskob dropped in for a game of gin rummy and a glass of beer with their father.

Tonight, the millionaire had a different game to play. He rose to his feet and opened a bottle of champagne. Their glasses filled, he led Riordan into his study. The climax of the evening was at hand.

A space had been cleared among the clutter of books. In it stood a draped object.

Solemnly, Raskob removed the cloth. Underneath was a scale model of the Empire State Building.

Silently, the two men toasted this vision of tomorrow.

Then, like a couple of schoolboys with a new toy, they knelt down and began to examine the model.

It had been a busy day for Charlton MacVeagh at the office; call money had leaped to 16 percent, but there was still considerable demand for United and Allegheny stock. Now, in the evening of Friday, April 26, shop talk was intruding into his private life. Every time his future father-in-law, banker Edwin Merrill, introduced him to a guest, the person almost immediately said to Charlton: "Ah yes, you work at J. P. Morgan and Company."

Time and again he was forced to discuss the market when all he wanted to do was be with Adele.

But she too was trapped. Convention demanded that though this was their engagement party, Adele should spend little time with her fiancé during the early part of the evening.

Escorted by her mother, Adelaide Merrill, Adele mingled with the hundred handpicked guests seated around the ballroom of the Colony Club on Park Avenue.

At every white-linened table were "the *crème* of the *Social Register,*" as well as bankers and diplomats from a dozen nations; the latter's presence was an indication of Charlton's father's standing in the diplomatic world. In quick succession, Adele was introduced to the ambassadors of France and Italy, and to MacVeagh's opposite number in Washington, the Japanese ambassador.

Charlton's father and mother had traveled specially from Japan to attend one of the most glittering private functions of the season. He had captivated Adele by saying he had always wanted a daughter like her. The MacVeaghs had seven sons; Adele felt none of them was as handsome as her Charlton.

But she found her fiancé's mother "formidable." Mrs. MacVeagh had asked her what she knew about the fountains of Rome. Adele confessed her ignorance. Charlton's mother fixed her with a beady stare and suggested they were well worth her study. In the few snatched words they had so far managed together, Charlton whispered to Adele that his mother was a renowned authority on Roman relics.

Moving among the tables, each glittering with silver and cut glass and decorated with spring flowers, Adelaide Merrill was in her element. She loved playing the hostess; for weeks she had pondered over the invitation list, adding an ambassador here, dropping a banker there to get what would be "the perfect blend." It had required tact and ruthlessness; she had lost old friends and made new ones by simply deciding who would, or would not, receive the gold-embossed invitations to the dinner and ball.

She left nothing to chance. She designed the place cards, chose the menu, hired the orchestra to play during the reception and for dancing.

And now Adelaide was behaving like a royal lady-in-waiting. As her daughter approached a table, she would murmur in Adele's ear a biosketch of each guest: "influential banker," "wife of important broker," "daughter of Spanish consul," "General Motors executive," "close friend of J. P. Morgan."

Adele tried hard to fit the faces to the details. She was glad of the two attributes Bryn Mawr had taught her—poise and the art of making small talk.

In her knee-length dress, bobbed brown hair set in marcel waves, she still felt very much a schoolgirl; she wondered how she would ever cope when she was married and herself had to entertain these people.

When she finally reached the top table, Charlton was waiting for her. Smiling proudly, he told her she was the "wow of the night."

Adele then knew that "everything would fall into place." The future no longer held any fears for the beautiful young socialite. She might not yet know how to boil an egg but, with her handsome broker beside her, Adele felt she could cope with anybody and anything.

Mike Meehan was feeling even more restless than usual. Six weeks after his hugely successful Radio pool, the specialist in RCA stock could see no immediate prospect of mounting a similar spectacular operation. Worse, the pool in Anaconda Copper was not doing well. Even with the financial support of Percy Rockefeller, John J. Raskob, and Billy Durant, pool managers Bragg and Smith found themselves powerless to stop the declining value of Anaconda stock.

Originally the pair had accumulated for the pool nearly 200,000 Anaconda shares, costing on average $170 each. They had swiftly risen to $174. But then the price of copper unexpectedly fell from its high of 24 cents a pound a month before to its present value on this Monday, April 29, of just 18 cents. Inevitably, the price of Anaconda shares dropped. They now sold at around $160.

In consultation with Meehan, Bragg and Smith had to choose between retaining the stock they still held in the hope there would be a dramatic increase in world demand for copper, or selling it at a considerable loss. They chose to cut their losses.

Meehan agreed, and the pool managers were now attempting discreetly to rid themselves of thousands of Anaconda shares without causing a further fall in their value.

The continuing high call money rate also concerned Meehan. It stood at 15 percent.

Yet those other trusted indicators of future market trends—steel and auto production—seemed to suggest reason for optimism. Steel output, although less than in March, was 632,000 tons up on the corresponding figure for 1928. The projected auto production for April—over 621,000 cars—if reached would be a record.

And the public had just been given official encouragement to speculate. The morning newspapers quoted an unnamed Treasury official in Washington as saying he did "not consider stocks dangerously high."

To Mike Meehan the anonymous spokesman sounded suspiciously like Secretary Andrew Mellon, perhaps prompted by Charles Mitchell and Billy Durant.

Still feeling uneasy, Meehan walked away from the Radio post and into the Stock Exchange smoking room. Smoking was forbidden on the floor.

The room was a comfortable clublike place. Today, a sure sign the market was temporarily slack, it was crowded with members bent over backgammon boards or perusing newspapers and magazines.

Meehan settled down to read the New York *Times*. Though he did not share financial editor Alexander Noyes's view that the bull market must soon end, Meehan had a sound respect for the veteran financial journalist's integrity. Noyes's pages of hard fact and informed gossip were required reading for any Wall Streeter. Now he was again warning of the international dangers inherent in the flow of gold into the United States; this month's import would total over $24 million.

A proportion of that gold, Meehan knew, had already come over on the Cunard liner *Berengaria*.

A few months before, he had read a similar report. Tacked on as a footnote to the main story was a paragraph reporting that on the six-day voyage from Southampton to New York, passengers on the ship had bought and sold 50,000 shares of stock, using the *Berengaria*'s wireless to transmit orders.

The report had given Meehan an idea. He had telephoned Cunard's Manhattan office promising he would guarantee the line $100,000 a year for the exclusive right to run a floating brokerage business aboard the *Berengaria*. The offer was quickly accepted.

Next, Meehan had put the proposition to the Board of Governors of the New York Stock Exchange. They had not yet given their answer. Reading Noyes's column spurred Meehan into action. He hurried to his office at 61 Broadway, and telephoned Exchange Vice-president Richard Whitney. He was told to call Whitney at home in the evening. Before then, Meehan had an appointment with David Sarnoff, executive vice-president of the Radio Corporation of America.

Sarnoff and Meehan were old friends. Indeed, Mrs. Sarnoff, like James Riordan, had made a profit in Meehan's Radio pool of $58,342.15 without putting up a penny.

By midafternoon, Meehan was seated in Sarnoff's office.

Seventeen years before, in 1912, when he was a Marconi operator, Sarnoff had reported the news of the *Titanic* sinking, become famous overnight, and awakened the world to the importance of radio telegraphy. In 1919 he had helped found RCA. A year later he predicted vast profits were to be made from the sale of "radio music boxes." Since then he had been in the van of the burgeoning radio industry.

Sarnoff saw immediately the possibilities in Meehan's floating brokerage service. He promised to assign Arthur Costigan, "the best wireless man in the world," to help make the project technically feasible.

Returning home, Meehan telephoned Richard Whitney. The Stock Exchange vice-president was stiff and formal. He told Meehan the Board of Governors had given their qualified approval for the operation, with the proviso that "the security of transmissions between ship and shore was guaranteed, that continuous quotations would be provided, and that the entire operation would be conducted like a proper brokerage house."

Surrounded by waxed wood, thick pile carpets, and brocade seat covers, Henry Ford and his family were being pulled smoothly through the early May countryside aboard his private rail car. It was hitched to the *Detroiter* express bound for New York. With Henry were Clara, Edsel and his wife, Eleanor, and their son, twelve-year-old Henry, Jr.

Harry Bennett was also on board, jaunty as ever, sporting a polka-dot bow tie to match his vest. His pistols were in their special traveling case, handily placed beside his bunk. The trip was a welcome break for Bennett from the life he now led. Increasingly, and with justification, he felt "they" were out to kill him. Though "they" were never precisely identified, Bennett doubtless meant either that growing legion of Ford workers he had terrorized or members of the Detroit underworld he had alienated. Recently, it was said, five toughs in a car had tried to ram him off the road. Bennett produced his pistols and threatened to blow their heads off. They fled. On another occasion, a gunman had taken pot shots at one of his daughters. Since then, the Bennett family had flitted between their five mansions, trying to make it harder for hit men to locate them. In one mansion, Bennett had reportedly installed an escape hatch concealed in a shower stall which led to a forty-foot tunnel opening into a garage.

Aboard the train, the troubleshooter could relax. Short of dynamiting the track there was no real way anyone could harm him or the Fords; Bennett had stationed armed guards outside each of the locked doors connecting the car to the *Detroiter*'s Pullman coaches.

Inside the car, the atmosphere was convivial and relaxed.

Ford's sales for April had exceeded expectations; already May looked like being even better. Not even the news that General Motors had bought a 40 percent interest in Fokker Aircraft of Germany to challenge Ford in the air could dampen Edsel's mood. Long before Mott saw the possibility of diversifying into aircraft, Edsel, in spite of some grumbling from his father, had opened Ford Airport near Dearborn. It was part of his determined desire to push the company into new areas. Now, Ford-built all-metal trimotor planes carried mail around the Midwest. Edsel doubted whether Mott could ever wrest control of that contract.

Yet the threat on the ground from General Motors was real. The corporation was on target for producing a monumental billion and a half dollars' worth of cars this year. It was all very well for the press to report that Henry Ford's personal income would likely be $14 million in 1929; what concerned Edsel was the company's profits. Increasingly, his father seemed to be more concerned with other matters. Even now, when they might have been talking business, Henry Ford was tucked away in his private study adjoining the railway car's master bedroom.

Edsel turned to the financial pages of the morning newspapers. As usual, he looked first at the auto stocks; General Motors was riding high on a market that now, on this Thursday, May 9, was peaking again. Unlike his father, Edsel paid close attention to the stock market, convinced that the family fortunes were closely bound to its behavior. And while he also hated the sharks who, despite a thunderous protest from the company publicists, were still operating in Ford stock, Edsel did not share his father's blind hatred of Wall Street. Further, he believed that General Motors present position as market leader was due in part to the support it received in the Street.

Edsel wished his father would recognize that the Ford Motor Company was not some isolated giant, but an integral member of global industry. If there was a slump in Germany—as many were now predicting there would be—then Fords would be affected; the forthcoming election in England could also have a direct bearing on company profits. Edsel was due to turn the first sod of earth at the Dagenham site later in the month—a silver-plated shovel to do the job was tucked away in his baggage—but he did not for a moment believe this gesture was other than symbolic; the success of the Ford plant in Essex would depend almost totally on the British economic climate following the election.

Closer to home, if General Electric jumped a few points, if U. S. Steel continued its climb, Edsel knew that meant, ultimately, more money would be available for cars. Equally, a snap break in the market would mean a drop in car sales.

Edsel had tried hard to convince his father of this connection between market reaction and company prosperity. But Henry Ford still stubbornly refused to have any dealings with "that Wall Street gang of crooks."

In any case, as the train sped through lower Ontario, not far from his Canadian plant, Henry Ford's mind was not on Wall Street. Instead, he was immersed in updating an old theory. Seated in his small study, he was composing yet another attack on the eating habits of the nation.

Ford was confident reporters would be waiting at Grand Central Terminal to hear his latest thoughts.

His basic theme was familiar: "Bad food causes crime." If "people ate right, they would act right and think right"; if "clergymen would quit squabbling about evolution and give a series of good diet lectures, they would save more stomachs than they are now saving souls."

Further, Ford was prepared personally to support any campaign to rid the world of cows. He believed it possible to produce milk "commercially and get by without eating meat and so cut out these wasteful animals."

He had been researching cows for some time; they never stopped eating and they left their slurry everywhere. Cows were, in Henry Ford's opinion, in the same category as hospitals and jails—capable of being dispensed with once people learned "to eat the things they should." He had no doubt at all that crime and health were directly linked to diet. A person was more prone to steal if he filled himself with steak; more likely to fall sick if he included butter fats in his food.

People, he believed, should not only eat but also live in the Ford manner.

Most mornings he jogged three miles around his estate, swerving past the deer dung, keeping an eye open for bird droppings. He often shunned breakfast, believing a person worked better on an empty stomach. He liked to run up and down stairs, ignoring Clara's warning it was dangerous for his heart.

Though he would never say so publicly, Henry could not understand why his wife did not support his food and keep-fit fads; in every other way they were happily compatible. But Clara remained unconvinced of the nutritional quality of weeds, and stubbornly refused to help coax his staff into chomping on what they called "grass sandwiches." Now, as he prepared his statement for the expected reporters in New York, Ford was still searching for that little extra ingredient that would ensure he got front-page coverage.

He turned to a tried and trusted source. It was in a briefcase beside a well-thumbed copy of *The Old Farmer's Almanac*. Ford never traveled anywhere without his leather-bound Bible. There, in the New Testament, he had once found support for his belief in reincarnation. For some years now he had sustained himself with the thought that in a previous life he had been Leonardo da Vinci.

Once more the Bible offered support for his food-related-to-crime theory. Culling the Old Testament, he concluded that Jews, "in the heyday of their career, considered the right kind of food a prime essential. Moses and Aaron were dieticians. The basis of a good many official sanitary and health bureau regulations bears striking similarity to those observed by the pre-Christian children of Israel."

Their society, Ford knew, had been virtually crime-free.

He had found what he was looking for—an olive branch, a suitable sentiment with which to pave the way for his important approaching public reconciliation with American Jewry.

It was Edsel who had suggested his father should attend the forthcoming tesimonial dinner in New York to honor David A. Brown, chairman of the United Jewish Campaign. Edsel felt the occasion would be a perfect opportunity for Ford to show that his anti-Semitism, in public at least, was a thing of the past.

Henry Ford agreed.

Now, with those references to Aaron and Moses, he had found a way of associating the Jews with sensible eating. That should please them.

Relaxed and genial, dressed in pepper-and-salt tweeds and custom-made lattice-topped shoes, Ford rejoined his family.

Edsel's wife, Eleanor, was as usual polite but cool. After thirteen years of marriage she still insisted on addressing her in-laws as "Mr. and Mrs. Ford."

And Eleanor also had habits Ford found hard to endure. For instance: her fingernails. Ford had noticed that Eleanor wore her nails long, and painted them. He let the nail of the little finger on his left hand grow to almost an inch in the hope of persuading Eleanor "how silly women with nails like that looked." She had ignored the hint. Next, Ford lacquered his nail bright red. Again, Eleanor took no notice; her nails remained long and were varnished vivid crimson.

Henry, for once defeated, was forced to snip off his nail.

Nor could he understand Eleanor's fixation with good causes. He believed that "philanthropy, like everything else, ought to be productive." Though $200 was always kept available for him by Bennett, Ford himself never carried money—for charity or otherwise. He sometimes boasted he had no patience "with any kind of commercialized humanitarianism."

This attitude further widened the gap between his daughter-in-law and himself.

Conversely, he utterly spoiled Edsel's eldest boy, Henry.

He let the child run wild through the Rouge plant. Recently, young Henry had driven a Model T inside one of the factory buildings, zigzagging between the support pillars, seeing how close he could come without hitting. On another occasion, he mixed up employee's time cards, delaying a whole shift waiting to clock in. His grandfather had been much amused, as he was when the boy took over a cash register at the Rouge canteen and handed back to baffled workers money with their meals.

Eleanor could not have been altogether pleased when told by her father-in-law that her son was "a real Ford."

Claire Giannini always took it as a compliment when she was compared to her father; it made her feel "one of the team."

The Gianninis were again back in New York.

Ostensibly, her father had returned to consolidate the alliance with Blair and Company. Privately, Claire wondered whether he had come to keep a closer eye on Elisha Walker. Twice this month of May, trusted aides, long-serving Italians, had sent Giannini confidential reports stating that Walker was behaving arrogantly in his new position as president of the Bancamerica-Blair Corporation.

And yet, Claire had to admit that Walker's conduct was exemplary. He was courteous and attentive toward her, and he worked almost as hard as her father.

The new corporation began trading officially on Monday, May 20. Capitalized at $500 million, it was one of the largest private investment houses in operation, with offices in twenty-three American cities and also in Europe.

Two days later there was a stock market break, lopping between two and eighteen points off many shares. It was the third time this month the market had broken. The break was caused largely by the Federal Reserve Advisory Council—the ultimate federal fiscal authority—suggesting to the board "a definite recommendation" that it authorize the discount rate be raised to 6 percent.

The board, quite against its custom, published this recommendation while at the same time repeating its adamant opposition to it and to the request of the New York Federal Reserve Bank to raise its discount rate from 5 percent to 6.

Giannini, like other bankers, was asked for a reaction by the press. He declined; he did not wish to exacerbate what he correctly sensed was a bitter struggle going on in Washington and New York.

Next day the market rallied following inspired leaks that there would be no increase in interest rates.

But on Monday, May 27, there was a fourth and most severe slump in shares. General Electric fell 13¼, Case Threshing 25. In all, more than two hundred stocks hit a new low for the year.

Then, once more, the market lurched upward.

Giannini was now deeply troubled. Like his friend, banker Paul Warburg—who believed the market "had shown unmistakable symptoms of its intrinsic weakness"—Giannini felt the collapse of May 27 clearly demonstrated stocks had advanced far beyond their true value.

Giannini told Claire the situation was "chillingly reminiscent" of early 1928 when speculators, adopting the same tactics as now, almost ruined him.

He had spoken out then—and been ignored. Instinctively, he felt he would suffer the same fate if he spoke out now.

The media were voraciously feeding the stock market, urging it again upward to record levels. The reporters who daily called on Giannini were interested only in hearing optimistic statements from him.

Realizing he had no other choice, Giannini seized an opportunity to rekindle his favorie theme—branch banking. The press lapped it up.

CHAPTER TWELVE

THE CHINESE CONNECTION

All day the crowd gathered on the pavement opposite what was probably the most famous doorway in the land, Number 10 Downing Street, the official residence of Britain's Prime Minister. In many ways, noted the reporter from the *Daily Express,* the watchers reflected the split in the nation on this Thursday, May 30.

To one side, grouped together, were some of the year's most publicized people—the Gay Young Things, the mainstay of thousands of newspaper stories. Like their New York counterparts, these London flappers wore skimpy dresses, beads, and close-fitting hats; their escorts wore tight jackets, and trousers cut so wide they looked like split skirts.

Outnumbering them by far were those who represented a great nation's discontent. In their cloth caps, shiny serge suits, and worn shoes, they were part of the growing ranks of unemployed; they were the men who were learning to live in idleness and poverty. They had come to Downing Street seeking a miracle; they hoped for a change of government to relieve the apathy in which they felt trapped.

For the past month the British unemployed had been a vast malleable force in the hands of the politicians. All three parties—Conservative, Labour, and Liberal—had promised relief from a torpid economy coping with outdated industries. Their manifestos spoke of a brave new world, of "turning the corner." Britain, in the words of one politician, would soon be booming like America.

In just a few hours, the crowd outside the simple wooden frame door of Number 10, along with the rest of the waiting nation, would know whether they had a new government or whether there would be a further term of Conservatism under Baldwin.

Baldwin, more than any other Tory, epitomized everything the workless resented. They thought him indifferent to their plight; that his indolence was contagious; and that he shrunk from new thoughts, preferring instead the stagnant remedies that had totally failed to cure the terrible disease of unemployment.

The number out of work was well over a million—it had never during the decade dropped below that figure—and the sight of seedy men, worried-looking women, and obviously underfed children walking the streets was commonplace in many parts of the country.

They were baffled, and then angry, with Conservative talk of a better world based on empire trade, business, "the City," the stock market. They did not care whether, in this election month, the Bank of England, on Treasury orders, had shipped no gold to America, thus temporarily improving the gold reserve position; bars of gold in Bank of England vaults had not brought down the price of bread and potatoes. Nor did the unemployed care about Conservative promises to clean up the bucket shops which had turned London's financial district—the maze of streets around Throgmorton—into a dangerous place for the unwary. The poor did not have a penny to risk in such dives. Talk of stabilizing the market, improving the balance of payments, and regulating foreign exchange rates had little impact on people who felt humiliated, degraded, and intimidated by their circumstances.

Old class issues—which in many cases were thought to have withered away—were viciously revived by both sides before the election; the triumph of Russia's Bolshevism heartened the Left and frightened the Right. The police were given new powers to search and detain; foreigners found Britain a nation that was becoming unfriendly and restrictive.

But it was the workless who felt most alienated. The average unemployed man could not relate his personal suffering to the economic conditions of the time. Churchill's budget, with its concessions on tea and betting taxes, did little to alleviate that feeling. The workless, in the words of one newspaper leader, felt betrayed.

The voting would decide how deep that feeling went. But, judging the mood of those gathered outside Number 10, the *Express* reporter felt the chance of a Conservative victory was not good. He doubted whether these hungry-looking men had been much impressed by the carefully orchestrated splurge of publicity Edsel Ford received when he dug the first sod at Dagenham a few days ago. The Conservative press had played up his promise of hundreds of new jobs; it was a chance for some old-fashioned jingoism, a reminder that even the all-powerful United States could see the wisdom of investing in an about-to-be-reborn Britain.

Yet, the reporter knew, it would need more than promises to bring vitality into the back-to-back ghettos of London's dockland, the arid workless North, and the coalfields of Wales. And, in the *Express* man's eyes, the contrast between the grim, joyless men in their make-do and mended clothes, and the feckless flappers, was a story his newspaper would never run. The *Express,* as always, liked only to report the buoyant side of Britain.

The newspaper's beliefs were exemplified by the first cabinet minister to arrive at Number 10 after the polls closed.

Sir William Joynson-Hicks—"Jix" to his many critics—managed to do something that had not happened all day: unite the crowd. The flappers and the unemployed were equally vehement in their booing of the Home Secretary. His appointment to the Home Office in 1924 was seen as the "greatest compliment the forces of reaction could pay to the progressive spirit of the Twenties."

Jix had enthroned DORA—the Defence of the Realm Act—as the Big Auntie of England. DORA was a rallying figure for those politicians, bishops, and sermonizing generals who wanted a return to Victorian days when the working classes knew their place and a gentleman could play bowls and the stock market all day.

And so Jix and DORA, hand in hand, had set out to turn back the clock. The forces of reaction swept to their assistance. The police pursued homosexuals and unlicensed drinking clubs with a fury never before seen. Vigilante committees hounded all aliens and especially Jews—the particular *bête noire* of Jix. And each Sunday the clergy urged England to repent before it was too late.

The Gay Young Set went its way: Older men drowned their memories of the Great War in a queasy river of manhattans, bronxes, and martinis; the younger Charlestoned and black-bottomed with their scantily clad girls.

At this election, those happy flappers had newfound status; Jix, in a moment of weakness, had given women under thirty the vote for the first time in Britain. Now, making his way into Number 10, he had reason to regret that decision.

Seated in the rear of his official car, still on the way to Number 10, Chancellor of the Exchequer Winston Churchill had no regrets. He had fought a typically tough election campaign; he had been uncompromising and determined to cling to his Conservatism while at the same time hardly concealing his contempt for Jix and his bigotry. But above all Churchill was concerned about unemployment. He did not believe that Labour's Ramsay MacDonald was the man to bring about an improvement.

And, in spite of the ranks of workless, there was much in Britain for

Churchill to admire. The country's proud boast was still true; even now, at sunset, as Big Ben's chimes rang out over London, somewhere in the British Empire a Union Jack was being raised up a flagpole to herald the morrow. Britain, through her empire, was the most powerful nation on earth, and London the capital of the world.

As Churchill's car sped down the Mall, he could reflect on the innumerable triumphs that had been celebrated along this route. Queen Victoria's coach had been drawn down its length in the breathtaking procession which marked the zenith of her reign, the Diamond Jubilee. The Mall itself seemed a reassuring symbol that the age of imperialism was still alive. A Conservative victory, Churchill believed, would ensure the old ideals and traditions remained intact.

He genuinely feared that Ramsay MacDonald—whom he had repeatedly attacked at the hustings for his wartime pacifism—would change the very fabric of a Britain he loved passionately.

Churchill did not share the opposition of many of his colleagues to the flapper generation. He accepted them as part of an ongoing process. They were new, just as radio was new; that did not mean either was bad.

The Chancellor had himself brilliantly exploited radio during the election. He had used it to deliver an electrifying party political broadcast. Churchill remembered how, three years earlier, during the 1926 general strike, Prime Minister Baldwin had employed radio to help settle the dispute.

Churchill also believed his own role in the general strike, and that of the BBC's, had been misunderstood. In part, he blamed the BBC's managing director, Sir John Reith, for this. The thirty-nine-year-old Scot, six feet six inches tall, rawboned and craggy-faced, had been dubbed, in typical Churchill fashion, "that Wuthering Height." Yet Reith had been the first to recognize Churchill's mastery of the microphone. He told friends that if the Chancellor lost his post, he could always get a job at the BBC.

Churchill had other plans if the Conservatives were defeated—though the smile on his face as he entered Number 10 gave no hint there was such a thought in his mind.

Inside the large, rambling residence, he seated himself by the desk of Baldwin's private secretary, Charles Patrick Duff, and waited for the first results to come in on the Press Association tape which Baldwin had installed especially for the occasion.

Churchill had firmly decided that if he was defeated he would make a coat-to-coast tour of America. He loved the country and its people second only to his own. His mother was born in Brooklyn and her father had been a member of the New York Stock Exchange; Churchill himself held American shares. He would be able to get firsthand specialist advice on his investments from wily old friends like Percy Rockefeller and Bernard Baruch; and in Wall Street Churchill could assess on the spot whether the fears of Montagu Norman, governor of the Bank of England, were realistic. The two men disliked and distrusted each other.

Already, behind the scenes in the bank, there was growing agreement with Norman that the constant bickering between the Federal Reserve Board and its banks, especially the one in New York, was an "obstacle" to realization of the dangers of the stock market boom and also "an obstacle to prompt action to meet them."

Norman had even offered to lend the Federal Reserve Bank of New York $50 million to "assist it in controlling the market." The offer had been politely refused. To Norman, studying American conditions from the vantage point of Europe, the need for "a drastic tightening" of credit in New York was plain.

Earlier in the year, the governor had visited Washington hoping to be given a "clearer view of monetary conditions there." Instead, he had returned home "baffled," with an "even deeper feeling of confusion and obscurity."

Throughout the spring months, Norman was in close contact with Europe's finance ministers to try to persuade them to join him in pressuring the Federal Reserve to be firm. Norman wanted to see a controlled slowing down of the American boom. He thought it should have been done in January, and again in March. Now he feared it could be too late. This very day, as Britain was going to the polls, he had drafted a letter to the governor of the Swedish Riksbank stating that they "must expect to go through the summer with a Federal Reserve Bank rate out of relation with the effective rate of interest in New York." Norman predicted this would have "the worst consequences," attracting "short funds to New York while preventing the issue of long-term foreign loans in that market."

Norman, better than anybody, knew he was fighting an uphill battle in seeking European cooperation. Political ill-feeling between France and Germany—being exploited by Hitler to broaden his political platform—and between Italy and Hungary was affecting the possibility of a common European fiscal policy.

Norman had just warned the French—sublimely secure behind their hoarded gold—that elsewhere in Europe the exchange position was growing steadily worse and reserves were falling.

His fears for the future were succinctly summed up in an earlier letter to his counterparts in several countries in Europe. Norman laid most of the blame for the fiscal problems they faced squarely on an American monetary policy that allowed an "apparently inexhaustible demand for funds" to be met and fed into the market. He wrote that he felt "strongly that a complete adjustment by some means or other must somehow come about and will before long impose itself upon us all. The strain to which our own monetary system is being exposed will then become manifest to everyone."

So far the Federal Reserve had not acted on Norman's outspoken warnings.

This high-level unease had not reached the floor of the London Stock Exchange, where there was great activity in all shares and especially in the new-issue market. The sterling-dollar exchange was strong; there was no embargo on foreign issues, nor was there any objection to subscriptions to French funding loans, previously a sore point with the London traders.

And the buoyant American stock market played its part in boosting the London market—which had not been seriously disturbed by the election campaign. Nevertheless, there was one American import that was causing concern in the city. The London market was still bedeviled by bucket shops, operating on American lines; during the election there had been several references to the "Thieves Kitchen" as a synonym for the Stock Exchange.

All three parties had promised a cleanup—though privately, the politicians recognized it would be hard totally to clamp down on dubious prospectuses and "information bulletins."

Winston Churchill, as Chancellor, knew that if the Conservatives were returned, there might well have to be a probe into the City.

But tonight, in the tense atmosphere inside Number 10, was not the time to be thinking of such matters. All eyes were on the tape. Soon it began to punch out the first results. They announced one Labour victory after another. Churchill's language, in the words of one observer, became unprintable.

Financier Clarence Hatry heard the first election results over his dressing room's radio set late in the evening. He was not unduly worried about these early Labour victories. He told Dolly, his wife, that the Socialist wins would soon be overtaken by a solid mass of Conservative successes in the shires. His carefully laid plans were not endangered by these initial returns.

Hatry continued fixing his black tie. He could have asked his valet to help him, but he preferred to tie it himself. Besides, Hatry guessed that the fourteen staff who ran his elegant mansion in Stanhope Gate, off London's Park Lane, were probably all down in the basement listening to the radio there. Their master had fitted out the cellar as a replica of an Elizabethan pub, calling it "Ye Olde Stanhope Arms"; when it was not filled with guests, the staff liked to group around the wireless, still a relatively new innovation for them.

The house contained another of Hatry's imaginative touches. On the second floor was a swimming pool which allowed him virtually to dive straight out of bed into the water. It was quirks like this that made Dolly adore her dapper Chaplin-like spouse with his toothbrush mustache and lank black hair combed close to his scalp. She had also become accustomed to his slight limp, the legacy of childhood rheumatic fever.

Dolly had yet to meet anybody able to match her husband's drive, vision, and foresight. Because of these attributes, she forgave such extravagances as the pub and pool.

Hatry was generous by nature. Often, after dinner, he would stroll along the Thames Embankment and give away five-pound notes to tramps. Occasionally he lavished expensive presents on his staff in a desire to compensate them for the almost impossible demands he made. The previous Christmas he had given his secretary a gold mesh evening bag from Aspreys stuffed with twenty-pound notes.

It was a small thing for a man who lived the life-style of the multimillionaire he was, with a string of fine racehorses, a country manor in Sussex, and the world's largest racing yacht, needing a permanent crew of forty, including two chefs, to staff her.

The press said that even Jack Morgan envied Hatry this floating palace; there was speculation that when he came to London in the summer, Morgan might meet Hatry to discuss common financial interests.

The Englishman would welcome an opportunity to talk to Morgan, even if then, as now, Hatry was hard-pressed for time; he was working fifteen hours daily, seven days a week, on his plans to achieve a substantial hold on the steel industry of Britain.

For the past five months he had been engrossed in a complicated and delicate piece of business maneuvering.

First he had merged some hundred different iron foundries into one unit, Allied Ironfounders Limited. That gave him a base from which to advance toward his next goal—acquiring control of a large number of heavy steel companies by purchasing the stock of their holding company, United Steel Limited.

Typically, Hatry reduced the complicated strategy to a few words: "If I could acquire the share capital, I could use United Steel as the nucleus for acquiring and amalgamating yet more steel companies. They would prosper. So would I."

Eventually, like some industrialized Topsy, the nucleus would grow and grow, all the time absorbing more steel companies, until Hatry alone would dominate Britain's steel industry. Among other things, it would make him the equal of the American steel barons. It was a satisfying thought; Hatry had an intense feeling of competition with his rivals in the United States. His proposal was every bit as bold and dramatic as any Billy Durant had conceived.

As a first move, Hatry had circulated the forty thousand stockholders of United Steel, offering to buy from them their individual holdings for something over the market value of the shares. Already a large number of stockholders had accepted his offer; they were now awaiting payment from Hatry for the shares he had agreed would be made within a specified period. Hatry had also undertaken to pay off United Steel's £3 million bank overdraft.

United Steel was in a financial mess. Its stock had slipped from an initial market value of £27 million to around £5 million; it was in arrears with its payments to preferential stockholders; it had requested a moratorium with its creditors. As Hatry saw it, "they were in a mess, but the business itself was sound."

As with most takeover bids Hatry required bridging finance, money to help pay for the stock he had already agreed to purchase—and further acceptances of his offer were coming in every day—and to tide the company over until the group's shares could be traded on the London Stock Exchange under its new name—Steel Industries of Great Britain.

All told, Hatry needed some £8 million to back up his offer to United Steel's stockholders and to pay off the company's overdraft. He personally had immediately available "in cash and securities about £1,000,000"; he was confident he could easily raise another 2 million or so from his contacts in the City.

But for the remainder, some £4 million, Hatry relied on Lord Bearsted, a director of Montagu Samuel, one of London's most prestigious private bankers. Twice before, Bearsted had loaned Hatry similar large amounts; each time the money was repaid.

On this latest deal there had been several meetings between the two men; after the most recent, Hatry left Bearsted's office convinced the £4 million would be forthcoming when needed. He and the banker had "discussed it from all angles. I was to go ahead with my plans and he would make his portion of the money available when the shareholders began to take up my offer and my million had been absorbed."

In this happy, confident mood, Hatry set off with Dolly for one of the most lavish election night parties in London.

Driving through the West End, he could sense the mounting excitement. Crowds were gathering at the traditional election night sites, around Eros in Piccadilly Circus and in Trafalgar Square. Among them might well be investors waiting for Hatry's money to pay for their

United Steel stock; he had already committed the bulk of his own ready cash and would need Bearsted's funds fairly soon now.

As the car swept down Oxford Street, Hatry could hear cheers for a Conservative gain. He was pleased.

The chauffeur dropped them outside Selfridge's department store. Flunkies hurried forward to guide Hatry and Dolly past the display counters; an elevator whisked them to an upper floor. Waiting to greet them was tycoon Gordon Selfridge who had chosen to hold the party in his store.

Hatry could see that his old friend had prepared everything in anticipation of a Conservative victory. Waiters were circulating with magnums of iced champagne, trays of caviar, smoked salmon, and savories. There was an orchestra, playing hits from the Great War and the twenties. Above their rostrum was a large screen, similar to those used in the New York and London stock exchanges. On it, election results flashed every few moments.

The guests—show business figures, peers, financiers, sportsmen, bishops, the élite of the Establishment—stared intently at the screen.

Results were coming in more frequently now.

Hatry had one other quality that Dolly admired. Better than almost any of the reporters who wrote about him, her husband could take in a scene, reduce it to its essentials, and file it away in his memory for writing up later.

First he made a mental note of the general ambience. "Champagne bubbles winked in the goblets and cigar-smoke hung like incense on the air."

Then he got down to the detail. "There were cheers when some Tory stalwart regained his seat, mock-boos and groans as a Labour name appeared on the screen. But as the evening drew on, faint gasps of surprise showed that the Conservative facade was cracking. The crack became an ominous split and then a chasm. What had appeared safe majorities were slipping and tumbling under the Labour onslaught. The parties were running neck and neck, with the Liberals a poor third, and then slowly, inevitably, the Tories dropped back in the race. And all the sparkle went out of the evening. The champagne, sipped in silence, tasted flat. Labour was back—and back to stay."

Finally, feeling "strangely depressed," he left the party with Dolly in the early hours of May 31.

Arm in arm they walked down Oxford Street.

Dolly, concerned by her husband's silence, asked if the Socialist victory was worrying him.

"It's a bad omen," said Hatry morosely. "A very bad omen."

The cold night air did nothing to lift his "sense of brooding depression."

Nor had Hatry's sense of the dramatic deserted him. "I felt that everything was curiously unreal. It was like walking across a deserted stage when the players had taken their bows and the cheering audience had left the theater. In the pale light the bulk of my house seemed flat, two-dimensional. As I let myself in through the front door, it was almost as though I were stepping into nothing."

Hatry slept little during what was left of the night, trying to assess what the Labour victory would mean for Great Britain—and for him.

Early next morning, Winston Churchill learned that, although he had retained his seat, the overall result was a blow to the Conservatives. They had won only 260 seats against Labour's 288. The Liberals, with 59, held the balance of power. He could begin to plan his trip to America.

The London Stock Exchange reacted immediately to the Socialist victory. Shares tumbled. Finance houses moved to a liquid position. The big banks battened down their financial hatches.

In Europe, the return in Britain of a second Labour Government within five years was greeted with indifference in France, concern in Germany, and surprise in Italy, Belgium, and Holland.

On the U.S. stock exchanges, the news would scarcely cause a ripple.

By noon of this same Friday, Clarence Hatry was in Lord Bearsted's office in the City.

The financier's predawn fears that he had "stepped into nothing" had grown. A Socialist victory *was* a bad omen. His depression *was* still there. His sense of doom *would not* go away.*

For the rest of his life, Clarence Hatry vividly remembered his conversation with Bearsted.

He began by posing a question. "I suppose this political upset makes no difference to our agreement?"

Bearsted looked at Hatry steadily and then replied. "What agreement? I have no agreement with you."

Hatry was stupefied. "I could hardly believe my ears."

He reminded the banker of "our plans to take over the steel companies, all those conferences, your share in the purchase price."

Hatry would remember how he gabbled on, finally slithering to a stop, gripped by "a nightmare from which I would soon wake up."

The awakening was even more painful.

* See Source Notes.

Bearsted spoke slowly. Hatry sat quite still, mesmerized, noting how the banker was "weighing every word."

In measured terms, Bearsted reviewed the position as he saw it.

"Certainly we have discussed this operation of yours. In some detail indeed. As a spectator I have been interested in it. But I have never, *never,* said that I would back it financially. You must be mistaken."

Stunned into total silence, unable even to ask what made Bearsted change his mind—for Hatry was totally convinced they had previously reached a complete understanding—he left the banker's office.

He felt himself to be on the edge of some bottomless void that threatened to engulf his family, his homes, his racehorses and luxury yacht—everything he had worked so hard for. Now he must choose either to renege on the deal he had already made with many United Steel stockholders—in which case he might be sued by them or, more likely, be ruined by lack of confidence in him, which would cause a disastrous drop in the share value of his other companies—or he could attempt to raise the necessary money in some other way.

Hatry was an immodest man. He would not give up easily.

On Thursday, June 6, Stanley Baldwin traveled by special train to Windsor where the King was convalescing from his long illness. With Baldwin went his cabinet colleagues, Winston Churchill among them. They handed the King their seals of office and bade him formal farewell. Next day Ramsay MacDonald arrived with his Labour Ministers to collect those seals. Thus government continued in a uniquely British manner.

Ramsay MacDonald was taking office for the second time. And for the third time in twenty-one years, Churchill was without a political post. His great admirer, T. E. Lawrence—who had recently returned to England from Karachi to satisfy the Left that he was not after all planning a revolution in the Orient—wrote that Churchill was "a fighter, and will come back in a stronger position than before. I want him to be Prime Minister."

The changeover of government did little to affect Britain's far-flung empire and dominions.

Churchill's departure was given pride of place in the South African press; he was still a controversial figure in the country because of his Boer War escapades. In Johannesburg's Holland Street, the center of the nation's financial and business district, the rumblings from London about a Socialist victory barely affected the stocks being traded. The most important of all, gold, remained steady.

To the east, in Australia, the return of the Labour Government was welcomed with quiet satisfaction in many quarters. There, significant social progress in the past had been achieved under Labour. Australia was unique in its trade-union movement, which had grown rapidly from the 1850s.

In 1856 Australia became the first country in the world to introduce the eight-hour day; in Europe and America people were then working fourteen-hour shifts. The strength of the trade unions and the Labour party, their supporters said, was responsible for the absence of social discontent in the country.

But now Australia was being governed by a coalition government, and the country was in the grip of a growing economic crisis; there had already been a serious slump in exports, the coal industry was in trouble, the price of both wheat and wool was falling while unemployment was rising. The stock market, behaving erratically, accurately reflected the situation.

In the election due later in the year, there was little doubt Australia would follow Britain's lead and elect a Labour Government in the hope it would succeed in reversing the depressing incline.

Far to the north, Japan, too, was caught in a national crisis, now in its second year. Its roots went back even further, to the great earthquake of 1923 which left much of Tokyo in ruins. The banks had been ordered to help subsidize relief and rebuilding. In 1927 the Watanabe Bank failed, driven out of business by the demands made upon it. This had touched off a widespread financial panic in which thirty-seven other banks—including the important Bank of Taiwan, and the Fifteenth Bank—either went bankrupt or suspended operations. The collapse of Suzuki Shōten, a powerful trading company engaged in highly speculative ventures, caused further consternation.

With rampant inflation, weakened exports, and endless political scandals at home, Japan's stock markets in Tokyo and Osaka were in a constant state of unease. Japanese traders could only envy their colleagues working in the most exotic of all the world's stock exchanges—those in Shanghai.

Shanghai had three thriving main exchanges. There was the Shanghai Stock Exchange, dealing largely in shares of foreign companies and run mainly by British expatriates almost as a private club. At 429 Jiu Jiang Road was the Shanghai Chinese Merchants Stock Exchange, trading in native stocks. It had opened in 1911 with fifty-five brokers; now it had eighty. And at 1 Szechuan Road was the city's Stocks and Commodities Exchange, with 350 brokers. There were also four other markets that dealt in commodities.

The Shanghai exchanges were still adjusting to the effects of a sudden currency devaluation in China's northeast provinces which had led to the issue of a new silver-backed currency in the region.

Since June 1, business had picked up with the opening of the restructured U.S.-owned Chung Kuo Hen Yeh Bank in Shanghai. By American standards its assets were small, a mere $2.5 million.

But the bank, like many others in Shanghai, planned to improve its situation by placing its spare cash in the most lucrative of all markets. The mandarins of Shanghai were hoping for a quick killing in the low-risk, high-return call money market operating in New York.

CHAPTER THIRTEEN

A FRAUD IS BORN

Viewed from his Fifth Avenue aerie in New York, Jesse Livermore saw Wall Street, on this fine summer's Tuesday of June 11, as "a colossal suction pump," steadily draining the world of capital, and "the suction is fast producing a vacuum in Europe."

With his domestic life for a change running smoothly—Dorothy had cut back on her drinking and he had given up chasing girls—Livermore was able to concentrate his full attention on the market.

During the past week his staff had monitored the financial scene in Europe and Canada for any indication that the time was ripe for another of Livermore's celebrated assaults on the New York stock market.

They discovered the newspaper reports were true; in spirit of the serious market break in late May, an uninterrupted and unprecedented absorption of European funds by the United States had made Wall Street, in the words of a London weekly, "the financial capital of the world." The great European banks, with the exception of the Bank of England and the Bank of France, were in danger of becoming "dependencies of the Federal Reserve Bank of New York." Americans were said to be "rich not in units, but in droves. The man with a million dollar fortune is now an insignificant cipher in the American hierarchy of wealth."

Livermore himself felt that with "trade depressions hanging like a cloud over many European exchanges," it was not surprising that money, "the most sensitive and mobile commodity we use, should fly to the fairer field of America, which today is the goal of refugee capital, just as a generation ago, she was the goal for political fugitives."

The movement of European funds into Wall Street, particularly from a Britain still edgy about its new Labour Government, had reached "full flood."

Studying the reports his aides brought him, Livermore permitted himself a rare joke: "The Gulf Stream may go one way across the Atlantic, but the Gold Stream goes the other."

For already the first June shipment of what by the end of the month would amount to over $9 million worth of gold had arrived in New York from England; a further $29 million was on its way from London to Berlin. This huge drain from Great Britain was now reinforced by a related phenomenon: Thousands more American shares were being bought daily in London by investors made nervous by the Socialist victory.

Nor, Livermore learned, was the situation much different in Berlin, Brussels, or Amsterdam. The orders for American stocks placed in those cities had reached such a level that the question was being seriously asked: "Will Wall Street swallow Europe?"

An Italian newspaper reported that "with more authority than the League of Nations, and with more subtlety than Bolshevism, another world power is making a direct appeal to the strongest instinct of human nature. The new power is Wall Street."

Usually Livermore distrusted such reports; he was inured to the flummery of the press. Even now he doubted there was any real basis for stories that Paris "was going mad for U.S. auto stocks." His common sense told him the proud French would prefer to invest in their own shares than plunge into a market three thousand miles away.

Nevertheless, the newspaper reports could not be entirely discounted. Exaggerated and biased perhaps, but collectively they represented a trend. Trapped between its traditional fear of the "American money monopoly" and admiration for the "greatest financial phenomenon of the age," Europe's media, like the American press, had finally turned Wall Street into a burning talking point.

Livermore's staff believed they had established a definite relationship between favorable publicity in Europe and surges in certain stocks in Wall Street. Earlier in June, the London *Daily Mail* and the Paris *Herald*—an English language newspaper which proudly boasted it was delivered to every village in Europe where an American lived—had each predicted particular U.S. stocks would rise. Forty-eight hours later, they had—doubtless coinciding with a spate of buy orders from all over Europe.

There was no comfort there for Jesse Livermore; ambitious little bulls in faraway places like Warsaw, Venice, and Lithuania made it hard for him to be an effective bear in New York.

The picture from north of the border was not quite so clear. Prices on Canadian exchanges were generally steady and had yet to reflect the recently renewed upturn on the New York Exchange. Even so, on the remote farms and ranches of Alberta and Saskatchewan, people no longer had to rely for their evening entertainment largely on radio programs like "Amos 'n' Andy"; many nowadays also listened avidly for news of share advances in Shredded Wheat, Simpson's, and the Cockshutt Plow Company.

Stock reports could be heard on the radio between morning prayers, time checks, and chest expansion exercises; they were an indispensable item in the daily routine for millions of listeners throughout North America. There was also a dramatic growth in newspapers' printing stock tables, market lists, and syndicated financial columns.

To Livermore these were "just bait for the minnows," aimed at small-time investors who had "no real idea why they were buying or selling."

Evidently the little fish were biting. Livermore's efficient staff had collated a neat pile of newspaper items which showed that the market had successfully hooked the most unlikely of persons. A Fifth Avenue household had just lost its cook because she had been refused her own personal ticker in the kitchen; a dowager in Queens bemoaned the fact that her chauffeur would not report for duty until the market had closed; a writer for *The Saturday Evening Post* announced that he discussed the quotations with his garbage man, and "the grocer's boy came in this morning to ask whether the May 27 break meant the end of the bull market or was it only a technical readjustment?"

There were hard-to-believe reports that some tracks were thinking of cutting out lengthier races because jockeys were complaining about being away too long from the ticker; that street cleaners in Brooklyn were refusing to pick up anything but financial papers; that a synogogue was considering installing a ticker at its entrance; that several movie houses had promised to place tickers in their foyers.

None of these stories surprised Livermore. He had just returned from a swift, unannounced trip to the Midwest where he had been stunned by what was happening in Chicago, Minneapolis–St. Paul, and half a dozen smaller cities he visited. In each place he dropped in on the branch offices of Wall Street brokerage firms. With their swinging doors and half-darkened windows, the offices looked to him like old-fashioned bars. Most had low ceilings, were filled with cigar smoke, and contained tall wicker baskets into which the ticker tape fell. On a wall, each office had a blackboard for posting the latest prices.

Livermore had observed "all manner of men, rubbing elbows in tolerant good fellowship. But the ticker tape passed uneasily through the hands of the amateur as he hunted halfheartedly among the strange

figures. Often he confused one share with another and had to go back
to check again. Then he would discover the stock he had bought with
such rosy hopes had dropped. And he was bust."

This image of sudden insolvency had remained with Livermore. He
felt little compassion for those who gambled and lost, believing as he
did that amateurs had no place in the market.

Now, back in New York, as he evaluated the reports on his desk, the
visit to the Midwest was a reminder that the popular slogan he had so
often heard, that it was safe to "buy AOT"—buy Any Old Thing—was
not at all true.

People did buy—and lose.

Briefing his staff, Jesse Livermore ordered a different sort of market
analysis.

His employees compared current stock prices on the New York Exchange with those for earlier in the year. They showed significant losses
in some of the most prominent stocks traded. Issues like U. S. Steel,
General Electric, and Kennecott had dropped between twenty and
thirty points in the past two months; this June, many others were still
below their January position.

On the Curb Exchange—among the so-called unlisted securities—the
losses were truly staggering. In May alone, a fact verified by the New
York *Times,* the paper value of 240 stocks shrank $3 billion.

More significantly, one of Livermore's sources had made available to
him in advance the contents of a survey by the Midland Bank of
Cleveland. It had studied the behavior of 1,002 stocks listed on the
New York Exchange. More than 60 percent, 614 shares, were lower
now than they had been in January; only 338 stocks had shown any
real and sustained advance during the past six months.

Significantly, too, after twenty years of annual increase, the total of
savings held on deposit throughout the country was now in decline. The
American Bankers' Association report, due to be made public at the
end of June, would show that savings were $195,305,000 below what
they had been a year previously. The ABA believed the withdrawals
were largely attributable to "the lure of profits to be made in stocks."

For Livermore, the most telling factor of all was the way the market
was daily attracting yet more small investors; he felt he could not better
Harper's Magazine, who reported that investing was "becoming a children's crusade, not an adventure for a few hard-boned knights; a place
for the butcher and the barber and the candle-stick-maker."

By the end of the day Livermore had confirmed what he suspected:
This new get-rich-quick game was being played at an increasingly
breakneck pace right across America. The Chicago Stock Exchange's
volume was now seventeen times greater than it had been ten years ago.

During that same period, the annual volume on the St. Louis Stock Exchange had grown from 80,000 to 1 million. The Los Angeles Curb Exchange, conveniently sited in the basement of the city's Stock Exchange building, had been founded only in 1928; in its first year of trading it had handled no fewer than 18 million shares. The whole country seemed to be buying and selling stocks, assessing profits and loss, covering close margin with fresh capital.

In Livermore's view it had become "a new national sport which can be played for the price of an evening paper."

That this was changing the ethical and economic mores of America did not interest him. He was not concerned by "those highbrow magazines" which, alongside dissertations about Freud, Proust, and psychoanalysis, were starting to question the morality of the stock market.

But his instincts told him that, with this mass of untutored people "joining in the game," the chance of a sudden change in the market was greater than before. The "minnows" lacked the essential qualities that helped a professional speculator to survive—steely nerves, an ability to read in advance a stock's behavior, the knack of sitting tight when "everybody else is running wild."

The "minnows" would panic.

Livermore knew that in the May market breaks, thousands of people had been wiped out.

Yet those tremors had done nothing to dissuade thousands more newcomers, small-timers, from trying their luck. The odd-lot brokers who specialized in handling their business had never been busier.

But for how long?

It was a question to which Jesse Livermore now thought he could perceive the glimmer of an answer.

Waiting in the outer office of the president of the New York Stock Exchange, Richard Whitney knew on this Thursday morning of June 13 that his only real hope of survival depended on the economy continuing to climb.

Whitney had borrowed so much, invested so unwisely, that he was firmly impaled on the sort of stocks never accepted for listing on the Stock Exchange. But, instead of switching even to some of the more doubtful listed shares, he continued to pour borrowed good money after bad into the obscure issues of companies dealing with mineral colloids and peat humus.

Despised for his snobbishness by big-time operators like Meehan, Bragg, and Smith, attempt as he might, Whitney was excluded from their pools in Radio and Anaconda Copper. Even his overtures to join with Joe Kennedy had been spurned. True to form, Whitney was finding it impossible to exploit the unique opportunity his position presented at a time when the financial world was at his feet.

Exactly a month ago to the day, May 13, he had been invited to this office and quietly told by the Exchange president, Edward Henry Harriman Simmons, that he and his fellow governors had decided Whitney would be the only candidate in the ballot for next president. His election seemed assured.

Whitney knew the governors would make their usual discreet inquiries. He thought he had covered his tracks well. Now he was not certain.

Uneasily, the smooth-shaven, ruddy-faced Whitney—even a good barber could not hide the signs of his fondness for whiskey—wondered if this summons to see Simmons was the first stage in his unmasking. Was he about to be told he would face trial by his own peers, the prelude to being drummed out of Wall Street for conduct unbecoming an officer and gentleman of the Stock Exchange?

The shame would have serious repercussions on his marriage; his wife was close to the Morgan and Vanderbilt families; his father-in-law was a former president of the Union League Club and treasurer of the Republican National Committee.

And what of his own family? His forebears had emigrated from England on the *Arabelle,* the ship that in 1630 followed the *Mayflower* to the New World. The Whitneys 299 years later were still one of the top families in America, with influential links to the upper echelons of politics and finance.

Yet none of these important connections had been asked to help avert the financial mess that Richard Whitney was in; fear of public shame stopped him approaching any of his well-connected relatives, except his brother George.

For the sake of the family name and J. P. Morgan and Company, George Whitney continued to help his brother. Now, Richard suspected, even that source was drying up. He felt, increasingly, that he was the unfair victim of circumstances. He still could not admit he was the product of his own overbearing arrogance and stupidity.

Filled with foreboding, he went in to see Simmons.

The president was seated behind his desk in the center of an office that lovingly preserved the spirit of a bygone age. The room was furnished in authentic eighteenth-century style; its walls were lined with original portraits of Washington, Jefferson, and Franklin. In one corner stood a stock ticker, spewing out tape.

Simmons invited Whitney to be seated. Then the Stock Exchange president solemnly announced he planned to marry in the fall, probably early October. His bride would be Beatrice Vanderpoel Bogert, whose second marriage had recently ended in a Reno divorce. An elegant, regal woman, she was a fitting companion for Simmons, a widower these past nine years.

The highly relieved Whitney listened in silence as Simmons went on to explain that immediately after his marriage he would be taking an extended honeymoon in Hawaii. During that time, Whitney would be in charge of the Exchange.

For one of the few times in his life, the smooth-tongued Whitney found himself almost at a loss for words as he stuttered his congratulations and thanks.

By Friday, June 14, Edith Stone's search for a heroine for her play about Wall Street had narrowed to a couple of choices; a "lady bull," knowing nothing of the market, but still making one killing after another; or a woman broker, well versed in the wiles of Wall Street, who would guide Edith's hero—loosely based on a discarded boyfriend—to a fortune. The young dramatist now dreamed of imitating one of those sophisticated comedies with which Noël Coward was having such success.

But where Coward played upon drawing-room manners for his characters' words, Edith planned to give her stars speeches peppered with talk about the *rails,* the *industrials, grangers* and *coalers* and the *oils.* She hoped she had it right; that *rails* referred to railroad stocks; *industrials* were shares in large producing and manufacturing companies; a *granger* was a railroad that served the grain belt; a *coaler* the minefields; that groups of stocks were known by the industries they represented—the *oils,* the *motors,* the *sugars.*

In one scene Edith intended to have her hero tangle with a *short*—a man who sold stock he did not yet own in the hope its price would drop before he had to buy the shares he had promised to sell. Her hero would force the *short* to "run to cover," market jargon for making him buy when prices are rising; he would "squeeze the shorts," compelling them to cover at a loss.

To devise a suitable heroine to play opposite her tough *operator*—market slang for a professional speculator—was not easy.

There was in Edith's view undoubtedly something attractive about having a "dizzy dame" lead. She guessed many women in the audience might identify with such a person; after all, tens of thousands "of real-life lambs were every day mixing among the bulls and bears."

Consulting a recent survey, aimed at discovering why women had in the past month entered the market in even greater numbers, Edith learned that "financial ignorance is largely responsible for the feeling many women have of waning social popularity."

Baffled but intrigued by the strange language men used to describe market situations, according to the article women then set out to learn for themselves why General Motors was not a military figure, or call money not something needed for pay phones, or how it came to be that Seaboard Airlines was actually a railroad.

Edith could see possibilities there. Her heroine could ask cryptic crazy questions like "What do you think of Amalgamated Whiffets buying into Wingle Mattresses?" or "See what happened to Bifurcated Gulf today?"

Equally, the young playwright knew if she chose a lady broker as her heroine she could also make a social comment.

What the newsmagazines were calling "positively the newest phenomenon" was gathering momentum. In Wall Street, there were now twenty-two firms with women partners; while none of them yet traded on the floor of the New York Exchange, they wielded considerable influence behind the scenes.

Basing her character on one of these women, Edith could explore the common male criticism that women were "bad losers," "stubborn as mules," "nagging investors," and "when they lost, they fired their broker."

Perhaps, Edith felt, she could make her leading lady talk like that about men.

The ultimate decision—what kind of heroine to create—was complicated by another problem with dramatizing the stock market; its constant vagaries made it hard to keep the plot straight. Every time she thought her story line was settled, the market seemed to call for some new twist.

Edith decided to postpone actual writing until after her trip to Europe. There was bound to be interesting material there to include. She was due to sail on the *Berengaria* in just three weeks' time.

She was also highly relieved to see that the latest batch of German newspapers contained only brief references to Hitler. Perhaps, Edith hoped, he and his Nazis were merely a passing phase.

At three o'clock sharp on Saturday afternoon, June 15, the train steamed into the picturesque station at Bedford Hills. It had been chartered by banker Edwin Merrill to bring from New York many of the five hundred guests for the wedding of his daughter, Adele, to Charlton MacVeagh.

The station, like the engine and coaches, was decorated with white chiffon bunting. It provided a perfect backdrop for the distinguished passengers. The men wore black or gray cutaways, silk hats, and carnation boutonnieres; the women were elegantly dressed and often ravishingly beautiful in a variety of large picture hats.

Merrill and his wife, Adelaide, moved smilingly among the arrivals. With all the skill of a hunter culling a deer herd, Adelaide separated the hundred most carefully chosen guests who would attend the actual wedding service. The rest were directed to refresh themselves at the MacVeagh family house, within walking distance of the station.

One of the many reporters covering the event said it looked as though "Wall Street was transplanted to the backwoods."

Among the fifteen ushers Charlton had chosen were a number of young colleagues from Morgan's, and Corliss Lamont, son of Thomas Lamont, the senior Morgan partner.

Edwin Merrill's diverse business interests were represented by fellow directors from banks, insurance companies, and hospital boards.

His wife's social status was firmly confirmed by the presence of many of the leading families of the eastern seaboard: the Van Rensselaers, the Reynals, the Curtises, the Ahlefeldts and Coolidges. Between them these first families would ensure the newspapers described the occasion as one of the great society weddings of the year.

The MacVeagh side of the family was reinforced by foreign diplomats and senior State Department officials; there were also partners from several of New York's leading corporate law firms.

Outwardly, Adelaide Merrill was relaxed and friendly. Inwardly, she seethed. The morning newspapers had announced "Ambassador's Son to Marry Miss Adele Merrill." She thought it should have read "Banker's Daughter to Marry Ambassador's Son."

She told her daughter that it was "probably an attempt by Charlton's mother to establish her superiority." In the prewedding planning, both mothers had clashed several times; finally Adelaide Merrill had pointedly ignored Mrs. MacVeagh's views on seating and floral decorations. Adele felt they "were scared to death of each other. They liked to be dictatorial. Each one wanted to be a grande dame."

Now, living up to this image, both women surrounded themselves with their own friends. In two definite groups they moved out of the station and up the road to St. Matthew's, the pretty yellow-and-white-painted church where generations of Merrills had worshiped.

Charlton and his best man were already standing before the flower-banked altar.

In the Merrill home, close to the church, Adele took one last look at the tables piled high with presents, then turned to her father.

He checked his fob watch and nodded. A maid stepped forward and adjusted Adele's veil. A footman handed her a bouquet of lilies.

Arms linked, Edwin Merrill and his daughter walked from the house into brilliant sunshine, through the lines of well-wishers, past the ranks of photographers and reporters, and on into St. Matthew's. As they crossed the flower-bedecked threshold of the church, the organist struck up Wagner's Wedding March.

Later, to the music of Mendelssohn, the new Mrs. MacVeagh emerged on the arm of her husband and returned to the house. There, they kissed and promised again to love each other for the rest of their lives. Then they moved to the rear of the old farmhouse. On the spacious lawn, a huge red-and-white-striped marquee had been erected for the reception.

While the guests waited to congratulate the couple, the men exchanged the latest market gossip. Some predicted that the merger of leading New York utilities which Morgan had sponsored to consolidate its hold on United Corporation would bring still further profits to stockholders. Others said that the forthcoming merger between the Chase National and National Park banks would settle the market. All agreed the panic of late May was a thing of the past.

Listening to the hub of conversation, Adele sensed that many of the guests wished soon to be back in New York "where the real action was."

She mentioned this to Charlton. He said he was sure there were just as many others who would hang on until the last drop of Prohibition liquor ran out. Charlton himself had arranged for the booze to be bought from "a trusted source in Wall Street."

In a roundabout way, that source was Michael Levine, a garrulous thirty-seven-year-old Russian Jew who had made his fortune running the financial district's first messenger service. His two thousand "boys" —most of them in reality old men—brought him a personal income of $25,000 a week. He earned almost as much again from his shrewd market investments, "tossing coins for $1,000 a spin" and "providing all kinds of personal services."

Levine and his boys knew where to lay their hands in the financial district on a hooker for a broker; knew the nearby hotels where a banker could take his secretary on the lunch hour; knew the best local brothels, the abortionists, the speakeasy owners who had bought off the police, the gambling dens "where some of the biggest names in the Street played for $5,000 a card." Above all, when he had to, Levine knew how to keep his mouth shut.

Contacts of Levine had arranged, on "a no-questions-asked basis," for delivery of the vintage French champagne, whiskey, and gin now being quaffed by the guests.

It was Adele who first noticed that some of the waiters were crouched behind the tables and "tippling faster than anyone else."

Shrugging helplessly, Charlton led Adele away. He knew there was no point in remonstrating—if he did, "the waiters were quite likely to disappear taking all the drink with them!" By late afternoon several of them were swaying drunkenly. Even the glacial stare of Adelaide Merrill could not halt their unsteady progress among the guests.

Charlton's main concern was whether he had bought enough moonshine to survive to the toasts.

He had not anticipated that here, in select Bedford Hills, he might have to look out for a bootlegger.

In Flint, in the stifling basement where the bootleg alcohol fumes were "almost thick enough to drink," Jolan struggled to absorb what Steve was saying. But the bubbling of the copper vats, the sounds of liquid gurgling through pipes, the low steady keenings of a Hungarian hymn sung by her mother and stepfather as they poured whiskey into gallon jars, made it difficult for the just-turned-sixteen-year-old to hear.

Besides, there was something very disturbing and, she was coming to realize, exciting about the physical presence of Steve. He was standing close to her, shirt unbuttoned, sweat glistening on his skin as he helped stir the fermenting mash. She could sense his manliness and, although she would never have admitted as much, it aroused her. For the first time the prospect of marriage, and making love, seemed acceptable to Jolan.

She still did not love Steve Vargo, but she had developed a real respect for his knowledge. She was coming to the conclusion that had she been given a choice—instead of having her parents choose for her—she could have found "a worse catch by far" than Steve. He was kind, straightforward, considerate—and he never seemed to be short of a dime to buy her a vanilla ice. He had even promised she could have ice cream every day after they were married.

The Saturday night ritual of preparing moonshine had taken on a new excitement for Jolan since Steve had been helping. He not only proved adept at blending but showed himself an expert in many other matters. He had impressed her stepfather by signing up a dozen new customers for the liquor. Jolan's mother was pleased with the magazines Steve regularly brought her. He avidly read newspapers and periodicals and listened to the radio. To Jolan he seemed to be "a living encyclopedia."

Tonight, prompted by a headline that Detroit auto shares had reached a new peak on Wall Street, Steve was giving Jolan her first lesson in economics. He asked if she knew what the stock market was. She wondered if it was a place where cattle were sold. Steve's explanation was one a New York Stock Exchange guide could hardly have bettered.

Jolan, interested, asked more questions. Why, if the market was "that good," had not her father invested her money in shares instead of in the Union Industrial Bank.

Steve explained that, in "all probability" the bank had reinvested her money in the market: "All banks do that. It's another way they make money."

Jolan was worried about her money "getting lost." Again Steve reassured her, explaining that banks never invested "in anything but the best stock. And because it's a bank, you can always be sure that your money is safe."

Steve's grasp of economics did not take into account the behavior of the "league of gentlemen," still busily embezzling at the Union Industrial Bank.

On Friday, June 21, Grant Brown received news that Charles Stewart Mott was leaving for a "delayed honeymoon" in Europe. The bank president took that as a good omen; he informed his staff the reason for the board chairman's absence and hoped they would "pass the word," that, contrary to rumor, the Motts were happily married.

Undoubtedly Grant Brown would have been surprised to learn Mrs. Mott was taking her attorney along on the trip.

Brown himself was off to a bankers' conference in San Francisco. He hoped for a chance there to meet A. P. Giannini, a man he admired, to discuss "matters of mutual interest."

Like any other banker, Grant Brown was concerned by the increasing number of cases of trusted bank staff embezzling. Only recently he had told the local Elks Club how proud he was that, in his long association with Flint banking, there had never been a case of serious theft among the staffs of the city's banks. It was a record, he insisted, few other cities in the country could match.

Frank Montague welcomed the news that the two men most likely to discover the discrepancies in the Union Industrial—Mott and Grant Brown—would be absent from Michigan for some time.

The strain was beginning to show on the vice-president. Montague was eating and sleeping badly, had lost weight and developed an uncomfortable nervous eczema. Several times recently his wife, Louise, had asked what was worrying him.

Once, when he had returned home after a particularly hard day for the syndicate, he had been tempted to confess to Louise. At the last moment something stopped him. Montague knew she would have urged him to go to the police and admit his complicity. While Louise would be sympathetic, her husband doubted whether the police would take such a lenient view. The prospect of even a night in the cells was more than he could bear. He remained silent.

In their many years of happy marriage there had never before been a secret between them. But, he told himself, he was doing what was best for her, showing husbandly concern that she should not be further burdened. Louise had her hands full with the children and a household budget that never seemed to balance.

It was to alleviate that situation that Montague remained in the syndicate. He would insist later he was "acting from the highest motives, the welfare of my family." He saw nothing criminal in his behavior.

Now, as if to support this view, for the first time in many months the consortium of crooks was making money.

In early June they had recovered most of what they had lost when they bought too late into Radio in March. One successful investment had followed another; recycled call money was placed in air and auto stocks which, in a matter of days, made the embezzlers almost $200,000 profit. On Wednesday, June 19, acting on a "hot tip," Milton Pollock had invested in food company shares. Next day came the news that J. P. Morgan and Company were backing a forthcoming merger of a number of brand leaders in the food industry. The shares Pollock invested in jumped thirty points.

Every morning when he led his family in prayer, the deeply religious vice-president privately asked God to intercede and "give the money" he so badly needed to pay medical bills for his sick wife, Elizabeth, and to meet the needs of his growing family. Every evening, as he walked back home after a long day at the bank, Pollock offered up another prayer for heavenly help.

He was convinced that the change of fortune—the latest being the jump in food stocks—was directly attributable to the praying he had done. In his mind, he was not a thief but the victim of "a situation which was easy to get into and hard to escape from."

Pollock realized he had been weak to become involved in the first place, but he constantly vowed he would repay all the money he had "borrowed." A thief, in his view, would never do that.

The success they were at last having was especially welcomed by Elton Graham, the bank's senior cashier. Once more he hoped he, too, would soon be able to disentangle himself from "the unholy mess" he was in.

Now, late this Friday morning, that possibility came closer still.

At eleven o'clock Senior Vice-president John de Camp placed a substantial amount of money with a Flint broker for investment in wheat. The broker thought the money was being placed for a client of the bank. De Camp did not disabuse him.

Unlike Montague and others of the conspirators who showed increasing signs of frayed nerves, De Camp had remained his churchy, rock-solid self, with a soft smile for favored customers and a sharp word for members of the staff who were lax in any way. These past months of almost continuous embezzlement had, outwardly at least, left De Camp totally unaffected.

Others, among them Ivan Christensen, did not bother to conceal their excitement.

For Christensen, the bank's assistant cashier, this further turn in fortune came at a most opportune time. The building of his spacious mansion was demanding more money; his cut from the wheat profits would help ensure that construction deadlines were met.

In one way or another every one of the fifteen men involved in what was already one of the longest-running swindles in banking history had profited from this spate of successes. Some, like the tellers, made comparatively small profits of a few hundred dollars on each deal; the more senior officers picked up thousands.

More important for all of them, they had succeeded in reducing by half the $2.5 million of purloined money outstanding at the end of May.

They still had a lot of leeway to make up. But recouping just over a million dollars was not an insurmountable task in a rapidly rising market. The newspapers regularly reported such feats.

Even cautious Frank Montague conceded that within "a week, a month, three at the most," they would all be "in the clear." For once he could agree with the ebullient Christensen that "the tide was turning."

In London, on the morning of Sunday, June 23, Clarence Hatry included a similar feeling of optimism in his many calculations. He and his staff had worked hard to overcome the disastrous blow that Lord Bearsted delivered when he refused to loan the £4 million Hatry hoped would ensure he became Britain's first steel baron.

Edmund Daniels, the personable young managing director of Austin Friars Trust, Hatry's issuing house which had circulated the offer for United Steel's stock, confirmed Hatry's own instinct that "I had to fight on, even if it seemed a hopeless cause."

As so often in the past, Hatry was impressed by the calculated risk in the plan Daniels proposed.

Shortly after he returned from the fateful meeting with Bearsted, Daniels had told him: "We're not beaten yet. By the law of averages, not all the shareholders will sell up their shares in the first few days. Some of them will be on holiday, or abroad, on business perhaps. Some just won't answer letters unless they're reminded. From my experience I reckon it will take at least a month, even two, to get all the replies in. A month or so—there's our chance."

It was advice like that which had taken Daniels to the top of the Hatry pyramid. Looking and dressing like an ad man's idea of a city gentleman, Daniels had joined Hatry's organization as a clerk in 1920. The first time Hatry became aware of him was when he spotted his signature on an office memorandum. Hatry was appalled by the scrawl and ordered Daniels be instantly dismissed. Then, because the order was so clearly unfair, he relented.

Hatry soon discovered that, in spite of his poor handwriting, Daniels was charming and dedicated, spending his little free time as scoutmaster to a local troop near his home in Surrey.

Unknown to his boss, Daniels used his charm to winkle secrets from Hatry's secretaries. In a short time he had learned a great deal about his employer—and used the information to his own advantage. He patronized Hatry's tailor, copied his mannerisms, spoke and even tried to think like the financier. In almost every way, Edmund Daniels became a carbon copy of Hatry. It was virtually inevitable that Hatry, always susceptible to such hero worship, should make Daniels his personal assistant, and later managing director of the most important of his many companies.

It was Daniels who brought John Gialdini into the organization. He, too, was handsome and amusing, with the quick, agile mind that was a prerequisite for admission into Hatry's inner circle.

Gialdini, who was Daniel's assistant, had endorsed the view there was still time to raise the money to buy the United Steel shares.

And now, Hatry admitted what had started as "a ray of hope" was a distinct possibility. He doubted whether anybody else could have overcome the obstacles he had faced these past three weeks. With his usual sense of melodrama, he detailed them.

"Everyone was sitting tight on his money, reluctant to let it out until the Socialist programme was known. Furthermore, an old adversary of mine, Montagu Norman, Governor of the Bank of England, was privately exerting his very considerable influence against my plan. To him I was, perhaps rightly, a dangerous upstart, an interloper in the well-regulated affairs of the City of London. Now was the chance to teach me a crushing and merited lesson. Days flickered into nights and back into days as I and my associates worked the clock round in our efforts. There were conferences, interviews with syndicates and banks, correspondence and telephone calls in a never-ending stream. And all the time, despite the intense strain, we had to keep up a bold front. The City is a delicate sounding-board and the slightest whisper reverberates into a booming roar. If once a rumour had spread that we were overextended in resources, we would be finished. So, in spite of being at my desk before eight in the morning, having a sandwich sent in instead of breaking for lunch, and working on into the night until the columns of figures danced before my aching eyes, I still had to put in appearances at social functions, laugh and joke and appear unconcerned although every nerve in me was shrieking for rest. Gradually the money was coming in and just keeping ahead of the replies to the circulars. As the shares were brought in, we sometimes managed to use them as security for borrowing money with which to pay for more incoming shares. But the process was like lifting oneself off the ground by pulling one's bootlaces."

Even tonight, when the rest of London was relaxing, Hatry had scheduled yet another meeting, at his home in Stanhope Gate.

The moment Daniels arrived, Hatry sensed trouble. His senior executive was "brooding and depressed."

Worse was to follow.

Two more aides and then Gialdini arrived. The Italian, "always emotional appeared at his wits end."

The men sat around the table and compared notes.*

They had managed to arrange for nearly 90 percent of the money they would soon need to purchase all the United Steel shares.

But, as Hatry would recall, "that last fateful fraction, £900,000, was missing. And we had exhausted our resources."

He tried to put on a bold front, "to look cool and collected. But it was a poor masquerade."

Then, according to Hatry's account, a new element intervened.

"Gialdini broke under the strain. He sprang up and began to rave, swearing that he would blow his brains out. Somehow we quietened him. And then Daniels spoke. He had an idea. He explained it rapidly, the words tumbling out. My brain, muzzy with fatigue and confused with Gialdini's emotional outburst, grasped that it meant borrowing money on the security of the Corporation Loans [involving another Hatry company] and repaying it inside a few days. I shook my head. 'I don't like it,' I said. Then Gialdini broke down again. He made for the door. He had a pistol at his flat. He was off to shoot himself. He shouted that I would be his moral murderer. The tears were streaming down his face. 'You must agree,' he pleaded, 'you must agree. It's our only chance.' Daniels joined his urging. I was becoming overwrought myself. I turned to the silent Dixon [another aide]. He nodded. 'They're right, Clarence,' he murmured. 'There's no other way.' And so, reluctantly and against my better judgment, I agreed to Daniels' plan."

Whether Hatry was yet aware of it or not, what he had agreed to would involve him in a gigantic criminal fraud, one that would soon seriously shake the sensitive international world of high finance.

* See Source Notes.

CHAPTER FOURTEEN

GATHERING CLOUDS

For the hard-pressed staff of the Plaza Hotel, Saturday, June 29, was like the "good old days"; everybody in New York who mattered seemed to be passing through the hotel's magnificent entrance on Fifth Avenue across from Central Park. For years there had been intense rivalry between the Plaza and the Waldorf-Astoria. But now that the Waldorf had finally closed its doors on May 3 and was waiting for the wrecking crews to move in, the Plaza was the undisputed flagship in a city of fine hotels.

The oak dining room where Elisha Walker had taken the Gianninis to dinner was booked solid. The hotel's suites were all occupied. There was not a vacant bedroom in the house on this weekend before Independence Day.

Since early morning a steady flow of departing guests had kept the bellboys busy; by midmorning the process was being reversed as the first arrivals checked in.

Many of them were out-of-towners, real-life Babbitts dressing and behaving like characters out of Sinclair Lewis' best seller. They were in town for the weekend with wives and mistresses. The hotel staff welcomed them warmly, not least because many guests openly announced they were celebrating spectacular wins on the stock market.

Bellhop Eddie Mullighan would long remember the fat man who arrived with a beautiful blonde on his arm and said he'd just made "a half million on a rail deal and wanted the best suite in the house." The bellboy received a twenty-dollar tip for showing the couple to their rooms.

At 9:30 A.M. waiter Norman Shiegle received his first order for champagne and realized it was going to be "a helluva day." In a Prohibition city, Shiegle, like many of the other hotel waiters, would, for a price, conjure up vintage French bubbly; crates of it were stored in a basement cellar, its door locked and disguised from the eyes of prying federal agents.

Shortly before ten o'clock, an assistant manager greeted his "regulars"—a group of fashionably dressed women traipsing across the luxurious lobby in a cloud of exotic perfumes and Turkish cigarette smoke. He let them into the suite specially reserved for women who wished to invest in the market. Nowadays, nearly all the leading hotels had suites set aside for this purpose.

This morning the women had something fresh to talk about, the reports that Western Union was going to install new high-speed stock tickers throughout the country. They were urgently needed to cope with the huge increase in volume of shares traded. Two years' research and more than $2 million dollars had so far been put into the project, jointly sponsored by Western Union, the New York Stock Exchange, and the Teletype Corporation of Chicago. The new tickers would operate at twice the speed of the present ones. It was going to cost, all told, over $4.5 million to link up 350 American and Canadian cities to the system.

Customers' rooms in New York, like this ladies' club, would be among the first to have the equipment installed.

The women welcomed that news, but had reservations about the symbols that would be introduced with the system; there was bound to be confusion, at least initially. American Telephone and Telegraph, listed for thirty years as ATT, would become simply T—the letter now used to denote Texas and Pacific Railroad. Standard Brands, a new listing would, under the revised code, be known as SB—presently used by Seaboard Airlines. Fox Films, whose stock was flashing across the tape this morning as FOX, would be reduced to the letter F, a symbol that Fleischmann Foods had used for many years.

The lady speculators in the room—like investors everywhere—would have to learn a completely new language.

For many of these Saturday morning market players, the trip to the Plaza was worthwhile. By noon, when the Exchange closed for the weekend, a number of the women were celebrating their wins with splits of champagne. Soon they were tipsily testing each other on the proposed changes in symbols.

The new code would have no effect on the market predictions of Evangeline Adams. In the past month another 25,000 subscribers had signed up for the astrologer's newsletter, eager to know what effect a rising Taurus had on Transamerica's fortunes, or whether being born on the cusp was a signal "to get into rails."

Evangeline's fame rocketed in May when she predicted that month's market breaks with uncanny accuracy. The tabloids hailed her as "the wonder of Wall Street" and "the stock market's seer."

Now, escorted by admiring young men who surrounded her like acolytes attending a high priestess, the square-jawed Miss Adams, in one of her famous black suits, strode boldly across the lobby to a reserved table in the dining room. A waiter who cheekily asked her for a market tip was firmly crushed. "You do not work for nothing. Why expect me to?"

Shortly afterward, the maître d' led the corpulent figure of banker Charles Mitchell and the skinny-framed Billy Durant to a table far removed from the flow of traffic and the orchestra.

The two men had met several times since Durant's still-secret visit to the White House and his subsequent, well-publicized networked broadcast attacking the Federal Reserve.

Their entrance had not gone unnoticed. Even here, in the main dining room of the Plaza, long used to entertaining Wall Street giants, the presence of two of the most powerful men in the market drew inquisitive eyes to their secluded table.

Mitchell basked in the limelight; he also regarded as a practical example of his salesmanship the fact he persuaded his taciturn, introverted guest to sit down for a meal in the sort of place Durant normally gave a wide berth.

Even so, Durant stuck fastidiously to his standard fare for those rare occasions when he was forced to eat away from his hermetically sealed smoke-free office: mineral water and salad.

Mitchell, a renowned trencherman, ordered his usual substantial meal.

The banker said he had suggested lunch in order to discuss the Federal Reserve Board and to see whether there was any common ground between them with regard to what the federal authorities in Washington should do. Though both men were strongly critical of the board's continuing inaction, during the meal they could not agree on what needed to be done. Mitchell still thought the rediscount rate should be raised in New York; Durant believed it was already too high. They did agree, however, that unless the Reserve Board provided strong leadership of one sort or another very soon, Wall Street would continue to drift onward dangerously out of control.

Durant was not surprised that he and Mitchell had held to their positions. He sensed there was something else on his host's mind. He wondered how long it would be before Mitchell raised the real reason for their meeting.

The Plaza's dining room was almost full. The activity and sound increased as waiters moved from kitchen to tables at a faster tempo and the orchestra tried hard to be heard above the clamor of conversation and the clink of cutlery and china.

Into this busy scene came John J. Raskob and party. Between them, Raskob, the Du Pont brothers, former presidential candidate Alfred E. Smith, and James Riordan represented several fortunes; they were lunching together to hear Raskob's plans of how he intended to make another.

The financier was in expansive mood. The press had been enthusiastic about his Equities Security Company, the corporation he proposed to launch to buy stocks for "proletarians who could invest $200 a head."

Raskob was being widely hailed as another financial visionary, in the mold of Giannini.

Riordan promised he would recommend the scheme to customers of his bank. The Du Ponts and Smith felt there should be a national campaign to attract the thousands of "proletarians" needed.

Raskob said he hoped to launch his investment trust in the fall; he was concerned about the present high cost of shares and thought it best to wait until "the stock market has got back to normal."

He was also worried about unemployment. For weeks now, the unemployment figures across the nation had been creeping upward. In spite of a booming market, production lines were slowing down, the public were beginning to resist salesmanship and the temptation to buy on credit. A few people were starting to say that maybe Alexander Noyes of the New York *Times* was right—that the market could suddenly collapse.

It was this possibility that lay behind the reason Charles Mitchell had invited Billy Durant for lunch. He liked and trusted the promoter. Even so, what he had to discuss was delicate. He came to the point carefully.

As Durant well knew, the pool in Anaconda Copper, conceived by Meehan and masterminded by Bragg and Smith, had now been disbanded. It had been a financial disaster for all its participants; Bragg himself, who gambled $500,000 on his own ability to make the pool pay, had lost $400,000. Durant had lost nearly as much. And so had Percy Rockefeller, the Fisher brothers, and John J. Raskob, whom Mitchell could see holding court at a table on the other side of the room.

Some 300,000 Anaconda shares had originally been bought by Bragg for Mitchell's National City Bank, and sold by the enthusiastic salesmen of its handy subsidiary, the National City Company, to thousands of small-time investors. Most of the shares had been bought for the bank near their high of 174 and been sold to the public at a loss for much less. They were still dropping in value, and were now around 120.

Mitchell told Durant he had yet to unload many thousand Anaconda Copper shares. He could do that easily. The question was one of timing. His field salesmen reported there was still a healthy demand for the stock, but Mitchell had noted a worrying tightening of purse strings in rural America. He did not know whether this was only a temporary slowing down or the precursor of something more serious. He wanted Durant's advice.

Durant had no doubt. It was temporary. The boom would go on. In his opinion, what was needed was for "ten or twenty of the leaders in the market" to maintain well-publicized bullish positions, and the nation would continue to buy. There was no reason for the bull market to end.

His advice to Mitchell was to wait. In the coming weeks, copper could well bottom out and begin to rise. Speculators would then remember the days when the stock soared to 174. It would not need much persuasion from Mitchell's salesmen to suggest that could happen to Anaconda again.

Mitchell was relieved. What he had kept from Durant was the fact that Tom Bragg, the audacious market manipulator, had recently telephoned him from his office at W. E. Hutton and Company. It was an astonishing call. Bragg had said to Mitchell: "Congratulations. You have just bought the Anaconda Copper Company. The stock is on its way over to you now."

Before Mitchell could refuse, the certificates for over 1 million shares had been delivered to his bank. It was the end of the great pool in Anaconda Copper, but so far as Mitchell was concerned it was for him only a beginning.

On this stifling hot Monday, July 1, Homer Dowdy was certain that thunderstorms would sweep across Michigan before nightfall. The postman was also sure of something else. Judging from the large numbers of identical buff-colored envelopes in his mail pouch, it seemed that "a lot of Flint folk were winning in the market." The envelopes contained checks from brokerage firms.

Even the cautious old man who ran a corner store on Dowdy's mail round was speculating. He gleefully displayed to Dowdy the check in his envelope. He had, he boasted, made more from a single investment in General Motors than he could expect from a month's hard work in the store.

Dowdy trudged on, concealing behind his smile the knowledge that Gladys was getting worse every day. The doctor had now told him his wife had about six months to live.

Her husband was coming to terms with her impending death; he was forming his own rules for coping with the situation when it came. He had banished self-pity and recrimination of any kind. He blamed nobody. Instead he drew great comfort from the help and support he received from his neighbors, his church, and his three small children. Homer Dowdy believed that more than anything his wife's incurable illness had brought them closer together as a family.

Gladys never once complained, but bore her pain stoically. And the children scrimped and saved whatever they could to buy that little "extra something" for their mother.

He still had not told them how ill she was, but he had started to prepare them for her death. Recently, he had informed the girls that "Jesus is probably going to call Mommy one day."

The children said nothing and asked no questions. But that night he overheard them telling their little brother that "sometimes Jesus takes those he loves most from us."

Walking from one mail drop to another, Homer Dowdy doubted there was any family in Flint who could better cope with the situation.

Having totally accepted the inevitable, he had started to look beyond Gladys' death. He would need some of the money deposited in the Union Industrial Bank to employ a housekeeper. The balance he would divide between his three children, opening for each of them an account at the bank. They might find the money useful in the future for their education.

Even now, hours later, staring down at the body of her small brother, seven-year-old Frank, Jolan could not accept his death.

The strangely doll-like figure lying in the cheap, plain-deal coffin was not the brother she remembered—tough and robust, full of fun, generous to his last piece of candy. This waxen-faced stranger, hidden beneath embalming cosmetics, was not *her* Frank, but a replica of one of those statues at the church, unreal, a travesty of life.

She moved back from the coffin, resting on two trestles. In the terrible silence, she could clearly hear the gurgling from the basement. Slowly, with that familiar sound of distilling liquid, the sequence of events that had brought her here came into focus.

Jolan had been at her new job, working as a maid in Mrs. Baum's house, when Mr. Goldberger arrived. Her reaction at his arrival was one of panic; Jolan thought he had come to tell her she was not, after all, suitable to be Mrs. Baum's domestic at three dollars a week. But instead, Mrs. Baum had rushed up to her, thrown her arms around Jolan, and said she "must be brave."

Confused, and not a little frightened, Jolan was escorted by Mr. Goldberger from Mrs. Baum's house.

In the car he told her. Frank had been killed instantly by a truck.

By the time they reached home, Frank's coffin was already in the living room and Jolan's mother had hung a big black wreath on the front door, signifying there was a death in the house.

Mr. Goldberger had left her alone with the body. Now he returned with the rest of the family to join them in the opening ritual of a Hungarian wake. First, the young children filed past the coffin. When they had left the room, neighbors took their place, joining Jolan, her two elder brothers, and her mother and stepfather in a vigil; soon there was hardly an inch of spare space around the bier.

One by one, and then in haunting harmony, the mourners started to keen, chanting hymns and prayers for the dead. As they sang, a bottle of home-brewed whiskey was passed reverently from mouth to mouth. Soon a second bottle was called for.

The mood of stifling oppressiveness lifted as the mourners began to relax. Tears came, loud, unceasing sobbing punctuating the keening.

Suddenly, Jolan sensed Steve by her side, whispering. She could not hear him above the singing and crying. He tugged at her arm. She followed him out of the house.

Steve said they must get a wreath for Frank's coffin.

"But how? Mrs. Baum hasn't paid me—"

"The bank! We'll go there!"

Jolan nodded. Together, holding hands, they ran through the streets to the Union Industrial Bank.

When they arrived, it was closed. They pounded on the doors. It made no difference. No one came.

Exhausted by their run, emotionally drained, the young couple walked back to the house.

Two days later, they stood together as Frank's coffin was lowered into the ground of Grace Lawn Cemetery in Flint.

It did not seem to matter then that they had still not got him a wreath.

Leaning over the deck rail, Edith Stone watched the bunch of carnations bobbing in the *Berengaria*'s wake and wondered why people always threw flowers after a departing ship. Behind her, as the gap be-

‚tween shore and liner widened, a fusillade of champagne corks popped in all parts of the Promenade Deck as passengers celebrated freedom from Prohibition.

A young man, handsome in homburg and slung binoculars, looking like a character from one of the Sunday rotogravures, thrust a glass into her hand. Edith turned back to the shore and toasted the policemen on Pier 54 whose job it was to enforce the Volstead Act while the *Berengaria* was in port. They waved friendly farewells.

Edith continued to watch as the ship's four huge screws bit into the murky water of the Hudson River, driving her gleaming black hull with gently increasing speed toward the Statue of Liberty. Far above, smoke poured from her three crimson stacks, black trails in a cloudless sky whose sun was already warming the creamy-white superstructure and glinting from every porthole and window of the ship which had been chosen by Mike Meehan to carry the world's first floating brokerage office. A few yards from where Edith sipped her champagne, the ship's radio staff prepared for the first of a series of test transmissions designed to establish whether stock quotations could be transmitted to and from sea within the rules laid down by the New York Stock Exchange; the tests would continue for the next four transatlantic crossings.

The liner, with her more than seven hundred passengers, slipped smoothly by the concrete canyons of Manhattan, passed between the Narrows separating Staten Island from Brooklyn, and in a surprisingly short time was cutting through the cold, glass-green Atlantic, bound for Europe. The ship's next landfall would be Cherbourg Light in almost six days' time.

From Cherbourg Edith would travel by train to Paris and then spend the next two months "doing the Continent."

Her schedule was not entirely frivolous; as well as going to art galleries and cathedrals, this time she intended to visit the stock exchanges of Paris and Berlin in order to absorb local color for her proposed stage play.

As the great liner settled down for the crossing, Edith went to her suite on D Deck. The latest European newspapers available in New York had been delivered. She saw that the Paris newspapers were speculating on whether President Raymond Poincaré's continuing ill health would shortly force him to resign and hand over to a younger man, probably Aristide Briand.

Poincaré could give up the burden of office secure in the knowledge that France was in almost perfect financial shape. Nineteen twenty-eight's exports had exceeded imports by 1 billion francs; unemployment amounted to a trifling 13,000 in a work force of 20 million. The newspapers reported that business and banking were optimistic the 1929/30 budget of 64.2 billion francs would not be fully needed. France's largest bank, the Banque de Paris et des Pays Bas, was paying a 20 percent dividend and had just increased its capital from 200 million francs to 300 million.

Yet Edith remembered her father bitterly criticizing what he regarded as France's "outrageously deflationist and selfish economic policy." The French, he had told her, were playing a "dangerous game," one "so subtle and devious" that Edith could never hope to encompass it in her stage play. Edward Stone believed that France's gold-hoarding policy was going to wreck Europe's plans for rebuilding after the Great War. In his opinion Germany, Austria, and Italy were now economically defenseless.

Turning to the German press, Edith saw once again Hitler was railing against Poincaré's insistence that Germany pay its war debts in full, on time, down to the last Reichsmark. In rejecting this, it seemed to Edith that Hitler was stirring German xenophobia in the same way Poincaré's outbursts aroused French opinion.

She could readily accept her father's view that "Europe may be heading for trouble." But she firmly believed he was wrong on one issue. The "financial horn-locking" between France and Germany had the ingredients of high drama and could be woven into her plot. She clipped the papers and placed the cuttings in her file of press reports.

While her cabin maid unpacked her trunk, Edith sipped more champagne, a farewell gift from her father, and received her first shipboard mail. A steward brought her an embossed invitation to cocktails with the captain, Sir Arthur Henry Rostron, K.B.E., R.N.R., and commodore of the Cunard Fleet. Rostron had been master of the Cunard liner *Carpathia* the night she heard the *Titanic*'s S.O.S., in April 1912. He had arrived at the scene first and rescued more than seven hundred passengers. Her father had told Edith that short of meeting a member of the royal family, the next greatest honor would be meeting Captain Rostron.

There were also invitations to several private parties in adjoining suites. Edith scribbled acceptances for her steward to deliver. It looked like it was going to be a memorable voyage.

Henry Ford was telling the press about his latest trip. Reporters were in his office to hear his impressions of a car journey he had recently completed with his long-suffering chauffeur, Burns. They had traveled in a single long day from New Jersey to Detroit.

It was an event Ford decided worthy enough to mark with yet another press conference.

His obsession with publicity had reached new proportions since his tribute to the Jews in New York on May 24; a highly sentimental statement about a race he had bitterly maligned for years received national coverage. More headlines quickly followed, the result of a luncheon with President Hoover at the White House and Ford's latest comment on the stock market: "I don't know a thing about it. I never looked at a stock quotation in my life." The admission did not noticeably restrain him from continued criticism of Wall Street.

Throughout June, Ford's name had appeared in a variety of bold typefaces as, in quick succession, he announced the planning of a plant in Portugal, that he would continue to fight for his "rights" in Brazil, that he was opening a factory in Russia.

Anything was grist to a grateful press mill. When he attacked the medical profession for its "curtain of secrecy," it made the front pages; when he trundled out his views on cows, he got generous space. An attack on horses and pigs—"parasites"—put him on the front pages again. If he had a cough, the media printed his remedy; if he bought a new necktie, the store was described; any angle that could drag in Ford, or his name, was guaranteed space.

He had also managed to convey to millions of readers that, in spite of his eccentricity, the Ford Motor Company was still one of the world's most powerful corporations. It was now producing 8,000 cars a day, had a surplus fund of $582 million and a cash balance of $275 million.

Money, as Henry Ford liked to say, "talks." It was the power his money represented that brought the reporters into his office this Saturday, July 6.

He told them that, on his car journey with Burns, they had seen "many new houses. With new paint on them. Paint is a good sign of prosperity. For both the people and the paint concerns."

And so, for the next hour, in his familiar, disjointed delivery, Ford rambled on. Flowers were "evidence of a good state of mind among our people"; highways—"there is more history on our roads than there is in our books"; people should "write our history in highways."

From anyone else it would have sounded inane. From Henry Ford it sounded profound.

Finally he turned to Burns. In his gray livery and highly polished boots, the chauffeur had sat motionless as a window display model during his master's recital. Ford employees knew Henry disliked fidgets; for a while the ubiquitous Harry Bennett had carried a cane to smartly rap those who could not keep still.

Today, as usual, Bennett was seated in a corner of the office keeping a watchful eye on the journalists. He had warned the photographers "all hell will break loose" if a recent incident was repeated when a flash bulb had showered Henry as he posed following one of his habitual announcements.

Ford nudged Burns. "Go on, tell them about that new Ford sedan we saw. The one with the mother and eight children. Negroes. A lad about sixteen at the wheel."

The chauffeur picked up the story, detailing how his employer had signaled the sedan to a stop. "I guess they thought somebody was going to read them a lecture about something they hadn't done. Mr. Ford said, 'How do you do? I just wanted to congratulate you on keeping your car looking so nice.' Well, their faces didn't quite look so long then. But when Mr. Ford told them his name, the mother asked, 'You Henry Ford, the automobile man of Detroit?' He told them he was the man who made the car they were driving. That was why he was interested in seeing it carrying a family of nine. And he shook hands with everyone in the car. Well, you should have seen their faces then— regular water-melon smile on every one."

The newsmen would write the incident up as another example of "Ford's human side."

But there was more in store. During the trip, Ford, as usual without a dime in his pockets, had borrowed two cents from a J. F. Quinlan to purchase a stamp.

In return Henry had given Mr. Quinlan a check for two cents to cover the amount. It did not take reporters long to work out that during the time required by Ford to write out his check—the first personal check he had signed in five years—his income had increased by $6.32, or 316 times the amount payable. The New York *Times* announced the computation was "based on reports that Mr Ford had $1,000,000,000, which at 5% would yield him an income of $136,986 a day, $5,707 an hour, $95 a minute and $1.58 a second."

The *Times* estimated it had taken Ford four seconds to write out the check.

Ford and the reporters parted happily. Both sides had what they wanted—another clutch of headlines.

For probably only the second time in his life, A. P. Giannini was furious with the press. Claire knew there was no point in trying to pacify her father. It was far better he was allowed to "blow himself out like a tropical storm."

She sat calmly as Giannini pounded the piano in the Ritz Hotel suite. It would hardly have surprised her if the keyboard had collapsed under his attack.

Still smoldering, Giannini left the piano and began to pace the hotel room, cursing the latest newspaper stories.

Twice in the past month the press had published a "heap of garbage" about his intentions. On June 19 the usually reliable San Francisco *Examiner* ran a totally fictitious story stating Giannini intended to invest in a $100 million deal with the Fox Film Company and Western Electric to run "talkie" theaters. As a result he had been inundated with calls from Hollywood offering all sorts of wild schemes. He had patiently explained to producers and studio heads that, for the moment, he had no further plans to invest in the motion-picture industry. His courteous denials fed further stories. Finally, Giannini erupted, grabbed the nearest telephone, and roared at the Associated Press to kill the rumor.

Now, San Francisco's other main newspaper, the *Chronicle,* had run a story reporting he had "abandoned his European trip" in order to handle "further acquisition of banks, possible split-ups of stock, etc.," and also due to the "fact that Elisha Walker could not accompany him."

The trip to Europe had never been certain. The talk of buying more banks and the split-up of stock was an old newspaper standby which Giannini had not expected to see in the *Chronicle.*

These references, he knew, would cause further speculation. Like Henry Ford, Giannini "had only to cough for some newspaper to report he had pneumonia."

What made the banker mad was the reference to Walker.

At face value, the mention was innocent enough and would probably go unremarked by most readers. But to those on the inside, the long-serving executives who helped Giannini run Transamerica and his other corporations, the report would be read differently.

Giannini, always highly attuned to atmosphere, had picked up whispers that Walker was creating friction within Transamerica. More than one Italian old-timer had come to share Claire's view that her father's new aide was a "cold fish." Giannini was keeping a discreet, watchful eye on developments. For him to interfere now could create more problems than the action might resolve. At Blair, Walker had been used to being autocractic; perhaps he just needed to settle into the teamlike atmosphere that Giannini encouraged. The situation was delicate—and not helped at all by a newspaper report that Giannini would not go to Europe without Walker. Giannini thought that in the ultrasensitive atmosphere of Transamerica's offices in San Francisco the story would be interpreted as a further sign of what Claire openly called "the danger of Wasp domination."

Her father respected her views; in the past year she had shown herself, time and again, to possess a formidable business brain And yet, when she made pronouncements like this, Giannini's twenty-four-year-old daughter reminded him only of his "little girl." He had reassured her he could handle any threat—WASP or otherwise.

Meantime Giannini continued publicly to emphasize the skilled role Walker was playing in expanding Transamerica. Privately, he was beginning to wonder whether, in the end, his aide's reported failings could outweigh his undoubted professional skills.

In this second week of July, Giannini decided he would let matters ride for another three months. Then, if there was no improvement, he would take whatever steps were needed. He made a note in his diary to review matters in the last week of October.

Jesse Livermore rarely lost his temper—and until now, Tuesday, July 16, nobody could remember him ever having done so over a newspaper report.

But the New York *Times* story sent him raging out of his apartment, leaving Dorothy behind in tears. Her husband stormed into his office complex, scattering staff waiting to brief him on the latest market trends. Livermore sent for his attorneys.

They assured him there was nothing to be done about the *Times* report. It had stated that the "Wall Street speculator was directed by Supreme Court Justice Walsh to testify before trial against him for $525,000 for alleged breach of an agreement."

Outraged by what he regarded as little more than blatant extortion, Livermore had previously refused to appear in court to answer allegations made by the Carbonite Corporation of America. Despite its impressive name, the company was a dubious concern whose stocks, it was said, Livermore had promised to peddle on an unsuspecting public. The company lodged suit alleging Livermore had reneged on his agreement.

This accusation was the latest in a stream of writs served upon Livermore. Each time, rather than face further costly, time-consuming litigation, he settled out of court. The most spectacular settlement concerned what the press had called the "Boca Raton Crash" of 1926. Ninety-three survivors from that Florida land-investment deal had just sued Livermore and his associates, who included the Du Pont brothers, for $1.45 million. The plaintiffs, led by Maximilian Morgenthau, son of a former U.S. ambassador to Turkey, lodged the longest complaint so far filed in an American court. Morgenthau's complaint alone ran to 870 pages.

That action had been settled; part of the settlement included a proviso that the plaintiffs would not reveal details to the press.

Now, after he calmed down, his attorneys advised Livermore that the safest way to avoid further unwelcome publicity over the latest case was to seek a similar out-of-court settlement with the Carbonite Corporation.

After all, said one of his lawyers, Livermore would then be free to recoup the costs of that settlement from just a few hours' work in the market.

For the first time in hours Livermore smiled.

The loyal staff he had earlier brushed aside in his fury were called into his office. He listened carefully as, one by one, they made their reports.

His specialist on foreign currency movements reported that approximately $10 million worth of gold from Great Britain had been received by this mid-July, making a total for the year so far of $48 million. More serious for Britain was the shipment of $41 million to Paris and $36 million to Berlin. The Bank of England's gold holding had now decreased to over $30 million below the minimum recommended figure. If the pattern continued, Livermore knew the likelihood was that interest rates in Britain would soon have to be raised. In that case, money earmarked for Wall Street could well be diverted to London.

Another cause for concern was the result of the huge demand by the public to acquire the new, small-size currency introduced on July 10. All denominations of dollar bills were reduced in size by one-third and printed on paper "with a higher folding endurance." People were assured that, although their money was now smaller in size, even $10,000 bills were worth the same as before.

It seemed to Livermore ironic that, just when most Americans were making more money than ever, the government had decided to print money smaller.

The curiosity demand for the currency right across the country would cause, as Livermore knew, a large withdrawal of funds from New York by out-of-town banks. That, too, might lessen the flow of money for investment in the New York market.

He turned his attention to industrial production. The monthly output of steel, Livermore's specialist reported, continued close to the year's high figure, and would likely exceed by about 1 million tons the output for July 1928.

But, significantly, automobile production was down. And freight-car loadings were only marginally up on last month's figure. Here was a clear pointer that the home and export markets were starting to lose impetus.

Clicking his fingers, a trick of Livermore's when he was nervous, he listened as his other experts reported: house building contracts had fallen by almost a billion dollars since 1928; inventories had grown alarmingly from $500 million to $18,000 million. Most worrying of all, agriculture, which for many years had been the weak link in the flourishing American economy, was now being severely affected by the worldwide fall in commodity prices.

Livermore turned to the stock market itself. There, everything was still at it booming best. July looked like being a record month for new security issues on Wall Street and prices had already advanced during the month by an average of about 7 percent, despite the erratic behavior of money on call, which had fluctuated between 6 and 15 percent.

Wall Street was going on its giddy way. But Livermore realized the situation in America was not what most people thought. And in any case, the rest of the world was slipping steadily out of economic alignment. The further apart they grew, the greater the strain one imposed upon the other. And, in Livermore's inelegant phrase, "there's gotta be a snapping time sometime."

On this sunny mid-July day in New York, Jesse Livermore was probably one of the first men to interpret correctly the gathering clouds. Typically, he would keep his views to himself until after he had acted.

CHAPTER FIFTEEN

DIVORCE DETROIT STYLE

Charlton MacVeagh, hurrying as usual to be inside Number 23 Wall before the Morgan partners arrived, was one of the first to spot Joe Kennedy. The Irishman was standing in the shadow of Trinity Church as MacVeagh strode into the Street. Before turning the corner, he noticed that Kennedy looked fitter, leaner, deeply suntanned—and much more relaxed than the morning Charlton had witnessed his humiliation at the hands of Jack Morgan. These signs of a rejuvenated Kennedy confirmed the story Charlton had heard, that the Bostonian was nowadays leading a life of leisure. Charlton briefly wondered what had brought Kennedy back to his old stomping ground on such a glorious day as this Wednesday, July 17. The young broker put it down to nostalgia.

He could understand that. Already, as he repeatedly told Adele, "Wall Street is in my blood." She accepted without protest the extra hours her husband worked at the office, the papers he brought home, the time he spent most evenings poring over them. At breakfast Charlton talked excitedly to her about some huge deal he expected to be involved in that day. When they entertained, it was similarly dedicated young men who sat at their table with their wives. Adele was openly proud of the way his colleagues respected Charlton's views and judgments. Once, when they were guests at the Thomas Lamonts, another of the Morgan partners present murmured to Adele that Charlton could be destined to become the youngest partner in the firm. To prepare herself, Adele was trying hard to grasp the ramifications of high finance.

Glimpsing Joe Kennedy, her husband could be forgiven for feeling a twinge of sympathy at the sight of "one of the great figures of yesterday" having seemingly nothing to do while others went about their business.

Charlton's sympathies were misplaced. Joe Kennedy was not idling. He was working to a carefully predetermined plan.

He had prepared it soon after burying his father in May. Patrick Kennedy had died at the age of seventy-one. The list of pallbearers read like a roll call of Boston politicians. Aside from insurance, the elder Kennedy's estate amounted to a humble $55,000. It included a $25 bond issued in 1920 in Ireland. Acting as executor of his father's estate, Joe Kennedy had assigned the bond the realistic value of nothing.

Newly rich but still driven by an almost messianic desire for the power and position he believed only a truly vast fortune could achieve, Joe Kennedy was nowadays, as part of his plan to increase his wealth, monitoring the stock market with great care.

For weeks he had been able to read and evaluate the trends well away from the influence of those most actively involved. He had gradually come to the conclusion there was a danger that many of the people he could now see hurrying to work in Wall Street might in some degree be victims of their own propaganda, self-hypnotized spellbinders, unable any longer realistically to assess the market's probable future behavior.

He had come to the Street to regain at firsthand his own sense of "feel," and also to hear the views of some of the most intelligent "old pros." He would talk to them later; he had deliberately come early to give him time to wander through the Street and to savor its mood. Kennedy, like Thomas Lamont, had a strong belief in the "instinct of ordinary folk"—and what his own eyes and ears could pick up.

Moving briskly, he joined the crowds pouring from all sides into the financial district.

Michael Levine, the millionaire owner of the district's longest-established messenger service, recognized the tall, loping-striding Kennedy. Levine was not surprised to see the Irishman giving the House of Morgan a miss: "He'd been badly treated by that crowd and Joe Kennedy never forgot nothing."

Kennedy was also greatly disliked by his peers. Too often in the past they had been fooled by his charm before realizing behind his banter there was, in John J. Raskob's view, "a ruthless, razor-sharp mind."

Raskob was one of those who forgave Kennedy his dog-eat-dog tactics; he recognized the Irishman was a product of his background. Raskob once confided to banker James Riordan that "beneath all his smooth talk Joe is a pick-and-shovel Paddy." Riordan, himself fiercely proud of his Irish ancestry, smilingly told Raskob that if anybody else had said that about Kennedy he would have flattened him.

Today, the two men greeted Kennedy warmly when he joined them in the Wall Street office of an old friend of Raskob's, Arthur Cutten.

Raskob had arranged for them to meet there after Kennedy had asked to see him; he knew Kennedy wanted to talk about the market and he intended this meeting to provide him with any reassurance needed. Like Billy Durant, Raskob, too, thought now was the time for "all the big names to make their views known."

Few were bigger, or less known to the public, than Cutten. Shy and introspective, he had the dry, reedy voice of a college professor. Unlike his friend, Charles Mitchell, Cutten had rarely been photographed or interviewed; he had once told A. P. Giannini there was "no money in seeing your name in the paper."

Cutten was probably the country's most successful commodity speculator. Born in Guelph, Ontario, until the middle of 1924 he was totally unknown around the stock markets of America. Then, in July of that year, he quietly took $1.5 million out of the corn pit of Chicago. Six months later he reaped a further fabulous harvest from wheat, making "at least" $10 million. Nobody knew the exact figure—and Cutten wasn't telling, not even Richard Whitney, who had tried once to team up with him. Whitney's advances had been coldly rejected.

Late in 1925, a multimillionaire at fifty-five, Cutten came to Wall Street. He moved in on Radio, just as Mike Meehan was starting in the stock. Both men made fortunes from RCA—and established a friendly long-running rivalry.

Subsequently, Cutten plunged from one stock to another. Each time he made money and returned home to Chicago. His enemies said he was a modern Midas.

In 1928 he finally moved his business base to New York, running the entire operation from a modest office a few yards away from the Morgan fortress. Now the Canadian was reportedly within striking distance of Jack Morgan's $500 million personal fortune.

Cutten made all his money by being, one of his rivals said, "the most bullish in the bull market."

He preferred to style himself a "cash grain expert."

When in New York he put up at his nephew's apartment, went to bed early with a pile of stock investment guides, and enjoyed sniffing cigars, a habit he had caught from Billy Durant.

Like Jesse Livermore's, Cutten's office in Wall Street was a discreet hideaway. The men had one more thing in common—they hated each other. Theirs was one of the few real feuds Wall Street had known. Its origins were now obscure but probably stemmed from the time in Chicago when Livermore had sold wheat short and Cutten, away on vacation and unable to fight back, lost millions. Whether that was the reason or not, their mutual enmity remained as virulent as ever.

Exploiting the situation, Raskob told Cutten that Livermore was again being bearish, making people like Kennedy hesitant about investing.

That had been enough for the bespectacled, middle-aged Cutten to agree to this meeting.

It was a relaxed, informal affair, in which first Raskob, then Riordan, and finally Cutten reviewed events familiar enough to Joe Kennedy. And, he could concede, there was a great deal of truth in what they said. Yet, Kennedy felt the view from Wall Street was a narrow one; there was a real possibility the people working within its confines could be constricted in their thinking.

The more he probed, the more he perceived that, for all their financial expertise, Raskob, Riordan, and Cutten were not really aware—or perhaps did not care—there was a greater world beyond their immediate ken.

Finally, when he had exhausted his questions, Kennedy thanked them, and continued on his way.

The meeting troubled him. If men of this caliber staunchly believed there was no end to the boom in sight, he would be a fool to ignore them. Quite possibly they were right.

And, as he went from one brokerage house to another, questioning and listening with equal care, he heard only statements confirming what they had said. AT&T *had* gone up. U. S. Steel *was* still climbing. So *was* Consolidated Gas. Although wheat had fallen, *most* of the shares on the New York Exchange *had* moved up. There *were* record queues for the visitors' gallery. *More* brokers than ever before were actually on the floor. On July 13 the Curb Exchange *had* reached a new Saturday record—1,832,200 transactions. This morning, as call money dropped from 12 to 8 percent, stocks were showing another general increase.

From all sides, Joe Kennedy was assailed by optimism. Yet somehow that inner, nagging force, well concealed and trusted, which had taken him out of the market earlier in the year, urged him still to stay out.

Noon found him, as so often in the past, standing among the crowd listening to one of the preachers in his portable pulpit on the sidewalk.

The evangelist was attacking the new smaller-size currency, saying it was "evil," that it made the public "more money conscious."

Kennedy, a devout Catholic, was amused at the curbside prophet's claim that the Scriptures warned of dire perils for those who found

President Herbert Hoover. Could he have done more? Should he have intervened earlier? Will he always be remembered as the leader who, at the height of America's greatest financial disaster, pronounced that "the fundamental business of the country . . . is on a sound and prosperous basis"? *United Press International.*

John D. Rockefeller, Sr., attempted to help—and earned a bitter riposte from comedian Eddie Cantor. *United Press International.*

The public face of a private crook. Richard Whitney, president of the New York Stock Exchange. On the fateful day before the Crash he had forsaken his office for the racetrack. *International News Photo.*

The man who saved the bank—and kept a romance secret. Charles Stewart Mott, one of the magnificent millionaires whose fortune was linked to the Great Crash. *Courtesy Mott Foundation, Flint.*

Jesse L. Livermore, the great bear and womanizer of Wall Street. His financial prowess was only matched by his sexual escapades. Here he is with his third wife, Harriet, from whom he borrowed money to stay in the market. Livermore died the way he lived—sensationally. *United Press International.*

Mammon more attractive than God; on this basis everybody in Wall Street should have been struck dead long ago.

Wearied by the familiar rantings of the itinerant minister, Kennedy retraced his steps up Wall Street. When he reached Number 60, he stopped.

Shoeblack Pat Bologna was momentarily without a customer and reading *The Wall Street Journal.* Kennedy climbed into his wooden chair with its protruding footrests.

"How's the market, Pat?"

Bologna put aside his newspaper and picked up his brushes.

"Booming, Mr. K. Just booming."

"Yeah? You making much?"

"Sure, you wanna tip?"

Kennedy smiled and nodded.

"Buy oils and rails. They're gonna hit the sky. Had a guy here today with inside knowledge."

"Thank you, Pat."

Kennedy slipped the bootboy a quarter. That night, he told his wife, Rose, that a market everyone could play, and a shoeshine boy predict, was no market for Joe Kennedy.

This Friday, July 26, Edith Stone wrote later to her father, was "the sort of perfect day God reserves for Paris." The sun shone in a cloudless sky; a breeze blew gently off the Seine, beside which Parisians walked, sat in outdoor cafés, or sprawled lazily along the banks of the majestic river.

For a moment Edith was tempted to change her mind, to join the crowds by the Seine instead of going to la Bourse, the Paris Stock Exchange. But the French relations with whom she was staying had gone to considerable trouble to arrange the visit and it would be unthinkable for her to disappoint them now. Besides, this was her last day in France; tonight she was going by train to Germany.

So far the trip had exceeded Edith's expectations. On the *Berengaria,* she had sipped cocktails, and later dined with Captain Rostron. With his courtly manners and wisdom he reminded her of her own father. The voyage itself had been a succession of parties, each increasingly uninhibited. Paris had been equally gay, with an endless round of late lunches, elegant dinners, visits to the theater, and intimate suppers.

It was almost as an afterthought that Edith had told her French uncle of her aspiration to write a play about the stock market. He had seized enthusiastically on the subject and spoke knowledgeably about France stockpiling its gold, refusing to expand its industry, housing, schools, and hospitals. He was reflecting the view of André Kostolany, one of the most respected financial journalists in Europe, who likened France to an old miser "who has accumulated a huge treasure in the cellar of his dilapidated house. Instead of spending some money on building a new house, he prefers to sit in his ruinous shack, watching his treasure grow."

As Edith left for la Bourse, her uncle jokingly reminded her not to get trapped by any of the miser's assistants; the *agents de change,* like their New York counterparts, were renowned womanizers.

Edith's first reaction on seeing la Bourse was that it resembled an ancient Greek temple, surrounded by Corinthian columns. The perfectly square central building had at each corner a large statue of a woman, seated, dominating those who passed through its portals. The statues represented Justice, Industry, Agriculture, and Commerce.

Awed by the majesty of the building, Edith walked toward its sixteen broad entrance steps. The scene on the steps was, she imagined, similar to what it must have been in ancient Rome when the money-changers had gathered outside the Senate to ply their trade. Each step of la Bourse was occupied by members of the *coulisse,* the unofficial market. It was, she discovered, an altogether livelier and more informal trading center than the one inside the building.

Passing through one of the eleven entrance doors, Edith found herself in arguably the most ornate Stock Exchange in the world. The huge trading floor was capped by a magnificent glass-domed roof decorated with monochrome frescoes framed in carved wood. The floor was surrounded by an arcade in which were the booths of the *agents de change.*

After the frenetic atmosphere she had seen on the New York Exchange, Edith was disappointed by the lack of activity; perhaps, she thought, it was another example of what the French liked to call their "civilized way of doing things."

The seventy brokers in those booths were the only people allowed to deal in the official stock market. And they dealt only in French stocks and bonds. Outside, in the unofficial market on the steps, the *coulissiers* traded in a few foreign stocks in addition, the most important being South African gold mines and Royal Dutch Shell. No American bonds or stocks were on offer.

Standing in her skimpy summer dress, conscious of "the masculinity of the place," Edith was reminded of a recent experience she'd had. That was when she visited Rheims Cathedral and found that her guide, "after undressing me with his eyes," had gone on to tell her "there was probably more gold in the Cathedral's altar than the average American bank had in its vaults."

It was a line she knew she must include in her play. But she had yet to think of a way of using la Bourse.

Some three hundred miles, and light-years, away from where Edith Stone stood in Paris contemplating the indestructible high temple of French finance, Clarence Hatry, in London, realized the structure he was creating was built on shifting sands. The foundations had been laid at the fateful Sunday night meeting at his home on June 23. Now, on Wednesday, July 31, they were starting to crumble, threatening to drag Hatry further into the morass of what would be the greatest single financial fraud of the century.

Staring moodily out of the window of his office in the heart of the City, Hatry watched a news vendor hawking the noon editions of London's three evening newspapers. The *Star, News,* and *Standard* all reported Britain was fighting hard for economic survival. Hatry firmly believed his own plight was directly linked to the return to power of Labour. The Socialist victory had produced a clamp-down on borrowing. Hatry saw this as the reason for Lord Bearsted's change of mind about lending him £4 million as bridging finance to buy United Steel's stock.

Britain, and Hatry, were being squeezed harder financially every day. The financier wondered if this was why Ramsay MacDonald was rumored to be planning a trip to America—to try to borrow funds to keep Britain afloat. The press, of course, talked simply of a possible goodwill visit by the new Prime Minister. They used the same largely meaningless phrase to announce Winston Churchill's forthcoming journey to North America. The defeated Chancellor was going with his brother and their two sons on a combined business and pleasure trip to Canada and the United States. He intended to reach New York in late October and to visit Wall Street.

Hatry had made overtures to Wall Street for the bridging finance he needed. But the problem proved insurmountable. Those approached had been unwilling to put up the money immediately; they, too, were waiting to see how Labour would handle the sagging economy. Hatry had considered going to New York and using his own considerable persuasive powers to drum up the cash. In the end that idea had also been abandoned; there was no way Hatry could spare the minimum ten days needed to go to and fro across the Atlantic.

America, at least for the moment, was out.

He was still trying the great European finance houses. But they, like those in Wall Street, were reluctant to become involved in a country that showed few signs of being revitalized under socialism.

Worst of all for Hatry, intimations of his difficulties were circulating in the City. On the London Stock Exchange, the value of shares in some of his companies began to fall. As a result, he and his associates were forced to purchase these shares to keep their price from falling further. This disastrous additional drain on his nonexistent reserves made Hatry more and more desperate. He found he was unable to make payments on time to the bulk of the 40,000 stockholders in United Steel who were looking to him to honor his promise to buy their shares. He seemed trapped.

And yet, in those balmy days of late June and early July, it had all seemed so possible. Gialdini and Daniels were as gifted as Hatry in making the impossible sound reasonable. He had listened as they told him how simple it was to pick their way through the City's minefield of high finance and company law. They had told Hatry what he wanted to hear.

He would always maintain he had no detailed knowledge of what they were doing; his associates would say he had been an eager participant from the outset in as bold a piece of chicanery as the financial world had known. The truth was they had devised, argued, schemed, and planned behind closed doors. No notes were made of these most secret deliberations.

But finally, for whatever reason, Hatry's scruples were brushed aside. Doubtless motivated by many emotions—among them pride and a misplaced desire, he would claim, not to let anyone down—Clarence Hatry allowed himself to become involved with actions more usually associated with a common crook.

For the past six weeks he had supported a fraudulent scheme to issue scrip certificates with which to raise funds to buy the total stock of United Steel. He hoped that company would be his springboard to eventual control of British steel.

Daniels devised the initial plan; Gialdini supported it. And Hatry's gambler's instinct told him the risk was acceptable. Between them, they set out to perpetrate a deliberate and calculated swindle. It should only have lasted a few days. The need to support in the market the falling shares of other Hatry companies meant the fraud had to go on.

The scrip—Hatry company receipts in certificate form issued for money received which in normal circumstances would be exchanged for proper stock certificates later—was being deposited in banks by Hatry's staff as security for loans. That was normal enough. And, as a matter of course, Hatry's associates had thousands of scrip certificates in various denominations already printed. But what they were now doing was issuing that scrip for fictitious amounts far in excess of the stock they were thought to represent in order to raise more money at the banks.

It was a criminal offense. Banks in many parts of Britain had been duped. So far about £1 million worth of fabricated scrip had been issued.

Even so, Hatry realized he had not raised enough to buy all the outstanding United Steel shares he was pledged to purchase. Steadily—by the scrip frauds on one side and on the other pressure from United's stockholders to settle—he was being gripped in a pincer movement.

He knew it must only be a matter of time before the banks he was misleading began to ask questions.

The only way to avoid that was by bold action.

Turning back to the window, Clarence Hatry could think of nothing bolder than carrying the fight to his old enemy. A few blocks away was the Bank of England—and the one man Hatry believed could still save him, his familiar foe, Montagu Norman.

Charles Stewart Mott knew by the evening of this stifling Thursday, August 1, in Detroit, that nothing could now save his 153-day-old marriage. For most of that time he had gone on forgiving Dee her frequent "excesses." At fifty-three years of age, multimillionaire Mott believed he had shown tolerance toward Dee, a full, vivacious, twenty-four years younger than he was.

Looking back, thumbing through the notes he had made cataloguing the collapse of their marriage, he saw it had probably been doomed from that moment the plane crash-landed near Anderson on the first day of their honeymoon. Later, they had traveled by train to Arizona. There, in the week they spent at the ranch, Mott noticed that "all the time Mrs. Mott showed she preferred the company of almost anybody but me."

In his notes he always referred to her as "Mrs. Mott"; there is no record of what she called him.

After only a week Dee had suggested divorce and, according to Mott's later sworn testimony,* "began to make overtures for a property settlement and for money."

Mott dated the first serious rift in their relationship from then, when he "discovered Mrs. Mott felt nothing for me personally; she was cold and only wanted money."

The rest of their honeymoon was a disaster. Dee insisted querulously that a woman stranger she had met at the ranch should accompany them to California. Mott protested. Dee flared. The woman came.

In California the Motts's squabbling became daily set pieces. Once, Mott recorded, Dee had even said she hated him.

Despite this, back in Detroit, he tried hard to patch up matters. He

* See Source Notes.

permitted Dee to spend $35,000 remodeling their apartment. He bought her a $2,500 piano and paid, he noted, "several large bills of personal wearing apparel, a coat, dishes and coffee." He also gave her 5,000 shares in General Motors.

None of these gifts improved the marriage. Their rows became longer and more acrimonious. Mott, like Jesse Livermore—whom he met during Livermore's recent visit to the Midwest—sought refuge in his office. Dee, unlike Dorothy Livermore, did not resort to hard drink, preferring instead endless cups of coffee to sustain her for the next battle.

Mott suggested the trip to Europe, calling it "a second honeymoon." That hope evaporated when Dee insisted her attorney, Prewitt Semmes, accompany them.

Motoring through England, France, and Germany, Semmes sat in on one row after another. According to Mott, "a substantial gift of property" he had made over to Dee shortly after their marriage was considered by her not nearly enough. She dismissed his gifts of jewelry as derisory.

Mott returned with Dee to Detroit bitterly disillusioned.

His son, Harding, and his two daughters, Aimee and Elsa, were dismayed by how unhappy their father was. Harding, a sensitive teenager, was convinced "they were incompatible and it was only going to be a matter of time before they split up."

Mott clung stubbornly to the belief the marriage might be saved. He went on lavishing presents on his wife.

But then he discovered Dee was lying to him. In spite of her denials, he was certain she was secretly speculating in Wall Street. He thought, remembered Harding, "that was no thing for a lady to do; my father was very old-fashioned in some ways."

Worst of all, Mott also discovered his wife had tried to cheat him. Returning from Europe, Dee underwent an unspecified operation in Battle Creek Sanatorium. She presented her husband with a bill for $2,000. On checking with the clinic, Mott found the cost came to only $1,000.

He was bitterly hurt that, after all he had given her, Dee had tried to take him for $1,000. It was a further sign her "entry into the marital relationship was not actuated by love." Now, on August 1, reviewing these past months of tension, Charles Mott applied the same ruthless principles he used in business. He would cut his losses, end the marriage, and attempt to keep the whole thing quiet.

What had also helped to destroy the union was Dee's refusal ever to set foot in Applewood, Mott's home in Flint. She had no interest in inspecting the trophies bestowed upon him for his public generosity which were on display there; nor had she any desire to meet his friends in Flint and hear yet again the role her husband had played in developing the city.

Because of Dee's attitude, Mott had stayed away from Flint for many months. He knew that to go alone would be to create gossip within the community.

Having made up his mind to end his marriage, he no longer felt such constraint.

He would not tell anyone he was coming. He would enjoy surprising them—especially the poker-faced Grant Brown at the Union Industrial Bank. Mott could not wait to see Brown struggling to hide his surprise as he walked through the bank's entrance.

The letter giving the New York Exchange's formal permission for Michael Meehan to initiate his floating brokerage on the *Berengaria* had been handed to him personally on July 25 by Richard Whitney. Prior to that Meehan had sent Whitney a detailed report showing the test transmissions from the liner had proven entirely satisfactory.

Since receiving the go-ahead, Meehan had been waiting to break the story to the media. And now, on Saurday, August 3, radio and newspaper reporters began arriving at his office well before noon, the scheduled start for one of the largest press conferences Wall Street had known this year. Meehan was a popular figure with the press. Even Henry Ford had not commanded more attention during his visit to New York.

Swelling the ranks of newsmen were many of Meehan's business friends. Percy Rockefeller was there, dashing as ever in tweeds, fending off reporters' questions about his private life. John J. Raskob was in a huddle with a group of journalists, mysteriously promising them he would soon have "a very tall story to tell—and a true one." He would not be drawn further. Charles Mitchell had sent an aide to keep an eye on things; Jesse Livermore, too, typically, had slipped in an assistant. Billy Durant was a late arrival. The man from the New York *Telegram* noted the promoter hesitated between standing by an open window or going deeper into the smoke-filled room. Durant decided to stick by the window.

Grouped in one corner were "Meehan's Mafia": the pugnacious Tom Bragg, the inscrutable Ben Smith, and the studious Bradford Ellsworth, curious like the rest to hear Meehan speak.

Sharp at noon, accompanied by Arthur Costigan, the RCA expert who had supervised the radio test transmissions, Meehan walked into the room and opened the press conference.

Nodding toward Alexander Noyes, financial editor of the New York *Times*—his presence was a sign of the importance attached to the conference—the broker explained how a *Times* story had first fired his imagination. Noyes smiled. The other reporters groaned; nowadays everybody tried to begin a press briefing with a suitable tribute to the media.

Meehan quickly showed there was more to his conference than puffery; moving through the background, he deftly outlined the various stages involved in setting up the floating brokerage service. An English newspaper correspondent noted he appeared to be "enjoying his role as an entrepreneur."

Meehan was also generous enough to pay full tribute to the help and encouragement he had received from David Sarnoff at RCA, and from Cunard.

His prepared statement over, he turned the first question over to Costigan. The engineer carefully explained the technical problems he had overcome before successfully setting up a "stock-circuit headquarters" at Tuckerton, New Jersey, and a "backup station" at Chatham on Cape Cod. He talked of call signs, time differencs, radio frequencies, amps, ohms, shortwaves, and static.

The Hearst reporter finally cut through the technical talk. "How many securities will you handle?"

Meehan took over. "One hundred. Twenty blue chip and what you guys call 'glamour' stocks will be quoted every fifteen minutes. Forty less active stocks every thirty minutes. The balance every hour."

An interviewer from station WABC wanted the complete list of stocks. Meehan read them rapidly from a pad. They included his own specialties: RCA, National Cash Register, International Match, Cuba Company, Lehn & Fink, and Utility Power & Light.

The *Wall Street Journal* representative had a question about costs.

"Dollar minimum for the wireless charge. No other extras beyond the normal commission."

"What about splitting?"

"No problem. I expect about three quarters of our trading at sea to be give-up."

The financial journalist nodded knowingly. The man from the Associated Press, like many of the reporters, was puzzled. "What's give-up?"

Meehan explained it was sharing commission with another brokerage house.

The questions came thick and fast, those from the back of the room often drowned by the clicking cameras near Meehan.

"Are you going to use a code?"

"Yes."

"What kind?"

"Secret. Undecipherable."

"What if a bucket shop breaks it?"

"That's impossible." Meehan then read aloud the letter he had received from the Stock Exchange with its request that "all quotations which are to be supplied by high-speed telegraphy shall be safe-guarded in every way."

"Gentlemen, I assure you we have done that. Next question."

"What happens if you get a share shark on board?"

"We'll throw him over the side!"

An appreciative laugh came from the reporters.

The New York *Telegram* man wanted to know what the position would be if the broker on the ship became seasick and couldn't open the floating office.

"No chance. We're equipping all our staff with special sea legs!"

The journalists roared happily.

The New York *World* reporter asked whether this now meant "the American businessman will be able to take a vacation in Europe without stopping for a single day his market transactions during the crossing?"

"Yes."

Meehan had the hard-boiled reporters in his palm.

Only the Philadelphia *Inquirer* correspondent struck a sour note, suggesting the operation "will rob ocean voyages of their greatest charm, getting away from the office."

Meehan appeared to consider the statement seriously. Then with a broad grin he replied. "I'd just like to remind you all it's my floating brokerage service that's got you out of your offices today!"

The reporters whooped.

It took some time for the correspondent of a Paris daily to make himself heard. As the noise died, he asked Meehan whether he was aware of the fact that the French brokerage firm of Saint-Phalle and Company was also planning a brokerage service on the Atlantic: "due to begin very soon aboard the liner *Ile de France*."

There was sudden silence in the room. The reporters sensed Mike Meehan's reaction to the prospect of being unexpectedly pipped by a rival. Smiling broadly, he hid any disappointment. "I have heard that rumor. There is room for both of us."

It had not previously occurred to him that the French might beat him at his own game.

CHAPTER SIXTEEN

EVERYBODY OUGHT TO BE RICH

At nine o'clock sharp, highly pleased, William Crawford turned into Wall Street, his faith in journalism restored on this Monday morning of August 5. On the subway the Stock Exchange superintendent had read the current issue of *American Magazine*. It contained an article on Wall Street by John T. Flynn, one of the most respected financial writers in America.

Flynn had consulted Crawford during his research, and the superintendent was gratified to see the journalist had kept his promise to be "responsible." Crawford felt, with the stock market getting daily front-page treatment, too many journalists wrote "tabloid trash about little old ladies winning fortunes by blindly choosing stocks."

While Crawford accepted that could well be true, it was not the image of Wall Street he wanted to foster. Flynn's article was refreshingly different, with its imagery of the Street as "a web which spreads over the whole country, its filaments finding their center in New York and running out in countless spokes fastened upon every bank, every trust company, every great industry, every financial establishment."

Striding down its short narrow length not far from the Battery, historic landing point for so many settlers, Crawford agreed with another of the journalist's observations: "almost the first step an immigrant takes in America is into Wall Street. A few of them have never gotten beyond it."

Some of their descendants this morning were doubtless among the thousands of people crisscrossing the Street—clerks, guards, stenographers, telephonists, pages, peddlers, bankers, brokers, and, most numerous of all, the messenger boys.

Messengers were joined together chain-gang fashion; in a long line, with an armed guard front and rear, they carried locked metal boxes filled with securities, each messenger holding with one hand the handle of the box ahead and with his other the handle of the box behind. Sometimes as many as twenty boys formed the line moving between banks and brokerage houses.

Not long before, as Crawford clearly recalled, a horse had run amuck in the Street, broken through a line of boys and boxes, and ended up spread-eagle across the hood of a banker's Rolls-Royce.

Looking ahead of him now, Crawford could see, towering over the crowd, the bulky figure of a banker who seldom used his car. Charles Mitchell completed his seven-mile walk to work by bounding up the steps of the National City Bank. His limousine, which had shadowed him from his home in uptown Manhattan, slid into the curb and the chauffeur carried Mitchell's bulgy attaché case into the bank.

Crawford wondered whether the walk did Mitchell much good. He had seen him lunching in the Stock Exchange Club and been "absolutely astonished" by the amount of food Mitchell shovelled into his mouth.

Turning off Wall at "The Corner"—the Street's junction with Broad Street—Crawford watched the doormen outside Number 23 brace themselves to greet the first Morgan partners. The superintendent was a strong believer in "the Morgan tradition"; he wished more journalists would concern themselves with that rather than writing so much "tittle-tattle" about Jack Morgan's life-style.

The tabloids were again full of Morgan's latest doings; he had commissioned the largest yacht in the world, one that would even outstrip those owned by Vincent Astor and Clarence Hatry; he had bought a Tintoretto and a number of rare manuscripts for the library he inherited from his father; he had given $2 million to New York Hospital and a similar amount to the city's Lying-in Hospital, his father's old charity. Now, said one of the Sundays, Jack Morgan was off to England to shoot grouse with the royal family. Crawford hoped the British press would have the good manners to let Mr. Morgan bag his grouse in peace.

Once the superintendent entered the Stock Exchange, he had little time to muse on the intrusions, real or imagined, of the American media.

The early August market had taken up where July had left off; shares were bounding forward in a greater-than-ever-before upsurge. Records had been broken almost every hour the Exchange was open in these past few days of a normally quiet month.

This morning, Crawford estimated by ten o'clock there would be close to 1,000 members on the floor waiting impatiently for his gavel to open trading. Since February the 1929 membership had been increased from 1,100 to 1,375. A seat now cost $625,000.

Already the telephonists in their booths around the edge of the floor were fully stretched. So, too, were the page boys.

And, just before the beginning of another week's trading, mechanics were again at work on the tickers. They were trying to eliminate a problem that Crawford realized could only be resolved finally when the new ticker system was introduced. The present tickers were totally inadequate to cope with the ever-increasing listings and volume of trading. The wheels off which the ticker tape spilled were able to revolve only at a certain speed; it was physically impossible to make them go faster.

Swamped by the unprecedented amount of business, the tickers frequently ran an hour late reporting transactions on the floor. Crawford's mail included a growing number of complaints about the service from brokerage houses all over the country.

Often he and his engineers worked into the night trying all sorts of makeshift solutions. They experimented with shortening some of the symbols used to codify stocks. That brought more complaints. They tried changing the actual ticker paper. They even switched the printing ink. None of these made any difference. Nothing further could be done but soldier on until the new system arrived, capable of printing 900 characters a minute, enough even to cope with 7-million-share days.

Pausing only to remind his mechanics that they had less than thirty minutes before the market opened, Crawford hurried to the basement of the Exchange.

There, amid a maze of wheels, belts, cogs, wires, batteries, dynamos, and magnetos, Crawford found still more engineers checking the machines and cables which provided the power for driving the 3,000 tickers in the financial district; there were some 2,000 others dotted about the city and a further 4,500 sited around the country.

Here, in the jam-packed basement—it had a greater variety of equipment than would be found in most large factories—elaborate arrangements ensured the tickers would not stop during the 300 minutes of trading on each weekday and the 120 minutes trading on Saturdays.

Duplicates of most mechanical parts were readily at hand. If one of the "master" tickers, installed in a special gallery of the Exchange, broke down, technicians on duty in the basement would be able instantly to switch to a standby machine. All told, there were a dozen standby tickers interconnected and ready to be brought into action. Each was a marvel of ingenuity, capable of selecting the symbols and processing them into a running order; this order was then fed onto a master tape. In turn, the output of this tape was turned into a series of electrical impulses and tapped out on tickers all across America.

Crawford believed he had some of the best technicians in the country working in this basement. He also knew they were powerless to control the tidal wave of trading that sometimes swamped them. All he could do was wish them good luck and then hurry back to the floor.

Making his morning round among the horsehoe-shaped trading posts, Crawford sensed more than ever that "every factory, every store, every business of every kind is in some way represented here in the form of securities."

Pausing for a few words, eavesdropping on a conversation, overhearing a snippet of gossip, Crawford always amassed a respectable store of information during his walkabout.

At Post One he picked up the tidbit that a seat on the Boston Exchange had just sold for $45,000 while one on the Los Angeles Exchange had gone for $150,000. Five years ago those seats could have been bought for under $5,000 each. Even on the eight-month-old Twin Cities Exchange—that of Minneapolis–St. Paul—seats costing $1,000 in January were now selling at over $6,000.

William Wadsworth, the doyen at Post Five, told Crawford he predicted another "bull day" on the Chicago Exchange because Samuel Insull, the utility magnate, was in the midst of an immense operation to add about $100 million to his Middle West Utilities enterprise. There were men out there in La Salle Street, said Wadsworth, who believed the day would come when Chicago would supplant New York as the national financial capital.

Both men agreed this talk was "pure nonsense." They took more seriously A. P. Giannini's latest remarks. He was insisting again that San Francisco could eventually become the new banking headquarters of America.

Prompted by Giannini's remarks in the past, Crawford had recently compiled a report on the San Francisco Stock Exchange. He was surprised to discover that this year some 50 million shares in oils, banks, sugars, and industrials were expected to be traded there. Significantly, the volume of business had doubled every year in the past three; if that continued, San Franciscans calculated that by 1940 they could have the nation's busiest exchange. And already, next to New York, a seat on the San Francisco Stock Exchange was the costliest in the country— $500,000. Crawford felt that, if Giannini "really got behind things," the San Franciscans might be right.

At Post Eleven, the talk before opening was, understandably, not restricted to business. Only eight days before, July 28, Jack Bouvier had become a father for the first time. He had agreed with his wife they should name their baby daughter Jacqueline, after himself. Crawford told Jack's great-uncle, eighty-two-year-old Michael Bouvier, that he entirely approved of the choice.

At Post Twelve Mike Meehan could be heard talking animatedly to his young Radio clerk, Ed Schnell, about his plans to launch the brokerage service on the *Berengaria*. Crawford thought the idea "a trifle flash"—again, not quite the sort of image he would like for the New York Exchange.

But there was nothing he could do about it; he knew the press would play up the venture. Crawford walked past Posts Four and Eight and mounted his rostrum. Standing on the podium, looking down at the milling mass, he could imagine how difficult it was for journalists to capture in words the thrill he felt every morning as, at ten o'clock, with a final quick glance at the chronometer, he opened the market.

Crawford suspected most visitors to the public gallery thought his work consisted solely of ceremoniously opening and closing each trading day. If that was so, he regretted their ignorance, just as he could not forgive those journalists who dismissed him as an archaic figure. He had given interviews to the press and told them of his many responsibilities—"the mechanics," looking after the page boys, supervising all permanent staff and generally "keeping the Exchange ship-shape"—but the reporters wrote little about him.

Crawford had toyed with the thought of getting the gallery guides to mention his functions in their commentaries, but he dropped the idea for fear of being thought too pushy. Behind his stern, unbending stare he was a kindly, avuncular man whose great love in life was the Stock Exchange. More than anyone else he jealously guarded its reputation.

One of his tasks was keeping an eye on the guides, making sure, by their "words and demeanor," they did nothing to bring the Exchange into disgrace.

Satisfied that, for the moment, the ticker was keeping up with the market, Crawford went to the visitors' gallery.

He reached it just as Exchange President Edward Simmons and Richard Whitney arrived with James Joseph Walker, mayor of New York.

When Crawford had been told of Walker's visit, he had understood it would be private; the sight of a posse of newsmen around the mayor made him angry. He felt the Stock Exchange was being exploited as part of Walker's preparations for his forthcoming reelection campaign. In November Walker was due to go to the polls to meet a challenge from Fiorello La Guardia. This visit to the Exchange was doubtless designed to help the mayor's image of being a hardworking interested executive.

Watching him at close hand, the conservatively minded Crawford felt repelled by the wisecracking Walker. In the flesh the mayor looked less handsome, more theatrical than he did in his newspaper photographs. His jacket was a loud check, clashing with a brightly colored shirt. His feet were encased in flashy pointed shoes. He appeared as if dressed more for the racetrack than the New York Stock Exchange.

Trailing in the wake of his cavalcade came Walker's wife, Janet. When the entourage stopped in the center of the gallery, Walker hailed her to his side.

Crawford wondered whether the tabloids were right, that there really was nothing left between the mayor and his wife. Ever since his election to office in 1926, they had regularly reported on Jimmy's gallivanting around New York in the early hours with a succession of exotic women. Today, for the benefit of tomorrow's papers, he was calculatingly creating an impression of seriousness and husbandly concern.

He announced his visit to the Exchange was to see for himself "the eighth wonder of the world—the continuing bull market on the Big Board." He had brought his wife along so she could learn about the bulls and the bears—in the hope she "will never get cornered by either."

Corny speeches like this always went down well with the city's media.

At a nod from Crawford a guide began to explain the working of the Exchange to Walker. He spoke clearly and fluently, detailing how stocks were traded, how the ticker worked, and much else.

Walker grinned continuously for the cameramen and frequently interrupted the lecture with jokes. Simmons and Whitney smiled bravely. Janet Walker looked forlorn.

Finally, with an angry shake of his head, Crawford cut short the guide.

Walker did not even notice. He delivered an exit gag to the gallery and swept out on his way to another stage-managed appearance.

Minutes after the mayor had left the Exchange—roaring up Wall Street in his custom-built limousine, hotly pursued by press cars— William Crawford heard that the ticker was starting to fall behind.

Resignedly, he hurried to his office again to chase up Western Union about advancing the date for installing the new system.

Grouped together around the ticker in his office, Billy Durant and his visitors were unaware the tape was running late, but they were in no doubt the market was experiencing the busiest August any of them could remember. Oris Van Sweringen tore off a strip of tape and put it in his pocket; it would survive as a memento of a morning when, in his brother Mantis' view, "the market was going mad."

Durant, the Van Sweringens, and John J. Raskob, the fourth man in the room, instantly and silently translated the coded symbols. Almost every reported stock was gaining ground.

Durant turned away from the ticker and led his guests to the grouped armchairs. He had invited them to his office as part of his policy of talking to fellow speculators and reminding them, as he had done with Charles Mitchell, of the continued need to be seen to be bullish.

Raskob, as usual, was volubly enthusiastic. An interview with him had just appeared in the *Ladies' Home Journal* under the title "Everybody Ought to Be Rich"; it was a blatant plea for increased investment in the stock market.

Durant said he welcomed the article; he was also interested to hear the intentions of the Van Sweringens. The bachelor brothers had built a $3 billion railroad empire by trading in securities on a vast scale.

They assured him they planned to remain active in the market for the rest of the year.

The conversation moved on to other topics. Durant casually inquired about the prospects for General Motors; the auto stock was at a new high.

The others sensed what might lie behind the question. Each had heard the whispers from Detroit about Mott's marriage heading for the divorce courts. That could mean Mott would be increasingly occupied with his domestic crisis and unable to devote his full attention to General Motors.

All four men knew that while Alfred Sloan was still very much in command at GM, anything could happen should Mott's personal problems become public during the coming months. A company's shares had slipped in the past because some private trauma of a key executive became known.

The situation at General Motors was worth watching carefully. If its shares began to fall, there might be a need for quick support action to avert any overall drop in the market.

At 6:30 A.M. precisely, on Tuesday, August 6, as it did every weekday morning he was at home, the ringing telephone broke the silence of the Giannini household in San Mateo.

The banker bounded out of bed and padded across the floor in his nightshirt to a washstand. He doused his head in cold water and dried himself.

Three days before, he, Clorinda, and Claire had returned from New York to California. It had been a particularly long and tiring journey;

the *Overland Express* was almost nine hours late in completing the four-day trip. At each stop reporters had filled Giannini's compartment. They no longer sought his views mainly on the market but probed for new angles. Was it true he was about to buy Goldman, Sachs and Company, the New York financial house? Was he buying a chain of banks in Italy? France? Giannini had grown weary of denying the stories. But his frustration finally boiled over when he reached San Francisco and found his hometown reporters asking the same questions. He had angrily told them to stop wasting his time.

Clorinda was alarmed by his outburst. Before leaving New York, a doctor friend had quietly advised her to try to make her husband relax. At fifty-nine he was working far harder than most men half his age. The doctor warned Clorinda of the danger of a heart attack.

But now, watching her husband, she felt reassured. The fatigue was gone from his face; a few days of California sun had brought back his color. Physically, he had never looked better. There was not an ounce of spare fat on his husky body.

"The phone, A.P.," she said. "You'll wake up the street."

"Save them the price of an alarm clock!"

They had virtually the same conversation at the start of each weekday; it was one of the hundreds of small, private, trivial things they shared. Clorinda called it "verbal cement"; it bound them, and their marriage, ever more firmly together. Their relationship was built on old-fashioned trust and respect; it had never soured.

Giannini hurried out of the bedroom. Clorinda rose and began to dress. In an adjoining bedroom, Claire was also getting up.

Bounding down the stairs, fully awake and exuding energy, Giannini finally answered the telephone.

The caller was his brother, Attilio—"Doc" to the family—phoning from his office in the Bank of America building in Wall Street. He was making his first report of the day. In the hours to come he would make other calls to A.P. at his office in San Francisco, regularly bringing him up to date on financial events three thousand miles away.

Even the appointment of Elisha Walker had not interrupted this close contact between the brothers. Doc, A.P. told Claire, "is my eyes, ears and nose back East; he can see a potential merger or sniff out trouble before anybody suspects it exists."

Giannini was relieved that, after a cool start, the relationship between Doc and Walker was improving. Encouraged by him, both men were making a real effort to temper their different personalities to the common good of Transamerica and the growing Bank of America. Walker had become less starchy; Doc tried hard to appear as if he was born for Wall Street. More important, as Giannini had hoped, the complaints about Walker's autocracy within the organization had died away. Secure that his two key lieutenants in the East were in harmony, he felt free to return to the West Coast.

Giannini hoped to complete Walker's "reeducation" by having him spend time at the home office in San Francisco. The visit was scheduled for the last week of October. By then Walker "expected everything to be running smoothly in the East."

Giannini planned to have Doc travel with Walker; he felt the enforced intimacy of a long train journey would break down any remaining barriers between the two men. And from past experience he knew there was nobody better as a traveling companion than Doc.

Over the crackling line he could feel the warmth in his brother's voice, asking solicitously about Clorinda, his two sons, and Claire. For a few minutes they discussed family matters. Then Doc began a general report on market expectations in New York. There was likely to be no slackening of activity in the Street. Stock market averages were expected to go on climbing. The advance in particular of certain high-priced stocks that had started in July would continue throughout August. Public utility stocks were expected to jump a few points today following a bad break yesterday in Chicago.

Giannini listened carefully, evaluating Doc's words against what they both already knew. Toward the end of July the market had once more reacted nervously, and there had been several sharp bouts of selling. At one stage there were signs a fairly strong short interest was developing. Wall Street had been filled with rumors that "some big operators" were losing heavily. Then, at the end of the month, U. S. Steel had reported earnings per share of $11.72 for the first half of the year. It was a peacetime record. It soothed the market's nerves. Now, in Doc's view, the market was being "bulled hard again."

The news concerned Giannini. During July brokers' loans had reached a new high level, despite generally high call loan rates. Rival banks, corporations—even wealthy individuals with excess cash like the Shanghai mandarins Doc had recently heard about—had joined foreign bankers in supplying the extra funds needed to feed the market. This influx of cash was another sign the Federal Reserve Board was failing to prevent the increasing use of credit in the stock market. And the trend to buy on margin had been carried over into August.

What concerned Giannini most of all was the burgeoning of investment trusts. They were being promoted at the rate of almost one every day and some of them were doubtless designed specifically to fleece the unwary. For small-time investors they appeared ideal. But whereas the most respectable were backed by the best brains in Wall Street, helping the uninformed to invest their money in the most sensible, safe manner, the worst were run by slick operators who knew little more about what they were doing than those whose moneys they were using. Giannini knew that in the present bull market investment trusts could hardly go wrong, no matter how badly managed. Equally, in a falling market their losses could be compounded. Small investors who put all their spare cash into buying on margin would find themselves all too quickly being called upon to put up more margin; unless they could get more cash from somewhere to meet the continuing demand for margin, their shares would be sold at a loss and they might well have to go bankrupt. Although most did not realize it, they were playing a very dangerous game.

Giannini urged Doc once again to remind all their smaller customers on the East Coast of the dangers of buying stocks "of any kind in any way" on margin. He knew that, contrary to so much published opinion, it was folly to believe as so many did that "this market can continue to go up forever and ever."

The conversation turned to specifics. The present market leaders— American Telephone, General Electric, Western Union, and Consolidated Gas—were likely to maintain their present positions.

But wheat—which among other things had enabled the Flint bankers to pay back an appreciable amount of the money they had embezzled— had fallen 6½ cents a bushel in the past two days. The break had come so suddenly it was said neither Livermore nor Cutten had been able to take advantage of it. Doc reported that some of the morning newspapers were suggesting it was only a matter of time before one of the speculators took wheat "in hand." Other writers were keeping up the carping campaign against the Federal Reserve Board that Charles Mitchell and others had first inspired back in February; there were strong rumors "the men in Washington" were at last about to act. And finally, some financial pages were tipping a record dividend from Transamerica.

That did not please Giannini; he knew it was bound to attract more people to dabble on margin in the stock. He suspected when the actual size of the dividend was made public—it would be a record 150 percent—there would be an avalanche of "those trying to get rich quick with us."

It was a theme he continued over breakfast. Claire would clearly remember how troubled her father was: "There was simply no way he could stop people buying his stock on margin."

Her solution was to "go to the press and issue a warning against *all* margin buying."

Virgil and Mario—Claire's brothers who had joined them for

breakfast—were uncertain. They felt the press could report a serious warning by their father as just another market-related sensation.

Giannini sat back, listening intently as his children debated the issue. He admired their financial grasp and the way they had so readily accepted his own rigid business ethics. The tone of the discussion reflected their different personalities; Claire, as usual, was forceful and articulate, advancing her case on several simultaneous fronts. Virgil tended to say very little. Mario was more like his sister, voluble and persuasive.

But the question of how best to warn off small-time margin buyers was still unresolved when chauffeur Joe Garcia arrived. His presence was a signal for the domestic tempo immediately to increase. The discussion was put aside in the rush to gather up files and work papers.

Then, followed by their father, the children embraced and kissed their mother.

Outside, Garcia sat behind the wheel of the Rolls-Royce, its engine idling and its red fire light winking in the morning light.

Formerly the chauffeur had stood on the curb, ready to close the car doors behind his passengers. Giannini had dispensed with this courtesy as "too time wasting."

Now, with his employer seated beside him and Claire squeezed between her two brothers in the back, Garcia gunned the car forward for the thirty-minute drive to San Francisco.

The journey to work also had its ritual. Garcia had picked up the *Chronicle* on the way to the house. Giannini divided it up and handed sections to the children. While they perused the paper for items of financial interest, he talked to Garcia.

In the chauffeur's view, "this was one way for A.P. to try and get a man-in-the-street reaction."

For the third time this morning, Giannini raised the issue of small investors. He asked Garcia if he speculated.

"No, boss."

"Why not?"

"Simple. A big guy gets caught—he can afford it. A little guy like me could be ruined for life. If I wanna gamble, I go to the tracks."

"What would you do about the little guys who are gambling on the market?"

Garcia answered at once. "Boss, I'd tell them they were fools. They wouldn't listen to me. But sure as hell they'd listen to you!"

Giannini turned and smiled broadly at Claire, grinning in the back seat. Her father asked her to hand him a scratch pad. For the rest of the drive Giannini made notes.

By the time he reached his office he had made up his mind. What he planned would probably once more arouse his enemies in Wall Street; Giannini could imagine how the Morgan grapevine would discreetly pass the word that "the West Coast Italian"—as he was still disparagingly referred to by the eastern establishment—was losing his nerve.

Even his friends might be aghast at his stand. But nothing would dissuade him. He would do what his old jousting partner in the media, Henry Ford, was always doing. He would seek out trusted newspapermen and ask them to publicize his views, that, while it was one thing for "the professional trader" to stand a loss, it was quite another matter for a family man to risk being ruined. He would urge the reporters to write the story as a warning that tens of thousands of their fellow Americans were in danger from what might happen in the market.

Escorted by Harry Bennett, Henry Ford walked briskly into the cavernous assembly shed in the Rouge plant. Above and beside them, moving inexorably, stretching endlessly, rolled the clanking production line. At their stations on either side of the line were thousands of workers. They, too, never stopped moving, continuously positioning, bolting down, adding to, and checking the various components which, together, formed the new Model A's coming off the end of the line.

To the waiting group of perspiring reporters and photographers, and a newsreel crew lugging its cumbersome equipment, the constant noise and heat in the shed was nearly overpowering.

The newsmen received only a cursory glance from the workers. They did not welcome the arrival of Ford. His regulation forbidding smoking in the plant led many of the men to take up chewing tobacco. Some of them had contrived to spit it out in such a fine spray it was entirely undetectable.

For the past month the Rouge had been visited almost daily by a press anxious to chronicle all aspects of the company and to report a succession of celebrations. They had come to record the moment the two millionth Model A rolled off the conveyor. They had returned to hear Ford detail his expansion plans for Europe, Brazil, and Mexico.

They returned again to hear him announce car manufacturing was now ahead of all other American industries in sheer dollar value. They listened, open-mouthed, as Ford reeled off figures in support of his claim. His company was again leading the home market, and Ford predicted by the year's end he would have almost half a million more customers for his Model A than its nearest rival, Chevrolet, could muster. And, he reminded them, it was all being done without a cent's help from Wall Street.

On Thursday, July 30, scores of reporters and photographers had arrived to hear Ford, on his sixty-sixth birthday, expound his familiar thoughts on food, diet, clothes, youth, progress, religion, history, reincarnation, cows, pigs, transport, and Wall Street.

They had asked him to comment on Wall Street reports that he planned to go public, planned to let more company shares onto the market, planned to retire, planned to hand over his empire to Edsel.

Ford snorted. He expected, he said, to be running his company when he was one hundred years old. He planned, he added, to live to "around 150," helped, he explained, by copious draughts of carrot juice, some of which he promptly drank for the benefit of the photographers.

The massive newspaper coverage his birthday received—in column inches it would be greater than that accorded the birthday celebrations of either President Hoover or the King of England—did little to satisfy his appetite for publicity.

The press had been called back to the Rouge day after day, to hear his thoughts on communism—"okay for Russia, bad for Detroit"—on Mother's Day, and on the Sermon on the Mount.

They had been there when he announced the latest progress on his "American Village": A few minutes' walk from Ford Airport, a full-scale replica of Philadelphia's Independence Hall was rising, complete with reproduction Liberty Bell, at the entrance to acres of museum floor space which would hold Ford's magpie collection of Americana. The village would be a pantheon to the heroes and virtues he worshiped. Reporters were given a glimpse of the site. They heard how Ford had bought and uprooted "a shepherd's cottage from the Cotswold Hills of England" to show how the Pilgrim fathers lived before they set sail, and a Cape Cod windmill to demonstrate what they did after they landed. They had learned it would not be long before the entire $20 million extravaganza would be open to the public.

But now, herded beside the Rouge assembly lines, the photographers in particular were becoming genuinely concerned about getting a fresh angle. They felt they had already photographed Ford in virtually every position possible.

The reporters well knew the reason they had been summoned this Friday. The Harvard Business School had yesterday voted Ford *second* in a poll for best businessman in America. Publicly, Ford accepted the award with a smile. Privately, he was said to be furious over not being voted top. Ray Priest of the Detroit *Times* felt he and his fellow journalists had been summoned as a "typical Henry gesture" to show that the Harvard dons had boobed.

Ford had chosen his ground well. He was completely at home among the whirring cogs and belts of the assembly line. There was no telephone or other unwelcome intrusion to distract him; here, he was surrounded by comfortably familiar nuts, bolts, and grease. He came to the plant regularly; it allowed him to see, and be seen by, his workers. His presence was a reminder to them that, in spite of his age, he was still capable of doing many of their jobs.

Now, never once referring to the Harvard award, Ford demonstrated his undeniable command of business mores.

Cool and relaxed, oblivious of the noise and heat, he moved steadily down the production line, expertly fixing, adjusting, and checking. He talked with complete fluency the language of electricians, welders, and assemblers.

And all the time, as the reporters wrote and the photographers snapped, Bennett reminded them that throughout the decade Ford had topped more polls than any other person in America.

In turn, Ford had been voted the nation's wealthiest personal income earner; the world's greatest newsmaker; the greatest living businessman. He had also been voted one of the four greatest men of the century; placed second, to Mussolini, as "the greatest living man in the world"; selected as one of the world's "twelve living immortals"—this time beating the Italian dictator comfortably.

Abroad, intoned Bennett, Ford was more highly regarded than any other American. Even in the Soviet Union only Lenin was more popular with the masses.

Coming toward the end of the line, Ford engagingly explained he never spoke to any worker too long for fear production would be halted. The loss could never be retrieved. A five-minute stoppage would cost the company more than any of the journalists earned in a year.

Ford's grass-roots grasp of business finance would, in the opinion of Priest, make him "a match for all the professors at Harvard."

The newsmen reached the end of the line. Ford climbed into a shiny new Model A, waved farewell to the cameramen, and drove out of the factory.

He did not have to wait for the newspaper reports to know he had pulled off another virtuoso public relations performance.

Charlton MacVeagh was one of the many regulars who arrived early for work in Wall Street on the morning of Monday, August 12. He wanted to see for himself a sight that a month ago even the most optimistic would have thought impossible.

Mid-August was by tradition Wall Street's vacation period, when the market was quiet and traders slipped away for at least a few days to Long Island or Atlantic City, there to refresh themselves before the renewed activity expected after September's Labor Day.

But the weekend newspapers and radio bulletins reported many brokers were in their offices, preparing to meet an unseasonal onslaught by small investors.

All through the past week, these speculators had drifted into the financial district. On Monday, August 5, after Mayor Jimmy Walker had left, some of them stood dumbfounded in the Exchange's public gallery as Insull Utility shares had collapsed in Chicago, dropping a full 19 points, and call money had jumped, again, to 12 percent. They had cheered when, next day, it fell back to 8 percent. On Wednesday, August 7, the aftershocks of the Insull collapse continued and caused breaks in many other stocks. Next day, the market rallied strongly, and there had been a carnival atmosphere in Wall Street with vendors and peddlers of all kinds descending on the district. At noon there were more itinerant preachers in the area than anybody could remember. Nobody took much notice of their hell-and-brimstone warnings. But for many investors the preachers' predictions seemed about to come true just after the Exchange closed that day: The news broke then that the Federal Reserve Board had finally allowed its New York Reserve Bank to raise its rate a point to 6 percent. There was "a general wail of dismay" throughout Wall Street which carried over to Friday, when there was an immediate and wide break in stocks the moment the market opened. The *Times* Industrial Average dropped 15¼ points; American Telephone 10½; General Electric lost 19 points; Commercial Solvents fell 30 points. By the end of the day 5 million shares had changed hands, the highest single day's figure since March. On the Curb, Marconi International fell 20¼ points in 100 minutes. On Saturday morning, August 10, however, the market partially recovered. The news was flashed across the country. It acted as a signal. People began to head from many parts of America for Wall Street to see what would happen on Monday. Most expected the market to forge ahead again.

By Sunday night every hotel within striking distance of the financial district was full. People tried to bed down in the precincts of Trinity Church; some even attempted to spend the night in the graveyard. Extra police patrolled the area. Its cafés and restaurants remained open to cope with the influx.

Journalists hurried to discover what had brought about this situation. An Ohio schoolteacher explained to NBC that he had come because he "wanted a piece of the bull market." He told the interviewer he didn't want much: Once he had made $50,000 he would leave, buy his wife a fur coat, and retire to Florida. Another newcomer said he was there simply because "Wall Street is the only place to be." A third explained that back home the ticker in his broker's office was "generally an hour late with the news. I want news of my winnings as it happens."

They were typical reactions.

William Crapo Durant, creator of General Motors and market plunger extraordinary. At the start of 1929 he was a multimillionaire. A year later he was on the verge of penury, one of the many victims of the Age of Illusion. *United Press International.*

Banker James J. Riordan. He had so much
to live for. His death created a sensation. He
became one of the most celebrated victims
of the Crash. *Courtesy Elizabeth Riordan
Porter*.

A visionary young broker, W. E. (Hut
Hutton-Miller, sensed what was coming. H
words of caution went unheeded. And in th
end, he too lost a sizable fortune from
Crash that changed his, and everybody else'
life. *Courtesy W. E. Hutton-Miller*.

The head office of the Union Industrial Bank, Flint, Michigan. Here in 1929, the biggest bank fraud the world had known was carefully planned and executed. It was almost foolproof—but the Crash laid bare the monumental swindle. *Courtesy Alfred P. Sloan, Jr., Museum, Flint.*

One of the Flint embezzlers, Milton Polloc[k]
a vice-president of the Union Industri[al]
Bank. Like the other members of the em[-]
bezzling gang, Pollock saw himself as part [of]
a "league of gentlemen," stealing for human[i-]
tarian reasons. *Courtesy Bruce Pollock.*

The public image of the most corrupted bank in America. *Courtesy General Motors Institute, Flint.*

Now, on this pleasant Monday morning of August 12, ever since 7 A.M.—an hour when the financial district was normally as silent as the graveyard of Trinity—people had been arriving by bus and by subway.

They told newsmen they came from the Midwest, from the Deep South, even from Canada. One claimed to have traveled from Alaska. Another said he had spent the past week on the train from Mexico. There were lumberjacks from Montana, cowboys from Texas, homesteaders from Arizona, and shopkeepers from Pennsylvania. A Delaware man said he had given up his vacation to be here in Wall Street. An Ohio clerk admitted he'd thrown up his job to make the journey. A housewife from Connecticut confessed she had left her children in the care of relatives; a husband from Milwaukee said he had told his wife that when she next saw him, he would "be on his way to being a financial somebody."

At eight o'clock, William Crawford turned into Wall Street a full sixty minutes earlier than usual. He had not really believed the weekend reports. Now, he saw that, if anything, they had understated the position.

His practiced eye estimated there were at least a thousand people in Wall Street itself. He pushed past the Exchange to The Corner. Nassau and Broad were similarly thronged. He walked further along Wall and looked up and down William. It was packed. At 55 Wall a crowd stood patiently outside the National City Bank. Across the street other groups stood outside the smaller Bank of Montreal and the Bank of the United States.

Pearl and Warren streets were almost jam-packed; it was virtually the same as far down as Front and South streets.

All told, Crawford thought at least 5,000 people had come to the area around Wall. On that basis there might be as many as 10,000 in the district.

The Stock Exchange superintendent turned and walked back up Wall. This was something beyond any previous experience; he had no way of assessing what it meant, except "that the whole world for some reason wanted to be here."

As Crawford reached the National City Bank building, the crowd outside started to cheer and formed a corridor. Down it, smiling, acknowledging the acclamation, came Charles Mitchell, perspiring freely after his long walk to work. Behind him, as usual, came his chauffeur, clutching Mitchell's attaché case. The driver had prudently left his car parked on Broadway.

A few in the crowd actually reached out to touch Mitchell's jacket, as if by doing so they might themselves be invested with his magical powers. Others asked for market tips. Beaming broadly, the banker told them to put their trust in National City Company issues.

Once he disappeared inside the monolothic building, the crowd dispersed, some of them no doubt to join the lines forming outside practically every customers' room in the district.

Clerks moved down the queues, handing out the brokerage houses' "morning letters." These predicted with confidence which stocks would rise and by how much this Monday, and which shares would "be taken in hand" by a pool or big operator during the 300 minutes of trading time. Whenever Crawford asked anyone why he or she was standing in line, he received the same answer: They wanted to get the best position in the customers' rooms from which to see the quotation boards.

Baffled and somewhat bewildered by all he had seen and heard, Crawford retreated to the Stock Exchange to supervise preparations for opening the market.

To Charlton MacVeagh the lines outside the brokerage offices were a reminder of the long queues of unemployed he had seen in Great Britain during the 1926 general strike. But, whereas in Britain it was often hunger that had brought them into those lines, here, in Wall Street, it was greed.

People exchanged their "morning letters," pored over the financial pages of the daily papers, read and reread magazines, especially this month's *Ladies' Home Journal* with its provocative claim by John J. Raskob that "Everybody Ought to Be Rich." They found no flaw in his argument that fifteen dollars a month, "wisely invested," would make them wealthy within twenty years—except, perhaps, that twenty years was a long time to wait.

The air was thick with talk of company dividends and new pools. People spoke of "luck" and "the breaks." On this August morning, the mentality of Wall Street seemed to owe more to a monster midway than serious finance.

For the first time, MacVeagh felt uneasy about the "constant and unhealthy preoccupation with money."

He turned and made his way into the House of Morgan.

Outside, Michael Levine was on the way to his office where he would direct his army of messengers, numbering 2,000, during what looked to him as if it would be one of the busiest Mondays he had known. With ninety minutes to go before the market opened, tipsters and sharks were already battening off the men and women standing patiently in lines. The touts offered all kinds of shady deals at a price. Levine felt "many a gullible dollar was changing hands for a piece of paper or a few words, both of which weren't worth nothing."

What struck him especially was that most of the newcomers were "not obviously wealthy." And, listening to snatches of their conversation, he thought they had little grip on "the realities of the market."

Levine, like all of the Street's professionals and many of its visitors, had spent the weekend wondering whether the action of the Federal Reserve Board would bring the bull market to an end—as indeed it was intended to do. In just over an hour Levine would learn he need not have worried. Raising the rediscount rate, which had been argued over ever since February, would cause little more than Friday's market hiccough; everything would now continue as before, only more so.

At 9 A.M. pool manager Tom Bragg stood at the foot of Wall with W. E. Hutton-Miller, "Hut" to his colleagues at the distinguished brokerage house of W. E. Hutton and Company, founded by his grandfather. The firm had played a central role in Mike Meehan's Radio pool back in March. Hut had come from the West Coast to join W. E. Hutton full-time not long after the pool ended. The twenty-six-year-old broker had astounded his seniors with his ready grasp of the complex financial maneuvering done in the district.

Looking up the crowded street, Hut told Bragg "maybe the Exchange should be moved to Yankee Stadium."

The poker-faced Bragg almost grinned. Hut's wit had endeared him to those in the firm during the four months he had been there. The well-connected young broker was handsome, sharp, and highly popular. Articulate and hardworking, Hut had already been tabbed as one of the most promising new professionals in the Street. Bragg felt it would only be a matter of time before his companion had a seat on the Exchange.

The two men worked their way up Wall. The further they went, the longer grew the lines of gossiping, gesticulating, and excited people.

Hut sensed that for many, it was enough to be physically present; "It made them insiders. It gave them an edge."

The New York *Times* estimated some 2 million investors across American were now playing the market. Judging by the linesmen he had seen stringing wires, Hut—an expert on cross-country communications—knew that an increasing number of private lines were being installed to ensure "no fashionable resort, no small town, however remote, was without its hook-up to Wall."

To Hut, still living in wonder at his new surroundings, "the air was filled with talk. There was talk of the fortunes made, of fortunes about to be made, of fortunes reinvested to create even larger fortunes. But never talk of money lost."

He and Bragg reached the top of Wall just as the chauffeured car bringing Thomas Lamont turned into the Street.

Hut would always relish, and remember, the "look of absolute astonishment on Lamont's face as he saw the scene."

By the time the car inched to a stop outside Number 23, Lamont had regained his poise. Glancing neither left nor right, immaculate as ever, he walked quickly up the steps and through the opened glass doors. Inside nothing had changed; the usual orderly calm prevailed.

By 9:30 A.M., shoeblack Pat Bologna had practically abandoned his calling to conduct a spirited appraisal of market trends before a growing group of admirers.

Judiciously dropping the names of Joe Kennedy, Charles Mitchell, and other of his distinguished clients, Bologna offered tips and market wisdom to his listeners. In return, some of them gratefully pressed dimes and quarters into his hand. On good mornings like this, Bologna could make as much in an hour from talking as he earned during a day shining shoes.

Mike Meehan's clerk, Ed Schnell, turned into Wall Street and felt he had "strayed into a carnival. People were behaving like they were at the racetrack."

Coupled with their shouting was the din of new office-block construction, the clatter from open-air food counters, mobile vendors hawking their wares, newsboys peddling the morning papers, cars and trucks honking, and ships hooting on the East River.

Inside Number 23, Charlton MacVeagh watched the Morgan partners grouped around Thomas Lamont. With Jack Morgan away on his annual vacation in England, Lamont was effectively in charge of the far-flung Morgan empire.

The brief morning conference over, the partners returned to their desks. Lamont left the enclosure for his private office on the second floor. There he could review without interruption the continuing upward progress of Morgan's flourishing investment trusts—United and Allegheny Corporation.

They were only two of many hundreds. In total, some billion and a half dollars' worth of new investment trust stock had come on the market since the beginning of the year; companies whose activities and composition varied widely, but whose main function in many cases was to invest on margin in the securities of other companies—who in turn were often investing on margin in the stock of yet other companies. According to the accepted mythology, this operation gave investment trusts the magic of "leverage," the ability to increase profits geometrically. It was a tantalizing prospect for small-time investors.

But, like Giannini, Charlton MacVeagh thought many of the trusts were unsound and overspeculative, not at all like the two gilt-edged giants masterminded by the House of Morgan.

Around noon another newcomer arrived in the Street. Nobody gave him a second glance. He was young, barely thirty, stocky, handsome, and very German. He had just arrived from Hamburg. He came with the highest references from the German Ministry of Finance.

Already he had a considerable reputation back home in Augsburg, Bavaria, for designing airplanes. Recently he had established a business footing in the United States. He had granted a manufacturing license to the Eastern Aircraft Corporation of Pawtucket, Rhode Island, to build one of his latest designs, code-named M-18.

But he had more ambitious plans. To make them work he needed money. He was in Wall Street to try to raise it. He would say the money would be used for peaceful means, to design still better passenger and freight planes. In reality, he would eventually help build a secret air force, one intended to avenge the defeats of the World War. His friend, Freiherr Wolfram Von Richthofen, who had just taken up the post of air attaché in the German Embassy in Rome, encouraged him.

The visitor was even more gratified to receive the enthusiastic support from a man he was coming openly to admire—Adolf Hitler. Not long ago, Hitler had told him his planes could help forge a new Germany.

This trip to Wall Street was one of the first positive steps Willy Messerschmitt was taking toward that goal.

CHAPTER SEVENTEEN

HIGH NOON

Edith Stone had come to the conclusion that the distinguished German playwright she met at dinner the night before, Carl Zuckmayer, *was* right. People *did* discuss Berlin as if the city were a highly desirable woman. They called her proud, snobbish, *nouveau riche,* uncultured, and crude.

She could still remember the passion in Zuckmayer's voice as he quoted to her one of his famous passages about the city: "Some see her as hefty, full breasted, in lace underwear; others as a mere wisp of a thing, with boyish legs in black silk stockings."

Zuckmayer had told Edith that to conquer Berlin was to conquer the world. He urged her to abandon her play about Wall Street and instead to fashion a scenario set in Berlin. If she must write a financial drama, then, he had boomed at her, she would find the Berliner Börse certainly as stimulating as the New York Stock Exchange.

He went on to confide that he himself had recently completed a movie script reflecting Berlin's decadence and depravity. Intrigued, Edith decided to visit the film set, on location at Berlin's Zoo Station, on her way to the Börse.

Zuckmayer had warned her he would not be present; he hinted darkly about feuds over his script with the film's director, and gave the impression he did not wish to suffer further seeing it rewritten on location.

When Edith learned the film director's name, she was not surprised the way Zuckmayer felt. From her own brief association with the movie industry, she knew that Josef von Sternberg was highly temperamental, arrogant, and iron-willed. He was said to be "hell on earth to work for."

Nevertheless, watching the preparations for filming going ahead, Edith felt a pang of regret at having abandoned a promising acting career for the lonely slog of writing. She was, she had to admit to herself, finding it increasingly difficult to keep her Wall Street theme to the fore. Here, more than three thousand miles away from the financial district, other, fresher thoughts constantly crowded her original ideas. In a letter home to her parents, she encapsulated her problems perfectly: "Too many vivid impressions and strong characters, all demanding my attention in Paris, in Lucerne and now in Berlin."

And, on this morning in mid-August—fifteen years to the month since the World War had broken out—Edith again sensed something she dare not tell her parents about, for fear her father would insist she returned home at once.

Here, "in the reality of the situation," Hitler was no longer a figure to be discarded with the days-old newspapers that reached New York by ship. In the week she had been in Berlin, Edith saw "his menace was everywhere. It was there in the photographs the newspapers published. It was there in his portraits some shop windows displayed. It was there in the swastika banners, armbands and lapel badges his followers wore. Above all, it was there in his brown-shirted, jack-booted troops who were roaming the streets."

Many were in Berlin for the first time; simple, country-oaf boys with the broad accents of southern Germany, brought into the city by Hitler to maintain "a presence."

Over dinner Zuckmayer had castigated them as "fine examples of the perfect definition of a beast—a Bavarian crossed with an Austrian." Their crudity and loudness disgusted Edith. But their rabid anti-Semitism frightened her. Almost for the first time in her life was she "aware that I was Jewish, and somehow different in the eyes of these people."

A group of uniformed Nazis were watching the filming, staring fixedly at Von Sternberg positioning his actors.

Edith recognized, and was surprised to see, Emil Jannings in the cast. She still vividly recalled the very public quarrel between the actor and Von Sternberg during the last film they had made together in Hollywood. It was called *The Last Command,* produced in 1927 when Jannings had been the highest paid silent movie star in America. He was getting $400,000 a year, plus substantial perks. Then, with the arrival of talkies, Jannings, as German as sauerkraut, refused to learn English. His contract was canceled. He returned to Berlin and vanished from the world's movie screens.

Now, looking older and fatter than Edith remembered, Jannings was trying for a comeback. He had swallowed his considerable pride and persuaded Von Sternberg to direct him again.

Edith watched Jannings' costar standing on her chalked cue line. Von Sternberg had originally rejected the tall, svelte young actress for the part: *"Der Popo ist nicht schlecht, aber brauchen wir nicht auch ein Gesicht?"* (Her bottom is not at all bad, but don't we also need a face?)

Later, he had been persuaded to change his mind. Marlene Dietrich not only had a stunning figure, she also had a haunting face.

Watching the actress walk through her scene, Edith knew she was witnessing a potential world star at work. Fraulein Dietrich was an inspired choice to express the decadent eroticism of *The Blue Angel*.

During a break in the shooting, Edith noticed the swastika emblem in Jannings' jacket lapel. And, as if to confirm her worst fears, before leaving, the group of young Nazis raised their arms in the party salute. Jannings solemnly clicked his heels and returned the salute in similar fashion.

Sickened, and saddened, by what she had seen, Edith left the location.

A few blocks away from the Börse toward which Edith now walked, Louis Lochner was preparing another European financial round-up-and-reaction story to the Wall Street bull market. His report in January had, together with a number of other old-fashioned journalistic scoops, paved the way for the energetic Lochner to become the Associated Press's Berlin Bureau chief, a key post in the wire service network.

Checking through his notes for the earlier story, Lochner was astonished how far attitudes throughout Europe had changed.

Eight months before, apart from Swiss readers, few Europeans were remotely aware of American high finance. Now, from Brussels to Belgrade, news of Wall Street frequently received front-page treatment. Even in Moscow, thanks to the pioneer marketing of Henry Ford—he was building tractors for Stalin's Five-year Plan—Russians were interested in the relationship between American industry and stocks and shares.

While French newspaper still stubbornly resisted the idea of publishing the closing prices in New York, in Belgium, Holland, Sweden, and half a dozen other countries, Wall Street quotations were regularly reported.

The Italian press found events in the United States a welcome relief from the growing economic confusion at home. Trading on the Milan Exchange was as sluggish as ever. Foreign investment had reached a new low; hard-pressed Italian businessmen had no lira left to speculate in Wall Street. Fundamentally an agrarian society, Italy was not greatly helped by what was described as "Mussolini's day-to-day muddling through" economic policy. The price index continued to fall; unemployment was starting to climb sharply as industrial production slowed down.

Italy's neighbor, France, had never been stronger economically. The nation's huge gold reserves continued to grow; many Frenchmen believed that one day soon France would replace America as the world's leading depository for the metal. Unemployment was almost nonexistent. The country's budget balanced easily. Immensely successful, confident, unrelenting in her pursuit of war reparations from Germany, the republic continued on its serene course under the new guiding hand of President Aristide Briand.

Lochner read his old German notes. One thing struck him at once. Hitler was now a factor to be reckoned with. He claimed some half a million followers, and more were joining the party every day. His rallies in Bavaria and the Rhineland attracted large crowds. Hitler had never yet referred specifically to the economic policies he planned for Germany, although he frequently criticized the "Jews of Wall Street" for ruining America. Germany's Jewish population had made no effective move to rebuff his anti-Semitism; it was as if by not confronting Hitler, they hoped he would go away. The reverse, as Lochner realized, was true. And Lochner believed Hitler's adherents were hypnotized. The reporter wondered how a man whose diction was scarcely faultless, who fumed and stomped, so successfully impressed even young intellectuals. Canvassing opinions for a story, Lochner had put the question to an assistant professor at the Berlin Institute of Technology. Albert Speer explained he was attracted by Hitler's "reasonable modesty. To me there was something engaging about it—all the more so since it ran counter to everything the propaganda of his opponents had led me to expect."

But Lochner knew that, in fact, relatively few people in Berlin took the little Austrian seriously. Berliners seldom paid serious attention to politics of any kind. Hedonism was rife in a city steeped in narcissistic self-indulgence to a point probably unequaled since the days of ancient Rome.

There was a determined purging of bourgeois standards; every vice was available, on demand, round the clock. There were brothels for the crippled of the World War, for pederasts, for the elderly. There was nude sunbathing and nude stage shows. Couples fornicated in the parks and on the shores of the city's lakes and in the Brandenburg woods. Apart from sexual titillation, speed excited Berliners. Lochner felt they "worshipped the triumph of the machine age." Two years before, they had rapturously hailed the transatlantic flight of Charles Lindbergh. Three weeks before, it was the record-breaking crossing of the *Bremen*. Now Berliners were following enthusiastically the exploits of Dr. Hugo Eckener, attempting to circumnavigate the globe in his *Graf Zeppelin*.

Lochner could be forgiven for wishing he was on the airship, rather than sorting out the complicated financial picture in Germany.

Gustav Stresemann was proving it was possible for the German Government to pay billions of dollars in war reparations to the Allies, by borrowing those billions from those very same countries. Stresemann was determined this system could go on for another fifty-nine years—when the time limit on reparations ran out.

Lochner had come to know and admire Stresemann; the German Foreign Minister was devoted to peace and democracy. Until recently the reporter believed, with Stresemann in control, there was nothing to fear from the rantings of Hitler.

But Lochner had learned it was only a matter of time before Stresemann's influence vanished. The Minister had an incurable kidney disease; his doctors did not expect him to live out the year.

Stresemann's impending death was one factor for the reporter to consider when shaping his story.

There were others. Renewed inflation was threatening Germany. There were bitter wrangles over wages in the Ruhr iron industry. Some 200,000 were facing a lockout. In the countryside of Bavaria and the Black Forest—where Hitler recruited his most willing battalions—the peasants, who had received little benefit from the foreign loans Germany attracted through high interest rates, were facing poverty in growing numbers. And yet in Berlin, in this tenth year of the Weimar Republic, everything was bustling. The shops displayed some of the finest goods in Europe. The theaters played to full houses. The Berliner Börse was, in the words of one broker, "as busy as a beehive." But one of the city's leading financial journalists, Georg Tischert, had posed a question in reply to Lochner's own question about the future. Tischert had asked: "Does anybody know how long this can continue?" Tischert's response would serve as a wrap-up to Lochner's story. What the reporter needed was a striking introduction. Scanning through his notes, he came across a quote from a banker: "We have had our high point. Things will never be the same again. They can only get worse."

Lochner had his opening.

Edith regained her composure by the time she reached Burgstrasse 25, the home of the Börse. The gray-stoned, rectangular, three-storied building faced the river Spree, filled as usual this lunchtime with lumbering barge traffic.

Her father had arranged for a business associate of his, one of the two thousand stockholders trading on the Börse, to show her around. She disliked her guide from the moment they met by the Doric columns supporting the entrance to the Börse.

It was not just the way he clung too long to her hand, or held her arm close as he escorted her into the building. Soon her middle-aged escort was making suggestive innuendos. Edith had become accustomed to such advances in Berlin. She quickly made it clear she had no physical interest in any man so much older than herself. But, apart from his crude approaches, there was something else about her escort Edith disliked. For the moment she could not identify what it was.

Yet, she had to admit, as a guide he was excellent. He explained first the history of the building, how it had been completed in 1864 and remodeled and expanded in 1922 when the produce and bond markets were added.

Inside, the building seemed even busier than Edith remembered the New York Exchange being; brokers were queueing to get to the rows of telephones fixed to each wall of the room.

Her companion explained that trading had begun at noon; now, nearing 1 P.M., it was reaching its peak. The market profile for the day was taking shape and the exchange rates for foreign currencies fixed. By 1:30 the market would be closed and members would adjourn to the Stock Exchange restaurant to continue their business over bowls of steaming goulash and glasses of Weisse, the fruit-based beer beloved of Berliners.

To Edith the trading floor looked similar to the one she had seen in Paris. But unlike the Parisian *agents de change,* the Berlin *Börsenmaklers* were deeply suntanned.

Her escort laughed and squeezed her arm yet again.

He explained a suntan was a mark of affluence. Many brokers spent their weekends at resorts near Berlin cultivating their tans. He knew a resort that was modeled on American lines. Perhaps Edith would like to visit it this weekend?

She ignored the suggestion. Instead Edith pointed to the profusion of "no spitting" and "no smoking" signs on the walls.

In his harsh Prussian accent, her escort explained. "Not all our members are gentlemen. Some are Jews."

Edith felt suddenly sickened. She now knew the reason for her instinctive dislike of this man.

"Are you a Nazi?"

"*Ja.*"

Her fury boiled over. "I am Jewish. And I'll promise you one thing. You'll never get another bit of business from my father. I'll see to that."

Eyes still blazing, she stormed out of the Börse, determined to leave Germany as soon as possible. She would take the next available passage on the *Berengaria* and report firsthand to her influential friends in New York just what was happening in Germany.

During the late afternoon of Friday, August 23, Michael Meehan, John J. Raskob, and James Riordan assembled in Captain Rostron's sitting room on the *Berengaria,* moored at Pier 54 in New York Harbor.

Flanking Rostron were his senior officers. In spite of Prohibition, stewards moved among the guests pouring champagne.

There was a good deal to celebrate.

A week before, on August 16, soon after departing Southampton, the *Berengaria*'s brokerage service had begun. Two days before that, much to Meehan's annoyance, on leaving Le Havre the liner *Île de France* had started its service for the French firm of Saint-Phalle and Company. But the office on the *Île de France* ran into transmitting troubles and had to relay orders through London, causing a delay of twenty-five minutes before its trading transactions were confirmed. Meehan took comfort in the fact that orders from his shipboard office were sent by shortwave direct to the U.S. mainland; investors on the *Berengaria* had their orders executed in just five minutes. Further, Meehan now had a second office afloat, aboard the *Leviathan* of the United States Lines. He was well ahead of his competitors, even though the newspapers reported other brokerage firms were about to follow his lead. Meehan did not mind. He approved of any moves that made the public more "stock conscious."

Today, he was at his ebullient best, carrying on where the newspapers left off; he was happy to encourage the massive amount of journalistic speculation floating brokerages had attracted. He answered Rostron's question by saying he saw no reason why there shouldn't be a ticker installed on the *Berengaria*. Meehan confided RCA engineers had said it was technically possible, that it could be only a matter of time before shipboard tickers became as commonplace as those on the land. One tabloid had even gone so far as to suggest that the *Graf Zeppelin*—now crossing the Pacific and nearing California—might also be equipped with its own special ticker.

Meehan visualized the time when no place on earth was out of range of the New York Stock Exchange.

Nobody dismissed the idea as farfetched. Mike Meehan, by his drive and determination, had shown anything was possible.

Listening to his friend, James Riordan thought that, if Meehan really put his mind to it, he could "place a ticker on the moon." Riordan had never been happier. His bank business was booming, his investment portfolio with Meehan was growing, his social calendar was crowded with invitations to dinners and balls. And, on this balmy Friday afternoon, he could toast again in champagne the twentieth birthday of his daughter Florence. As well as giving her a snappy new Chevrolet Roadster, four days earlier Riordan had presented Florence with an expensive diamond necklace. He intended to do the same for his younger daughter, Elizabeth, on her nineteenth birthday in early November.

Raskob, too, happily joined in the toasts to the children. He gave no hint he was engaged in a new, and even more bitter, battle with one of the most powerful religious leaders in America, Bishop James Cannon, as "dry" in drinking terms as Raskob was "wet." Cannon was the driving force in both the Anti-Saloon League and the dry Methodist Church. That alone put them on opposite sides of the social, religious, and political barriers.

But what had really sparked off their enmity was Cannon's speeches in support of Hoover during the presidential campaign of 1928. The bishop had bitterly attacked Raskob and Riordan's close friend, Al Smith. In openly racist speeches, Cannon had said that Smith "wants the Italians, the Sicilians, the Poles and the Russian Jews. That kind has given us a stomachache. We have been unable to assimilate such people in our national life, so we shut the door to them. But Smith says, 'give me that kind of dirty people.' He wants the kind of dirty people that you find today on the sidewalks of New York."

In subsequent speeches, Cannon returned to this theme and larded it still further with attacks on the dubious business ethics of this "ethnic rabble."

Raskob believed such smears had cost Smith the election.

But shortly after Hoover entered the White House, a scandal broke over Cannon's head—one that linked him directly to those "dirty people" he had railed against.

It emerged that for months he had been secretly playing the stock market through a brokerage house which even Richard Whitney avoided. Kable and Company was a bucket shop of the worst kind. In a memorable phrase, Raskob described it as "not so much a bucket, more a leaking sewer pipe."

The firm had been selling stock to speculators on precariously narrow margins. And, anticipating a market drop, in its own special version of selling short, the company had actually withheld purchase of several million dollars' worth of shares already paid for by clients. If the market had broken, the firm would then have been able to fill its clients' orders at prices lower than they had paid—and made a substantial profit for itself.

But the market continued to rise—and Kable and Company had been caught red-handed.

It had now declared itself bankrupt—and was under investigation by the Stock Exchange, the police, and the press.

These inquiries revealed Bishop Cannon, one of the firm's favored customers, had actually profited while others had lost. During an eight-month period, Kable had bought in his name stocks worth $477,000 and resold them for $486,000. Cannon had only invested $2,500 on margin to realize a profit of nearly $9,000.

The sums involved were trifling compared to the sort of deals Livermore, Durant, Cutten, and Raskob regularly pulled off. But, sensing a scandal, the press pounced on Cannon. His private life was also discovered to be blemished. He had what the newspapers euphemistically called "a close friend," an attractive socialite, Helen McCallum. A few days after his own wife died suddenly from a paralytic stroke, Cannon had hurried to Mrs. McCallum in quest of consolation.

Raskob wished no part of this seedy business. Yet Cannon was convinced the newspapers were being encouraged by the financier. In an extraordinarily virulent attack, Cannon spoke of "Raskobism" trying to ruin his life.

Mike Meehan had advised Raskob not to respond to Cannon's wild charges of a "wet" plot. Riordan was not sure this was the best course. He felt his friend's silence could be misconstrued. Better perhaps to go to the press with a clear-cut statement. Raskob was still trying to make up his mind. This visit to the *Berengaria* was a welcome break from a difficult problem.

Led by Captain Rostron, the visitors inspected the ship's brokerage office. One of the *Berengaria*'s staterooms on the Promenade Deck had been turned into a replica of a Wall Street customers' room. Even the portholes had been draped to give clients the familiar low-lit, smoky atmosphere.

Already, hours before the liner sailed, and with the market closed until tomorrow, a number of passengers bound for Europe were standing in the salon, staring at the prices on the quotation boards, wishing it were Saturday.

Before going ashore—having completely satisfied himself the brokerage operation was free of any teething problems—Mike Meehan accepted an invitation from Captain Rostron to make a crossing and see firsthand how his brainchild actually functioned at sea. Depending on the market, Meehan hoped to make the trip "next year sometime"; he would like to visit England again and take his wife and four children with him.

Riordan and Raskob said they, too, would be interested in making a voyage to see the ship's brokerage office at work.

Further, Raskob wanted to go to London soon because, among other things, he wished to check for himself a rumor which a colleague, who had just returned from there, had passed on.

There was said to be some sort of serious financial trouble brewing in the City.

Curious, Rostron asked if anyone in particular was involved.

Raskob hesitated. He disliked gossip. And he knew how dangerous it could be in a delicately poised financial situation.

Raskob told Captain Rostron he preferred not to say more until he had been to London to investigate the rumor in person.

Clarence Hatry presented himself at a side entrance to the Bank of England precisely at the time he had been requested. He wore his usual dark gray pinstripe suit, stiffly starched shirt, and a gray tie. He appeared relaxed, confident, and every inch the brilliant City millionaire the newspapers had so often described. Hatry could well imagine the headlines Fleet Street would roll out if the truth of his present position emerged—that he was head of a gigantic £20 million empire now tottering precariously under the domino effect of his failure to pull off the United Steel deal.

To avoid that collapse, Hatry had asked for this meeting with Montagu Norman, governor of the bank.

Hatry had been surprised how simple it was to arrange matters. A telephone call, a mention of "something important to discuss," and the meeting had been set.

The fact Norman had agreed to see him was a good sign. And there seemed no reason why the governor should not accede to his proposal. There was almost no financial risk; the amount involved was small for Britain's central bank. And later, when the deal was done and Hatry had acquired, with Norman's help, control of United Steel, the governor could take satisfaction from knowing the role he had played.

Traveling up in Norman's private elevator to his first-floor office, Hatry again reviewed in his mind how Norman might respond. Perhaps, after all, the governor would show himself not to be the enemy Hatry thought he was. But there was no way of knowing how Norman would react. He was a law unto himself; he had quarreled with Churchill and half the Cabinet and survived. There were those in the City who said he spoke to God as an equal. There was no doubting his towering intellect. And ever since he had been appointed governor, the strongly handsome, white-goateed Norman had attracted two other descriptions— controversial and eccentric.

Still pondering on how to exploit either, or both, of these conditions, Hatry was shown into Norman's office for his ten o'clock appointment.

Norman rose from behind the flat antique table which, like his friend Thomas Lamont at Morgan's, he preferred to a desk.

He shook Hatry by the hand and courteously led him over to two armchairs by the windows which looked out onto a small paved courtyard.

Hatry noted the decor of the governor's private office. He was surprised to see the room was not paneled.*

It was the first, and only, time he let his concentration slip.

For ten minutes, in what Hatry would always believe was a totally frank and honest review, he explained the background to the United Steel bid. Circumstances had combined against him: There had been Labour's victory at the polls. There had been Lord Bearsted's change of mind. There had been . . .

"Mr. Hatry. I'm very sorry to hear about your troubles. But in my view you just paid too much for your steel companies."

For a long moment Hatry stared at the governor. Norman looked far more forbidding now than he had when Hatry walked into the room.

Attempting to hide his nervousness, he asked Norman whether he could smoke.

The governor nodded.

While lighting his Havana, Hatry tried hard to work out a new tack.

"Mr. Norman. My merger has the full knowledge and support of the City—"

"Clearly that is not so. Otherwise you would not be here."

"But the deal is a bargain—"

"Then take it."

Hatry tried again.

"The companies have been valued. By all accounts they are a bargain. By loaning me the money to complete the arrangements the Bank would be dealing in gilt-edged—"

Hatry would remember how he stopped speaking. He was suddenly conscious he was wasting his time. The eyes of the governor had "grown smaller, colder." Hatry now felt, after all, he "was in the presence of an enemy."

* See Source Notes.

But his desperation, his ego, and his fears drove him to make yet another appeal. Almost gabbling, he explained that if he failed to raise the money his empire could crash. He had tried everything. America was out. The prospects from Europe looked, at best, limited. He was only "temporarily overextended": He needed so little, yet so much depended on his getting it.

Norman could see he was facing a desperate, overwrought man. For a few more moments he let Hatry continue. Then he spoke.

"I'm sorry, Mr. Hatry."

"You mean . . . you mean you will not help me?"

"No, Mr. Hatry. I will not."

Norman rose to his feet and looked down at Hatry. The slightly built financier knew he was beaten. But he would not let go.

"That is your last word?"

"Yes."

The interview was finally over.

Numbed, unable to speak, Clarence Hatry walked in a daze to the door and out of the Bank of England.

In the Union Industrial Bank in Flint, some four thousand miles from the Bank of England, on the morning of August 26, Frank Montague experienced a similar stomach churning feeling to the one Clarence Hatry had felt. Shortly after 9 A.M., bank Vice-president Montague saw bank Chairman Charles Stewart Mott walk into the building.

Montague was flabbergasted. It had been months since Mott had visited the bank. The immediate reaction of the vice-president was: "He knows."

Montague thought the other conspirators in the bank were probably experiencing the same fear. The next emotion he remembered having was one of bitterness at the prospect of being unmasked "just when things were so close to being squared away."

Yesterday, he, Milton Pollock, and Robert Brown had met after the Sunday morning service in the church where they had all worshiped for years. The trio had agreed within a week they could be in the clear.

After a series of spectacular stock market coups, the embezzlers were now very close to replacing the fortune they had stolen earlier in the year. The money had flowed in so fast from Wall Street they had to work late juggling their books and forging account ledgers.

But, even with this continuing success, the strain was almost as great as before. There was the ever-present possibility some honest member of the staff might become suspicious and begin to investigate. There was also the constant threat the bank examiners could make a sudden unforeseen swoop.

And, at home, there was always the chance Montague and his colleagues might drop a careless remark that could alert their families.

Nowadays, Milton Pollock had admitted to Montague, he found it a relief to come to work; there, at least, he could discuss his actions with men who were similarly criminally involved.

Even John de Camp and Ivan Christensen, for so long the most optimistic of the embezzlers, were showing signs of stress as they, like the others, took stringent steps to cover their tracks and anticipate every danger.

But the thieves had put from their minds the possibility of Mott coming to call, especially on a Monday. The few times he had come in the past, Mott dropped in on a Saturday morning and stayed only a few minutes sipping coffee with Grant Brown before leaving for Applewood.

Frozen-faced, Frank Montague now saw that even Grant Brown seemed flustered at Mott's totally unexpected presence. Only later, when the bank president explained, would Montague learn the reason for Brown's visible confusion.

Like many people in Flint, Brown knew Mott's marriage was on the rocks. The private clubs in the city were full of spicy gossip; it was a recurring topic at fashionable dinner tables. Brown was glad at least the *Journal* had fastidiously refrained from publishing a word about the breakup; he wondered how long it would be before the raffish Flint *Saturday Night* ran an item. His concern was not merely over the pain such publicity would cause Mott. He feared, if the gossip was true, that the bank itself could suffer in the aftermath of what might very well be damaging divorce testimony. There could, he had told Montague, be a "loss of confidence."

Mott's presence, normally so welcomed by Brown, was now an acute embarrassment for the staid and starchy bank president. He showed clear relief when Mott suggested they adjourn to the boardroom.

As Mott had hoped, he had caught Brown and his staff totally by surprise. The look of astonishment on their faces as he had walked in was the only bright spot in this first visit to Flint in so long.

He had spent the weekend alone in his red-brick mansion on the outskirts of the city, notating all the events that signposted the end of his marriage. It was a depressing experience, putting on paper his version of the rows and clashes with Dee during the past seven months. Sexually a virile and demanding man, Mott had found it especially hard to cope with Dee's physical rejection of him. Yet his attorney insisted the most intimate details of these refusals be itemized so they could help fashion a watertight case for divorce. And, his lawyer had warned, a divorce was likely to cost Mott a great deal. The millionaire accepted this as the price he must pay to close the unhappiest period in his life. But he had made one stipulation: He would meet almost any demand Dee made except one. She would never have Applewood.

This Monday morning, instead of driving back to Detroit from the house that had been the one constant in his entangled emotional life, Mott had accepted an invitation to breakfast with his old friend, S. S. Stewart. Even after twenty years of friendship, Mott still addressed his fellow industrialist by his initials only.

Stewart was one of the forty directors on the Board of the Union Industrial Bank. The Board was larger than many of the great New York banks', and at least thirty of its directors were close personal friends of Mott; he had unashamedly used his position and voting power to put them there. Envious people said it was one way for Mott to reward favors without spending money. For all his wealth, his thriftiness was legendary. Other directors, like the attorney Goldberger, were on the Board to attract small investors into the bank. Goldberger held 320 shares in the Union Industrial; Stewart close to 2,000. Mott was by far the largest stockholder, with 5,767 shares. Between them, his friends on the Board held about 80 percent of the stock. Some 15 percent was in the hands of people who each held only a handful of votes. The remainder was held by members of the staff. Grant Brown had 3,259 shares; his deputy John de Camp, 1,237; Frank Montague, 266; Elton Graham, 138; and Ivan Christensen, 103 shares.

It was the financial affairs of Christensen that had prompted Mott to adjourn to the privacy of the boardroom.

Over breakfast, Stewart had mentioned the cashier was building a new house costing $75,000.

Stewart, whose wife, Margaret, would remember as "a very private and uncurious person," was "puzzled" how Christensen was able to afford such a palatial home on his modest salary.

When Stewart faced a problem, he frequently climbed into his open cockpit plane and roared round and round in circles over Flint. He found it "marvelously helpful in solving any puzzle."

This time, though, the Flint flight had not helped; Stewart still did not see how Christensen could pay for the house.

Mott had decided to find out.

Grant Brown had a ready answer. He told Mott that when he learned about the house, he had himself carefully questioned the cashier. Christensen calmly explained that his wife, Betty, like many other women in

Flint, played the stock market. She was so successful her winnings were paying for their new home.

Brown had accepted the story. So now did Mott. He left the bank to drive back to Detroit.

Shortly after he had gone, the relieved embezzlers made their first investment of the day. They bought $10,000 worth of railroad shares. Two days later they would sell them at a profit. By then the "league of gentlemen" in Flint would be within $60,000 of paying back the $2.5 million they had "borrowed" and lost in the market.

It looked as if they were going to get away with it.

CHAPTER EIGHTEEN

DOW JONES IS GOING TO HEAVEN

At eight-thirty on the morning of Tuesday, August 27, a chauffeured yellow Rolls-Royce slid into the curb at 730 Fifth Avenue. Jesse Livermore tumbled out of a rear door and entered the Heckscher Building.

His gray double-breasted suit, cut from the finest cloth and expensively tailored, was rumpled. His once spotless white shirt, with the new lay-down collar, looked as if he had slept in it; his costly red foulard was loose.

In the bright morning sunlight Livermore looked his fifty-two years. His hair, no longer carefully combed, while still predominantly blond, was shot through with telltale flecks of white; it receded straight back from his high forehead, somehow accentuating his large nose and ears. He wore pince-nez glasses.

Normally Livermore's slim figure suggested a quick-thinking and acting man. Today, the effect was curiously feminine; his dismissive gesture to the chauffeur had been almost effete. On his right little finger he wore a sapphire in a setting designed for a more masculine hand.

Unaware he was being watched, Livermore crossed the lobby toward the elevators.

Outside, on the sidewalk, one of Michael Levine's messengers, already on his way to work, quickened his pace, eager to report what he had seen.

For the past month Wall Street's brokerage houses had buzzed with rumors about Livermore's whereabouts and intentions. He was reported to have been seen at both Miami and Nice. He was said to have traveled secretly to Canada and to England for discussions with "leading financiers" about forming a consortium to attack the market. In many ways the most sensational of all the rumors was the one suggesting Jesse Livermore was about to become a bull, returning to those days when he and Billy Durant in tandem were believed to have pushed up the value of a wide variety of shares. It was repeated, with growing conviction, that Livermore had no alternative; that, with the market continuously climbing, he had to become bullish to show a profit.

But, until this morning, Livermore had not been positively spotted in public for over a month.

The messenger knew his sighting would lend credence to all those other rumors circulating about Livermore.

Having watched him stagger into the Heckscher Building, the messenger was convinced Livermore was still drunk after a night's carousing. That did not surprise him; it was common gossip Livermore drank "like a fish," preferably with a pretty girl for company and a stock ticker close-by. Malicious wags said that "when Livermore is speculating he is thinking of screwing; when he is screwing he is thinking of speculating."

For once, the gossips were wrong. Livermore had spent most of the night doing something he had not done for years—staying at home and having a calm and rational discussion with Dorothy.

Each of them realized that, despite the truce of past weeks, their marriage had reached a critical stage. They had agreed to try to talk through their problems. It was a painful experience for them both.

Dorothy had listed her catalogue of neglect and indifference, her feeling of rejection as a result of his behavior. Livermore had explained his objections to her drinking bouts and slovenly appearance.

The initial tension between them had slowly disappeared; gradually, they both admitted their faults. And eventually, with dawn breaking, they resolved to consider all they had said to see if there really could be a future together.

Dorothy had gone to bed. But Livermore was unable to sleep. His mind, he would say later, "was in a turmoil." He seriously doubted whether he could do what Dorothy wanted. He wondered, too, whether she could change habits that had become so ingrained.

Finally, he had dozed in a chair. His chauffeur had awoken him and reminded Livermore this was the morning he was to return to the office. For the past month, the speculator had been resting at his country estate outside New York, considering not only the future of his marriage but also that of the market.

Livermore was not swayed by the crowds cramming Wall Street and customers' rooms across America. They were "just a symptom; I was looking for the cause."

Yet there seemed not a cloud in sight. The newspapers, Livermore had to admit, were right; it surely was boom time. Yet his "gut reaction" told him beneath the surface "powerful hidden forces" were on the move. He had felt like this before—on the eve of the San Francisco earthquake in 1906, and the Great Panic a year later. But on both those occasions he had made a fortune by selling short. This time his "gut reaction" was telling him something different.

At 10 A.M.—shaved, showered, and dressed from the substantial wardrobe he always kept at the office—Livermore moved into action. He had decided, like the bankers in Flint, to buy railroad stock. But, whereas they had invested $10,000, Livermore purchased shares worth $250,000. Tomorrow, he too would take his profit.

Watching their mentor at work, Livermore's staff smiled approvingly. They were glad he was back. And it was good to see the most famous bear in Wall Street at last being bullish.

Winston Churchill was also pleased this Tuesday, August 27, and for similar reasons. All the signs pointed toward his tour of Canada and the United States being a financial success. In one of his regular letters home to his wife, Clementine, he provided a detailed breakdown of his earnings since leaving England.

In just over three weeks, from contracts, articles, and investments, Churchill had earned an extra £5,750. He told Clemmie he hoped to make further "successful investments here and in the United States, and am glad to be able to find a little capital for that purpose. So you do not need to worry about money. The more we can save the better, but there is enough for all of us."

Free now of the burdens of high office, Churchill had spent part of his time in Canada reflecting on the infighting going on within the defeated Conservative party in England. Neville Chamberlain was emerging as the obvious successor to former Prime Minister Baldwin. Churchill wrote Clemmie he had almost made up his mind to "clear out of politics and see if I cannot make you and the kittens a little more comfortable before I die."

He was, he frankly admitted, attracted to "pastures new"—Canada and a business career. He felt "there are fortunes to be made in many directions. The tide is flowing strongly."

Churchill and his party—his son Randolph, his brother Jack, and his nephew Johnny—were traveling across Canada aboard a magnificent private rail car, the *Mount Royal*. Randolph and Johnny were high-spirited undergraduates at Oxford, and had shown quick appreciation for the beautiful Canadian women they met. Churchill confided to Clemmie he was having problems trying to "enforce discipline" among his lively charges.

And in spite of the pace—"we have never ceased travelling, starting, stopping, packing, unpacking, scarcely ever two nights in any one bed except the train"—Winston Churchill was hugely enjoying himself in an endless round of speechmaking, sightseeing, banqueting, and handshaking.

In Winnipeg he had visited the Stock Exchange, where, so he wrote his wife, "frantic dealers screamed and gesticulated as the telegrams from all the world recorded the ceaseless fluctuations of wheat prices."

Now in Banff, one of Canada's great beauty spots, Churchill and party were about to move on. Ahead lay the United States. He had already written to his old friend, Bernard Baruch, that in America he wanted "to meet the leaders of its fortunes"; along the way he hoped to get some worthwhile tips about investing in Wall Street. To William Randolph Hearst, who would be his main host on the West Coast, Churchill wrote: "We must discuss the future of the world, even if we cannot decide it."

Randolph and Johnny Churchill had made it clear that when they reached the first major stop in their U.S. travels—Hearst's self-designed castle at San Simeon, near Hollywood—they would waste no time in appraising the charms of the young movie actresses they hoped to meet.

And, fully aware of the perils of United States Prohibition, Randolph Churchill wrote in his diary before leaving Canada that "we are well equipped. My big flask is full of whisky and the little one contains brandy. I have reserves of both in medicine bottles. It is almost certain that we shall have no trouble. Still, if we do, Papa pays the fine, and I get the publicity."

Publicity was very much on John J. Raskob's mind. On Thursday, August 29, the New York *Times* broke the story about the Empire State Building; the financier had finally decided to beat the drum for his attempt to win the skyscraper stakes. He had given the *Times* an exclusive, shrewdly realizing the rest of the media would soon follow up. The *Times* had confined itself to a straightforward report of the expected cost and proposed dimensions of the new tower. The wire services widened the scope of the story; the Associated Press was carrying an account of how the operation was being financed; United Press had an interview with architect William Lamb about the staggering variety of materials involved in the project. All three radio networks had interviewed Raskob. He told his friend Mike Meehan that, newspaper storywise, his buoyant brokerage was "no match for my big building."

And Raskob had not finished. A retinue of reporters and photographers were gathering outside the Fifth Avenue entrance to the Waldorf-Astoria Hotel, now derelict. The last of the carpets and furniture had been trundled out and stored, ready eventually to grace a rebuilt Waldorf on Park Avenue. The front doors of the hotel—through which kings and emperors once passed—had also been removed, leaving in their place a yawning gap.

At a signal from a foreman, a multiwheeled truck roared up the broad marble steps, through the gap, down the empty cavernous lobby, and turned into the columned passage known to Waldorf-Astorians the world over as "Peacock Alley."

Momentarily lost in the gloomy interior, the driver changed gears and began to back up the truck, its tires grinding over the once highly polished floor of the lobby where Edward, Prince of Wales, had nodded to King Carol of Romania before sitting down to supper with Kitchener of Khartoum.

Down the lobby toward the truck came a gaggle of reporters, their voices echoing in the emptiness of a hotel where Prince Henry of Prussia had tippled with Buffalo Bill, and Teddy Roosevelt had hosted an intimate luncheon for ninety in honor of the King and Queen of Belgium.

At the far end of Peacock Alley stood Raskob and James Riordan.

Like flagmen, they caught the truck driver's eye and motioned him toward them. Its engine noise reverberating in the confined space, the vehicle finally came to a halt.

From the truck's cabin jumped a crew of white-overalled stonemasons, equipped with special marble-cutting hand saws.

Pointing to the row of imposing pillars, Raskob proudly announced to the reporters he intended to preserve the priceless columns in his country house in Maryland as a permanent reminder of the hotel.

The workmen fixed ropes to the first of the pillars, and, on a nod from Raskob, one of the stonemasons started to saw.

The blade cut into the delicately veined column—and sent a spray of plaster powder into the air. The pillars, carefully painted to look like ancient marble, had for years successfully fooled the Waldorf's select clientele.

But all was not lost. A workman appeared from the rear of the hotel. He whispered something in Raskob's ear.

Raskob motioned for Riordan and the reporters to follow him.

They descended through an old kitchen area to a subbasement.

There, at the end of a long-forgotten passage, the workman pointed to a padlocked steel door which had been hidden for years behind an accumulation of hotel bric-a-brac.

Determined to retrieve at least something from the fiasco of the faked columns, Raskob sent for William Lamb to bring the original site plans of the hotel.

Watched by the impatient reporters, the architect soon traced the passageway on the faded blueprints. He quietly explained to Raskob the original purpose of the room behind the padlocked door.

Eyes glinting in expectation, Raskob ordered the workman to break open the padlock.

He and Riordan then gently prized open the door.

It was the entrance to a wine cellar which had probably been locked since the earliest days of the hotel.

The cellar contained five huge hogsheads of whiskey, each barrel dating from the Spanish-American War, and cases of fine French wines and champagne.

A reporter asked Raskob what he intended to do with his find.

The financier looked at him solemnly. "I'll impound it, of course. What else can I do? There's Prohibition."

He ordered the workman to round up reinforcements. They quickly hefted the barrels and cases onto the truck still in the lobby. It drove out of the hotel and, like so many other consignments of forbidden alcohol, this one disappeared.*

The stock ticker in Billy Durant's sealed and spotless office was silent on September 2. This was Labor Day, and the market was officially on holiday. It did not keep away the crowds from Wall Street, or speculators like Durant from their offices. He was at his desk early, preparing his strategy for the fall.

There now appeared no foreseeable need for the Van Sweringen brothers, John J. Raskob, and him to come together to support General Motors stock; the corporation's shares were climbing steadily; Mott had not allowed his private life to interfere with his work at GM. The Van Sweringens had indicated they preferred to operate alone; Raskob seemed totally preoccupied with his Empire State Building.

For the past two weeks Durant had in fact been considering reactivating his famous and feared consortium consisting of some twenty fellow multimillionaires. Last year, between them, they had invested an estimated $4 billion in the market.

On Tuesday, August 20, an important day for Wall Street analysts like Durant, stocks had risen even more briskly through the list than they had previously. At 2 P.M. rails and utilities "took fire." Durant had agreed with *The Wall Street Journal* that it "reestablishes the major upward trend . . . the outlook for the fall months seems brighter than at any time in recent years."

Like Joe Kennedy, Durant took a wide view, relating even the inter-

* When Prohibition was repealed on December 5, 1933, Raskob produced the liquor for a celebration party. But he never revealed where it had been hidden.

national scene to the New York Stock Market. Yesterday's *Times* had carried the headline: "Arabs Invade Palestine from Three Directions. Fighting Reported in Haifa." But that was unlikely to affect American share prices. Closer to home, the Sunday editions had also reviewed Hoover's first six months in office. The papers gave him cautious approval, though one commentator thought "the real test of his political strength has yet to come."

A number of writers credited Hoover with maintaining economic confidence, so helping to keep Wall Street humming.

Durant was not so certain. Looking back on his visit to the White House, he doubted he had achieved much. Hoover may have delayed but he had not stopped the Fed from raising the rediscount rate. Nor did he appear to Durant to be curtailing the frequent Reserve Board announcements criticizing speculation in the Street. Perhaps the President had acquired a knack so many politicians do when they assume high office: an ability to say what people want to hear.

Durant scanned the financial pages. Sterling, at $4.84⅝, was at its lowest since 1926, the year of the general strike. He could imagine the feeling of consternation in London at this latest drop; he guessed the Bank of England might well raise its interest rate to coax money back to Britain.

But, at the end of his deliberations, Billy Durant concluded nothing could now stop the bull market continuing.

Having decided that, he could move forward with confidence. He would begin laying the groundwork for a new, full-scale plunge into the market.

It would, he knew, take several weeks of meetings and discussions to settle just who would join him in the syndicate. He would like to introduce some new blood. Joe Kennedy was one man he had in mind; he admired his professionalism, the way he kept his emotions under careful control and never panicked or, just as important, became overexultant when things were going well. And perhaps James Riordan would join in. The banker was known to be "enthusiastic and popular." Durant considered Mike Meehan. The Radio specialist strongly impressed him by the way he had established the Radio pool in March. And, almost as important, with Meehan might come the services of Bragg and Smith, whose skills would be an asset to any consortium.

But before any new members could be recruited, Durant would need to obtain at least the tacit blessing of the main founder members of his original group—the seven Fisher brothers from Detroit, Percy Rockefeller, and one or two others. That, too, would take time. The Fishers were a dour, cautious lot; they would not be pushed into accepting partners until they were sure they could be trusted.

Once the consortium's composition was settled, still more time would be needed to agree which stocks should be manipulated. The duration of the operation, when it should begin, the cutoff point, the split afterward—all these important matters must be settled in advance. Durant thought a massive, wide-ranging assault appropriate. The outlay might even exceed the estimated $4 billion used in 1928; raising that sort of money would also take time. It seemed to Durant it would probably be late October before his pool was in action. He provisionally set the start date for Monday, October 28.

Late in the afternoon on Labor Day a reporter from WJZ, NBC's New York flagship station, telephoned astrologist Evangeline Adams for an offbeat view of the stock market in the coming months. She briskly replied that "the Dow Jones could climb to Heaven."

Her prediction, broadcast on the evening news, cheered tens of thousands of motorists whose cars, newly equipped with radios, crawled along roads clogged for miles around New York with homeward-bound holiday traffic.

Next morning, Tuesday, September 3, one ear cocked to the radio, Charlton MacVeagh bolted his breakfast, kissed Adele, and hurried to Wall Street. The three-day holiday had been an unwelcome intrusion for the young broker. Adele believed her husband was nowadays "like a champion horse anxious to get on with the race."

The downtown subway was crowded and stifling; the Weather Bureau forecast this would be the hottest day of the year so far. A temperature in New York of 95° was expected.

To take his mind off conditions on the train, Charlton tried to recall highlights from the morning news bulletin. With the market closed, there had been no mention of stocks and shares. It was the first Tuesday morning newscast he could remember devoid of such information. Even so, Charlton was able to relate almost anything he heard to the market. There had been a report from Europe that disarmament was being discussed in its usual desultory fashion; that would do no harm to stocks. The *Graf Zeppelin* had safely completed its round-the-world flight and was now flying home from Lakewood, New Jersey; its success would be good for those companies promoting global airship travel. Eight people had died in an air crash in New Mexico; bad for air stocks. *All Quiet on the Western Front* was still comfortably ahead of *Dodsworth* on the best-seller lists; both books would help boost publishing and printing company stocks. Women's dresses were going to emphasize an even flatter look this fall; another fillip for the shares of rag-trade companies.

Coming into Wall Street by train from another part of the city,

William Crawford also had time to catch up with the day's news—and place it in context with the stock market.

His morning paper reported it was going to be a bitter three-way mayoralty race in November; the outcome could affect local utility issues.

Jimmy Walker was again denying charges by the socialist candidate, Norman Thomas, that he was a "Tango Mayor"; Walker claimed he had been in nightclubs only three times since assuming office in 1926, and that on each occasion it was to celebrate his wedding anniversary. Remembering the unhappy Janet Walker he had seen in the Exchange's public gallery, Crawford doubted the mayor's wife had much enjoyed the outings.

Fiorello La Guardia was predicting a landslide victory for himself. He promised when he got into office one of the first things he would do was pass a city ordinance forbidding aircraft from flying too close to skyscrapers like the proposed Empire State Building.†

Crawford fully approved of La Guardia's proposal. In the past year, New York had become a favorite playground for joy-riding amateur and military pilots. During recent weeks planes had actually cavorted through the canyons of the financial district, chased each other around the spire of the Woolworth Building, still the city's tallest skyscraper, and flown under the Brooklyn Bridge. Their daredevil antics caught the public's imagination, and so helped to boost the stocks of airplane manufacturers and airlines.

The superintendent deplored this almost as much as he resented some of the more fanciful claims involving Wall Street being made on this opening day of the fall advertising campaign.

More firms than ever were peddling securities of all kinds. Many of the claims smacked of rank huckstering. And the slightest connection with the market was enough for an advertiser. Investors who spent their day in smoky customers' rooms were advised to buy a gargle that "killed 200,000 germs in 15 seconds"; the refreshed speculators were reminded a clear throat went "a long way" toward a clear head, so necessary when playing the market. Businessmen were urged to smoke a certain cigar which was both "elegant and long enough to encourage a feeling of wealth."

Paid testimonials by society figures abounded. A French princess claimed she would only ever serve one brand of ginger ale to her broker and banker friends; an Austrian baron said he believed that by buy-

† In July 1945 a twin-engined B-25 army bomber, lost in blinding fog, crashed into the Empire State Building. Thirteen people were killed in the disaster. The first flier ever to crash into a New York City building did so on November 20, 1929. His two passengers died with him.

ing particular bonds he was ensuring the future of all his estates back home; an Italian count pushed another issue for a similar reason.

And, as might be expected, the funeral industry had cast its beady eye on the market-makers. In a message radiant with good tidings—and aimed specifically at bankers like Charles Mitchell and partners of the House of Morgan—a New York burial firm made known its willingness to provide a mausoleum with a suite of luxurious rooms for the dead, where the private papers relating to their business deals could be kept by them, neatly stored, presumably pending the Day of Judgment; then, perhaps, a greater deity even than Jack Morgan would decide the merits of those deals. The burial firm reminded its potential customers: "From the Pyramids of Ancient Egypt, down the corridors of time, to the tomb of the unknown soldier, the mausoleum has always been chosen as the final resting place of kings and queens, statesmen and famous generals."

Now successful brokers could have a similar tomb, "nestling in the beautiful hills of Westchester County, within an hour's ride of the crossroads of America's greatest center of population, a fitting monument, a symphony in marble."

Crawford felt it was just the sort of edifice Richard Whitney might purchase.

These days the vice-president of the Stock Exchange was more officious than ever, meddling in areas he knew little or nothing about. Recently Whitney had imperiously demanded that the ticker should keep up with trading. Crawford had tried to explain the problems. Whitney cut him off with an icy "I've no time for excuse makers."

Now that Simmons was preparing to marry in just over a month, Whitney had practically assumed the presidential mantle.

And already there were renewed rumors he was using the powers of his office to attempt to horn in on deals. A story was circulating that Whitney would welcome an offer to participate in a pool; in return, the President-elect of the New York Stock Exchange would make known his approval of the pool stock concerned.

To the outraged Crawford, it sounded even more blatant than some of the tricks performed by Madison Avenue publicists.

Shoeblack Pat Bologna, on the other hand, approved of the closer-than-ever links between Madison Avenue and the financial world; anything that focused attention on Wall Street was fine by Bologna. His fame was spreading. Every day more people came to his stand for market consultations. He had never been busier—or better off. The dimes and nickels he collected he invested in stocks. Bologna liked to say, "My money never leaves the Street. It's the best place in the world for it to be."

Not far from Bologna, in his basement office, Michael Levine knew by nine-thirty this was going to be "a helluva day." His two thousand messengers, running between banks, brokerage houses, and Wall Street's exchanges were unable to keep up with the flow of envelopes containing order slips, share certificates, and checks waiting to be messengered around the financial district.

At one minute past ten, sixty seconds after Crawford had banged his gavel to open trading, Levine felt he and his boys were in danger of "sinking in a sea of paper. Everybody in the whole damned district was buying and selling."

Around eleven o'clock, Jesse Livermore's team of analysts and statisticians confirmed what their employer already knew from the stock ticker. The market, in the words of one aide, was "being pushed up as if propelled by a financial volcano."

Livermore turned back to reading the New York *Times* entertainment guide. He told his secretary to book him seats for tonight's performance of Eddie Cantor's *Whoopee*. But he cautioned his staff not to relax. Exactly a week ago, for a short period, he had been a bull. Now he was awaiting another informed "gut reaction" before making his next move.

By noon, Billy Durant regarded the marked strength of the first 120 minutes of trading which had flashed across his office ticker as an exceedingly favorable portent. After only the briefest period of consolidation, the market had then moved on to even higher ground.

About 2 P.M., Mike Meehan felt it safe to snatch a quick lunch away from the hurly-burly around Post Twelve, where, for the past four hours, there had been "tremendous activity" in RCA stock; Radio, having not yet paid a dividend, and after its five-for-one split, was hovering around the $101 a share mark.

Elsewhere on the jam-packed Exchange trading floor, public utilities were especially strong, as were the stocks of amusement companies. Copper was making a comeback, led by Anaconda; to the great relief of Charles Mitchell, his super National City Company salesmen were now getting rid of the last of the stock so unceremoniously dumped on him by Tom Bragg back in June.

In America's other exchanges a similar across-the-board upward trend to that in New York was also clearly evident.

At 3 P.M., when Crawford banged his gavel for the second time in five hours, the New York stock market stopped, 4,438,910 shares having been traded during the day.

American Tel and Tel had risen to 304; U. S. Steel stood at 262;

General Electric was 396; J. I. Case, 350; New York Central, 256; RCA closed at 100.

The Dow Jones Average of industrial stock prices was 381.17, confirming, as Evangeline Adams had predicted the day before, it was indeed climbing to the heavens.

Already *The Wall Street Journal* editor responsible for pulling together the market information his reporters had filed was shaping his story for tomorrow.

It read: "Wall Street entered the autumn financial season in a definitely optimistic frame of mind. With railroad traffic showing steady gains, and production in the major branches of industry continuing at a high rate, the earnings prospects of the principal corporations with shares listed on the Stock Exchange were looked upon as extremely promising. Sentiment regarding the credit outlook was reassured by the activities of the Federal Reserve authorities in placing funds at the disposal of business through bill purchases in the open market. With trade and credit conditions favorable, buying orders accumulated in large volume over Labor Day, and the forward movement in the main body of stocks was vigorously resumed in the early dealings. . . . While irregularity cropped out from time to time during the day, due to profit-taking attracted by the sweeping character of the recent gains, the main upward trend was fairly well sustained throughout the session. Bullish enthusiasm was stimulated by the return of United States Steel to leadership of the industrial division."

It was prose to match the torrid weather; the temperature in New York, as expected, came close to 95°, a record for early September.

And, although no one could possibly know it at the time, another record was set on this Tuesday, September 3. The Great Bull Market had reached its high point.

Jesse Livermore, the notorious bear, eighteen floors up in his Fifth Avenue office, somehow sensed "events were at a decisive stage." He was still sniffing the air for signs and clues. But he decided to abandon all his private pursuits and remain at his desk. His staff had been promised bonuses if they could give him concrete evidence to confirm his intuitive feelings. Livermore's office was, in the words of an aide, "at battle stations."

The first warning shell was lobbed from across the Atlantic.

CHAPTER NINETEEN

CONFESSION TIME

It fell on Livermore's desk some time in the afternoon of Wednesday, September 4. It came in the form of a message from London. Whether it was by transatlantic telephone—introduced two years before and still an innovation—or by one of the coded telegrams that regularly arrived at his office remained unknown. So did the name of his informant.

Livermore took great pains to protect his sources; it was the only way he could continue to receive the sort of information that reached him this morning.

The message came in three separate parts.

The first part said a "high official" in the Bank of England reportedly told associates over lunch in the City this very day—London was five hours ahead of New York—that "the American bubble has burst."

Several times in the past month, Livermore had heard similar assertions from sources in Europe.

The second part quoted the same official as saying there were strong rumors Governor Montagu Norman of the Bank of England was looking for an excuse to raise the interest rate before the end of the month. That *was* significant, and made sense. The outflow of gold from Great Britain in July and August had been huge, the major portion of which was taken by France. The bullion stock of the Bank was now a mere £137 million. There was an obvious need to reestablish faith in sterling. And, as the Federal Reserve had raised the New York rediscount rate by 1 percent, there was reason to expect England to retaliate. If Norman did raise his discount rate, money earmarked for Wall Street would likely be diverted to London. That would be bad for the home market.

The third part of the message was also thought-provoking. It stated that Clarence Hatry was in serious financial trouble.

Livermore knew Hatry by reputation as an able and skilled financier. One thing puzzled him: If Hatry was endangered in London, why had he not turned to Wall Street for help?

Livermore did not know the answer. But he decided to keep a careful eye on what sounded like a fast-developing situation.

He turned to a report from another trusted source—one with access to the Federal Reserve Board.

This Washington source did not expect the board to take "any further definite steps" in September; it had made its big move in August. The board would remain as sluggish as the Potomac which it overlooked.

It was a generally quiet day. The market closed with many prices having receded somewhat in what was described as an overdue "technical correction." But General Motors, with a three-point gain, and RCA, up a full ten points, moved against the day's downward trend.

Radio had increased fourteen dollars a share in three days of trading. Livermore, like many operators, wondered whether Mike Meehan was backing another pool. By early evening he knew Meehan was as baffled as anybody why Radio, which had shown little movement in weeks, had now sprung so dramatically back to life. The stock was one of the public's favorites; it seemed for no reason suddenly to have taken their fancy again.

Livermore remained until midnight at his office trying to piece together "a jigsaw which did not have all the pieces."

Next morning, Thursday, long before his weary staff returned to their calculations, he was back at his desk, phoning, checking, cross-checking. He got people out of bed on the West Coast; out of meetings in London, Paris, and Berlin. Nothing really gelled.

At 8 A.M., talking to a contact in Boston, he was reminded that today's luncheon speaker at the annual National Business Conference was economist Roger W. Babson, who had been bearish about the market for the past two years.

Impulsively, Livermore asked his secretary to bring him Babson's file. Livermore kept dossiers on a wide number of people; fellow speculators like Kennedy, Cutten, Raskob, and Durant; journalists like Alexander Noyes of the *Times;* bankers like Giannini and Mitchell. The files were regularly updated and assessed.

The folder on Babson was slim, but revealing. The economist had first come to the notice of Livermore's staff during the "panic" of March 1926 when the market slumped sharply. Babson, however, had not thought the decline sufficient to "create any real stock bargains."

He urged investors to subscribe to his "long-swing-area method," a system Livermore dismissed as "designed purely for bearish minnows."

Babson had gone on being a bear, offering through 1927 and the boom year of 1928 a bleak blanket forecast that "any major movement should be on the downward side."

A year ago, at the same conference he was to address this lunchtime, Babson proclaimed that, if Al Smith and the Democrats were elected, "we are almost certain to have a resulting business depression in 1929."

Smith lost to Hoover, so there was no way to test Babson's belief.

Livermore looked again at the file on the economist. This was the third year running he had been invited to speak at the business conference. His previous speeches had not been widely reported, perhaps because Babson was a dull speaker who "doggedly confined himself to his familiar bearish bandwagon."

In any case, as Livermore quickly established, his public utterances had made no detectable impression on the market.

Livermore put aside the Babson file and called for others. He checked the Giannini folder. The latest entry showed that, on August 24, the banker had issued a statement attacking margin buying. Livermore glanced at Paul Warburg's folder. Again, when the distinguished banker had spoken out earlier in the year about overvalued shares, the response was less than enthusiastic.

He turned to the morning editions; it was a slack day for news. Livermore, Henry Ford apart, was probably unequaled in his ability to "read" the media; he knew, instinctively, the sort of story they would go for. For months now, the newspapers had vied with one another to run boom stories about the market. Now Livermore sensed they could be ready for a change. On such a slow day for news, the press would be looking for something "different." Babson, on previous record, could be just the person to give it to them.

By midmorning, every major New York and Boston newspaper, wire service desk, and the radio networks had received tip-off calls that Babson was to deliver a major financial speech at the conference. The tipster said the *Times* was sending Alexander Noyes to cover the occasion; Noyes was told rival financial editors were heading for the conference. Playing off one newspaper against the next was an old trick; seldom had it been more effective.

Soon Babson was receiving calls from reporters seeking an advance of his text.

The economist sensed that for reasons he could not fathom, the media this year were going to give him "the full treatment." He told callers there would be no advance leaks.

Press interest grew. Reporters knew a refusal to provide an advance generally meant a speaker had something important to say. In growing numbers they headed for the conference.

Professor Irving Fisher, of Yale University, one of the nation's leading economists, received a call from a *Herald Tribune* reporter in New York saying he might be needed to respond to Babson's speech. Fisher agreed to be ready to comment.

By noon, Jesse Livermore had completed his plans. Using thirty brokers so as to maintain secrecy, he had gone short of some $300,000 worth of stock.

At 12:30 P.M., the Associated Press bells rang on their machines across America with a news flash: "ECONOMIST PREDICTS 60 TO 80 POINTS STOCKMARKET CRASH."

A minute later United Press began to punch out the crucial words of Babson's speech. "Sooner or later a crash is coming which will take in the leading stocks and cause a decline of from 60 to 80 points in the Dow Jones barometer."

It was enough. Nearly every afternoon newspaper in America replated its front page to carry the sensational news.

Babson, unknown to the masses, was given the distinctive tabloid treatment. He was called "one of the world's great economists" and "a famous financial prophet." One, with a neat play on words, called him "the Prophet of Loss."

Radio programs interrupted their schedules to bring news of his forecast.

The specialist financial wire services in Wall Street fed Babson's statement into brokerage houses around the country.

William Hutton-Miller was just about to go for a late lunch when the Babson news flash "went off like a bomb" in W. E. Hutton's. Within minutes the telephones were ringing with investors wanting to sell. Hut, like every other employee in the firm, found himself pressed into handling increasingly hysterical calls from all over the country.

John J. Raskob was on his way for a game of cards with James Riordan; leaving his Park Avenue office, he stopped by the closet holding his private ticker. One glance at the tape and Raskob was running back to his desk.

He reached it as Riordan telephoned. The banker had also seen the ticker. The two men agreed Babson's speech could do "irreparable harm."

Billy Durant was just about to telephone Joe Kennedy and suggest a further meeting to resume their discussions over Kennedy joining the consortium when Durant's secretary burst into his office, without knocking, saying, "The U.P. is on the telephone with terrible news. The bull market is over and will Mr. Durant comment."

He shook his head and rushed to the ticker in the corner of his office. Westinghouse, Woolworth, Consolidated Gas, Adams Express, and Coca-Cola were all starting to slip.

At Radio's Post Twelve, Mike Meehan watched the sell orders coming at him from all sides. His clerk, Ed Schnell, felt they were in danger of drowning "in a blizzard of paper."

Almost every other post in the Stock Exchange was under similar siege.

Several miles away from Wall Street, but sensing the mood of panic that was beginning to sweep the financial district, Jesse Livermore, in his office complex, moved from one desk to another, from one aide to the next, issuing words of encouragement, oblivious to the shrill of telephones and the clatter of tickers. He was in his element.

In San Francisco, A. P. Giannini was interrupted at a company board meeting to hear the news Transamerica was falling.

He swore loudly, abandoned the meeting, and grabbed the nearest telephone to speak to his brother, Doc, in Wall Street.

A few yards from Doc's office in the Bank of America building, Pat Bologna found himself surrounded by fearful men and women. "They were out-of-towners, part of the crowds in the customers' rooms. Just because I worked in the Street, they thought I might know something." He tried to reassure them. But, when he saw a man run out of a brokerage house shouting he was ruined, young Bologna himself began to feel fearful.

At 2 P.M. Professor Fisher issued a measured retort to Babson through the *Herald Tribune*. Fisher rejected any possibility of a crash coming. In turn, the story was fed to the A.P. and U.P. Now the media had what it always thrived on—confrontation between two figures it had largely created as symbols in the public's mind of good and evil.

In Boston a hoarse and dazed Babson took yet another call, from a New York tabloid, offering him $100 a week to sign a financial column. He accepted.

Livermore continued to go short in his orders right up until the moment William Crawford banged his gavel.

The *Times* industrials had dropped ten points, and many individual stocks much more. All told, 5,565,280 shares had been traded.

By 4 P.M., with news of Fisher's rebuttal becoming ever-more widely known, Livermore sensed that tomorrow the market would start to recover. He told his staff he would cover his short position first thing in the morning.

Livermore was right. Within an hour of the opening gong on Friday, September 6, stocks recovered much of the previous day's losses. Industrials led the revival with an average gain of over $10 a share.

And by Saturday, in the relieved words of Pat Bologna, "everything was just as before."

Pat was almost right.

Wreathed in cigar smoke and bristling with anger, Winston Churchill faced the agents of the U. S. Customs Service on the deck of the ship which had brought the Churchills from Vancouver to Puget Sound, their entry point into the United States from Canada on this Saturday, September 7.

The three other members of what the Canadian press had dubbed the "Churchill Expedition to North America" watched expectantly. Previous experience had taught them how to spot the danger signs: Churchill's mouth was clamped bulldog tight around his cigar; his nostrils flared; there was a glint in his eye. He was very close to boiling point.

Only Randolph felt really nervous. His luggage bulged with bottles of whiskey and brandy—a flagrant breach of Prohibition.

He hoped his father's diplomatic visa and the letter of introduction he was waving in the face of the agents would stop their "dozens of questions." The letter was signed by former U. S. Vice-president, now American ambassador in London, Charles Dawes.

Instead, the agents stoically continued probing. Randolph was dumbfounded that "when they heard we had some camera plates, [they] gave us to understand that ordinarily they would have been subjected to the closest scrutiny to discover if any of them were of an obscene nature."

Winston Churchill began to rumble; the fuse to his temper was shortening by the second. A great gray cloud of smoke wafted into the air.

The local chief of Customs and the British vice-consul stared benignly at the agents. One of them asked yet another question. "How many cigars?"

Winston Churchill erupted. In the thunderous voice that had so often stilled the House of Commons he roared at the officers. "What are you looking for? I have already told you that we have nothing to declare. The point of this letter from the ambassador is to assure you of my integrity."

His nephew John would remember that "my uncle got so angry I thought he would explode."

A boot-faced agent finally replied. "We are looking for guns and ammunition."

Even Churchill was momentarily silenced by such an unexpected response. Then came a further outburst. "Monstrous! Absolutely monstrous."

Concerned suddenly that he might have a major diplomatic incident on his hands, the Customs chief ordered the Churchills be allowed ashore.

On the pier, a pretty young girl reporter asked Winston to comment on Prohibition.

He smiled broadly, his anger gone. "We realize £100 million a year from our liquor taxes, which amount, I understand, you give to your bootleggers!"

He led his party to a nearby hotel. Padding along behind, cowed and docile, came the Customs chief.

Inside, he astonished the Churchills by leading them to a table laden with beer and champagne.

He invited them to help themselves and explained that "the government took little interest in the ultimate consumer, but concentrated its warfare on the bootlegger."

Not even Winston Churchill had the heart to ask the official why then they had been subjected to the scene on the boat.

The incident was a fitting reintroduction to a nation Churchill would find in coming weeks both familiar and baffling in its customs and mores. And nothing would cause him greater confusion than the American attitude toward money. To the careful, husbanding Englishman, the average American seemed to have a much too casual attitude toward the commodity.

For months Steve Vargo carefully saved most of his salary from "the Buick" for a momentous moment. That moment had finally arrived.

Sunday lunch over, he and Jolan had sat in rockers on the porch of her clapboard home in Flint. Even on the porch the reek of fermenting alcohol was strong—"it was like sitting in the neck of a bottle." The first sign something unusual was about to happen had occurred when Jolan's mother joined them. Normally, on Sunday afternoons, "Mother and my step-dad went upstairs and closed the bedroom door."

The next out-of-the-ordinary occurrence was the arrival of Steve's parents, dressed in their Sunday best. Everybody sat and waited for Jolan's stepfather. He finally emerged from the basement in singlet and trousers, carrying a bottle of whiskey and cups. He poured the adults drinks. Then, "as if he had plucked the date out of the year," without any preamble at all he asked if Saturday, October 19, was agreeable. Jolan's mother quickly explained that would give them sufficient time to "brew something special." Steve's parents said the date was good for them because they would have time to buy some new clothes. Jolan's stepfather said he would make do with his present suit.

Mystified, Jolan and Steve had listened to even more cryptic exchanges. Finally she had turned to her mother. "What's happening on the nineteenth?"

Surprised at her daughter's question, Mrs. Arvay replied.

"That's the date you two are gonna get married."

Now, trundling the baby carriage through the Monday morning streets of Flint—with Margaret as usual perched on top of a fresh consignment of bootleg liquor—Jolan and Steve reenacted the "whole crazy business" of setting the wedding date.

Partly because he felt they were "being treated like a coupla kids," nineteen-year-old Steve had not previously told Jolan or his parents about his nest egg.

As they hurried through downtown Flint, he now let Jolan know.

"Gee, Steve. You could buy a lot of vanilla ice cream with all that money."

He grinned. "Maybe when we're married, I'll buy you an ice cream machine."

"Where's the money now?"

Steve patted his jacket pocket.

Jolan looked worried. If they were stopped by a Prohibition patrol, the money could be confiscated. The agents would never believe Steve had come by it honestly. These days they were everywhere, swooping at all hours, smashing up stills and throwing the whiskey mash into the streets. To outwit them, Jolan always made her deliveries at different times. But her greatest protection was baby Margaret. Nobody would ever suspect that the child was sprawled on top of a cache any agent would love to impound.

This morning's run was timed so that Steve could be with Jolan before he clocked on at "the Buick." After the last delivery had been made, Jolan would push Margaret home and then go on to Mrs. Baum's for another full day of domestic duties.

"Steve, if they stop us, you must say you don't know me—"

"But Jolan—"

"Listen. That money could get us both out of Flint."

Steve nodded. He shared Jolan's desire to escape from the drudgery of their present life. He explained he was carrying the money with him in order to deposit it in an account he had already opened at the Union Industrial Bank.

"Steve Vargo. You never told me you had a bank account!"

Steve grinned. "Lots of things you don't know!"

"Yes? Like what?"

"Like maybe my money'll cosy up to your money in there, just like we'll soon be cosying up!"

"Steve Vargo!"

Laughing happily, they raced down the street with the pram.

The last of Jolan's doubts about marrying Steve had gone the night they had "spooned" together in the back of a car. Steve, by his gentleness and patience, had shown himself to "be just the finest man a girl could want."

They reached the bank. After lifting Margaret out of the carriage and making sure the liquor was still concealed by a blanket, they walked inside.

Jolan had never been in a bank before. She was impressed by the size of the main hall and the gleaming brass on the cages.

It took Steve only a few minutes to deposit his money. They returned to the baby carriage.

Standing beside it was a policeman.

"This your buggy?"

Jolan nodded, terrified.

The policeman pointed at a wheel; its tread was almost bare and several spokes were missing. "Needs fixing."

Steve spoke. "I'll fix it."

The policeman nodded and walked on.

Edith Stone wished there was a policeman present to control the shoving press of reporters and photographers on the *Berengaria*'s Promenade Deck. They had boarded with the ship's pilot as the Cunarder entered New York Harbor. On the *Berengaria* was Bishop James Cannon, returning from Europe to face mounting criticism for his involvement with the now-closed-down Wall Street bucket shop of Kable and Company.

Throughout the homeward journey from Cherbourg, the Methodist minister had bored fellow passengers with his diatribes against drinking. Partly to avoid the bishop's constant wail about the evils he associated with even a glass of wine, and partly in search of material for her play, Edith had sought refuge in the ship's brokerage office. She was impressed by the speed and efficiency of the operation. Cannon had resolutely refused to set foot there, in case he was "misunderstood."

From what Edith now heard, there was no mistaking the attitude of the reporters: Their questions were hostile and probing, seeking to uncover just how deeply Cannon was implicated in the Kable fraud and conspiracy scandal. She enjoyed a certain satisfaction as she watched the unctuous bishop wriggling. But neither she nor the reporters were ready for his next move.

Cannon raised his hands high above his head and appealed "to God for the right to speak."

Gradually, silence settled. Motioning for the newsmen to stand back,

Cannon—with a flair even Henry Ford might have admired—seized his opportunity. He moved from one reporter to the next, peering into each face, murmuring that he wanted "to remember you all, just as I want you to remember well what I am about to say."

Edith had seen "similar performances in off-Broadway tryouts." The press were mesmerized by Cannon's outrageous posturing.

Raising his voice, puffing out his chest, the cleric began to speak.

"Gentlemen. Let us not waste time on old issues. I believe there is only one issue in this city at this moment that needs my attention. And that is the matter of whether District Attorney Banton and Police Commissioner Whalen should be impeached."

Edith was conscious of "a real thrill of excitement" running through the corps of reporters.

Cannon bored on.

He wanted both officials impeached because they had failed to close down the city's estimated 32,000 speakeasies.

The shenanigans of Kable were forgotten as Cannon went on in his bellicose public manner, repeating his familiar accusations about the evils of drink.

Then, without waiting for any questions, he swept off the ship. He had totally outmaneuvered the reporters.

It was, Edith told her parents, a show "guaranteed to make Cannon win any ham-of-the-year award."

Edward and Mabel Stone were relieved to see their daughter so cheerful as she traipsed past the Customs barrier, leaving a nonplussed agent staring after her. The Customs man had asked her if she had anything to declare. Smiling sweetly, Edith replied: "Only I love you."

Her parents had been anxiously awaiting Edith's arrival ever since receiving the terse telegram she had sent from Berlin: "CUTTING TRIP SHORT. RETURNING BERENGARIA SEPTEMBER THIRTEEN."

As the family chauffeur loaded her trunks, she quietly recounted her experiences in Germany.

Her father kept shaking his head in shocked silence. Then he told the chauffeur to drive them to the nearest post office. There, Edward Stone sent a telegram to his contact in Berlin, firing him.

Somewhat mollified, he slumped back in his seat and listened to Edith's recital of Nazi bully-boy tactics and the growing influence Hitler was having on his fellow countrymen.

Mabel Stone had a question. "Why haven't we read more of this in our newspapers?"

Edith shrugged. She thought the reason might be that Americans "don't care about what happens to a bunch of Jews in Europe."

Her father said people must be made aware. He turned to his daughter. "You want to be a writer. Write about this. Make people aware!"

Edith had yet another thread for her play.

From a hotel bedroom balcony in the center of Paris, Clarence Hatry stared down into the darkness of the night. Far below, the traffic moved along the Champs-Élysées in a ribbon of moving light; it was as though some endless ticker was spewing out vehicles onto the majestic boulevard. Hatry envied the occupants of the cars their freedom. And, unlike them, he had an overpowering feeling of doom.

It was September 14. Twenty-four hours had passed since his secret arrival in the city with Daniels and Gialdini to make a further desperate attempt to raise the money needed to fend off the impending collapse of his empire.

The journey had been uneventful except for Gialdini's behavior.

When he first heard about the trip, the voluble young Italian announced that after Paris he would "snatch a few days" with his wife in Switzerland. Hatry agreed. He hoped the holiday would help Gialdini regain his strength; he seemed to be on the verge of a nervous collapse.

When Gialdini boarded the boat train at London's Victoria Station, Hatry had been surprised by his appearance. His aide was bowed under "with a great deal of luggage for a small trip." It included a new suitcase. Gialdini strongly resisted Hatry's suggestion that the case be "put in the guard's van." He kept it close by him. Even stranger, the Italian insisted on clutching his folded umbrella tightly to his side.

Hatry had wondered briefly about Gialdini's peculiar behavior, but in the frenetic hours they had spent together in Paris it was quickly forgotten. There had been no time to think of anything except how to find and pry open the doors of just one friendly bank. But Hatry's French connections had firmly refused to loan anything.

Finally, this Saturday evening, Gialdini, more tense than ever, had said that he must catch his train to Switzerland.

Hatry and Daniels had seen him off, still clutching his case and umbrella.

It was only as the train steamed out of the station that Hatry put into words his suspicions. He turned to Daniels and asked: "Will we ever see him again?"

Unknown to Hatry, now staring out over the roofs of Paris, he would not only never see his trusted aide again, but in Gialdini's case were probably some £400,000 he had discreetly stolen from one of Hatry's companies. The umbrella almost certainly contained still more cash, wound around the ferrule. From Switzerland, Gialdini would slip into

Italy. There he would be safe; there was no extradition treaty between Italy and England.

Aware only that his French mission had failed, Clarence Hatry told Daniels to book them two seats on the night ferry to Britain.

Sensing his employer's mood, Daniels asked whether he should make second-class reservations.

"Good God, no! Time enough for that!"

Daniels smiled. Clarence Hatry still had his greatest asset—the will to fight. Perhaps, even now, there might yet be a chance.

Late Wednesday afternoon, September 18, Charles Mitchell sat in his office in Wall Street and studied the figures on brokers' loans and the weekly "condition" statement from the New York Federal Reserve Bank.

Both sources indicated that during the two weeks after what the media dubbed the Babson Break, the market had rallied magnificently.

The *Times* Averages stood 9 points above what they had been on August 31, and a staggering 81 higher than at the end of 1928.

The percentage rise since the beginning of the year had been nearly 36; since the end of 1927 it had gone up by almost 72; compared to 1926, it showed a climb of over 123.

There were, of course, worrying signs. Most important, steel output was down in August and so too was auto production. Although figures for freight car loadings were marginally up on a year ago, railway net income was down for the first time this year.

Mitchell discounted such facts as of "no lasting consequence" when measured against what was happening in Wall Street. The issue of new securities this month was expected to break all known records, as were sales of investment trust stocks.

The banker intended to tell reporters who would see him off as he sailed for a month's vacation in Europe in two days' time that "things have never been better." He would have a familiar message for all readers: "be a bull on America."

He was going to Europe to spread the glad news that America was ready, able, and willing to take on the financial challenges of the world. And should any reporter need reassuring about the country's fiscal health, Mitchell had his answer ready. "There is nothing to worry about in the financial situation in the United States."

If the best-known banker in America was pressed to make a forecast, he would say the boom could last at least another year—maybe much longer.

At 10 A.M. on Thursday, September 19, Clarence Hatry, Edmund Daniels, and two other directors of Hatry's empire were shown into the spacious office of Gilbert Garnsey, one of the most respected chartered accountants in the City of London.

Garnsey had recently been retained by Lloyds Bank to investigate the credit worthiness of Hatry's group. Hatry had approached Lloyds the previous day in a last-ditch attempt to borrow the money he needed to stop his huge empire from going under.

His request for help had been refused.

Now, the newspapers, led by the *Daily Express,* were snapping at his heels, seeking explanations as to why Hatry company share prices had plummeted £2.5 million in just two days. In Paris, his Photomaton shares had collapsed equally dramatically when news of his abortive visit leaked out.

The time had come when Hatry could only admit the full extent of the fraud he had been a party to. Scrip to the value of £1.6 million had been issued, of which only some £789,000 could be exchanged for genuine stock. And it was impossible for him to meet his obligations to the United Steel stockholders.

Hatry realized nothing could now save him. But even as he calmly confessed the facts to Garnsey, the financier still saw it as a giant gamble in which he had pledged his liberty and reputation and "everything that made life worth living," so he could save from ruin a "great many innocent people." He insisted there had never been any thought of ultimate fraud.

Referring to his colleagues, Hatry told Garnsey they "had undertaken the scheme out of loyalty to me and my companies." He readily shouldered the entire blame. "As their chief it is my duty to accept responsibility for the actions of my subordinates."

Garnsey sat, "in appalled silence," as Hatry admitted being "guilty of very serious offences." It appeared his companies had liabilities of some £19 million and total assets of only about £4 million.

Hatry concluded his explanations with a request. "Sir Gilbert, will you take me to the nearest police station so I can give myself into custody?"

Garnsey made a counterproposal. He would go at once to see Montagu Norman at the Bank of England. Perhaps, even now, a way out could be found which would avert an appalling financial catastrophe.

The accountant had no doubt the ramifications of a Hatry collapse would not only rock the City but could affect Wall Street and other stock markets. A crash on this scale would produce, in his opinion, an immediate and depressing reaction on many exchanges around the world. That, he told Hatry, would be the basis for his intercession with Norman.

In the meantime he advised Hatry to see his solicitor and "make a clean breast." Hatry and his aides should return to his office later in the day.

The financier smiled reassuringly at Daniels, who was "shaking like a leaf." Hatry was relieved his associate was at least sober; since returning from Paris, for much of the time Daniels appeared to be in an alcoholic daze.

Over lunch, the four men were joined by Stanley Passmore, Hatry's solicitor for many years. He, too, was appalled when he heard Hatry's admissions. Passmore did not consider himself qualified to take on the case. And a criminal lawyer friend of Hatry's who would have been ideal, was ill.

Hatry knew he was badly lacking a barrister he could trust, but he felt too shattered to do anything about it.

After eating, Hatry and his colleagues returned to Garnsey's office.

The accountant was grim-faced. He said his visit to the Bank of England had failed. What he did not reveal was that Montagu Norman had immediately informed the chairman of the London Stock Exchange of these recent developments; it was agreed dealing in Hatry shares would be suspended tomorrow.

Garnsey had only one piece of advice for Hatry and his associates: "Gentlemen, you must give yourselves up to the law."

He then telephoned an old friend, Sir Archibald Bodkin, Britain's director of Public Prosecutions. Garnsey told Bodkin he wanted to "send over a group of City men who wish to see you urgently."

Bodkin asked why.

"To confess to fraud."

"Fraud? What sort of fraud? What have they done?"

Garnsey explained. "It is fraud and forgery, as far as I can see. And the amount involved is stupendous."

"How much?"

"It may be in the order of £20 million."

With commendable restraint, Bodkin said he would "see them in the morning. Ten sharp in my office."

Around the time that appointment was being fixed, another meeting was being arranged in Flint. Late this Thursday morning, word was passed from one embezzler to another in the Union Industrial Bank they were to gather in the director's boardroom that night.

Frank Montague spent the rest of his day on "tenterhooks." This would be the first meeting since the Babson Break. When he had previously asked Ivan Christensen why his practice of calling weekly meetings of the "league of gentlemen" had been discontinued, Montague was told to stop worrying.

It was bad advice for the highly strung and hyperanxious vice-president. His old fears and doubts returned stronger than ever. At night, while Louise lay asleep beside him, he spent hours staring at the ceiling "praying for some way out of this terrible mess."

Milton Pollock and Robert Brown had both told him they, too, offered up similar prayers.

Montague had tried to question his fellow conspirators about what was happening; nobody seemed to know what the present position was. John de Camp and Christensen had "clammed up."

When the rest of the bank's staff had gone home, the fifteen embezzlers assembled in the boardroom.

De Camp came straight to the point. The Babson Break of September 5 had hit them hard. Their $60,000 "deficit" had jumped to $300,000.

Montague groaned loudly.

De Camp was not finished. There had been another sharp market break on September 10. They had been caught there, too, losing nearly another $400,000.

All told, in less then two disastrous weeks, they had stolen and squandered $700,000.

A shocked and "very frightened" Montague would never remember precisely who said what in the debate that followed. He doubted anybody present could make "much sense" of what had happened.

But at the end of the meeting, the majority of those present decided they had no option but to continue with their fraudulent operations.

At ten sharp on Friday, September 20, in well-pressed City suits, Hatry and his associates presented themselves at Sir Archibald Bodkin's waiting room. Hatry had spent the night in a hotel. He slept well. Over breakfast he had studied the newspapers. News of the collapse was on every front page.

After a lengthy wait, the four men were escorted into Bodkin's office. He did not invite them to sit down. They stood awkwardly before his desk.

He looked them over. In a cold voice he asked them to explain their presence.

Hatry again acted as spokesman, carefully sketching in the background, leaving nothing out of the "financial difficulties" he had encountered these past months. Then, in a slow, purposeful voice, he added: "I wish to say there are irregularities."

Bodkin pressed the buzzer on his desk. A Scotland Yard detective who had been waiting in the outer office entered the room.

Bodkin nodded toward the four men. "They wish to make a statement."

The detective nodded. He listened as Hatry briefly repeated what he had told Bodkin, again admitting there had been "irregularities," and adding, to his subsequent great regret, that he had raised money on "fictitious" scrip.

Bodkin waved toward the door. "Take them away."

In silence Hatry and his colleagues walked out of the room. Behind them came the detective.

Outside Bodkin's sanctuary, the policeman's manner thawed. He was almost friendly as he suggested Hatry might like to "adjourn" to nearby Charing Cross Hotel while he obtained a warrant for their arrest.

Hatry looked at his watch. "It's almost lunchtime."

The detective was equable. "Then by all means have lunch."

"That's very kind of you."

On the street, the afternoon newspaper vendors were shouting out news of the "Big City Scandal."

Hatry winced.

Before leaving, the police detective, according to Hatry's later recall, made an astounding proposal. The financier would maintain that the officer said: "I should catch a train. I can't stop you."

Hatry declined the offer.

The detective went to pick up his warrant; Hatry led his associates into the Charing Cross Hotel, where he bought them a "damned fine lunch" while they waited to be arrested.

Within a few hours they were all behind bars.

CHAPTER TWENTY

THE PEAK OF ILLUSION

At about the time Clarence Hatry was being taken to the cells, in New York Thomas Lamont sat in his private office at the House of Morgan and signed a confidential letter to President Hoover.

On Wednesday the two men had met in Washington. Hoover had asked Lamont for his opinion of Ramsay MacDonald, the British Prime Minister who was due to arrive in America early next month.

Lamont had been frank, almost brutal, in his criticism of Mac-Donald. The memory of their meetings in London five years ago was still clear in his mind. Then, MacDonald had given the impression of "lacking thoroughness in his handling of even very important matters."

Nothing MacDonald had reportedly done subsequently led Lamont to alter his assessment.

The Prime Minister's forthcoming visit to the United States was being publicized as another milestone in the "special relationship" existing between the two countries.

Lamont had little doubt that MacDonald's glad-handing would be a determined attempt to make his brand of socialism acceptable to Americans.

The Morgan partner knew how important this was to the new, but already struggling, Labour Government. Only huge injections of foreign capital—and decisions like Henry Ford's to build a plant at Dagenham —could really enable the Socialists to deliver their election promises.

In his communication to Hoover, Lamont was determined the President should be left in no doubt about what he should watch for in the man he would officially welcome to the United States as an honored guest. "I think he is apt to 'kiss' a thing through if he possibly can . . .

you ought not to be surprised if he seems at times rather vague and even seems to shift his ground."

For the usually discreet Lamont these were strong words. His letter boded ill for MacDonald's chances of going home with anything more than a farewell handshake.

Writing steadily at the carved antique desk in the library of his New York apartment, pausing only to sip whiskey and chomp on a Havana, Jesse Livermore found it surprisingly easy to begin putting on paper his vast accumulation of market experience.

Edwin Lefevre, the doyen of Wall Street journalists whose contributions to *The Saturday Evening Post* helped explain the intricacies of high finance to the masses, had been responsible for persuading Livermore to attempt a guide to investing. Lefevre had even offered to act as ghostwriter. Livermore refused him; he was concerned nobody should learn all his secrets.

Lefevre argued that the thousands of petty speculators "cluttering up" Wall Street were "a menace to themselves and the professionals in the market."

He maintained the public needed a simple, clear-cut guide and that Livermore was the man to write it.

Now, on this Sunday evening of September 22, Livermore had embarked on the task.

He told Dorothy the "mood" in the apartment was ideal for creative purposes. It was another way of expressing his almost boyish satisfaction that since their night-long discussion of a month ago they were both enjoying a tranquillity rare in their ten turbulent years of marriage.

During the past weeks they had been closer than either could remember since the balmy days of their honeymoon. They regularly dined alone at home or in one of the many fine neighborhood restaurants. They refused almost all invitations to parties, content instead to remain in the apartment listening to the radio or phonograph. Sometimes they danced, and afterward made love in the huge double bed that dominated the apartment's master bedroom.

Dorothy had rationed her drinking and the bloom was returning to her cheeks. Her voice had lost much of its whining harshness and she looked fitter and younger than in years.

Livermore had cut out his wenching and carousing. In every sense he was a model faithful husband, telephoning Dorothy from the office when he worked late and bringing her gifts of candy and flowers.

Both experienced the unspoken need to rebuild their marriage.

Dorothy was now curled up in one of the library's leather armchairs watching her husband write. The pad of legal paper in front of him was filled with his scrawl.

Livermore looked up at Dorothy and in a soft, suprisingly uncertain voice, asked if she wanted to hear what he'd written.

She nodded eagerly.

He began by reading one of his cardinal rules for all investors: "Take small losses. Profits always take care of themselves. But losses never do. The speculator has to insure himself against considerable losses, by taking the first small loss. In doing so he keeps his account in order, so that at some future time, when he has a constructive idea, he will be in a position to go into another deal, taking on the same amount of stock as he had when he was wrong."

As he read on, Dorothy occasionally interrupted with sensible questions which delighted her husband. He had forgotten his wife had such a sound grounding in market strategy until she gently reminded him that in the first years of their marriage she had spent most of her time at his side.

Dorothy listened carefully as he read her another of his principles. "Don't trade every day. There are only a few times every year, possibly four or five, when you should allow yourself to make any commitment at all."

She smilingly reminded him that in this past month he himself had already used up his own suggested trading quota for the entire year.

It was true. These last few weeks—one moment going short, the next buying long—Livermore had enjoyed one of the best runs he could remember. At peace with the world, he was able to devote all his energy and skills to the market. His timing was faultless, his choice of stocks uncanny, his rewards staggering.

By this Sunday night he could relax in the knowledge that since the by-now-notorious Babson Break of September 5, he had cleared some $1 million from the market.

Yet, despite his success, he was still unable to discover any lasting, overall pattern. One day the market was up; the next, often for no apparent reason, it plunged. Then, just as quickly, it climbed again.

In a note on his pad Livermore scrawled: "For the professional, the most dangerous time of all is when the market see-saws under the influence of unknown forces. It is no place for the amateur."

Dorothy pointed to the weekend newspapers lying on the floor and asked her husband why he had ringed reports of Clarence Hatry's arrest and arraignment in London.

He told her about the secret message he had received eighteen days before. Since then Livermore had been carefully monitoring developments in London.

Three days earlier, Thursday, September 19—the day Hatry saw Sir Gilbert Garnsey—Livermore had decided to move. Even his loyal staff had raised their eyebrows when he issued orders to go short of U. S. Steel, General Electric, and Radio.

Next day, Livermore sat in his office watching the ticker as prices began to fall, led by the bellwether U. S. Steel. General Electric and Radio also dropped a few points. Although not a large break, it had been enough for Livermore substantially to increase his takings.

He resumed reading to his wife. "The stock market is a mirror whose function it is to provide an image of the underlying or fundamental situation. Cause and effect run from the economy to the stock market, never the reverse. An unstable economy can be disturbed by all kinds of incidents that on the surface appear extraneous."

He told Dorothy the Hatry collapse might fall into this category. *The Wall Street Journal* reported the British financier was charged with "conspiring to attain money under false pretenses." If the defalcations turned out to be large, there could be a wave of liquidations which would not only further shake the London Stock Exchange and other exchanges where there was a strong British influence—Shanghai, Johannesburg, Sydney, Montreal, and Toronto—but could also spill over to New York. The exchanges in Paris, Berlin, and Amsterdam, following London's lead, had already been badly hit.

Even the skimpy details released so far were enough to give Livermore food for thought. He turned back to his writing.

"One major mistake of all speculators is the urge to enrich themselves in too short a time. Instead of taking two or three years to make 500% on their capital, they try to do it in two or three months."

Livermore wondered whether the reason Clarence Hatry had gambled and lost was because he had tried for too much too quickly.

John J. Raskob offered James Riordan another possible perspective on the Hatry failure. Serious though it was for all those directly involved, he doubted there would be any long-term or widespread effect on the English or American markets; "knowing the British," Raskob believed the London Stock Exchange would act swiftly, taking "suitable steps" to reestablish confidence in the integrity of the financial community.*

* On January 10, 1930, the London Stock Exchange announced: "The investing public will receive in full whatever is due to them." For this purpose, a £1 million fund was created from the contributions of jobbers and brokers and Stock Exchange members.

The two men were seated in the living room of Riordan's large brownstone on Twelfth Street. Raskob had not managed to get away to his family at their country retreat in Maryland because of "teething troubles" with the Empire State Building. For reasons that the financier still could not fathom, the demolition crews would be moving into the Waldorf-Astoria a week late. But William Lamb had assured Raskob it would not delay the completion date.

On hearing their adopted uncle was staying in town, Elizabeth and Florence Riordan had insisted he join them for a family Sunday supper.

It was formal, as usual, but beforehand the girls had carefully discussed the menu with the cook. Raskob brought a bottle of vintage wine and another of cognac.

Florence had asked whether he was not worried about being stopped by Prohibition agents.

Raskob had shaken his head; he carried a note from his doctor saying he required alcohol for medicinal purposes.

It was responses like this that made the girls adore him. Elizabeth always felt Raskob drew out the best in her father. Dissimilar in so many ways, she could see each genuinely liked and respected the other.

Supper over, their father and Raskob settled down for one of their lively postdinner discussions. The conversation soon turned to the market. Both agreed that, in Riordan's words, "things are not normal."

Riordan felt there were "too many small people playing for big stakes and not knowing the rules." Every day he was getting requests from customers at his bank to loan money for speculative purposes.

"And do you?"

"Not always."

"But that is what banks are for. To lend money for people to make more money."

Elizabeth would remember how Raskob "always made things sound simple."

He persisted. Every banker had "a solemn duty" to encourage investment in the market. It was the only way to keep America strong. The market could "climb for another twenty years"; he thought that by 1949, "when I might well be dead and forgotten but for the Empire State Building, people would still be playing the bull market."

Elizabeth was not entirely convinced. "Not everybody can get rich."

"Yes, they can! Yes, they can!"

Sensing a slight difference of opinion, Riordan moved the conversation to safer ground. He began to draw from his daughters the progress they were making at college.

Raskob was delighted the girls were doing well; he reminded them a good education was the best guarantee they could have for their future.

"Look at your papa! Look at me. And we didn't even have the benefit of your fine education. You can always get ahead in this country if you're willing to work hard."

The girls smiled. They had long become accustomed to Raskob's patriotism. They also felt with men like their father and Raskob helping to shape the destiny of America, the nation had little to fear.

Traveling into Wall Street on the subway on Monday, September 23, Charlton MacVeagh listened to the gossip of his fellow passengers and got the impression the Hatry collapse had done little so far to shake the average person's faith in the American market.†

The train was filled with optimistic talk. The conviction was stronger than ever in the public's mind that the market was now the personal instrument of mysterious but omnipotent men who could "take" even the most powerful share "in hand" and make it bend to their will.

Charlton knew, from his own experience at Morgan, it was possible to manipulate stocks—though nobody used such a vulgar term in the hallowed confines of 23 Wall.

He also accepted, with reluctance, there was no way of confining shop talk to the office. Raised in the conservative tradition of the founding fathers, he had been taught never to discuss business on social occasions; in particular, never to raise it in the presence of women. But now women themselves led conversations into the realms of the stock market.

Adele had explained to him stock market talk was no longer regarded as unfeminine. Consequently, at every dinner party he and Adele gave or attended, the talk swiftly turned to the market; it was, since Labor Day, the one great, unifying fashionable social conversation.

And it had spilled over to the public transport system. A wag wanted to know why the subway didn't have a ticker in each carriage. It was not so farfetched. In a Boston factory prices were being posted on a blackboard from hour to hour to please the workers. On a Texas ranch, a radio hooked to a loudspeaker blared out quotations for the cowpunchers.

Charlton drew wry amusement from listening to his fellow passengers; much of what they said was ill-informed nonsense, culled from the worst of the tip sheets.

Emerging from the subway, he found himself immersed in the now familiar crowds hurrying to join the lines outside the customers' rooms. The air was filled with the latest "rags to riches" stories. Charlton had

† See Source Notes.

no doubt some of them were true. Successful players, through the popular press, urged everybody to "get in on the game."

Yet most of the new millionaires the bull market created were rich on paper only. To buy stock on margin was easy; in fact it was hard not to do so once a brokerage connection was established. But to sell the stock, to collect the profit, and perhaps become a millionaire in reality was more difficult. The temptation was to hang on, to wait for the market to go higher, as it had most days for so long, and then to reap an even larger profit. The thought was self-perpetuating. And since investors were reluctant to sell the securities they had, new securities had to be produced to fulfill the demands of those still wanting to buy. That was no problem. Further stoking the Stock Exchange fire, this month the securities issued would be nearly $1 billion *more* than in any previous September.

There were stocks and shares available for everyone. And whether the market was up or down, virtually everyone without exception believed it was booming.

It was this certainty that again brought the public in large numbers to Wall Street this Monday morning. Their appetite for securities seemed insatiable. Almost every person carried some sort of newssheet giving stock guidance and financial information. Those who did not were sought out by touts who signed up subscribers as they stood in line outside the brokerage houses.

Of more immediate concern to Charlton as he turned into Wall Street was the sight of Thomas Lamont's car easing away from the curb as the patrician figure of Lamont himself hurried up the steps of 23 Wall.

With Jack Morgan away on vacation, Lamont was by tradition the last partner to arrive. But it was not yet 9 A.M. Something extraordinary must have happened.

Charlton MacVeagh, forgetting his Morgan training, broke into a run and shouldered his way through the throng.

Walking along Wall Street toward the brokerage offices of W. E. Hutton and Company, Hut Hutton-Miller, the highly regarded junior broker in the firm, pondered anew the dangers of "the stock market cult."

The sight of several thousand speculators hoping this Monday would be *the day* for them disturbed him. He knew that by the close of trading, inevitably, a good many would have to leave Wall Street disappointed.

In spite of his mere twenty-six years, Hut was a mature and sensitive man; behind his wisecracking facade was a compassionate and deep-thinking person.

He had come to fear that the euphoria which had gripped Wall Street since the market's recovery from the Babson Break really masked only blind overconfidence. And, sitting in W. E. Hutton, he had ample opportunity to realize the truth of a market maxim that had been forgotten in the boom: For every buyer of stock there is a seller; for every purchase that leads to a profit, there has been a sale at a loss of that profit.

Hut knew many of his customers watched the prices of stocks they had recently sold just as attentively as they watched the prices of those they still owned. To the perceptive broker, it was another example that, when it came to the market, people were "more involved in fantasy than in reality, more concerned with justifying past actions than planning future ones." And while he conceded this was human, he also knew a number of persons who, as far back as 1928, had got out of the market; since then they had good reason to curse themselves for not having come back "into the game."

At the slightest provocation they telephoned Hut. It only needed John J. Raskob to say a few words to a popular magazine, or a new edition of John Barton's book to appear, for the calls almost to swamp the young broker. He had read Barton's *The Man Nobody Knows* and found it tasteless, with its presentation of Jesus as the "first businessman," whose parables "were the most powerful advertisement of all time." It was still selling well.

He tried to be honest with all who telephoned him. To those who sought advice on whether they should return to the market, he urged they read the words of the brilliant British economist John Maynard Keynes. Hut could quote Keynes virtually verbatim.

"Amid the rapid fluctuations of his fortunes, the businessman loses his conservative instincts, and begins to think more of the large gains of the moment than of the lesser, but permanent, profits of normal business. The welfare of his enterprise in the relatively distant future weighs less with him than before, and thoughts are excited of a quick fortune and clearing out."

Hut counseled those who had "cleared out" to stay out; the market was becoming increasingly difficult to fathom, even for dedicated professionals like himself.

For those who were in, and insisted on remaining so, he strongly urged a cautious approach, reminding them of the dangers of the margin calls that would immediately come when stocks plunged, and which could wipe them out if they were unable to put up more money.

He knew he was not always listened to; that in the eyes of some colleagues he was far too conservative.

But the real problem for Hut was that he found it quite impossible to follow his own good advice.

Charlton MacVeagh watched the morning conference of the Morgan partners run on well past its normal time. Like most of the staff, he now knew the partners had arrived especially early and assembled immediately around Thomas Lamont's desk for a meeting.

Why it had been called Charlton could only guess. Presumably an important message had arrived from Jack Morgan in Britain, assessing the possible repercussions of the Hatry collapse.

Only the charmed circle around Thomas Lamont knew whether that was true or not. And, in keeping with normal House of Morgan policy, no notes were made of their deliberations.

What is sure is that Jack Morgan would later claim Hatry's fall had a direct bearing on all that was about to occur.

Billy Durant thought the Hatry "business" was being overplayed by the media. He believed the press should be concentrating its attention on "the good side of the market."

It was a view Durant tried to promote to Bernard Baruch. He and Baruch had known and respected each other for years; Durant believed the financier would be an ideal member for the new consortium he was planning.

Baruch had politely declined the offer to join. Durant's wife, Catherine, would remember her husband arguing passionately for Baruch to issue a suitable public statement that would encourage investment.

Again, Baruch politely refused.

And, for the first time in weeks, Durant felt a twinge of unease. At the back of his mind, a question was forming. Was he right to pursue his plan? Or did Bernard Baruch know something even wily Billy Durant did not yet suspect?

As so often recently, Joe Garcia found the drive on Tuesday morning, September 24, unusually quiet. Hunched beside the chauffeur, A. P. Giannini hardly spoke on the journey from San Mateo to San Francisco. Claire, seated in the rear of the Rolls, sharing her father's thoughts, was also silent.

Garcia believed Giannini was still smarting from the poor public response to his warning about the dangers of buying unwisely on margin.

But Giannini, as Claire knew, was concerned with even more serious matters.

The two market breaks in the early part of the month had greatly disturbed him. He had not joined in ridiculing Babson when prices recovered after his prediction. Giannini felt the market's initial reaction to the economist's prophecy indicated its vulnerability. And, following the second break on September 10, the market had been alternately strong and weak.

Only this morning Doc, in his regular early call from New York reported there appeared to be more bearish traders in the district than he could remember. Some were saying a "shake-out" was overdue.

Studying the latest batch of weekly market letters sent out by various East Coast brokerages, Giannini detected an ambivalent mood.

"They're covering themselves," he had said over breakfast. "They're taking up positions from which they can jump either way."

Claire felt news of the Hatry fiasco had further deepened her father's fears.

And Elisha Walker—well established as a bull—had said the high level of stock price averages was deceptive. He thought it might be that the sustained strength of a few score "favorites" was distorting the true picture. Walker was now trying to substantiate his theory.

Even if it was proven wrong, Giannini would still be concerned; he could see for himself many listed stocks were lagging behind their prices of earlier in the year.

He was still brooding as Garcia entered the city limits.

Claire reminded the chauffeur to drop her father at the nearest barbershop to San Francisco's Chinatown.

"And don't forget the flowers," she added.

Giannini suddenly smiled. He remembered how Claire had insisted a bouquet was the most appropriate present for his newest bank manager. From this morning pretty Dorothy Gee would be the only Chinese woman manager of a bank in the entire country. She was running the Chinatown branch of the Bank of America at 1009 Grant Avenue. Assisting her would be a staff of ten Chinese, all women.

Later, shaved and barbered, clutching the flowers, Giannini walked into the branch. A fusillade of photographers' flashbulbs greeted him. The staff, all dressed in kimonos, bowed deeply.

Towering over the slim, pretty Miss Gee, Giannini presented her with the bouquet.

He was about to launch into an impromptu speech when the telephone rang on Dorothy's desk. It was Doc in New York.

"A.P. There's been a sharp break. We're losing ground."

Giannini gave orders to support Transamerica. He sounded relaxed and confident. One of the reporters, Ed Gleeson, felt he had never seen the banker "in better shape." Gleeson did not suspect what Claire did

—"the news had blown my father off course. He was reacting instinctively."

After making his speech, he left the branch with his daughter. Only when they were inside the Rolls did Giannini refer to the matter again. "Things are bad, Claire, and they could get worse."

The speed of the break caught even Jesse Livermore unprepared. The market had been climbing one minute; the next it started to crumble. All he could do was watch the ticker in his office spell out the collapse. American Can tumbled $5.12 a share; General Electric dropped $5; Montgomery Ward, $4.20; Radio, $3.50; and U. S. Steel in its downward spiral lost $5.25 a share.

Livermore attributed the break to the aftershocks of the Hatry collapse. But he still believed there might be more fundamental "forces" at work. He likened them to the strain on an earthquake fault; despite the numerous breaks since May, perhaps the strain had not yet been relieved. The signs were beginning to suggest to Livermore there could be a gigantic financial trembler coming.

The break cast a pall of gloom over all fifteen embattled embezzlers in the Union Industrial Bank in Flint. This very morning of September 24 they had "diverted" a substantial amount of stolen money into the market. They had chosen only blue-chip stocks—U. S. Steel, General Electric, the major rails—convinced that even if these investments did not produce spectacular returns, the money would at least be safe.

Each of their stocks had dropped. The "league of gentlemen" suffered an average decline of over $5 on every share they bought.

They had now embezzled and lost $1.5 million in less than a month.

Pat Bologna viewed the break without great concern. He could not believe that the hordes of people roaming the financial district were wrong. He had seen no evidence of panic; those who had lost "knew they would make it all back tomorrow."

The bullish Bologna agreed with them.

The break worried William Crawford. Because of the sudden splurge of sell orders, the ticker had fallen rapidly behind; at close of trade it was running almost thirty minutes late.

Crawford received an icy rebuke from Richard Whitney.

Whitney's reaction was probably prompted in part by the break having resulted in his losing still more money; the will-o'-the-wisp stocks he dabbled in dropped along with the rest.

The Exchange's vice-president dreaded the prospect of going again to his brother; George was likely this time to refuse to advance further funds.

If George declined, Richard Whitney would be in much the same position as Clarence Hatry had been—forced by circumstances he had helped to create, and could no longer control, to become a common crook.

Whether by accident or design, coincidental with the time of the Clarence Hatry collapse, some of the biggest market players decided either to withdraw from "the game" altogether or to begin going short.

By this Tuesday evening, the august Bernard Baruch had started "to sell everything I could"; Baruch's son, an up-and-coming young broker, was also getting rid of his shares.

Eighty-two-year-old broker Michael Bouvier "had unloaded almost all the common stocks" in his portfolio; Jack Bouvier, specialist at Post Eleven and father of two-month-old Jacqueline, emulated his granduncle and converted most of his holdings into cash.

Joe Kennedy remained as before, steadfastly out, biding his time before going short.

Among those who had already begun to sell short—who would make money if the market fell—were veteran manipulator Tom Bragg of W. E. Hutton and Company, and Albert Wiggin, chairman of the Board of Directors of the Chase National Bank.

Wiggin had a wrinkle no one could have guessed; he was selling short shares in the huge bank of which he himself was the head. It was a decision that would increase his personal fortune by $4 million.

But those who now became bears were part of a very small minority. The great majority of investors, big and small, all across America, continued to speculate, mainly on margin, seduced into believing Wall Street was a never-ending path paved with gold.

CHAPTER TWENTY-ONE

THE EVE OF REALITY

On Wednesday, September 25, the London *Daily Express* switched its emphasis from Hatry and, under a banner front-page headline, addressed an "open letter" to Montagu Norman, governor of the Bank of England. It was a well-worn device used by Britain's popular press to infiltrate editorial opinion into the news columns. The *Express* "letter" warned Norman that if he raised the bank rate, as it was rumored he was about to do, "the whole onward march of British industry will be cruelly and unnecessarily checked."

The "letter" spoke darkly of colleagues of Norman's, "closely identified with large foreign interests who may be tempted to consider questions of current policy from the standpoint of international finance." The *Express* urged Norman to think firstly of Britain's interests.

On a quiet day for news, London correspondents of the U.S. wire services did follow-ups on the *Express* warning. Amplified by statements from unidentified "sources" in the City, stories were quickly cobbled together about Britain being on the verge of a major financial decision that could have a serious effect on Wall Street.

For the second time in a month—the notorious Babson Break being the first—sections of the U.S. media were poised with reports that could directly influence performance on the New York and other of America's stock exchanges.

Shortly before the New York market opened on this Wednesday, the wire services carried the news that tomorrow, the Bank of England's Court of Governors were to meet; "informed opinion" was they would seize on the opportunity presented by the Hatry collapse as a reason for raising the discount rate.

In Wall Street's keyed-up mood following the sharp break of yesterday afternoon, which had caught even Jesse Livermore by surprise, it was enough. During the first 120 minutes of trading there was urgent selling. More bad news came from London: The value of the pound sterling was rising, suggesting funds were being withdrawn from other countries—including the United States—in anticipation of the higher interest rates soon to be paid in Britain.

Share prices tumbled.

Inside the Union Industrial Bank, the fifteen embezzlers listened in despair to the succession of telephone calls Ivan Christensen was receiving. Since just after 10 A.M. his telephone had rung almost nonstop. The calls were substantially the same; they came from the three Flint branch offices of Wall Street brokerage firms, passing on repeated requests from New York for more margin.

In spite of their losses of yesterday afternoon, earlier this morning, Christensen and John de Camp had put up another $100,000 of "borrowed" money to buy yet more blue-chip stocks.

The local brokers believed, as always, that Christensen and De Camp were investing on behalf of wealthy customers of the bank. It was a fiction the embezzlers had relied upon for a year; there was, they believed, little chance of the subterfuge being discovered. This morning, in a piquant choice, they told the brokers they were investing on behalf of, among others, a local judge and district attorney.

The immediate spate of margin calls stunned the thieves, particularly the bank's vice-president, Frank Montague.

Since the market breaks began earlier in the month, his nerves had worsened. He had lost weight, and also his temper with Louise and the children. Tormented by his eczema, he had been unable to sleep. And he was tortured by the memory of something he had done without the others knowing—"borrowed" over $50,000 from the bank for his own use. He had then invested the money in Wall Street; he intended to hand over the profit direct to De Camp, along with his formal resignation from the "league of gentlemen."

He had made no profit. He had lost the entire $50,000.

Montague turned to his closest friend in the ring of thieves, the devout Milton Pollock, and confessed. Pollock prayed for the vice-president.

But despite Pollock's prayers, Montague's physical, financial, and mental state had not improved. And now, following directly on from yesterday's disaster, the new demands for margin worsened matters. A sense of despondency, which had never been far away these past weeks, welled up inside Montague. He felt almost suicidal.

The nine tellers involved in the fraud had no time to dwell on their feelings. They were too busy diverting funds to meet the margin calls. Robert Brown felt events had reached "a war footing—we had to break out of our position or perish."

Brown, like his colleagues, believed he had no option but to continue embezzling. The gifted and articulate young teller saw himself and the others as "victims of our time—seduced by the dream of easy money."

He was also driven by another compulsion; he wanted the bank repaid in full before his father discovered what was happening. Robert felt if the bank's president learned his son was a thief it might kill him.

As prices continued to fall, a number of the bank's customers who had requested the bank to invest their surplus cash in the New York call money market demanded the funds be recalled in order to cover the calls for margin which they were receiving. The bank was bound to give them their money. But it, of course, had long ago been "diverted" for the embezzlers' own use. To provide the cash while covering their tracks required complex juggling of the Union Industrial's $32 million assets.

During the morning, the sober-faced Elton Graham and Russell Runyon swiftly laundered money through their ledgers. It was skilled and demanding work, ideally suited to the phlegmatic temperament of both men.

Then Grant Brown intervened.

Normally, after a routine daily inspection before the bank opened, Brown left the building to keep various appointments. Flint's other banks had launched a determined drive to topple the Union Industrial from its premier position; Brown retaliated by calling upon businessmen and reminding them of his bank's proud claim to be "the safest and most trusted in all Michigan."

As part of his strategy, he planned to launch an intensive local advertising campaign early in October. Every business premise and domestic dwelling in the city would receive a pamphlet showing the impressive financial resources of the Union Industrial, backed up by "consolidated sworn statements."

To prepare his brochure, Brown needed to check the bank's ledgers. He chose this Wednesday morning to do so.

John de Camp immediately offered to perform the task for him.

Brown refused the offer. He explained to his deputy that later he would have to swear to the accuracy of the statements before the Banking Commission in Lansing. He could only do so if he personally had checked the books.

A white-faced Milton Pollock brought the first ledger to the president's desk.

Frank Montague sensed even the crooked tellers in their cages, a full forty feet from Brown, "were probably holding their breath."

Brown approved the first ledger and called for a second.

He had hardly begun to peruse it when Christensen acted. He walked smartly up to the president's desk and said he needed the ledger to check whether there was enough money in a customer's account to meet a call for margin.

Montague listened, open-mouthed, as Christensen addressed Brown in an urgent but confident voice.

"Sir, the market's slipping. We've got our hands full with margin calls. I need to keep the ledgers by me to make sure our customers have enough cash to meet the calls. We've got to look after our customers!"

Grant Brown immediately handed over the ledger, commending Christensen for his foresight. It was staff like this, Brown would later tell customers, that enabled the Union Industrial to live up to its proud claim of being "the bank that watches over your money."

For the rest of the morning, the doctored ledgers remained firmly on Ivan Christensen's desk.

At one o'clock—after Grant Brown had gone for the day—the assistant cashier gave John de Camp the latest grim picture. The blue-chip issues they had chosen were, on average, now down $7 each.

The news was passed to the other embezzlers. They stared in desperation at Christensen. He continued to maintain his poise and nerve.

At 2 P.M. Christensen received another phone call from one of the Flint brokers. For the first time he revealed the great tension he was under. Oblivious of the customers in the bank, he shouted out the news.

"It's over!"

De Camp told him to check with New York. There it was rumored the National City had joined with other banks to mount a hasty and spectacular buying operation to "keep the market in balance."

The support was concentrated on pivotal stocks—U. S. Steel, General Electric, United Aircraft, and Standard Oil—issues in which the embezzlers had a large investment.

By 2:45 P.M. Christensen was able to report the downward trend had been arrested; there was every possibility tomorrow would see the market "begin to boil again." They had been right to hang on.

Frank Montague recalled "a number of the boys gulping with relief —there was quite a procession to the bathroom."

Milton Pollock reminded him the "power of prayer had got us out of a hole."

Once more Montague decided, despite all his fears, "just to sit tight and pray some more."

On Thursday, September 26, the Bank of England advanced its discount rate to 6½ percent—a full ½ percent above New York's.

Within forty-eight hours the central bank rates would also be raised in Austria, Denmark, Norway, Sweden, and the Irish Republic.

Reactions on the whole were predictable.

Jesse Livermore saw the Bank of England's purpose as a determined attempt to reverse the flow of gold to France, Germany, and the United States. He felt it must cause a weakening of the U.S. position, and planned accordingly.

John J. Raskob was incensed by the timing of the new London rate. Liquid capital would be attracted away from the United States at the very moment the usual seasonal need for funds was on the increase.

Billy Durant, after taking careful soundings, decided the British hike would have no lasting influence on the U.S. stock market. Even so he decided to maintain caution.

Henry Ford worried whether the increase in bank rate would affect his Dagenham plant. Edsel offered reassurance. His father turned his attention again to finalizing the details for his dream "American Village," due to open in three weeks.

A. P. Giannini welcomed the news from London. It confirmed in his view the propriety of the rise in August of the New York Federal Reserve rate.

The New York Stock Exchange, in common with the other U.S. exchanges, gave no public reaction to the Bank of England's decision. And during the day, prices throughout the market remained generally steady, with a few stocks advancing moderately.

Late in the afternoon, Richard Whitney announced that during the past week there had been an increase of $192 million in brokers' loans, bringing the total now borrowed—and therefore owed—to a staggering $6.8 billion.

Hutton-Miller found a surprising mood of elation over the news among his colleagues; they interpreted the huge sum as clear proof more people were investing more than ever. Hut saw it differently: "The investors were small-timers, having to borrow to buy, and probably borrowing beyond their means. A puff of wind—and they and their stocks bought on margin could be blown away forever."

Charlton MacVeagh was much too occupied at work to come up with any theory. He told his wife, Adele, that tonight, as usual, he expected to be at Morgan's until very late. The firm had never been busier.

Whitney's announcement stunned both Billy Durant and John J.

Raskob. They realized the increase in brokers' loans was totally at variance with the market's recent performance. As prices declined, so in parallel should brokers' loans have fallen. That they had not might be an indication stock was passing from the stronger hands of big investors into the weaker ones of small speculators.

Like Hutton-Miller, these older stalwarts of the bull market felt there could be a definite danger in so many untutored people feeding so voraciously on shares bought with money borrowed on an unprecedented scale.

In another of his laconic observations, Raskob told James Riordan, "things look like getting mighty interesting."

Next morning, Friday, September 27, the market went into an immediate decline, as it had the past three mornings out of four. During the day, Westinghouse slipped $11 a share; Allied Chemical, $10.75; General Electric dropped almost $13; Columbia Carbon ended $17.25 down on its opening price.

The day's trading left the Flint embezzlers some $100,000 worse off.

Pat Bologna thought he lost "a coupla hundred."

On September 28 Saturday's market again opened weakly; then, in the last forty minutes of trading, it recovered sufficiently to show a modest gain for the day.

It was enough to rekindle the optimism of the crowds thronging Wall Street. On all sides, Hutton-Miller heard the same argument restated. "People thought prices were so low, now was the time to get smart, move in and be set for the next upward surge."

Hut was not sure. During the morning hundreds of calls for more margin had gone out from W. E. Hutton to overextended buyers: Hut suspected similar calls were being made from many other New York brokerage offices. Some stocks purchased on margin had fallen so far they were barely worth the money borrowed for their purchase in the first place. If speculators could not meet the demand for margin, their shares were sold. In many cases, Hut knew "investors who faced financial ruin because they had bought to the hilt on margin, and found it impossible to provide more money when asked."

This Saturday night millionaire businessman Edward Stone hosted a black-tie dinner party in honor of his daughter, Edith. It was the first he had been able to have since her return from Europe, for the decorators had only just vacated the elegant new custom-built apartment overlooking Central Park. A dozen tuxedoed men and their gowned ladies were seated around the dinner table in the room Mabel Stone was most proud of; its stained-glass windows faced onto the park, the imported Italian furniture was of hand-carved gray ash, and the sideboard and tabletops were in green Italian marble. With its glittering silver and cut glass, the room reflected the opulent standard of living Edward Stone's wealth was able to provide.

Over dinner, Edith described what she had seen of the rise of Hitler and Nazism in Germany.

Edith was a good speaker with a fine flair for the dramatic, but she found it difficult to reach her audience. Although attentive, their interest only became total when she talked of the Berlin Börse. And then the questions were not so much concerned with Nazi influences as with the volume and types of stocks traded there. When the guests exhausted their queries about the Börse, they switched to the Paris Exchange as a topic.

She did not know whether to be outraged or amused.

Later, when they retired for coffee, leaving the men with their brandies, it was the ladies' turn to discuss the market with Edith.

Finally she could stand it no longer. She asked the women whether their lives were so narrow they could only gossip about stocks.

Edith was asked icily by one woman what she would prefer to talk about.

"About Hitler and what he's doing to our people."

There was an embarrassed silence. Then an aged dowager spoke.

"I've Jewish friends in Germany. They haven't mentioned the man once in their letters to me. Don't you think you're worrying unduly?"

Without bothering to wait for an answer, the elderly lady turned to her neighbor and resumed a discussion about investments.

If nothing else, Edith realized the reactions she had received showed she was on to a sure thing with her Wall Street-based play.

Pat Bologna was accosted on all sides by the new phrase, which, by Monday, September 30, the last day of the month, swept reassuringly through the financial district.

It passed from mouth to mouth; along the lines outside brokerage houses, the queues waiting to get into coffee shops, banks, and the Exchange visitors' gallery. It traveled from Broadway to the East River, at the foot of Wall Street.

It could be heard in warm Italian voices inside the Bank of America Building; in a mishmash of accents in the National City Bank; and in the merest of refined whispers in the House of Morgan.

Tipsters spread it. Hut heard his colleagues use it in telephone calls. It was, recalled the young broker, "as though the words had come from some financial Moses as holy writ."

The magical new phrase was: "organized buying support."
It sounded good.

The phrase had sprung into prominence following an extraordinary intervention by the usually circumspect Arthur Cutten. In an interview published yesterday, the speculator declared himself "a bull on stocks —a bull on the United States." He had also said he would not be disturbed if brokers' loans rose to an unbelievable $12 billion—almost double what they were now. Cutten felt such a figure "would not be unduly large."

To hundreds of thousands of people in crowded customers' rooms across America and in Wall Street this Monday, Cutten's words were a positive encouragement to borrow money from brokers to invest on margin in stocks. It was seen also as "a sign" that he and other big operators were ready, by "organized buying support," to move prices up if they went dangerously down.

Not even the New York *Times* could dampen the enthusiasm. Financial editor Alexander Noyes's criticism of Cutten was washed away in a tidal wave of optimism.

"Organized buying support" was the new guarantee for the individual investor that he was no longer operating alone.

Hut, along with most brokers, believed the big bankers and speculators would not let the bull market end. He perceived a change of mood in the Street. "A few days earlier we feared it was all over. Now everything was okay again."

Messenger boss Michael Levine agreed. He told the two bouncers he employed to stand outside his office "to let in any decent guys looking for work."

Jesse Livermore was furious with Cutten's pronouncement. Like Joe Kennedy, he decided all he could do was wait and watch, and be ready to pounce.

By noon, with trading volume low and prices slipping, a rumor flared through the financial district: Unnamed operators were quietly buying better quality stocks—"organized support" was on the way.

As Pat Bologna told a customer: "What goes down can always come up. With help."

Fluently marshaling his arguments, counting off his points on the tip of one manicured finger after another, John J. Raskob explained to his luncheon guests why he was maintaining his allegiance to the bull market. Wearing one of his vivid shirts, tanned from a weekend's sailing, Raskob looked like a nut-brown garden gnome—a striking contrast to his pale-faced, conservatively dressed guests.

His alert, clear eyes moved steadily around the table as he spoke, settling first on Billy Durant, then moving on to Arthur Cutten, James Riordan, Percy Rockefeller, the Du Pont brothers, and Oris and Mantis van Sweringen, before finally coming to rest on William Lamb, the architect for the Empire State Building.

Satisfied he had their undivided attention, the financier continued speaking.

The nine guests at the table in Raskob's New York book-strewn suite in Carlton House appeared to have just one common link—they were friends of their host. The refined Du Ponts socially had little in common with the homespun Van Sweringens; Percy Rockefeller had not met Lamb before; Cutten and Durant, both by nature reclusive, were on barely more than nodding terms with the others.

Riordan was the only one who knew how carefully Raskob had chosen the guests for this lunch.

Billy Durant was there because Raskob was concerned the speculator might be "drawing in his horns" in relation to the market. Durant sat impassively, eating little, sipping his mineral water. As Raskob warmed to his theme, Durant started to sniff a cigar thoughtfully—a gesture that did not noticeably affect his host's concentration.

Cutten was there, because, Raskob apart, he was now the greatest publicly acclaimed bull in the market.

Rockefeller, like the Du Pont brothers, was invited because he represented "the top end of the scale." The Van Sweringens were there for their specialized knowledge of railways and close connection with Morgan.

Ostensibly, they had been asked to lunch to hear Lamb deliver a progress report on the $60 million skyscraper project.

In reality, Riordan knew Raskob was using the lunch as a platform from which to expound his latest views on the market. The banker realized that every nuance, every gesture Raskob made, was carefully prepared; several hours earlier, Raskob had outlined his strategy to Riordan. But even now, watching him, Riordan could only marvel at the apparent spontaneity of Raskob's presentation.

Abandoning his familiar dogmatic ebullience, the financier chose instead to be calmly authoritative, determined to impress his listeners by the sheer logic of his argument.

He told them powerful "factors" were giving "unfavorable attention" to Wall Street. This was having a direct bearing on the way the market was behaving. To ignore either the "factors" or the "attention" would be a mistake. They must be met face on.

The surest and best way to do that was to maintain "a positive belief" in the market.

Once more his eyes swept the table, alighting on Cutten.

Raskob was certain he spoke for them all when he said how welcome Cutten's intervention had been.

There was a murmur of agreement.

Raskob went on to remind them that only two days after Cutten's effort, an attempt had been made to negate it completely. On October 1 the president of the American Bankers' Association, addressing its annual convention in San Francisco, expressed "grave alarm" at the ever-increasing total of outstanding loans to small borrowers. The president said there was "a limit beyond which bank credit in this country must not be expanded" and alluded to the overuse of credit for the purchase of stock.

One of the guests growled there was nothing new in that.

Nevertheless, Raskob said, the convention had adopted a resolution urging the Federal Reserve Board to investigate the "whole situation" involving brokers' loans.

Someone murmured the Fed would likely pigeonhole the resolution; since raising the rediscount rate in August it seemed to have slumped back into inactivity.

Raskob insisted that to ignore the threat was a mistake—just as it would be to attack publicly the ABA or its president.

But all of them, he went on, knew what had happened after the ABA president's speech was reported: On October 1 prices had moved downward until the final hour. Then U. S. Steel led a small rally.

Raskob surprised even Riordan by dismissing the rally as unimportant.

Percy Rockefeller said steel's sudden recovery at the end of the day had been widely interpreted, even within the industry itself, as heralding an unexpected increase in steel production to meet new demands for more rolling stock.

Raskob looked to the Van Sweringens.

Oris, the elder brother, thought the rumors untrue. He knew of no American railroad that was about to give the steel industry substantial orders.

Triumphantly, Raskob hammered home his argument. Steel led the recovery because the market had refused to be intimidated by "outside forces" in the way it had allowed itself to be throughout September.

The "pernicious pessimist, Babson" had been "able to do his mischief" largely because the climate was created for him by talk of the market's lack of "snap and buoyancy," and the "regrettable absence of enthusiasm" shown in some boardrooms.

There was only one way to stop the rot of September returning—by remembering certain "basic factors."

Raskob counted them off on his fingers. There should be a determined drive to end the growing practice of using rallies as an excuse to reduce what should remain long-term holdings; such reductions only paved the way for further market declines. Equal determination must be used to curb the tendency for speculators to accept small profits on stocks purchased during a break. They, too, should be encouraged to maintain their holdings.

Since May, Raskob told his listeners, there had been no fewer than nine major breaks in which millions of shares of "well managed, growing companies" had been cashed in by investors fearful of being caught in a bear trap. Inevitably, some of those speculators had not returned to the market.

He paused and glanced around the table. Percy Rockefeller, the Du Ponts, the Van Sweringens—none of them actively courted publicity. Their host urged them to put aside their personal prejudices and vigorously promote the market in the media. The message to push was simple: Many stocks, in years to come, would sell for "ten times their present price, and brokers' loans will be billions more than they are now."

Raskob reminded his guests that a few weeks ago he had caused a national stir with his widely publicized claim that everybody could eventually be rich if they invested sensibly in the market. Despite "all the ups and downs" of September, he still fervently believed in his credo.

But he had come to the conclusion that for the masses—who he was glad to see were still flocking by the tens of thousands into the market —to reap their promised reward, the market must have the continuing strong support of big investors.

Once more he glanced at his guests. Each of them, he continued, probably knew at least one such financier who was about to pull out or had already done so.

Raskob felt they all had a solemn duty to attempt to persuade those people to change their minds.

Again a murmur of assent came from his listeners. Between them, they represented, controlled, or held interests worth many billions of dollars. And those dollars were directly linked to the stock market.

Making no apology for stating the obvious, Raskob reminded them, "in a healthy market we prosper; in a sick market we suffer."

He rose to his feet and motioned to William Lamb. The two men hurried from the dining room to return carrying the model of the Empire State Building which James Riordan had been the first to see just over five months ago.

They placed the structure on a side table. In a voice filled with emotion, Raskob spoke. "Gentlemen, this is part of what I have at stake. A monument to the future."

He sat down again and watched, satisfied, as his guests stared, fascinated, at the model. Even the Van Sweringens, known for their lack of aesthetic taste, admitted it was "a powerful piece of work."

Raskob explained the skyscraper would symbolize the America he believed in—"a land which reached for the sky with its feet on the ground." Nodding toward his partners in the enterprise, the Du Ponts, he reminded the others the hugely expensive project had been made possible largely because "the faith in the future reflected in the stock market enabled us to raise the money without trouble."

He turned to Lamb and invited him to give details of the superstructure's construction.

The architect explained orders had already been placed with mills in Pittsburgh for more than 60,000 tons of steel—enough to lay a railroad track from New York to Miami. Each girder would be given a code number tied to a date. Exactly seventy hours from the moment a girder was shaped, it would be in the hands of the riveters working on the shell of the skyscraper. The building would have 6,800 windows, set in 10 million bricks, which in turn would be faced with 200,000 cubic feet of limestone. A full year before delivery, factory staff were braiding the more than 1,000 miles of steel wire needed to hold the sixty-seven elevators in their seven miles of shafts. Bell Telephone had diverted scores of its New York staff to begin work on the planning and installation of 15 million feet of telephone cable which would eventually connect 3,000 office switchboards in the building. Other firms were working on the thousands of miles of conduit tubing needed to carry light and power cables.

Lamb ended his dissertation by saying he had calculated if all the material needed to build the edifice arrived in one shipment, it would require a train fifty-seven miles long to carry it.

The men around the table—many of them used to mammoth projects—shook their heads in wonder.

Raskob rose to his feet, crossed the room, and stood beside the perfectly scaled model.

"Gentlemen, a country which can provide the vision, the resources, the money and the people to build such an edifice as this, surely cannot be allowed to crash through lack of support from the likes of you and me."

His passionate plea did not fall on deaf ears.

CHAPTER TWENTY-TWO

TOP HATS AND CZARDAS

Gray top hat placed squarely on his head, Edward Henry Harriman Simmons stepped briskly out of his home at 812 Park Avenue. The forbidding figure of the president of the New York Stock Exchange—in his dark suit and stiffly starched white shirt—was dressed as for any other day in Wall Street.

Those neighbors who had read their Friday morning newspapers this October 4 could only marvel at his sangfroid. Clearly, if Simmons had seen the deck of headlines in the New York *Times,* he had not been affected by them.

YEAR'S WORST BREAK
HITS STOCK MARKET

Trading of 1,500,000 Shares
in Final Hour Swamps
the Whole List

STEEL DROPS 10 POINTS

Incredibly, in spite of the *Times* headlines, the Stock Exchange president appeared to onlookers as if he did not have a care in the world.

In fact, Simmons was acting, determined nothing would disrupt his most carefully laid plans. He did not want anybody who saw him coming out of his handsome town house to believe anything untoward was afoot.

The same pose was adopted by his companion, Allen Lindley. The two men had been friends since those far-off days when Simmons trained as a doctor at Columbia University. Later, Lindley supported Simmons' decision to give up medicine for a career in finance. Soon, Simmons had his own brokerage business and was a director of the Harriman National Bank.

Lindley had been present at the celebrations marking his colleague's progress in the financial world: a seat on the Stock Exchange in 1900; appointed a governor in 1909; vice-president in 1921; president from 1924. Now Lindley was to play a role in yet another celebration.

This morning, Edward Simmons was getting married.

As they had done on many other mornings, the two men casually settled in the back of Simmons' chauffeured limousine. Once the car was moving through the traffic, they inserted carnation boutonnieres in their lapels.

A few minutes later they were hurrying into Park Avenue's Presbyterian Church.

Only a few close friends and relatives had been invited to see Simmons wed divorcee Beatrice Vanderpoel Bogert.

They all returned to a reception at Simmons' house. There the bridegroom announced that on the following day he and his bride would leave for a honeymoon in Honolulu. They would not be returning for two months.

There was no mention of the stock market.

The president was particularly pleased he had managed to avoid the press. He genuinely disliked contact with the media. He could not understand the desire his deputy displayed to see his name in print.

Simmons was concerned by Richard Whitney's attitude; he felt it was not at all in keeping with the way the acting president should behave. Partly because of Whitney's appetite for publicity, Simmons had not invited him to the wedding. He feared his deputy might have leaked the news to the press. It was easy to imagine what reporters would have made of the decision by the head of the world's busiest Stock Exchange to leave his post for two months just at this time.

If Richard Whitney was upset at being excluded from Simmons' wedding, he hid it from the Exchange staff. Whitney knew they did not like him. He had no wish to antagonize them further by criticizing the absent president; he would need their cooperation while he was in charge.

Some of the staff and Exchange members said that at forty-one, Whitney was fulfilling a long-held dream—to be the youngest man ever to sit in the president's office. But Whitney's main motive in coveting the position was closer to cupidity; from the security of the president's office he could wheel-and-deal with new freedom.

And Whitney quickly discovered the president was privy to more highly confidential information than even he had suspected.

The president regularly received secret reports on companies and banks across the United States; he also was serviced with information from other exchanges in the United States and abroad, giving privileged news of local market conditions.

More important to Whitney were the technical reports on various stocks, prepared by New York Exchange experts. The stocks' past performances were carefully analyzed to help ascertain future potential. These assessments were also part of the Exchange's determined effort to ensure no new issue was offered to the public which was known to be in any way suspect.

Whitney knew in reality a number of stocks were being traded which had no place in the Exchange. Only recently he had allowed to be listed a stock that a technical expert warned was "not above suspicion and contrary to the public interest."

The tragedy for Whitney was that he could not see just how dubious were the stocks that he himself continued to buy in a frantic attempt to recoup the fortune he had borrowed from his brother and lost.

But with all these secret reports to peruse, Whitney was in a new situation. He could hardly fail to profit from the wealth of information now at his disposal.

Armed with such knowledge, he was not unduly alarmed by what was happening six floors below on the floor of the Exchange.

On this day of Simmons' marriage, the market continued the way it had closed yesterday—plunging downward.

Even so, Whitney insisted the market was basically sound; the present breaks, he told a reporter who telephoned for a reaction, were no more than aftershocks from September.

Whitney's opinion concurred with that expressed by John J. Raskob to his guests a few days before. Since then, as part of their promise to Raskob, they had been making their views known.

The acting president, whose arrogance was equaled by his gullibility, accepted the prognosis. After all, men such as Raskob spoke with the great authority only long experience of the market could give. And, in fact, the market would rally strongly tomorrow.

But, like many others, the acting president was capable of self-delusion. He *wanted* to believe the bull market would continue, and therefore accepted *only* that information that supported the belief.

In an ordinary speculator it was bad enough; in Richard Whitney the weakness made him more desperate and dangerous to himself and to those who trusted his judgment and integrity.

A few people were coming to doubt these qualities in the acting pres-

ident. They were the ones who had loaned him money and were waiting
to be reimbursed.

Nobody yet dared to question Whitney openly. He was allowed to go
on shamelessly using his office, his connections with J. P. Morgan and
Company, his friends and relatives. His position as acting president of
the world's most important stock exchange made him, for the moment,
inviolate.

At noon on Sunday, October 6, Bernard Baruch's private rail car,
hooked to the express from Chicago, glided into Grand Central Station
in New York. Baruch had traveled to Chicago to collect the Churchills,
all four of whom were now suntanned following their stay in California.
There they had been guests of William Randolph Hearst, who mesmerized them with the opulence and eccentricity of his life-style.

In a letter home to Clemmie, Winston Churchill described Hearst to
his wife as "a grave simple child—with no doubt a nasty temper—playing with the most costly toys," including "two charming wives," a reference to Mrs. Hearst and Marion Davies, Hearst's mistress.

As usual, Churchill had kept Clemmie fully informed on his financial
affairs. In one "windfall," resulting from his New York broker investing
for him on margin instead of purchasing shares outright as Churchill
expected, he made £5,000. In another whim, he made £1,000
by speculating in the stock of a furniture firm called Simmons; Churchill was particularly taken by its advertising slogan: "You can't go
wrong on a Simmons mattress."

Between amusing Baruch with his perceptive observations on Hollywood and its stars—Churchill thought Charlie Chaplin "bolshy in politics and delightful in conversation"—he carefully questioned his host
about dabbling further in the market.

Baruch explained why he had adopted a cautious position.

And yet, just as Richard Whitney had predicted to the reporter, the
Great Bull Market had now seemingly shaken off its fetters and was
rampaging on more strongly than ever.

On the New York Stock Exchange on Saturday, U. S. Steel had
leaped ahead almost $8 a share. General Electric's surge was even more
dramatic; it went up 10 points. American Tobacco achieved one of the
most spectacular rises of all—a wondrous $38 a share. The Dow
Jones industrial average regained more than 16 points during the dramatic turnabout.

In San Francisco there was near-record trading in Transamerica and
other issues. In Chicago some brokers were said to have sent their
clerks out to buy gargles to ease throats sore from shouting. Baltimore,

Boston, and Hartford were swept by a wave of trading that often equaled the volume of earlier in the year.

In St. Louis, Los Angeles, Philadelphia, and Minneapolis–St. Paul, the urge "to get into the market" reached what one hard-pressed broker described as "an epidemic."

Along thousands of miles of private wires went the cheerful news "the big boys" were behind this new wave of buying.

With a flair few could match, John J. Raskob encouraged the thought. Throughout Saturday he talked up his media contacts. Percy Rockefeller, the Du Ponts, Van Sweringens, and Billy Durant helped reinforce his message.

After Saturday's market closed there were few Americans unaware that, in the words of one reporter, "a financial revival equal in fervor to anything the Bible Belt can produce" was under way.

Across the nation, still more hopefuls threw up their jobs, packed their bags, bid their families and friends farewell, and headed for New York.

A radio commentator said, with considerable justification, Wall Street had "taken on the appearance of a Gold Rush."

The train that brought Baruch's private car into Grand Central no doubt carried at least a few more speculators who quickly headed downtown to get the first glimpse of their Klondike.

Even an investor as seasoned as Baruch could not but be surprised by the amazing about-face the market had made.

Some Wall Street brokerage houses called in their staff this Sunday to change the tone of their market letters from somber caution to renewed optimism. And once again the phrase "organized support" was heard in the Street.

The shrewd and prudent Winston Churchill was not the only potential investor in New York who believed the stock market was still the quickest, and possibly easiest, way to become rich.

Writing carefully, A. P. Giannini in San Francisco prepared the announcement he hoped would not only alter radically the stockholding structure of Transamerica but also the role of all small investors in major corporations. At its simplest he hoped to encourage the public in large numbers to hold modest, individual blocks of shares in Transamerica. They could be paid for "in monthly installments of $5 per share per month for a period of ten months."

In this way Giannini meant "the little fellah" to have a new and important voice in the running of Transamerica. It was a plan he wished to see all big companies follow.

The idea had taken root after Giannini read, and enthusiastically endorsed, John J. Raskob's proposed Equities Security Company, designed to buy stocks for "proletarians who could invest $200 a head." Giannini was surprised Raskob had not yet launched his corporation; he assumed the financier was preoccupied with his Empire State Building.

Months of careful thought and planning had gone into Giannini's proposal. Often working late at the office, snatching hours from his weekends, working in the car to and from work, he gradually improved on what Raskob had outlined. Claire and his sons warmly approved of his plan. They urged him to launch it as soon as possible. He told them he wanted the market to settle and stabilize first.

For days, the regular telephone calls from his brother, Doc, in New York had been concerned largely with the situation there. The rocketlike rebirth of the market on Saturday, October 5, had not immediately impressed Giannini. He wondered at first whether it was another flash-in-the-pan, the kind of inexplicable spurt, followed by an equally abrupt dip, that had characterized September and the first days of October.

But gradually, as prices moved forward steadily, without any sudden surge in either direction—a sign Giannini always took as a warning—his fears faded. All the indications, he told Claire, did point to a period of consolidation; the market seemed "at its sanest for months."

Call money hovered around the 6 percent mark; on October 9 it had dropped to 5 percent, the lowest level for fourteen months.

Next day, the market showed its appreciation; the *Times* Industrial Average rose nearly 7 points.

On October 15 call money edged to 7 percent. And 6,000 miles from banker Giannini in San Francisco, in London, banker Charles Mitchell, ending his European trip, delivered his considered judgment on events in America. He boldly announced that throughout the country, the stock market was "in a healthy condition."

No one asked on precisely what information the president of the National City Bank based his diagnosis. It did not matter; it was seized upon as holy writ by the American media.

Not to be outdone, Professor Irving Fisher of Yale, still poohpoohing Babson, stepped in nimbly with: "I expect to see the stock market a good deal higher than it is today, within a few months."

Giannini did not pay much attention to the pronouncement of either man. He was well aware of their mutual penchant for publicity.

Nevertheless, the general financial picture seemed far better than it had been two weeks before. There were some, like Alexander Noyes of the New York *Times,* who hinted this was the calm before the storm. Noyes pointed to the decline in industrial output. Giannini was willing to believe this regression was temporary, that with the market holding steady, production would pick up. He was more worried about the investment trusts. They continued to multiply like locusts. There were now said to be nearly 500 of them, with a total paid-up capital of some $3 billion. While many were honestly and intelligently managed, others troubled Giannini; he suspected they were wildly speculative and so poorly capitalized they could not even pay their preferred dividends out of the income from the securities they held. Even worse were those trusts, often backed by banks, whose main purpose was the absorption of securities that would otherwise have been difficult to sell.

Now that the market was bulling along nicely, the newspapers were full of new stories of people who had just got rich overnight. A broker's valet was reported to have made "nearly $250,000"; a nurse $30,000 "following the tips of grateful patients." A Wyoming cattleman, thirty miles from the nearest railroad, bought and sold 1,000 shares a day, it was said—getting his market information from the radio and telephoning his orders to the nearest large town to be transmitted to New York by telegram. An ex-actress, rumored to have been a girl friend of Jesse Livermore, had fitted her Park Avenue apartment as an office and, like the archbear himself, surrounded herself with charts, graphs, and financial reports; she was reported to be playing the market with increasing abandon. A young banker boasted how he had placed every dollar he possessed into Niles-Bement-Pond, and was now "fixed for life." A widow told a Hearst tabloid she had just bought a large country house with her winnings in Kennecott.

Thousands speculated—and were again winning—without the slightest knowledge of the nature of the shares they invested in.

It was these people, more than anybody else, Giannini hoped to attract into his scheme. He accepted it was "part of the American way of life" for delivery boys, motormen, plumbers, seamstresses, and speakeasy waiters to play the market. Equally, he felt it was his duty to protect these "small fellahs and gals" from making mistakes. He had founded his banking philosophy on that premise.

Tomorrow, October 17, Giannini would celebrate his once tiny Bank of Italy's twenty-fifth anniversary. He planned then to unfold his scheme as a perfect climax to the birthday celebrations.

At about the time Giannini was finalizing his statement, the Committee of Investment Bankers Association in New York announced that speculation in public service stocks "has reached danger point and many stocks are selling far above their intrinsic value."

Almost immediately the market broke; General Electric fell 12 points, Westinghouse over 11, U. S. Steel nearly 10.

Next day, October 17, the market recovered.

Giannini was pleased Transamerica had escaped unscathed. He went ahead with his announcement at the twenty-fifth anniversary celebrations for the Bank of Italy in San Francisco that night.

Jolan and her elder brother, Michael, walked hesitantly into the Union Industrial Bank in Flint shortly before closing time on Friday, October 18. They had waited until now in the hope the bank would be empty, so they could complete their business "before anybody got a good sniff at us." Jolan was conscious she and Michael reeked "like a distillery." For days they had been helping to brew the extra-potent beverage that would be served at Jolan's wedding breakfast the next morning.

The teenage bride-to-be knew her stepfather and mother expected her to assist in their alcoholic endeavors until the very last moment. Just this morning, to reduce the escape of fumes from the vats in the basement—fumes were a telltale sign to Prohibition agents searching for stills—Jolan had pressed freshly kneaded dough around the vat lids and joints. The dough soon became impregnated with alcohol, and the pretty bootlegger wondered whether there might not be a market "for the only bread in the world which could make you drunk."

Michael had persuaded Jolan to leave her work in the basement temporarily in order to come with him to the bank.

The temperature was below freezing outside, but once in the bank, Jolan became uncomfortably aware of the pungent aroma radiating from her brother and herself.

Mustering her confidence—trying to appear unconcerned about her patched and worn clothes which were in total contrast to the way customers dressed in the bank's glossy brochure—Jolan marched forward and stopped at the first teller's cage she came to, the one occupied by Russell Runyon. She smiled sweetly at the teller.

He stared back in surprise at the two youngsters smelling strongly of spirits who faced him.

Jolan said they wanted to talk about her brother's account.

Runyon could barely disguise his astonishment. "You have an account *here?*"

Jolan, for all her tender years, was capable of handling "snooty folk." Affecting the manner of Mr. Goldberger, she addressed the teller in the way of an attorney. "This *is* the Union Industrial Bank?"

Runyon agreed that it was.

"Then you should know we have our accounts here."

Michael explained about the trust fund their father had set up before his death. Now he was eighteen, he wanted to withdraw his money.

The teller hurried from the cage to the trust department across the floor.

Jolan leaned nonchalantly against the counter. She and her brother were the only customers in the bank.

Runyon returned. He said Michael could not have his money "right now."

Jolan asked why.

The teller explained it would "take time" to organize the withdrawal.

Michael turned to his sister and shrugged. "I guess I won't be able to buy me a new car—or get you and Steve that wedding present."

This time Runyon did not bother to hide his surprise. He looked at Jolan. *"You're* getting married?"

"Sure. And after I am, I'll want *my* money. That's how Dad arranged things."

"But you're just a child!"

"Sixteen. Old enough. And you better have my money ready when I come for it next week. Otherwise I'll send Mr. Goldberger here!"

"You *know* Mr. Goldberger?"

"Sure. He handles all our affairs!"

Jolan motioned to her brother and walked serenely out of the bank.

The first flakes of snow were falling when they reached home.

Inside, arrangements for the wedding were in full swing.

Gallon jars of freshly brewed alcohol were being brought up from the basement by Andrew Arvay and Steve; a full pint of raw liquor had been allowed for each adult among the three hundred guests.

Jolan's and Steve's mothers, assisted by women from the surrounding blocks, were creating a variety of special Hungarian concoctions to supplement those being prepared by other neighbors in the basement of the nearby St. Joseph's Catholic Church.

There, trestle tables had been set up and covered with borrowed white bed sheets. Crockery and cutlery, also borrowed from neighbors, were laid on top of the sheets.

At dusk John Bokr, the local grocer, arrived at the house. Some believed Bokr was even better connected than Goldberger. A short, sprightly man, the grocer was said to have a direct channel to the city's mayor.

Bokr held a whispered consultation with Andrew Arvay, who smiled broadly and then turned to his wife. "Ma, ain't gonna be no problems with the Prohibition boys."

The grocer had arranged that throughout the entire wedding reception, the approaches to the church would be patrolled by the local police department with specific instructions to turn away any snooping Prohibition agents.

Barbara Arvay had one question: What would happened if the federal agents still insisted on raiding the church premises?

Mr. Bokr had a comforting answer. "They'll be arrested on a charge of sacrilege."

Reassured, Jolan and Steve, with baby Margaret seated in the baby carriage, began to ferry flagons of alcohol to the church hall. The liquor was stored behind bottles of communion wine and boxes of wafers.

At midnight Jolan was packed off to bed. Too excited to sleep, she lay awake in her bunk and tried to imagine what it was going to be like to have somebody beside her. All she could think of was whether Steve might have cold feet or snored.

Next morning, Saturday, dawned crisp and clear. The snowing had stopped.

By 7 A.M., Jolan was up and bathed. Then she joined her mother in her bedroom. On the large double bed, Barbara Arvay had laid out her daughter's wedding ensemble—a modish dress, veil, headdress, and a train that would sweep to the ground.

The outfit had cost a princely $100—money Mrs. Arvay had saved from the profits of bootlegging.

Slipping into new underwear, for the first time in her life Jolan experienced the feel of proper panties instead of those fashioned from flour bags.

While she dressed, her mother gently warned her not to "expect too much" on her wedding night. It was the sum total of Mrs. Arvay's advice to her daughter on sexual matters.

At nine o'clock the ushers and bridesmaids started to arrive. There were a dozen of each; the girls wore their best frocks, the boys were scrubbed clean and in shiny dark suits.

Soon every downstairs room in the house was filled with guests.

At nine-thirty, Mr. Goldberger and Mr. Bokr, in line with their preeminent status in the community, arrived last to wish the bride good luck.

Goldberger had one piece of news. He solemnly told Jolan any plans she had for honeymooning with Steve on J. P. Morgan's yacht, *Corsair,* now entrusted to the nation by the millionaire financier, would have to be shelved. Goldberger had just heard the government was having trouble finding the $100,000 needed to keep the yacht afloat.

Everybody laughed; Goldberger was renowned for taking a topical item and making a quip about it.

The joke was lost on Jolan. She had never heard of J. P. Morgan.

Mr. Bokr shooed the guests to the church. Then he and Mr. Goldberger escorted Barbara Arvay to St. Joseph's.

Finally, shortly after ten o'clock, Jolan walked up the aisle on the arm of her beaming stepfather.

Minutes later, on the New York Stock Exchange, the market began to break. In the day's 120 minutes of trading, stocks would plunge as much as $40. Shares in the Simmons Company fell 11 points; Churchill had taken his £1,000 profit just in time. Otis Elevators dropped from 401 to 396; General Electric from 347 to 339; Auburn Auto from 390 to 375. During the week, U. S. Steel had declined from a high of 223 to its present 209.

When the news from New York became known, some of the embezzlers in the Union Industrial again appealed to the Almighty to intervene and make the market right itself. They now knew not only their own fortunes but those of a great many people in Flint depended on that happening.

Blissfully unaware their modest bank deposits were in jeopardy, Jolan and Steve watched "a small fortune" in dollar bills being thrown into the large copper kettle on the table in the basement of St. Joseph's. It was the Hungarian community's traditional way of giving to a bridal couple.

Steve felt the money should be placed as soon as possible in the Union Industrial.

Jolan was not certain. She was still puzzled why Michael had been unable to withdraw his money on demand. She mentioned the incident to Mr. Goldberger. The attorney promised to look into the matter during the coming week. In the meantime he agreed to store the kettle of dollars in his office safe.

The wedding breakfast over, the music began. Dancers whirled around the floor to a Hungarian czardas. At the tables, bootleg booze flowed as freely as the talk.

And, at regular intervals, the policemen "guarding" the hall dropped in for a drink.

In the Flint post office, as in post offices all across America, clerks were processing telegrams from New York brokerage houses, demanding more margin. The telegrams' bad tidings let speculators know their speculative favorites had taken a nose-dive.

At midnight, the wedding festivities showed no signs of a letup. Another kettle had been filled to the brim with money, including this time a generous splash of ten- and twenty-dollar bills.

A fresh meal was served. New flagons of spirits were opened. The music grew louder, the dancing more abandoned.

A relief team of policemen came to join in the celebrations. They brought Sunday editions of the newspapers. Like the *Times* in New York, the Detroit press made the Saturday market break front-page news.

The guests balled up the newspapers to pelt the dancers.

In the early hours of the morning Jolan took Steve aside. There was something she had been wondering about all night. The innocent sixteen-year-old wanted to know whether when she became pregnant, "the baby will come out of my belly button."

Gently, Steve told her she would learn "in good time" about such matters. He did not want to admit he, too, had no idea how babies were born. Instead he fetched another scoop of the special vanilla ice cream he had reserved for his virginal young bride.

CHAPTER TWENTY-THREE

ALL AT SEA

Twenty-four hours out of Cherbourg, the passengers on the New York bound *Berengaria* had found their sea legs and were paying little attention to the sixteen-foot combers, driven by a nor'wester, now smashing against the liner's quarter.

Captain Rostron found the storm timely. He had enjoyed Sunday dinner—salmon steaks and sliced roast duck—at his table in the first-class dining room. But over coffee he became uneasy when a passenger started to talk about his part in the *Titanic* drama. Rostron nowadays tended to minimize his hero's role in the tragedy. He used the storm as an excuse to leave for the bridge. Behind him an animated conversation commenced about the stock market.

Ever since the ship's brokerage service had opened, such discussions had filled endless hours at sea. Rostron, an affirmed nonspeculator, was astonished how far some of his passengers were prepared to go to keep in close touch with Wall Street. On this voyage, one of them had already spent a tidy sum bombarding his broker with wireless messages; another requested he receive personal daily reports on all aspects of the market during the crossing.

Even some of Rostron's officers were bitten by the investment bug. Forbidden by company regulations to speculate directly, they did so through passengers. Rostron suspected a number of his crew were financially better off from these ventures than he was from his salary as commodore of the Cunard Fleet. The possibility did not trouble him unduly.

Nor did the problem he faced tonight when he reached the bridge. The watch officer reported a porthole light, shining from a stateroom, was hindering the helmsman. A steward was sent to close and curtain the porthole. The stateroom's occupant was an obdurate fresh-air lover who insisted she needed to inhale sea breezes to prepare herself for the long daytime hours she anticipated spending in the ship's brokerage room. A compromise was reached; a piece of sailcloth was rigged over the porthole, letting in air without allowing the light to escape.

There were no illumination restrictions in the softly lamplit smoke room on A Deck. There, Helena Rubinstein, who proclaimed herself "the world's greatest beauty specialist," was playing bridge. The fifty-eight-year-old millionairess, traveling with four steamer trunks of *haute couture* clothes and jewel cases of rubies—real and fake—was playing bridge in a game where the stakes were a twelfth of a cent a point. What kept her at the card table was her companions' talk of stocks and shares. Madame Rubinstein, too, meant to visit the ship's broker tomorrow.

In the ballroom, the orchestra rendered the latest hits from Paris and New York, and a new song from Havana, "Siboney"; rumor had it the Cuban composer had given up music for the market.

In a salon, Charlie Goudiss, watched by his assistant, Stanley Moore, was playing no-limit poker. His fellow gamblers did not really mind if he won; Goudiss ran the ship's brokerage, and they were there in the hope of receiving one of his carefully dispensed tips.

They were not disappointed. Goudiss sincerely believed the serious Saturday morning break would be balanced on Monday by "organized support." He passed on this view to the players.

Goudiss was fully informed of the latest news from Wall Street through his close connection with the ship's wireless room staff; the *Berengaria* carried six operators plus two specially retained by Michael Meehan exclusively to receive stock market quotations and to transmit the buy and sell orders.

After dinner, Goudiss—a Yale dropout, class of '25, and one of Meehan's best customers' men—had picked up from the wireless room the special news digest that Marconi radioed to ships at sea. The New York Sundays reported the increase in margin calls, but that did not trouble Goudiss or shake his faith in the market's ability to recover. It had always done so before.

Both Goudiss and Moore had noted the unusually large number of millionaires aboard on this trip. The two brokers expected when they opened their office for trading at two o'clock the next afternoon—coinciding with the 10 A.M. Monday opening in New York—they would be exceptionally busy.

Another of those who intended to call on them was now entertaining in her private suite on B Deck. Anna de Koven, secure in her position as one of society's grandest dames, presided over the end of a dinner party. During the meal there had been no talk of business. But over liqueurs and coffee, a spirited discussion developed about which shares would show the greatest profit before the liner docked at New York on Friday.

All over the great ship in these last hours of Sunday, passengers were laying plans to play, and beat, the market.

At midnight, the two crew members responsible for the *Berengaria*'s daily newspaper began to rewrite the latest Marconi news bulletin. John Durham and Bill Judd operated their "city desk" from a cubbyhole near the print shop on A Deck; there, along with the ship's paper, menus, and official bulletins, the printers were frequently asked to run off embossed invitations to parties given by passengers celebrating a stock market win at sea.

Durham and Judd had chosen as their "splash" story the report that Prime Minister Ramsay MacDonald—having met with President Hoover in Washington and shared his birthday cake with Winston Churchill in New York—was now on his way to Montreal. From London came the news the Prince of Wales had agreed to preside over a dinner in Parliament on November 3 for all living holders of the Victoria Cross; only 185 VC's had so far accepted—it was assumed many could not afford the expense of traveling to London. In Havana four men had been arrested for issuing a political manifesto against President Machado's regime. In New York Dr. Clarence True Wilson had attacked American World War veterans for importing European ideals "with their lewd conception of social life never before experienced on American soil."

And from Paris came the report of a series of searing attacks in the French press against Wall Street. The Paris newspapers blamed the Street for the sudden depression that had hit the city's Bourse. Socialist Léon Blum thundered that French Treasury deposits in New York were being used to encourage speculation on the Stock Exchange. Claimed Blum: "Wall Street's call-money needs are draining to New York all the world's floating balances, with a resultant depression everywhere."

By 4 A.M., Monday, October 21, Durham and Judd had their newspaper written and printed. Three hours later, 1,000 copies were being slipped noiselessly under stateroom and cabin doors by the ship's corps of page boys.

At about the same local time in New York, Jesse Livermore scanned the New York *Times*. The Monday edition had done no detailed followup to the previous day's page-one, column-one story. The Sunday edition ran a headline that had stunned Livermore:

J. L. LIVERMORE REPORTED TO BE
HEADING GROUP HAMMERING
HIGH-PRICED SECURITIES

The story bluntly asserted Livermore was leader of "the bear clique," and that Saturday's decline could be attributed, at least in part, to his "brilliantly executed drives."

The *Times* reminded its readers Livermore was "the Wall Street Wonder"—the "Boy Plunger" who had been barred from the Boston bucket shops when in his teens and was now "the best man on the stockmarket tape the speculative world has ever known."

His first reaction was one of fury. The story brought back unhappy memories of the previous one the newspaper published about his legal battles. But there was nothing in the Sunday *Times* article that was actionable. And, when he calmed down, Livermore had to admit it wasn't every day America's most influential popular newspaper gave such prominence to a market operator. He could imagine the envy such publicity would create in Arthur Cutten, whom the *Times* described as his archrival, "the recognized leader of the bull party."

Livermore began to work out how he might exploit the story.

Almost every word it contained about him was either misleading or untrue. He telephoned one of the *Times* editors and told him he was going to hold a press conference, "to set the record straight."

The *Times* agreed to send a reporter.

What the *Times* did not know was that Livermore had deliberately restricted the "press conference" to them. Just as John J. Raskob had used the technique back in August to get the maximum coverage for his announcement about the Empire State Building, so Livermore hoped the rest of the media would swiftly purloin what he told the *Times,* thus ensuring the widest coverage for his views.

Jesse Livermore intended to demonstrate he was just as capable of manipulating the media as he was of mounting a bear raid.

He planned to talk to the *Times* in his office in the Heckscher Building on Fifth Avenue. When he informed Dorothy of this intention, his wife accused him of trying to exclude her further from his life. Their weeks of fragile bliss were coming to an end; the strain of papering over the cracks in their marriage was too great. He had started to chase girls; she was back on the bottle.

Livermore would take care the *Times* learned nothing of his domestic misery—just as he would ensure the newspaper was left in no doubt as to his thoughts on the market.

By nine-thirty he was safely ensconced behind the huge mahogany desk which was the centerpiece of his private office inside the secret complex he maintained at the top of the Heckscher Building.

Thirty minutes later his chief clerk showed the *Times* reporter in.

The journalist scribbled his first observation of Livermore: "Sphinx-like, imperturbable and rigid . . . he reached for the telephone resting on a ledge to his left, and carefully covering the mouthpiece with his delicate fingers, began to whisper market orders to an unidentified ally, somewhere deep in the financial district."

Livermore was playing up to the *Times* description of yesterday that he was again "one of the foremost market plungers of the day."

The reporter stood respectfully while Livermore continued his confidential conversation. Carefully appraising his interviewee, memorizing the minutiae about Livermore that *Times* readers would love, the journalist saw that a fine gold chain hung across the speculator's chest.

Aware of the newsman's interest, Livermore obligingly "fished out a slim gold pencil hanging from one end of the chain. The ever-present secretary automatically slid a pad of paper before his boss who quickly covered the pad with coded markings."

Suddenly, Livermore tucked the pencil back into his vest pocket, replaced the receiver, and yanked out a little gold knife attached to the other end of the chain.

Only then did he acknowledge the presence of the reporter. He casually waved him toward a chair. The *Times* man committed to memory Livermore's "warm friendly smile . . . did not offer to shake hands, abhors physical contact with any male . . . carefully controls his agitation."

It was a reasonable assessment of the speculator's complex public facade.

The formal interview began by the reporter asking Livermore whether he was, as reported, the leader of a gigantic bear consortium.

Livermore handed the newsman a single sheet of neatly typed paper. He still had not spoken.

The puzzled reporter tried again. He repeated his question.

Livermore finally spoke, "in a hushed voice ripping the air like a stiletto."

He told the reporter to read his typed statement.

It was a well-written denial of the allegations in Sunday's *Times*.

Livermore had completed the first stage of the interview he was so carefully stage-managing.

The *Times* man gave him the opening to move to the second stage.

He asked why stocks were declining.

Livermore replied many issues were now, and had been for a long time, "selling at ridiculously high prices."

Digesting this answer, the reporter noted how Livermore "pushed back against his padded swivel chair, while twirling the little pen-knife furiously between his ever-moving fingers."

He reminded Livermore that Professor Fisher claimed stocks were still cheap.

Livermore slammed forward in his chair and snapped out his answer. "What can a professor know about speculation or stock markets? Did he ever trade on margin? Does he have a single cent in any of these bubbles he talks are cheap? Beware of inside information—*all* inside information. How can the public possibly rely on information coming from a classroom? I tell you the market never stands still. It acts like the ocean. There are waves of accumulation and distribution. The market always tells you when you are wrong. So let's leave it to the market to tell its own story—with or without help from college professors."

He had achieved the second part of his plan—demolishing Fisher and his buoyant attitude to the market.

But before he could move to the next stage—establishing his own position—the reporter surprised him.

So far, the *Times* man had given the impression of being little more than an uncritical cipher for Livermore's views. Now he displayed unsuspected mettle. He asked Livermore directly whether he was not "on the short side since you believe the market will break?"

Livermore's answer was quick, glib—and evasive. He read from his prepared statement.

"What little business I do in the stock market has always been as an individual and will continue to be done on such a basis. It is very foolish to think that any individual or combination of individuals could artificially bring about a decline in the stock market in a country so large and so prosperous as the United States."

For many years Livermore had grown rich by conducting bear raids.

Now, uncertain in the reporter's presence, he cut short the interview. This line of questioning was not what he had intended. His carefully prepared attempt to bamboozle the *Times* might, after all, rebound.

By noon, aboard the *Berengaria,* Goudiss and Moore could see the ship's newspaper had heightened interest in the market. On the decks and in the public rooms, conversation buzzed about the expected opening prices in New York.

Goudiss and Moore encouraged such discussions; it was part of the role Mike Meehan originally envisaged for them. Impeccably dressed and groomed, glowing from their morning sessions in the ship's Turkish bath and gymnasium, they circulated among the preluncheon crowd in the smoke room, having a quiet word with carefully selected potential investors. By early afternoon they had spoken to a score of multi-millionaires, millionaires, and the merely very wealthy.

At a few minutes before 2 P.M., with a tray of sandwiches and coffee for lunch, the two men stood by to open shop.

Their brokerage office was not quite so "spacious and clublike" as Meehan had described it to the press. But it was comfortable enough, with twenty easy chairs for clients, a desk apiece for Goudiss and Moore, and a "cage" with two smaller desks for the radio operators whose equipment was patched through to the main wireless room behind the bridge. Entirely covering one wall was a blackboard where prices would be chalked by a young clerk.

One of the radiomen tapped out a test message to Tuckerton, New Jersey, still over 2,000 miles away. The response was clear and immediate.

The radio operators had by now so refined their procedures, a buy or sell order from ship to shore could be executed in two minutes.

At a few seconds past 2 P.M., Tuckerton tapped out STOX—the signal that the New York Stock Exchange had opened.

Almost immediately there followed the first opening quotations. Thirty minutes later all the prices for the hundred selected stocks were on the ship's blackboard.

Soon both Goudiss and Moore were busy with orders.

At 6:30 P.M. ship's time—thirty minutes before the 3 P.M. closing in New York—news of a bullish upsurge on Wall Street reached the floating brokerage. Passengers assured each other this late rally toward the close of an up-and-down day was a certain sign "tomorrow will bring full recovery." Some placed buy orders on that basis.

At 7 P.M. Goudiss ended the day's trading. The last person to leave the room was Helena Rubinstein. So far she had made no investment. But the experienced Goudiss sensed it was only a matter of time before the beautician did so in a big way.

Goudiss knew there would be a guaranteed spin-off if Madame Rubinstein won. With her great flair for publicity, she would ensure further coverage for Mike Meehan's innovation, thus furthering his wish to see all the world's important liners equipped with similar brokerages. Goudiss told Stanley Moore that, when Miss Rubinstein chose her moment to invest, they must give her the best advice possible, guiding her to those stocks most likely to give a high return for a low risk.

The one risk that Harry Herbert Bennett had feared all day—some lunatic or extremist attempting to harm Henry Ford or his distinguished guests—continued to haunt him in the evening as the celebrations moved to their climax. Since 9:30 A.M. this Monday, America and, through radio, the world beyond, had gawped at a public relations classic in which President Hoover, Will Rogers, Madame Curie, Orville Wright, and Albert Einstein had all been given carefully timed and designed walk-on parts in a pageant planned, some thought, for the greater glory of Henry Ford.

Today, October 21, was "dedication day" for Ford's "American Village," sited in the Detroit suburb of Dearborn. It was also—almost but not quite—fifty years to the day since Thomas Edison had first demonstrated a practical electric light. Ford had arranged for the inventor's laboratories, machine shops, and library to be removed from their original setting at Menlo Park, New Jersey, and to be transported and put in another place, his village, for posterity. Along with the cluster of structures came an acre of New Jersey clay for them to stand on; scattered around the buildings were large stones, thoughtfully collected and brought with the clay. Nearby stood the resited boardinghouse where a number of Edison's unmarried associates had once lived, and to which wires had been strung fifty years before for the first flickering of the inventor's lamp outside his laboratory.

The buildings added further luster to the astonishing collection of brick and clapboard edifices that dominated the two-hundred-acre site.

The climax of the day's celebrations would come when the eighty-two-year-old Edison reenacted the lighting of his incandescent lamp.

Weeks of intensive work had gone into masterminding what journalist Stanley Walker would dismiss as "simply a publicity stunt, representing powerful and rich interests, to exploit the uses of electric light."

The majority of journalists were far less critical. The presence of Hoover gave the event a veneer. And, hopefully, Henry Ford might say or do something spectacular. To make sure they did not miss anything, the newsmen ignored orders to stay behind barriers. Instead, they milled all day around Ford as he guided the coterie of luminaries through his village.

Augmenting the men of the Secret Service, Bennett had deployed his guards, many of them armed as he was, in and around the historic buildings on the site. They occupied Longfellow's blacksmith's shop, uprooted from Uxbridge, Massachusetts, and the courthouse from Logan County, Illinois, where Abe Lincoln practiced law. Bennett's heavies could be seen in the old country inn, a log cabin, a general store, the office of Luther Burbank, and in a building that appeared somewhat incongruous—Ford's spanking new chemical laboratory where he planned to build car bodies out of soybeans.

When Ford reached the small house in which Stephen Foster had been born, he revealed a disappointment. He had hoped to have ex- humed and stuffed the body of Old Dog Tray, to lie forever in the dwelling of his master's birth. But that had proven impossible. Ford had reluctantly accepted a living substitute, another setter, who now lolled outside the pauper composer's cottage. He hoped the hound carried the same canine spirit as Old Dog Tray.

The story was an opportunity for reporters to quiz Ford about his latest views on reincarnation. The magnate confided he no longer believed he was Leonardo da Vinci in a previous life; he now ap- parently thought he had been King Midas. As King Midas, he had, "of course," known Bacchus, "that god of intoxicating beverages. No doubt my animosity towards liquor drinking comes as an inheritance from my King Midas existence."

Ford, the gleeful reporters saw, was living up to form. The revelation about King Midas was the latest headline-grabber the auto king had delivered. He had recently collected thousands of column inches and hours of radio time by speculating about building an airplane for "the common man"—an aerial Tin Lizzie; proposing a scheme to convert city garbage into compost for dust-bowl farmers; predicting that women would never have a place in industry; announcing he was going into "partnership" with Archbishop Dobrecic, Catholic primate of Serbia, to market cars in Yugoslavia; banning workers on his rubber plantation in Brazil from drinking rum; promising to produce 175,000 cars this month; setting the Mexican Government "right" on its labor policies.

But even publicity-hungry Ford must have been satisfied to see so many reporters assembled in one place as there were at his Village this Monday. Running into hundreds, they represented the media of forty countries. Like their readers, the newsmen were agog at Ford's determi- nation to re-create his past.

Tourists in the future would be able to view the original transplanted farmhouse where he had been born, the schoolhouse he attended, the coal shed where he built his first invention.

After lunch Hoover lit a fire in the hearth of Lincoln's courthouse and Edison one in the boiler of the brick machine shop. The fires, "symbolizing government and home and science and industry," were designated by Ford "eternal flames."

And not even the continuous rain could quench the enthusiasm of the distinguished guests.

The few who had been invited with Wall Street connections included Walter Chrysler, the Fisher Brothers, and John D. Rockefeller, Jr. Each of them took care not to raise in the hearing of their host such a sensitive matter as the stock market.

Only once did the harsh outside world of Wall Street intrude into Ford's expensively refurbished oasis of tranquillity.

Early afternoon, newsmen asked Hoover for a reaction to the latest news from Wall Street. The market had broken again. Hoover smoothly turned away the press with the suggestion they wait and see what developed. Thirty minutes before closing, the market rallied; a record 920 stocks had been dealt in during the 6,091,000-share day.

At Dearborn, after touring the Village even the most cynical journalist had to admit Ford had re-created a striking record of America's heritage.

Now, close to 7:30 this Monday evening, the climax was at hand.

During the day, while colleagues covered the spot news, Graham McNamee, one of the most experienced commentators NBC employed, had spent much of his time in Thomas Edison's old laboratory, seeping up the atmosphere, preparing notes to carry him through a worldwide broadcast. An estimated 100 million would hear McNamee describing Edison reproducing his historic experiment.

Now, primed and ready, wearing a tuxedo as were all other male guests, McNamee sat at a table in a corner of the faithful reproduction of Philadelphia's Independence Hall, ready to set the scene for his huge audience.

At 7:30 precisely, NBC's local affiliate plugged the reporter into the network. From NBC's studios in New York, the broadcast was relayed to Europe—where although it was already early Tuesday morning, tens of thousands of listeners were grouped around their radios.

In San Francisco, where it was 4:30 in the afternoon, A. P. Giannini snatched time from work to listen to McNamee speak from his place in the hall.

". . . I have just been thinking that the world could not celebrate its emancipation from darkness more fittingly than in this building, which is associated in the minds of all of us with freedom and progress. . . ."

In New York, John J. Raskob and James Riordan sat by candlelight in Raskob's apartment listening to the broadcast. Millions of others had also turned off their lights at McNamee's behest, and now, in near darkness, were attempting to recall what the world was like before Edison's invention.

". . . to the right and left of the main rotunda, where a statue of Thomas Edison will soon stand, two long wings stretch away filled with some five hundred of the most distinguished people in America. The high, wide halls are aglow with the light of thousands of candles, their golden brilliance dancing like sunlight on falling water as the facets of the great crystal chandeliers sway and twist. An interesting sidelight of this lighting is the fact that all the candles used here tonight were hand-dipped today in the village. . . ."

Alone in his Fifth Avenue aerie, Jesse Livermore paused in his calculations to listen to the dulcet-voiced McNamee, who, during a brief musical interlude, had sprinted from the mock-up of Independence Hall to Edison's authentic laboratory.

". . . from the upper windows I can see Mr. Edison approaching in an old-fashioned horse-drawn carriage. He has just passed the old saw mill and turned from Main Street into Washington Street. The streets now have exactly the same appearance as they had in the old Menlo Park days. Let me give you the setting for this unique drama of a half-century ago. Here is the old laboratory where the first incandescent lamp was born. . . ."

In their luxurious apartment, Edith Stone and her parents were raptly following the commentary. Seated side by side, Edward and Mabel Stone held hands and reminded their daughter that when they were born, electricity was still very much an innovation.

". . . below me, on the first floor, is the old office, the darkroom, and the little room filled with retorts, scales and old bottles. Just a word about the stairs we just raced up, ladies and gentlemen. This afternoon I noticed a little cubbyhole leading under them, and I am told that this dark little recess was one of Mr. Edison's favorite spots when he found it necessary to take a quiet nap from sheer exhaustion. You could always tell when he was taking a nap, because his feet stuck out through the doorway. . . ."

The anecdote still made Billy Durant smile, even though, when they had been close, he heard it many times from Henry Ford. The rift between them—stemming from the day Durant offered to absorb the Ford Motor Company into General Motors—had precluded any chance of him being invited to Dearborn for tonight's celebrations. Durant and his wife had to rely on McNamee's vivid commentary.

". . . here comes Mr. Edison, followed by President Hoover and the rest of the party. He is coming directly to the table behind the old vacuum pump. There is a notebook on the table. It was in a book such as this, I am told, that the records of the various lamp tests were kept. . . ."

In Flint, Frank Montague sat with his wife, Louise, hearing but not taking in the words. He had other things on his mind.

". . . can you imagine how this grand old man must feel as he is carried back half a century to the moment of his great triumph? Now he is taking up two small wires which lead from the main group of wet batteries, and he is touching them to other wires. . . ."

Jolan Vargo was glad of the darkness in her new in-laws' living room; it made it easy for her husband of two days to sneak a quick kiss without anyone else in the room knowing.

". . . you may close your eyes, ladies and gentlemen, and imagine you are one of this anxious little group of half a century ago, waiting, hoping. Mr. Edison is slouched back into a comfortable position, and as he sits calmly waiting for the old pump to complete its work, we will listen to his favorite air, 'Oh Susannah,' and then 'Take Me Home Again, Kathleen.'"

The sound of music, cued in from the NBC studios a few blocks from where he lived in New York, did nothing to relieve the tiredness W. E. Hutton-Miller felt. It had been a harrowing day on Wall Street for Hut as the market had dipped and then climbed as if it had a life of its own. The strain of coping with its vagaries was taxing even his capacity for work.

The Irish ballad "Kathleen" perfectly suited Michael Meehan's mood of nostalgia. Surrounded by his family in their comfortable apartment, the Radio specialist could remember the days when his own mother crooned the song to send him to sleep as a child.

In Edison's laboratory, listening to the music being faded out in his earphones, Graham McNamee pressed the microphone close against his lips and pitched his voice lower and softer to match the unfolding drama taking place a few feet way.

"And now, Mr. Edison is again on his feet, ready to test the lamp. Now he holds the wires to the bulb. This test is evidently satisfactory."

Pat Bologna sat, unseeing, staring toward a friend's radio amid the clutter of a Brooklyn apartment. In common with most others in the block, it was in darkness; without candles, the occupants had nevertheless switched off the lights. The young Italian believed the blackout helped lend authenticity to McNamee's words.

". . . I miss the lights. There are no lights on the wide boulevard which stretches away before this building. The only visible illumination is the flickering yellow flames from the kerosene lamps that here and there dot the streets of Greenfield. All you have to do is to imagine the shadowy, waiting mass to get an accurate picture of what night lighting must have looked like half a century ago. . . ."

Joe Kennedy had marshaled Rose and the children to hear this momentous broadcast. Later, the young ones would probably have umpteen questions for him to answer. But now they were silent, listening carefully to McNamee's commentary.

". . . the lamp is now ready, as it was ready half a century ago, for the critical test. Will it light? Will it burn? Or will it flicker and die, as so many previous lamps had died? Oh, you could hear a pin drop in this long room. Mr. Edison has two wires in his hand. Now he is reaching up to the old lamp. Now he is making the connection. It lights!"

Thomas Edison had successfully reenacted the scene when, at the age of thirty-two, he had demonstrated a new means of banishing darkness.

All over America lights were switched back on. Although no one could know it then, it would be a long time before they ever seemed to glow quite so brightly again.

Next day, wind-tanned and fit following an Atlantic crossing, Charles Mitchell set foot in New York in typical fashion—surrounded by newsmen. He was in optimistic form and had instant views to impart.

The banker told reporters he totally endorsed Professor Irving Fisher's pronouncement of the previous day that the recent decline represented only "a shaking out of the lunatic fringe." Fisher felt, "even in the present high markets, the price of stocks have not yet caught up with their real values." Nor, the prescient professor added, had the market "yet reflected the beneficent effects of Prohibition which has made American workers more productive and dependable."

Mitchell reinforced Fisher's remarks, claiming the sagging market "has carried prices of many issues below their true values," and that the fall "has gone too far." He believed the ever-increasing volume of brokers' loans "is nothing to become alarmed about; the situation is one which will correct itself if left alone."

The head of the National City Bank had pressing, albeit still secret, personal reasons for the boom to go on. His words were flashed to the financial district, lending impetus to a stock exchange rally. By the close of trading, Western Union would be up $18; Columbia Carbon $16.75; Hershey Chocolate over $10.

Roger Babson remained pessimistic—"the rebound will probably be only temporary"—but in comparison with the attention the optimistic Mitchell and Fisher received, he was virtually ignored by the media.

Not long after Mitchell had finished delivering his message to the press in New York, in Cincinnati, Ohio, President Herbert Hoover was handed a large envelope by an emissary of Thomas Lamont, senior partner at the House of Morgan. The envelope contained a twenty-page memorandum and letter which outlined Lamont's authoritative views on the present and future American investment situation.

Hoover began immediately to read the report, putting off an important appointment with the governor of Ohio in order to do so.

The combined talents of Lamont's fellow partners in the most powerful private banking house in the world had helped him prepare and then to put elegantly and persuasively on paper his well-argued case.

He started by conceding no one could *"know"* all the answers, and that there were "elements in the situation" that had given him and his colleagues real cause for concern. Nevertheless, stated Lamont, "there is nothing in the present situation to suggest that the normal economic forces, working to correct excesses and to restore the proper balance of affairs, are not still operative and adequate."

He raised the bull market, explaining and excusing its extremes in one eloquent sentence after another. Then he posed a question for the President.

"Is it not just possible that the improved machinery of the Stock Exchanges and the new investment trusts are attracting the savings of small investors all over the country who, induced in the first instance perhaps by merely the hope of a quick speculative profit or by stories of others' winnings, may become in time investors in the best stocks of the best companies?"

Lamont left his question unanswered, but he had a good deal more to say.

"In the not yet forgotten days when such things were possible, a jaded appetite was sometimes stimulated by a cocktail to the enjoyment of a hearty meal. If it should turn out that the speculative interest in stocks and the investment trusts are drawing the savings of the American people into partnership in the great and successful American industries, then the problem of waste of capital through the issue of fraudulent securities is being solved by making good stocks available to everyone.

"If that should turn out to be true a greater problem still is being solved. The wide distribution of the ownership of our greater industries among tens or hundreds of thousands of stockholders, should go a long way to solve the problem of social unrest and of conflict or imagined conflict between the corporations and the people."

The President could only approve of Lamont's articulate defense of the very principles that had helped to elect him.

Casting a critical eye overseas, Lamont poured scorn on Britain's "ill-informed" Chancellor Snowden, who, "three times in a recent speech held the 'American speculative orgy' as responsible for Great Britain's economic ills." He next chided newspapers for exaggerating "gossip about speculation," claiming their front-page stories were "generally quite misrepresentative."

Above all, Lamont dreaded "by premature action of any kind, to throw a monkey wrench into financial and economic machinery which appears to be functioning, on the whole, for the greater good of the people, and of a greater proportion of all the people, than ever before in the history of this or any other country."

In the dignified prose that had distinguished him as a young newspaperman, Lamont summed up.

"The future appears brilliant. It is this future which the stock market has been discounting . . . we have the greatest and soundest prosperity, and the best material prospects of any country in the world. Our national resources, our selected population, our great domestic market, our efficiency and our capital supplies make our securities the most desirable in the world. The whole world (including notably, and on a large scale, Chancellor Snowden's British compatriots) has wished to buy our stocks and is pleased to lend money at attractive rates."

Lamont made his conclusion crystal-clear. "Corrective action on the part of public authorities or individuals need not at this time be contemplated."

Eight months after Hoover entered the White House, he had the word of one of America's most distinguished bankers that the millennium had not only arrived but could continue throughout his presidency—*if,* and in Lamont's view only if, Hoover followed the lead of his predecessor and agreed "not to rock the boat."

Hoover agreed.

And within forty-eight hours, Lamont himself would be thrust center-stage as events dramatically negated his report to the President.

Richard Whitney felt relaxed and secure. His investments were showing some improvement. There had also been an improvement in his relations with Exchange staff. Initial hostility had given way to grudging admiration as Whitney displayed unexpected qualities of fair play and firmness. The acting president seemed to be growing into the job; no longer did he have to be supercilious or a bully; he *was* master and everyone accepted it.

Whitney had come to realize just how powerful was the position he now held; until he had actually sat in the president's office, the subtleties of the influence it commanded 'had eluded him. But he had learned to sit back and let people come to him. He began to dispense largess without seeking any immediate return; favors bestowed now could be reclaimed later.

Such pleasant thoughts helped him decide to take this Wednesday, October 23, away from Wall Street to participate in his favorite field sport—horse racing.

On this chilly fall day he was one of the two stewards presiding over the program of the Essex Fox Hounds at Far Hills, New Jersey.

The meeting attracted many figures from New York society. A number of them kept in touch with the market either by telephone or through the radio in the clubhouse.

Out on the turf, Whitney's main duties were confined to deciding one race a dead heat and settling an argument between owners over another.

In the New York Stock Exchange—with its president on honeymoon and his deputy at the horses—just after noon prices started to plummet. At the close, Adams Express had dropped a catastrophic $96 a share; Commercial Solvents, $70; Otis Elevator, $43; Westinghouse, $35; and General Electric, $20.

By 3 P.M., 6,374,960 shares had been traded, the second largest figure in history.

It was only the beginning.

CHAPTER TWENTY-FOUR

CRASH

Six-thirty A.M., Thursday, October 24: The time, date, and his actions would remain forever in Frank Montague's memory.

Unable to maintain the pretense of sleep, he had slipped out of bed. It was still dark, cold, and well before the tall, rawboned vice-president of the Union Industrial Bank normally rose.

Montague fumbled for his clothes and left the bedroom, relieved he had not disturbed his wife, Louise. Outside, the tail end of a blizzard that had raged through the Midwest left the ground coated with snow.

Montague wondered whether the long-distance telephone lines were still down, leaving Flint virtually cut off; and whether he would again have to rely on the radio to know what was happening in New York.

The night before, all three networks had devoted considerable time to the day's break. Detroit stations supplemented national coverage with specific details of how auto stocks had fared. Even rock-solid General Motors had been hit.

It was the series of telephone calls he had received about that particular piece of news that had stopped Montague from sleeping. John de Camp, Ivan Christensen, and Elton Graham—the only other embezzlers with telephones—had sounded frightened men. Shortly before Wednesday's break they had placed "a pile of money" on GM. Montague recalled the almost hysterical tone of those calls. Christensen had kept mumbling, "We've all gotta stick together"; De Camp had repeated, "It's a calamity"; Graham spoke of "being repaid for our sins."

Sipping coffee, he examined again the two choices he faced. He could continue deeper into the "quagmire." Or he could quit, and try to persuade the others to join him.

Montague loved his family. He knew they not only returned that love but also admired and trusted him. With Louise's support, he had tried to foster Christian ideals in his elder children; he rejoiced at the way they pointed out to their young friends his position as a vestryman and member of various church committees; he was delighted by the pride Louise showed in his position at the bank.

The shock they would all suffer if they learned what he had done kept him from ending his involvement with the "league of gentlemen."

He chose to plunge further into his "quagmire."

He suspected Christensen and De Camp would do the same, whatever today's news from New York. Elton Graham would probably accept the majority

Milton Pollock's reaction was one Montague felt he could also safely predict. The two men had much in common: strong family ties, deep religious commitments; mutual ground for stealing. Both men liked to believe they embezzled in order to provide their loved ones with the comfort and security absent from their own childhood. Montague thought it could be even harder for Pollock to face his wife with the truth. Elizabeth Pollock was a sick woman and her husband feared the discovery of his part in the massive speculation would kill her.

Robert Brown, Montague guessed, would continue to "move heaven and earth" to get the money back into the bank to protect his father, and the family name, from scandal.

But, with a sense of dread, Montague realized, despite many months of collaboration, he had no clear idea how the other thieves might behave if the crisis got worse.

Some of the tellers were little more than names to the vice-president. One, Clifford Plumb, was "simply not the sort of person I had socially much in common with." Montague regarded Plumb as a bore.

He was still pondering the appalling situation when Louise joined him in the kitchen.

Thirteen years of marriage, of struggling to raise four children while maintaining "a certain social position" on her husband's $350 a month salary, had not diminished her girlish good looks or her intuition.

Louise realized "something serious" was troubling her husband; she had suspected as much for months. Physically, he was clearly in poor shape; he came home tense and tired, especially after one of those "boardroom meetings." Louise could not understand why he had to attend, unless it was because he was being groomed for promotion. Yet, if that was true, why was he so nervous?

Even this morning he seemed to her tense as he sat hunched beside the radio.

The early bulletin quoted Wall Street "sources" as saying the market was about to receive "positive organized support."

Montague turned to his wife: "It looks like being a heavy day at the bank. Don't expect me home until late."

Seven A.M. A bitter wind dogged Homer Dowdy as he trudged along his round.

Unlike any other late fall morning in Flint he remembered, many people were standing on their doorsteps awaiting his arrival.

They snatched the telltale brown envelopes that staff in the city brokerage offices had prepared and sent out yesterday. The envelopes contained demands for more margin. Those who would not or could not meet them within a few hours knew their shares would be sold.

Dowdy found it difficult to feel sympathetic toward the letters' recipients. He possessed very little money; what he had was deposited in the Union Industrial Bank, "the safest place in town."

For months now people on his round had said he was foolish to work so hard when he could grow rich through investing.

Occasionally—when he wanted to buy something for his dying wife, Gladys, or their three small children—he had been tempted to dabble in the market.

Each time he resisted the idea. When he glimpsed the newspaper headlines this morning, he was glad his common sense had prevailed.

The newspaper reported that all over America people were failing to meet margin calls.

The mailman knew little about high finance. But he assumed most of the margin calls he was delivering would be met by borrowing from banks. If a "real panic set in," there was every chance money from his own modest account might be used to meet such demands. He began to think seriously about withdrawing his small deposit from the Union Industrial.

Seven-thirty A.M. Six hours after leaving Wall Street, Hutton-Miller was back to resume the task which exhaustion had forced him to halt in the early hours of this Thursday—ensuring after yesterday's hectic trading that all the thousands of buy and sell orders executed through W. E. Hutton and Company actually matched.

Walking along Wall, Hut realized the lines outside the customers' rooms and banks were longer than he could ever recall. He didn't like what he saw or heard.

Some people were still drunk from overnight sessions in speakeasies. Others were rumpled from sleeping in nearby hotel lobbies. A few were stiff-boned from sleeping on the streets.

The talk was heavy with rumors. President Hoover was "going to act." The Stock Exchange would remain closed. Jack Morgan had pledged $5 million from London. Other financial leaders were in secret conclave to raise billions more. John J. Raskob was about to "unveil a plan." Charles Mitchell had "a scheme."

A crowd was forming outside 23 Wall, drawn there by the knowledge of how Pierpont Morgan had stemmed the Great Panic of 1907 with a few well-chosen words.

Another gathering, mostly Italians, stood outside the Bank of America building, asking for "Papa" Doc Giannini and Elisha Walker. Both men were unreachable—almost 3,000 miles away, aboard the *Overland Express,* heading toward San Francisco.

Outside every building involved with the stock market knots of anxious people were gathering.

Hut could sense their anxiety. He was not prepared for their animosity.

A group of men and women almost blocked the entrance to W. E. Hutton. At first they thought the broad-shouldered young broker was another speculator trying to get into the building; burly doormen were keeping everybody at bay. When one of the guards recognized Hut and pulled him inside, the crowd became hostile. "I was a representative of those who were breaking their dreams."

He was not surprised to see that many of his colleagues had spent the night catnapping in the office. Bleary-eyed and disheveled, they were continuing to calculate and dispatch demands for margin. As a precaution against what might lie ahead, he had brought a clean shirt and several collars. Hut had a growing feeling it could be a long time before he again saw his own bedroom.

By 8 A.M. Charles Stewart Mott had accomplished more than many of his executives would achieve in a day. Alternately reading memorandums and drafting replies, he approved or rejected, allocated priorities and downgraded projects. Nothing was too small to escape his attention.

Pragmatic and ruthless, General Motors' chief of advisory staff allowed no one to stand in the way of the corporation. His few close friends said this attitude had contributed to the end of his marriage.

This morning, for perhaps the first and only time, his professional commitments and private life mingled on his desk. Among reports on yesterday's market break was a statement Mott's attorney had drafted announcing his client and Dee Mott were divorcing.

Mott quickly initialed approval of the statement, marking it for public release on Tuesday, October 29. By then he hoped the crisis in the market would have eased. Now, faced with hours of difficult decision-making, he did not want to be hounded by reporters.

The signs were bad—but GM was prepared. On October 4 Alfred Sloan, the autocratic chief executive officer, had predicted "the end of expansion" and promulgated a new policy of economy for the corporation.

Mott gave orders to implement that policy. GM was going to "batten down the hatches" until the future became clearer.

At 9 A.M. E. C. Delafield, senior executive in the Bank of America at 44 Wall, placed a call to A. P. Giannini, still asleep in San Mateo, California. There it was barely six o'clock in the morning—a full thirty minutes before Giannini was normally aroused by the first call of the day from New York.

Delafield described the siegelike conditions developing in the financial district. The crowd outside 44 Wall had grown to several hundreds —waiters, cooks, small shopkeepers, housemaids, seamstresses, some Chinese. They were all demanding to know if their money was safe. Delafield sounded distraught.

Giannini calmed him. He told the executive he should promise the crowd their savings were secure. Delafield was then to brief the staff, ordering them to discount all rumors and "take things as they develop."

Privately Giannini wished Doc and Walker were in New York; both would arrive in San Francisco in a few hours. He decided to send them straight back on the next express train—unless they could be persuaded to fly. He would not order them to; he shared their dislike of flying.

Giannini was not confident of Delafield's ability to cope on his own. A few days ago he had to upbraid him for refusing to open an account for a customer with $200 to deposit. The man had complained. Giannini wired Delafield: "You cannot expect to build up much of a savings business if you are going to adhere to any limit; you should take savings deposits of one dollar up."

After his call from Delafield, Giannini roused Clorinda and Claire. He told them it "could be '28 all over again."

He guessed a similar crowd to the one Delafield described would soon be forming outside Transamerica's head office in San Francisco. Normally Giannini was happy to see customers; but in the hours ahead he believed they could prove a serious distraction.

Giannini resolved they should know he was in San Francisco, unlike 1928 when he had been 6,000 miles away in Italy, but they should not be told where he was—in a special command post secretly prepared for just such an emergency.

His hideout was a top-floor suite in the Mark Hopkins Hotel on San

Francisco's Nob Hill. Only Clorinda, Claire, and a handful of key executives would be able to reach him, and then only in the direst emergency. The command post was designed so the banker could make out-
going calls, whereas incoming ones would be barred; in theory he could
have access to anybody he wanted without being bothered. Joe Garcia
would guard the suite's entrance door round-the-clock.

While Clorinda packed a suitcase for her husband, Claire warned the
hotel to expect her father.

Soon afterward, Garcia drove his employer into San Francisco. Giannini told him to go slowly and to leave the fire light switched off. He
did not want anybody to notice them arrive at their destination.

Nine-thirty A.M. saw Jesse Livermore moving restlessly around his
office complex, chain-smoking cigars and repeatedly asking one question: Had everything been checked?

The answer was always the same: It had.

Yet no one on Livermore's staff dared predict with confidence how
the market would behave today after yesterday's break; his impressive
network, able to reach virtually any major financial center in the world,
was providing no conclusive pointers. Livermore was forced to fall
back on his famed "gut reaction," that strange, intuitive feeling in the
pit of his stomach that only he could interpret.

Twenty-two years ago to this day—at the peak of the Great Panic of
1907—he had made a killing by correctly understanding what the combination of churning juices and tightening muscles in his abdomen
meant. That day, October 24, he had sold short and made $250,000.

It was again October 24; perhaps he should again go into action
when the market opened, again with little more than his intuition to
guide him.

His brain warned him to hold back.

While the conflict within Livermore raged, an assistant handed him
the morning mail. As on so many days lately, despite his statement to
the *Times,* it contained letters from people threatening to kill him if he
continued to force prices down by short selling.

The letters disturbed Livermore. Although he believed the address of
his hideaway was still largely unknown—most of the letters he received
had been redirected to him—he had felt it necessary to take on a full-
time bodyguard.

The continuing receipt of the menacing communications was yet another complicating factor affecting Livermore's attitude to the market.

Nine forty-five A.M. found John J. Raskob staring intuitively toward
the stock market ticker in its new position—close to his desk. He was

no longer concerned it be hidden out of sight in the cubbyhole down the corridor; he wanted it within easy access. "I was up to *here* in the market. My life, my future and that of my family depended on what the ticker told."

It now dominated his private office at 230 Park Avenue. The ticker stood on an antique table between two crystal floor lamps James Riordan had given Raskob for his fiftieth birthday, just celebrated.

Raskob urged other members of the consortium financing the Empire State Building to have their tickers close by them.

It was another sign the bullish financier was worried. Earlier, he had surprised his valet by slipping on a wristwatch—the first he had worn in many years—and astonished his chauffeur by asking to be driven to the office. With a touch of humor, Raskob had explained, "I need to know the time—and I haven't the time to walk."

Timing, he suspected, was going to be crucial in the upcoming 300 minutes of trading. One miscalculation could see his skyscraper dream collapse before the structure was put up. The $60 million needed to raise it depended in large measure on market profits. The financier feared the money could be lost or diverted in an attempt to stop prices falling further.

Raskob's ticker was handily placed in preparation for the next five hours. Now, in spite of his huge personal fortune, his political and financial power and his great social influence, there was nothing he could do except impatiently monitor the hands on his watch creeping toward ten o'clock.

In other offices, Joe Kennedy, Billy Durant, Arthur Cutten, and Charles Mitchell were among those who had also positioned themselves close to stock tickers.

Pat Bologna, in Wall Street itself, fancied he heard an expectant hush fall across the crowds. "People just stood there, stopped talking, and looked towards the Stock Exchange. It was like the silence before the off at a big race."

The sense of impending melodrama was heightened by the arrival of police wagons. They parked across the narrow entrance to Wall from Broadway, effectively blocking all traffic from entering. From the wagons came scores of policemen who began to fan out purposefully through the financial district.

One of Michael Levine's perspiring messengers asked a policeman why he was there. The reply was laconic and menacing. "In case there's trouble."

Levine had just posted an order-of-the-day for his hard-pressed work force: "Nobody Goes Home Until I Say So."

The millionaire messenger boss had been on the telephone since dawn, taking his own special soundings, making his own special plans.

He had come to the conclusion that today could be the busiest in the history of the Street.

Brokerage houses served by Levine's boys said that their staffs were already working almost round-the-clock. All told, that could mean up to 100,000 men and women would have to be fed and bedded down for days. Folded cots would be wanted for hundreds of offices; the district's restaurants would need extra staff and food; those who required hard liquor had also to be catered for. Sharp operators were quick to book every available hotel room within walking distance of Wall Street; these could be quickly relet as dormitories for telephonists and clerks.

The shrewd, hard-grafting Levine had made a substantial sum well before the market opened. He did not intend to invest the money or to place it in a bank. He would keep the cash by him, "in a fluid position."

Whether the market went up or down, Levine was sure of one thing further. By nightfall he would be considerably richer.

At 9:50 A.M. William Crawford—crossing a trading floor more crowded and apprehensive than any he could remember—received his first jolt of the day. One of Richard Whitney's aides brought a message from the acting president. The superintendent was to prepare to receive a distinguished visitor. Whitney had just learned Winston Churchill was likely to visit Wall Street later in the morning; Crawford must see he was properly looked after in the Exchange.

From his newspapers, Crawford knew Churchill, next to Ramsay MacDonald, was the most popular and important Englishman to visit New York for many years. He only wished the statesman had chosen a different morning to visit the financial district.

The mood of the previous day—a curious combination of dejection and near hysteria—had carried over.

Brokers and clerks arrived on the floor early to cope with the unprecedented backlog of orders received overnight. Many brokers had instructions to buy only at prices below—often much below—those prevailing at yesterday's close.

Well before he was due to reopen the market, Crawford had detected a tenseness in many of the men bustling around the stockadelike trading counters.

At Post Twelve, Michael Meehan, who kept concealed any fear he might be feeling, was constantly on the move, talking to fellow brokers and specialists; his team was fully stretched as orders flowed to their post from the telephonists around the periphery.

William Wadsworth, at Post Five, found no time for the pleasantries he usually exchanged with Crawford each morning. The oldest broker on the floor was "working like a boy demon," busy already with a spate of railroad orders.

The Exchange superintendent could only marvel at the attitude of the Bouviers, clustered together at Post Eleven. A close-knit group, they showed little sign of the grief that must still be hurting deeply. Two weeks before, Bud Bouvier had died from alcoholism in California. His brother Jack, the darkly handsome specialist at Post Eleven and father of baby Jacqueline, was filled with remorse over the way he had treated Bud. But none of that showed; egotistical and aggressive, "Black Jack" seemed in his element in the hurly-burly developing around the Post.

Aware of the hundreds of pairs of eyes watching him, of "electricity in the air so thick you could cut it," William Crawford approached the podium.

There he received a second shock. Richard Whitney was waiting. He told the superintendent that, apart from attending upon Churchill, he was to remain near the rostrum throughout the day. Steeped in Exchange lore, Crawford knew the reason: He must be ready at all times to interrupt trading so that Whitney might make an important announcement.

Climbing the podium steps, the superintendent could imagine what Whitney's announcement would order: the closure of the New York Stock Exchange. Crawford watched the chronometer reach ten o'clock and gave the gong an extra hard whang. It was one way of expressing his determination that the market must never close.

Three minutes after ten would remain forever in Hut's memory as the moment an excited shout swept through W. E. Hutton. "She's trading big and brisk!"

The market had opened "like a bolt out of hell."

Kennecott Copper, which had slumped just before yesterday's close, leaped $11 on a 20,000-share transaction. Sinclair Oil jumped fifty cents on a 15,000-share deal. Standard Brands rose almost forty cents after a block of 15,000 shares was traded.

Hut moved to the point of greatest need, the trading table, a huge desk bristling with telephones. His colleagues around it could not keep up with the calls; every unanswered phone was ringing. Hut joined in the general scramble. As soon as a phone was put down, it rang again. The time each call was received, and its message, was carefully noted.

Many callers begged for an extension of their margin deadlines now that the market showed signs of reviving. A few were granted extensions; the majority were told the deadlines stood.

At 10:10 a buy order for 13,000 shares of Packard Motors added further hope the market really was in a mood to recover.

For the next fifteen minutes, prices remained generally steady. Apart from the unusually large number of leading stocks changing hands in big blocks, there was no particular pattern or trend to the trading.

Then, at 10:25, a 20,000 block of General Motors showed a loss of eighty cents a share.

Four minutes later, at 10:29, Hut picked up the phone.

In a hysterical voice, desperate to accept any price offered, the caller shrieked a phrase beginning to be heard in brokerage houses throughout the district:

"Sell at the market."

Ten-fifty A.M.—again the moment was fixed in his memory—Pat Bologna achieved what he had been trying to do for the past twenty minutes: force his way into the customers' room close to his pitch. The young shoeblack had his entire savings of $5,000 invested on margin.

The scene Bologna saw was typical of those that would serve as the basis for numerous "eyewitness accounts" written later by journalists. None of them would quite capture the raw impact the room had on Bologna.

"In the crowd there's a Chinaman wearing a hat which rests on his ears. He's got a dead cigar in a mouth of dead teeth. He's standing on tip-toe to see over the shoulders of a woman wearing a big fancy hat. She's holding out her wedding ring and shouting 'you want more margin—you can't have more margin.' He's drunk as a lord. Everybody is shouting. They're all trying to reach the glass booth where the clerks are. Everybody wants to sell out. The boy at the quotation board is running scared. He can't keep up with the speed of the way stocks are dropping. The board's painted green. The guy who runs it is Irish. He's standing at the back of the booth, on the telephone. I can't hear what he's saying. But a guy near me shouts, 'the sonofabitch has sold me out!'"

The remark made Bologna hesitate. He had come to the room expecting to receive help; clearly, in these crazed conditions, that was impossible.

Bologna could not make up his mind whether to sell the stock he held in Charles Mitchell's National City Bank. He recalled the advice the master banker had once given him after he had finished shining his shoes. Mitchell, along with his usual dollar tip, had passed on guidance. "A wise man never sells out at the first sign of trouble. That's for the pikers."

Acting on the multimillionaire's words, Bologna turned and elbowed his way out of the melee. He had decided to retain his holdings a little longer.

Close to 11:00 A.M., Charles Stewart Mott at his office in Detroit received some unwelcome information. The specialist in General Motors on the New York Exchange had taken a moment away from Post Four to let Mott know there was nothing he could do to stop the company's stock falling.

Nor had there been time for Mott to ask questions or give orders before the long-distance connection was broken.

The tremendous activity in the market was beginning to impose a severe strain on the entire communication network linking Wall Street to the outside world. Brokers whose private wires were already overworked were being forced to fall back on ordinary commercial telegraph lines; in turn, those lines were also becoming clogged with the unaccustomed traffic. The Bell Telephone Company announced it was busier than it had ever been during the previous peak periods of the Great War. Overseas calls doubled.

Mott summoned his executives into emergency session. His secretary was given strict instructions to disturb him only if more news came in from Wall Street.

At about the same time, Thomas Lamont's secretary, on the second floor of 23 Wall, finally got through to Charles Mitchell's offices on the second floor of the National City Bank at 55 Wall. It had taken her almost ten minutes telephonically to connect two offices only one block apart. The switchboards at Morgan's and the bank were almost jammed.

Lamont's secretary inquired whether Mitchell could join a meeting of bankers just after midday, "to exchange information on the stock-market situation."

Mitchell's secretary, having checked, said Mitchell would be pleased to attend.

By 11:30, William Crawford could see that, increasingly, the proprieties of normal Exchange behavior were being disregarded. The rules specifically stated traders should not "run, curse, push or go coatless."

All around him men were doing precisely that. Since eleven o'clock, "panic had prevailed on the Stock Exchange floor—there was no other word for it."

The confusion was compounded by the minute as the ticker lagged further and further behind. No one could tell what the true trading situation was.

Ordered to remain in the vicinity of the rostrum, the superintendent could only phone or send runners urging the engineers in the basement to try everything possible to improve matters.

Meanwhile, Crawford paced between the four trading stockades closest to his podium.

At Post One—where Borden, Du Pont, Electric Power and Light, St. Paul Railroad, Sinclair Oil, and United Aircraft were traded—floor brokers were literally being pinned against the trading counter by the overwrought throng.

At Post Three—Allegheny, Columbia Gas, Erie Railroad, Macy & Company—the position was equally frenzied.

But the center of "a kind of madness" was Post Two. Everyone there appeared to be "bellowing like a lunatic." The object of their attention was General Oliver Bridgeman, specialist for U. S. Steel. He knew if steel continued to plunge, it could "carry everything else down the chute with it." Bridgeman was surrounded by a waving, roaring rabble. Every so often he would crouch, scribble some figures on a pad, then leap up and shout even louder than the rest as he tried frantically to stop steel's paper value melting before his horrified eyes.

Suddenly, at Post Four—Anaconda, Caterpillar Tractor, Southern Pacific, U. S. Pipe and Foundry, General Motors—Crawford saw "a fat, perspiring man become almost hysterical, yelling orders that made no sense until some friends seized him by the arm and and led him away."

The panic had claimed one of its first recorded casualties.

Eleven thirty-five A.M. found Hut yelling into his telephone for "quotes as of this moment." He was talking to one of W. E. Hutton's clerks on the Exchange floor.

Hut had spoken to the man by phone many times each day since joining the firm; he knew his voice and vocabulary intimately, "though as so often happens in this business, I wouldn't have recognized him if I saw him."

Over the tie line, the clerk always gave the impression of being calm and collected; now, his demeanor had cracked. He sounded "like a kid close to tears."

Hut asked him for quotations for half a dozen shares.

The clerk wailed. "I can't get them. I can't get any information! The whole place is falling apart!"

It was not so much the words that stunned Hut; it was the tone of utter despondency in the clerk's voice.

Eleven forty-five A.M. found Winston Churchill looking down on the trading floor of the Exchange from the visitors' gallery.

He had received a brief official welcome and then chosen to observe the activity from this high vantage point. The reporter in him quickly came to the surface; the view would provide interesting material for one of the articles in the series he planned to write for the London *Daily Telegraph.*

Most of the people around him were too dazed by what was happening on the floor to give the Englishman a second glance.

Not unaccustomed to being present at moments of high drama, Churchill coolly observed a scene that seemed to him "one of surprising calm and orderliness . . . there they were . . . . offering each other enormous blocks of securities at a third of their old prices and half their present value, and for many minutes together finding no one strong enough to pick up the sure fortunes they were compelled to offer."

Winston Churchill left Wall Street, his faith in America apparently totally unshaken.

But whatever he thought about the day's decline in the value of the American stock he himself held, or what he may have said about his loss to Percy Rockefeller, whose guest he now was, Churchill decided never to put into public print.

At 11:50, Ivan Christensen and the other embezzlers heard the news they had always dreaded: A wave of liquidation was sweeping the New York Stock Exchange, overwhelming what little buying resistance was left. With so few buyers for so many stocks, great gaps developed between each successively lower bid.

The ticker was now running fifty-five minutes late. As a result, the thieves, like millions of honest Americans, could not know that the current position was even worse than they believed it to be.

About noon in Wall Street, Claud Cockburn, one of the dozens of reporters, photographers, and newsreel cameramen now there, was trying to absorb the atmosphere.

Cockburn, a gifted Irishman working for the New York *Sun,* had been admonished by a colleague that when he wrote his story, "the word 'panic' is not to be used."

In the Street, Cockburn found "an enormous murmuring crowd, and the people pressed close around us were talking, when one listened to them, almost in whispers. Every now and then you could hear quite distinctly a hysterical laugh. As time passed the crowd grew thicker and noisier, and then there was an eddy in the middle of it and a man in shirtsleeves was pushing his way across the street in the direction of the Morgan offices."

Charles Mitchell was on the way to his appointment with Thomas Lamont. Head high, the huge body of the banker seemed impervious to the stiff breeze blowing up Wall from the river.

Some five hundred miles away in the Atlantic, that same wind blew ragged scud over the *Berengaria*. At a speed of twenty-three knots through choppy seas, the Cunarder was carrying her 1,415 passengers toward New York. Already the first birds had wheeled over the liner. There was now only an hour's difference between ship's time and that in New York—a further sign the voyage was nearing its end.

At one o'clock—noon in New York—the first-class dining room should have been filled. It was half empty. Many passengers stood dazed, their appetites gone, either rooted to the spot in the ship's brokerage office or standing in the crowded corridor outside.

Yesterday had been bad enough. Today looked like being even worse.

Those close enough to be heard yelled at Charlie Goudiss. In the low-ceilinged, steel-walled, converted stateroom, the noise was deafening.

"Sell at the market!"

"Get me out!"

"Sell!"

Passengers surrounded Goudiss at his desk, tugged at his jacket for attention, bellowed in his ear. He found it difficult to write out orders legibly before passing them—again with difficulty—to the hard-pressed radiomen in their "cage" to transmit.

Goudiss was doing his best to stay calm, feeding the slips of paper as fast as he could to the wireless operators. In the circumstances he could do no more.

The youth at the blackboard was also being jostled. Stanley Moore, who had been steadily ripping sell orders from his pad since the opening prices were posted, moved to help the clerk. In a bold-chalked scrawl, he wrote out the latest news from Wall Street.

General Electric was down $25 a share; Westinghouse had dropped $20. Other key issues were falling.

For a few moments there was a "curious calm," like "a death watch."

Then the roar of the crowd intensified.

"Get me *out!*"

"Sell!"

"The bottom's dropping out!"

As the word spread through first class, to Goudiss and Moore it seemed nearly every one of its 529 passengers began to converge on their office. The crowd backed up into the lounge and the ladies' writing salon.

"Communication chains" were set up, allowing an investor at the rear of the crowd to pass his request forward.

"What's Steel?"

"Eastman!"

"General Motors—*sell*—five hundred at the market!"

Often by the time an order reached Goudiss, the stock's price had dropped even further.

To improve ventilation, Moore pushed back the drapes on the portholes opening onto the Promenade Deck. Soon people on the deck stood eight deep trying to see—or call—into the stateroom.

There, close to Moore's desk, oblivious to the frantic clamoring around her, Helena Rubinstein sat serenely in an armchair. Davenport Pogue, her trusted financial adviser, crouched at her side, scribbling figures and frequently whispering animatedly into her ear.

Madame Rubinstein showed no reaction. Moore thought she "looked like a little Buddha," expressionless as her favorite blue chips tumbled five and ten points at a time.

She sold some shares; others she held. Her market strategy was as mysterious to Moore as the secret ingredients in her cosmetics.

He noticed she never let her eyes stray from the board when a new price for Westinghouse was chalked. Stock in the electrical manufacturer seemed "destined to drop out of sight"; in the past hour it had plunged from $190 a share to $173.

Suddenly, imperiously, Madame raised a bejeweled finger to Moore. He pushed his way to the woman he thought of as "brilliant, but rather vulgar-looking with all those rings."

Calmly she gave her order. "Sell fifty thousand Westinghouse at the market."

There was a gasp from those who overheard her. Equally astounded, Moore hurried to the cage. The largest single order by far that the floating brokerage had ever handled was given top priority.

When confirmation of the sale was received, it showed the Westinghouse shares had been sold at $168 each.

Helena Rubinstein was poorer by more than $1 million.

With no outward sign of reaction, she got up and walked steadily through the respectful gap made for her by the ranks of now-silent fellow speculators.

At 12:20 P.M. Charlton MacVeagh had finally abandoned any appearance of working.

For the past three hours he and his colleagues had found themselves increasingly distracted by events outside the House of Morgan. Even the thick walls of 23 Wall could not exclude the insistent murmuring of the great crowd gathered in front of the Stock Exchange just a few feet away, across narrow Broad Street.

Morgan doormen politely but firmly kept the public from entering the hallowed banking hall. They were joined around midmorning by policemen.

Charlton and his colleagues had come to recognize the changing mood outside by the variance in noise level. Initially, the murmuring had been low, interspersed with the odd burst of laughter. As the morning wore on, the mood changed. The murmur became more menacing.

Rumors swept the throng: The position was worse in other exchanges; the Chicago and Buffalo stock exchanges had closed; the San Francisco Exchange was about to.

Fed on fiction, anxious for action, most of the crowd saw trouble in everything. The sight of a coatless Charles Mitchell walking into Morgan's was taken by many as a "sure sign things must be bad." Optimists wondered whether they were witnessing "organized support" in the making.

The immaculate young Morgan brokers were surprised to see Mitchell in his shirt sleeves. They became even more astonished as other famous financial figures filed in to assemble around Thomas Lamont's rolltop desk.

Besides Mitchell there were Albert Wiggin, chairman of the Chase National Bank; William Potter, president of the Guaranty Trust Company; and Seward Prosser, chairman of the Bankers Trust Company.

The New York *Times* later reported the illustrious group "represented more than $6 billion of massed banking resources"—which figure, the *Times* was careful to point out, did not include the vast, but unrevealed, wealth of the House of Morgan. And, in the classic Morgan manner, precisely what the group were now discussing or deciding was kept a close secret. No notes were taken. Voices were deliberately pitched low so nobody outside the enclosure could hear what was being said.

However, news that the meeting was taking place at all was enough to steady prices on the Stock Exchange floor.

There, traders with a sense of history recalled a similar meeting on

October 24, 1907, when J. P. Morgan, E. H. Harriman, James Stillman, Henry Frick, and other titans of the time had reportedly created a $25 million pool to prevent a market panic continuing. They had succeeded. The elder Morgan was dead and his son was in Europe. But the firm's name was sufficient to raise hopes everywhere that, twenty-two years later, the Morgan magic was as potent as ever.

While the men were meeting, Whitney ordered Crawford to close the visitors' gallery to the public.

In Wall Street, word spread like a bush fire that the Exchange itself was about to close. Hundreds more began to converge on The Corner. Crowd control became a major concern for the policemen patrolling the area.

Edwin Lefevre of *The Saturday Evening Post* felt he was surrounded by "dying men counting their own last pulse beats."

Those leaving the visitors' gallery brought the news that the dreaded "no bid" was becoming commonplace on the trading floor: Brokers desperate to sell could not find brokers willing to buy.

Inside Morgan's the meeting broke up. Lamont escorted his fellow bankers to the door. There were handshakes all round. Then, led by a confident-looking Mitchell, the men left the calm of 23 Wall to brave the crowd.

Mitchell's relaxed dress and demeanor worked like a potion on the people; the crowd's good humor gradually returned. On all sides the cry was taken up. "It's going to be all right."

Word spread that Lamont and his colleagues had established a multimillion-dollar pool to "steady the market." The size of the fund varied from mouth to mouth, from one office to another. It was put as high as $240 million, seldom less than $100 million. In reality it was probably around $50 million. It was almost immediately put to good use.

At 1:30 Richard Whitney walked onto the floor of the New York Stock Exchange.

Superintendent Crawford braced himself. The moment he most feared seemed to have come. He prepared to climb the rostrum to interrupt trading and introduce Whitney.

The acting president walked past him before Crawford realized what was happening.

Whitney stopped at Post Two. He was there in his capacity as the official broker for Morgan's. In a loud, clear voice, he asked Bridgeman what had been the last bid he had received for Steel.

"195."

Even more loudly, Whitney promptly raised the bid by a full ten points, "10,000 at 205"—the price of the last sale.

For an instant there was silence around the post. Then a cheer broke out, grew in intensity, and spread across the floor.

Smiling broadly, Whitney marched from one post to another, placing further big orders for other important stocks.

His confidence was contagious. Prices steadied. Whitney was carrying out the instructions of the pool formed at Lamont's behest. In minutes he had spent millions. It was his finest hour. It was "organized support" in action. Its like would not be seen again.

By 2 P.M. Frank Montague realized he and his coconspirators were "down maybe two million dollars."

Since early afternoon, aware but no longer caring that their actions were attracting attention from other bank staff, many of the "league of gentlemen" had gathered around Ivan Christensen's desk. He had kept a telephone line open to a local broker's office.

John de Camp, Milton Pollock, and Elton Graham continued the endless calculations to try to keep track of their present position. It was a hopeless task. With the ticker now running over two hours late, they could not know the true situation; whereas Westinghouse was shown at 160, it was now in fact at about 172; General Electric read 283 when it should have been nearer 300.

The swindlers were aware the ticker was behind, but they could only surmise that prices were lower, not higher, than on the tape.

The position seemed so impossible that Frank Montague, at last, urged the time had finally come when they "had to get out."

The reaction which his suggestion produced was not the one he expected. His colleagues laughed at him.

Montague fainted.

Revived, he found himself stretched out on a couch in the boardroom with several of his cohorts standing sympathetically over him.

De Camp spoke, not unkindly; he might have been discussing a routine banking matter. He told Montague they would continue to invest in the market. Now was their opportunity to make a "killing"—stocks were bound to go up.

Once again Montague fainted.

When he next recovered, he learned that Elton Graham had "diverted" $350,000 of bank funds to cover margins and buy yet more stock.

Christensen was particularly bullish. By now the local brokerage concern had made contact with its main office in Wall Street and passed on the news that the market's downward momentum had stopped and was being turned into something approaching a rally; stocks in which Graham had just invested were already showing a modest gain—though the embezzlers would not have confirmation of this on the ticker for several hours.

And, possibly anxious to cheer up the depressed Montague, De Camp offered him another happy tidbit. Even if what they were doing was discovered, they had nothing to fear. With so many key employees involved, he was confident they would not be arrested and removed from their jobs, as "that would interfere with the operation of the bank."

Frank Montague seriously wondered whether the senior vice-president had become temporarily deranged under the strain.

After the market closed at three o'clock, Thomas Lamont greeted the press at the entrance to 23 Wall. He had called a rare conference: No one could remember when the House of Morgan had last opened its doors to reporters.

Among those who entered 23 was Claud Cockburn. He thought Lamont had the "manner of the man who comes on the stage of a burning theater and urges everyone to keep perfectly cool, stating there is no cause for alarm."

Lamont led the noisy newsmen past the surprised staff in the usually silent central salon, up one flight of stairs, across a spacious reception area furnished with antiques, and into the beautifully paneled room which served as his office. The journalists positioned themselves against the drapes and beside the handsome gray marble fireplace; some settled comfortably in deep armchairs and on the settees. Few, if any, of the reporters had previously been privileged to see Lamont's famous, flat, Spanish ex-monastery desk.

He waited for the newsmen to bring out their pads. Then, with one of the most remarkable understatements of all time, he addressed them.

"There has been a little distress selling on the Stock Exchange, and we have held a meeting of the heads of several financial institutions to discuss the situation. We have found that there are no houses in difficulty and reports from brokers indicate that margins are being maintained satisfactorily."

While accepting "the situation is susceptible of betterment," Lamont thought what had happened was "due to a technical condition of the market, rather than to any fundamental cause."

He would have been less than human if he did not still have in mind the reassuring words of his confidential report delivered to President Hoover only two days before.

Six P.M. found Edith Stone hovering between her bedroom and the radio in the living room. Several times during the afternoon she had paused in her writing to listen to the latest bulletin from Wall Street.

The financial district was said to resemble an armed camp, with four hundred policemen on duty. A reporter had broadcast a graphic picture of brokers with sweat pouring down their faces, their collars and shirts torn to shreds. Edith particularly liked one of his phrases—"they were like shell-shocked soldiers, crazily flinging handfuls of torn ticker tape and order pads in the air."

Perhaps her father had been right when he had forbidden her to set foot in the area today.

The latest news report stated that, in spite of the traumatic first three hours of trading, the market had closed on an upward beat. It was said that U. S. Steel had even shown a gain on yesterday's close. There was growing belief the rally would continue tomorrow.

Edith was relieved. Her father had gone to work apprehensive. She suspected yesterday's break had been a bad one for him.

When Edward Stone opened the front door of the apartment, his daughter saw immediately that something was seriously wrong.

She started to move toward him.

"Stop! Stop everything! We've got to move out!"

Frightened by the hysteria in his voice, certain her father was acutely ill, Edith remained still.

Slowly, as if to memorize every detail, Edward Stone's staring eyes scanned the room, taking in the expensive paintings, the new furnishings, the crystal wall lights, the hand-sewn carpets and drapes.

Once more his voice broke the silence. "We can't keep any of it. I haven't a penny. The market's crashed. We're wiped out. Nothing!"

Edith gasped. As she turned toward the kitchen and called to her mother, her father lunged past her.

"I'm going to kill myself! It's the only way. You'll have the insurance. . . ."

Screaming, also close to hysteria, Edith chased after her father.

Mabel Stone rushed from the kitchen.

"Ed, for God's sake!"

Her husband reached the french doors leading onto the apartment's terrace. They were closed.

It gave Edith and her mother the chance to catch up. Edith grabbed her father around the waist; his wife tried to pull his hands from the door.

He broke their hold, turned the key, and wrenched open the door.

For a moment Edward Stone stood in the doorway. Then, panting, he turned to his wife and daughter.

Edith would never forget how he kept repeating "the same terrible words, he wouldn't stop saying them."

Banker in a hurry. A. P. Giannini, founder of the Bank of America, discovered a new use for his Rolls-Royce—he turned it into a fire truck. It enabled him to travel faster—and buy more banks. *Courtesy Bank of America Archives.*

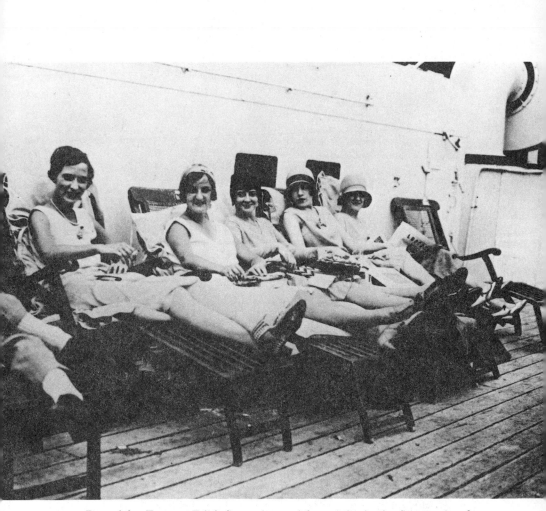

Bound for Europe, Edith Stone (second from left) in the flapper rig of the day. Life for Edith looked pleasant. Soon it would change forever from the cataclysmic effect of the Crash. *Courtesy Edith Stone.*

Edward and Màbel Stone. They never talked business at home. The shock of its intrusion on the night of the Great Crash altered their relationship irrevocably. In a few hours he had lost $5 million. He tried to pay for it with his life. *Courtesy Edith Stone.*

Edith Stone, one of the most beautiful flappers in a city of flappers. But she had another string to her bow—a plan to write a drama about Wall Street. Finally, her own private trauma stopped her. *Courtesy Edith Stone.*

Homer and Gladys Dowdy. They both knew the truth. They both, in the end, became victims of the Crash. *Courtesy Homer Dowdy.*

The brothers-in-law. Michael Slezsak (right) and Steve Vargo. Linked by a marriage and bootlegging, they became victims of the "league of gentlemen" in the Union Industrial Bank. Fifty years later, Steve and his wife, Jolan, were still waiting for their money. *Courtesy Steve Vargo.*

Jolan Vargo on her wedding day. The sixteen-year-old bride helped
brew the bootleg liquor for the celebration. *Courtesy Jolan Vargo.*

Ensuring a plentiful supply of liquor was a problem when one of Wall Street's brightest young scions, Charlton MacVeagh, wed his beautiful young teenage bride, Adele. *Courtesy Adele MacVeagh.*

The MacVeagh wedding was one of the last glittering society weddings before the Crash. When it came, Adele, protected by her family wealth and her husband's position at the House of Morgan, was able to cushion herself from the reality of the event. *Courtesy Adele MacVeagh.*

"The money's gone. All of it. We can't get it back. You'll have the insurance. . . ."

"Ed, for God's sake, you have a wife and family . . . !"

"Get back!"

He turned and took hold of the balcony's railing. The street was twenty floors below.

Edith and her mother simultaneously lunged at him. This time Edith did not let go. She hooked both arms around her father's neck and pulled, determined if necessary to choke him into unconsciousness. Mabel Stone tackled her husband around the knees.

The force of their combined assault brought Edward Stone to the floor.

For a moment they were locked in an impasse.

"Please. Listen . . ."

Edith loosened her grip.

It was a mistake. Her father broke his wife's hold on his legs, got away from his daughter, and leaped again to his feet.

"Mama! We've got to stop him! He's going to jump!"

Even as she shouted, Edith managed to get a grasp on his foot. Twisting it savagely, she toppled her father back to the ground.

She dived on him, helping her mother pinion him to the terrace. Edith would remember his eyes bulging, his mouth opening and shutting but now saying nothing, as if driven by compulsion to suicide.

Close to breaking herself, the slimly built Edith knew she could not physically restrain him much longer. She fell back on the only weapon she had: words. "I called him a sissy, yelled at him, reviled him, hated him for what he was making me say and do."

Edward Stone began to cry.

His wife slapped him twice—hard on each cheek.

He whimpered on for some moments. Then he slowly came to his senses.

One of the servants arrived.

Mabel Stone rose to her feet and, in a controlled voice, told him that her husband had suffered a fall.

In silence they led Edward Stone inside. Only there was he able to tell them the facts. He had lost close to $5 million. They would have to fire the staff, move out at once from their new apartment, and completely readjust their life-style.

"Ed, it doesn't matter. We'll manage somehow."

Edith thought her mother was the "most magnificent person in the whole rotten world."

Together, she was certain they had saved her father's life. She also knew what had happened would now make it impossible for her to contemplate further any play about Wall Street.

At 7:08 P.M., 248 minutes late, the ticker finally finished recording the day's story. Brokers had traded in 974 different stocks during a Crash which saw 12,894,650 shares change hands—a record.

But the morning's losses of $6 billion had been halved during the afternoon.

It was enough to provide comfort.

After the last stock price had stuttered out, there followed a brief news item.

Representatives of thirty-five of the largest wire houses in Wall Street issued a joint statement saying the market was "fundamentally sound" and "technically in better condition than it has been in months."

The statement ended with four unforgettable words: "The worst has passed."

CHAPTER TWENTY-FIVE

DELUSIONS SUSTAIN ILLUSIONS

Late Thursday evening, astrologer Evangeline Adams abandoned private consultations in favor of mass sessions in the waiting room of her studio over Carnegie Hall. It was the only way she could cope with the long line of clients waiting to hear her next prediction for the market.

Twenty-four hours before, whether by canny deduction or some more extraordinary force, Evangeline had forseen the Crash with amazing accuracy, even pinpointing the prenoon period as its peak.

It was another triumph for a seer who claimed correctly to have forecast Lindbergh's transatlantic flight to within twenty-two minutes of actual duration; foretold Rudolf Valentino's death to within a few hours; and prophesied the 1923 Tokyo earthquake to within a few days: the aftermath of that particular disaster was still directly, and direly, affecting the Japanese economy.

The hundreds of people flocking to Evangeline's studio were mostly small investors; men and women now overcommitted to depreciated securities. They had met the calls for margin throughout this Thursday. What they wanted to know from Evangeline was whether or for how long the decline would go on—whether they should continue to commit the capital and collateral they still had in order to hold their stocks in the expectation of a rise.

Evangeline knew they wished to be told that, in spite of its tremendous pummeling, the market would recover.

Some of her wealthier clients, those with ample liquid funds, seemed almost pleased by what had happened. In the past, great fortunes had grown from opportunities seized when prices collapsed; the Rothschild empire had been founded in London when they bought huge blocks of shares after a market break based wrongly on the belief that the Battle of Waterloo was lost. And Evangeline, a keen student of native financial history, herself knew that, in previous American market declines, many of the already wealthy had managed to become even richer by buying when share prices were at rock bottom. But were prices at rock bottom now?

For all her clients, Evangeline had an answer. Having divined that the conjunction and interrelation of certain planets were creating "spheres of influence over susceptible groups, who in turn will continue to influence the market," Evangeline saw good times ahead. Friday and Saturday would witness a substantial swing upward. She would go no further; perhaps, like any good forecaster, she wanted to see the way the wind blew.

But the "forecast" was enough for her followers. They spread the word. In their own small way they helped rekindle optimism; delusions sustained illusions.

All over America this evening the Crash was assessed. Brutal though it had been, the market had responded to the ministrations of the pool that Thomas Lamont had set in motion; "organized support," like the cavalry, had arrived in the nick of time.

The bruised public took comfort from the fact some shares had actually ended the day worth more than they were twenty-four hours before; Western Union was up $8; U. S. Steel $2. Other stocks, while still down on yesterday, were climbing at today's close.

Some of the best informed in the land, and also those who had swallowed Evangeline's "forecast," believed the crisis was over.

It was late evening before the last of Evangeline's clients trooped out of her studio. She then turned to a market matter of more personal concern. However accurate her past predictions had been, her broker now told the seer she was $100,000 down. In a monumental display of lack of confidence in her own foresight, she told him to sell her out first thing tomorrow.

Jesse Livermore calculated it was mainly "the minnows" who had suffered so far. His staff had analyzed the trading pattern throughout the day. The greater proportion of shares had been sold in bundles of a few hundred.

The big operators—those holding large blocks of stock in one issue —had, like Livermore, kept their nerve and maintained their margins.

Livermore, in spite of his initial "gut reaction," had done little more than support his position. He had neither lost nor made money yet.

John J. Raskob was also relieved. Glued to his ticker all morning— he had even lunched at his desk—he relaxed once news reached him of the bankers' consortium. Financial backing from such august sources was the best balm for the most frayed of nerves.

When the market closed, Raskob went into action. By dusk he had completed his telephoning. Each call brought assurance the money he needed to build the Empire State Building was safe and still forthcoming.

In San Francisco's Mark Hopkins Hotel, it was 4:08 P.M. when the last price clattered on the ticker in A. P. Giannini's command-post suite.

Several times during the day Transamerica stock had been hit. But like many others it recovered, closing only $1 down.

Reviewing events, the banker could be well pleased; his efforts had not been in vain. And he had worked entirely on his own. Doc and Elisha Walker were on their way back to New York; overcoming their trepidation of flying, they were on board a United airliner.

After fifteen hours of exertion, Giannini ordered up his favorite meal of spaghetti, and invited Joe Garcia to join him. Then, fed and content, he fell asleep while the chauffeur continued his vigil outside the suite door—determined to let nobody disturb his master's rest.

On paper, Billy Durant had lost money—although not as much as he anticipated at one stage. The late rally had covered most of his earlier losses. He expected tomorrow to be in profit again. His wife, Catherine, marveled at the way her husband survived under such pressure. The crisis seemed to bring out the best in him—and to sharpen his appetite. That night he ate a dinner substantial enough for Charles Mitchell.

Edwin Lefevre of *The Saturday Evening Post* had no time for food this Thursday night. He was moving systematically from one brokerage house to another, collecting "case histories" which might challenge the veracity of Thomas Lamont's statement about limited "distress selling." Some of the facts he found did not fit that premise.

He interviewed a number of investors who had lost substantial sums; none of them appeared unduly distressed. A baker said he was $250,000 down; he'd cheerfully go back to work to earn a crust another way. A grocer was $300,000 poorer "on paper"; as this profit had only been "on paper" in the first place, he wasn't in reality worse off; it was money he *could* have had if he had sold out at the market's peak. He told Lefevre he intended to continue investing.

A similar attitude prevailed in many of the customers' rooms for women. Few "lady bulls" had showed signs of hysteria during the Crash. In marked contrast to the scenes he had observed earlier in Wall

Street, the mood in these rooms had apparently remained remarkably calm. A broker told Lefevre women were "good losers."

Striking confirmation of this came when the reporter walked into one brokerage office and was introduced to a pretty young widow sipping coffee and smoking. She calmly admitted losing $1 million in five hours.

Lefevre commiserated.

She shrugged. "I had a perfectly stunning time while it lasted. I never knew before what fun it was to make money. No wonder you men want to monopolize the business."

It would make a nice payoff for one of the articles Lefevre was planning. But the veteran journalist was in no hurry to rush into print. The story would keep.

On the editorial floor of the New York *Times* there was no time to wait. Deadlines had to be met, tomorrow's paper printed.

In an outstanding feat of journalistic enterprise, Alexander Noyes and his staff produced a masterful account of "Black Thursday's" events.

They not only covered the drama in Wall Street but pulled together reactions from many other places.

In Los Angeles, they reported, shares valued at $8,743,000 had changed hands; in San Francisco the figure was $21,068,782. Boston, Philadelphia, Baltimore, Cincinnati—prices on all of America's stock exchanges had fallen. But, as in New York, they closed, climbing.

Times reporters in Canada filed similar accounts: Rallies in Montreal and Toronto recovered much of the early losses.

From London the *Times* man wired a graphic account. "The wild day in Wall Street caused the London Street Market to keep open exceptionally late tonight, and some popular Anglo-American securities broke sharply. American stocks were dumped wholesale into Shorters Court, where dealers in Anglo-American securities assemble after the Stock Exchange closes at 4 o'clock. The uproar was deafening, while hatless, rain-soaked brokers cried "Sell!" "Sell!" "Nickels—sell!" "Columbias—sell!" "Tractions—sell!"

From Paris the *Times* correspondent quoted the influential *Journal des Débats:* "We have long believed this débâcle to be inevitable." The *Journal* also declared the Bourse could benefit from the probable repatriation of French capital from New York.

From Germany came a report the Berlin Börse had first reacted badly to the news from Wall Street. Stocks had dropped up to ten points. Then, when traders heard of the New York rally, the Börse had "speedily recovered."

News columns trimmed to the last line, Noyes's thoughtful analysis of an eventful day set in type, there were only the decks of headlines to write. For once the usually cautious financial editor let himself go.

WORST STOCK CRASH STEMMED BY BANKS; 12,894,650-SHARE DAY SWAMPS MARKET; LEADERS CONFER, FIND CONDITIONS SOUND

FINANCIERS EASE TENSION

Call Break 'Technical'

Wall Street Optimistic After Stormy Day

Noyes accurately summed up the feeling in Wall Street in one paragraph. "The opinion of brokers was unanimous that the selling had got out of hand not because of any inherent weakness in the market but because the public had become alarmed over the steady liquidation of the past few weeks. Over their private wires these brokers counseled their customers against further thoughtless selling at sacrifice prices."

And there, on the front page, was the by-now obligatory quote from Charles Mitchell. "I am still of the opinion that this reaction has badly overrun itself."

There was no hint in those words that Mitchell was himself nearing the end of his personal financial rope.

As chief executive of the National City Bank, Mitchell's salary was a paltry $25,000. However, the bank, with his hearty approval, had set up a most generous management fund, into which a staggering 20 percent of the total net profits of both the bank and its security affiliate, the National City Company, were paid. This money was divided twice a year between the principal officers. The unusual method of apportioning the fund was again looked upon with favor by Mitchell.

While he stood aside, the other officers each placed in a hat an unsigned slip suggesting the amount Mitchell should receive. Then each submitted a second ballot, this one signed, indicating the proportion of the fund each other officer, excluding himself, should have.

These past two years had been good for National City—and for Mitchell. In 1927 his cut from the fund was $1,056,000 In 1928 it went up to $1,316,000. But 1929 looked like being the best year yet; he had already received $1,108,000—and that was only for the first half of the year. Dividends and numerous other investments would doubtless further enhance his total income.

Clearly the avaricious banker would have a serious tax liability at the end of 1929.

One way to remove that would be to sell to his wife National City stock he held—its value had declined considerably since he bought it—thereby establishing a tax loss on the sale. Dubious—but legal. The real problem was that Mitchell no longer held much of his stock. It was lodged with Morgan's, pledged as collateral for personal loans he had from the firm.

That small detail did not stop Mitchell. Without telling Morgan's, he would soon "sell" the stock pledged to them to his wife, creating a loss on paper, for tax purposes, of $2,872,305.50.

This maneuver would eliminate Mitchell's entire tax liability for 1929—a most satisfactory state for a man whose income was upwards of $2 million a year.

Now that he was on a slippery slope, just like the Flint embezzlers and Clarence Hatry, Mitchell began to slide faster.

For weeks he had been paving the way for National City to complete a merger with the Corn Exchange Bank. Holders of Corn Exchange stock could choose to receive either four fifths of a share of National City stock—or $360 in cash.

When the deal was proposed, the price of National City stock stood at over $500 but, since September, it had frittered downward, a few points at a time. No reason for the drop was discernible. Today's Crash had worsened the position. National City now stood at around $440 a share. At any price below $450 a share—four fifths of which equaled $360 in cash—the stockholders of the Corn Exchange would obviously opt for the money instead of the shares.

To buy out all of them with cash would cost the National City some $200 million. That was too much to fork out even for the wealthiest bank in America.

Charles Mitchell—just as Clarence Hatry had tried to do—decided to support his own bank by purchasing more of its stock in an attempt to push its price up.

Precisely when the idea came to him would remain a matter of conjecture, but, by his own later account, this Thursday night he had concluded he would need about $12 million to launch the scheme.

Mitchell did not personally have such money available. But he thought he knew where he could get it—from the House of Morgan, the same private bank he would hoodwink to remove his 1929 tax liability.

On Friday morning, October 25, after Charlton had gone to the office, Adele MacVeagh settled down to read the *Times*. When she had finished, she felt a sense of wifely pride. The newspaper reports confirmed what Charlton had told her: Things *were* going to be all right.

Hutton-Miller sensed a similar mood of optimism when he returned to Wall Street after a short rest in a nearby hotel. Despite his clean shirt and collar, his appearance was somewhat spoiled by the stubble on his chin; he had forgotten to pack his razor and there were long queues outside the barbershops.

Michael Levine examined, and rejected as impractical, several ideas for cashing in on the sudden tonsorial need. It was a sideline the ingenious self-made millionaire was unable to exploit. Yet during the night some of his messengers had successfully delivered booze and supplies in the district, easily avoiding patrolling policemen. Their employer was, nevertheless, relieved to see that the police presence had been reduced by daylight; it was another sign the crisis was over.

Levine fell asleep in his office, totally ignoring the ringing telephones.

Since early morning, they had also been ringing in the surrounding brokerage houses. Customers, some as far away as Alaska and California, having spent a sleepless night figuring out their financial position, were coming back into the market with a vengeance.

Pat Bologna saw there were again lines forming outside the customers' rooms. Rumors ran rife among them as before, but today the shoeblack detected one difference: The people were in much better humor. The first jokes began to do the rounds; there were gags about brokers buying stock in gas companies and bankers investing in those manufacturing red ink.

Sustained cheers greeted Thomas Lamont and the other Morgan partners when they arrived at 23 Wall. They appeared embarrassed by their sudden popularity.

Charles Mitchell took it as his due. Dogged by his faithful chauffeur toting his valise, the banker strode down Wall Street radiating confidence and good cheer.

By nine-thirty the crowd had formed an avenue outside the Stock Exchange entrance, down which the last of the brokers hurried.

One of the many newsmen present saw the traders as "newly seasoned combat troops going back up the line, knowing that some of them could be wiped out, but all determined to survive. It's the mentality which wins wars—and overcomes financial panics."

William Crawford detected a similar fierce determination when he opened the market at ten.

Minutes later the tension gave way to visible relief as the first prices for many stocks showed immediate, if modest, gains.

They set the standard for the day's trading.

The only real sensation was a jump of $11 in the shares of American bank note; most thought this was probably due to the great increase in stock transfers, which required the printing of new certificates. At the other extreme was a drop of $18.50 in J. I. Case. Apart from those who had invested in the stock, few were unduly concerned; the company's shares had seesawed for months.

The day closed with the Dow Jones industrial and railroad averages both up, 1.75 points and 1.01 points respectively. In all, nearly 6 million shares had been traded, half the number traded yesterday, but still a very high figure.

Workers emerged from the Exchange with the feeling that the crisis had been successfully weathered.

There were other reasons for renewed confidence.

George Baker of the First National Bank had joined the Lamont pool; there had been a further meeting of the bankers at Morgan's. They had not thought it necessary to issue a statement.

President Hoover did. "The fundamental business of the country, that is production and distribution of commodities, is on a sound and prosperous basis."

It was a pronouncement that carefully avoided any attempt to predict the future trend of stock prices.

Arthur Loasby, president of the Equitable Trust Company, was rather more specific. "There will be no repetition of the break of yesterday. The market fell of its own weight without regard to fundamental business conditions, which are sound. I have no fear of another, comparable decline."

One market expert was conspicuous by his absence, Edward Harriman Simmons, president of the Stock Exchange, tracked down by a reporter at his honeymoon hotel in Honolulu, stolidly refused to comment about the Crash—or to contemplate returning to New York.

His deputy, Richard Whitney, continued to bask in the unexpected warmth of popularity. A stream of telephone messages, telegrams, and personal callers brought congratulations for his market-saving actions of yesterday.

Whitney was glad, now, that he had resisted those who wanted to suspend trading on Saturday in order to give exhausted clerical staff a chance to catch up over a long weekend. Whitney argued that such a move could disturb public confidence just as it was being restored.

Late Friday evening, Hut and his colleagues were still totting up the casualty figures. Hundreds of accounts—a few that had been large and many that were small—had to be closed.

It was agonizing talking to clients. When they were unable to put up the margin required, they often abused the broker, blaming him for not having sold their shares sooner when prices had been higher, or bemoaning the fact they might now receive nothing at all. Hut was left in no doubt, "much human misery followed in the wake of those calls." But compassionate as he was, he was too busy, and too tired, to spend time dwelling on such matters.

For the second night running, Hut staggered to bed in a cheerless hotel room. He arranged for an extra early call in the morning so that he could go home and clean up before returning to work.

On Saturday, before the market opened, newspaper readers received further words of comfort from many leading financial figures in the country.

Charles Schwab, chairman of Bethlehem Steel, friend of Henry Ford and client of Evangeline Adams, said he saw no reason in principle why prosperity should not continue "indefinitely."

James Farrell, president of U. S. Steel, concurred.

Alfred Sloan, chairman of General Motors, reportedly declared Thursday's Crash was "healthy," a diagnosis that startled not only GM shareholders who had seen their stock drop but also Charles Stewart Mott, who, for the past two days, had remained virtually full-time at his office.

Walter Teagle, president of Standard Oil, announced: "There has been no fundamental change in the petroleum industry."

Samuel Vauclain of Baldwin Locomotive believed that America was back on track, on time and steaming along at full speed.

Even Doc Giannini was ready with a word of comfort—to add to the thousands already dispensed by his fellow luminaries. But Doc, in common with other bankers, was quietly revising downward the estimates of the lending value of stocks.

And out-of-town banks and corporations continued to call back their deposits from Wall Street.

New York banks were plugging the gaping hole left by these "summer financiers." So far, $1 billion had been used for this purpose.

John J. Raskob saw this bank support as a bold stroke. The banks were ensuring there would be no shortage of money for investors, that stocks would not have to be dumped because their owners could not borrow money at any price to keep them.

Raskob, like many other bulls, also drew comfort from call money being freely available this Saturday at an attractive 6 percent.

The two-hour trading period, in spite of this, was reported "uneventful," average prices falling very slightly.

William Crawford was one of many who worked late into the afternoon; the superintendent was supervising a complete overhaul of the Exchange's ticker system.

It continued through Sunday, October 27, when the financial district, usually deserted, teemed with people and traffic.

Trinity Church was packed; among the worshipers was Hut. He "asked the Lord to bless my loved ones, and then I mentioned the market." Hut had now put almost all his savings into sustaining his stocks.

From noon on Sunday, sightseers' buses toured the district.

Michael Levine was amused to hear guides intoning that this was "where millions of dollars were lost last Thursday." Since that day, he had continued to increase his fortune by every possible legal means. He only wished he had thought of the bright idea one Wall Streeter had dreamed up: He was selling copies of Thursday's historical ticker tape to tourists at fifty cents a strip.

Monday, October 28, dawned in a swirl of optimism which enveloped many people in the financial district. Thousands of newcomers —rubbernecks, some with money to invest—converged on the area. Many were drawn by reports that "a mountain" of buy orders had accumulated in brokers' offices over the weekend.

Mike Meehan did not share this enthusiasm. He was nervous. Radio had slumped badly from those halcyon days of six months before when it had been over 100; on Thursday it dropped to only 44, but had recovered since then and was now just under 60.

The astute Meehan was concerned about another aspect, one that had no direct link with Radio but could have a strong indirect bearing on the performance of the stock. It was the erroneous, and growing, conviction among the speculating public that the purpose of Lamont's bankers' pool was to push up prices. Meehan knew this was not so. The bankers' fund was intended only to stabilize the market—to "stop the bottom falling out entirely"—and to prepare the way for an orderly liquidation if that should be necessary.

Meehan did not know how long the bankers intended to provide money to buy stock; he did know that when they stopped, it would be dangerous. He could only do what he had done since Thursday, "attempt to maintain an orderly and fair market in Radio."

Still tucked away in his command post, A. P. Giannini surprised his brother, Doc, in New York, by calling him at 8:30 A.M.—5:30 in the morning in San Francisco.

Giannini, too, well understood the role the bankers' pool was intended to play.

While he would do everything possible to help stabilize the market by making the "right noises," he had no illusions as to the reality of the situation.

Giannini told Doc there was no reason to suppose the market would get more support from the pool if everybody wanted to sell and no one wanted to buy.

Nor was he yet certain it would be sensible for him and his brother to continue supporting Transamerica; perhaps the stock should be allowed to find its own level.

A somber Doc, like millions of investors and staff in every board-room in the country, waited tensely for the market to open.

William Crawford hardly had time to step from his podium before trouble erupted.

At Post Two U. S. Steel opened at $202.25, a full $1.25 off its closing price of Saturday.

At Post Seventeen there was a greater dip as International Tel and Tel started $3 down on Saturday's price.

The biggest drop of all in these opening moments was at Post Six: General Electric fell $7.50.

The ticker started to lag behind. Everywhere the panic of "Black Thursday" seemed destined to be repeated.

By 10:30 Steel had crashed through the mythical 200 barrier; other blue chips followed in a wave of selling which successively knocked prices down from one low level to another.

By 1 P.M. the ticker was ninety minutes late.

The news agency tapes were up to the minute: Within seconds of each other, AP and UPI reported that Charles Mitchell had entered 23 Wall.

The rumor was born and nurtured that Mitchell was placing his bank's vast reserves behind a new move to stop the rot, reminiscent of the day in late March when he had bucked the Federal Reserve and saved the bull market virtually single-handedly. But this time the shoe was on the other foot; it is almost certain that Mitchell went there to borrow the $12 million he wanted to support his own bank stock. He spent less than twenty minutes inside J. P. Morgan and Company. He walked out smiling—Morgan's would loan him $10 million this week.

The market steadied when news of Mitchell's smile reached the trad-ing floor.

Soon afterward, a broker acting for Morgan's began bidding for Steel. It quickly rose from 193½ to 198. The broker was not Whitney, and his effort did not have the effect Whitney's had had on Thursday. Steel soon slipped back to 190.

As the afternoon wore on, the selling became even more urgent. In the final *hour,* nearly 3 million shares changed hands—a figure that in other, calmer times would have been good for a *day.*

When Crawford sounded the closing gong, 9,212,800 shares had been traded. It was less than on Black Thursday. But the fall in prices was far more severe: The *Times* general average of stocks was down 29 points. This was the largest drop in prices during any day in the entire history of the New York Stock Exchange.

All told, securities had fallen in value an estimated $14 billion.

High above Times Square, Alexander Noyes began to shape the story of the day's events. He blamed the "decline" on a number of factors: lack of support, exhaustion of margins; "selling by many frightened persons who had owned their stocks outright and a re-creation of the wave of fright which swept the speculative markets last week."

Noyes identified the "acute weakness" of the blue chips that had "spread terror" through the ranks of stockholders, leading to the "slaughter of market values."

Emotive words—likely to put fear into any but the bravest of bulls.

Once more Jesse Livermore had escaped comparatively lightly. He and his staff began yet another analysis of this latest tremendous break which had left so many shares so low.

The figures were an indication that the "snap," "resilience," and ability to make a "comeback" had been sapped from the market.

That was chilling enough.

Even more ominous was that most damage had been done in the last few minutes of trading.

That was the worst possible omen for the opening next day.

CHAPTER TWENTY-SIX

THE DAY THE BUBBLE BURST

The chatter of a news ticker awoke Hut. He ached from the brief nap in a cot on the floor of the customers' room at W. E. Hutton. Around him exhausted colleagues slept on. As a result of yesterday's break, they had all worked until the early hours of the morning, Tuesday, October 29, before snatching a short rest.

Picking his way past the slumbering men, Hut reached the ticker. It had been installed at the height of the bull market to keep clients abreast of the outside world while they invested.

Unable to switch off the machine, he slumped down beside it and began to read the information being tapped out.

Much of it was overnight news from abroad.

King Zog of Albania, whose Queen was reputedly an American heiress with Wall Street connections, had received a deputation protesting about Albania's economic conditions; Zog jailed the delegation for spreading public unrest. From London came news that Edward, bachelor Prince of Wales, was renovating York House; all the windowpanes were being reglazed with special glass said to attract ultraviolet rays. In Rome, Benito Mussolini, who had so far managed to make the trains run on time and the economy grind to a halt, had delivered another peroration about fascism sweeping the world. Stalin was saying the same about communism. In Shanghai, Chiang Kai-shek announced— again—that communism would never gain ground in China. From Berlin came news Hitler was attracting thousands of middle-class Germans into his ranks who were fearful of communism. In Tokyo, Emperor Hirohito was shocked by the death of a peasant who had leaped in front of his golden coach as it was taking him to open Parliament.

And, from the White House, came the announcement that President Hoover would be attending a funeral tomorrow afternoon.

Hut wondered whose funeral Hoover would be attending. And he could not understand why such unimportant news was being transmitted, "when the only story for Americans was what was happening in Wall Street."

There were four hours to go before the market opened.

The arrival of daylight heightened the tempo in the Stock Exchange. All through the night, William Crawford and his team had performed a second major overhaul of the ticker system.

At first light, tired and dirt-stained, almost unrecognizable in borrowed overalls, Crawford ordered it tested.

In an attempt to ensure the ticker would keep up with trading, he had recently obtained Richard Whitney's permission to omit on the tape all but the final digit from each stock's quotation. Those reading the tape now had to rely on their own memories or guesswork to supply the missing numbers preceding the final figure.

The test run showed everything was working perfectly.

Next to be checked were the private wire links with the other exchanges across the nation. They also were in order.

The circuits connecting the trading floor to the principal brokerage houses in the district were then certified as functioning properly.

Mechanically speaking, the New York Stock Exchange was as prepared as it ever could be to meet the coming day.

About the same time, wire men in every major brokerage house and bank in the district were transmitting tests over their private circuits to branch offices throughout America. At W. E. Hutton, Hut tested the lines from New York to offices in Cincinnati and California. Those firms with links overseas—with the markets of Canada, Europe, the British Empire, the Far East—established that these sources of communication were working effectively. Wall Street was, telephonically and telegraphically, plugged in to the world.

Some of the more enterprising of Michael Levine's 2,000 messengers, indefatigable as ever, had discovered another way of augmenting their incomes. Since dawn they had been rushing around the city, calling at the homes of hundreds of workers who had been forced to spend their fifth night in a row at the office or in hotels. For fifty cents a delivery, a person had clean clothes brought from home to his place of work.

Not to be outdone, Levine himself had arranged to lay in a stock of smelling salts after he heard the local drugstores were running short.

He thought there could be a need for the stimulant once the stock market opened.

John J. Raskob had scheduled a meeting over breakfast at the Plaza Hotel in order to be back at his office before trading began. The financier was his usual gregarious self. His jovial mood carried to those around the table: Alfred Smith, Pierre du Pont, and other directors of Empire State, Inc., the company founded to finance and build the tallest building in the world.

Suddenly that claim had been challenged by Walter Chrysler's building, rising on Lexington Avenue. Raskob had discovered that Chrysler, as competitive as he was rich, planned secretly to build an ornate art deco spire inside his building and, at the last moment, elevate it through the roof. At 1,146 feet, the Chrysler Building would then dominate Raskob's proposed structure.

At first the news had thrown Raskob and architect William Lamb into a panic.

Although the Empire State Building would have three times the volume of the Chrysler Building, its height had been fixed at slightly below 1,050 feet; there would be eighty-five floors for offices and an observation tower.

To arrange to add more stories at this late stage would be almost impossible—more so as the promised date of completion, April 1931, was already imposing a strain on Lamb and the builders.

And yet Raskob knew unless the Empire State Building *was* the tallest in the world, it would become just another skyscraper: Prospective tenants would withdraw; the structure's value as a tourist attraction would be minimal.

Raskob, in an inspired moment, had put forward a plan to solve the problem. It would not only increase the height of the building, but also its earning potential. He would add a two-hundred-foot-tall mooring mast for dirigibles—a soaring tower where giant airships like the *Graf Zeppelin* could tie up; the mast would be placed on top of the Empire State Building, its tip a comfortable hundred feet above the Chrysler spire.

The breakfast meeting this morning was to discuss progress on the proposal.

Al Smith reported he had received enthusiastic support from navy dirigible experts and officials of the Goodyear Zeppelin Corporation. They had assured him the mast could be made strong enough structurally.

Pierre du Pont said there would be no problem with city ordinances: Mayor Jimmy Walker had welcomed the idea of transatlantic passengers landing a quarter of a mile above Fifth Avenue. No other city in the world could boast of such a thing.

Most important of all, the mooring tower was not expensive, and could be built within the existing timetable.

The decision to proceed made, the men departed, pleased with progress on the unique undertaking. Their deliberations had also been unusual for another reason: No one had actually mentioned the stock market, now due to open in two hours.

Traveling into Wall Street, Pat Bologna was assailed on all sides by market talk. He was astonished to hear how good-natured were his fellow passengers. Bologna put it down to the surprisingly optimistic tone of the morning papers; apart from the *Times,* most of the papers predicted that the situation would today be retrieved by "banking support." Bologna felt the subway train was "like the *Titanic,*" with his fellow passengers putting on the same brave face as those on the great liner had reportedly done as she was sinking.

One of the subway passengers, a night manager in a Manhattan hotel, had a captive audience for his tale about a wealthy Midwest industrialist who had checked in the night before. The guest was a regular, with a standing order for a magnum of champagne and a call girl. As soon as he'd settled into his suite, the champagne was delivered—but the girl failed to materialize. The man rang the night manager, who promised to send a girl up. Moments later there was a knock on the suite door—and, when he opened it, the guest was confronted by a beautiful blonde. The impatient industrialist yanked her inside and told her to undress. The girl icily told him she was his broker's secretary. She handed the dumbfounded man a margin call for $400,000 and departed. Minutes later, the desolate guest checked out, his sexual appetite, like his fortune, suddenly diminished.

Bologna was still chuckling over the story when he reached Wall Street.

There he found the mood pensive and somber. "People who had battled through Thursday's Crash, who had been hit again hard by Monday's break, looked like they couldn't take any more. They were at the end of their resistance."

Already the police, who had returned to patrol the district in large numbers, were directing the more obviously distressed to the Stock Exchange's medical department, a well-equipped office near the trading floor.

Normally, the department only treated Exchange members and their staff. After touring the district early this morning, its medical director,

Dr. Francis Glazebrook, decided to open the facility to anyone who needed attention. Soon a number of cases of exhaustion and disorientation were being treated. The normally quiet medical department had become a busy frontline casualty station, its small team of doctors and nurses prescribing sedatives and medicines before sending the more serious cases to one of the city hospitals for further treatment.

As the morning wore on, Dr. Glazebrook, a wiry, iron-gray man with the snap and precision of a military commander, realized he had potentially the busiest practice in Manhattan. The fifty-one-year-old doctor, who had treated shell-shock cases in the Great War, had seen enough in his tour of the district and the Exchange floor to recognize markedly similar symptoms in a number of people. He warned his staff they would probably become even busier when the market opened in an hour's time.

By nine o'clock the predicted drizzle cast a pall over the city—but did nothing to dampen Jesse Livermore's creative flow. He continued to dictate to a secretary in his top-floor office on Fifth Avenue. She would transcribe the notes so they could eventually be included in his guide for investors.

Gripped in the first flush of authorship, Livermore set aside a full hour every day before trading began to dictate his thoughts. He preferred that to actually putting the words down on paper himself. He had also found it impossible to write at home. His wife's renewed drunken behavior was unsettling; there were increasingly bitter arguments between them. Finally, to avoid further acrimony, Livermore had all but moved out of the apartment.

In the past five days—except for brief forays to some show girl's apartment—Livermore had barely left the office. The sequence of events that had caused countless thousands of "minnows" to be ruined and billions of dollars lost excited him more than anything, or anybody, could. He relished having to call into play his unsurpassed market skills.

Livermore had been driven at times to the very edge of disaster; on each occasion, using brilliant financial ringcraft, he had fought his way out of trouble. When others predicted prices would rise, he kept his nerve and remained on the short side of the market: Prices fell, and Livermore collected. On other occasions he had been long, buying through a large number of brokers, to avoid arousing suspicion, blocks of shares in anticipation of a rally. He had been more often right than wrong, and managed to maintain his financial equilibrium while lesser operators had seen their fortunes virtually vanish.

Supported by his tired but elated staff—to whom he had given bonuses for the work done since Thursday—Jesse Livermore had spent most of the night gearing himself up to move again into the attack. His "gut" told him that this Tuesday was the "time to move out of the trenches and through the wire." Having readied himself, he could relax and concentrate on his book.

Unusually, when he tried, Livermore could speak as well as he could write; despite his lack of sophistication and social polish, he possessed a natural command of the language. Much of what he dictated was good enough to go straight into print.

"A speculator should make it a rule each time he closes out a successful deal to take one half of his profits and lock this sum up in a safe deposit box. The only money that is ever taken out of Wall Street by speculators is the money they draw out of their accounts after closing a successful deal."

Livermore had also decided his guide would contain homespun advice; for all his contempt for the "minnows," he knew they were far likelier to buy the book than professional investors.

"I know but one sure tip from a broker. It is your margin call. When it reaches you, close your account. You are on the wrong side of the market."

For this morning, he had one last piece of advice to dictate.

"There is no sense in trying to anticipate the next big movement, whether it is going to be up or down. The thing to do is to watch the market to determine the limits of the get-nowhere prices and make up your mind that you will not take an interest until prices break through the limits in either direction."

Those words would serve as Jesse Livermore's battle order for a trading day only minutes from starting.

On the floor of the New York Stock Exchange, the mood around Post Twelve, Mike Meehan's Radio Post, had changed dramatically since the arrival of the gifted, mercurial Irishman and his team.

He had dressed in his "lucky" blue suit; a pearl pin held his tie in place. His shoes were burnished. He looked "like several million dollars—or a man going to a funeral."

Meehan's staff were equally smartly turned out. Heads had turned as they crossed the floor in a phalanx to their horseshoe-shaped trading enclave.

Incredibly, "the Irish Contingent"—the affectionate phrase used for the Radio specialist and his team—had never looked more relaxed or confident. They reminded one broker of "men about to lead the light brigade into that valley, and come out unscathed." Another felt, "if the Exchange ever struck a medal for coolness under fire, then Mike and his boys deserved one apiece."

Radio had taken a nose-dive. During yesterday it had been battered down nearly $19, crashing to a close of just $40.25 a share.

Overnight, thousands of sell orders for the stock had come in. Those who had bought Radio at the peak of $114.75 had subsequently watched their holdings fritter downward until yesterday's collapse. Now they wanted, or were forced, to get out before the stock fell still further.

Meehan, sensing the unspoken concern of his staff, put on a typically rousing performance to encourage them; he traded jokes with fellow brokers, gossiped about the drama of the *Berengaria* crossing when Helena Rubinstein had calmly written off a millionaire's ransom as if it were chicken feed. Madame Rubinstein's loss could have been worse; Westinghouse shares were now worth some $20 less than when she had sold hers.

The *Berengaria* would soon again be heading for Europe. Meehan expected his floating broker's office to show another considerable profit from the crossing. He was not so sure about the ship's return journey to New York. He had heard Americans were queueing up to come home; they were ones wiped out by Thursday's Crash. He doubted they would have a cent to spare, or the inclination, to visit Goudiss and Moore's office.

Here, on some of the most expensive land in the world—a square foot of Wall Street now commanded $900—Mike Meehan could still look forward to profits; in spite of the drastic decline in Radio, his firm had a huge income resulting from the record trading volume. The company's commission for executing orders was running at about $3,000 each hour the Exchange was open.

But as prices fell, so Meehan's personal fortune in his private investments was also falling. He was already down well over $1 million. The pressure on him was enormous.

To maintain his appearance of almost total unconcern, Meehan left Post Twelve to tour the floor.

When he returned, he was still smiling. But Ed Schnell fancied he detected a change in his employer. He did not have to think hard for the reason. Schnell knew that Meehan had invested millions in the market, that Meehan's fortune, the security of his wife and children, even to some extent the future of his firm, were tied to the stocks he held.

Schnell did not know the extent of Meehan's personal loss so far, but even a brief tour of the trading floor was enough for his employer to learn his shares were more at risk than ever.

Yet, "typically, Mike didn't dwell on his own private problems. He just put everything he had into looking after Radio."

Now, as William Crawford climbed the podium, Ed Schnell and his colleagues inside their stockadelike booth knew what it "must have been like for the defenders of the Alamo as they waited to be overrun."

Crawford's eyes swept the Exchange. Instinctively, he glanced toward the visitors' gallery. It was empty; it had not been reopened since its closure midday on Thursday. The superintendent was relieved reporters were unable to peer down on the bedlam already developing on the floor. Veteran traders, clerks, and page boys were running wildly around the perimeter before darting into the jostling mass in the center. The floor was littered with discarded pieces of paper.

And, even as Crawford raised his gavel, the din from below increased to a "baying roar." The sound of the gong was lost.

"Twenty thousand at the market!"
"Thirty thousand—sell!"
"Fifty thousand! Sell at the market!"

General Oliver Bridgeman, U. S. Steel's battle-scarred specialist, flinched at the hammer blows. Steel plunged through yesterday's ruinous close of $186 a share with girderlike force.

The rest of the market tumbled with it, sucked swiftly down by the uncontrollable crowd besieging Post Two.

During the first three minutes of trading 650,000 Steel shares were dumped on the market. At the end of those three minutes, few buyers were interested in the stock at $179. It seemed a lifetime since Whitney had bid 205.

Steel's collapse created ugly panic. Men swore, shoved, and mauled, clawing at Bridgeman, forcing him to take refuge inside Post Two.

A messenger struggling through the crowd suddenly found himself yanked by his hair off his feet. The man who held him kept screaming he had been ruined. He would not let the boy go. The terrified youth at last broke free, leaving the man holding tufts of his hair. Crying in pain, the messenger fled the Exchange. His hair never regrew.

Behind, he left a scene of increasing pandemonium. As huge blocks of shares continued to be dumped at all seventeen trading posts, 1,000 brokers and a support army of 2,000 page boys, clerks, telephonists, operators of pneumatic message tubes, and official recorders could sense this was going to be the "day of the millionaire's slaughter."

William Crawford, swept along helplessly by the great tide of people, would always remember how "they roared like a lot of lions and tigers.

They hollered and screamed, they clawed at one another's collars. It was like a bunch of crazy men."

By the time he found himself at Post Seven, in the center of the floor, the superintendent realized that something else was seriously wrong: The huge Translux screens, strategically placed around the vast hall, were blank. That meant the ticker was not running at all.

Crawford knew immediately what had happened. The panic selling had completely disrupted the flow of information about the buy and sell orders that traveled from the trading posts to the ticker staff.

Stunned, crushed in the crowd near Post Seven—where Air Reduction and Allied Chemical were leading the rout of stocks traded there—the superintendent was powerless to intervene.

Then, almost miraculously, the first share quotations began to judder across the screens; brokerage offices throughout the country were now receiving confirmation of the calamity occurring in New York.

A few feet away, at Post Twelve, Crawford could see Mike Meehan's mouth moving, but he could not hear what the broker was saying because of the noise.

Radio had fallen dizzily. In the first frantic moments of trading, its value had depreciated $10.25 a share. The stock was selling now for $30.

At the far end of the hall, at Post Seventeen, men were literally charging into the crowd in an effort to get to the specialist in International Telephone and Telegraph, whose stock had fallen $17 and showed no sign of stopping.

Suddenly a broker pitched to the floor and began to scramble about wildly. Before he was trampled underfoot he was dragged to the side. A nurse rushed to his aid; "the man was spluttering incoherencies." Convinced he was deranged, she sent for Dr. Glazebrook; he could commit the broker to Bellevue, the nearest mental hospital.

The medical director stooped beside his gibbering patient, pressing his ear close to the man's mouth. Then the doctor rose and smiled grimly; he told the nurse the man wasn't mad. He was incoherent because he had lost his false teeth while shouting an order. He had simply dropped to the floor in a vain attempt to find his dentures.

At Post Twelve—Ed Schnell's Alamo—the defenses were breached as sell orders for Radio poured in to the post. It seemed to Schnell, "the heavens had opened up, the stock was being pounded, down, down, right down to 26."

The young clerk marveled at the way Meehan conducted himself— accepting, never challenging anyone as the avalanche of orders spelled the demise of one of the most popular stocks of the Great Bull Market.

Many of the brokers who had seen Steel smashed to smithereens moved across to Post Twelve, there to witness the onslaught against that equally sacred stock, the pride of the House of Morgan, Allegheny. It fell 4⅞ from 28⅛ on a single block sale of 50,000 shares. It was a knockout blow. Allegheny had been one of the investment trusts that optimists claimed would give the market strength.

At Post Six, a fight broke out as a scramble developed to sell American Can. Two clerks, possibly rendered momentarily senseless by the noise, lashed out at each other. The Specialist in General Electric swiftly separated them, and returned to the fray. His stock had dropped at the rate of a dollar every ten seconds during the first six minutes of trading.

Post Fifteen—the home of some of the most prestigious stocks—found Westinghouse wilting under the bombardment. It dropped $2 a minute between the time the market opened and 10:15 A.M. At its present rate of decline it could be worthless by noon. Another of the post's stocks, Timken Roller Bearing, was skeetering toward oblivion even sooner, driven there by a 25,000-sell order which lopped $19.75 off its value.

William Crawford, pushing ruthlessly to get to the edge of the floor, reached Post Four in time to hear a strangled shout to sell 50,000 shares of General Motors, again "at the market." The order was executed for a drop of $2.25 below its previous price.

Now Crawford heard a new sound. High and wailing, the words were indistinguishable at first, their source somewhere inside that same mob around Post Four, where Anaconda Copper was toppling even faster than Southern Pacific—the railroad stock whose collapse had led the 1907 panic.

Then Crawford saw him; middle-aged, collarless, a rent in his jacket —"he looked more like a Bowery bum than a broker." The man struck out blindly from the melee, moaning, "I'm sold out! Sold out! Out!"

Before Crawford could reach him, the broker was swept along in the huge overspill surging around Post Eight, where shares in Montgomery Ward were "falling quicker than cans off a supermarket shelf."

The superintendent reached the comparative sanctuary of the New Street side of the Exchange. One of the guides who normally would have been on duty in the visitors' gallery pointed toward a Translux screen. The figures sliding across continued to tell a story of total disaster.

Blue Ridge, yet another investment trust, was on the floor. It had opened at $10. Now it was $3. Not long ago it had traded at $24; there was confident talk then it would go higher.

A sale of 50,000 shares in United Corporation saw the stock slither drunkenly from its opening price of $26 to $19.30.

Crawford knew Blue Ridge and United had been favorites among small investors.

The "dream stocks"—Paramount, Fox, and Warner Bros.—were also taking a trouncing.

Ed Schnell felt as if he had been working for hours. His throat ached, his hands were grubby from handling so much paper. And all the time sell orders streamed to Post Twelve; he began to fear every share ever issued in Radio was going to be dumped.

At the adjoining Post Eleven—where the Bouviers could not stop American Smelting from melting away almost as fast as Kennecott Copper—suddenly, for no discernible reason, the crowd turned their fury against Woolworth shares. The chain-store stock had held firm since the opening; now, against a great, sustained roar of "sell, sell, sell," it too gave way.

Dotted around the trading floor were some forty governors of the Stock Exchange. On heavy selling days in the past, it was said they had sometimes joined forces to create the basis for a rally by using the tens of millions of dollars they controlled to force some stability into the situation.

In today's selling maelstrom they were flotsam; out of touch with each other, separated by groups of near-demented men, the governors could do nothing to stem the ferocious waves of liquidation.

Richard Whitney was also on the floor. Pushed and shoved, like everyone else, the acting president was being almost totally ignored.

His appearance had at first raised the hope he had arrived to again make the saving gesture by bidding for a big block of U. S. Steel. But Whitney made no such move, and it was assumed the bankers' consortium had been disbanded. It had not, but the injection of funds it fed into the market for the purchase of shares was insufficient to make any noticeable difference. Whitney could only stand to the side and watch as the institution for which he was temporarily responsible transformed itself into a madhouse.

Superintendent Crawford eased himself down to the vicinity of Post Sixteen. There, Warner Bros' zigzag downward was being overhauled by the plunge in Safeway Stores and Simmons—the mattress company stock which had taken Winston Churchill's fancy.

A man, a complete stranger to Crawford, broke out of the crowd and lunged at another stranger—who sidestepped. The man careened on out of the main entrance into Wall Street, "screaming like a lunatic."

Shaken, feeling he was in the presence of "hunted things"—a phrase Whitney would also use later—William Crawford backed toward the staircase leading down to the basement.

He looked at his watch.

It was barely ten-thirty.

In all, 3,259,800 shares had been sold for a combined loss of over $2 billion in just thirty minutes.

Hut could sense it was "no longer just alarm but a feeling of real horror" that was permeating the offices in W. E. Hutton and Company. It was "a live, tangible thing." It seeped out of the customers' room, up on through the wire room, the directors' room, and into the large work area where Hut helped his colleagues man the trading table.

The room had taken on the semblance of a beleaguered command post. Blackboards had been set up on which a team of boys were trying —and failing—to keep pace with the collapsing prices. In another corner was the shiny screen across which marched a procession of figures—each group spelling out further disaster. Every minute Hut felt the emotion around him being "notched up a peg."

He was too busy to allow his own fears to surface; the sheer pressure of work acted as a very necessary safety valve for the broker.

Grabbing a telephone, he found himself speaking to one of the firm's clerks on the New York Curb Exchange.

The man sounded as if he was having hysterics. Hut shouted at him to pull himself together. The clerk modified his speech to an "understandable gabble."

He reported the cave-in of prices on the Curb was just as disastrous as the one occurring on the senior Exchange.

In the past half hour's trading on the Curb, accounts that had survived the severe pressure of yesterday were wiped out.

As Hut put down the phone, he could hear the office manager give the despairing order to sell off "at once" any account for which the margin call had not been met.

Pat Bologna waited anxiously for an answer over the pay telephone he was using close to his shoeshine stand. Unable to force his way into the nearby customers' room, he had requested by phone that the shares he held in National City be sold. He could not afford to put up the margin to keep them.

A clerk came on the line. Bologna's stock had been sold. Of the $5,000 the shoeblack had invested, he would get back $1,700.

In San Francisco, by 7:30 A.M. local time, A. P. Giannini knew his dreams had been shattered. Transamerica, which he resolutely believed to be inviolate, had dropped $32 a share on the San Francisco Exchange, itself gripped "in a whirl of frenzied selling." Worse still, in New York the stock had sunk $42.50; on offer now at $20.25 a share, it was awaiting a bid.

Giannini issued an immediate statement to the press. "The fact Transamerica was the last stock to resist affords a fair appraisal of its investment value. This is a period that calls for clear heads and bold hearts." He then gave instructions that the value of Transamerica's shares was not to be artificially supported. The stock would be left to find its own level in the bereft market.

Every telephone in Jesse Livermore's complex was constantly in use as his staff struggled to follow events in Wall Street and further afield.

Livermore, in the memory of one of his staff, "was like a dervish," alternately feeding buy and sell orders into the market.

He would go short in one issue at the same time as he was long in another, a will-o'-the-wisp figure, switching his attention from broker to broker, from stock to stock.

Livermore dumped his rubber and coffee holdings just before prices in both commodities broke. Coffee slumped because of a quite separate internal panic sweeping the coffee exchanges in Brazil.

He bought wheat on the strength of a tip that the Farm Board was about to pronounce grain prices too low.

Aware that telephone, telegraph, and cable facilities into New York were clogging under the volume of orders pouring in from all over the country, as well as from abroad, Livermore had clerks keep his crucial private lines permanently open to key contacts in the great trading centers of Los Angeles, San Francisco, Chicago, and London.

Thousands of dollars an hour were being added to his telephone bill. The investment was worth every cent: Livermore was keeping his head above water.

At eleven o'clock the roar of voices raised in anger, desperation, and defeat continued to dominate the New York Exchange.

Large blocks of stock were being offered for whatever they would fetch; sales were running at an unbelievable 33-million-a-day rate.

At post after post there was a plethora of sell orders for which there were a diminishing number of buyers.

Forcing his way through the shouting crowd, the indefatigable William Crawford was tracking down the Exchange governors and bellowing in their ears—the only way he could make himself understood—a message that was supposed to be secret.

Richard Whitney was summoning them to an extraordinary emergency session at noon. It would not be held in the Exchange's splendid boardroom. Instead, the governors were discreetly to make their way down to the basement office of the president of the Stock Exchange Corporation, directly beneath the trading floor.

Hut saw that the ticker was falling behind; the prices flickering across the screen bore no relationship to those he was being quoted over the telephone.

All over the financial district the biggest communication jam in its entire history was happening. And those in London, Paris, Berlin, and Milan who did not have an open line to someone in Wall Street were virtually isolated from events in New York; the Transatlantic undersea cable could not possibly cope with the traffic. A system for restricting the length of overseas calls was introduced. It made little difference.

In New York Western Union hired a fleet of taxis to help with telegram deliveries of margin calls. As a result of those demands, a commonplace sight developed of people on their way from banks to brokerage offices, carrying stock certificates and bonds taken from strongboxes. Insurance companies had a rush of people wanting to cash in or borrow on their policies.

Hut at last decided his shares must be sold. He could no longer cover his margin. At age twenty-six, he found himself well over $100,000 the poorer.

Richard Whitney looked around at his fellow governors. He had put to them the proposal the Exchange be closed forthwith.

It was not easy for him to hear their responses. The tumult from the trading floor immediately above was deafening; herds of wild buffalo appeared to be thundering across the ceiling, obliterating all normal conversation.

Whitney's graphic account—the only one to survive—caught the atmosphere in the small, poky room, its entrance watched over by Crawford and several other guards.

"Panic was raging overhead on the floor. Every few minutes the latest prices were announced, with quotations moving swiftly and irresistibly downward. The feeling of those present was revealed by their habit of continually lighting cigarettes, taking a puff or two, putting them out and lighting new ones—a practice that soon made the narrow room blue with smoke and extremely stuffy."

The governors, visibly shaken and dazed by their own experiences, were filled with "apprehension for the future."

It was decided two Morgan partners—almost certainly Thomas

Lamont and Richard Whitney's brother, George—should join the deliberations.

"The gentlemen naturally wished to arrive at the meeting as unobtrusively as possible, lest a new crop of rumors be started. But as they attempted to slip quietly in, they were detected by one of the stalwart guards and sternly refused admittance."

One of the governors went to the rescue of the men from Morgan. Soon afterward a decision was taken against closing the Exchange.

The unspoken hope was that matters would improve.

The panic carried uninterrupted into the early afternoon.

Steel was sinking toward $170. General Bridgeman and his staff were ankle-deep in paper.

At Post Five, eighty-six-year-old William Wadsworth—who had endured the 1907 panic and even earlier ones in the previous century—had never experienced such sustained fury. Men who normally treated the oldest broker on the floor with the deference his age and service demanded now hurled abuse at Wadsworth as they dumped rail stocks "by the bucketful."

Nearly all of the 751 investment trusts had been virtually wiped out; the trusts had been founded, one bitter critic was to write, "on the same solid economic principles as the promotions of the Middle Ages financing the alchemists attempting to transmute base metal into gold. They were designed mainly to attract the spare dollars poor people had saved."

Most of those savings had now vanished in the whirlwind of selling.

Steel, the rails, the coals, the motors were swept away with the stocks of corporations, oil companies, and the other giants of industry.

Men wept openly in the Exchange. A few, doubtless for the first time in years, were driven to prayer, kneeling in impromptu supplication at the edge of the floor. Many went to nearby Trinity Church. It had totally filled for the thirty-minute service that began at noon, and would remain so for the rest of the day. For the first, and possibly only, time until now, Protestants, Catholics, and some Jews gathered together in Trinity, oblivious of its denomination, drawn there simply because it was a place of worship.

By early afternoon, Wall Street was blocked almost solid from Broadway to the river by an estimated ten thousand men and women. Rumors passed up and down the Street, bounced into adjoining streets, were enlarged, and bounced back into Wall.

Nobody knew what to believe; nobody knew how to behave.

There was no precedent for such a disaster.

By one o'clock, the orgy of selling on the Stock Exchange had risen to 12,652,000 shares.

It showed no sign of stopping.

Since early morning Homer Dowdy had been delivering telegrams along his route in Flint. In the past four hours he had dropped off more demands for margin than he had delivered altogether since Black Thursday.

Throughout the city every other available mailman was engaged in a similar task.

It was the same in each city, town, and hamlet in America. The flood of telegrams had increased as the market crisis escalated.

In Flint, most of the margin demands were to cover the tumbling value of auto stocks.

Hundreds of employees in the body-building and assembly plants that surrounded the city had invested during the summer of 1929 in such shares. Many had bought individual $1,000 blocks for the minimum 10 percent deposit. Others formed consortiums, the members putting up $1,000 between them to buy $10,000 worth of stock in GM or Chrysler. Housewives had bought on margin. Businessmen extended their credit to speculate.

Seventeen-year-old Ed Love, whose uncle, Grant Brown, was president of the Union Industrial Bank, had recently asked his father whether he was worth a million dollars. His father said he was. And he was—on paper.

The boy's father was one of the first of the city's "margin millionaires" to be wiped out.

Others followed.

By midmorning, Flint doctors—in common with physicians right across America—were having to treat cases of stroke and even heart attacks, brought on by the tension of "being caught in the market."

On Saginaw Street, where Billy Durant had first ridden a mechanically propelled cart, Homer Dowdy observed men actually "wailing like lunatics, saying they wished the motor car had never been invented. They were ruined from their losses in GM."

Outside brokerage offices he saw lines of "white-faced men who already knew what misery lay ahead."

Dowdy had his own problems. His wife, Gladys, was now close to death; the burden of nursing a dying woman and bringing up three small children was taxing his resources. The world outside had come to mean less and less to the shy, lonely mailman locked into his own tragedy.

Then Dowdy heard something that jerked him back into that world and made him temporarily abandon his deliveries.

Someone ran past him shouting the Union Industrial Bank had closed its doors.

Jolan and Steve Vargo saw the doors shut when they were still a couple of hundred yards away from them. They started to run, joining the many others converging on the building.

Married just ten days, the young couple had put off going to the bank until now because "we had so many other things to do."

And Steve had been "too busy" to ask Goldberger whether the attorney had learned why Jolan's brother had been unable to withdraw his share of the trust fund.

Today, after lunch, Jolan and Steve had decided to go to the bank and settle what Steve assured his bride was a simple matter.

They arrived to find that the doors were firmly locked, a full hour before normal closing time. Steve had a ready explanation.

Several of his friends at work had received margin calls. He sympathized with them. Privately, he felt relieved he had the foresight to have placed his money in the bank.

Steve told Jolan the doors had undoubtedly been closed "on account of the trouble in New York."

He led his wife away from the Union Industrial with the promise they would return another day; in the meantime, he insisted, their money was safer in the bank than anywhere.

It had been just before two o'clock when Frank Montague had finally decided what he must do. All morning he had followed news of the collapse in New York being relayed by telephone to Ivan Christensen.

At one-thirty Montague had estimated they owed the bank "around three million."

Montague was short—and not for the first time—in his calculations. All told, he and his fellow conspirators had looted the bank for $3,592,000.

For thirty minutes Montague had agonized over what was the best course of action open to him. He had come to believe he had been "duped by the others. I had no idea we were in so deep "

Montague decided there was no point in appealing to his coconspirators again. The moment had come.

As purposefully as he could, he walked the few feet to the desk of bank president Grant Brown.

In a halting voice Montague requested a private word with the president.

Brown led Montague into the directors' room—where for so many months the "league of gentlemen" had planned their strategy at the strictly unofficial and very private late evening "board meetings."

Montague began to confess.

Brown stopped him the moment Montague mentioned embezzling.

The president walked back into the bank.

The few customers there were quickly shown out. It was then that the bank doors were locked.

Standing in the center of the main banking hall, the stern-faced Grant Brown ordered all those who knew anything of the embezzlement to come to the directors' room.

He rejoined Montague.

Behind him, Ivan Christensen quietly replaced the telephone receiver which, for almost four continuous hours, he had held to his ear.

Brown and Montague sat in total silence, watching the closed door of the boardoom.

There was a hesitant knock.

"Enter."

Into the room stepped Milton Pollock, ashen-faced, looking far older than his thirty-nine years.

Pollock closed the door and remained standing until Brown motioned him to sit. Pollock chose the chair he had always occupied at the illicit meetings.

There was another knock.

"Enter."

Russell Runyon and Elton Graham came in and also took up their usual places.

Next came a group of tellers: James Barron, Farrell Thompson, Robert McDonald, George Woodhouse, Clifford Plumb, Mark Kelly, David McGregor, and Arthur Schlosser.

They, too, silently took their accustomed seats.

There was a pause.

Then, without knocking, Ivan Christensen and John de Camp entered.

Grant Brown stared frozen-faced at his deputy.

In strained silence the embezzlers waited.

There was another knock.

"Enter."

Robert Brown, the president's own son, the young teller widely tipped eventually to succeed his father to the bank presidency, stood, head down, in the doorway.

His father's mouth fell open. In a low voice he spoke to his son.

"You, too, Robert?"

He nodded, eyes brimming, and walked into the room.

The distressing silence stretched on.

Finally Grant Brown asked whether there were any more to come.

John de Camp shook his head.

The president rose to his feet and walked back into the bank.

He told one of the staff to reopen the doors. Brown assured the anxious crowd outside that all was well; Flint's only bank "panic" was over.

He returned to the boardroom. He locked its doors behind him and resumed his seat.

In a calm, clear voice he asked each man the same question. "Are you involved?"

Each time he received the identical answer: Yes.

Grant Brown said nothing further. He went to a telephone on a side table and asked to be connected to Charles Stewart Mott in the General Motors Building in Detroit.

When he got through, Brown's first words matched his magnificent control. "Mr. Mott, we have a problem here."

Once Brown had identified that "problem" to the chairman of the bank's Board of Directors, Mott immediately responded in similar fashion.

"Mr. Brown, I'll be with you in no time."

In New York the ticker kept running long after Crawford's closing gong at 3 P.M. Every falling share it recorded helped sound the death knell of the New Era.

America, the richest nation in the world, indeed the richest in all history—its 125 million people possessed more real wealth and real income, per person and in total, than the people of any other country—was now paying the price for accepting too many get-rich-quick schemes, the damaging duels fought between bulls and bears, pool operations and manipulations, buying on overly slim margins securities of low and even fraudulent quality. The indecisive and sometimes misleading leadership from the business and political world had contributed to the nationwide stampede to unload.

At 5:32 P.M. the final quotation clicked across the tickers of a numbed nation. The tape's operator signed off: TOTAL SALES TODAY 16,383,700. GOOD NIGHT.

Those millions of sales represented a loss in share value on the New York Exchange alone of some $10 billion. That was twice the amount of currency in circulation in the entire country at the time.

Eventually, the total lost in the financial pandemic would be put at a staggering $50 billion—all stemming from a virus that proved fatal on October 29, 1929: the day the bubble burst.

CHAPTER TWENTY-SEVEN

THE PARTY'S OVER

By five o'clock next morning, Charles Stewart Mott had heard a full account of their defalcations from the embezzlers. They had spent all night in the bank's boardroom.

Mott demanded each man's resignation. Then he sent them home. There was no talk of prosecution.

After a brief rest at his local mansion, Mott summoned Flint's public prosecutor, Charles Beagle.

Precisely what transpired between the two men is even today a matter of dispute.

Mott's son, Harding, who was not present, stoutly insists his father gave Beagle the facts and made no attempt to influence the prosecutor.

Beagle's son, John, who was also not present, believes Mott asked his father not to prosecute because he feared publicity could embarrass him and his friends on the bank's Board. John Beagle feels his father's refusal to bend the law was directly responsible for the political campaign Mott subsequently ran which eventually forced his father from office.

One matter not in dispute is what Mott did after seeing the public prosecutor. He returned to Detroit and withdrew from his own private bank account $3,592,000—the exact amount stolen.

He brought the money to Flint, driving at the head of three armored cars carrying the cash.

Mott placed the money on well-publicized display in the Union Industrial Bank.

The Flint *Journal* led the paean of praise for "the man who saved the bank."

Mott was quickly turned into the first post-Crash hero.

Steve Vargo, Jolan, and her brother Michael made several further visits to the bank in an attempt to get their money. Each time they were brushed aside. In the end they gave up. As Jolan says: "We were small folks. That was a big bank. They could do what they liked." The couple never moved from Flint, where they now enjoy a life of happy retirement.

Homer Dowdy was still trying to withdraw his savings when his wife, Gladys, died. His pressing domestic problems left him little time to pursue the matter. Later, he remarried; his son became a senior executive in the Mott Foundation, the splendid building in downtown Flint originally erected to house the now-defunct Union Industrial Bank.

The Vargos and Dowdy were among several small depositors who, despite Mott's well-intentioned action, never recovered their hard-earned savings.

On Friday, November 15, warrants were issued charging the "league of gentlemen" with embezzlement.

Just over a month later, on Monday, December 16—by a curious coincidence the very day Clarence Hatry was committed for trial at the Old Bailey in London—nine of the Flint bankers pleaded guilty. The others "stood mute," and were committed for trial in January 1930.

Shortly after Hatry received his fourteen-year prison sentence, judgment was passed on the embezzlers.

Their sentencing took place in the Flint court, where, on December 3, 1929, Mott's divorce was granted on his promise to pay his wife nearly $2 million in settlement. Afterward Mott married for a fourth time. He died in February 1973, aged ninety-seven.

Mott was not present to hear John de Camp receive ten years; Ivan Christensen seven and a half years; Frank Montague three and a half years.

Grant Brown saw his son, Robert, sent down for six months.

The other embezzlers also drew short sentences.

The "league of gentlemen" remained intact; they were given adjoining cells in Michigan State Prison. They were model prisoners, soon working together to bring order to the prison's records. Later, seven of them returned to the Flint area, some to work until retirement in local banks. Several were still alive in 1978. Frank Montague retired to live in a trailer far from Flint; he remains convinced he was "exploited by the others."

The Flint crooks had, in part, been enticed to embezzle by the temptations of a blossoming market.

It had collapsed, some argue, partly as an indirect result of Clarence Hatry's misdemeanors in London.

Jack Morgan, for one, did not doubt that Hatry's demise "precipitated the panic of 1929"; he testified as much later before a Senate inquiry.

To say that Hatry caused the Wall Street Crash would be to put it far too strongly. But to say that his downfall played no part in it whatsoever would possibly be equally misleading.

Hatry was released from prison in 1939. Soon he was again a respected financial tycoon. He died June 19, 1965, aged seventy-six.

At least a million Americans—some would put the figure as high as 3 million—were immediately and directly affected by the Crash, many of them financially almost totally wiped out. Yet in some ways the most tragic and longest lasting result was the total loss of trust within families: Husbands could no longer trust wives who they discovered had been secretly using housekeeping money to play the market; children no longer trusted fathers who had squandered their savings to try to get rich quick.

Even so, on the day after the greatest financial disaster in history until then, men and women still grabbed what were in many cases their very last dollars and rushed to a broker. They were drawn by the hope stocks would pick themselves up off the floor and return to at least a semblance of their former glory.

And, on October 30, many had actually started to climb as Winston Churchill boarded the *Berengaria* for home, somewhat poorer from dabbling in the American market but wiser about the wiles of Wall Street.

In the following week, a brave cry was sometimes heard: "Buy at the market."

John D. Rockefeller announced he and his son were "purchasing sound common stocks." It brought the sour raspberry from singer Eddie Cantor that only the Rockefellers had any money left. Cantor, like so many of his show business colleagues, had lost everything in the Crash.

From Thursday's closing on October 31, the New York Stock Exchange remained closed for trading until the following Monday, November 4. The holiday was warmly welcomed by exhausted Wall Streeters; many of them had been almost a week without proper sleep.

The newspapers began to talk of "recovery." Readers smiled at *Variety*'s thumb-at-nose handling of the Crash: "Wall Street Lays an Egg."

The same tireless experts who for two years had calculated the gains in the Great Bull Market now counted the cost at its end.

In the five hours the market had gone mad on October 29, it was later estimated that almost as much money in capital value vanished into thin air as the United States had spent on World War I. The loss was around ten times the budget of the Union in the entire Civil War.

A great portion of the loss represented money that ordinary people had already spent as *income* during the dizzy days of the climb; when, in the words of astrologer Evangeline Adams, Dow Jones seemed set to reach heaven.

On the day the bubble burst, the land was dotted with houses bought on part payments; cars bought on credit; clothes, jewelry, vacations, luxury goods of every kind acquired on the promise to pay in the future —often when stock profits came in.

Now, for too many, the money would never come.

In New York there was an immediate and huge increase in requests for aid from the charitable organizations. Domestic staff were among the first to be hit. Just as Edward Stone was forced to fire his establishment, thousands of others, the *nouveaux pauvres,* had to dismiss their chauffeurs, butlers, and maids.

One exception was Adele MacVeagh. For her the Crash caused no more than a momentary "tinkling of the tea cups." She and Charlton continued as before, comfortably cosseted from the new realities of life.

Those realities grew starker by the day. Faced with a sudden decline in buying, manufacturers cut back on production; workers were laid off in droves.

On Friday, November 1, the $20 million Foshay enterprise of Minneapolis collapsed. It was also the day Alfred Sloan of General Motors chose to pronounce that "business is sound," and Henry Ford to cut the price of all his cars as a "contribution to the continuation of good business."

This time it was not only Eddie Cantor who made rude noises.

On November 4, the Monday morning the market opened again, Professor Irving Fisher determinedly continued with his series of magnificent miscalculations. He insisted prices were absurdly low. They swiftly went lower; the *Times* industrials dropped 22 points for the day.

Next day the market closed, this time to let New Yorkers go to the polls in the mayoralty race. Fiorello La Guardia was trounced as they overwhelmingly returned the Democrat dandy, James Walker.

Roger Babson issued a statement calling for "poise, discernment, judicious courage and old-fashioned common sense."

Nobody knew what he was driving at—or much cared. His sojourn in the public eye was over. Other prophets of doom were waiting in the wings to take over.

At 5:50 P.M. on Friday, November 8, James Riordan sat in a chair, placed a revolver to his head, and pulled the trigger. He fell, still conscious, to the floor of his home in New York. Shortly before he died, he whispered to his valet, "What's going to happen to my girls?"

They both recall speaking to him on the telephone two days before, on the nineteenth birthday of his younger daughter, Elizabeth. She remembers assuring him that, "if things were tight," he should not concern himself about providing a present. Elizabeth thinks her father was preoccupied with the financial problems of his friends; he mentioned on the telephone in particular his fear that one of them might be driven to suicide.

Indeed, the very day he spoke to his daughters, many newspapers carried a gruesome report of a woman who had plunged forty stories to her death from the roof of the Equitable Building. Her death was a direct result of the Crash.

News of Riordan's suicide was kept from Elizabeth and her sister, Florence, until the next morning and from the rest of the world for twenty-four hours while urgent steps were taken to verify that his bank was solvent.

It was.

John J. Raskob, his closest friend, became the second man since the Crash to find himself suddenly at the helm of a bank. Like Mott, he did a workmanlike job in keeping Riordan's bank running smoothly.

Bishop John Dunn found himself in a dilemma. The Catholic Church insisted that suicides could not be buried in consecrated ground unless there were special extenuating circumstances. The bishop found them. After due inquiry he ruled that Riordan had taken his life while in a state of "mental aberration caused by his own losses in Wall Street and the losses of his friends for which he perhaps felt a moral responsibility."

Among the creditors of Riordan's estate were former New York Governor Al Smith, with whom Riordan had been the afternoon of his death, and Michael Meehan.

Riordan's suicide was one of many. But there was no "rush" of suicides. In the months following the Crash, actuarial figures show only a small increase in the average of the number of suicides expected. Nevertheless, that distraught speculators and others did take their lives because of the Crash there can be no doubt.

The market continued to slump downward until it reached its nadir —at least for the time being—on November 13.

Thereafter it began a sluggish climb.

Richard Whitney wrote his own requiem for the Crash. "A thing compounded of both wisdom and folly, of both heroism and fright, of stubborn persistence and impatient irresolution, of tragically shattered hopes and ambitions and of incongruous and unique episodes not without at times a certain humorous aspect."

He could have been describing his own behavior.

The aftereffects of the Crash were worldwide, and far-reaching.

In Augsburg, southern Germany, Willy Messerschmitt swiftly learned that the Eastern Aircraft Corporation of Pawtucket, Rhode Island, which he had planned to use as a springboard into U.S. aviation, was bankrupted by the Crash. And his hopes of finding the finance to help build a secret air force to prepare Germany for another war had, so far as America went, died with the bull market.

Messerschmitt found himself facing financial ruin as a result of an event on the other side of the world. But he was kept going by government subsidies, and the encouragement of Hitler who promised that when he came to power, there would be all the money necessary for the brilliant designer to make whatever aircraft the New Order needed.

The Crash caused Germany's growing economic crisis, which had begun about a year before, to quicken in pace—just as it improved and accelerated Hitler's chance of gaining office. The Reich was tied to the American economy more closely than almost any other country in Europe. Massive loans had come from Wall Street to help finance the German reparations payments and the beguiling postwar reconstruction projects that had, for a time, led some Germans to believe they were heading for Utopia. After the Crash aid stopped coming.

With Gustav Stresemann's death in early October at the age of fifty-one, there was no one of his stature left effectively to challenge and counter the demagogic statements of Hitler.

Unemployment grew. By the end of November, almost 2.5 million Germans were jobless. Money became so short banks offered 8¾ percent interest on three-month deposits. Corporations lucky enough to find a bank with money to lend paid up to 15 percent interest for short-term loans; private individuals could be charged 25 percent.

Even so, banks began to fail.

In this economic doldrum Hitler prospered. His attentive disciple, Albert Speer, does not remember the Führer ever dwelling unduly upon the Wall Street Crash. Hitler did not have to; the result was there for any German to see. The nation faced bankruptcy largely because of its dependency upon outside help. Hitler—stepping into a political, social, and economic vacuum—promised to make Germany strong and self-sufficient; he promised, in short, an external collapse would never again seriously affect the internal affairs of the Reich. His message was readily embraced. He grew stronger, more popular.

Indirectly, the Crash paved the way for World War II.

In France, and especially by its insular press, the Crash was initially, to all intents and purposes, ignored. The nation was gripped in the turmoil of its own political crisis. On October 22, President Aristide Briand's cabinet had fallen over a minor foreign policy matter. La Bourse reacted sharply; the tremors that shook the neo-Greek temple in Paris were as violent—although they lasted but briefly—as those that later swept the New York Stock Exchange.

Only as the full magnitude of the Wall Street collapse finally penetrated the French financial world did the press begin to react. Its attitude was smug and self-centered.

Having waspishly attacked Wall Street on the eve of the disaster, the media now maintained an almost amused attitude to "the scrabbling" going on across the Atlantic.

By early November, with a new government in power and La Bourse trading strongly, France was back to normal. Wall Street and its panic receded even further; in the later considered verdict of one of the nation's foremost economists, Alfred Sauvy, the Crash could be dismissed as "not having had the slightest effect."

France, in fact, benefited. La Bourse attracted floating capital which would otherwise have gone to Wall Street. Throughout 1929 French industrial output increased while that of the other major nations declined. Unemployment figures fell even further; France was the only country in the world able to claim such an achievement. Some 483 new companies, each with a capital of at least 1 million francs, were registered. As France entered the thirties, on the country's horizon there appeared not a cloud.

While the Italian press gave reasonably informed accounts of the Crash, the collapse had little immediate effect, one way or another, on the country. Mussolini, a journalist and not an economist, seemed unconcerned. Trading on the Milan Stock Exchange was already stagnating. Most Italians simply "took note of the Crash, and carried on as before."

The Amsterdam Stock Exchange, the financial hub of the Netherlands, was quickly affected. Already disturbed by the Hatry collapse— which had caused certain Dutch shares to tumble in September— following the news from Wall Street in late October one of Amsterdam's best-known brokerage houses went into bankruptcy; the firm had close trading links with New York. Other closures followed.

But few commentators foresaw the serious economic slump facing Holland in the near future.

The rock-solid financial fortress of Switzerland was hardly shaken by the Crash. The country had "a normal business year"; although "alarming signals had been received," New York was still "a far-away world, threatened by dark powers."

Members of Belgium's Palais de la Bourse, founded in Brussels by Napoleonic decree in 1801, recall the Crash in similar picturesque terms: "like the distant rumble of thunder on a summer's day, it was a portent of more troubled times to come. We were shaken like plums in a tree."

But there was no panic selling.

Black Tuesday marked the onset of a deepening epoch of economic severity for Belgium. Within weeks the secondary effects of the Crash were biting ever deeper into its balance of payments. By the end of the year shares had slumped dramatically in leading Belgian stocks.

In Lithuania the sizable American expatriate community, mostly retired businessmen and their wives, found themselves considerably poorer after the Crash. Many of them had been plunging on Wall Street to boost their pensions. A few were almost bankrupted.

Spain, on the other hand, displayed almost total indifference to the Crash. Nobody could see how it would affect the ambitious program of public works which gave the dictatorship of General Primo de Rivera the appearance of prosperity.

But the days of Spain's economic upsurge, like De Rivera's rule, were numbered.

In 1930 he fell from grace, driven from office, appropriately enough, by the case of *la Caoba*—the mahogany girl—an Andalusian courtesan convicted in a drug scandal.

De Rivera ordered her conviction be quashed. A constitutional crisis developed. He resigned.

Simultaneously—there was no direct connection—the peseta dropped as the world slump came to Spain.

Devoid of sound economic planning, the gross national product fell, and with it went any prospect of foreign investment. American finance, often hinted at, remained a myth. Economic collapse led to political instability; the seeds of revolution were sown; the path was cleared for bloody civil war—though even in their wildest *pronunciamientos,* the Left restrained from blaming the conflict on Wall Street.

The Crash immediately rocked the London Stock Exchange, still sensitive after the Hatry scandal. London had become a huge—if not the largest—overseas market for American shares; inevitably there was a swift sag in values, an increase in lending money rates and a clampdown on credit. The official position was described as "unsettled."

On November 2 *The Times* reassuringly reported "hysteria has now disappeared from Wall Street." The news lifted spirits in London.

So, briefly, did the forecast of American economist Stuart Chase: "We have probably three more years of prosperity ahead of us before we enter the cyclic tailspin which has occurred in the eleventh year of the four great previous periods of commercial prosperity."

Professor Irving Fisher could hardly have put it better.

By the end of the year business activity had begun its decline toward The Slump.

Unemployment continued to rise.

The socialist promises of recovery in the depressed industries were swept aside by the consequences—both direct and indirect—of the Wall Street Crash.

Britain's far-flung Empire responded predictably to the Crash.

In New Zealand it had almost no immediate impact; the collapse in share value of faraway companies had little bearing on the agricultural economy of the two distant islands.

In South Africa the mood was predominantly that "the overexuberant Yankees" had received their comeuppance.

Johannesburgers thought they were immune as they studied the sustained price levels on their own booming Exchange. As the largest producer of gold in the world, no nation felt more secure or safeguarded.

Later, South Africans realized that the evil day had only been postponed; when Great Britain and a host of other countries went off the Gold Standard in 1931, it had a shattering and lasting economic impact on the entire Union.

Australia, like the United States, had had its boom, helped by the discovery in 1923 of the rich Mount Isa silver-lead lode. Even so, Australian State Governments, as rashly as any Wall Street speculator, were borrowing up to the hilt against future hopes.

The Crash ended that dream. The country's economy depended on loans from overseas, and her ability to export. Both declined drastically in the latter part of 1929. The fall in the world price of wheat and wool was disastrous for Australia. The country proceeded to plunge toward its own peculiarly savage Depression.

In India, those members of the British Raj with investments in Wall Street salvaged what they could and switched to the now far safer and lucrative Shanghai market.

There, the Chinese Connection continued to flourish.

The market Crash in New York had an instant impact on the stock exchanges of Canada. The prices of Canadian shares traded on the New York Exchange collapsed along with the prices of American stocks traded in Toronto and Montreal. A well-known broker in Toronto described the domino effect between the exchanges of the two countries at the time: "When you raid a whore house, you take all of the inmates."

But the consequences did not seem catastrophic to Canada. Prime Minister Mackenzie King saw no need to change his policies; they would sustain him during the coming election. At the hustings the threat from proposed American tariff restrictions would loom larger than any sorry tale of decline from Wall Street.

Even economically sophisticated Canadians failed fully to realize how precarious their country's situation now was. Canada, like Australia, needed to export to survive. But the purchasing power of European countries, apart from France, was shrinking. And the Crash meant that the lucrative market on Canada's doorstep was being swiftly closed off.

As if as a signal of what was to come, a drought in the prairies had reduced the wheat crop in 1929 to half the yield of the previous year.

Canada's "hungry thirties" were just around the corner.

In America the weeks following the Crash saw a steady deterioration in steel production, freight loadings, automobile manufacturing.

The government tried to restore confidence. A cut in income tax was introduced. It gave a man supporting a family of two children on $4,000 a year a full $6 a year extra to spend.

The benefit was derisory, but in any case there were few men earning that sort of salary.

Public works budgets were increased by $175 million to be spread over ten years. It did little to restrain the growing army of workless.

President Hoover sent for Henry Ford and asked if he could help.

Ford promised he would raise wages from $6 to $7 a day. The gesture cost him about $20 million a year.

Most failed to realize that the automobile market was saturated; a million used vehicles crammed the nation's secondhand lots.

Bank deposits shrank. Gold flowed out of the country. Speakeasy prices fell; illicit champagne dropped from $100 to $75 a bottle. There were few takers.

By December, New York stores were reporting a 50 percent drop in the sale of radios. The stock itself languished on the market.

Charles Mitchell's National City reneged on its agreement with the Corn Exchange Bank, but hounded its own employees to maintain salary-deduction payments on National City stock bought in the boom.

The New York Stock Exchange publicly called for a daily report on short sales—an attempt to warn off those making money out of a declining market—and secretly set up a black list of welshers who had refused to honor verbal promises not to sell short. Trust, the essential lubricant of the market, like so many other things, was disappearing.

But the long-absent Exchange president, Edward Simmons, at last returned from his Honolulu honeymoon on December 2. He did not feel able to make any comment to the press on the Crash.

The Christmas season opened with the bankruptcy of the Stutz Motor Car Company; its Bearcat runabouts had been the flagships of the coonskin-coated escorts of flappers like Edith Stone.

For Edith and her parents, in common with millions of others, Christmas was a cheerless pause in the midst of a drastically reduced life-style.

Yet the New York Stock Exchange seemed determined to act as if nothing had changed.

William Crawford was told to prepare for the biggest and loudest New Year's Eve party ever, on Tuesday, December 31.

Before the opening that morning, he supervised the erection of a bandstand in the center of the trading floor.

At one-thirty the 369th Infantry Band—thirty Negro musicians—assembled on the stand and started to play ragtime and hits from the Roaring Twenties.

There were still ninety minutes to go before trading ended.

A new joke was doing the rounds.

Investor, to another who's looking distinctly unwell:

"What's the matter with you?"

"I've got diabetes at thirty-five."

"Don't worry. I've got Chrysler at 98."

Confetti started to fly. Solo dancing broke out.

A watchful reporter from the New York *Times*—the newspaper that had chronicled so well so many of the Exchange's idiosyncrasies during the boom—now recorded its last moments at the close of an unforgettable decade.

"Soon the brokers had forgotten trading for sport. Dances were interrupted to close trades which had to be made, but the main endeavor of those around each post was to originate some form of impromptu entertainment that would surpass that given at other posts.

"Noise-makers had been supplied to everyone on the floor and the galleries were crowded with visitors who had procured the few invitations available for the families and friends of the members of the Exchange.

"Even the staidest of the floor traders became frivolous under the influence of the band. Pinning tails on the traders became the popular sport of the afternoon. At one of the trading posts the newspaper record of the trading on the 16,000,000-share day was burned as an indication of desiring never to be reminded of it again.

"E. H. Simmons, president of the Exchange, personally sounded the gong at 3 o'clock to announce the end of trading for 1929. As the gong was still reverberating, the members broke into a pandemonium of noise, everything in the Exchange that had noisemaking possibilities being utilized. The din could be heard as far away as Broadway. This outburst in celebration of the passing of the year lasted over five minutes, members yelling until they were hoarse."

New Year forecasts were bright. The market would assuredly climb.

In Washington the Department of Labor predicted that 1930 would be a "splendid employment year."

The party was over, but the age of illusion was not quite dead.

CHAPTER TWENTY-EIGHT

AFTERMATH

In the early part of 1930, the residue of the Crash silted up large areas of America's economy. Bankruptcies increased. So did bank failures.

As the year wore on, extraordinary measures for economizing were introduced. Newspapers disconnected electric clocks to save current. Paper mills requested employees to use wood shavings for toilet purposes. Bethlehem Steel sacked 6,000 of its work force and ordered them evicted from company houses so that these could be torn down to save property taxes.

Conrad Hilton offered long-staying guests hotel rooms at rates below actual running cost, closed whole floors to save heat, removed guest telephones to save fifteen cents a month in rental charges, and ordered clerks to dole out stationery sheet by sheet.

The Plaza Hotel, where so many stock market deals had been discussed, could no longer afford to clean its marble, tapestries, bronze, and the panels in the Oak Room.

Everyone felt the Depression deepening. A few were able to lighten it.

John J. Raskob decided the erection of the Empire State Building would act as a symbol of hope in a dark and troubling time.

On St. Patrick's Day, March 17, 1930, in the full glare of publicity, the first steel piers were sunk into position to support the building's eventual 365,000 tons of steel, stone, concrete, and glass.

From then on, nobody was allowed to forget the project. For those who could stop off at the site—and as many as 5,000 did some days with double the number on Sundays—he arranged observation stands all around the area. It allowed the legions of "sidewalk superintendents" to watch the building go up.

For those too far away to pay a visit, he ordered that newsreel and still cameras record every day's headway. Regular bulletins were published in hundreds of newspapers; radio networks devoted prime time to reporting progress. The Empire State Building diverted a nation's attention from its agony—and in so doing made it more bearable.

People cheered when the 57,000-ton steel skeleton was topped out in twenty-three weeks—twelve days ahead of schedule—the first of many construction records to be broken. There were more cheers as the 3,000 workmen pushed the building up floor by floor at the rate of a story a day.

It took, in all, 7 million man-hours and the lives of fourteen workmen before the record-breaking building was finished, towering a proud 1,250 feet over New York.

On May 1, 1931, President Hoover officially opened it.

John J. Raskob told anyone who would listen that his Empire State Building was visible proof "the good times" would return.

They were a long time coming.

But that, seemingly, did not trouble Raskob. He was still a multimillionaire—although no one ever knew for sure exactly how rich he was.

He adamantly refused to discuss reports that shortly before the Crash he had quietly sold off thousands of shares bought on margin—making a handsome profit.

There were other reports, also unverified, that he had thousands more shares stashed away in his bank vault, ready for the day when the market regained its strength.

More credible was the third, less-widely reported story that the Crash had cost him several million dollars.

Even so, Raskob's remaining fortune would sustain him in comfort for the rest of his life. A devoted husband and father, churchgoer and contributor to charity, he became one of the elder statesmen of American finance. He died in October 1950, aged seventy-one. Right to the end he was as confident as ever in the strength of America.

In 1951 his estate sold off the Empire State Building for $34 million.

Billy Durant's dogged determination to stay in a dying bull market left him badly mauled by the Crash. A large portion of his savings went; some reports put his losses as high as $40 million. He was sued by several brokerage houses for unpaid commissions. He counterclaimed that he had been sold out without consultation.

In 1930, trying to get back into a market he thought showed a flicker of bullishness, Durant took 187,000 shares of General Motors stock from the trust fund he had set up for his wife. Catherine Durant parted with them without demur; she still had implicit faith in her husband's market ability. She never saw the stocks again; they disappeared into the great maw of Wall Street. This left Catherine Durant without any securities of her own, and resulted in her later impoverishment when she could have been one of the wealthiest women in America.

Her husband, his magical touch almost gone, plunged on. He sold their large holdings in the Whittier Corporation, a family-owned investment fund, to cover his further market losses.

He began to show signs of increasing eccentricity. He offered a "Durant Prize" of $25,000 for the best plan to keep Prohibition going, just before it was repealed in 1933. He supported the "World Peace League," urging the nation's children to donate their pennies to "buy a brick" to help build the league's headquarters.

He made a last, pathetic stab at a comeback in the auto industry, taking personal charge of the almost moribund Durant Motor Car Company. It was liquidated in 1933.

Three years later he filed for voluntary bankruptcy. He listed his debts at $914,231, his total assets as "clothing, valued at $250."

He opened a lunchroom in Asbury Park, New Jersey. For the next four years he lived an almost hand-to-mouth existence, only really happy when he could return to Flint. There, in 1940, the man who had created General Motors opened a bowling alley. Almost eighty, he talked bravely of chains of bowling alleys and all manner of other ambitious ventures. They never materialized. In October 1942—thirteen years to the month after the Crash that had changed his life—he suffered a severe stroke. He rallied, but his health, like his spirit, had finally broken. For five more years he lived on, confined to a wheelchair; his mind remained active but his speech was increasingly slurred. Catherine Durant sold off her jewelry, piece by piece, to pay living costs and medical bills. Charles Stewart Mott, Alfred Sloan, and Walter Chrysler, all still multimillionaires, slipped him handouts during their occasional visits to Durant at his modest New York apartment. There on March 18, 1947, at the age of eighty-five, William Crapo Durant died.

After considerable discussion, Flint—the bush town which he had turned into a booming city—finally put up a memorial to Durant; a chunk of marble, handsome enough, acting as a base for flagpoles. It is not easy to find—or to understand its symbolism.

On November 13, 1929—sixteen days after he had managed a brilliant coup at the height of the Crash—Jesse Livermore, showing no signs of losing his uncanny market sense, was reported as saying that many leading stocks had been driven down too far: "this situation should go no further."

It didn't. As if in response to Livermore's command, next day the market began its recovery.

Throughout 1930, he continued to make money out of the hesitant market.

Then in 1931, like Billy Durant, Livermore plunged heavily—and lost. He plunged again—and lost even more. By the end of the year half his fortune was gone. Most of the remainder went in a series of ill-conceived, poorly researched, and largely unnecessary market gambles in 1932. There was no financial need for Livermore to speculate so rashly. But, in two years, he squandered an estimated $30 million.

The most likely explanation is that Livermore's sensitive judgment was knocked off balance when he discovered that his wife, Dorothy—by then a mumbling alcoholic—was having an affair with a Prohibition agent. In September 1932 the Livermores were divorced in Reno, Nevada.

In March 1933, aged fifty-eight, still eerily handsome, youthful, and trim, Livermore married for the third time. His bride was Harriet Metz Noble, a thirty-eight-year-old concert pianist—a regal lady far removed from the slaggy showgirls who had been his constant companions in the past.

Livermore asked Harriet for a loan of $136,000 in securities to be used as collateral. They were not returned.

He had to sell his estate and his yellow Rolls-Royce. His market losses grew. His creditors became more demanding. Old enemies threatened to call in the underworld to make Livermore pay up.

Finally, pursued by mobsters, process servers, summonses, and court officers, Livermore fled, hiding out in a dingy hotel he had used as a "love nest" before the Crash. There, he drank himself into a stupor, a round-the-clock binge which aged him overnight.

He returned to face his creditors, appealing for time, promising them and himself he would make "a killing" and wipe out his debts.

The memory of his old magic brought him a respite. But Livermore—like so many of the pre-Crash operators—found irreversible changes were taking place in Wall Street.

His triumphs had been based on the old Roman maxim—*Caveat emptor,* Buyer beware.

But in May 1933 the Securities Act effectively made it mandatory, in all stock dealings, for the seller to beware.

The new, tough legislation—and there was more to come—which restricted the short-selling practices Livermore had for so long enjoyed made it almost impossible for him to make a comeback.

He closed down his complex; many of the staff were quickly snapped up by Wall Street brokerage firms.

Throughout the Depression, Livermore was entangled in one lawsuit after another, resulting from disputed market deals and loans.

Former associates, his lawyers, even old friends, all bled him dry.

Finally, on March 4, 1934, he filed for bankruptcy. His debts amounted to $2,259,212. His assets, many questionable, even so amounted to a mere $184,000.

From time to time he returned to his book. Eventually, after innumerable rewrites, it was published in March 1940. He called it *How to Trade in Stocks*. It was a flop.

One fall afternoon eight months later, Livermore went to the men's bar in the Sherry-Netherland Hotel. He downed two stiff martinis in ten minutes, then dug into his vest pocket and fished out the same gold pencil that had fascinated the *Times* reporter shortly before the Crash. From another pocket he took a notebook. He began to tot up his debts. They came to $365,000.

Livermore began to write, repeating himself time and again. In bold capitals he penned a verdict: MY LIFE HAS BEEN A FAILURE. MY LIFE HAS BEEN A FAILURE. MY LIFE . . .

He paused and looked in the bar mirror. He was, as always, immaculately attired—a gray flannel suit, navy foulard tied in a fashionable dimple knot.

He got off his barstool and walked to the men's room. There he drew a pistol, held it to his forehead, and pulled the trigger, dying instantly at the age of sixty-three on Thursday, November 28.

Jack Morgan duly returned to New York from the grouse moors of Scotland and following tea at Buckingham Palace with the royal family. He resumed running the firm. Its losses during and after the Crash were said to have been between 20 and 60 million dollars. Nobody really knew—and Morgan was not telling.

But there was a clue: On November 31, 1929, the net worth of the partnership was put at $118 million; three years later it had shrunk to $53 million.

Yet Morgan sincerely believed that in spite of the Crash, nothing fundamental had changed; that the firm would continue, unhampered and unchecked, to go about its business of making money just as before.

He apparently saw no reason why, at the time the first bread lines were forming, he should not launch the largest private yacht in the world costing all of $2.5 million. Nor did he see why his vast estate on Long Island should be valued as high as $1,121,000 for the purpose of taxation. And he saw nothing improper—when it was pointed out to him in public—in the fact that he himself had not personally paid any income tax at all for the years 1930, 1931, or 1932; such details were beneath him. If he had paid no tax, he said, then much as he regretted that, it must have been because his losses were greater than his income.

Behind the scenes, sensing the mounting pressure in Washington againt all big bankers, Jack Morgan fought a vigorous, refined, always polite and well-argued case to maintain the status quo.

He failed.

Finally, along with other giants of Wall Street, he was ordered to appear before the Senate Banking and Currency Committee in 1933.

On June 1, surrounded by his partners, lawyers, and their assistants, Jack Morgan, a shy, avuncular, sixty-two-year-old, sat in a leather-upholstered armchair in the Senate Caucus Room, waiting to testify.

He felt uncomfortable in the presence of the reporters, photographers, and spectators milling around him. He paid no attention to a man pushing his way through the crowd, one arm trailing oddly behind him.

The stranger reached Morgan, swung his arm forward, and promptly plopped a midget girl into the lap of the most distinguished banker in the world.

The man was a press agent for the Ringling Bros. and Barnum & Bailey Circus. The midget was a member of the circus troupe.

Her name was Lya Graf, a twenty-seven-inch-high, shapely, German-born brunet, with sparkling eyes and the face and charm of a Black Forest peasant. She looked like a doll in her flounced blue satin dress and red straw hat.

Jack Morgan's entourage were stunned. Richard Whitney thought to pluck her from the Morgan lap. Jack stopped him. The photographers were delighted. A cascade of bulbs exploded, catching the twinkle in Jack's eye as his face relaxed and the great businessman became the genial grandfather.

The conversation between banker and midget owed more to *Alice in Wonderland* than Wall Street.

"I have a grandson bigger than you."

"But I'm older."

"How old are you?"

"Twenty."

"You certainly don't look it."

The photographers asked Miss Graf to take off her hat.

Morgan intervened. "Don't take it off; it's pretty."

Then he gently lifted Miss Graf from his lap and set her on the floor.

Given the almost unbearable situation Morgan had been placed in, he carried it off well.

But the picture of the financial giant and the circus midget became an overnight classic around the world, treated by many as another version of Beauty and the Beast.

Yet, in some ways, Morgan and even Wall Street, benefited from the photograph. It "humanized" them.

Miss Graf became a celebrity—and hated it. In 1935, hounded by fame, she returned to her native Germany. She did not realize until too late that as a Jewish midget she was doubly blighted. The Nazis shipped her to Auschwitz as a "useless person."

Soon after the Senate investigation, Jack Morgan retired from active life. Thomas Lamont became the effective head of the firm.

But Wall Street was no longer the place it had been: In the repercussions of the Crash, the government moved in; it became a tightly regulated enclave. The power of the House of Morgan, while still great, was drained in a series of bills and regulations; its very function was changed when it was forbidden any longer to be involved in underwriting the issue of securities.

In February 1943 Jack Morgan suffered successive strokes at his Florida retirement home. He died on March 12, aged seventy-five.

Thomas Lamont died five years later.

All told, the Crash cost Richard Whitney around $2 million in lost security values. That was about balanced by the value of the free publicity he received. He was the tabloids' hero who had "saved" Steel on October 24. Whether that was true or not—and it was not—the hour needed a hero; Whitney was the best available.

In the aftermath he played the part well. He showed leadership—some recall it as bullying—on the floor; the press was filled with his demulcent declamations that all was well.

The return of the aging Simmons from honeymoon did nothing to diminish Whitney's status. In April 1930 he was elected President of the New York Stock Exchange.

Publicly, he cast himself in the role of Wall Street's ambassador to the world. One of his favorite lectures was titled: "Business Honesty." He read it against the background of a severely falling market and rising unemployment; by the end of 1931, the *Times* averages were more than 50 percent below their 1929 low; unemployment was close to 10 million.

Privately, Whitney was sinking in his own financial quicksands. To survive, he had increasingly to dispense with his last remnants of business honesty.

By June 30, 1931, the total worth of his firm—which yearly handled millions of dollars—was $36,000.

The House of Morgan—where his brother, George, was seen as the most likely heir apparent one day to succeed Thomas Lamont—arranged for $500,000 to be loaned to its errant broker. Whitney took the money on a ninety-day unsecured loan at 5 percent.

But he was so enmeshed in his pie-in-the-sky stocks that the money was squandered away. In all, he had squandered $1.5 million on senseless speculations.

Once more George covered for him.

When the Senate hearings were convened in April 1932, Whitney was the first to sit in the witness chair. Fortunately for him, he was called upon to explain the practices of the Stock Exchange, not his own.

He gave a brilliantly sustained display of arrogance, indifference, disdain; he was patronizing, dismissive, rude, at times angry and always aloof.

Many in Wall Street felt he had seen off its enemies. He returned triumphantly to the financial district.

The ensuing President Roosevelt-approved restrictions, framed in the 1933 Securities Bill, were an even greater shock to those who believed most fervently that Richard, their lion-hearted White Knight, had won the day in Washington.

By now Whitney was submerging fast in a series of increasingly juvenile but nevertheless dishonest moves. They were not just criminal; they were stupid. Appalling financial judgment, rather than basic crookedness, drove him on.

He began to do what the hapless Flint embezzlers had done—take the funds and securities of his customers and use them for his own speculations. And lose them.

He mortgaged everything he owned not already pledged—his estate and racehorses fetched close to half a million dollars—to pay off his mounting debts.

It was not enough.

He plunged ever deeper into the market. And lost even more money.

He was now beyond redemption, rushing from one potential source to another for money. One after another the doors were slammed in his face. Wall Street's memory was long; there were many who had waited for, and savored, this moment of revenge on a man who had trampled on them for so many years.

By early 1938 Richard Whitney had exhausted every avenue for raising money.

Only then did he admit to a decade of cheese-paring crookedness that had been allowed to grow—and by their silence was condoned by his peers—into something approaching grand larceny.

Whitney's trial was a New York sensation.

At nine o'clock on the morning of April 11, 1938, he left 115 East Seventy-third Street, his magnificent Manhattan home. As always he was escorted to the door by his liveried butler. The servant bowed ceremoniously low.

Two hours later, the ruined former president of the New York Stock Exchange was roughly motioned into a precinct cell, pending his transfer to Sing Sing to serve a five-to-ten-year sentence.

In Sing Sing he had his own cell and was unfailingly called "Mr. Whitney" by both staff and inmates.

He was paroled in 1941.

He never returned to business life; some said he was supported in his early retirement by his brother George's munificence.

Richard's devoted wife, Gertrude, remained loyally with him. In 1968, at the age of eighty, her husband was still able to charm the ladies. One described him on his birthday as "a twinkly old man."

It was a generous epitaph for a man who was born with so much—and achieved so little.

In October 1929—before, during, and after the Crash—shares in National City dropped in three weeks from $577 to $270. There were rumors Charles Mitchell would resign.

He was still chairman, still walking to work every morning, when, on March 21, 1933—with shares in the bank slumped to around $20—he was arrested for income tax evasions.

Eighteen days previously, President Roosevelt in his inauguration address had promised to drive the money changers out of the temple. Mitchell was one of the first to be driven.

His trial in May and June, although a sensation, was necessarily subservient to the even greater sensations simultaneously unfolding at the Senate hearings.

Mitchell put up a spirited defense. It did not stop the press from excoriating him. Novelist Edmund Wilson, in particular, in a savage piece of journalism, flayed "Sunshine Charley" in the June issue of *The New Republic*.

The jury acquitted Mitchell on all counts; the unusual financial intercourse indulged in between him and his wife, if unethical, was apparently not illegal.

Mitchell, who had resigned from the bank, returned to Wall Street as head of Blyth and Company.

The government tried again, this time winning judgment of $1.1 million. A long legal wrangle followed. Mitchell lost his final appeal to the

Supreme Court. He made an undisclosed settlement with the government on December 27, 1938.

He faded from public life, living comfortably from his still vast private fortune.

There were many who said that, for all his faults, Wall Street was the poorer by his absence.

Michael Meehan's Irish spunkiness was enhanced further at the height of the Crash when he was reported to have said to a colleague: "Well, I understand I'm broke. Guess we'd better give all the boys in the office a two weeks' bonus to prove it."

The story was true, and perfectly in keeping with the character of the most flamboyant and famous broker in Wall Street.

The Crash cost him heavily. How much exactly is uncertain. His son, William, will only go so far as to say it was "in the tens of millions."

Others suggest Meehan's losses ran out at over $40 million, but that he nevertheless had some $20 million of his fortune intact.

By 1932 Radio had descended to $2.50 a share, a far cry from those days in March 1929 when the Radio pool pushed the price of the stock to $109 before pulling the plug.

Even so, in late 1935, on William's twenty-first birthday, Michael Meehan still showed a trace of his old style. He gave his son a seat on the Exchange which cost $130,000.

Before then, like so many others, Meehan found it hard to adapt, to understand that times were a-changing, that what had been entirely legal in 1929 was no longer so. He was accused of taking part in a pool to raise the price of a stock long after the Securities Exchange Act had outlawed the practice. The SEC began to investigate his alleged manipulations in Bellanca Aircraft.

Meehan protested his innocence. Then, in the midst of the hearings, he vanished.

In November 1936 he was discovered in Bloomingdale, the exclusive private hospital for the disturbed rich near New York.

It was said visitors were surprised to find him so sane. One report spoke of him "strutting the grounds, puffing on cigars, and shouting greetings with all his old cockiness and elan."

But *Time* magazine reported in its December 7, 1936, issue: "The SEC challenge had changed him into a tense, excitable, nervous case. He drank frequently and had a tendency towards rambling talk. He was *not* under restraint in the sanatorium."

When Meehan left Bloomingdale in June 1937 the SEC pounced.

That August he faced accusations of violation of the Securities Exchange Act in the Bellanca pool. He was ordered to be expelled from all of America's stock exchanges.

His sons would always believe that their father had been harshly, even wrongly treated. There are many today who would agree with them.

Michael Meehan died on February 2, 1948 at the age of fifty-six.

His firm remains an honorable, highly respected and honest brokerage concern led by its extremely hard-working head, William Meehan.

A. P. Giannini's Transamerica was hurt badly by the Crash. Elisha Walker sold off its New York operations to Charles Mitchell's bank for cash and a 9 percent shareholding in National City.

Giannini was furious over the action of his handpicked successor.

The clash that had been long in the making erupted. Walker chose to challenge Giannini for control of Transamerica.

A classic, bitter battle developed.

Walker mobilized the support of the elite of the banking world.

Giannini turned to the "little fellahs," the farmers, bakers, waiters, produce men; the grass-roots backbone of his banking empire.

These small holders tipped the proxy fight his way.

Walker and his supporters were out.

During the Depression Giannini got rid of his Rolls-Royce with its fire alarm. He kept on chauffeur Joe Garcia to drive an American car; in late 1978 Garcia was running a local bartenders' union, a sprightly old man with "the best memories any guy could want of the most wonderful boss in the world."

Claire married. Like her brothers, she continued to take an active part in the bank. In 1978 she was still going to the office most days, a strikingly strong-faced old lady of seventy-five, fiercely proud of her father—and not always happy with the way his ideas have been transmuted.

Soon after his proxy battle with Walker, Giannini renamed Transamerica, the Bank of America. It became the biggest bank in the world.

Giannini died, still dreaming of nationwide branch banking, at the age of eighty in 1949. He left $489,278. In practical terms he was worth less than he had been when he opened the Bank of Italy, shortly before the San Francisco earthquake of 1906—the tremor that launched him on his dazzling career.

Joseph Kennedy survived the Crash with his wealth intact, his family secure, his future bright. From 1930 onward in a series of bold, resourceful, and often merciless deals, he considerably increased his fortune picking up Depression-forced bargains.

At first he made money in the market, mainly by short selling, taking his profit as prices fell. The total Kennedy picked up in this way is variously estimated between $1 million and $15 million. He collected again when Prohibition ended, having cleverly filled warehouses with imported booze in preparation for the day the country went wet. He went on to make most out of real estate. His close friend and confidant, property broker John J. Reynolds, once indiscreetly admitted that Kennedy had made $100 million from realty.

It is one of the few times a tag was put on any part of Joe Kennedy's wealth.

In July 1934 he was appointed the first chairman of the newly formed SEC by Roosevelt. Many saw it as an inspired move, to get one of Wall Street's most ruthless speculators to police it; others, among them influential Streeters, were soon furious.

Some said Kennedy launched himself into the task with such enthusiasm because the memory of the public slighting he had received from Jack Morgan early in 1929 was still fresh in his mind.

Most dispassionate observers felt he did a good job at the SEC, stopping stock manipulation and enforcing the new laws about the issuing of securities. His role at the SEC helped pave the way for a wider political career, one that eventually saw a Kennedy ensconced in the White House.

On November 18, 1969, knowing he had founded a political dynasty, Joe Kennedy died peacefully at his home in Hyannis Port. He was eighty-one.

The Crash had no immediate effect on Henry Ford's fortunes; he saw it as no more than Wall Street deserved.

He did not think the Depression would last very long; he insisted "today is better than yesterday."

His company survived the bleak years of the 1930s, but it was a close thing. Detroit was a ghost of its former self. Across the nation cars stood idle because their owners could not afford to run them.

The price of Texas oil dropped to four cents a barrel.

Industrial unrest swept the Rouge. Harry Bennett led the fight against the unions. There was bloodshed and death.

World War II came—and Ford's fortunes revived.

By then Henry Ford was a back-seat driver; Edsel was at the wheel. Ford looked back down the long tunnel of memory, living in a world of his own, making plans for the next.

At times he liked to strum a Jew's harp.

On April 7, 1947, he died of a brain hemorrhage. He was eighty-four years old—a long way short of the life-span he had promised himself.

Fifty years after the Crash, Pat Bologna, a sixty-nine-year-old shoe-shine boy, and Michael Levine, an eighty-seven-year-old messenger boss, were still going strong, still at work in Wall Street.

Inevitably, when the shock of the Crash subsided, when its af-tereffects had been dissipated and then merged into the debilitating Depression, two questions remained.

Why had it happened?

Could it occur again?

The questions provided fuel for market analysts, economists, histo-rians, investors, speculators, and almost any two people who met to dis-cuss the merits of a stock.

There was a great deal of talk about the market being the ultimate gambler's den; about it being the world's first example of financial mass-psychology manipulation in action; about it being the product of a unique era, the Roaring Twenties.

Seeking a historical explanation, some intellectuals traced the origin of the Crash back as far as World War I and to the merry-go-round of money that resulted from the war reparations imposed on a defeated Germany. Many saw the Boom which had to precede the Crash as an integral part of the times; church leaders later pointed to the fact that the arrival of the bull market coincided with a national relaxing in morals, a reduction in religious worship, the emergence of the Ku Klux Klan, and much else.

Such post-mortems were a very reassuring and necessary salve to a still basically puritanical national conscience. On reflection, there were millions of ordinary men and women who decided the "stock market craze" had resulted from breaking faith with the great Puritan tradition that an honest day's pay came only from an honest day's work. They came to the comforting conclusion the Crash was the inevitable product of a craze spawned by the belief that money no longer had actually to be earned; that the stock market, for a brief period of time, had acted as a substitute for the normal method of acquiring wealth.

Later, the Federal Reserve Board came to be criticized from all quar-ters. It was, and is, said to have set the Boom straight on course in mid-1927 when it reduced interest rates and made money easier—some say as a result of British persuasion; almost everyone agrees that the board muffed the last opportunity to avert the coming Crash when, in March 1929, it "warned" and "appealed" for a cutback in the supply of money for speculation but did nothing to reinforce its words with strong action. So, it is said, uncontrolled, the "orgy" was allowed to go on getting worse.

Some pundits take swipes at individuals as the real bogeymen in the story: Mitchell, for thumbing his nose at the Federal Reserve in March 1929 by making more money available when the board had just appealed for it to be reduced; Churchill, who returned Great Britain to the gold standard in 1925 and to an exchange rate which, by overvaluing the pound, unrolled a fiscal line leading directly to the Crash; President Coolidge, President Hoover, Thomas Lamont, Clarence Hatry, Professor Fisher . . . man's greed.

Pool operations, manipulating stock prices, bucket shops, pyramiding, leverage, shoddy shares, selling short . . . the media.

An article in *The Wall Street Journal* in late 1977 claimed it was possible to argue convincingly that the market at its peak in 1929 "was exactly where it should have been, and that the Crash resulted from some stupendous political error"; the "error" being the Smoot-Hawley Tariff Act of 1930, the consequences of which, the writer stated, a sensitive market anticipated before the bill became law.

In truth, it is impossible to single out any one person or event as the sole cause of the Crash.

Could it—will it—occur again?

It cannot happen again for the same reasons: Too many of Wall Street's barn doors were closed by the mass of legislation introduced as a direct result of the Crash. But only a fool would say that other circumstances could not contrive to make another crash occur.

Others go further.

Professor Kenneth Galbraith, secure in the position of preeminent financial Cassandra, believes that many of the lessons, having been digested, are in danger of being forgotten; or that, even if never forgotten, man may be incapable of taking corrective action in the present to offset financial disaster in the future.

Most Wall Streeters dismiss talk of another great crash as mischievous speculation. They have faith in America, and in an old Street dictum about the market: It is like a dog's tail; its wagging is controlled by the economic-cum-political body of the nation it is joined to—but it does not cause the body to wag.

There are others to be found in the Street, respected elder statesmen, who say quite definitely that another crash *is* coming. And there are still others who emphatically state that the Stock Exchange itself is now, as it was in 1929, only a glorified switchboard, "obsolete, unnecessary, should be done away with."

And, of course, there are those, equally eminent, who believe the market is on the eve of the "biggest and strongest economic boom in history."

There is only one thing to worry about in those words. They have been used before. On the eve of the day when the bubble burst.

APPENDIXES

SOURCES

In a sense the Crash was the most recorded financial event in history. As it touched millions, not only in America but around the world, a great many felt the need, for one reason or another, to record their participation.

For the news media it produced an endless source of copy. But, as with so many cataclysmic events, a large part of the story proved impossible to evaluate properly under the pressure of deadlines. Consequently, much of the contemporary coverage was confused and contradictory. Statements were taken at face value, and often couched in the somewhat flowery doublespeak of the era. Recondite phrases, allusions, and euphemisms—the language of the insider—buried the truth from immediate view.

Now that time has passed, allowing those directly involved no longer to feel the heat of the headlines, it has been possible at least to move through the tangle of wheeling-dealing which, in the end, was responsible for the Crash.

Given the essential time, secrets that had been carefully buried, surfaced, often of their own volition; people talked about the peccadilloes surrounding the Crash.

For the first time the now-aged Flint embezzlers revealed how and why they had engineered what was then, and still remains, one of the largest bank frauds in history; as Frank Montague told us, "I'm close to dying and it's time to put the record straight." The recall of men like Montague enabled us to go beyond the faded news clips, to come to know a group of gamy characters which a historian couldn't and a novelist probably wouldn't invent.

Again, the private papers made available to us by Claire Giannini and the Bank of America—letters, interbank memos, contracts, telegrams, receipts, audit reports—coupled with her own detailed recollections enabled us to understand her father's attitude far more clearly than all the millions of words published about him.

The Ford archives were richly revealing on the remarkable Henry. Though, here again, the archival material was by no means the only source material we used. Ford employees, past and present, provided minute recollections carefully stored over half a century, ready to be tapped for the asking.

Some asked to remain anonymous, and have remained so; others did not seek anonymity, but will nevertheless be protected by it.

The event itself spread across the world. It would have been impossible for us, indeed for anyone, to have conducted the research on such a global scale without support.

As before we owe a considerable debt to the worldwide facilities of the *Reader's Digest*. Under the guidance of Walter Hunt and Margaret Furniss, *Digest* editors and researchers in many countries did an invaluable job in preparing the groundwork for us.

They served as an adjunct to our own research efforts, spread across the United States, Canada, Europe, and the British Isles.

In Wall Street itself, we might have been lost without the gentle guidance of Bill Close, to whom we owe a large debt of gratitude; he and, indeed, all others who cooperated with us should not, however, be thought to have endorsed, or directly influenced in any way, our portrayal of events.

We should also like to acknowledge the generous help of Michael Pearson, who allowed us access to his notes made for an unfinished authorized biography of Clarence Hatry.

In all we amassed some 14.5 million words of published and unpublished material. The crucial portion, again as before, came from the meetings and original interviews we conducted with key eyewitnesses. Over the research period a total of 438 persons were contacted around the world. Subsequently a number—ranging from Albert Speer to Pat Bologna—were interviewed at length.

Some interviews, with just one person, were spread over a period of weeks, allowing checks and double checks to be made on what was said.

In the chapter notes that follow, documents and reports that to the best of our knowledge have until now remained unpublished are designated as such. Contemporary private papers have always proven a rich source of material for us. We were not disappointed this time. A wealth of invaluable, and often unsuspected, information about the period has come from personal diaries, aide-mémoire, letters, manuscripts, billets-doux. Even the messages on Christmas and birthday cards provided revealing insights which helped us to set an eyewitness in time, context, and character.

Such documents provided a useful aid in prompting memory. So, too, did the large number of published books, newspaper and magazine accounts. Rereading them, a number of witnesses found it easy to return to that time when they and the world were younger than it can ever be again.

Our main sources are listed, chapter by chapter, as follows:

AI	=	Authors' interviews
OI	=	Other interviews
B	=	Books
C	=	Correspondence
D	=	Documents and reports
UD	=	Unpublished documents and reports
M	=	Magazines, periodicals, and booklets
PP	=	Private papers
T	=	Transcripts

A list of all books and magazines consulted will be found in the Bibliography; the list of interviewees is in the Special Thanks section.

Chapter One

AI: Bologna, Fisher (W), Frank, Garcia, Giannini, Hatry, Kahn, Levy, Lewis, MacVeagh (C), Mann, Meehan, Schnell.

B: *The Lawless Decade* (Sann); *The House of Morgan* (Hoyt); *Once in Golconda* (Brooks); *Biography of a Bank* (James); *The Long Thirst* (Coffey); *Building the Bank of America* (Rink); *Ardent Spirits* (Kobler); *The World Almanac* (Lyman, ed.); *More Essays of Today* (Pritchard, ed.); *The Bootleggers* (Allsop); *The Prohibition Mania* (Darrow).

D: Menus and Recipes, various, Stock Exchange Luncheon Club (1929–30); Report on Prohibition Violations (NYPD, 1929); Stock Exchange Practices (1934).

UD: Bank of America Boxes (1921–28).

M: *Saturday Evening Post* (December 28, 1928; July 4, 1929; July 24, 1930) *World's Work* (April 1929; July 1930; April 1932); *Woman's Home Companion* (July 1930); *Fortune* (March 1930); *New Republic* (July 1930); *American Heritage* (March 1930).

N: New York *Times* (December 1, 1928–January 1, 1929).

PP: Levy, Giannini.

Chapter Two

AI: Hatry.

OI: Ausenda, Boucher, Chelma, Kostolany, Pagani, Rutschmann, Speer, Warren.

B: *Slump and Recovery* (Hodson); *Winston S. Churchill*, Vol. 5 (Gilbert); *The General Strike* (Renshaw); *Before the Deluge* (Friedrich); *Always the Unexpected* (Lochner); *Mussolini* (Hibbert); *The Manipulators* (Sobel); *Inside the Third Reich* (Speer); *The Spanish Civil War* (Thomas); *Man of the World* (Lewis); *Adolf Hitler* (Toland); *Hitler* (Fest); *The Millionaire Mentality* (Pearson); *Nascita Dello Stato Imprenditore in Italia* (Cianci); *Light out of the Darkness* (Hatry); *Europe of the Dictators* (Wiskemann); *Churchill in America* (Pilpel); *Stationen Deutscher Bankgeschichte* (Wagner); *Geld-Banken-Borsen* (Webber); *Gustav Stresemann* (Stresemann); *La Bataille Économique* (Hersent).

C: Jurgens, Ostroff, Wisner.

N: *Daily Mail* (January 1–31, 1929); *Daily Herald* (January 1–31, 1929); *Sunday Telegraph* (August 1, 8, 1965); *British Gazette* (May 1926).

PP: Hatry.

Chapter Three

AI: Barry, Brown, Fisher (R), Love, Mott (H), Mott (R), Overly, Schlaff, Stewart.

B: *The Legend of Henry Ford* (Sward); *The Public Image of Henry Ford* (Lewis); *My Years with General Motors* (Sloan); *Mystery Men of Wall Street* (Sparling); *Billy Durant* (Gustin) *The Plungers and the Peacocks* (Thomas); *Foundations for Living* (Young and Quinn); *We Never Called Him Henry* (Bennett); *The Ford Dynasty* (Brough); *The Turning Wheel* (Pond); *The Age of the Moguls* (Holbrook); *The Lawless Decade* (Sann); *The Secret Life of Henry Ford* (Dahlinger).

M: *Collier's* (January 19, 1929); Detroit *Saturday Night* (various, 1929)

N: New York *Times* (January 1–31, December 31, 1929); New York *Post* (December 13, 1967); Dearborn *Independent* (all issues).

Chapter Four

AI: Garcia, Giannini, Hatry, Hutton-Miller, Levine, Lewis, Mac-Veagh (C).

OI: Chelma.

B: *Wall Street* (Mayer); *A. P. Giannini* (Dana); *Biography of a Bank* (James); *Building the Bank of America* (Rink); *Panic in Wall Street* (Sobel); *The Founding Father* (Whalen); *Once in Golconda* (Brooks); *Times to Remember* (Kennedy); *The Plungers and the Peacocks* (Thomas); *Mystery Men of Wall Street* (Sparling); *A Monetary History of the United States* (Friedman and Schwartz); *The Great Crash* (Galbraith); *Jesse Livermore* (Sarnoff); *Lord Norman* (Clay); *A History of Economic Change* and *Modern Banking* (Sayers); *Reminiscences of a Stock Operator* (Lefevre).

C: O'Brian.

D: Federal Reserve Bank of New York *Monthly Review* (various); Federal Reserve Board *Monthly Bulletin* (various).

UD: Bank of America (Boxes January–March 1929).

M: *Fortune* (September 1937; January 1963).

N: New York *Post* (December 14, 1967).

PP: Giannini, Collins (Chas W), Hutton-Miller.

Chapter Five

AI: Druyan.

B: *The Sky Is Falling* (Weingarten); *Postscript to Yesterday* (Morris); *The Great Crash* (Galbraith); *The Shocking History of Advertising*

(Turner); *Middletown* (Lynd); *We're in the Money* (Bergman); *The Life of an American Workman* (Chrysler).

D: Empire State Building, Inc. (various).

M: *Woman's Home Companion* (January 1930); *Collier's* (August 11, 1928); *Saturday Evening Post* (November 17, 1928; February 2, 1929; March 23, 1929; March 8, 1930); *Literary Digest* (November 17, 1928); *North American Review* (April 1929); *Ladies' Home Journal* (August 1929); *Delineator* (May 1929); *American Magazine* (July 1929).

N: *Daily News* (February 1–28, 1929); *Poor's Weekly Business and Investment Letter* (February 1929); *Commercial and Financial Chronicle* (February 1929); New York *Times* (December 31, 1929).

Chapter Six

AI: Baron, Beagle, Brown, De Camp, Dowdy, Love, Montague (F), Montague (L), Mott (H), Mott (R), Pollock, Stewart, Transue, Vargo (J), Vargo (S), Zimmermann.

OI: Bonbright, Carey, Fullerton, Gary, Largent, Peckham, Travers.

B: *The Great Crash* (Galbraith); *The Federal Reserve System* (Warburg); *Once in Golconda* (Brooks); *The Lords of Creation* (Allen); *Billy Durant* (Gustin); *Halfway to Yesterday and Well Do I Remember* (Lethbridge); *Turning Wheel* (Pond).

M: *New Republic* (January 28, 1933); Flint *Saturday Night* (various, 1929).

N: Flint *Journal* (various, 1929); Detroit *Times* (various, 1929).

PP: Dort (family letters), Montague, Beagle.

Chapter Seven

AI: Barry, Dowdy, Fisher (F), Lowell, MacVeagh (A), MacVeagh (C), Mott (H), Mott (R), Schlaff, Vargo (J), Vargo (S), Zawacki, Zimmermann, Zlatec.

OI: Howard, Largent, Love, Stewart, Travers.

B: *The Ford Dynasty* (Brough); *My Years with General Motors* (Sloan); *High and Low Financiers* (Washburn and De Long); *The Legend of Henry Ford* (Sward); *The Public Image of Henry Ford* (Lewis); *The Secret Life of Henry Ford* (Dahlinger); *Foundation for Living* (Mott); *The Big Change* (Allen); *Ford—Expansion and Challenge* (Nevins and Hill); *My Forty Years with Ford* (Sorensen); *We Never Called Him Henry* (Bennett).

M: *Old Farmer's Almanac* (various, 1928–29).

N: *British Gazette* (May 1926).

PP: MacVeagh, Vargo.

Chapter Eight

AI: Fisher (W), Flynn, Frank, Garcia, Hutton-Miller, Meehan, Mills, Mott (H), Mott (R), Schnell.

OI: Baker, Coolard, Davis, Fullerton, Howard (J), Servis, Stewart.

B: *A. P. Giannini* (Rink); *Biography of a Bank* (James); *Giant in the West* (Dana); *Only Yesterday* and *The Great Change* (Allen); *The Great Crash* (Galbraith); *Jesse Livermore* (Sarnoff); *Times to Remember* (Kennedy); *The Hoover Memoirs*, Vol. 3 (Hoover); *The Bootleggers* (Allsop); *The World Almanac* (Lyman, ed.); *The Growth of the U.S.A.* (Nye and Morpugo); *The American Presidents* (Whitney); *The Bouviers* (Davis); *The Plungers and the Peacocks* (Thomas); *The History of the United States* (Friedman and Schwartz); *The Lawless Decade* (Sann); *Mystery Men of Wall Street* (Sparling); *The Perils of Prosperity* (Leuchtenburg); *The Weeds of Wall Street* (Wickwire); *Babbitt* (Lewis); *Billy Durant* (Gustin); *The Sky Is Falling* (Weingarten); *Life of an American Workman* (Chrysler).

D: Stock Exchange Practices (1934).

UD: Bank of America (Boxes March–May 1929).

M: *Army Training Manual* (1928); *Harper's Magazine* (August 1930); *Collier's* (May 2, 1952); *Time* (October 30, 1964); *American Mercury* (October 1930); *North American Review* (March 1929); *Saturday Evening Post* (March 27, 1926); *American Magazine* (August 1929).

N: Detroit *Free Press* (March 1, 2, 1929); *Wall Street Journal* (March 9, 11, 12, 22, 1929); *Daily News* (March 11, 1929); New York *Times* (December 31, 1929).

PP: Giannini, Hutton-Miller, Sutro & Co.

Chapter Nine

* Authors in the past have disagreed on whether this meeting took place; economist Galbraith, on balance, is dubious; journalist Sparling, who regularly met such speculators as Durant during the period, describes the meeting in some detail. Since Sparling's account tends to be confirmed in the biography of Durant by Gustin, who not only interviewed Durant's widow but also had access to unpublished manuscripts and documents, we have decided, on balance, that it likely took place and in the manner presented. Whether it did or not, there is no doubt that Durant felt as described, and that Hoover was aware of his views.

AI: Dito, Fisher (W), Garcia, Giannini, Hutton-Miller, Mann, Wong (W).

B: *Billy Durant* (Gustin); *The Great Crash* (Galbraith); *Mystery Men* of *Wall Street* (Sparling); *The Hoover Memoirs,* Vol. 3 (Hoover); *The Great Bull Market* (Sobel); *The Great Slump* (Rees); *A Monetary History of the United States* (Friedman and Schwartz); *The Plungers and the Peacocks* (Thomas); *Wall Street Under Oath* (Pecora).

D: Federal Reserve Bank of New York *Monthly Review* (April 1929).

M: *Saturday Evening Post* (June 22, 1929).

N: *Wall Street Journal* (March 9–22, 1929; October 29, 1977); New York *Evening Mail* (March 9–22, 1929); New York *Herald Tribune* (March 9–22, 1929); New York *Times* (March 9–22, April 2, 1929); New York *Telegram* (December 13, 1929).

PP: Durant, Giannini, GMI Institute, Hutton-Miller, Scharchburg.

Chapter Ten

AI: Bologna, Brown, Dowdy, Lamont (C), Love, MacVeagh (A), Mac-Veagh (C), Montague (F), Montague (L), Peckham, Pollock, Vargo (J), Vargo (S).

OI: Davis, Noble, Norman, Rankin, Stewart, Travers.

B: *Wall Street Under Oath* (Pecora); *My Boyhood in a Parsonage* (Lamont, T); *The Thomas Lamonts in America* (Lamont, C, ed.); *Lords of Creation* (Allen); *Once in Golconda* (Brooks); *The House of Morgan* (Hoyt); *Fleecing the Lambs* (Elias).

D: Stock Exchange Practices (1934).

M: Flint *Saturday Night* (October 1929–January 1930).

N: Flint *Journal* (October 1929–January 1930); Detroit *Times* (October 1929–January 1930).

PP: Bologna, Thomas Lamont (at Baker Library, Harvard Business School), MacVeagh, Montague, Wallace.

Chapter Eleven

AI: Garcia, Giannini, Hutton-Miller, MacVeagh (A), MacVeagh (C), Meehan, Riordan (E), Riordan (F), Stone.

OI: Arnold, Warren.

B: *Winston S. Churchill,* Vol. 5 (Gilbert); *The Manipulators* (Sobel); *Adolf Hitler* (Toland); *Before the Deluge* (Friedrich); *The Berengaria Exchange* (Knapp); *The Ford Dynasty* (Brough); *The Public Image of Henry Ford* (Lewis); *The Federal Reserve System* (Warburg); *Ford—the Times, the Man, the Company* (Nevins and Hill), *The Last Billionaire* (Richards); *We Never Called Him Henry* (Bennett); *The Legend of Henry Ford* (Sward); *Young Henry Ford* (Olsen); *The First Henry Ford* (Jardin).

D: Stock Exchange Practices (1934).

M: *American Magazine* (August 1929).

N: Detroit *News* (May 25, 1929); Detroit *Times* (May 14, 25, 1929);
       New York *Evening Mail* (May 16, 1929).
PP: Hutton-Miller, Stone.

Chapter Twelve

* For fifty years the accuracy of Hatry's version of what happened
at this meeting has troubled historians. Until recently no record was
known to exist. We have had access to certain of Hatry's private
papers through the generosity of Michael Pearson, and have spoken
at length to Hatry's son. From these prime sources, we conclude
there is no reason to doubt his account of events. Lord Bearsted is
dead, and he has left no record of this fateful meeting. But Hatry,
for all his faults, appears to have been a truthful reporter. A full
account of his confrontation with Bearsted, written up in Hatry's
usual vivid style, was discovered in his papers; his son verified the
accuracy of his father's recall.

AI: Hatry.
B: *The Slump* (Stevenson and Cook); *Winston S. Churchill*, Vol. 5
       (Gilbert); *The Age of Illusion* (Blythe); *Lord Norman* (Clay);
       Montagu Norman (Boyle); *The Millionaire Mentality* (Pearson);
       The Hatry Case (Hatry); *A History of Shanghai* (Pin); *The New
       York Money Market* (Myers); *The World in Depression* (Kindle-
       berger); *Showa Keizaishi* (Yoshiaki); *Showa Kyoko to Keizai
       Seisaku* (Takafusa); *Kyoko* (Katsuto); *The Aspirin Age* (Leighton,
       ed.).
D: Shanghai Stock Exchange Reports (various, 1929); Shanghai Chinese
       Merchant's Stock Exchange Reports (various, 1929).
N: *Daily Express* (May 29, 31, 1929); *The Times* (May 29–31, 1929);
       Daily Mail (May 29–31, 1929); *Star* (May 29, 30, 1929); *Evening
       News* (May 29, 30, 1929); *Evening Standard* (May 29, 30, 1929);
       Sheffield *Telegraph* (May 30, 1929); *Sunday Despatch* (June 22,
       1929); *Sunday Express* (June 2, 1929); *The Observer* (June 2,
       1929); *Sunday Telegraph* (June 2, 1929; August 1, 1965); *North-
       China Herald* (Shanghai, various, June 1929).
PP: Hatry.
T: Hatry interviews (Pearson).

Chapter Thirteen

* Again, we must take Hatry's word for what happened at this
meeting; no written record of the others present has survived.

AI: Beagle, De Camp, Hatry, Hutton-Miller, Levine, Levy, MacVeagh
       (A), MacVeagh (C), Montague (F), Montague (L), Mott (R),
       Osthaus, Peckham, Pollock (B), Stone, Vargo (J), Vargo (S).
B: *The World in Depression* (Kindleberger); *The Roar of the Twenties*
       (Gray); *Who Controls Industry?* (Lunberg); *The Market Place*

(Noyes); *Once in Golconda* (Brooks); *Eight Current Misconceptions* (Hatry); *The Millionaire Mentality* (Pearson); *Right People* (Birmingham); *Jesse Livermore* (Sarnoff); *The Plungers and the Peacocks* (Thomas); *Mystery Men of Wall Street* (Sparling).

C: Gauthier, Gillman, Hillier, Johnson, Lee, Monroe.

D: Federal Reserve Bank of New York *Monthly Report* (June 1929).

M: *Literary Digest* (August 24, November 30, 1929); *Nation* (June 19, 1929); *Harper's Magazine* (April 1929); *Saturday Evening Post* (February 2, 1929); *New Republic* (July 13, 1928); *Literary Digest* (April 1929); *North American Review* (April 1929); *Saturday Evening Post* (March 23, 1929; March 8, 1930); *American Magazine* (July 1929); *Woman's Home Companion* (January 1930).

N: New York *Times* (April 27, 1929; June 16, 1929; June 30, 1940); *Sunday Pictorial* (June 2, 1929); *Sunday Despatch* (June 16, 1929); *Sunday News* (June 23, 1929).

PP: Hatry, Hutton-Miller, Stone.

Chapter Fourteen

AI: Dowdy, Giannini, Hutton-Miller, Lewis, Stone, Vargo (J), Vargo (S).

OI: Arnold.

B: *Billy Durant* (Gustin); *The Great Crash* (Galbraith); *Only Yesterday* (Allen); *Wall Street Under Oath* (Pecora); *The Berengaria Exchange* (Knapp); *Biography of a Bank* (James); *A. P. Giannini* (Dana); *Jesse Livermore* (Sarnoff); *Modern Banking* (Sayers); *The Age of Roosevelt* (Schlesinger).

C: Barrington, Mullingham, O'Brian, Shiegle.

D: Stock Exchange Practices (1934); Federal Reserve Bank of New York *Monthly Report* (August 1, 1929); Annual Report on the State of Finance for the year ended June 30, 1929 (Secretary of the Treasury).

M: *Collier's* (December 15, 1928); *Scientific American* (December 1929); *Literary Digest* (June 1, 1929); *Saturday Evening Post* (June 2, 1929).

N: Portland (Maine) *Telegram* (July 7, 1929); Detroit *News* (July 7, 1929); Nashville (Tennessee) *Banner* (April 24, 1929); Detroit *Times* (May 24, 1929); New York *Times* (July 13, 1978); San Francisco *Examiner* (June 19, 1929); San Francisco *Chronicle* (July 2, 1929).

PP: Hutton-Miller, Stone.

Chapter Fifteen

*Mott made determined efforts to suppress details of his divorce. Even to this day the Mott Foundation and the GMI in Flint have no records available, at least to the public. Mott's fourth wife, Ruth, offers a likely explanation: "The whole experience was very upsetting for my husband." The Flint *Journal* had "no details available on the divorce." The only full reports appear to be in the archives of the Detroit *Free Press,* who made them freely available to us. Those reports were amplified by a number of Mott's friends, to whom he confided; although Mott is dead, they still prefer to remain anonymous.

AI: Bologna, Hatry, Hutton-Miller, Levine, MacVeagh (A), MacVeagh (C), Meehan, Mott (H), Mott (R), Riordan (E), Riordan (F), Schnell, Stone.

OI: Arnold, Chemla, Kostolany, Pagani, Saint-Phalle, Stewart, Warren.

B: *The Founding Father* (Whalen); *Jesse Livermore* (Sarnoff); *The Plungers and the Peacocks* (Thomas); *Times to Remember* (Kennedy); *1929: La Grande Crise* (Roy); *La Prodigieuse Histoire de la Bourse* (Colling); *Winston S. Churchill,* Vol. 5 (Gilbert); *Mr. Justice Birkett* (Bardens); *The Hatry Case* (Hatry); *Norman Birkett* (Hyde); *The Berengaria Exchange* (Knapp).

C: Anglan, Largent.

D: Letter, New York Stock Exchange to Meehan (July 25, 1929).

M: *Collier's* (June 19, 1929); *News-Week* (November 18, 1933).

N: New York *Times* (July 24, August 4, 1929); New York *Telegram* (August 4, 1929); New York *World* (August 4, 1929); Philadelphia *Inquirer* (August 4, 1929); *Wall Street Journal* (August 6, 1929); *Star, Evening News, Evening Standard* (all July 31, 1929); Detroit *Free Press* (October 29, 1929); Detroit *Times* (October 29, 1929).

PP: Bologna, Hutton-Miller, Stone.

Chapter Sixteen

AI: Bologna, Druyan, Fisher (W), Garcia, Giannini, Hutton-Miller, Levine, Levy, MacVeagh (A), MacVeagh (C), Meehan, Messerschmitt, Mills, Overly, Schnell.

OI: Speer.

B: *House of Morgan* (Hoyt); *The Bouviers* (Davis); *The Lawless Decade* (Sann); *Biography of a Bank* (James); *A. P. Giannini* (Dana); *Building the Bank of America* (Rink); *The Big Board* (Sobel); *Once in Golconda* (Brooks); *The Great Crash* (Galbraith); *The Ford Dynasty* (Brough); *Ford—the Times, the Man, the Company* (Nevins and Hill); *A Monetary History of the United States* (Friedman and Schwartz); *The World in Depression* (Kindleberger); *Messerschmitt* (Ishoven); *The First Henry Ford* (Jardin); *We Never Called Him Henry* (Bennett); *The Legend of Henry Ford* (Sward); *Tin Lizzie* (Stern).

C: Frick, Ostroff, O'Neill.

M: *American Magazine* (August 1929); *Ladies' Home Journal* (August 1929); *Woman's Home Companion* (January 1920); *Saturday Evening Post* (January 2, February 2, 1929); *Collier's* (December 15, 1928; March 8, May 31, 1930).

N: New York *Times* (December 31, 1929); San Francisco *Bulletin* (August 24, 1929); Sacramento *Bee* (August 24, 1929); Detroit *Times* (July 28, 1929); New York *Telegram,* New York *Herald,* New York *Journal,* New York *American,* New York *Sun,* New York *Herald Tribune,* New York *Times* (all for August 1929).

PP: Bologna, Hutton-Miller, Lamont (T).

Chapter Seventeen

* Our description of this important meeting is based largely on the private papers and notes of Clarence Hatry, confirmed in interview and correspondence with his son and also Michael Pearson, with whom Hatry collaborated for a time on a proposed biography.

AI: Arnold, Brown, De Camp, Hatry, Meehan, Montague (F), Montague (L), Mott (H), Mott (R), Pollock, Riordan (E), Riordan (F), Schnell, Stone.

OI: Davis, Largent, Pagani, Saint-Phalle, Speer, Stewart, Warren.

B: *Before the Deluge* (Friedrich); *Always the Unexpected* (Lochner); *Europe of the Dictators* (Wiskemann); *Fun in a Chinese Laundry* (Sternberg); *Berlin: Schicksal einer Weltstadt* (Kiaulehn); *Bishop Cannon's Own Story* (Cannon); *The Long Thirst* (Coffey); *Lord Norman* (Clay); *Silver Spoon* (Norton); *Montagu Norman* (Boyle); *The Berengaria Exchange* (Knapp); *Inside the Third Reich* (Speer); *Hitler* (Fest); *When Money Dies* (Fergusson); *Adolf Hitler* (Toland); *Citizen Hearst* (Swanberg); *Als war's ein Stuck von mir* (Zuckmayer); *Well Do I Remember* and *Halfway to Yesterday* (Lethbridge); *Geld-Banken-Borsen* (Weber); *Staatssekretar unter Ebert, Hindenburg, Hitler* (Meissner).

C: Gauthier, Gillman, Johnson (D).

UD: Union Industrial Bank Record of Shareholders; share ledgers, various brochures.

M: Flint *Saturday Night* (January–December 1929; January–March 1930).

N: New York *Times* (June 21, 25, 26, 28, August 5, 1929); *Sunday Telegraph* (August 5, 1929).

PP: Hatry (Pearson), Stone.

Chapter Eighteen

AI: Bologna, Hutton-Miller, Levine, Levy, MacVeagh (A), MacVeagh (C), Meehan, Riordan (E), Riordan (F), Schnell.

B: *Mystery Men of Wall Street* (Sparling); *Jesse Livermore* (Sarnoff); *Once in Golconda* (Brooks); *Winston S. Churchill,* Vol. 5 (Gilbert); *Twenty-one Years* (Churchill, R); *Crowded Canvas* (Churchill, J); *The Sky Is Falling* (Weingarten); *The Plungers and the Peacocks* (Thomas); *The Great Bull Market* (Sobel); *Citizen Hearst* (Swanberg); *Only Yesterday* and *Lords of Creation* (Allen); *Airships* (Jackson); *The Great Crash* (Galbraith); *Billy Durant* (Gustin); *The Shocking History of Advertising* (Turner); *Wall Street Under Oath* (Pecora).

D: *Winston S. Churchill,* Companion Vol. 5, Part 2 (Gilbert); Stock Exchange Practices (1934).

M: *Harper's* (November 1937); *Time* (September 9, 1929).

N: New York *Times* (August 29, 30, September 1–3, 1929); *Wall Street Journal* (August 21, September 24, 1929).

PP: Bologna, Hutton-Miller, Levy.

Chapter Nineteen

AI: Bologna, Brown, De Camp, Fisher (W), Hatry, Hutton-Miller, LaBranche, Levine, Levy, Meehan, Pollock, Schnell, Stone, Vargo (J), Vargo (S).

OI: Davis, Stewart.

B: *Jesse Livermore* (Sarnoff); *Mystery Men of Wall Street* (Sparling); *The Plungers and the Peacocks* (Thomas); *Lord Norman* (Clay); *Once in Golconda* (Brooks); *The Great Crash* (Galbraith); *The Big Board* (Sobel); *A Monetary History of the United States* (Friedman); *Oh Yeah!* (Angly); *The Stock Market Crash—and After* (Fisher); *Winston S. Churchill,* Vol. 5 (Gilbert); *Churchill in America* (Pilpel); *Twenty-one Years* (Churchill, R); *Crowded Canvas* (Churchill, J); *Bishop Cannon's Own Story* (Cannon); *The Long Thirst* (Coffey); *Ardent Spirits* (Kobler); *The Market Place* (Noyes); *Mr. Justice Avory* (Jackson); *Norman Birkett* (Hyde); *Case for the Prosecution* (Jackson); *The Trials of Mr. Justice Avory* (O'Donnell); *The Hatry Case* (Hatry).

C: Ackley, Augustine, Raymond, Rushlow (R).

D: *Winston S. Churchill,* Companion Vol. 5, Part 2 (Gilbert); Federal Reserve Bank of New York *Monthly Review* (September 1, 1929).

M: *Nation* (March 26, 1930); *Literary Digest* (October 3, 1931).

N: *Commercial and Financial Chronicle* (September 7, 1929); *Wall Street Journal* (September 6, 11, 21, 1929); New York *Herald Tribune* (September 6, 14–18, 1929); *Barron's* (September 9, 1929); New York *Times* (September 14–18, 21, December 31, 1929); *Daily Express* (September 20, 24, 1929); *Evening Standard* (September 20, 1929; July 6, 1935; September 16, 1954); *Daily News* (September 25, 1929); *Sunday Telegraph* (August 1, 8, 1965); New York *World* (September 14–18, 1929); *Sunday Telegraph* (August 1, 8, 1965); New York *World* (September 14–18, 1929); New York *Sun* (September 14–18, 1929).

PP: Bologna, Hatry, Hutton-Miller, Stone.

T: Hatry Interview (Pearson, 1957).

Chapter Twenty

* Economic historians disagree on the ultimate strength of impact the Hatry demise had on the American market. We believe it was not great; it may have been the stone that started the avalanche, but one should blame the snow, not the stone, for the storm.

AI: Bologna, Bongard, De Camp, Garcia, Giannini, Hutton-Miller, Lee, MacVeagh (A), MacVeagh (C), Montague (F), Riordan (E), Riordan (F), Stollery, Wong (H), Wong (M), Wong (K), Ying.

OI: Stewart.

B: *Reminiscences of a Stock Operator* (Lefevre); *How to Trade in Stocks* (Livermore); *A Treasury of Wall Street Wisdom* (Schultz and Coslow); *Jesse Livermore* (Sarnoff); *Mystery Men of Wall Street* (Sparling); *The Stock Exchange Story* (Jenkins); *Once in Golconda* (Brooks); *Reprints of Statements* (Morgan); *Billy Durant* (Gustin); *Wall Street Under Oath* (Pecora); *The Hatry Case* (Hatry); *The Bouviers* (Davis); *The Public Years* (Baruch).

D: Stock Exchange Practices (1934).

M: *Saturday Evening Post* (February 2, August 23, September 7, 14, 28, 1929; January 4, 1930; February 20, April 2, 1932); *Harper's Magazine* (September 1929); *Ladies' Home Journal* (September 1929).

N: New York *Times* (September 1–30, December 31, 1929; January 16, 1930); *Wall Street Journal* (September 21, 1929); *The Times* (January 11, 1930); San Francisco *News* (September 26, 1929); New York *Herald Tribune* (September 1–30, 1929); New York *Daily News* (September 1–30, 1929); San Francisco *Chronicle* (September 1, 11, 21, 27, 29, 1929); San Francisco *Examiner* September 2, 12, 22, 28, 30, 1929); Los Angeles *Times* (September 4, 16, 17, 22–30, 1929); Chicago *Tribune* (September 14–30, 1929); *Daily Express, Daily Herald, Daily Mail* (all September 1–30, 1929); Detroit *Free Press,* Detroit *Times,* (September 1–30, 1929); Flint *Journal* (September 14, 22, 1929).

UD: Lamont, Thomas (letter to Hoover, September 20, 1929).

PP: Bologna, Durant (Scharchburg), Durant files (GMI), Durant files (Sloan Museum), Hutton-Miller.

Chapter Twenty-One

AI: Bologna, Brown, De Camp, Frank, Giannini, Hutton-Miller, Levine, Levy, Love, MacVeagh (A), MacVeagh (C), Meehan, Montague (F), Montague (L), Mott (H), Riordan (E), Riordan (F), Schnell, Stone, Vargo (J), Vargo (S).

OI: Baker, Conway, Kimmel, Largent, Rodgers, Servis.

B: *Slump and Recovery* (Hodson); *Prosperity Decade* (Soule); *The*

Plungers and the Peacocks (Thomas); *The Great Boom and Panic* (Patterson); *Lords of Creation* (Allen); *The Sky Is Falling* (Weingarten); *Mystery Men of Wall Street* (Sparling); *Billy Durant* (Gustin).

D: Federal Reserve Bank of New York *Monthly Review* (October 1929); Federal Reserve Board *Bulletin* (October 1929).

M: *Saturday Evening Post* (January 11, 1930); *Newsweek* (November 18, 1933; November 12, 1951); *Collier's* (May 31, 1930); *American Magazine* (July 1928).

N: New York *Times,* Los Angeles *Times,* San Francisco *Chronicle,* Chicago *Tribune, Daily Express* (all for September 20–30, 1929); New York *Times* (October 1, December 31, 1929); *Wall Street Journal* (October 3, 1929).

PP: Bologna, Durant (Scharchburg), files (GMI), files (Sloan Museum), Hutton-Miller, Stone.

Chapter Twenty-Two

AI: Dowdy, Fisher (W), Garcia, Giannini, Hutton-Miller, Vargo (J), Vargo (S), Zawacki, Zimmermann, Zlatec.

B: *Wall Street Under Oath* (Pecora); *Winston S. Churchill,* Vol. 5 (Gilbert); *Twenty-one Years* (Churchill, R); *The Public Years* (Baruch); *The Great Boom and Panic* (Patterson); *Once in Golconda* (Brooks); *Who Controls Industry?* (Lunberg); *The Market Place* (Noyes); *My Autobiography* (Chaplin); *The Principal Causes of the Stock Market Crisis* (Simmons); *Building the Bank of America* (Rink); *Biography of a Bank* (James); *Only Yesterday* (Allen).

D: *Investment Bankers' Association Report* (Oct. 1929); *Winston S. Churchill,* Companion Vol. 5, Part 2 (Gilbert); *The Wilderness Years* (letters to Clementine, September 1929); Stock Exchange Practices.

UD: Lamont (T) (letter to Hoover, Baker Library).

M: *Literary Digest* (April 23, 1932); *Saturday Evening Post* (June 11, 1938); *New Republic* (July 13, 1938).

N: San Francisco *Examiner* (October 17, 1929); *Wall Street Journal* (October 18, 1929); San Francisco *Call Bulletin* (October 17, 1929); New York *Times* (October 4, 5, 16, December 3, 31, 1929); New York *Herald Tribune,* New York *Sun,* New York *Daily News* (all October 4–19, 1929).

Chapter Twenty-Three

AI: Barry, Bologna, Fisher (W), Garcia, Giannini, Montague (F), Overly, Riordan (E), Riordan (F), Schlaff, Stone.

OI: Arnold, Largent, Meynial, Rodgers, Speer, Strohmier.

B: *Ford Dynasty* (Brough); *The First Henry Ford* (Jardin); *Young Henry Ford* (Olsen); *We Never Called Him Henry* (Bennett); *Forty Years with Ford* (Sorensen); *The Legend of Henry Ford* (Sward); *The Berengaria Exchange* (Knapp); *Jesse Livermore* (Sarnoff); *Henry Ford and Greenfield Village* (Simonds); *The Public Image of Henry Ford* (Lewis); *The Great Crash* (Galbraith); *Once in Golconda* (Brooks); *O America!* (Barzini); *The Memoirs of Herbert Hoover,* Vol. 3 (Hoover).

C: O'Brian (M), O'Brian (N), Ostroff.

D: Manual for Guides (Greenfield Village).

UD: Lamont (T) (letter to Hoover, October 19, 1929); Egan (M) (memo to Thomas Lamont, October 23, 1929).

M: *Justice* (September 1929); *Time* (October 1929); *Ladies' Home Journal* (October 1929).

N: New York *Times,* New York *Herald Tribune,* New York *Daily News,* Boston *Globe,* Chicago *Tribune,* San Francisco *Chronicle,* San Francisco *Examiner,* St. Louis *Post Dispatch,* Detroit *News,* Detroit *Times,* Detroit *Free Press* (all October 10–20, 1929); New York *Times* (October 21, 22, 25, December 31, 1929); Detroit *Free Press* (September 5, October 21, 1929); *Sunday Graphic* (October 13, 1929).

PP: Durant (Scharchburg), files (Ford Achives), files (Greenfield Village).

T: NBC/WWJ Radio broadcast October 21, 1929.

Chapter Twenty-Four

AI: Bologna, Bongard, Brown, Champion, De Camp, Dowdy, Fisher (W), Garcia, Giannini, Hutton-Miller, Lamont (E), Levine, Levy, MacVeagh (A), MacVeagh (C), Mills, Montague (F), Montague (L), Mott (H), Mott (R), Plate, Pollock (B), Riordan (E), Riordan (F), Stollery, Stone.

OI: Arnold, Atchison (C), Atchison (W), Bird, Burton, Carey (H), Carey (J), Ferrington (P), Johnson (D), Largent, Parker, Servis, Sullivan, Whitcomb.

B: *Once in Golconda* (Brooks); *Only Yesterday* (Allen); *My Years with General Motors* (Sloan); *Biography of a Bank* (James); *Jesse Livermore* (Sarnoff); *The Plungers and the Peacocks* (Thomas); *The Great Bull Market* and *The Big Board* (Sobel); *The Bouviers* (Davis); *Panic!* (Alexander); *The Great Crash* (Galbraith): *In Time of Trouble* (Cockburn); *The Berengaria Exchange* (Knapp); *O America!* (Barzini); *Winston S. Churchill,* Vol. 5 (Gilbert); *The Great Boom and Panic* (Patterson); *The Public Years* (Baruch); *Jeudi Noir* (Gigon).

C: Alper, Annglan, Baringrow, Barrington, Brinkman, Coite, Gilbertson, Hickman, Jurgens, Kent, Leary, Lyons, Moss, O'Neill, Orlins.

D: Stock Exchange Practices (1934).

UD: Letters Giannini to Delafield (October 22, 1929); memos, Giannini to Walker; Giannini to Giannini (M) and Giannini (C); memos Giannini to Delafield (all October 1929); memos, letters of Thomas Lamont (various, all relating to October 24, 1929).

M: *Literary Digest* (December 7, 1929); *World's Work* (April 1932); *Fortune* (March 1930); *New Republic* (October 29, 1930); *American Mercury* (November 1949); *Saturday Evening Post* (October 29, December 28, 1929; January 4, 1930); *American Heritage* (March 30, 1930).

N: New York *Times,* New York *Herald Tribune,* New York *Daily News,* New York *Daily Mirror,* New York *American,* New York *World Telegram,* New York *Evening Journal, Wall Street Journal,* Los Angeles *Times,* San Francisco *Chronicle,* San Francisco *Examiner,* Chicago *Tribune,* Boston *Globe,* St. Louis *Post Dispatch, The Times, Daily Express, Daily Mail, Daily Herald, Daily Telegraph* (all for October 25, 1929); *Daily Telegraph* (December 9, 1929); New York *Post* (June 28, 1960).

PP: Bologna, Durant (Scharchburg), Hutton-Miller, Mott (Mott Foundation), Mott (GMI), Mott (Sloan Foundation), Stone.

T: Voice tapes of C. S. Mott (Scharchburg-GMI).

Chapter Twenty-Five

AI: Bologna, Garcia, Giannini, Hutton-Miller, Levine, Levy, MacVeagh, (C), Meehan, Schnell.

OI: Saint-Phalle.

B: *Postscript to Yesterday* (Morris); *The Great Crash* (Galbraith); *The Great Boom and Panic* (Patterson); *Once in Golconda* (Brooks); *The Plungers and the Peacocks* (Thomas); *The Merchant Bankers* (Wechsburg); *Jesse Livermore* (Sarnoff); *Wall Street Under Oath* (Pecora); *Lords of Creation* (Allen); *The Market Place* (Noyes); *The Stock Market Crash—and After* (Fisher); *The Great Slump* (Rees).

D: Letter Snyder to Giannini (October 10, 1929); telegram Snyder to Giannini (October 15, 1929); telegram Giannini to Snyder (October 15, 1929); letter Snyder to Giannini (October 17, 1929); memo McGinnis to Giannini (October 17, 1929); letter Preston to Giannini (October 17, 1929); interoffice memo Giannini to Walker (October 29, 1929); telegram Giannini to Barrett (December 20, 1929).

M: *Nation's Business* (June 1937); *New Republic* (October 29, 1930; January 28, 1933); *American Mercury* (November 1949); *Saturday Evening Post* (December 28, 1929; February 1, March 8, 1930; January 31, 1931).

N: New York *Times* (October 25–29, December 31, 1929); *The Times* October 25, 26, 1929); *Barron's* (October 28, 1929); *Wall Street Journal* (October 26, 1929).

PP: Bologna, Hutton-Miller.

Chapter Twenty-Six

AI: Beagle, Bologna, Brown, Champion, De Camp, Dowdy, Fisher (W), Frank, Giannini, Hutton-Miller, Kahn, La Branche, Lamont (C), Lamont (E), Levine, Levy, Love, Marshall Meehan, Mills, Montague (F), Montague (L), Osthaus, Schnell.

OI: Arnold, Atchison (C), Atchison (W), Bird, Boffito, Burton (A), Burton (D), Carey (H), Carey (J), Carey (K), Chemla, Conway, Ferrington, Halls, Harper, Healy, Held, Largent, Murphy, Parker, Rodgers, Thompson.

B: *Panic!* (Alexander); *Once in Golconda* (Brooks); *The Great Boom and Panic* (Patterson); *Only Yesterday* (Allen); *The Great Crash* (Galbraith); *The Sky Is Falling* (Weingarten); *Jesse Livermore* (Sarnoff); *The Plungers and the Peacocks* (Thomas); *Mystery Men of Wall Street* (Sparling); *A Treasury of Wall Street Wisdom* (Schultz and Coslow); *Fleecing the Lambs* (Elias); *Middleton* (2 vols., Lynd); *The Stock Market Crash—and After* (Fisher); *A Monetary History of the United States* (Friedman and Schwartz); *How to Trade in Stocks* (Livermore); *Churchill in America* (Pilpel).

C: Baer, Blocher, Brackett, Breen, Castleden, Cox, Ellis, Fox, Gibbs, Harris, Jurgens, Kent, Leary, Lee, Lyons, Mailer, Marshall, Mellincoff, Monroe, Moore, O'Brian (M), O'Brian (O), O'Donnel (P), O'Neill (P), Ostroff, Perryman, Quarry, Reagan, Roberts, Welsh, Woods.

D: The Work of the Stock Exchange in the Panic of 1929 (Whitney address, June 10, 1930); papers, records (Trinity Church); interoffice memos, Giannini to Walker, Pedrini, Delafield (October 30–November 8, 1929).

M: *American History Illustrated* (December 1969); *Saturday Evening Post* (February 2, December 28, 1929; January 4, 1930); *The World Tomorrow* (January 1930): *American Magazine* (August 1931).

N: New York *Times,* New York *Herald Tribune,* New York *Daily News,* New York *Daily Mirror,* New York *American,* New York *World Telegram,* New York *Evening Journal,* Wall Street Journal, Los Angeles *Times,* San Francisco *Examiner,* San Francisco *Chronicle,* Chicago *Tribune,* Boston *Globe,* St. Louis *Post Dispatch,* The Times, *Daily Express, Daily Mail, Daily Herald, Daily Telegraph* (all for October 30, 1929); New York *Times* (November 12, 1929); Los Angeles *Times* (October 30, 1929).

PP: Bologna, Hutton-Miller, Thomas Lamont (Baker Library).

Chapter Twenty-Seven

AI: Beagle, Bongard, Brown, Champion, De Camp, Dowdy, Druyan, Hatry, Lee, Love, MacVeagh (A), MacVeagh (C), Messerschmitt,

Montague (F), Montague (L), Mott (H), Mott (R), Plate, Pola, Pollock (B), Riordan (E), Riordan (F), Schnell, Stollery, Stone.

OI: Chemla, Friedman, Fullerton, Meynial, Saint-Phalle, Speer, Vermuelen, Warren.

B: *Lords of Creation* and *Only Yesterday* (Allen); *The Great Crash* (Galbraith); *The Millionaire Mentality* (Pearson); *The Invisible Scar* (Bird); *Churchill in America* (Pilpel); *Messerschmitt* (Ishoven); *La Crise de 1929* (Bere); *1929: La Grand Crise* (Roy); *The Great Depression Revisited* (Wee); *Als wars eni Stuck von Mir* (Zuckmayer); *Geld-Banken-Borsen* (Weber); *Always the Unexpected* (Lochner); *The Spanish Civil War* (Thomas); *The Stock Exchange Story* (Jenkins); *Gold Bricks and Mortar* (Rosenthal); *Before the Deluge* (Friedrich); *William Lyon Mackenzie King* (Neatby); *The Great Slump* (Rees); *The Great Depression* (Hoover); *A Monetary History of the United States* (Friedman and Schwartz); *Nascita Dello Stato Imprenditore in Italia* (Cianci); *Fascismo e Societa Italiana* (Quazza); *The Hungry Thirties* (Braithwaite); *Ordeal by Fire* (Allen); *The Canadians* (Careless and Brown); *The Hatry Case* (Hatry); *Reprints of Statements* (Morgan); *Slump and Recovery* (Hodson); *The Market Place* (Noyes).

C: Castleden, Gordon, Marshall, Munroe, Ristori, Roberts, Waters.

D. Annual Reports: Charity Organisation Society (October 1928–September 30, 1929; 1930–31); New York Association for Improving the Conditions of the Poor (1928–29, 1929–30, 1930–31); Reports (Disconte-Gesellschaft); Reports (Credit-Anstalt); Reports (Dresdner Bank); Reports (Die Geschichte der Zurcher Borse, November–December 1929).

N: *The Times* (November 2, 1929); New York *Times* (November 10, December 31, 1929; January 1, 1930); *Variety* (October 30, 1929); Sydney *Morning Herald* (October 31, 1929); *L'Humanité* and *Le Populaire* (both October 24–November 2, 1929), *Le Figaro* (October 15–November 10, 1929); *Le Temps* (October 15–November 4, 1929); *Der Tag, Deutsche Allgameine Zeitung, Frankfurter Zeitung, Berlin Kreuz Zeitung, Germania, Vossische* (all for October 20–November 8, 1929); *Corriere Della Sera* (October 4, December 20, 1929); *Schweizerische Handelszeitung, Neue Zurcher Zeitung* (October 29–November 8, 1929); *North-China Herald* (September 7–November 9, 1929); Flint *Journal* (January 1–30, October 24–December 31, 1929); Flint *Saturday Night* (October–December, 1929; January–March, 1930); *Daily Mirror, Sunday Pictorial, Sunday Express, Sunday Empire News* (November 2–10, 1929); *Zurich Finanz-Revue* (October 24–December 1929); Paris *Herald* (October 30, 1929); Toronto *Globe and Mail,* Winnipeg *Free Press* (October 16–December 2, 1929).

Chapter Twenty-Eight

AI: Bologna, Champion, Druyan, Fisher (W), Frank, Garcia, Giannini, Hutton-Miller, Kahn, Levine, Levy, MacVeagh (A), MacVeagh (C), Meehan, Schnell.

B: *Billy Durant* (Gustin); *The Plungers and the Peacocks* (Thomas); *The Invisible Scar* (Bird); *Lords of Creation* (Allen); *Reprints of Statements* (Morgan); *Bank of America* (Rink); *The Founding Father* (Whalen); *Mystery Men of Wall Street* (Sparling); *Once in Golconda* (Brooks); *The Great Boom and Panic* (Patterson); *The Age of Roosevelt* (Schlesinger); *The Sky Is Falling* (Weingarten); *The Great Depression* (Hoover); *Wall Street Under Oath* (Pecora); *Jesse Livermore* (Sarnoff); *The House of Morgan* (Hoyt); *The Thomas Lamonts in America* (Lamont, C); *Who Controls Industry?* (Lunberg); *Hard Times* (Terkel).

C: Maloney.

D: Annual Reports; Charity Organisation Society; New York Association for Improving the Conditions for the Poor.

M: *Forbes* (March 6, 1978); *New Republic* (June 1933); *Time* (December 7, 1936; October 23, 1950); *Life* (January 25, 1963).

N: New York *Times* (November 13, 1929); *Wall Street Journal* (October 28, 1977).

PP: Hutton-Miller, Thomas Lamont (Baker Library).

SPECIAL THANKS

Authors' Interviewees

Ackley, Edward
Augustine, Pat
Baron, James
Barry, James
Beagle, John
Bohen, William
Bologna, Pat
Bongard, Gordon
Brown, Beryl
Champion, George
Collard, Frank
Collard, Hazel
Cook, Fred
De Camp, Virginia
Dito, Salvador
Dowdy, Doris
Dowdy, Homer
Dowdy, Homer, Jr.
Druyan, Pearl
Faugh, Gerry
Fisher, Rudy
Fisher, William
Flyn, Hope
Frank, Walter
Freeman, Ralph
Garcia, Joe
Gary, Francis
Giannini, Claire
Greene, Howard
Hatry, Cecil
Howard, Isabel
Howard, Jason
Howard, Jay
Huang, Fred

Hutton-Miller, William E.
Kahn, Herman H.
Kramm, Alfred
La Branche, George M. L.
Lamb, Dana
Lamont, Corliss
Lee, Bob
Lee, S. Charles
Lethbridge, Alice
Levine, Michael
Levy, Dan
Lewis, Maxine
Lewis, Salim
Love, Ed
MacVeagh, Adele
MacVeagh, Charlton
Mann, Russell
Marshall, David
Maloney, E. Burke
Meehan, William M.
Messerschmitt, Willy
Mills, Dudley H.
Mott, Harding
Mott, Ruth
Montague, Frank
Montague, Louise
Nielsen, Neil
Noble, Ollie
Norman, William
Osthaus, Franz
Overly, Lowell
Page, Eurico

Park, Arthur
Peckham, Gail
Plate, George F.
Pola, Eddie
Pollock, Bruce
Pollock, Milton
Pollock, Stuart
Quadland, H. P.
Redenger, Jack
Riordan, Elizabeth
Riordan, Florence
Rushlow, Floyd
Rushlow, Ruth
Russell, George
Russell, Ishaw
Ryan, Patrick
Schoenfeld, Joe
Schlaff, Don H.
Schnell, Edward
Simms, Ami
Simms, Steve
Smith, Russell
Stewart, Margaret
Stollery, William
Stone, Edith
Transue, Andrew
Travers, Linda
Vargo, Jolan
Vargo, Steve
Walter, Carl
Walter, Lena
Wilson, Louise
Wong, Howard

Wong, Michael K.
Wong, Philip
Wong, Wilfred

Yager, George
Ying, Lee

Zawacki, John
Zimmermann, Joseph
Zlatec, John

Other Interviewees

Arnold, Stanley A.
Atchison, Clara
Atchison, William
Ausenda, Dorothy
Baker, Dora
Bird, Vera
Boffito, Carlo
Boucher, Victor
Burton, Alice
Burton, Darwin
Carey, Harry
Carey, Joanne
Carey, Kitty
Chemla, Lucien
Conway, Marilyn
Cookie, William R.
Dake, Lillian
Davis, Keith
Dayer, Roberta

Ferrington, Ann
Ferrington, Percy
Fullerton, Hugh
Garance, Gaston
Halls, Priscilla
Harper, Sarah
Healy, Gerald
Held, Charles W.
Johnson, Donald
Kahan, Jacques
Keller, James
Kimmel, Charles
Kostolany, André
Largent, Robert
Lenti, Libero
McElderry, Andrea
Merrichella, Donato
Merrill, Earl

Meynial, Pierre
Molho, Max
Murphy, Thomas
Paganini, Bruno
Parker, Aida
Rodgers, Clara
Rutschmann, Arthur
Saint-Phalle, Count
  Alexandre de
Saraceno, Pasquale
Servis, Arthur
Speer, Albert
Strohmeier, Werner
Sullivan, Elizabeth
Thompson, Jacey
Warren, Lansing
Whitcombe, Philip
Witke, Roxanne

Correspondents

Alper, Benedict
Annglan, Annie
Baer, Arthur
Balling, Marshall
Barrington, Barry
Blocher, Margaret
Bokent, Lewis
Brackett, Edward T.
Breen, Ernest
Brinkman, E. H.
Brown, Margaret
Castleden, John R.
Coite, William
Cox, E. Van Dyke
Croll, Mrs. Leslie
Eldridge, John
Ellis, Jack
Farelly, Phillip
Fischer, Jake
Fitzgerald, Thomas

Fox, Laurie
Fricke, Arnold
Gauthier, Elaine
Gibbs, Richard
Gilbertson, S. K.
Gillman, Judson
Gordon, Richard
Harris, Robert
Hibberd, Stuart
Hickman, D. F.
Hillier, Helen
Johnson, Donald
Johnson, L. F. E.
Jurgens, Rodney
Kent, Leviw
Kucewicz, Joseph
Lea, Ivy
Leary, Raymond
Lynch, Frank
Lyons, Doloris

McGalliard, Mrs. Alex
Mailer, Louis
Marshall, C. R.
Mellincoff, Abe
Monro, W. P.
Monroe, Frederick H.
Moore, Donald S.
Mullingham, Eddie
O'Brien, Michael D.
O'Brien, Noreen
O'Brion, Oliver
O'Donnell, Patrick
O'Neill, Pamela
Orlins, Scott
Ostroff, Sidney
Perryman, A. C.
Pickett, John
Pugh, Roger
Quarry, Raymond
Ranger, Francis

Regan, Patricia
Ristori, Bridget
Roberts, E. C.
Ross, Justin
Sargent, Mary
Sarin, Jose

Saunders, K. C.
Shiegle, Norman
Silvester, Evelyn
Thomas, S. L.
Thompson, Tommy
Turley, Robert

Turner, Gordon
Walsh, Edward
Williamson, Charles
Wilson, Austin
Wisner, Carl V.
Woods, W. A.

Research

Admundson, Aluth
Bartholomes, Martina
Barzini, Ludina
Besaw, Vicki
Bessell-Browne,
  Elizabeth
Bohrensen, Renate
Bosshard, Hans
Bright, Anne
Carberry, Sean
Cheng, Annie
Davis, Steve
DiBlasio, Gloria

Eldridge, John
Fodor, Denis
Furniss, Margaret
Greaves, Margaret
Kudo, Alice
Lin, Joseph
McDonald, Colin
Moss, Leonard
Myers, Patricia
Naccache, Ursula
Nishizaki, Colette
Ohta, Kiyoshi

Olmos, Victor
Puffer, K. Hart
Redman, Chris
Royce, George
Ryser, Jeff
Schmid, Hans Rudolf
Schmitt-Thomas,
  Hilary
Tai-yi, Lai Lin
Tazawa, Tadahiko
Walta, Jan
Weiss, Ingeborg
Wood, Pamela

And the editors and staff of Reader's Digest Bureaus around the world.

Stenography

Albaladejo, Ana
Bennett, Mary
Grogan, Kathleen

Laughton, Heather
Morphew, Penelope
Rubinowitz, Susan

Trone, Mary
Wormer, Laura Van

ACKNOWLEDGMENTS

Individuals

Many, not directly associated with the Wall Street Crash, gave us generous help. We should like to thank in particular:

Brian Freemantle
Martin Gilbert
Simon Knott
Bill Maxwell
Simon Tooth
Malcolm Turner

Aitkens, Ronnie
Atchison, Clara
Atchison, William
Auti, Keith
Baker, Marilyn
Cole, Anthony
Dobie, Marian
Donaldson, John
Dribben, Elizabeth
Dumont, Giles
Dunn, Lee
Emanuel, Eric D.
Field, Joyce
Fildes, Christopher
Florida, Joe
Foster, Marion
Lounsbury
Friedlander, Albert

Gorringe, Victor
Greenfield, George
Healy, Ellen
Hephern, Sue
Hickey, Des
Hutton, R. S.
Jenkinson, Pat
Jordan, A. E.
Karetsky, David
Keto, Yaeko
Lamb, Robert
Lamont, Edward M.
Lamont, Lansing
McDonough, William J.
McGough, Sheila
Montet, Madame de
O'Griafa, Cathal
Parker, Selwyn
Payn, Graham
Perry, Merrill
Phipps, Beatrice
Pizarro, Dottie
Poole, Duane
Pond, Thomas L.

Recanati, Harry
Rendall, Mrs. Olie
Rush, Jim
Satterfield, Archie
Scharchburg, Richard
Shioya, Ko
Simmons, Dawn
Langley
Small, Anthony
Swindell, Harold L.
Syracuse, Angelo
Taha, Susa
Thompson-Noel, Michael
Tomoko, Takahama
Van Bolt, Roger
Vizard, David
Wallace, Diana
Wallace, Kenneth
Weigall, Michael
Whittam-Smith, Andreas
Xamadu, Oriole
Xuereb, George
Young, Howard

Organizations, Societies, Institutions

Associated Press
Auckland *Star*
Baker Library, Harvard Business School (Robert Lovett)

Bank of America, San Francisco (James Babbitt), London (Mary Mackenzie)
Barclay's Bank, London (K. Bryan)
Barron's
British Broadcasting Corporation
British Library Reading Room and Newspaper Library
British Shipping Defence League (A. Mackay)
Brooklyn Business Library (Sylvia Mechanic)
Carnegie Institution of Washington (Sheila McGough)
Chase Manhattan Bank, Paris
City Business Library, London
Collins, William (Africa) Pty. Ltd. (John Donaldson, Pamela Wood)
Community Services Society, New York (Margaret Knowles)
Detroit *Free Press* (Neil Shine)
Discount Corporation of New York (Ralph Peters, Doug Fairchild, Donald Brodie)
Federal Reserve Bank of New York (Richard Hoenig)
Financial Times, London (David Dixie)
Flint Public Library
Ford Motor Co. (Gerry Sloan); Ford Guest Center (Dave Dowling); Greenfield Village (Don Adams, Gary Hoffman); Ford Archives, Henry Ford Museum (Douglas A. Bakken)
General Motors, London (John McCormack), Detroit
General Register and Record Office of Shipping and Seamen, Cardiff (D. I. Cook)
Guildhall Library, London
Hammersmith Books, London (Ronald Gray)
Hodder & Stoughton, Ltd., New Zealand (Ronald J. Coombes, Pam Nemie)
Hornblower & Weeks, Paris
Hutton, E. F. & Co., Inc., New York (Ronald Miller)
Institute of Bankers, London (Pamela Jilks)
Johannesburg *Star*
Liverpool University (M. A. Cooke)
London School of Economics
Morgan, J. P., & Co. (James Brugger)
Morgan Guaranty Trust Co. of New York (Russell Everett)
Mott Foundation, Flint
Municipal Archives & Record Center, New York (Garcia Pena)
Municipal Reference Library, New York
Natal Mercury, Durban
National Archives & Record Service, Washington, D.C. (John E. Taylor)
National Broadcasting Corporation
National Union of Seamen
Nelson, Thos. (Aust) Pty. Ltd. (Caroline Lurie)
New York City Fire Department (Anne Pol)
New York, City of, Police Academy Museum (Alfred J. Young)
New-York Historical Society
New York, City of, Police Department (Ellen Fleysher)
New York Public Library
New York *Times*

Princeton University, Seeley G. Mudd Manuscript Library (Frances Chen)
Public Record Office, Richmond
Reuters
Rockefeller Archives Center, North Tarrytown (Joseph Ernst)
Roosevelt, Franklin D., Library, Hyde Park (William R. Emerson)
Sea Breezes, Liverpool
Signal
Stock Exchanges: Amsterdam, Chicago, Frankfurt, Hong Kong, Johannesburg, London, Los Angeles, Madrid, Milan, Montreal, New York, Paris, San Francisco, Tokyo, Toronto, Zurich
Trinity Church (Phylis Barr)
UCLA Research Library
United Press International
Wall Street District Messenger Co., Inc. (Israel Kaver)
Wall Street Journal
Warburg Institute, University of London

BIBLIOGRAPHY

Books

Abels, Jules. *The Rockefeller Millions.* London: Frederick Muller, 1967.

Adams, William S. *Henry Ford and Greenfield Village.* New York: A. Stokes Co., 1938.

Aldrich, Winthrop W. *Suggestions for Improving the Banking System.* New York: Privately printed, Chase National Bank, 1933.

Alexander, David. *Panic! The Day the Money Stopped.* Evanston, Ill.: Regency Books, 1962.

Allen, Frederick Lewis. *Only Yesterday.* New York: Harper & Bros., 1931.

———. *The Lords of Creation.* New York: Harper & Bros., 1935.

———. *Since Yesterday.* New York: Harper Bros., 1939.

———. *The Great Pierpont Morgan.* New York: Harper Bros., 1949.

———. *The Big Change: 1900–1950.* New York: Harper Bros., 1952.

Allen, Ralph. *Ordeal by Fire.* Toronto: Doubleday, 1961.

Allen, Trevor. *Ivar Kreuger.* London: John Long Ltd., 1932.

Allsop, Kenneth. *The Bootleggers.* London: Hutchinson & Co., 1961.

Amory, C., and Bradlee, F. *A Cavalcade of the 1920's and 30's.* London: Bodley Head, 1961.

Angly, Edward. *Oh Yeah?* New York: The Viking Press, 1932.

Armstrong, F. E. *The Book of the Stock Exchange.* London: Sir Isaac Pitman & Sons Ltd., 1934.

Ashley, F. W. *My Sixty Years in the Law.* London: The Bodley Head, 1936.

Bardens, Dennis. *Lord Justice Birkett.* London: Robert Hale Ltd., 1962.

Baruch, Bernard. *The Public Years.* New York: Holt, Rinehart & Winston, 1960.

Barzini, Luigi. *O America!* London: Hamish Hamilton Ltd., 1977.

Bennett, Harry Herbert. *We Never Called Him Henry.* New York: Gold Medal Books, 1951.

Bird, Caroline. *The Invisible Scar.* New York: David McKay & Co., 1966.

Birmingham, Stephen. *Right People.* Boston: Little, Brown & Co., 1958.

———. *Our Crowd.* New York: Harper & Row, 1967.

Blythe, Ronald. *The Age of Illusion—England in the Twenties and Thirties.* London: Hamish Hamilton Ltd., 1963.

Boyle, Andrew. *Montagu Norman.* London: Cassell & Co., 1967.

Braithwaite, Max. *The Hungry Thirties.* Toronto: McClelland Co., 1977.

Broadfoot, Barry. *Ten Lost Years, 1929–1939.* Toronto: Doubleday Ltd., 1973.

Brogan, Denis W. *The Era of Franklin D. Roosevelt*, Vol. 52. New Haven: Yale University Press, 1950.

Brooks, John Nixon. *The Seven Fat Years*. London: Victor Gollancz, 1959.

————. *Once in Golconda*. New York: Harper & Row, 1969.

————. *The Go-Go Years*. New York: Weybright & Talley, 1973.

Brough, James. *The Ford Dynasty—an American Story*. Garden City, N.Y.: Doubleday & Co., 1977.

Bullock, Hugh. *The Story of Investment Companies*. New York: Columbia University Press, 1959.

Cannon, James, Jr. *Bishop Cannon's Own Story*. Durham, N.C.: Duke University Press, 1955.

Cantor, Eddie. *Caught Short!* New York: Simon & Schuster, 1929.

Careless, J. M. J., and Brown, R. Craig, eds. *The Canadians, 1867–1967*. Toronto: The Macmillan Co., 1967.

Chandler, Lester V. *Benjamin Strong—Central Banker*. Washington, D.C.: The Brookings Institution, 1958.

————. *America's Greatest Depression*. New York: Harper & Row, 1970.

Chaplin, Charles. *My Autobiography*. London: The Bodley Head, 1964.

Ching, Choukai, ed. *An Economic History of the Republic of China*. Taiwan: Jin Hua Books Co.

Chrysler, Walter P. *The Life of an American Workman*. New York: Dodd, Mead & Co., 1950.

Churchill, Allen. *The Incredible Ivan Kreuger*. London: Weidenfeld & Nicolson, 1957.

Churchill, John G. S. *Crowded Canvas*. London: Odhams Press, 1961.

Churchill, Randolph. *Twenty-one Years*. London: Weidenfeld & Nicolson, 1962.

Cianci, Ernesto. *Noseita Dello Stato Imprenditore in Italia*. Mursia, 1977.

Clay, Henry. *Lord Norman*. London: Macmillan & Co., 1957.

Coblentz, Edmond D. *William Randolph Hearst—A Portrait in His Own Hands*. New York: Simon & Schuster, 1952.

Cockburn, Claud. *In Time of Trouble*. London: Rupert Hart-Davis, 1956.

Coffey, Thomas M. *The Long Thirst*. New York: W. W. Norton & Co., 1975.

Coit, Margaret L. *Mr. Baruch*. Boston: Houghton Mifflin & Co., 1957.

Collier, Peter, and Horowitz, David. *The Rockefellers—An American Dynasty*. London: Jonathan Cape, 1976.

Colling, Alfred. *La Prodigieuse Histoire de la Bourse de Paris*. Paris: Société d'Éditions Économiques et Financières, 1949.

Coward, Noël. *Present Indicative*. London: William Heinemann Ltd., 1937.

————. *Future Indefinite*. London: William Heinemann Ltd., 1954.

Dabney, Virginius. *Dry Messiah—The Life of Bishop James Cannon, Jr.* New York: Alfred A. Knopf, 1949.

Dahlinger, John Cote. *The Secret Life of Henry Ford*. New York: The Bobbs-Merrill Co., 1978.

Dana, Julian. *A. P. Giannini—Giant in the West*. New York: Prentice-Hall, 1947.

Darrow, Clarence, and Yarros, V. S. *The Prohibition Mania*. New York: Boni & Liveright, 1927.

Davis, John H. *The Bouviers*. New York: Farrar, Straus & Giroux, 1969.

Dawson, Robert MacGregor. *William Lyon Mackenzie King*. London: Methuen & Co., 1959.

Dew, Walter. *I Caught Crippen*. London: Blackie & Son, 1938.

Dice, Charles Amos. *New Levels in the Stockmarket*. New York: McGraw-Hill, 1929.

Doctorow, E. L. *Ragtime*. London: Macmillan, 1976.

Elias, Christopher. *Fleecing the Lambs*. Chicago: Henry Regnery Co., 1971.

Ellis, Edward Robb. *The Epic of New York City*. New York: Coward-McCann, 1966.

Feis, Herbert. *1933: Characters in Crisis*. Boston: Little, Brown & Co., 1966.

Fergusson, Adam. *When Money Dies—The Nightmare of the Weimer Collapse*. London: William Kimber, 1975.

Fest, Joachim C. *Hitler*. London: Weidenfeld & Nicolson, 1974.

Field, Carter. *Bernard Baruch*. New York: Whittlesey House, 1944.

Fisher, Irving. *The Stock Market Crash—and After*. New York: Macmillan, 1930.

Flynn, John T. *Security Speculation—Its Economic Effects*. New York: Harcourt, Brace & Co., 1934.

Fowler, Gene. *Beau James*. New York: The Viking Press, 1949.

Friedman, Milton, and Schwartz, Anna J. *A Monetary History of the United States, 1867–1960*. Princeton, N.J.: Princeton University Press, 1963.

Friedrich, Otto. *Before the Deluge—A Portrait of Berlin in the 1920's*. New York: Harper & Row, 1972.

Galbraith, John Kenneth. *The Great Crash*. New York: Houghton Mifflin, 1954.

Gifford, Denis. *Chaplin*. Garden City, N.Y.: Doubleday & Co., 1974.

Gigon, Fernand. *Jeudi Noir*. Paris: Laffont, 1976.

Gilbert, Martin. *Winston S. Churchill*, Vol. 5. London: Heinemann, 1976.

———. *Winston S. Churchill*, Companion Vol. 5, Part 2. London: Heinemann, 1979.

Gilbert, Michael F. *Dr. Crippen*. London: Odhams Press Ltd., 1953.

Gray, James H. *The Winter Years*. Toronto: The Macmillan Co., 1966.

———. *The Roar of the Twenties*. Toronto: The Macmillan Co., 1975.

Guiles, Fred Lawrence. *Marion Davies*. London: W. H. Allen, 1973.

Gustin, Lawrence R. *Billy Durant*. Grand Rapids, Mich.: William B. Eerdmans Publishing Co., 1973.

Hackett, Alice Payne. *Fifty Years of Best Sellers*. New York: R. R. Bowker Co., 1945.

Harris, Seymour E. *Twenty Years of Federal Reserve Policy*. Cambridge, Mass.: Harvard University Press, 1933.

Hartmann, Johannes. *Das Geschichtsbuch*. Frankfurt: 1955.

Hatch, Alden P. *Citizen of the World—Franklin D. Roosevelt*. London: Skeffington & Son Ltd., 1948.

Hatry, Cecil. *The Hatry Case—Eight Current Misconceptions*. London: privately printed, 1938.

Hatry, Clarence C. *Light out of the Darkness*. London: Rich and Cowan Ltd., 1939.

Hellerman, Michael, with Renner, Thomas C. *Wall Street Swindler*. Garden City, N.Y.: Doubleday & Co., 1977.

Hersent, Georges. *La Bataille Économique*. Paris: Payot, 1934.

Hibbert, Christopher. *Benito Mussolini*. London: Longmans, Green & Co., 1962.

Hilton, Conrad. *Be My Guest*. Englewood Cliffs, N.J.: Prentice-Hall, 1957.

Hodson, H. V. *Slump and Recovery, 1929–1937*. Oxford University Press, 1938.

Holbrook, Stewart H. *The Age of the Moguls*. Garden City, N.Y.: Doubleday & Co., 1954.

Hoover, Herbert. *The Memoirs of Herbert Hoover—The Great Depression, 1929–1941*. New York: Macmillan & Co., 1941.

Hoyt, Edwin P. *The House of Morgan*. London: Frederick Muller, 1968.

Hyde, H. Montgomery. *Norman Birkett—The Life of Lord Birkett, of Ulverston*. London: Hamish Hamilton Ltd., 1964.

Ishoven, Armand Van. *Messerschmitt—Aircraft Designer*. Garden City, N.Y.: Doubleday & Co., 1975.

Jackson, Robert. *Case for the Prosecution—A Biography of Sir Archibald Bodkin, Director of Public Prosecutions, 1920–1930*. London: Arthur Barket Ltd., 1962.

——. *Airships*. Garden City, N.Y.: Doubleday & Co., 1973.

Jackson, Stanley. *Mr. Justice Avory*. London: Victor Gollancz Ltd., 1935.

James, Marquis and Jessie. *Biography of a Bank*. New York: Harper & Row, 1954.

Jardin, Anne. *The First Henry Ford*. Cambridge, Mass.: MIT Press, 1970.

Jenkins, Alan. *The Stock Exchange Story*. London: William Heinemann Ltd., 1973.

Kennedy, Joseph Patrick. *The Story of the Films*. New York: A. W. Shaw Co., 1927.

Kennedy, Rose Fitzgerald. *Times to Remember*, Garden City, N.Y.: Doubleday & Co., Inc., 1974.

Keynes, John Maynard. *A Treatise on Money*. London: Macmillan & Co., 1930.

——. *The Means to Prosperity*. London: Macmillan, 1933.

——. *The General Theory of Employment, Interest and Money*. London: Macmillan, 1936.

Kiaulehn, Walter. *Berlin: Schicksal einer Weltstadt*. Munich: 1968.

Kindleberger, Charles. *The World in Depression: 1929–1930*. London: Allen Lane, The Penguin Press, 1973.

Knapp, Paul. *The Berengaria Exchange*. New York: The Dial Press, 1972.

Kobler, John. *Ardent Spirits—The Rise and Fall of Prohibition*. New York: G. P. Putnam's Sons, 1973.

Kostolany, André. *Geld das Grosse Abenteuer*. Bastei, Lübbe, 1977.

Lamont, Corliss, ed. *The Thomas Lamonts in America*. New York: A. S. Barnes & Co., 1971.

Lamont, Thomas W. *My Boyhood in a Parsonage*. New York: Harper & Bros., 1946.

——. *Across World Frontiers*. New York: Harcourt, Brace & Co., 1951.

Lang, Gordon. *Mr. Justice Avory*. London: Herbert Jenkins Ltd., 1935.

Lawrence, Joseph Stagg. *Wall Street and Washington*. Princeton, N.J.: Princeton University Press, 1929.

Lefevre, Edwin. *Reminiscences of a Stock Operator*. Garden City, N.Y.: Doubleday, Doran & Co., 1931.

———. *Stock Market Manipulator*. New York: Traders Press, 1967.

Leighton, Isabel. *The Aspirin Age*. London: The Bodley Head, 1950.

Lethbridge, Alice. *Halfway to Yesterday*. Privately published, 1974.

———. *Well Do I Remember*. Bodwin-London Publishers of Michigan, 1976.

Leuchtenburg, William E. *The Perils of Prosperity, 1914–1932*. Chicago: University of Chicago Press, 1958.

Lewis, David L. *The Public Image of Henry Ford*. Detroit: Wayne State University Press, 1976.

Lewis, Sinclair. *Babbitt*. London: Jonathan Cape, 1932.

Livermore, Jesse Lauriston. *How to Trade in Stocks*. New York: Duell, Sloan & Pearce, 1940.

Lochner, Louis Paul. *Always the Unexpected*. New York: The Macmillan Co., 1956.

Lunberg, Ferdinand. *America's 60 Families*. New York: The Vanguard Press, 1937.

———. *Who Controls Industry?* New York: The Vanguard Press, 1938.

Lyman, Robert Hunt, ed. *The World Almanac*. New York: New York World, 1930.

Lynd, Robert S. and Helen M. *Middletown—A Study in Contemporary American Culture*. London: Constable & Co., 1929.

———. *Middletown in Transition—A Study in Cultural Conflicts*. London: Constable & Co., 1937.

McAdoo, William G. *Crowded Years*. London: Jonathan Cape, 1932.

McCabe, John. *Charlie Chaplin*. Garden City, N.Y.: Doubleday & Co., 1978.

McDonald, Forrest. *Insull*. University of Chicago Press, 1962.

MacDonald, James Ramsay. *American Speeches*. London: Jonathan Cape, 1930.

McElderry, Andrea Lee. *Shanghai Old-style Banks, 1800–1935*. Ann Arbor: University of Michigan Press, 1935.

Manchester, William. *Portrait of a President—John F. Kennedy in Profile*. Boston: Little, Brown & Co., 1962.

Marcus, Edward. *Canada and the International Business Cycle, 1927–1939*. New York: Brookman Associates, 1954.

Mavity, Nancy Barr. *Sister Aimee*. Garden City, N.Y.: Doubleday, Doran & Co., 1931.

Mayer, Martin. *Wall Street—The Inside Story of American Finance*. London: The Bodley Head, 1959.

Meekes, J. Edward. *The Work of the Stock Exchange*. New York: The Ronald Press Co., 1930.

Meissner, Otto. *Staatssekretar unter Ebert, Hindenburg, Hitler*. Hamburg, 1950.

Moggeridge, D. E. *The Return to Gold, 1925: The Formulation of Policy and Its Critics*. Cambridge University Press, 1969.

———. *Britain Monetary Policy, 1924–1931*. Cambridge University Press, 1972.

Morehouse, Clifford P., ed. *A History of Trinity Church in the City of New York*, Part 7. New York: The Seaburg Press, 1978.

Morgan, John P. *Reprints of Statements Submitted by Members of J. P. Morgan and Company to Senate Committee on Banking and Currency at Its Hearings in Washington, May 23 to 9 June 1933*. Privately printed, 1933.

Morris, Joe Alex. *What a Year!* New York: Harper Bros., 1956.

Morris, Lloyd. *Postscript to Yesterday*. New York: Random House, 1947.

———. *Incredible New York*. New York: Random House, 1951.

Moscow, Alvin. *The Rockefeller Inheritance*. Garden City, N.Y.: Doubleday & Co., 1977.

Mowat, C. L. *Britain Between the Wars*. London: Methuen & Co., 1955.

Muggeridge, Malcolm. *The Thirties*. London: Hamish Hamilton Ltd., 1940.

Mugglebee, Ruth. *Father Coughlin of the Shrine of the Little Flower*. Boston: L. C. Page & Co., 1933.

Murray, George. *The Legacy of Al Capone*. New York: G. P. Putnam's Sons, 1975.

Myers, Margaret G. *The New York Money Market*, Vol. 1. New York: Columbia University Press, 1931.

Myers, Starr, and Newton, Walter H. *The Hoover Administration*. New York: Charles Scribner's Sons, 1936.

Neatby, H. Blair. *Mackenzie King, Vol. II, 1924–1932*. London: Methuen & Co., 1963

———. *The Politics of Chaos*. Toronto: The Macmillan Co., 1972.

Nère, Jacques. *La Crise de 1929*. A. Colin, 1968.

Nevins, Allan, and Hill, Frank E. *Ford—The Times, the Man, the Company*. New York: Charles Scribner's Sons, 1950.

———. *Ford—Expansion and Challenge, 1915–1933*. New York: Charles Scribner's Sons, 1957.

———. *Ford—Decline and Rebirth, 1933–1962*. New York: Charles Scribner's Sons, 1963.

New York Stock Exchange *Year Book:* 1928–29, 1929–30.

Nichols, Beverley. *The Sweet and Twenties*. London: Weidenfeld & Nicolson, 1958.

Norton, Richard H. B. *Silver Spoon*. London: Hutchinson & Co., 1954.

Noyes, Alexander Dana. *The Market Place*. Boston: Little, Brown, 1938.

O'Connor, Harvey. *Mellon's Millions—The Life and Times of Andrew Mellon*. New York: The John Day Co., 1933.

O'Donnell, Bernard. *The Trials of Mr. Justice Avory*. London: Rich & Cowan, 1935.

Olsen, Sidney. *Young Henry Ford*. Detroit: Wayne State University Press, 1963.

Parker, John Lloyd. *Unmasking Wall Street*. Boston: The Stratford Co., 1932.

Patterson, Robert T. *The Great Boom and Panic*. Chicago: The Henry Regnery Co., 1965.

Pearson, Michael. *The Millionaire Mentality*. London: Secker & Warburg, 1961.

Pecora, Ferdinand. *Wall Street Under Oath*. New York: Simon & Schuster, 1939.

Pilpel, Robert H. *Churchill in America*. New York: Harcourt, Brace, Jovanovich, 1976.

Pin, Tao Hsu. *A History of Shanghai*. Taiwan: China Book Translation Co., 1968.

Pound, Arthur. *The Turning Wheel*. Garden City, N.Y.: Doubleday, Doran & Co., 1934.

Prescott, Marjorie Wiggin. *New England Son*. New York: Dodd, Mead & Co., 1949.

Pritchard, F. H., ed. *More Essays of Today*. London: George G. Harrup & Co., 1928.

Prothero, James Warren. *The Dollar Decade*. Baton Rouge: Louisiana State University Press, 1954.

Punder, Herman. *Von Preussen nach Europe*. Stuttgart, 1968.

Quazza, Guido, ed. *Fascismo e Societa Italiana*. Einaudi, 1973.

Rees, Goronwy. *The Great Slump—Capitalism in Crisis, 1929–1933*. London: Weidenfeld & Nicolson, 1970.

Renshaw, Patrick. *The General Strike*. London: Eyre & Methuen, 1975.

Richards, William C. *The Last Billionaire*. New York: Charles Scribner's Sons, 1948.

Rink, Paul. *Building the Bank of America—A. P. Giannini*. Chicago: Encyclopaedia Britannica Press, 1963.

Robbins, Lionel. *The Great Depression*. New York: Macmillan, 1934.

Roberts, Cecil. *The Bright Twenties*. London: Hodder & Stoughton, 1970.

Rosario, Romeo. *Breve Storia Della Grande Industria in Italia, 1861–1961*. Cappelli, 1961.

Rosenthal, Eric. *Gold Bricks and Mortar*. Johannesburg: Printing House, 1946.

Roy, Maurice. *1929: La Grande Crise*. Denoël, 1969.

Royster, Vermont. *A Pride of Prejudices*. New York: Alfred A. Knopf, 1968.

Samuel, Herbert Louis. *Memoirs*. London: The Cresset Press, 1945.

Sann, Paul. *The Lawless Decade*. New York: Crown Publishers, 1957.

Sarnoff, Paul. *Jesse Livermore—Speculator King*. Palisades Park, N.J.: Investors' Press, 1967.

Sauvy, Alfred. *Histoire Économique de la France Entre les Deux Guerres*. A. Fayard, 1965.

Sayers, R. C. *A History of Economic Change in England, 1880–1939*. Oxford University Press, 1967.

Sayers, Richard Sidney. *Modern Banking*. Oxford University Press, 1938.

Schacht, Hjalmar. *My First Seventy-six Years*. London: Allan Wingate, 1955.

Schlesinger, Arthur M. *The Age of Roosevelt, Vol. 1. The Crisis of the Old Order*. London: Heinemann, 1957.

Schultz, Harry D., and Coslow, Samson. *A Treasury of Wall Street Wisdom*. Palisades Park, N.J.: Investors' Press, 1966.

Serling, Robert J. *The Only Way to Fly*. Garden City, N.Y.: Doubleday & Co., 1976.

Shannon, David A. *The Great Depression*. Englewood Cliffs, N.J.: Prentice-Hall, 1960.

Sijthoff, A. W. *Nederland in de Crisitijd, 1929–1939*. Leyden.

Simmons, Edward Henry Harriman. *The Principal Causes of the Stock Market Crisis of Nineteen Twenty-nine*. Privately printed, 1930.

Simon, Kate. *Fifth Avenue*. New York: Harcourt Brace Jovanovich, 1978.

Simonds, William Adams. *Henry Ford and Greenfield Village.* New York: Frederick A. Stokes Co., 1938.

Sloan, Alfred P. *My Years with General Motors.* Garden City, N.Y.: Doubleday & Co., 1963.

Sobel, Robert. *The Big Board—A History of the New York Stock Market.* New York: The Free Press, Macmillan Co., 1965.

————. *The Great Bull Market—Wall Street in the 1920's.* New York: W. W. Norton & Co., 1968.

————. *The Age of Giant Corporations.* Westport, Conn.: Greenwood Press, 1972.

————. *Panic on Wall Street.* New York: The Macmillan Co., 1972.

————. *The Manipulators.* Garden City, N.Y.: Anchor Press/Doubleday, 1976.

Sorensen, Charles E. *My Forty Years with Ford.* New York: W. W. Norton & Co., 1956.

Soule, George Henry. *The Economic History of the United States, Vol. VIII. Prosperity Decade.* New York: Rinehart, 1947.

Sparling, Earl. *Mystery Men of Wall Street.* New York: Greenberg, 1930.

Speer, Albert. *Inside the Third Reich.* New York: The Macmillan Co., 1970.

Stagg, Lawrence Joseph. *Wall Street and Washington.* Princeton, N.J.: Princeton University Press, 1929.

Stern, Philipran Doren. *Tin Lizzie.* New York: Simon & Schuster, 1955.

Sternberg, Josef von. *Fun in a Chinese Laundry.* New York, 1965.

Stevenson, John, and Cook, Chris. *The Slump—Society and Politics During the Depression.* London: Jonathan Cape, 1977.

Stresemann, Wolfgang. *Gust Stresemann.* Berlin, 1978.

Strong, Benjamin. *Interpretations of Federal Reserve Policy.* New York: Harper & Bros., 1930.

Sullivan, Lawrence. *Prelude to Panic.* Washington, D.C.: Statesman Press, 1936.

Sullivan, Mark. *Our Times—The Twenties,* Vol. 4. New York: Charles Scribner's Sons Ltd., 1935.

Swanberg, W. A. *Citizen Hearst.* London: Longmans, 1962.

Sward, Keith. *The Legend of Henry Ford.* New York: Rinehart, 1948.

Tebbel, John W. *The Life and Good Times of William Randolph Hearst.* London: Victor Gollancz, 1953.

Terkel, Studs. *Hard Times.* New York: Pantheon Books, 1970.

Thomas, Dana L. *The Plungers and the Peacocks.* New York: G. P. Putnam's Sons, 1967.

Thomas, Hugh. *The Spanish Civil War.* London: Eyre & Spottiswoode, 1961.

Toland, John. *Adolf Hitler.* Garden City, N.Y.: Doubleday & Co., 1976.

Tuke, A. W., and Gillman, R. J. H. *Barclays Bank Ltd., 1926–1969.* London: Privately printed, 1972.

Turner, Ernest Sackville. *The Shocking History of Advertising.* London: Michael Joseph, 1952.

U. S. Congress. *Congressional Record,* 1933.

U. S. Senate. *Stock Exchange Practices: Report of the Committee on Banking and Currency, pursuant to Senate Resolution 84, 72nd Congress, and*

Senate Resolution 56 and 97, 73rd Congress: Report No. 1455. Senate, 73rd Cong., 2nd sess., 1934.

————. *Hearings Before the Committee, 1932–1934.*

Valette, Jacques. *Vie Économique et Sociale des Grande Pays de L'Europe Occidentale et des États Unis.* Paris: Société d'Éditions, 1976.

Wagner, Kurt. *Stationen Deutscher Bankgeschichte.* Koln, 1967.

Warburg, Paul M. *The Federal Reserve System—Its Origins and Growth.* Vol. 1. New York: Macmillan, 1930.

Washburton, Watson, and De Long, Edmund. *High and Low Financiers.* Indianapolis: Bobbs-Merrill Co., 1932.

Weber, Adolf. *Geld-Banken-Borsen.* München, 1951.

Wechsburg, Joseph. *The Merchant Bankers.* Boston: Little Brown & Co., 1966.

Wee, Herman van der. *The Great Depression, Revisited.* The Hague: M. Nijhoff, 1972.

Weingarten, Arthur. *The Sky Is Falling.* London: Hodder & Stoughton, 1977.

Whalen, Richard J. *The Founding Father—The Story of Joseph P. Kennedy.* New York: New American Library, 1964.

Whitney, David G. *The American President.* Garden City, N.Y.: Doubleday & Co., 1975.

Whitney, Richard. "The Work of the Stock Exchange in the Panic of 1929." Address before the Boston Association of Stock Exchange Firms, June 10, 1930.

Whitney, Richard, and Perkins, William R. *Short Selling—For and Against.* New York: D. Appleton & Co., 1932.

Wickwire, Arthur M. *The Weeds of Wall Street.* New York: Newcastle Press, 1933.

Winkleman, Barnie F. *Ten Years of Wall Street.* Philadelphia: The John C. Winston Co., 1932.

Wiskemann, Elizabeth. *Europe of the Dictators.* London: Collins (Fontana), 1966.

Woodhead, H. G. W. *China Yearbook.* Shanghai: North-China Daily News & Herald Co., 1931–1932.

Wyckoff, Richard D. *Wall Street Ventures and Adventures Through Forty Years.* New York: Harper Bros., 1930.

Zuckmayer, Carl. *Als wars ein Stück von Mir.* Frankfurt, 1966.

Magazines

Magazines in the 1920s through to the late 1950s held a public position similar to that which radio and television do today; they provide essential background and assessment. Magazines also offered a unique glimpse of the period they were published in—an invaluable asset when re-creating social history.

The American Magazine
Barton, Bruce. "The Future of American Business." June 1929.
Phillips, H. I. "My Stock Market Operations." March 1929.

Carroll, Edgar. "Wall Street's Family Doctor." August 1931.
Flynn, John T. "How Much Do You Know About Wall Street?" August 1929.
Singleton, John. "Stories of Winning and Losing in Wall Street" (an interview with John Moddy). June 1920.

The American Mercury
Lee, Henry. "1929: The Crash That Shook the World." November 1949.

The Atlantic Monthly
Carver, Thomas Nixon. "Selling Short: The Morals and Economics of Margins." February 1930.
Danielian, N. R. "The Stock Market and the Public." October 1933.
Spring, Samuel. "Whirlwinds of Speculation." April 1931.
Bundy, Harvey H. "Inside Information." March 1929.
Moddy, John. "The New Era in Wall Street." August 1928.
Holden, Arthur C. "Speculating in Homes." February 1928.

Business Week
"What Bull Market?" September 7, 1929.
"When It's a Man, Wall Street Doesn't Speculate." January 15, 1930.
"Wall Street Is Placing the Blame." November 27, 1929.
"In Praise of Speculation." March 12, 1930.
"Yes, Wall Street Really Is All In." November 9, 1929.
"What the Wall Street Crash Means." November 2, 1929.
"Rallying from the Whitney Blow." March 19, 1958.
"Looking Back at the Great Crash." April 23, 1955.

The Christian Century
"Business Must Clean House." May 4, 1932.
Whitney, Richard, "In Defence of the Stock Exchange." August 9, 1933.

Collier's
Flynn, John T. "Riders of the Whirlwind." January 19, 1929.
The Gentleman at the Keyhole. "The Inseparable Vans." May 31, 1930.
Uncle Henry. "The Stock Market." May 4, 1929.
Flynn, John T. "The Ticker's in a Jam." December 15, 1928.
"Two and Two Still Makes Four" (editorial). February 9, 1929.
"Are Women Pikers?" May 21, 1927.
Downey, Fairfax. "They Call Him Wall Street's Bishop." March 21, 1925.

The Commonweal
"The Call to Order." November 13, 1929.
McCabe, George. "Wall Street Goes Amateur." December 11, 1929.

Current History
Noyes, Alexander D. "The Stock Market Panic." December 1929.
Ellsworth, D. W. "Causes of the Stock Market Boom." December 1928.

Delineator
Laimbeer, Mrs. William. "The Story of Wall Street." May 1929.

Fortune
"The Map of Wall Street." March 1930.

Forum
Flynn, John T. "Taming the Great Bull." February 1929.
Flynn, John T. "Mobilizing Deflation." February 1930.

Flynn, John T. "The Birthday of the Slump." November 1930.
Hanson, Donald Rea. "The Financial Crisis." January 1930.

Good Housekeeping
Frazer, Elizabeth. "Wall Street Women." August 1931.
Frazer, Elizabeth. "Speculation and the Stock Exchange." September 1928.

Harper's Magazine
Allen, Frederick Lewis. "One Day in History." November 1937.
Flynn, John T. "Speculation and Gambling." January 1930.
Flynn, John T. "The Wall Street Debt Machine." July 1933.
Merz, Charles. "Bull Market." April 1929.

Journal of Political Economy
Eiteman, Wilford J. "The Economic Significance of Brokers' Loans." October 1932.

Ladies' Home Journal
Crowther, Samuel. "Everybody Ought to Be Rich." August 1929.

Life
Allen, Frederick Lewis. "Morgan the Great." April 25, 1949.

The Literary Digest
"The War Against Wall Street Speculation." April 13, 1929.
"What Smashed the Bull Market." November 9, 1929.
"Wall Street's Prosperity Panic." November 9, 1929.
"Beau Gestes." November 23, 1929.
"From Stock-Gambling to Embezzling." December 7, 1929.
"The Stock-speculating Mania." December 8, 1928.
"The Great Senate Bear Hunt." May 7, 1932.
"Two Years of the Bear Market." October 3, 1931.
"More and Bigger Stock Markets." March 2, 1929.
"Whitney's Defence of Wall Street." April 23, 1932.
"The Ticker's New Alphabet." June 28, 1930.
"The Brokers Take to the Sea." August 31, 1929.
"Stock-Market Aristocrats." March 2, 1929.
Meehan's Sky-rocketing Operations in Stock Market Under SEC Inquiry." December 26, 1936.
"Mr. Raskob's Poor Man's Investment Trust." June 1, 1929.
"Wall Street Bids for the Woman Speculator." November 17, 1928.
"The World-wide Fever of Speculation." June 9, 1928.
"Making New York the World's Financial Hub." October 29, 1927.

The Magazine of Business
Dice, Charles A. "Have Stocks Struck a New Holding Zone?" November 1928.

The Nation
"The Man Who Did It." November 13, 1929.
Hall, Henry. "The Money Market," June 19, 1929.
Anderson, Paul Y. "Sacred Bulls and Sinister Bears." May 11, 1932.
Bernheim, Alfred L. "Wall Street Upside Down." November 27, 1929.
Hodges, Charles. "Wall Street and the World." December 4, 1929.
"Wall Street's Crisis." November 6, 1929.
Harman, S. Palmer. "Facts About the Bears." November 4, 1931.
"Notes on Black Tuesday." October 30, 1937.
"Larceny in the Stock Exchange." November 12, 1938.

"Questions on the Whitney Case." January 14, 1939.
"Larceny in Wall Street." March 19, 1938.
Ryan, Robert. "Brokers and Suckers." August 15, 1928.

The New Republic
Rascoe, Burton. "The Grim Anniversary." October 29, 1930.
"The Call to Order." November 13, 1929.
Wilson, Edmund. "Sunshine Charley." June 28, 1933.
"Behind the Credit Battle." April 10, 1929.
Gorey, Lewis. "Who Gains by Speculation?" April 17, 1929.
Josephson, Matthew. "The 'New Era': Its Rise and Fall." November 4, 1931
    (Part 1).
Flynn, John T. "How Whitney Went Broke." July 13, 1938.
Flynn, John T. "Mr. Whitney Learns the Hard Way." March 23, 1938.
"How to Get out of the Stock Market." January 2, 1929.

North American Review
Jordan, Virgil. "The Era of Mad Illusions." January 1930.
Winkler, Max. "Paying the Piper." January 1930.
Barnard, Eunice Fuller. "Ladies of the Ticker." April 1929.
Garrett, Paul Willard. "The Jazz Age in Finance." February 1930.
Willis, H. Parker. "Who Caused the Panic of 1929?" February 1930.
Simmons, E. H. H. "Mechanics of the Stock Exchange." March 1929.
Bond, Frederic Drew. "The Common Stock Racket." April 1929.
Simmons, E. H. H. "Some International Aspects of the Stock Exchange."
    March 1927.

Outlook
Murphy, Charles J. V. "Wall Street Branches Out." September 18, 1929.
Scroggs, William O. "By-products of the Bull Market." May 8, 1929.
Scroggs, William O. "We Have Changed All That." December 25, 1929.

Overland Monthly
Selig, Trebor. "The State of Mind: The Day After the Big Crash." January
    1930.

The Review of Reviews
Economicus. "The Hatry Scandal." February 15, 1930.
Florance, Howard. "What Really Happened?" January 15, 1930.
Schwartz, Sidney L. "Our Second Largest Stock Market." January 1929.
Rukeyser, Merryle Stanley. "Eyes on the Stock Market." October 1928.

The Saturday Evening Post
Frazer, Elizabeth. "The Lady and the Ticker." March 8, 1930.
"A Trip on the Magic Carpet." February 1, 1930.
Lefevre, Edwin. "The Little Fellow in Wall Street." January 4, 1930.
Atwood, Albert W. "Men and Markets." April 27, 1929.
Garrett, Garet. "Wall Street and Washington." December 28, 1929.
Sparkes, Boyden. "The Retail Business of the Stock Exchange." December
    28, 1929.
Sparkes, Boyden. "A Career in Wall Street." March 8, 1930.
Atwood, Albert W. "Investment and Speculation." December 7, 1929.
Payne, Will. "A Reformed Speculator." August 10, 1929.
Lefevre, Edwin. "The Bigger They Are . . ." January 11, 1930.
Atwood, Albert W. "The Great Bull Market." January 12, 1929.
Dayton, Katharine. "This Little Pig Went to Market." March 23, 1929.

Garrett, Garet, "Speculation," May 4, 1929.

Atwood, Albert W. "The Future of Stock Speculation." September 13, 1930.

Lefevre, Edwin. "With Blue Chips This Time." February 2, 1929.

Payne, Will. "Deflation." May 3, 1930.

"The Dance of the Billions." December 22, 1928.

Lefevre, Edwin. "The Long and the Short of It." December 13, 1930.

Lefevre, Edwin. "The New Bears—Normal and Grizzly." December 27, 1930.

Lefevre, Edwin. "Speculation—Both Versions." April 2, 1932.

Lefevre, Edwin. "Blame the Broker." April 9, 1932.

Lefevre, Edwin. "Running Past the Signal." February 9, 1929.

Rinehart, Mary Roberts. "A Woman Goes to Market." January 31, 1931.

Lefevre, Edwin. "Bulls on America." February 16, 1929.

Payne, Will. "Paper Wheat." September 7, 1929.

Van Wyck, Frederick (as told to Boyden Sparkes). "Panic Profits." August 1, 1931.

Vanderkip, Frank A. "What About the Banks?" November 19, 1932.

Sparkes, Boyden. "Down and Up." March 25, 1933.

"Speculator's Wife." March 31, 1934.

"Some Other Stock Exchanges." April 28, 1934.

Lefevre, Edwin. "The Newest Era in Wall Street." September 28, 1935.

Schwed, Fred. "Twenty Years Ago This Week." October 29, 1949.

Lefevre, Edwin. "Stock Market Manipulation." February 24, 1923.

Lefevre, Edwin. "The Reminiscences of a Stock Operator." June 10, 1922.

Lefevre, Edwin. "The Reminiscences of a Stock Operator (Part 2)." June 17, 1922.

Scientific American

"High-speed Tickers to Serve Brokers." March 1930.

Scribner's Magazine

Sparling, Earl. "These Brokers." July 1930.

Noyes, Alexander Dana. "The Conflict over Credit Reaches a Climax." May 1929.

Sunset

Kemper, Lucrezia. "There Is a Tide—The Story of the San Francisco Stock Exchange." December 1928.

Time

Article on Michael J. Meehan. December 7, 1936.

Woman's Home Companion

Flynn, John T. "How to Make Money in Wall Street." January 1930.

The Woman's Journal

"Is It Safe to Buy on Margin?" February 1929.

World's Work

"The March of Events." June 1929.

Payne, Will. "Geatest of Bull Markets." January 1929.

"Wall Street at Close Range." December 1930–October 1931 (series).

"Another New High." May 1929.

"All's Quiet on the Exchange." April 1932.

Woolf, S. J. "The Man Behind the Ticker." March 1931.

Sparkes, Boyden. "Fifty for a Million." March 1930.

The World Tomorrow
Volkening, Henry T. "Wall Street—The Modern Mecca." April 1930.
Niebuhr, Reinhold. "The Speculation Mania." January 1930.
"The Stock Market Debacle." December 1929.

INDEX

Adams, Charles, 149
Adams, Evangeline, 70–71, 205–6, 274, 278, 369–70, 377, 403
Adams Express, 114, 283, 346
Adams family, 57
Advertisements: dubious types of, 75–76; paid testimonials by society figures, 275–76
Advocate, The (magazine), 100
Agents de change, 224, 257
Ahlefeldt family, 196
Airline industry, 54
Air Reduction Company, 389
Alexander I, King of Yugoslavia, 33
Allegheny Corporation, 148, 149, 250, 358, 390
Allied Chemical Corporation, 312, 389
Allied Ironfounders Limited, 181
All Quiet on the Western Front (Remarque), 274
America Commercial Corporation, 18
American Association of Wholesale Opticians, 76
American Bankers' Association (ABA), 191, 316
American Can Company, 135, 305, 390
American Institute of Banking, 110
American Magazine, 232
American Molasses Company, 12
American National Bank, 15
American Smelting Company, 391
American Sumatra Company, 65
American Telephone and Telegraph (AT&T), 73, 135,

205, 222, 241, 246, 277
American Tobacco Company, 322
"American Village," 99, 244, 311
American Woolen Company, 135
Amsterdam Stock Exchange, 298, 406–7
Anaconda Copper Corporation, 6, 7, 138, 277; price decline (October 1929), 358, 390
Anaconda Copper pool, 111, 112, 121, 130, 138, 167, 192, 207–8
Andes Copper Company, 138
Anti-Saloon League, 259
Anti-Semitism, x, 59, 255; of Henry Ford, 36, 40–42, 97, 172; in Germany, 34, 35, 36; *See also* Nazi party
Arabelle (ship), 193
Archmere (manor house), 20
Armour & Company, 6
Army Training Manual, The, 119
Arvay, Andrew, 102, 103, 104, 285, 327, 329
Arvay, Mrs. Barbara, 102–3, 104, 286, 328
Associated Press, 32, 127, 215, 254, 270, 282, 283, 379
Astor, Vincent, 233
Astrology, 71, 205–6, 274
Atlantic Building, 11
Atlantic Monthly, 12
Auburn Auto Company, 329
Auschwitz (concentration camp), 418
Auslandsdeutsche, 162
Austin Friars Trust, 201
Australia, 185–86, 408–9
Austria, 34, 83, 212, 311